# The Archaeology

**Publication of the Advanced Seminar Series
is made possible by generous support from
The Brown Foundation, Inc., of Houston, Texas.**

**The National Park Service generously supported the Chaco Synthesis.**

**School of American Research
Advanced Seminar Series**

James F. Brooks
*General Editor*

# The Archaeology of Chaco Canyon

**Contributors**

Nancy J. Akins
*Office of Archaeological Studies, Museum of New Mexico*

Linda S. Cordell
*University of Colorado Museum, University of Colorado, Boulder*

Jeffrey S. Dean
*Laboratory of Tree-Ring Research, University of Arizona*

Andrew I. Duff
*Department of Anthropology, Washington State University*

W. Derek Hamilton
*Department of Anthropology, University of Colorado, Boulder*

W. James Judge
*Department of Anthropology, Fort Lewis College*

John W. Kantner
*Department of Anthropology and Geography, Georgia State University*

Keith W. Kintigh
*School of Human Evolution and Social Change, Arizona State University*

Stephen H. Lekson
*University of Colorado Museum, University of Colorado, Boulder*

William D. Lipe
*Department of Anthropology, Washington State University*

Peter J. McKenna
*Bureau of Indian Affairs*

Ben A. Nelson
*School of Human Evolution and Social Change, Arizona State University*

Lynne Sebastian
*SRI Foundation*

H. Wolcott Toll
*Office of Archaeological Studies, Museum of New Mexico*

Mollie S. Toll
*Office of Archaeological Studies, Museum of New Mexico*

Ruth M. Van Dyke
*Department of Anthropology, Colorado College*

Carla R. Van West
*SRI Foundation*

R. Gwinn Vivian
*Arizona State Museum, University of Arizona*

Richard H. Wilshusen
*Archaeological consultant*

Thomas C. Windes
*National Park Service*

# The Archaeology of Chaco Canyon

*An Eleventh-Century Pueblo Regional Center*

*Edited by Stephen H. Lekson*

**School of American Research Press**

*Santa Fe*

# School of American Research Press

Post Office Box 2188
Santa Fe, New Mexico 87504-2188

Acting Director: Catherine Cocks
Manuscript Editor: Kate Talbot
Design and Production: Cynthia Dyer
Proofreader: Sarah Soliz
Indexer: Catherine Fox

**Library of Congress Cataloging-in-Publication Data:**
The archaeology of Chaco Canyon : an eleventh-century Pueblo regional center / edited by Stephen
H. Lekson.– 1st ed.
   p. cm. – (School of American Research advanced seminar series)
 Includes bibliographical references and index.
 ISBN 1-930618-47-6 (alk. paper) – ISBN 1-930618-48-4 (pbk. : alk. paper)
 1. Chaco culture–New Mexico–Chaco Culture National Historical Park. 2. Excavations
(Archaeology)–New Mexico–Chaco Culture National Historical Park–History. 3. Chaco Culture
National Historical Park (N.M.)–Antiquities. I. Lekson, Stephen H. II. Series.

E99.C37A73 2005
978.9'8201–dc22

                                        2005028433

Library of Congress Catalog Card Number 2005028433
International Standard Book Numbers 1-930618-47-6 (cloth); 1-930618-48-4 (paper).
5th paperback printing 2013.

This volume is one of two presenting the final scholarly publications of the Chaco Project. F. Joan
Mathien's *Culture and Ecology of Chaco Canyon and the San Juan Basin* (Santa Fe, NM: National Park
Service, 2005) reviews the archaeology of Chaco Canyon and the work of the Chaco Project in
admirable detail. Mathien's study and this book were originally planned as volumes I and II of a set.

Cover illustration: Pueblo Bonito © by Adriel Heisey, reprinted by permission.

# Contents

# Contents

# Figures

**Plates**   after page 152

# Foreword

This volume and its companion, *Culture and Ecology* of Chaco Canyon *and the San Juan Basin* by F. Joan Mathien (2005), are the final but by no means sole products of the Chaco Synthesis Project. Partially funded by the National Park Service and the Chaco Publication Fund and directed by Stephen H. Lekson, the Chaco Synthesis Project was conceived to evaluate, synthesize, and critique the results of the National Park Service's renowned Chaco Project. How the synthesis project came about is a long story, but one worth telling.

Established in cooperation with the University of New Mexico in 1969, the Chaco Project was the most ambitious, innovative, and productive archaeological research project ever directed and funded by the federal government (see chapters 1 and 10 for short histories of the project). Unfortunately, the Chaco Project ended prematurely in 1986, a victim of the ballooning federal deficit, an inflexible civil service system, and the waning support of National Park Service and university officials. Each institution had its own reasons for bringing the project to a close, but, for those of us who had lived and breathed Chaco for more than a decade, its end was a heartbreaking and sobering experience. Most of all, it was a troubling reminder that good intentions, hard work, and the idealistic pursuit of knowledge were no match against economic reality and bureaucratic intransigence.

Although none of us had the experience or influence to save the project, we did have one card in our favor, and that was our relative youth. The project's senior archaeologists, including Bob Lister, Al Hayes, Tom Lyons, and Tom Mathews, had retired by 1986, and our chief, Jim Judge, had resigned from the park service. The rest of us, including Nancy Akins, Cathy Cameron, Anne Cully, Bill Gillespie, Steve Lekson, Peter McKenna, Joan Mathien, Judy Miles, John Schelberg, Mollie Toll, Wolky Toll, Marcia Truell, Tom Windes, and me (for a complete list of Chaco Project staff, see Mathien 2005), were in our late thirties or early forties. As The Rolling Stones were fond of saying, we had time on our side.

As part of the Chaco Center's closure, most staff members were terminated (many as early as 1982), and those remaining were transferred to the National Park Service's regional office in Santa Fe. Under the prodding of a new chief, Larry Nordby, the park service agreed to allow Tom Windes and Joan Mathien to continue to work on and publish the series of reports planned during the project's heyday in the late 1970s. It was a highly ambitious list, twenty-four reports in all, several of which would be multiple-volume affairs. Eleven of the reports had been completed before the center's dissolution. The remaining thirteen, including the Pueblo Alto excavation report and a synthetic study of the artifacts from the project excavations, were far from complete. It seemed highly unlikely that the project's lofty publications goals would ever materialize.

Nineteen years later, our success still seems improbable. Yet, twenty of the twenty-four projected reports have been published or are in press, one is available as an unpublished thesis, one will soon be available on the Chaco Digital Archive web site, and another is nearing completion. Only one is unlikely to ever see the light of day. This turnabout is the happy result of several factors. First, many of the individuals listed above have, over the intervening decades, put in hundreds if not thousands of hours to complete their original project obligations. The park service has paid for some of their work, but they accomplished much of it after hours and on weekends. Second, the park service has, by and large, kept its promise to support publication of the project results. Larry Nordby, Ronald Ice, Richard Sellars, and Rick Smith of the former Southwest Regional Office supported and protected us and managed to find money when it was most needed. Dabney Ford, archaeologist at Chaco Culture National Historical Park, has also provided steadfast programmatic and much needed moral support over many years.

Third, and most important, Joan Mathien and Tom Windes kept producing reports. Joan was named the Chaco Center publications editor in 1984 and, since that date, has successfully designed, edited, and produced eleven of the project's twenty monographs. Joan's dedication to this mammoth task has been absolute, and her remarkable success is, in my opinion, due largely to her steely determination and unshakeable practicality. It is no exaggeration to say that the project would have died long ago without her.

The second pillar of our resurrection is embodied in the person of Tom Windes. Tom has been the heart and soul of the Chaco Project since he joined it in 1972. Over the intervening thirty-three years, he has been intimately involved with every aspect—from the original inventory survey of the park to the final excavations at Pueblo Alto and from the first published articles to these capstone volumes. Tom's unwavering commitment to ferreting out Chaco's past has put him in the spotlight and on the spot, in equal measure. From his claustrophobic, packed-to-the-gills office at the University of New Mexico, Tom has steadily produced Chaco report after report over the past nineteen years. Tom not only has inspired us but, through his resolve, has also helped bring the project and us ever closer to the finish line—exhausted, staggering, nearsighted, and graying, admittedly, but here nonetheless.

Having succeeded Larry Nordby in 1995 and seeing that a successful end to Tom and Joan's Sisyphean labors was increasingly likely, I felt that a final synthesis of the project's findings was essential. The astonishingly detailed but also daunting mass of data and interpretative material produced by project authors between 1975 and 1995 begged for synthesis and critical evaluation. A final volume synthesizing the project's work had been planned since the early 1980s, but I felt that our final effort needed to take into account more than our work. It also needed to feature the voices of other archaeologists, particularly the new generation of scholars whose work in Chaco and the surrounding San Juan Basin was testing the significance of our work.

Also, if the synthesis was to be the really valuable contribution I envisioned, it needed a leader whose Chaco credentials were impeccable, whose enthusiasm and boldness were unlimited (and brass plated), and whose ideas and quick intelligence would take this final phase of the project to places where staid bureaucrats would never dare to tread. We needed Steve Lekson!

Beyond the few goals just articulated, the synthesis project is Steve's brainchild. He conceived and planned it and also won financial and intellectual support for it from virtually every major university in the Southwest. He developed the conference themes, cajoled the right people into leading them, and helped publish their results. With the capable assistance of Lynne Sebastian, he organized the capstone conference, the results of which appear in this volume. Steve's extraordinary leadership of the synthesis effort has turned it into the crowning achievement I so very much hoped for.

Steve's efforts and the decades-long labors of Joan and Tom and the other Chaco Project hands have at long last, I believe, fulfilled the immense promise of the Chaco Project. They have also rekindled the tremendous pride that all of us felt in ourselves and in our work during our youth in Chaco.

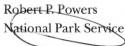

Robert P. Powers
National Park Service

# The Archaeology of Chaco Canyon

# 1

## Chaco Matters

### *An Introduction*

### Stephen H. Lekson

Chaco Canyon, in northwestern New Mexico, was a great Pueblo center of the eleventh and twelfth centuries A.D. (figures 1.1 and 1.2; refer to plate 2). Its ruins represent a decisive time and place in the history of "Anasazi," or Ancestral Pueblo peoples. Events at Chaco transformed the Pueblo world, with philosophical and practical implications for Pueblo descendents and for the rest of us. Modern views of Chaco vary: "a beautiful, serene place where everything was provided by the spirit helpers" (S. Ortiz 1994:72), "a dazzling show of wealth and power in a treeless desert" (Fernandez-Armesto 2001:61), "a self-inflicted ecological disaster" (Diamond 1992:332). १۹ ٦

Chaco, today, is a national park. Despite difficult access (20 miles of dirt roads), more than seventy-five thousand people visit every year. Chaco is featured in compendiums of must-see sights, from AAA tour books, to archaeology field guides such as *America's Ancient Treasures* (Folsom and Folsom 1993), to the *Encyclopedia of Mysterious Places* (Ingpen and Wilkinson 1990). In and beyond the Southwest, Chaco's fame manifests in more substantial, material ways. In Albuquerque, New Mexico, the structure of the Pueblo Indian Cultural

3

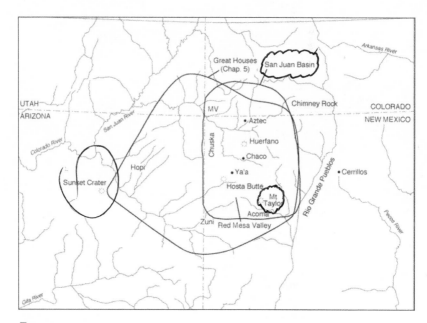

**FIGURE 1.1**

*The Chaco region.*

Center mimics precisely Pueblo Bonito, the most famous Chaco ruin. They sell Chaco (trademark!) sandals in Paonia, Colorado, and brew Chaco Canyon Ale (also trademark!) in Lincoln, Nebraska. The beer bottle features the Sun Dagger solstice marker, with three beams of light striking a spiral petroglyph, presumably indicating that it is five o'clock somewhere. Videos, books, New Age pilgrimages, décor in high-end Santa Fe restaurants—Chaco is a famous place, officially inscribed in the roll of UNESCO World Heritage sites.

Chaco was also an important place in the development of Southwestern and American archaeology (Lister and Lister 1981; Mills 2002; Wilshusen and Hamilton, chapter 11 of this volume). This book is about Chaco's archaeology: how it was done, what it tells us, how we should think about it. We have, perhaps, conducted more archaeology per square kilometer or per century of sequence at Chaco than at any comparable district in the United States—and far more, to be sure, than at many more impressive and important sites around the world. The last, largest, and most expensive field campaign at Chaco Canyon

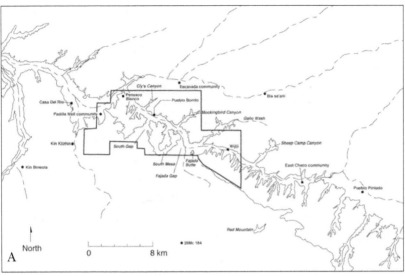

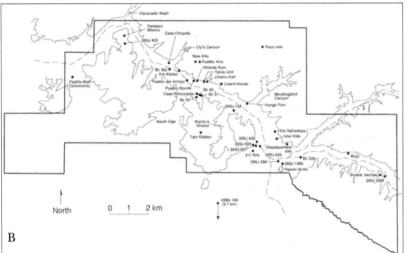

**FIGURE 1.2**

(a) *Chaco halo, or core (redrafted from Windes 1993:figure 1.1),* (b) *Chaco Canyon (redrafted from Windes 1993:figure 1.2).*

was the National Park Service's Chaco Project in the 1970s and early 1980s.

In this volume, you will find papers from our recent effort to synthesize the archaeology of Chaco Canyon, particularly the fieldwork of the Chaco Project (a list of participants, conferences, and products appears in appendix A, "Chaco Synthesis meetings"). The Chaco Synthesis—the results of which you are reading—was a series of small working conferences from March 1999 to October 2002, twenty years after fieldwork ended at Chaco. In addition to chapters from the Chaco Synthesis (chapters 2–6 and 12), chapters 7–11 provide temporal and spatial context for Chaco Canyon and its archaeology.

In this introduction, I briefly explain Chaco ("What Is Chaco?") and its marque archaeology ("The Bonito Phase"). I then describe the 1970s research that generated the data ("The Chaco Project") and our turn-of-the-millennium efforts to understand those data ("The Chaco Synthesis"). Finally, I address two issues, one of general interest and one of personal interest, respectively, in "Where Are the Indians?" and "Where Is Lekson?"

## WHAT IS CHACO?

Of the various phase or stage sequences proposed to describe Chaco's history, we seem to use the Pecos System most widely (figure 1.3). The term specific to Chaco Canyon at its height is the *Bonito phase*, divided into three subphases: Early Bonito phase (850–1040), Classic Bonito phase (1040–1100), and Late Bonito phase (1100–1140). The Bonito phase is roughly equivalent to the Pueblo II (PII) period of the Pecos System. In this volume, *Pueblo I (PI)* often describes the archaeology of Chaco Canyon before the Bonito phase, and *Pueblo III (PIII)*, the archaeology of the Four Corners region after Chaco. (For more extended treatments, see Lister and Lister 1981; Mathien 2005; Vivian 1990; for shorter, more accessible reviews, see Frazier 1999; Noble 2004; Vivian and Hilpert 2002. For an excellent review of recent research, see Mills 2002.)

*Anasazi* is an archaeological term, anglicized from a Navajo phrase, for the ancient peoples of the Four Corners region in New Mexico, Colorado, Utah, and Arizona. For many decades, technical and popular writing has widely used the word *Anasazi*; we use it here in its archaeological sense. Many archaeologists and Natives prefer *Ancestral Pueblo*, so that term appears here also.

A prime object produced by the Chaco Synthesis, specifically by its leader Lynne Sebastian, was a chronological chart dubbed "The Chaco

| Pecos Stage | Phase | Period | Ceramic Assemblage | Major Architectural Events | Demography |
|---|---|---|---|---|---|
| Late PIII | Mesa Verde | 1200–1300 | Mesa Verde B/w, indented corrugated (rock & sherd temper) |  | Major re-population. |
| PIII | McElmo | 1140–1200 | McElmo, indented corrugated (rock/sherd/sand temper) | Major population decrease. |  |
| Early PIII | Late Bonito | 1090–1140 | Chaco-McElmo/Gallup B/w, indented corrugated (sand temper) | Major Great House construction north of San Juan River. | Population increase, then decrease. |
| Late PII | Classic Bonito | 1040–1110 | Gallup B/w, indented corrugated (sand & trachyte temper) | Major Great House construction at Chaco. Kivas appear. | Population decrease. |
| Early PII | Early Bonito | 900–1040 | Red Mesa B/w, narrow neckbanded, neck corrugated (sand temper) | Small house aggregation & increase in number. | Major population increase. |
| Late PI Early PII | Early Bonito | 850–925 | Kiatuthlanna & Red Mesa B/w, Lino Gray & Kana'a Neckbanded | Aboveground slab house sites; small to moderate size. |  |
| PI | White Mound | 800–850 | White Mound B/w, Lino Gray | Aboveground slab row house sites; small to moderate size. Major Great Houses. Major increase in storage facilities. |  |
| Early PI | White Mound | 700–800 | White Mound B/w, Lino Gray | Deep pit houses, dispersed. Limited storage facilities? |  |
| Late BMIII | La Plata | 600–700 | La Plata B/w, Lino & Obelisk Grays | Shallow pit houses, dispersed. Storage facilities (cists). |  |
| BMIII | La Plata | 500–600 | La Plata B/w, Lino & Obelisk Grays | Shallow pit houses. Storage facilities (cists). |  |
| Late BMII | Brownware | 400–500 | Obelisk Gray & brownware | Two large, aggregated communities with Great Kivas. |  |
| Archaic | – | pre-A.D. 1 | none | Unknown. |  |

**FIGURE 1.3**
*Chaco chronology (Thomas Windes).*

Timeline" (following page 392). The timeline covers Chacoan prehistory from 800 to 1300, but in this volume we pay particular attention to the span from about 850 to 1140, the Bonito phase. During this phase, Chaco reached its height with the construction of Pueblo Bonito and the other Great Houses and with its development as a center place.

Archaeologists have excavated at Chaco Canyon for more than a century (Frazier 1999; Lister and Lister 1981; Mathien 2005). That large investment of time and money has returned remarkable results, multiplied and compounded by several factors: arid climate and consequent good preservation; visibility, with scant plant cover, minimal soil development, and almost no later cultural superimposition; tree-ring dating, making Chaco the best dated prehistoric site anywhere; and a short, simple sequence (compared with Troy or Copán). Doing archaeology at Chaco is relatively easy, and many excellent archaeologists worked there over a long time. With all that high-quality work at an advantageous site, we should know a *lot* about Chaco. Thanks to those early archaeologists and Chaco's remote location and aridity, we do.

Richard Wetherill, the cowboy-archaeologist who discovered Mesa Verde, initiated excavations at Chaco in 1896, at its marquee site of Pueblo Bonito. His was the first of several major field projects sponsored by a variety of institutions: the American Museum of Natural History (with Wetherill) at Pueblo Bonito (1896–1900), the Smithsonian Institution and National Geographic Society at Pueblo Bonito and Pueblo del Arroyo (1921–1927), the Museum of New Mexico and the University of New Mexico at Chetro Ketl (1920–1934), and the National Park Service (NPS) at Kin Kletso (1950–1951). The last major field program, the NPS's Chaco Project, worked at Chaco from 1971 to 1982. Subsequent analytical work ended about 1986, although report writing continues to this day.

Chaco Canyon is at approximate latitude 36 degrees north, 108 degrees west, in the northwestern quarter of New Mexico, a piece of old Mexico acquired by the United States in 1848 (see figures 1.1 and 1.2). At Pueblo Bonito, the elevation is about 1,865 m (6,125 ft) above sea level. The canyon is near the center of the San Juan Basin (see figure 1.1; refer to plate 1). Archaeology borrowed the canyon's name from geology and refashioned it to indicate a region about 100 km in radius around Chaco, comprising the Chaco River drainage and nearby portions of the San Juan River (into which the Chaco flows, when it flows at all). The San Juan Basin is centered in the southeastern quarter of the Colorado Plateau, a vast uplifted region of canyons and mesas around the Four Corners.

The very largest Great Houses were concentrated in a 2-km-diameter "downtown" zone at the center of Chaco Canyon (see figure 1.2b; refer to plate 4). These include Pueblo Bonito (described below), Pueblo Alto (Windes 1987a, 1987b), Chetro Ketl (Lekson, ed., 1983), Pueblo del Arroyo (Judd 1959), Kin Kletso (Vivian and Mathews 1965), and many other monuments and smaller structures (Stein, Ford, and Friedman 2003). Architecture extends beyond this central zone. Doyel, Breternitz, and Marshall (1984) have proposed the "Chaco Halo," an oval area with a maximum radius from Pueblo Bonito of about 8.5 km, for the Chaco area beyond the immediate confines of the canyon. Many archaeologists extend the halo to encompass Great Houses up to 15 km or more from the park boundaries. Gwinn Vivian and others, in chapter 2 of this volume (refer to figure 2.1), refer to this as the "Chaco core." Forty to fifty km beyond the Chaco halo, or core, lie the boundaries of the San Juan Basin (described above; see figure 1.1), often considered more or less coterminous with the Chaco region. The scale of geographic interest for the Chaco world is perhaps even larger, however, extending over much of the Four Corners region (see figure 1.1; Kantner and Kintigh, chapter 5 of this volume).

Chaco Canyon's environment was harsh—a description overused in Southwestern archaeology but singularly applicable here. Summers are blisteringly hot; winters are wretchedly cold. The growing season is short, and rainfall uncertain. Indeed, water for basic domestic needs is (and was) a concern. The canyon contained little wood for building or burning and no outstanding local resources besides sandstone. At the turnoff from paved to dirt road, miles away from the canyon, a park service sign warns, "No wood, no food, no services at Chaco Canyon." Other necessities could be added to that list.

Why did the Bonito phase flourish in this desert canyon, when well-watered valleys lay to the north and south, closer to mountains and forests? Chaco's environment seems an unlikely setting for what happened there. Opinions on its import range widely: some archaeologists feel that Chaco's particular environment more or less explains the

9

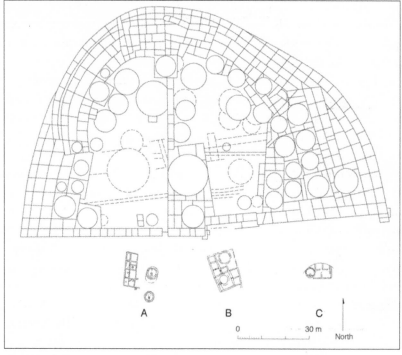

**FIGURE 1.4**

*Pueblo Bonito and unit pueblos: (a) Three C Site, early 1000s, (b) Bc 126, late 1000s to middle 1100s, and (c) Gallo Cliff Dwellings, 1200s. (Redrawn from plans in Lekson, ed., 1984a and McKenna and Truell 1986)*

Bonito phase, and others think that the Bonito phase shaped that environment to its needs. In any event, Chaco is a place where one cannot ignore nature. The environment, described in this volume by Gwinn Vivian and others (chapter 2), is critically important to our understanding of the Bonito phase.

## THE BONITO PHASE

The archaeology of Chaco Canyon centers on a dozen remarkable buildings called "Great Houses"—a motif of every chapter in this volume, but the particular theme of Lekson, Windes, and McKenna (chapter 3). Great Houses at Chaco (figures 1.4 and 3.1; see plates 5 and 6) began in the late ninth century as monumentally up-scaled versions of regular domestic structures—the small, single-family unit pueblos (see figure 1.4), also called "Prudden units" (Lipe, chapter 8) or "small sites" (McKenna, chapter 3), of the Pueblo I and Pueblo II periods. Shortly after 1000, Great Houses took a canonical turn in form and function that distinguished them thereafter from normal residences. An entire unit pueblo would fit in a single large room at a Chaco Great House.

In approximately one century, from 1020 to about 1125, the people at Chaco Canyon built the Great Houses, but each Great House has a unique construction history and several started much earlier. Pueblo Bonito was one of these early Great Houses (Judd 1954, 1964; Neitzel, ed., 2003; Pepper 1920) and is typical, perhaps archetypical, of Chaco Canyon Great Houses (see figure 1.4 and plate 5).

Pueblo Bonito took almost three centuries (850 to 1125) to build (Windes and Ford 1996). The "roads" of ancient Chaco (described later in this chapter) led viewers to the edge of Chaco's sheer sandstone cliffs, where they could behold the D-shaped ground plan. The building began as a huge version of Pueblo I unit pueblos, built three stories tall (normal unit pueblos were one short story). Pueblo I masonry was inadequate for multiple stories, so, when the rear wall of Pueblo Bonito began to fail in the early eleventh century, Chaco architects buttressed the old building by enveloping it in an exterior curtain wall of superior stonework. In many cases, they razed existing sections of Great Houses, including parts of Pueblo Bonito, to make way for new construction, but "Old Bonito" remained at the heart of the structure throughout its long history.

Beginning about 1020, the architects of Pueblo Bonito started a series of six major additions, each of which was enormously larger than anything previously built in the Pueblo world. At the culmination, about 1125, almost seven hundred rooms, stacked four and perhaps five stories tall, covered an area of about 0.8 ha. Only the outermost of Pueblo Bonito's rooms had sunlight; most of the interior rooms were dark and had limited access, suited (presumably) for storage. We now believe that only a score of families lived in this huge building (Bernardini 1999; Windes 1987a:383–392). They were very important families who controlled, or at least had access to, enormous numbers of large storage rooms.

Like other Great Houses, building Pueblo Bonito was expensive or laborious. That is, the labor-per-unit measure of floor area or roofed volume far exceeded that for unit pueblos. What distinguished Pueblo Bonito and the other Great Houses were site preparation (leveling and terracing); extensive foundations; massive, artfully coursed masonry walls; overtimbered roofs and ceilings (hundreds of thousands of large pine beams brought from distant forests); skillful carpentry, which can only be appreciated today from masonry remnants of elaborate wooden stairways, balconies, and porticos; and other features and furniture unique to these remarkable buildings. Among these last were colonnades (a Mesoamerican form, found at Chetro Ketl), unique raised platforms (for storage? sleeping?) within rooms at most Great Houses, and large sandstone disks (approximately 1 m diameter and 30 cm thick) stacked like pancakes as foundations or dedicatory monuments beneath major posts of Great Kivas (described later in this chapter).

Construction required a much larger, far more complex organization of labor than the family economy of unit pueblos. Life, too, was different. At Pueblo Bonito and other Great Houses, gangs of grinders prepared meals for larger groups in rooms devoted to batteries of corn-grinding *metates* fixed in bins. Archaeologists found huge ovens in Great House plazas where, presumably, people cooked for larger groups. The few families who actually lived in Pueblo Bonito could not have built it themselves. Likely, others built the huge structure and did much of the domestic work (grinding corn, cooking).

Pueblo Bonito was only one of a dozen Great Houses at Chaco. Great Houses were part of a large, sprawling, complex settlement. These massive buildings were clustered in downtown Chaco, and the cultural landscape included many other elements, such as roads, mounds, Great Kivas, and small sites.

Roads appear much as their name implies. Long, straight, wide (typically 9 m) engineered features linked sites to other sites and to natural places, simpler in construction but not unlike the causeways of La Quemada (Nelson, chapter 10 of this volume) and the *sacbe* of the ancient Maya. The Chacoans designed the roads for foot traffic. Where roads met cliffs, they constructed elaborate ramps or carved wide stairways out of the living rock. They valued the symbolic or monumental aspects of roads, however, as much as transportation. The dense network of roads in downtown Chaco, for example, created redundant, parallel routes clearly unnecessary for efficient pedestrian use. Roads were meant for something beyond simple transportation. This conclusion is probably also valid for roads running out from the canyon. Several are known to run many kilometers to the north, southwest, and west, but these roads may run to symbolically important natural features rather than to other sites (as Kantner and Kintigh note in chapter 5 of this volume; see plate 3). Other roads may be formally constructed only at their termini, where they approach or enter Great House complexes (Roney 1992).

Mounds encompassed a range of earthen structures with (presumably) a variety of purposes (figure 3.14). Most mounds are oval, sculpted accumulations of earth, trash, and construction debris. A few mounds have very formal geometric shapes. In front of Pueblo Bonito were two large, head-high, rectangular, masonry-walled, platform mounds, each larger than a basketball court. Stairs led up to their heavily plastered surfaces. We do not know what structures, if any, stood on these platforms. Other earthworks include large berms running alongside roads and huge "trash mounds" at some (but, importantly, not all) Great Houses (Windes 1987a, 1987b; Wills 2001).

Great Kivas were large, round, subterranean chambers up to 20 m or more in diameter; each was a single large room with an encircling bench, presumably to seat audiences for ritual or other performances (figure 3.8). Great Kivas had a very long history in Anasazi building, both before and after Chaco, but at Chaco Canyon and related sites they were built with the monumental technologies and scales of Great Houses. Great Kivas were not exclusive to Chaco, but Chacoan Great Kivas formed a class apart.

Small sites (unit pueblos, or Prudden units, and aggregates of several such units) were the final major element of Chaco Canyon architecture (see figures 1.4 and 3.11). Hundreds of small sites, clearly residential, line the canyon, particularly along the south cliffs. As discussed by Peter J. McKenna in chapter 3, the archaeology of small sites is critical to our understanding of the Bonito phase, and that archaeology is complex.

The artifacts of Chaco Canyon, with some very notable exceptions, resembled other contemporary Anasazi pottery and lithic industries. Chacoan artifacts and the organization of production are the themes of

Toll's chapter 4 in this volume. Many artifacts were actually manufactured in other Anasazi districts; for example, Chaco-related communities up to 50 to 60 km distant made most of the pottery found at certain Great Houses in Chaco. Conversely, at least one intriguing class of ceramic vessels existed almost exclusively at Chaco. Two rooms in Pueblo Bonito contained almost all of about two hundred known cylinder vases (resembling Mesoamerican forms; see Toll, chapter 4, and Nelson, chapter 10, of this volume).

Chaco Canyon, particularly Pueblo Bonito, is notable for long-distance imports, for example, about thirty-five copper bells and about thirty-five scarlet macaws, all presumably from western Mexico (Toll, chapter 4, and Nelson, chapter 10, of this volume). Chaco contains more of these "exotica" than any other eleventh-century Pueblo II site and, indeed, more than all other excavated Pueblo II sites combined. Turquoise, too, is conspicuous at Chaco Canyon and at Pueblo Bonito. Some estimates place the number of recovered pieces at more than one hundred thousand, mostly in the form of small discoidal beads. Many small and large sites at Chaco Canyon contained workshops for the manufacture of turquoise beads, but the source(s) of the stone was not local. The huge Cerrillos turquoise mines, 190 km southeast of Chaco near Santa Fe, New Mexico, are clearly implicated in Chacoan production of turquoise (Mathien 1986; Weigand and Harbottle 1993).

Whatever the nature of the Bonito phase, the context for our understanding must extend beyond the confines of Chaco Canyon. Chaco was the geographic (if not geometric) center of a large regional system marked by about two hundred smaller Great Houses (sometimes called "outliers") and roads (see figures 1.1 and 5.1). The nature of that regional system (even its reality) is a matter of much debate and the focus of Kantner and Kintigh's chapter 5 in this volume. The builders applied the same techniques and design principles for these smaller Great Houses, which are typically about one-twentieth the size of Pueblo Bonito or Chetro Ketl, as for the Chaco Canyon Great Houses. Usually, scattered communities of unit pueblos or small sites surround the Great Houses in this region.

At many outlier Great Houses, there are clear indications of roads, often pointing towards other Great Houses or to Chaco Canyon. Whether all road segments at outlier Great Houses actually continue the many miles to Chaco Canyon (or other destinations) is not clear, however. Most roads appear to be formally constructed only at their ends and are either less formal or completely absent in the stretches between termini (Roney 1992). Paralleling the roads (real and projected) was a remarkable network of fire-signal or mirror-signal stations, typically represented by large, formal masonry fireboxes placed on pinnacles or high spots (for example, Hayes and Windes 1975). This line-of-sight signaling network remains understudied but may extend (with one or two "repeater" stations) to the most distant Great Houses. The geographic distribution of Great Houses, Great House communities, road segments, and signaling stations extends over 80,000 sq km. Some archaeologists believe, however, that Chaco Canyon during the Bonito phase directly influenced only the immediate San Juan Basin or a small radius immediately around the canyon itself. Almost every chapter of this book discusses the nature of the Chacoan region and the canyon's role there.

What was the Bonito phase? How should we characterize it as a society and polity? Archaeological interpretations of the Bonito phase have altered greatly over the past hundred years. Interpretations change with new data, and we have indeed learned much about Chaco. But evolving interpretations also reflect the fluid nature of American archaeology. The intellectual framework of archaeology is not static; ideas about the past reflect the archaeological knowledge and theory of their times. Chapter 6, by Judge and Cordell, presents a reconstruction of Chaco that favors ritual over political (congruent with many archaeologists' current ideas). Other chapters in this volume offer views ranging from a centralized political hierarchy to a ceremonially based pilgrimage center, or even a hierarchically organized rituality.

In assessing our arguments, the reader should recall the history of changing interpretations of the Bonito phase. The first excavators of Pueblo Bonito and Chetro Ketl, working long before the development of tree-ring dating, looked on these sites as early versions of modern pueblos, that is, as prehistoric pueblos before colonial impacts. Neil Judd (at Pueblo Bonito) and Edgar Hewett (at Chetro Ketl) turned first and foremost to Pueblo colleagues for interpretive counsel. The equivalence of past and present was direct and unquestioned. During an era when archaeology was essentially culture history, the Bonito phase seemed to fit in to a steady historical progression of the Pecos System, within the "Great Pueblo" (Pueblo III) period. Great Houses compared well with the large sites of Pueblo III and Pueblo IV.

Tree-ring dating, developed in the 1920s, revealed that the Bonito phase dated instead to Pueblo II. That created a quandary. Compared with unit pueblos, Great Houses were remarkably, even disturbingly, large. Moreover, tree-ring dating demonstrated that the Bonito-phase Great Houses were contemporary with much smaller sites in Chaco Canyon. That is, at least two styles of architecture existed in Chaco Canyon during the Bonito phase: monumental Great Houses and smaller, less formal sites typical of Pueblo II throughout the Anasazi region. Some interpreted Chaco as a multiethnic community, with Great Houses representing one ethnic group (or more) and small houses, another (Kluckhohn 1939; Vivian and Mathews 1965; Vivian 1990).

The early dating of the Bonito phase (Pueblo II, not the expected Pueblo III) prompted other archaeologists in the 1950s and 1960s to question the Bonito phase's place in the Anasazi (Ancestral Pueblo) sequence. Was the Bonito phase the result of influence or import from the high civilizations of Mexico? Many archaeologists, including key Chaco Project archaeologists (Hayes 1981; Lister 1978), concluded that the Bonito phase was the result of Mesoamerican influences. Opinion was sharply divided, and James Judge (1989:233) could accurately summarize Chacoan thinking of that time as either "Mexicanist" or "indigenist."

The New Archaeology of the 1970s and early 1980s favored local adaptation over diffusion, migration, and extraregional influences. In that intellectual atmosphere, researchers rejected Mesoamerican explanations in favor of the evolution of the Bonito phase as a "complex cultural ecosystem" (Judge 1979). New Archaeology posited complex political structures, locally developed but still out of place in a gradual culture history from ancient Anasazi to modern Pueblo. Managerial elites, chiefs, and other complex political structures went far beyond conventional, egalitarian Pueblo models. Again, opinion was divided. The most heated debates centered on sites in Arizona; Chaco was (generally but not universally) accepted without undue cavil as a "complex" society, that is, a centralized political hierarchy (for example, pro: Schelberg 1984; Wilcox 1993, 1999; Vivian 1990).

Postprocessual approaches of the 1990s and early 2000s reconfigured Chaco to fit postmodern tastes. Influenced by European revision (and rejection) of Neolithic chiefdoms, Southwestern archaeologists began to explore and extol ceremony at Chaco, favoring rituality over polity (Mills 2002; Wills 2000, 2001; Yoffee 2001; and Judge and Cordell, chapter 6 of this volume). Postprocessual approaches also reestablished culture history and contingency as equally important as, or more important than, the evolutionary generalities of New Archaeology. As discussed in following sections of this introduction, regulatory requirements for "culture affiliation" reinforced historical interests. The congruence of postprocessual historicity and legally mandated affiliation studies encouraged an archaeology not unlike culture history of the 1940s and 1950s, but with greater methodological sophistication (we hope).

Below, I discuss the current division of opinion between rituality and polity at Chaco (see also Sebastian's concluding chapter 12 and several other chapters in this volume). Unlike the stark dichotomy of Mexicanists and indigenists in the 1970s, both ritual and political are important in understanding the Bonito phase. Few researchers would claim one to the exclusion of the other; it is a matter, rather, of degree. To view Chaco data with both ritual and political emphases is legitimate and appropriate, for the data sustains both interests.

We focus on the Bonito phase because the Chaco Culture National Historical Park was created to preserve and display the monumental ruins of the Bonito phase and because the Bonito phase and its contexts largely structured the Chaco Project's research. There would be no park and no Chaco Project absent Bonito-phase ruins. People used Chaco Canyon in the Archaic many centuries before Pueblo Bonito, and people called Chaco home long after, evidenced by Navajo homes and Navajo names for Bonito-phase ruins: Kin Kletso, Tsin Kletzin, Wijiji. The Chaco Project investigated earlier and later periods at Chaco but sought principally to understand Chaco's raison d'etre, the Bonito phase. And so do we, here.

## THE CHACO PROJECT

The Chaco Project was almost certainly the last major archaeological research program at Chaco of our lifetimes (or at least my lifetime—I am feeling pretty feeble, so, younger scholars, take hope). The NPS continues to do exemplary work at sites threatened by natural or human impacts, but the era of large-scale research programs—and particularly major excavations—has passed. This makes the Chaco Project's work all the more significant.

The Chaco Project spanned interesting times in American archaeology. It was conceived as culture history; the fieldwork and laboratory analyses developed as New Archaeology. The research was largely completed before the passage of the Native American Graves Protection and Repatriation Act (NAGPRA), but that law (discussed below) deeply affected the present volume. To varying degrees, the interpretations of Chaco (and of the Chaco Project) presented here reflect postprocessual sensibilities adapted to Southwestern practices (as exemplified by Hegmon 2003).

Because the history of the Chaco Project is well told by Joan Mathien (2005; see also Frazier 2005) and summarized by Wilshusen and Hamilton (chapter 11 of this volume), I give a very brief review of that story here. During the late 1960s, just as the huge Wetherill Mesa Project was winding down at Mesa Verde, NPS archaeologist John Corbett first advanced the idea of a large field project at Chaco. Corbett asked the School of American Research in Santa Fe to host a three-day planning conference, January 8–11, 1969. From that conference, Wilfred Logan and Zorro Bradley developed a research *Prospectus* (National Park Service 1969) for a multidisciplinary partnership between the University of New Mexico and the NPS. The *Prospectus* was wide ranging, addressing not only archaeological research but also NPS needs (for example, preservation of structures) and an admirable variety of natural science studies. The project began in 1970, intended to last ten years. It officially ended in 1986, and, thirty years after its inception, several reports are still in preparation.

Fieldwork began in 1971. Initially, Robert Lister and Alden Hayes directed the research. The project expanded significantly in scale with the excavation of Pueblo Alto (Windes 1987a, 1987b), which coincided roughly with the retirement of Lister and the arrival of W. James Judge as director. At one point (in 1977), more than thirty people were working on Chaco Project field research, including part-time field labor. Judge brought New Archaeology credentials to the Chaco Project and subsequently modified the research goals. Work at Pueblo Alto, the last major field project, ended in 1979. (Minor field projects continued sporadically and, even today, have not quite ceased.)

Analyses and writing reached a crescendo about 1986 when staffing was cut and the office moved from the University of New Mexico in Albuquerque to Santa Fe. But work still continues. A small but dedicated team of NPS archaeologists is completing technical reporting of the project. The cost of fieldwork, analysis, publication, curation, and other matters totaled more than six million dollars. $

The Chaco Project was a multifaceted affair including many natural science studies, remote sensing projects, Navajo archaeology and history, and cultural resource management in and around the park. We are concerned here with the archaeological program. After completing archaeological surveys, the Chaco Project excavated more than twenty prehistoric sites from all time periods, culminating in work at Pueblo Alto (one of the largest Bonito-phase sites). Excavations recovered 1.5 million artifacts and produced 150 linear feet of field notes, thousands of maps, and more than forty thousand photos. Twenty technical monographs were published in two series and sent to most university and many city libraries: *Reports of the Chaco Center* and NPS's *Publications in Archaeology*. (With the exception of two titles reprinted by the University of New Mexico Press and widely available, Chaco Project reports are of readier access than conventional "gray literature" but less widely distributed than real books.) Journal articles, book chapters, theses, dissertations, and other shorter, "official" Chaco Project contributions numbered more than sixty. During the Chaco Project's salad days, media coverage was heavy, including PBS documentaries and trade books (Frazier 1986, 1999). But there was never a final synthesis to evaluate and discuss the manifold findings of the Chaco Project.

## THE CHACO SYNTHESIS

In 1996 Robert Powers of the NPS asked me to consider how a final synthesis might look. My credentials were a ten-year association with the Chaco Project (1976–1986) and famously poor judgment regarding foolish risks. I accepted Bob's challenge, and the result is this book. A complementary effort was already underway. Joan Mathien's (2005) volume on the history and results of the Chaco Project detailed site excavations and what they produced. Mathien's book was to be volume one of a two-volume set, of which the present book is the second.

I suspect that Bob Powers anticipated my offering to author that second volume alone, much as Mathien authored volume one. But I felt strongly that I feel too strongly about Chaco Lekson's Chaco (despite the fact that it is gospel truth) is not widely accepted. The Chaco Project's work was too important for me to control, intellectually, a final synthetic effort. Instead, I proposed a series of small thematic conferences mixing Chaco Project staff and other Chaco "insiders" with interesting and/or influential "outsiders." From the beginning, I insisted that the conferences focus *inside the canyon* (because that is where the Chaco Project spent your money and did its work) and on the Bonito phase (the central matter of both park and project).

The Chaco Synthesis, as it ultimately evolved, was complex and moderately elaborate (refer to appendix A). After many meetings with Bob Powers, Dabney Ford, and NPS staff, after long conversations with Chaco specialists, and after planning palavers with several Distinguished Conference Organizers, we settled on structures and themes for the conferences: "Economy and Ecology" would deal with environment and subsistence; "Organization of Production" would cover artifacts; "Architecture" would go beyond the Bonito-phase buildings to consider the landscape; and "Society and Polity" would aim at these aspects of the Bonito phase. (There were other, ancillary conferences and activities, too, discussed below.) We added one more working conference, "Chaco World," addressing the Chaco beyond the canyon. Despite our focus inside the canyon, synthesizing Chaco without some formal reference to its region seemed reckless. The Chaco Project did a bit of work outside the canyon (and we wish that we had done more). More important, young scholars are currently paying much attention to the Chaco regional system and outliers, and those fresh voices should be heard (for example, Kantner and Mahoney 2000). Therefore, we decided to have a Chaco World conference, organized not by Chaco Project staff or senior Chaco scholars but by younger researchers conducting fieldwork on outliers.

For each conference, I recruited two insider organizers: Chaco specialists, usually but not always Chaco Project staff. To work, I thought, each conference should be small, six or seven people at most, ideally with three or four insiders and three outsiders (discussed below). I recused myself on the question of who would be invited, but in practice I was often consulted. I would then work with the organizers to support the logistics of their conference and the publication of the results. Each conference would produce a half-dozen papers, which we would financially support and assist into appropriate journals or books. Each conference would produce insights that were to be translated, somehow, up to a final capstone conference. The form of that translation and, indeed, the nature of the final conference itself (which generated this book) developed over many months. I will discuss the capstone after briefly evaluating the six working meetings that led up to the capstone, as well as the ancillary activities that paralleled those meetings.

The plan had political and geographic dimensions. I wanted to involve most or all major archaeological institutions in the Southwest as host institutions. We held sessions at Arizona State University, the University of Arizona, the University of New Mexico, Fort Lewis College, the University of Colorado, and the School of American Research (and, of course, at Chaco Canyon). I had hoped to have a session at the Museum of Northern Arizona, but that did not work out.

Although this volume focuses on the Chaco Project, it borrows heavily from other, earlier projects. Despite our program's name, *Chaco Synthesis*, we cannot synthesize (in a comprehensive sense) the Chaco Project, much less the enormous contributions of other Chaco research programs. Gratefully and humbly, we do acknowledge past research and the ongoing work of researchers not directly involved in this volume. A glance at our references will indicate the depth and breadth of our debt to other archaeologists.

I tried to include all the major thinkers on Chaco, in one capacity or another. The insiders were supposed to be Chaco Center staff (and, alas, only selected members of that staff, to keep things small), but we enlarged that list to include a few people who were obviously essential, such as Gwinn Vivian, Lynne Sebastian, and others who co-authored chapters here. A few very important Chaco scholars did not participate in the project; offers of various roles were made and (for various reasons) declined. Still, I knew that hurt feelings and annoyance were inevitable reactions, so I told conference organizers to blame exclusions on me and my insistence on small meetings. That avoided, I hoped, undue blame and calumny for hard-pressed conference organizers.

Outsiders were the key part of the program. I did not envision the customary discussant role; I wanted outsiders to really engage the data. Insider organizers would, ideally, lead our guests through the relevant publications long before the meeting. I wanted fresh eyes and fresh ideas to break us out of internal bickerings.

Also, I was quite open about using the project to advertise Chaco data to a larger world via outsiders. I hoped that they would broadcast the potential of these data to their personal circles and networks. Southwestern archaeology is choking on its own overabundant data (compared with other regions of the world) and is perhaps too provincial (we seldom compare our sites with other regions of the world). To me, exporting data or rumors of data via outsiders seemed to be one solution.

Outsiders certainly made things interesting for insiders. Many insiders were tired of Chaco (more accurately, bored to tears)—including me, perhaps particularly. The chance to work with interesting outsiders, though, revved up recalcitrant organizers for yet another round of Chaco.

Almost every working conference included open sessions or public presentations, which were well attended. For two reasons, I was also interested in extending the scope of the synthesis to the arts and humanities: first, this might move Chaco out of anthropology and Native American studies and into other disciplines, and, second, this might address humanistic yearnings so evident in contemporary American archaeology. I proposed two events, one focusing on words and another on arts. The former, titled (for political reasons) "Chaco, Mesa Verde and the Confrontation with Time," was organized by Patricia Limerick and me. It brought together essayists, historians, poets, and journalists. The session was great fun, but no product has appeared. A parallel event, tentatively titled "Seeing Chaco," would display and discuss fine art (photography, easel art, computer graphics, sculpture). I planned it as an adjunct activity for the capstone conference, but I ran out of time and energy. "Seeing Chaco" never happened, but it should.

Public representation of the Chaco Project was an important goal of the program from its very inception. Indeed, Powers and his NPS colleagues envisioned a single book that would simultaneously appeal to professional and public audiences. I disagreed, and in the end we produced this book, which (I hope) will have a large professional readership and perhaps appeal to Chaco fans of every stripe. But this is not a coffee table book. My attempts to entice several notable science writers to attend all the conferences came to naught (our schedule was unrealistic for high-caliber writers). We were extremely fortunate in having three parallel, collaborative projects that will provide excellent print products for larger audiences: books by David Noble, Kendrick Frazier, and Brian Fagan. Noble (1984), serendipitously, was considering a revision of his highly successful *New Light on Chaco Canyon*, a well illustrated, well edited collection of chapters by various Chaco scholars. Noble's interest coincided exactly with our capstone conference, from which he recruited many authors for his revision. Under Noble's excellent editorial guidance, these authors summarized their areas of interest in the Chaco Synthesis. (This was doubly happy in that Noble's publisher is the School of American Research, a party to the very beginnings of the Chaco Project and publisher of the present volume.) The resulting volume, *In Search of Chaco* (Noble 2004), is a superb blend of up-to-date archaeology and Native American insights. Ken Frazier (2005) was preparing a third edition of his excellent *People of Chaco* and included a new chapter on the Chaco Synthesis Project (Frazier 2005). At our invitation and with full support of our project, Brian Fagan has written an excellent book titled *Chaco Canyon: Archaeologists Explore the Lives of an Ancient Society* (2005).

Early in the project, Kim Malville (University of Colorado) and Dan Yankofsky began a web page, a "Chaco Virtual Conference." The aim was to engage broader archaeological and nonarchaeological audiences in the synthesis via the web; in the end, that did not happen to the extent we had hoped. Malville's web page remains a useful compendium of preconference and conference data. Another web resource resulted from the Chaco World conference, a web-accessible database of Great Houses (see Kantner and Kintigh, chapter 5 of this volume). Also, serendipitously, Steve Plog (University of Virginia) launched a Chaco Digital Archive project just as the synthesis was winding down. Although the synthesis is not directly involved, we anticipate transfer of our records to Plog's digital archive.

Lynne Sebastian organized the capstone conference. Like the sessions leading up to it, the capstone conference was intended to be small (fewer than a dozen participants), but, like those earlier sessions, it grew like Topsy. To keep any of the meetings as small as I had wanted was simply impossible. When the capstone finally convened in October 2002, there were at least forty people in the room, not including a large video team capturing it all on tape. With an audience so large, there was, inevitably, as much presentation as conversation. Sebastian managed it very well, however, and they accomplished much good work (as demonstrated by her chapter 12 in this volume). Understandably, as newly elected president of the Society of American Archaeology, Sebastian demurred from editing the present volume. At the capstone, I was charged to undertake that task.

When I approached the School of American Research about publishing this book, the idea arose of a smaller post-capstone conference at the school. The principals from the first capstone were understandably dubious—what *more* could we say about Chaco? With only one exception, they did agree to reconvene at the school and continue discussions curtailed or constrained by time and tide at the capstone. The School of American Research session—small, relaxed, conversational—was a delightful and extremely worthwhile coda to the long Chaco Synthesis.

The Chaco Synthesis was great fun and (I think) fruitful in its many activities and products. It cost a bit of money. The NPS supported the synthesis generously, to a total of about $216,000. That figure represents less than 4 percent of the six-million-dollar Chaco Project budget for fieldwork, analysis, and curation. If adjusted for inflation, that fraction would be much lower (dollars in 2000 were worth less than half their 1980 value). We more than doubled the NPS funding through contributions in cash and kind from the institutions that hosted sessions and from University of Colorado grants. Our total expenditures for the synthesis, NPS and contributed, probably represent about 3 percent, or less, of the total funds expended for the Chaco Project, adjusted for inflation.

The Chaco Synthesis's scholarly archaeological conferences were traditional in format and conduct. A new generation would do it differently, perhaps with greater use of the web. I believe that each conference worked very well in its own way; the reader must judge for himself. The papers representing the working conferences (chapters 2–6) and

Lynne Sebastian's "synthesis of the synthesis" (chapter 12) constitute the core of this volume. I solicited additional chapters on contexts of ancient Chaco (chapters 8–10) and the Chaco Project itself (chapter 11).

## WHERE ARE THE INDIANS?

None of the authors are Native American. Why not?

The Chaco Project began in the late 1960s. Archaeologists and Indians stood in a very different relationship then than they do today. Many Native Americans worked for the Chaco Project as laborers. Many were valued colleagues, and more than a few became good friends. But no Native Americans were involved in the development and direction of Chaco Project research. This is not a condemnation of the Chaco Project. Few, if any, archaeological programs incorporated Native Americans in the late 1960s and early 1970s. Today, that has changed, and archaeology is better for it.

To redress the past in the present was agonizingly difficult, and, in the end, impossible. Many Native Americans were involved in the synthesis, but I had hoped to have a Native American writer attend all the conferences and "report out" in a chapter or a separate book. That did not happen. I also planned to have a working conference of Native American tribal representatives, scholars, writers, and artists that would address two questions: what do you want the public to know about Chaco? and why? ("Nothing" and "None of your business" would have been acceptable answers, but I had higher hopes.) That did not happen either.

Native American involvement, or underinvolvement, was the single biggest flaw in the project, and the reason was this: a very difficult NAG-PRA dispute over Chaco broke out right at the start of the synthesis project. This is not the place to recount specifics; in brief, Hopis and other Pueblos objected to NPS's inclusion of the Navajo Nation in NAGPRA agreements. (My impression is that all concerned are doing the right thing, but the "right thing" is seen differently by the various groups and agencies.)

Because of the significant NPS funds and full NPS backing for the synthesis, our actions were (justifiably) seen as indicative, but not official. If I included Navajos, the Pueblos were alarmed at an evident expert opinion. If I excluded Navajos, the Navajos were understandably disturbed.

I proposed several individual writers for participation; all were Pueblo. The NPS was wary. I approached several excellent Native American historians from tribes not Southwestern. They were wary. I went several times before Chaco's large Native American Advisory Board, begging guidance. The board was wary. I spoke to individual tribes. The tribes were wary. No solution appeared that would not entangle the NAGPRA situation. After two years, I gave up trying.

In the end, the NAGPRA situation (unresolved even as I write) made it impossible to organize "official" Native American sessions or products. To nearly every conference, we invited Native Americans as individuals (botanists, poets, historians), not as tribal representatives. These people would have been invited in any event because their knowledge and intelligence would have added immeasurably to our work. All of us, though, would have welcomed more formal collaboration with the tribes, Pueblo and Navajo.

Finally, a solution materialized. In a happy coincidence (over three years of opportunistic planning, there were several happy coincidences!), Chaco National Park had collaborated with Gary Warriner of Camera One to create a new eponymous video about the canyon, *Chaco* (Warriner 2000). Production preceded the NAGPRA situation, and Warriner proceeded with a freedom we did not have. The voices on the video are almost entirely Native American. (Archaeology is conspicuous by its absence.) Members of Chaco's Native American Advisory Board appear, and appear very well indeed. *Chaco* is a superb presentation of Indian perspectives on the canyon. Perhaps this is the product my thwarted Native American conference would have produced. I like to think so. The video nearly fills the hole so evident in the synthesis project but was not affiliated in any way with our work. David Noble's (2004) *In Search of Chaco* includes excellent essays by Pueblo and Navajo writers, in addition to chapters by many Chaco Synthesis participants. Again, a happy coincidence.

## WHERE IS LEKSON?

A question far less important than participation of Native Americans, I admit, but still of some interest to your author. My role in the Chaco Synthesis was to raise and spend money, organize the organizers, and (for the architecture conference) step in when a proposed organizer became unavailable. I considered running the capstone conference (a carrot at the end of my personal stick), but I came to my senses and convinced a very busy Lynne Sebastian to do it (and she did a far better job than ever I would). I organized the post-capstone session at the School of American Research because I did not dare ask any of the principals to do that. I had solemnly promised that Sebastian's capstone was our last and final act. Also, I wrote two-thirds of "Architecture" (chapter 3) and a quarter of "Notes from the South" (chapter 9) in this book—the latter, again, after a planned contributor withdrew.[1]

Otherwise, I avoided (as far as possible) planning or staging individual meetings and conferences. Given my strong opinions about Chaco, I felt honor-bound not to load decks, rig juries, pull wires, and self-fulfill prophecies. While I helped to shape form, I tried not to meddle with content.

Consequently, I disagree with many statements, conclusions, and interpretations in the excellent chapters that follow (while I very much respect the authors of those opinions). Here is my chance, at last. The sessions are done, the chapters are finished, and what I say cannot bias the outcome. I conclude this introduction with a few calm, dispassionate observations on a Chacoan matter that seems, to me, important.

### Matters

What is important is this: Chaco had rulers, leaders, centralized hierarchical decision makers. Why flog that dead horse? Complexity is so seventies. Professors today were bored with complexity before their current students were even born. I drag this shibboleth out from under the carpet where it was swept, because it is important. Explaining why will take some exposition.

Recall Gregory Johnson's (1989) famous pronouncement that "Chaco data can support a basically egalitarian interpretation." I have always wondered what data Johnson was shown, but no matter; his was certainly not the last authoritative deflation of Chacoan hierarchy. Essays reaching similarly nonhierarchical conclusions include those by respected arbiters such as Norman Yoffee (2001; Yoffee, Fish, and Milner 1999; to be fair, Yoffee sees hierarchal structure at Chaco, but not the political hierarchy here termed "complexity") and Collin Renfrew (2001). Warren DeBoer (2001:24), a trenchant and insightful critic, mocked Southwestern pretensions: "Are Southwestern archaeologists still recovering from Johnson's devastating critique, trying to reinvent their own brand of home-grown complexity? Why does a regional archaeology wish to find complexity? Is complexity a positively valued polarity? Does it get grants?"

In the face of such formidable opposition, it would seem prudent now for pro-complexity Southwesternists to strike their tents. But I argue, below, that Southwestern complexity is not an empty exercise, a professional brass ring. Claims for complexity at Chaco have consequences for modern political philosophy and, in a small but real way, for the history of the twentieth century—gone these five years, but not forgotten.

Complexity has become unfashionable, out of step with our times. It definitely does not get grants. Many (most?) contemporary Southwesternists are not in sympathy with political hierarchy at Chaco (for example, Mills 2002; Saitta 1997; and Wills 2000, among others). Many favor reconstructions of Chaco that are nonhierarchical, decentralized, pleasantly un-complex. In an important volume on "alternative leadership strategies in the prehispanic Southwest" (Mills 2000), the lead essay is a new reading of Chaco by Chaco Project alumnus Chip Wills. He concludes that, while Chaco "involved leaders," its glory days were shaped and driven by "communitas or anti-structure" (Wills 2000:41, 43).

Is it that Great Houses happened, happily, communally? Have we come full circle, back to Edgar Hewett's "ants heaping up great mounds far in excess of actual needs"? No. Wills and other recent authors allow leaders to direct the formic heaping. Chaco was too big to just happen. It is the nature of leadership that is at issue: something political, permanent, and hierarchical or something ritual and ceremonial, spiritual, situational, and evanescent?

Ritual interests are, in part, homegrown (witness the 1980s discovery of a plethora of Southwestern cults) and, in part, an import from European and particularly British archaeologies that, in their Berg and Routledge manifestations, eschew hierarchy in favor of ceremony (witness the rise of Southwestern alternative leadership strategies in the 1990s). The appeal of ritual also owes something, un- or under-recognized, to the relentless, seemingly unstoppable teleology from the archaeological past toward the Pueblo present. To simplify (enormously), Pueblos in the present, we think, are ritual and not political; therefore, the past—and Chaco—should also be ritual and not political.

If modern Pueblos favor ritual and ceremony over political power, that is really interesting. How did that come about, historically? I think that Chaco played a role—a key role—but it was not a step or stage along a gradual road to an egalitarian Pueblo ethos. Pueblos did not *develop from* Chaco; rather, they represent a *reaction against* Chaco. To compress Pueblo accounts, Chaco was a wonderful, awful place where "people got power over people" (according to Paul Pino, in Sofaer 1999). What happened at Chaco was not right for Pueblo people  (today), and Chaco is remembered that way (today). The remarkable shifts in Pueblo architecture, settlement, iconography, and society around 1300, when sites begin to look like modern pueblos, represent Pueblo peoples' conscious, deliberate reaction to and rejection of Chaco, distancing themselves from that bad experience. Pueblos developed new ways and means to avoid anything like Chaco, ever again. These social and philosophical "leveling mechanisms" are remarkable, almost unique, in the anthropology of agricultural societies.

To paraphrase, with apologies, what I have learned from Pueblo people, Chaco was wrong. Modern Pueblos do not do it that way. Yet, many archaeologists look to modern Pueblos and historic accounts of Pueblos for insights, transportable models of how Chaco worked (for example, Stuart 2000; Vivian 1990; Ware 2001; and various chapters in this volume). My question, which comes from my first days of thinking about Chaco, is this: whatever archaeological inspiration may be found in modern Pueblos, east or west, *why did they never build anything like Chaco*? I think that they did not want to; they had been there and done that.

After 1300, Pueblos turned their energies to other matters and never again raised up a city. Later villages were larger than individual Great Houses—a point I made (graphically, two decades ago) by fitting Pueblo Bonito into Taos's plaza with room to spare—but the peoples of Hopi, Zuni, Acoma, and the Rio Grande chose not to build another Chaco. Chaco may have continued in city-size Aztec Ruins and Paquimé—a long story I will not retell here (Lekson 1999)—but that history is tangent or parallel to the path Pueblo peoples chose. Why seek models for Chaco among modern Pueblos? Histories, memories, lessons—yes, to be sure, all of those and more. But Pueblo people reject the incorrect actions and institutions of their errant ancestors at Chaco Canyon and created new, deliberately different societies. Pueblos do not have political leaders (at least, as we recognize political leaders), *but Chaco did.* I now look at three lines of evidence that support this assertion: high-status burials, elite residences, and regional primacy.

We have seen Chaco's rulers, archaeologically, in the high-status burials from Pueblo Bonito and, particularly, the very rich crypt burials of two middle-aged men (Akins 2001, 2003; Akins and Schelberg 1984). I interpret scores of additional bodies piled above these burials as "retainers." These two men were buried in the mid-eleventh century (in my opinion), deep in the much earlier rooms of the original, early tenth-century Old Bonito. Watch them closely; these burials tend to vanish in Chacoan debates. Barbara Mill's excellent summary of "Recent Research on Chaco" dismisses them as "a few unusual burials" (Mills 2002:66). Were there only two such rulers? Perhaps, over a century's span (Chaco's glory days, from 1020 to 1125) two "kings" might be all that were required. More high-status burials might exist in other, partially excavated Great Houses.

These two men may well have been the rulers remembered as "our kings"—a term used by a traditional Native American man from the Chaco area. They may have been principals among those "people at Chaco who gained power over people"—improperly, disastrously, in present Pueblo worldview—alluded to by Paul Pino from the Pueblo of Laguna. Pino said, "In our history we talk of things that occurred a long time ago [at Chaco], of people who had enormous amounts of power: spiritual power and power over people....These people were causing changes that were never meant to occur" (in Sofaer 1999). Other Pueblo accounts similarly describe stern political leaders and their city, which rose and fell in ancient times (summarized in Lekson 1999:143–150).

Pueblo people tell us that Chaco had political rulers, and Navajos concur. Archaeologists, however, demur. Found anywhere else in the world, the high-status burials of Pueblo Bonito would strongly suggest political power. High-status burials are ripe evidence of elites and leaders. At the capstone conference, I referred to these men as kings because a Native American colleague (at the Architecture working meeting) told me to call them kings. His point? Europeans have kings, but Indians are allowed only chiefs. I thought about medieval Irish kings and Mississippian chiefs and agreed; *chief* is iniquitous (and, in any event, anthropologically dubious). Let us call them kings and see where that leads. To riot. My use of *king* deeply annoyed my capstone colleagues. Why? We have to call these men something. *Chief* is not a Native American word, nor is *ruler, leader,* or *centralized, hierarchical decision maker,* or *shaman* or *priest,* for that matter. If we are to use European terms, why not *king*? If it looks like a duck, walks like a duck, and quacks like a duck....

They had rulers. Not only have we exhumed their bodies, but also we have turned their stately homes into a national park. My second set of evidence consists of Great Houses. The single, central fact of Chaco is Great *Houses,* not Great Temples. (Recall that the Great Kivas are not specific to Chaco; Lekson, Windes, and McKenna, chapter 3 of this volume.) Great Houses are among the most remarkable, unambiguous examples of pre-state stratified housing that I have found in the literatures of anthropology, geography, and architecture. Great Houses were first (tenth century) and foremost (through the eleventh century) elite residences (see also Neitzel 2003). That much of the Chacoan building was ritual and ceremonial I do not doubt (roads, platform mounds, Great Kivas, perhaps waterworks), but monumental elite residences dominated the landscape then (and do now). The same review that dismissed the kingly burials as "unusual" also disposed of Great Houses: "The construction of Great Houses was not accompanied by obvious signs of status and hierarchy, such as social ranking [or] palaces" (Mills 2002:66). Umm, excuse me, Great Houses *are* palaces. Great Houses—elite residences—are monumentally obvious signs of hierarchy, hidden in plain sight. As long as we are getting into trouble with *kings,* let us see what happens when we call them palaces (Lekson, McKenna, and Windes, chapter 3 of this volume). Outrage! *Palaces* imply states, and Native states are not allowed north of Mexico.

I will not fight that fight here. Fine (for now), no states north of Mexico. Perhaps palaces can exist without the state (cities can exist without the state; McIntosh and McIntosh 2003!) The 1980s and 1990s have seen the rejection of conventional, lock-step political taxonomies.

The old order of band, tribe, chiefdom, and state is confounded, deconstructed. Perhaps the various elements we have used in defining political stages can have lives and histories of their own. Perhaps palaces have a trajectory disentangled from surpluses or armies or writing. That happened, it seems, at Chaco: monumental elite residences, palaces without the state.

The third and final category of data that seems, to me, strong evidence for hierarchy is the regional system—Chaco's place in a region of Great Houses. (Please note that my views contrast in many regards with those of Kantner and Kintigh, chapter 5, and other chapters in this volume.) Chaco sits at the center of a region of remarkable clarity. I use *clarity* in two senses: archaeological observation and prehistoric vision. The Chacoan region is as clear an archaeological signature as we may hope to find in pre-state societies. Chacoan Great Houses are recognizable from Cedar Mesa in Utah to Quemado in New Mexico, from Hopi in Arizona to Guadalupe in New Mexico. It took a decade of hard argument to convince stubbornly local archaeologists that their "unusually large site" was, in fact, one of 150 Great Houses. Most archaeologists agreed, if grudgingly, that there was a pattern in the Pueblo region during the eleventh and twelfth centuries: Great House, mounds, roads, and associated communities of unit pueblos and Great Kivas. I called this pattern Chacoan (Lekson 1991), but it could be called anything if Chacoan offends (should we say ducky? or, more formally, anatidoid?). More important than the name is the reality, the empirical pattern of hundreds of small Great Houses, with Chaco at the center.

Roads are a famous part of the Chacoan regional pattern. Initially, we thought that roads formed a network, an infrastructure for the Chaco region; that does not seem to be the case. Much about the roads remains uncertain; their physical continuity and their functions have come into question (for example, Roney 1992). Some roads apparently are discontinuous; others run visibly for miles. As noted above, most roads were monuments, not solely (or even principally) transportation corridors. The Great North Road is trotted out (and trotted on) as an example of a ritual, nonfunctional road. It reputedly goes nowhere (at least in this world); it is said to end with a stairway into a deep canyon that represents a *shipap* or place of emergence (Marshall 1997). Chaco ritualists repeat this intriguingly symbolic interpretation as gospel. But it is a canard (speaking, as we were, of ducks). It is simply not true. The Great North Road continues beyond its legendary termination at the lip of Kutz Canyon. Twin Angels Pueblo is obviously a road-related Great House, on the alignment of the Great North Road as it doglegs down Kutz Canyon, more than a mile beyond its descent into the putative symbolic shipap.

Real, tangible evidence in the form of a Great House (with road features galore) demonstrates (as well as any evidence used to substantiate roads) that the North Road continues down Kutz Canyon beyond its famous but false termination at a purely symbolic shipap. Because Salmon Ruins sits a few miles farther down Kutz Canyon, it seems reasonable to project the road beyond Twin Angels to Salmon. For now, the important point is that the North Road does not end at "nowhere." Ritualists may prefer a road to nowhere, but the North Road's continuance down through Kutz Canyon is as much an archaeological fact as the North Road itself. I do not doubt that the North Road and all roads were heavily, even primarily symbolic, but the North Road, at least, went somewhere. Maybe other roads did too.

Now I will briefly revisit the history of road research (see Vivian 1997a and 1997b for details). Navajos reported roads to early archaeologists, who scoffed. Roads were then ignored for several decades. In the 1960s, a few intracanyon roads were mistakenly interpreted as canals and subsequently recognized as roads, sparking renewed interest in intracanyon roads. In the 1970s, work by the San Juan Valley Archaeological Project on the North Road, between Salmon and Chaco, drew attention to extracanyon roads. Research by the Remote Sensing Division of the Chaco Project and others put many possible (but unverified) roads on the map. Again, archaeologists scoffed, denouncing roads as pipelines, fence lines, wagon trails, and so on (importantly, some projected roads were later determined to be historic linearities). NPS research at Pueblo Alto confirmed the complex network of intracanyon roads within downtown Chaco and restored confidence in roads. In the 1980s, research by the Bureau of Land Management (BLM) and the Solstice Project confirmed the reality of the north and southwest regional roads. Notably, careful study by the BLM also failed to confirm several other projected roads (Nials, Stein, and Roney 1987); that is, the results were negative for several proposed roads.

The BLM's field research showed that, when the BLM used a variety of techniques (save excavation), some projected roads were not visible on the ground, so those projected roads were judged to be false. Of course, that same research showed that some roads were both visible and real (Nials, Stein, and Roney 1987). In an important paper, Roney (1992:130) concluded that ~~not all projected roads were real~~ and that many "real" roads were discontinuous and therefore not transportation corridors: "Some of the roads, such as the North Road and the South[west] Road, are regional in scale and are clearly associated with the regional center at Chaco Canyon. However, I believe that it is entirely possible that many other Chacoan roads are purely local phenomena. The 'roads,' if that is what we choose to call them, may be seen as but one more embellishment of the local integrative structures, complementing earthworks, Great Kivas, and the other trappings of these buildings [Great Houses]....They might have formalized preexisting routes of transportation and communication, but it is equally possible that they were raceways, avenues for ceremonial processions, or even cosmological expressions." Roney perceptively suggested major symbolic roles for road monuments, and his ideas fell on good ground. The 1990s were a happy time for symbolism.

I honor Roney's insights, but I worry that his conclusions, as interpreted by others, are used to deny the road network through *falsum in uno, falsum in omnibus* logic. Roney's careful observation that some projected roads are probably false has been elevated to a general assertion, negative to regional networks. We could not confirm a few regional roads; therefore, we regard all major regional roads as false—with the constant exception of the North and Southwest roads (the only regional roads intensively studied through their entire lengths). The orthodoxy today runs something like this: a regional road network does not exist, roads are almost purely symbolic, all roads (save two!) are fragmentary and local, and even the two "real" regional roads go to landscape features, not to settlements (for example, Kantner and Kintigh, chapter 5 in this volume). That seems a heavy penalty for two unconfirmed, projected roads, when, in fact, two other projected roads were confirmed (North and South) and several other extracanyon roads are widely accepted (for example, the Coyote Canyon or Southwest Road, and the Mud Springs or West Road.)[2]

It is critical to note that, since the BLM studies, no one has really looked at other regional roads. Full-scale research on regional roads is labor intensive and very costly; no one has mounted research necessary to evaluate major extracanyon roads comparable to earlier efforts on the North and Southwest roads. We have found and confirmed many new roads undreamt of in initial road research of the 1970s and early 1980s, but recent research on roads has been almost exclusively local in scale. Small scales inexorably lead to local interpretations. Therefore, I think it is safe to say of projected regional roads that (1) we know that some are real, (2) we think that at least a few are false, and (3) we need to research the rest. For most major roads, there is evidence, usually indirect, that they exist, and no solid knowledge that they do not. That is, we do not actually know that they are false. Given that at least two regional roads are almost universally accepted as true, it seems prudent to assume that at least some of the other regional roads are or may be real.

Outlying Great Houses themselves also have received welcome critical reevaluation. One result of recent research is that they do not all look alike. I applaud recent research, but, at the risk of curmudgeondom (a fair charge, to be sure), I note that from the earliest days of "outlier hunts" we recognized variability within those sites (for example, Lekson 1991:figures 3.3, 3.4, and 3.5, showing highly variable site plans compiled by many archaeologists). We could read maps and recognize that not all Great Houses looked exactly alike. We were impressed, however, that a strong pattern encompassed that significant variability, as any preindustrial archaeological pattern surely must. Today, the simple fact of variability is used to argue that the pattern is weak, the system insubstantial (Mills 2002:82–83; Kantner 1996, 2003a; papers in Kantner and Mahoney 2000; Neitzel 1989, 2000; Vivian 1996; Kantner and Kintigh, chapter 5 of this volume). Recognition of Great Houses is relative and relational, even within Chaco Canyon (Lekson, Windes, and McKenna, chapter 3 of this volume). Few archaeologists, however, who visit Great Houses in various quarters of the Chaco region doubt the reality of the pattern. Why hold Great Houses to an undefined but apparently quite high standard of standardization? After decades spent beating down barriers of antiquated "culture" areas, state lines, and personal research domains, I fear a return of provincialism to Chacoan studies, fracturing the region into small units, study areas perceived (as they must be) as wholly or largely independent.

In archaeology, there are (at least) seven sins. In the role of angry elder, I preach now against two in particular: *Mono-Arborolatry*, worshiping one particular tree above the forest, and *The Sin of Ockham*, misapplication of the Razor to the question of interest, rather than the logic of its answer. I adjure readers and researchers to see the forest, not the trees (and especially not their particular tree), and to cleave to the fundamental truth that human behaviors were always necessarily more complicated than the simplest account we can write from fragmentary archaeological remains. Trust, like your hope of heaven, that the past was (almost) always bigger than we think and more complicated than we will ever know.

Trust, but verify. One question often (and rightly) asked of the Chacoan regional system is, how could it possibly work? How could Chaco possibly affect, much less control, a Great House 240 km (eight days' walk) distant? This brings us to the second issue of regional clarity: the remarkable clearness of Southwestern skies, its open landscape and broad vistas, and a large, complex line-of-sight communications system postulated throughout the Chacoan region. Since the 1970s we have known about the existence of an elaborate line-of-sight system spanning large portions of the Chaco region (Hayes and Windes 1975); subsequent work has expanded our knowledge of this system to encompass most of the northern San Juan Basin and beyond (Thomas Windes, personal communication 2002). For example, Farview House, a Great House on Mesa Verde, is aptly named; from Far View, they could see Chaco, and Chaco could see them. Chimney Rock, at Pagosa Springs, is another excellent example. We know that the line-of-sight system extends over much of the northern San Juan Basin; I firmly believe that similar linkages existed between Chaco and the most distant outlier Great Houses in all directions. A thoughtful (and very smart) senior archaeologist, when considering this claim, replied, "This communication system would be easier to believe if it was linked to ritual." Why? Why this insistence on ritual over practical?

Many things moved into Chaco; communications moved out, and maybe that is how the regional system worked. I do not specify here *what* the regional system did, or *why*; those are research issues for the next several generations of archaeologists. We can research those issues *if* we can recognize the nature and scale of the questions. Still, some things are clear, at least to me. Chaco was the central place in a large, well-defined region. Moreover, it was a primary center, unmistakably larger, notably more elaborate, and incomparably more monumental than any other place in its territory. Architectural monuments, (probably) roads, and (perhaps) constant contact via a complex communication system integrated the region.

Alternative leadership strategies of every stripe and nuance undoubtedly characterized many Southwestern societies before and certainly after Chaco. In the rush to embrace ritualities and communitas, however, we risk losing one of the Pueblo world's few garden-variety chiefdoms or petty kingdoms or *cacicazgos* or whatever we want to call a centralized political hierarchy. And that is a big loss. My argument is not that all the ancient Southwest was politically complex but rather that, at least once (and perhaps several times, Lekson 1999), social formations developed in the Pueblo Southwest that mirrored or translated into Southwestern terms the political hierarchies so pervasive in North America. During Chaco's era, the Mississippi Valley and the Southeast were rife with chiefdoms (for example, Anderson 1999; Pauketat 2004), and Postclassic Mesoamerica was a complex patchwork of petty kingdoms, states, and empires (for example, Smith and Berdan 2003). Metaphorically, states and polities surrounded the Southwest. Is it so unthinkable that, at Chaco, Southwestern people experimented with centralized political hierarchy? The baby we just threw out with the bathwater might be the Lost Dauphin.

Taken together, kingly burials, palatial Great Houses, and a large (if gossamer) region in which Chaco was a city among villages suggest that Chaco was neither a Pueblo (in the "ethnographic parallel" sense) nor an egalitarian commune. Chaco was the center of a complex polity, suffused with ritual and ceremony but fundamentally political and hierarchical: a chiefdom, a petty kingdom, a cacicazgo.[4] Why harp on this? Because it matters. Chaco plays a role, both direct and diffuse, in modern thought and modern times. Eleventh-century Chaco impacts the twenty-first century (and our lives today) through the nineteenth-century works of Lewis Henry Morgan. Morgan anticipated our current dehierarchizing when he leveled New World monuments in his 1881 *Houses and House-Life of the American Aborigines*. As an anthropologist, Morgan corrected what he perceived as errors made by historians who improperly used European terms for Native formations. Their *kingdom* became his *confederacy*, *king* became *sachem*, and *palace* became *communal house*. Newark, Chaco, and Palenque were communal variations on a theme: "A common principle runs through all this architecture, from the Columbia River to the Saint Lawrence, to the Isthmus of Panama, namely, that of adaptation to communism in living" (Morgan [1881]1965:309).

Morgan made the Southwest and, in particular, Chaco Canyon the prime ur-commune, the source of "primitive communism" from whence came all other communes in ancient North America (Morgan [1881]1965). With regard to the monumental buildings of Chaco, Morgan (310) wrote, "It is evident that they were the work of the people, constructed for their own enjoyment and protection. Enforced labor never created them....they were raised by the Indians for their own use, with willing hands, and occupied by them on terms of entire equality. Liberty, equality, and fraternity are emphatically the three great principles of the gens [clans], and this architecture responds to these sentiments."

Ancient "primitive communism" was important (for a brief review of primitive communism in contemporary archaeology, see McGuire 1992:181–182). Morgan, of course, profoundly influenced Marx and Engels and the theoretical development of Marxism (Bloch 1983; Krader 1972; among others). In Morgan's ancient America, primitive communism proved that human beings could do great things and build great monuments (Chaco, Newark, Palenque) without kings. Alas, Morgan's primitive American communes—Aztec, Iroquois, and the rest—have not survived the scrutiny of more careful, later scholarship. Of all Morgan's primitive communes—from the Columbia, to the Saint Lawrence, to Panama—only the Pueblo Southwest survives. The (archaeologically) past and (ethnographically) present Pueblos remain astonishingly resistant to intimations of political power. Within both anthropology and the larger world of ideas, the pervasive view of Pueblo societies, past and present, is egalitarian, governmentless, and communal.

Chaco and the Pueblos were exceptions that proved the rule. Chaco justified our hopes for communal utopia, despite disasters in

Russia and China. I do not say that Morgan's mistakes (or Chaco) were responsible for Joseph Stalin and Mao Tsetung, but I do say that, when thinking people ponder the rehabilitation and perfectibility of Marxism, one thing that gives them hope is Morgan's Chaco and its extension into the Pueblos. Chacoan communes—liberty, equality, fraternity—are the answer to a Brave New World that unfortunately was not. (Indeed, in Huxley's novel of that name, a barely disguised Zuni was the antidote, albeit savage, to totalitarian modernity.)

These are simple statements about Marxism, as manifold an admixture of complex and conflicting beliefs as the Bible. Marxist scholarship is densely theoretical, profoundly academic, and staggeringly various. Let us hop the briar patch: engaging that vast literature is impossible and unnecessary. Instead of analysis, I offer anecdote. Edmund Wilson was a sympathetic critic of Marxism and a fan of its eponymous founder. In his influential study of revolutionary communism, *To the Finland Station,* Wilson ([1940]2003:298) discusses Engels's reliance on Morgan and other ethnographers and makes the point clearly: "Certainly, there is some plausibility in the assumption that a primitive community of equals is sounder within its limits than modern society—as the Pueblo Indian villages of the American Southwest have survived with their communist economy in the teeth of their more predatory nomad neighbors and of the massacres and bankruptcies of the white man; and that any society of the future which is to be stable must have gravitated to some such equilibrium."

If we are to credit Marxism as a political program, we must believe that human nature will allow communism. The record of modern Marxist states is not good. Primitive communism is the proof, the warrant, that the program is still possible. Coffee shop conversations with colleagues in political science, philosophy, literature, and the fine arts suggest that Pueblo primitive communism (emerging, unbeknownst to them, from Chaco) remains an inspiration. Morgan's communal Chaco —given new life by recent nonhierarchical, "alternative leadership" interpretations—floats as archetype above the hurly-burly of political philosophy. Whatever went wrong in Russia, we still hope for Hopi.

But a commune did not build Chaco; a complex, hierarchical government (however unsteady or short-lived) directed the construction of its monuments. Chaco had rulers—we have seen their burials and Great Houses. The Pueblos learned to live without rulers and Great Houses in historical reaction (and only in reaction) to this brilliant but troubled episode of complexity. Pueblo communism (insofar as it exists) springs not from an earlier primitive communism but emerges, instead, from a difficult history of hierarchy. The Pueblos figured out how to live without leaders because they had seen real rulers at Chaco and did not care for the situation. Monumental architecture at Chaco matters because Morgan's mistake continues to affect our intellectual climate and our thinking about right and wrong.

### Anti-Matters

What if I am wrong and ritualists are right? (I have been wrong before; I keep a list, which I consult when I am feeling too cheerful.) In the chapters of this book, you will find thoughtful, logical, and convincing arguments in favor of ritual community over political hierarchy at Chaco. Communitas over complexity, anti-structure over structure. Still, complexity *matters*, even in the breach. Southwestern complexity is not an antiquated, academic brass ring, uninteresting, undertheorized. If I am wrong, then Morgan is right and there is hope for humankind.

Removing tongue from cheek, Chacoan complexity and rituality matter, or should matter, through works that escape the confines of anthropological archaeology. Glancing admirations of ancient Pueblo society are myriad in social critiques of many disciplines; I decline to cite a sample here. Let Edmund Wilson (above) stand for all. Instead, I focus here on a single remarkable book written by an archaeologist for the thinking public, for voters, for policy makers: *Anasazi America* by David E. Stuart (2000) of the University of New Mexico. *Anasazi America* tells the story of "seventeen centuries on the road from center place" (its subtitle), and Chaco is the climax of the story, the defining episode. Stuart's Chaco is strongly ritual and communal, but he is not starry-eyed about Chaco's potential for the present: "Perfect egalitarianism in the Pueblo fashion is not achievable in a population of 260 million" (Stuart 2000:199). He draws solid conclusions and workable policies from the story of Chaco and Pueblo peoples. His closing chapters mix analyses of tax revenue and GDP with archaeologies of Chacoan society and Pueblo world formation.

Stuart and I part company in his acceptance of Chaco rituality: "Ritual and religion were *the* organizing principles of Chacoan society"

(Stuart 2000:119, original emphasis). It is possible to consider a society with ritual but no political (some models of Chaco approach that pole), but it is harder to conceive (outside science fiction) a society with political but no ritual. Neither Stuart nor I think that ritual and political are mutually exclusive. Chaco was a mix of both, entirely intermixed, but Stuart sees ritual far higher in the mix, subordinating the political, and he sees that as Chaco's strength—and its weakness. Chaco fell, in part, because its elites became greedy (Stuart recognizes Chacoan elites): "On Wall Street, veterans of the business cycle know that 'bulls get rich, bears get rich, pigs get slaughtered.' As Chacoans, too, discovered nearly a millennium ago, greed is not a badge of honor. It is the signature of a dying society" (Stuart 2000:201). Perhaps Stuart and I are not so far apart after all. I will not further summarize his excellent book. Buy it and read it. I hope that his book reaches its intended, wider audience, but I recommend it here for archaeologists.

I have heard *Anasazi America* criticized as undertheorized; Stuart does not cite our favorite Frenchman or the sociologist-du-jour. When theory hits the pavement, though, it is hard to argue with the idea of bears, bulls, and pigs. *Anasazi America* demonstrates what appeals to Bourdieu and Giddens and what Hodder and Binford cannot demonstrate: why archaeology should be suffered to live, why we should be allowed to practice on other people's pasts, why archaeology matters. This is how we should write archaeology, how we should use our work—not to replace site reports or articles in scholarly journals but to demonstrate that archaeology matters, beyond the narrow halls of peer review.

At the beginning of this chapter, I quoted Simon Ortiz, Felipe Fernandez-Armesto, and Jared Diamond. Chaco Canyon is more than the arcane focus of archaeologists or even the ancestral homeland of Native Americans. Chaco is a profoundly public place, a historical event increasingly known to poets and policy makers, a place of World Heritage. Chaco matters. It matters, of course, to Pueblo people, for it is their past. But Chaco also matters as a national park, a tourist destination, a New Age harmonic convergence, a setting for historical novels, an inspiration for fine art and essay. Chaco matters in the great wide world as a key episode in political history, a place where people achieved monumental things—with, or without, government. What was the nature of the Bonito phase?

## Notes

This was a long, complicated project and the work of many, many people. My thanks to all those named above and in Appendix A! I have not tried to count everyone involved in the Chaco Synthesis, but I always counted on their expertise, energies, and enthusiasm: thanks to you all, indeed! I particularly recognize and thank the following people and organizations: the National Park Service; the Chaco Culture National Historical Park, especially superintendents Butch Wilson and Stephanie Dubois, archaeologist Dabney Ford, and the wonderful people of the Park staff; and the National Park Service, Santa Fe, especially F. Joan Mathien and Robert Powers.

For financial and logistical support: the Chaco Culture National Historical Park; the University of Colorado, Boulder; Arizona State University; the University of Arizona; the University of New Mexico; and Fort Lewis College.

At the School of American Research, Richard Leventhal, James Brooks, Catherine Cocks, and Kate Talbot.

Thanks to Karen Burd Larkin and Gail Bleakney, graduate assistants at the University of Colorado. David Underwood at the University of Colorado drafted all illustrations unless otherwise indicated. And Marjorie Leggitt for last minute graphics! Thanks also to John R. Stein, Richard Friedman, and the Navajo Nation Chaco Sites Protection Program for permission to use color plate 8. Bluth Enterprises filmed the capstone conference.

For the Chaco Timeline (in this volume and also available on the web): Lynne Sebastian (SRI Foundation), R. Gwinn Vivian (Arizona State Museum), Carla R. Van West (Statistical Research, Inc., and SRI Foundation), and Cindy Elsner Hayward (Statistical Research, Inc.).

Catherine M. Cameron, for material and spiritual support.

And finally, to all the great people who worked with, for, and around the original Chaco Project: thanks!

1. My opinions and notions, as percentages of the total number of words in the text of the book, break down as follows: chapter 1, "Chaco Matters: An Introduction," about 4 percent; chapter 3, "Architecture," about 7 percent; and chapter 9, "Notes from the South," about 2 percent, for a total of about one-seventh of the book. This fraction could be adjusted downward, I suppose, because I use twice as many words to express a simple idea than do my more concise colleagues. Sorry.

2. Another, practical consideration suggests clemency for regional roads,

dismissed because they could not be seen. Archaeological sites are supposed to be difficult to see. That is why we dig. Should we despair if we cannot see projected roads from the surface? Most archaeologists around the world do not have high expectations for surface visibility of any feature. (If we relied on surface observation only, the archaeology of North America would be rather different than we think it to be.) And it is likely, to the point of certainty, that many roads or road segments, like roofs on Pueblo ruins, are gone. By the same logic, we might note how remarkable that almost no Great House was ever finished, because from the surface we can see no evidence of roofs. Originally, missing roads and road segments were relatively insubstantial (earthen, even subtle, but still monumental). The North Road is far from continuous *as it appears archaeologically*. There are big gaps in the North Road as it appears from surface indications, yet we accept its reality. I have stood right in the middle of (many) road alignments, between known segments, and have seen nothing. Others, far better than I at this business, have had identical experiences. After a thousand years of erosion and aggradation, two centuries of livestock's tender mercies and myriad obliterating "formation processes," roads may not be all that easy to see as we waltz across Totah, march through Chinle, and beat our feet on the San Juan Basin mud.

3. The Seven Sins of Archaeology: (1) *Mono-Arborolatry*: Worshiping one particular tree above the forest. (2) *Timidity*: Mistaking professional safety for good practice. (3) *Solemnity*: Confusing dourness with rigor, from which comes mortis. (4) *The Sin of Ockham*: Misapplication of the Razor to the question of interest, rather than the logic of its answer. To err cautiously in archaeology is to err egregiously. (5) *Jargon*: Babel, speaking in tongues, cabalistic verbiage. (6) *Verblessness*: Undue passivity in the predicate. (7) *Bad Graphics*. The *Apocrypha Archaeologica* lists two more: *xeno-idolatry*, praising prophets who speak French, British English, or German over prophets in one's own land, and *humanist error*, the practice of art history without training or initiation into its mysteries. Generally, we consider xeno-idolatry and humanist errors to be merely annoying and not fully or dangerously sinful.

Catechizing on this list, I see that I dare not toss the first stone (or any stones). Mea culpa.

4. In contemporary Southwestern archaeology, *especially at Chaco*, novel political and social formations spring up like weeds, welcomed like flowers *if they are nonhierarchical*. Anti-structure? Embedded communal hierarchies? Ritualities? Surely this garden of sociological delights has room for a few new hierarchies. Great Houses and rich burials suggest that Chaco was, at least in part, a political

system—perhaps fledgling, perhaps weak, perhaps not very successful, and perhaps even something new under our sun (doubtful), but a centralized, hierarchical decision-making structure all the same. What to call it, kinda-kings? quasi-caciques? distended political pathologies? *aggrandisements*? Something, *someone* ruled Chaco, lived in grand residences, and won friends and influenced people over a vast region.

# 2

## Ecology and Economy

**R. Gwinn Vivian, Carla R. Van West,**

**Jeffrey S. Dean, Nancy J. Akins, Mollie S. Toll,**

**and Thomas C. Windes**

This chapter synthesizes the major attributes of Chacoan environment through time and the consequences of environmental change for resource procurement and subsistence technology.[1] We present the results graphically in the "Chaco Timeline" and in detail in appendix B ("Chacoan Ecology and Economy"). The most pertinent aspects of the natural environment, agricultural strategies and technologies, subsistence resources, and fuel and construction wood use follow. The geographic scope of this synthesis comprises Chaco Canyon and the Chaco core.

If Chacoan culture is identified and defined architecturally, as it often is, the three-hundred-year evolution of that tradition was fostered and conditioned, to a remarkable degree, by a unique set of environmental circumstances that generated and then significantly altered that tradition. Although those environmental factors operated on regional (San Juan Basin), subregional (Chaco core), and local (Chaco Canyon) scales, their impacts on Chacoan populations were inexorably linked and cumulative. The effects were particularly relevant for subsistence goods, fuel, and construction timber. Before tracing those linked but changing conditions and the technological and social adjustments they engendered, we will summarize the most relevant environmental aspects of the San Juan Basin, the Chaco core, and Chaco Canyon.

The San Juan Basin occupies the northwestern corner of New Mexico, with bordering mountains on the west and north extending into Arizona and Colorado, respectively. The interior basin is essentially elliptical and covers an approximately 12,000-sq-km area, ranging in elevation from about 2,500 m in the north to less than 1,500 m in the south. Surrounding mountains rise to considerably greater height. With the exception of Chaco Canyon and the Chacra Mesa, broad plains and shallow valleys punctuated by occasional low mesas, buttes, and short canyons dominate the topography. The basin tilts to the northwest, and most drainages, including the Chaco Wash, flow in that direction. Permanent surface water is rare, however, and arroyos and washes carry only ephemeral water.

No major changes in climate have occurred over the past ten thousand years, but short-term and long-term fluctuations in temperature and precipitation have been common. High diurnal and annual variation, ranging in the interior basin from $-24°F$ to $106°F$, characterizes the temperature. Usually, the growing season for the San Juan Basin averages 150 days, but frost-free periods in valley bottoms can be 30 to 35 days shorter. Basin precipitation is conditioned by its position relative to seasonal air-mass movements, the location of surrounding mountain ranges, and the dryness of local low-level air. More specifically, the basin occupies a transitional position with respect to the tracking of winter and summer storms, resulting in significant precipitation differences when seasonal circulation routes shift to the north or south. Moreover, these patterns cause north-south seasonal distribution differences. Annual interior-basin averages of 20 cm, northern mountain averages of 50 cm, and southern mountain averages of 43 cm evidence a strong positive correlation between precipitation and elevation. Finally, westerly winds keep humidity low.

We expanded our analysis to the Chaco core (figure 2.1) because sites in this zone were tightly integrated with those in Chaco Canyon and shared a common history, though with some notable differences, including the morphology of water control systems. The core is roughly equivalent to Doyel, Breternitz, and Marshall's (1984) "Chaco Halo" and extends from the headwaters of the Chaco Wash at the Continental

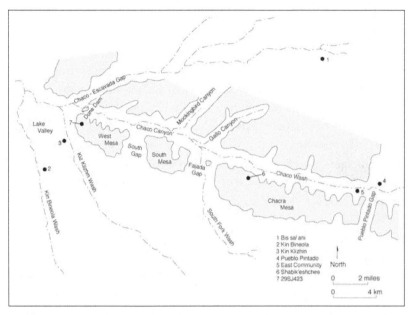

**FIGURE 2.1**

*The Chaco core. Northern, southern, and western boundaries are defined. The eastern*
*boundary extends several kilometers to the east. Major physiographic and hydrologic features*
*and several key sites are shown.*

Divide on the east, through and beyond Chaco Canyon, to the confluence of the Chaco and Kin Bineola washes at Lake Valley on the west.
The Escavada Wash marks the northern boundary. The core's southern
edge is less precise physiographically but roughly follows a line some 5
km south of the Chacra Mesa escarpment and includes the lower portions of the South Fork, Kin Klizhin, and Kin Bineola drainages.

Elevational variation within the core (excluding Chaco Canyon
and the Chacra Mesa) varies little to the north and south of the canyon,
averaging 1,900 m, but topography, soils, and vegetation differ to the
north and south of the canyon and the Chacra Mesa (refer to plate 2).
On the north, several large drainages flow from the northeast to the
southwest through long expanses of sagebrush-dominated rolling
plains and open, eroded badlands. Soils tend to have a higher clay
content than the sandier soils south of the canyon. Drainages on the
south flow more directly north through broad valleys, often marked by

47

outcropping sandstone ledges and low buttes, and badlands are rare. Various grasses and low shrubs replace sagebrush. Temperatures to the north and south of the canyon fall within the averages for the interior basin, but evening temperatures can be slightly warmer than within Chaco Canyon, where cold air drainage is a factor. Precipitation in the core also falls within the average for the interior basin, but summer moisture may be slightly greater to the south of the canyon as a result of summer storms entering the area from the southwest. Similarly, southern drainages may carry more runoff from higher source areas in the Dutton Plateau. The presence of far more Chacoan sites in the southern portion of the core, including several Great Houses, likely reflects better agricultural potential, as well as a wider range of useful wildplant resources.

Physically, and no doubt spiritually, Chaco Canyon and the Chacra Mesa were the heart of the Chacoan world and the Chacoan experience. The physiographic and hydraulic importance of these landforms for Chacoan populations is becoming increasingly apparent as studies (for example, Force et al. 2002) probe the complex interrelationship of the Chacoans and their immediate environment (refer to plate 2). Chaco Canyon ranges from 0.5 to 1 km wide and is about 30 km long from its head, near Pueblo Pintado, to the mouth, at the confluence of the Chaco and Escavada washes (see figure 2.1). It is bordered on the south for its entire length by the Chacra Mesa, which then continues to the east for an additional 35 km. The mesa varies roughly from 1.5 to 3 km in width and rises between 120 and 150 m above the canyon floor, although it terraces down to lower canyon walls on both sides.

Physiographically, the Chacra Mesa is the most dominant landform within the interior basin; its southern scarp, including the remnant Fajada Butte, is visible for miles from numerous points in the surrounding country to the south. Elevational differences between the mesa top and the canyon bottom, though relatively slight, were sufficient to create an upland life zone and microniche locales not found in the canyon. These supported multiple faunal and floral resources, including ponderosa pine and Douglas fir, largely absent in the canyon and the surrounding lowlands. Easy access to these resources could well have tipped the balance for subsistence in crop-poor years.

Hydraulically, three canyon-specific geomorphological features influenced the availability of rainfall, runoff, and groundwater within the canyon, thereby ameliorating fluctuations in regional precipitation. Summer storms carrying rainfall from the southwest toward Chaco Canyon encounter a barrier to their progress in the long, uplifted Chacra Mesa. Windes and others (2000:42) have determined, however, that four erosional breaks, or "gaps," in the Chacra Mesa funnel these storms into the canyon and keep them "localized for extended periods" (see plate 6). Rain gauges monitored by Windes show consistently higher annual precipitation in these locales, and warmer temperatures are also recorded for these zones. Within the lower canyon, three of these zones—Fajada Gap, South Gap, and the Chaco-Escavada Gap (figure 2.1)—were the loci of four early Great Houses: Una Vida, Kin Nahasbas, Pueblo Bonito, and Peñasco Blanco. The early East Community near the canyon head is situated not far from the fourth gap, Pueblo Pintado Canyon (figure 2.1).

When storms do enter Chaco Canyon, runoff varies significantly, relative to the topography on the north and south sides of the canyon (figure 2.2). Although both sides normally receive equal quantities of rainfall, even in localized storms, resulting runoff differs dramatically. Wide expanses of bedrock with limited terracing on the north are conducive to maximum discharge into numerous side canyons (see plate 4), whereas multiple short-stepped terraces, less exposure of bedrock, more sand cover, and long taluses at the cliff base on the south reduce runoff and encourage localized absorption of water (see plate 2). Following sufficient rainfall, much of the water on the canyon's north side drains rapidly through side canyons into the central-canyon Chaco Wash. Runoff on the south, however, moves more slowly as it soaks more abundant soils, and it almost never reaches the Chaco Wash. Soil moisture on the south side of the canyon is also increased in the winter because snow remains far longer than on the north side, which has greater exposure to the winter sun.

The presence of a natural sand-dune dam at the canyon's western end (see figures 2.1, 2.2, and plate 7) apparently conditioned the groundwater in the canyon for some time. Work by Force and others (2002) has shown that, at least twice during the Chacoan occupation of the canyon, the Chaco Wash was blocked at this location from reaching its confluence with the Escavada Wash. This not only created a shallow

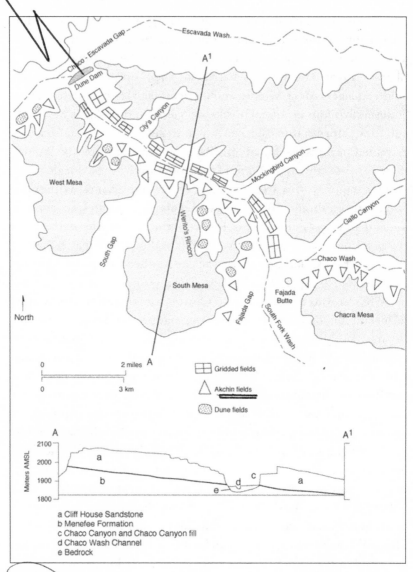

**Figure 2.2**

*Lower Chaco Canyon. Plan: Important physiographic and hydrologic features are shown. Known and hypothetical locations of gridded, akchin, and dune fields are plotted. Profile: A cross-section of the canyon and bordering mesas illustrates mesa drainage patterns and the importance of underlying geologic formations for canyon hydraulics.*

lake behind the dam but also raised the canyon floor some 4–5 m above the rest of its drainage network, thereby changing the base level. This caused erosional and aggradational processes in the canyon to be out of sync with regional trends, further stimulating the unique character of Chacoan cultural progression.

We used Force and others' (2002) four chronological periods for Chaco Canyon to organize synthesis data because Force's periods bracket episodes of channel cutting and filling and correspond, in part, to notable shifts in precipitation. Both precipitation and Chaco Wash dynamics could and did affect the Chacoan environment, natural resource base, and agricultural potential. In particular, significant changes in base-level variations in the canyon (Force et al. 2002) had beneficial or detrimental impacts on farming. To avoid confusion, we indicate the approximate equivalents of the culture-based periods and phases of the Chaco Center Revised Chaco phase system (Windes 1993: figure 1.4) for each Force period. Although the Chaco area has some of the most voluminous and precise archaeological dating in the Southwest, volume and precision can vary significantly between site types and their deposits. At times, this problem affected our ability to substantiate postulated, but not well-documented, links between data sets. For example, tying the appearance of runoff irrigation systems to periods of increased precipitation was difficult because Chaco lacked good temporal controls for dating its water control systems. Linking specific annual surges in rainfall to occasional catastrophic floods that destroyed gates and canals would be even more significant.

In 1924 Alfred V. Kidder (1924:54) spoke for many when he observed that it was "hard to see how life in the Chaco could have been anything but a continual struggle for bare existence." While acknowledging the power of the environment in our synthesis, we do not believe that Chacoans continually struggled for a "bare existence." Also, we do not believe that our analysis represents an overly environmentally deterministic interpretation of Chacoans' adaptation to their world. We accept the importance of decision making independent of environmental constraints and would argue that our analysis pays greater respect to the Chacoans' role in their history than recent scenarios that either deny the Pueblo nature of Chaco's Great Houses (Stein, Ford, and Friedman 2003:58) or characterize the Chacoan experience as "errant," "wrong," and "not right for Pueblo people" (Lekson, chapter 1 of this volume).

From our perspective, the long ecological and economic history of people dwelling in the often difficult environment of the Chaco core is a reflection of and testament to Pueblo resiliency, tenacity, and intimate familiarity with a landscape known from ancient times. Pueblo Bonito was not "an occult engine powered by the cycles of the cosmos" (Stein, Ford, and Friedman 2003:59). Rather, it was similar to "the historic Pueblos of Old Oraibi and Walpi" (Windes 2003:24), whose inhabitants were committed to a world order measured by the annual cycles of seasonal change. Therefore, we propose that the documented changes in farming technologies and macrobotanical, faunal, and wood resources over five centuries in the Chaco core reflect a rhythmic sequence of Pueblo adjustments to a continually fluctuating climate and an evolving social universe. The broad focus of that universe did not change, although overharvesting, catastrophic floods, and long periods of scant rainfall could jar the evolutionary process into alternative adaptations involving experimental technology or the use of social mechanisms. The remarkable duration of that process, coupled with increasing complexity, speaks to the deep roots of a Chacoan and, we believe, Pueblo lifeway that was perpetuated by others long after the Chacoan center ceased to be—but was not forgotten.

## EARLY AGGRADATION, A.D. 660–900 (CHACO CENTER = LATE BASKETMAKER III–PUEBLO I [LA PLATA AND WHITE MOUND PHASES])

Climatic and geomorphological data suggest that Chaco Canyon, and to some extent the Chaco core, may have been the best place to farm in the interior San Juan Basin during the Early Aggradation period. The unusual persistence of hydrologic and aggradation/degradation conditions in Chaco Canyon that had changed elsewhere in the Southern Colorado Plateau at ca. A.D. 750 may be attributed to the dune dam at the canyon's western end. This dam prevented the onset of a period of arroyo cutting and dropping water tables. Moreover, spring and summer storms funneling into the canyon through breaks in the Chacra Mesa (see figure 2.2) could have ameliorated the negative impacts of high temporal variability. Low spatial variability apparently precluded moving to other areas in the interior San Juan Basin, including the top of Chacra Mesa west of Pueblo Pintado. In effect, the established populations of Chaco Canyon were "trapped"—there was no better place to go.

There are no detailed studies of field areas and crop watering systems for this period, but macrobotanical remains and pollen undisputedly confirm the production and consumption of domesticated plants, particularly maize. Average annual precipitation in the interior San Juan Basin (8.5 in) is not sufficient for dry farming under most conditions. The Chacoans placed fields in locales with suitable soils that received runoff or that could be watered with runoff distributed by water control facilities. Floodplain farming along the Chaco Wash was feasible (see figure 2.2), although the potential for large center-canyon floods would represent a continual hazard during years of high summer moisture. Side drainages (*rincons*) had the advantage of more limited amounts of runoff, and those on the south were especially well suited for wide floodwater fan farming (*akchin*) that benefited from periods of increased effective moisture (see figure 2.2). Chacoans may have practiced a form of akchin on the canyon's north side, and measures to curb velocity of flow may have included relatively impermanent, low, earthen diversion dams, small canals, and simple gates—all precursors of later water-control facilities. Sand dunes located along the Escavada Wash, in shallow reentrants in the Fajada Gap, and in larger rincons on the canyon's south side, particularly Werito's Rincon (see figure 2.2), were well suited to dune farming. Dunes in Werito's Rincon produced maize in National Park Service experimental plots.

Initially, the Chacra Mesa may have been more important economically than the canyon. The two largest-known Basketmaker III settlements in the canyon (Shabik'eshchee Village and site 29SJ423) were on benches of the Chacra Mesa on the canyon's south side (see figure 2.1). Wills and Windes contend that large foraging areas were critical for adequate sustenance of groups practicing agriculture in small, scattered locations at some distance from the immediate settlement. They conclude that "the most common Basketmaker III settlement strategy probably was dispersal" (Wills and Windes 1989:365). That pattern characterized subsequent settlement on the canyon's south side, the location of most Chacoan "small house sites." Although the Pueblo I period brought a shift off the Chacra Mesa, critical mesa resources such as piñon nuts and some fauna were nearby, and the bottomlands of short side canyons were ideal for akchin fields. This land-use pattern persisted throughout the Chacoan occupation of the canyon.

Windes (n.d.) has proposed a different farming pattern for early Great House communities in the latter half of the Early Aggradation period. His data suggest that the Chaco Wash was a corridor for movement from the northern San Juan Basin into the central basin in the mid-ninth century—a route that ended in Chaco Canyon. Apparently, though, the canyon was not the preferred destination. Most of these early Great House communities (for example, Casa del Rio, Lake Valley, and Padilla Well) were located outside and to the west of the canyon, where Chacoans could farm the broad floodplain of the Chaco Wash or its tributaries. This was even true of Peñasco Blanco, which, although situated at the canyon's western end, was on the Chacra Mesa overlooking the wide floodplain at the confluence of the Chaco and Escavada washes (see figures 2.1 and 2.2; refer to plate 7). Seemingly, Chacoans at this time had not sufficiently developed floodwater technology capable of capturing runoff from northern side drainages in Chaco Canyon to realize the canyon's full agricultural potential. They established only four mid-ninth-century Great Houses within the canyon, and all were situated near or opposite breaks in the Chacra Mesa: Una Vida and Kin Nahasbas at Fajada Gap, Pueblo Bonito at South Gap, and Peñasco Blanco at the Chaco-Escavada Gap (see figure 2.2).

The dune dam at the western end of Chaco Canyon (see figures 2.1 and 2.2) may have modified the negative impacts of erosion, channel cutting, and a lowered water table after A.D. 750, but it did not influence the amount or frequency of rainfall. When both decreased, one viable option for improving farming strategies was to move out of the canyon proper. Small, widely spaced communities appeared after A.D. 800 in the Kin Klizhin and Kin Bineola drainages (Van Dyke, ed., n.d.) and along the South Fork of the Chaco Wash, south of Fajada Butte Gap. Relocating in better-watered zones, segments of the canyon population may have established all of these.

Macrobotanical remains from the Early Aggradation period carry indicators of farming and little else (Toll 1993). Sebastian's (1992a) simulated maize yields do not begin until A.D. 900, but Toll (1993) and others recovered abundant evidence for maize from late Basketmaker and early Pueblo sites and established that corn constituted the highest percentage (53 percent) of all economic occurrences at this time. Twelve-rowed cobs dominated Chacoan maize in this period, and the largest-diameter cobs of any period occurred in Chaco at this time. Cobs from contemporary sites to the west and south were primarily eight-rowed (Winter 1993) and diameters were smaller, suggesting that farming was more successful in the Chaco core. If true, the presence of maize in Pueblo Bonito that purportedly was grown in the Newcomb area to the west of Chaco (Benson et al. 2003) requires explanation. Assuming that the source area was correctly identified, dating remains a problem. Windes (personal communication 2003) cautions that assigning maize dates solely on its presence in early rooms at Bonito is problematic. Other domesticates are limited to cucurbit (*C. mixta*) recovered from one small-house site (29SJ724) that was identified as the cushaw type (Toll 1985).

The broad spectrum of economic annuals, grasses, and perennials so common in later Great Houses and small house sites was represented in only a scanty and patchy fashion during this period. Despite the early apparent scarcity of economic wild plants, the most salient aspect of their use in Chaco was its consistency from one era to the next. An array of weedy annuals utilized from Basketmaker times onward was present, including taxa with both edible greens and tiny seeds that typically grew in and around disturbed areas such as habitations and fields, suggesting that Chacoans encouraged their growth.

To place faunal use in temporal context, the Chaco area before the Early Aggradation period was marked by heavy dependence on small mammals (86 percent), particularly cottontail, whereas large mammal use was notably limited (6 percent). Apparently, Chacoans did not hunt turkeys. This earlier pattern continued into the first half of the Early Aggradation period with only a minimal (8.64 percent) increase in large mammals, primarily pronghorn. There was also a trace (.38 percent) of turkey. This early strong focus on small mammals, particularly cottontail, probably reflects a strategy of hunting in cultivated fields that increased crop protection and required limited travel. The faunal use pattern did not change significantly in the latter half of this period. An increase in jackrabbit bone probably represented a move towards communal rather than individual hunting, inspired by possible changes in habitat and larger human populations. Great Houses and small house sites exhibited no obvious distinctions in value. Late in this period, turkey bone increased slightly (1.71 percent).

Wood use during this period initiated a pattern that essentially continued throughout the Chacoan occupation of the canyon. By the end of this period, early Great Houses were marked by greater consumption of coniferous wood, particularly ponderosa pine and Douglas fir for construction. Juniper and piñon were the predominant species in small house sites. This difference, no doubt, reflects the need for longer beam spans in Great Houses. The ponderosa pine and Douglas fir may have come from small local stands, but builders quickly depleted most suitable wood, necessitating more distant travel to wood sources. Fuel use, on the other hand, consisting of locally derived shrubs, piñon, and juniper, was largely similar in both Great Houses and small house sites.

## CHANNEL CUTTING, A.D. 900–1025
## (CHACO CENTER = EARLY BONITO PHASE)

Three extremely wet years (A.D. 897–899) following a decade of unusually dry conditions may have triggered the breaching of the eolian dam at the western end of Chaco Canyon. This initiated arroyo cutting and a lowering water table in the canyon that contrasted with a regional trend toward aggradation and a rise in groundwater. A region-wide, gradual increase in effective moisture partially offset the deleterious effects of channel cutting in Chaco. Moreover, the canyon's position relative to seasonal storm circulation systems could have helped to counter the effects of high regional temporal variability. The Chaco core probably remained one of the best-watered locales in the interior San Juan Basin, and a continued pattern of low spatial variability reduced options for moving beyond the core.

Entrenchment of the Chaco Wash, however, would have placed floodwater fields on the canyon's north side in jeopardy; side tributaries would have eroded to the base of the main channel, thereby flushing water directly into the wash. Presumably, the hydrologic and geomorphic conditions on the canyon's south side "resisted entrenchment and...would have been far better than the northern margins for agriculture based on akchin methods" (Force et al. 2002:36). The effects of channel cutting were not felt immediately, but gradual head-ward erosion of the Chaco Wash ultimately impacted the central canyon and may well have delayed continued experimentation with water control devices useful for harnessing runoff in drainages on the north side of Chaco Canyon. This, in turn, may have slowed the establishment of new Great Houses. Lekson (1984a) defined a "hiatus" in Great House construction between A.D. 960 and 1020, but he also noted that it was unlikely that building stopped entirely, as may be evidenced by a few early dates from Hungo Pavi.

Dating is not precise, but there is evidence, particularly on the canyon's north side, for an early pattern of floodwater farming based on capture and diversion of runoff from short side canyons. Deeply buried (up to 1 m below present ground surface) masonry headgates and associated canals may date to this period. Gate morphology differs in several respects from later gates; gates are large, well constructed, and designed to handle major discharges of runoff, although floods destroyed several of them. The hydrologic and geomorphic conditions on the canyon's south side resisted arroyo cutting during this period, thereby permitting the continued use of multiple, diverse, and more flexible farming strategies. Channel entrenchment reduced the hydro-logic benefits of the canyon, and out-migration into the South Fork, Kin Klizhin, and Kin Bineola drainages presumably assumed greater importance. Although current evidence is slim, Windes (personal communication 2003) believes that the postulated tenth-century unit at the Kin Bineola Great House is larger than previously thought and may represent the first attempt to establish a Great House community in this drainage.

The macrobotanical record may reflect the effects of channel cutting. The lowest percentage of maize (26 percent) from all site samples occurred during this period and was coupled with a significant increase in a wide range of wild economic plant use. Departing markedly from the preceding period, cob diameters were much smaller at Chaco and other inner basin sites, compared with better-watered zones in the northern San Juan Basin, including La Plata Valley. Maize and wild plant taxa use patterns were largely similar in both Great Houses and small house sites.

The pattern of faunal consumption differed from the Early

Aggradation period only in terms of relatively minor changes in percentages of small and large mammals taken. Numbers of small mammals, including not only lagomorphs but also field mice, pocket gophers, kangaroo rats, and prairie dogs, continued to decline slightly (75–66.5 percent) throughout the period. A shift back to greater numbers of cottontail may represent use of smaller garden plots instead of larger open fields, a process that the maize record may reflect. Initially, large mammal use, represented by fairly equal quantities of pronghorn, deer, and bighorn, rose only slightly (8 percent) but then increased significantly (16.6 percent) by the end of the period. As usual, turkey consumption was extremely low, declining to less than 1 percent of faunal remains by the end of this period.

Species of construction timbers dated to this period in Chaco Canyon suggest that overharvesting of local trees, principally piñon and juniper, may have already occurred. This situation manifested best in small house sites where piñon and juniper declined notably and were replaced, in part, by ponderosa pine and Douglas fir. There was also an increase in ponderosa pine in Great Houses, but the most significant aspect of wood use in these structures was the sizeable (14 percent) utilization of spruce/fir that could only come from relatively distant sources. Shrubby plants continued as the dominant fuel in both Great Houses and small house sites, with minor additions of juniper, piñon, and cottonwood/willow.

## CHANNEL FILLING, A.D. 1025–1090
## (CHACO CENTER = CLASSIC BONITO PHASE)

Geomorphological and hydrological processes in Chaco Canyon "caught up" with regional trends in the early eleventh century following the out-of-sync channel-cutting episode initiated in the early tenth century. The construction of a "rock dam" in the breached portion of the earlier dune dam at the canyon's western end may have hastened and even initiated the cessation of entrenchment at approximately A.D. 1025 (Judd 1954:58). Regionally, longer periods between notable increases and decreases in moisture and an increase in spatial variability characterized the Channel Filling period. This pattern repeated locally with three periods of increasing precipitation (A.D. 1020–1030, 1040–1060, and 1070–1080) separated by dry spells. Dean and

Funkhouser (2002:41) point out that "the locally reduced variance and upward trending rainfall undoubtedly contributed to the environmental stability that allowed deposition to occur."

The relatively salubrious effects of low temporal variability, aggradation, rising water tables, and several periods of notably increased precipitation would have stimulated more agricultural production through water control systems. The best archaeological evidence for these systems and their related agricultural fields comes from this period in a zone on the north side of the canyon, from Gallo Canyon on the east, to the western end of the canyon (see figure 2.2). Two smaller systems are known on the canyon's south side, near Rinconada and Peñasco Blanco (see figure 2.2). Vivian (1990:305–313) has described and illustrated the process of capturing and channeling water from side tributaries through canals and masonry gates into gridded fields (figure 2.3). Three episodes of system construction were documented stratigraphically in canals, gates, and field levels, all of which were raised over time as runoff deposited heavy sediment loads in gridded fields (figure 2.4). Chacoans recognized the nutrient benefits of accumulating organic deposits on their fields, even though it meant modifying new canals and gates or constructing new ones. Morphological variation in headgates and in some canals also identified the three construction phases. Sometime during the Channel Filling period, severe flooding damaged or destroyed a number of middle-phase gates and canals throughout the canyon, but most were repaired or remodeled. Similar morphological changes have not been documented for gridded fields, although small gates in fields do show some variation over time. Chacoans employed morphologically similar water-control features for farming in the Kin Klizhin Valley and possibly in the Kin Bineola Valley, although the features in the latter valley may date to the Late Aggradation period. To suit local hydrologic conditions, Chacoans modified both of these Chaco core systems.

A good measure of the Chacoans' commitment to and investment in farming, despite occasional destruction of headgates and canals by flooding, is their intense manipulation of water in the canyon sometime after A.D. 1020. The growth of the East Community near the eastern head of Chaco Canyon after A.D. 1050 also may represent agricultural success, as well as the 1060s establishment of the Pueblo

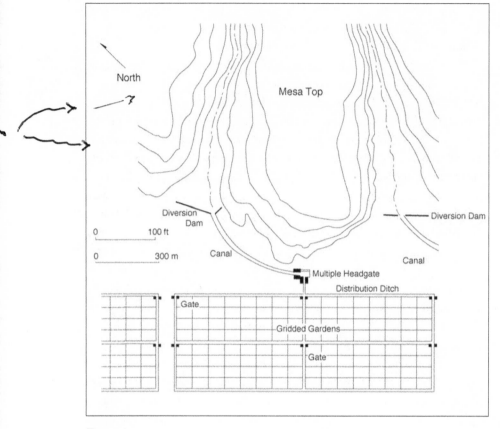

**Figure 2.3**

*A typical plan of water control systems in Chaco Canyon.*

Pintado Great House farther to the east but within the Chaco core. If good farmland was becoming scarce in the lower canyon, establishing settlements in agriculturally favorable locations in the Chaco core was an option. Small settlements in the Kin Klizhin and Kin Bineola valleys increased markedly during this period. The establishment of the Kin Klizhin Great House in the late 1080s, however, may have been a response to decreased moisture in the Chaco core during the last two decades of the eleventh century.

With aggradation and improving, though fluctuating, precipitation in the Channel Filling period, agriculture was often more successful, indicated by the rising ubiquity of maize in all canyon sites. At the

**FIGURE 2.4**

*Early and late gates in the Rinconada water control system. Bordering walls and stone paving of an early east-west gate in the foreground lie below a modified later gate that was oriented north-south. (Photo courtesy of G. Vivian)*

same time, simulated maize yields (Sebastian 1992a) suggest both surpluses and declines in production, and differences in cob size and cob rows may represent difficulties in producing consistently high-quality ears. Moreover, we may attribute possible differences in cob size between Great Houses to variation in field-watering systems. Tom Windes (personal communication 2003) cautions, however, that samples taken from early excavations at Pueblo Bonito, the Talus Unit at Chetro Ketl, and Pueblo del Arroyo may not be sufficiently well dated for us to draw any viable conclusions about maize differences in Great

Houses. Smaller, predominantly ten-rowed maize from small house sites may reflect use of akchin floodwater fields and microniche farming such as dunes. Squash and beans were recovered far less commonly than maize, but small house sites and Great Houses alike yielded similar species (Toll 1985). These sites also produced a wide variety of wild economic plants.

The general ratio of small to large mammal use characterizing earlier periods changed in the eleventh century, when the trend toward increasing large-mammal use became more pronounced. A shift from early preference for pronghorn to essentially equal exploitation of pronghorn, deer, and bighorn in the early 1000s changed again in the mid-1000s (Channel Filling period), when deer became the favored large mammal. Use of bighorn also increased then. These changes may represent a replacement of small group or individual hunting by communal hunting. The pattern of alternating cottontail and jackrabbit exploitation over time also continued, but the increasing frequency of these shifts may represent species exhaustion instead of hunting strategies related to types of agricultural fields. Turkey bone continued to represent less than 1 percent of all faunal bone in Great House and small house deposits.

The pattern of wood use for fuel and construction characterizing the preceding Channel Cutting period did not change. By the end of the Channel Filling period, importation of timbers for use in Great House construction increased dramatically. Ponderosa pine had become almost 60 percent of wood harvested for building, and spruce/fir had jumped to 14 percent. Meanwhile, local juniper and piñon decreased, as did Douglas fir, which Chacoans may have collected from small stands on the Chacra Mesa.

## LATE AGGRADATION, A.D. 1090–1125/1150 (CHACO CENTER = LATE BONITO PHASE)

The end date given by Force and others (2002) for this period (A.D. 1125) was extended to mid-century because researchers generally acknowledge continued Chacoan occupation of the canyon and Chaco core to at least A.D. 1150. Regional and local climatic conditions during the Late Aggradation period largely duplicated those of the preceding sixty-five years. A relatively long-term wet period from A.D. 1100 to 1130 ended with a major drought that, except for a short midway break, lasted from A.D. 1130 to 1180. Dean and Funkhouser (2002:41) concluded that "this drought, which may have been particularly severe in the summer (Dean 1992:37–38), would have been especially destructive to the Canyon food production system, which depended on summer rainfall and surface runoff." A concomitant shift to low spatial variability around A.D. 1130 could have radically altered a regional exchange system that may have developed in the preceding period. As total effective moisture decreased, a break occurred in the aggrading process, and water tables stabilized or dropped. Continued establishment of outlier Great Houses beyond the Chaco core suggests that outmigration was the ultimate option for many Chacoan farmers.

For those who stayed in the canyon, commitment to certain established agricultural strategies may have provided little leeway for adapting to changing climatic conditions in the twelfth century. The dedication of large tracts of land to a single method of crop watering compounded the heavy social, technological, and labor investment in water control systems on the canyon's north side. People may have practiced similar methods in other areas of the Chaco core, including the Kin Bineola, Kin Klizhin, and South Fork valleys. The best evidence for farming strategies in these valleys came from the Kin Bineola and Kin Klizhin drainages, where large-scale water-control systems utilized many of the same features characterizing water control in the canyon. These systems probably worked well between A.D. 1100 and 1130, when precipitation increased. Dry spells from A.D. 1080 to 1100 and from 1130 to 1180, however, could have resulted in no runoff or far fewer gridded fields being watered. The last structural changes in canals and headgates (late phase) strongly suggest that people were collecting and channeling far less water to fields.

Adjustments to fluctuating precipitation levels probably were easier on the canyon's south side, where, with the apparent exception of only two zones of gridded fields (see figure 2.2), farming strategies remained multidimensional and responsive to changing moisture sources. Fields were less rigidly confined to particular locales; people could take advantage of dunes and several floodplain niches. This method of farming also was practiced at the Bis sa'ani Great House on the Escavada Wash north of the canyon (see figure 2.1), where local geomorphology and runoff in the wash and from slopes bordering the wash created multiple, diverse crop zones (Cully et al. 1982). The severity of the mid-twelfth-century drought can be measured, in part, however, by the abandonment of small house sites and the apparent failure of ancient methods of small-scale microniche farming over large areas.

The significant fluctuations in precipitation in the Late Aggradation period had a clear effect on maize production, with high yields early in the period dropping dramatically after A.D. 1130. Benson and others (2003) report one late cob from Pueblo Bonito that may have been grown on the Animas River floodplain near Aztec, implying that people may have imported some maize into the canyon. Even during times of high yields, though, subregional climatic differences often resulted in stress on maize growth and maturation. The level of wild economic plant use remained constant in both Great Houses and small house sites, although detailed analysis in some sites, such as Pueblo Alto, showed slight variations in use of weedy annuals, grasses, and perennials. Increasing reliance on domesticates over three centuries precluded an easy reversal to wild plant use and, no doubt, contributed to the eventual cessation of farming in the Chaco area.

The most significant faunal change in the Late Aggradation period was the dramatic increase in turkeys, which were probably imported as a food item from the northern San Juan Basin (possibly with maize) as a substitute for declining numbers of small mammals. It is probably no coincidence that trade goods for this period indicate close ties with areas to the north where turkeys would have access to more natural foods and a greater abundance of agricultural crops. The continued swings between use of cottontail and jackrabbit, and the addition of prairie dogs, mark the decrease in small mammals. Large mammal consumption grew steadily, characterized by a slight decrease in deer but significant additions of pronghorn and bighorn. Many of these changes appear somewhat erratic and symptomatic of the uncertain times engendered by climatic conditions in the San Juan Basin.

In the Late Aggradation period, greater numbers of spruce/fir— and, for the first time, aspen—beams were carried into the canyon, reinforcing the past pattern of importing large numbers of construction timbers into Chaco Canyon. Windes (personal communication 2003) interprets shifts in species use as significantly greater harvesting of trees from higher elevations late in Chacoan prehistory. This same pattern was even represented in small house sites where spruce/fir accounted for 14 percent of construction wood, ponderosa pine actually increased slightly, and juniper and piñon continued to decline. Much greater use of conifers for fuel at both small house sites and Great Houses almost certainly represented the burning of construction timbers removed from abandoned rooms in habitation sites.

Agricultural strategies, combined with macrobotanical, faunal, and wood use in mid-1100s Great Houses and small house sites, appeared to represent a final, uneven, and tentative adjustment to climatic conditions that threatened Chacoan culture. Unlike the past, however, these adjustments were not sufficient for bringing order once again to the Chacoan world. Had the decline in moisture in the 1130s been brief, Great House and small house populations might have experienced a reprieve, and Chaco Canyon could have continued for a time as the center of the Chacoan world. But that did not happen. Ultimately, Chacoan populations resorted to the ancient practice of relocating in more favorable lands.

### Notes

1. The Chaco Ecology and Economy Synthesis Group met October 28–30, 1999, at the Desert Laboratory at the University of Arizona. Conference participants included Nancy Akins, Julio Betancourt, William E. Doolittle, Brian M. Fagan, Enrique Salmon, and Mollie Toll. National Park Service representatives and participants included Tom Windes, Joan Mathien, Dabney Ford, and Charles Wilson. Stephen H. Lekson (University of Colorado Museum) attended as the Chaco Synthesis representative. Papers for discussion were prepared by Akins (Faunal Resources), Dean (Paleoenvironmental Reconstruction), Toll (Macrobotanical Remains), Van West and Vivian (Agricultural Strategies and Technologies), Vivian (Hydraulic Technologies), and Windes (Wood Procurement). Betancourt, Doolittle, and Salmon served as discussants. Fagan provided an evaluation of the entire meeting. A summary of meeting results appeared in the Winter 2000 issue of *Archaeology Southwest* (vol. 14, no. 1).

# 3

## Architecture

**Stephen H. Lekson, Thomas C. Windes,
and Peter J. McKenna**

This chapter consists of five parts, with introductory words by Lekson: (1) "Pueblo I Great Houses" by Windes, (2) "Pueblo II Great Houses" by Lekson and Windes, (3) "Small Sites" by McKenna, (4) "After Chaco" by Lekson, and (5) "Cityscape" by Lekson.

Chaco is all about Great Houses (figure 3.1; refer to plates 4, 5, 6, and 7). That is, Chaco *today* is all about Great Houses. There would be no Chaco Culture National Historical Park, nor Chaco Project, nor Chaco Synthesis Project, without Great Houses. These large ruins caught scholarly and popular attention in the second half of the nineteenth century, and their appeal has only increased. Visitors bump over miles of dubious roads to see them; students toil over pages of dubious theses to explain them. Great Houses are Chaco's attraction and central matter.

There was, of course, much more to Chaco and its archaeology than a dozen oversized structures, built from 850 to 1150. A century of scientific research reveals impressive settlements at Chaco by A.D. 500: a long history of architectural development preceded, and a shorter period followed, the era of Great Houses (Mathien 2005; McKenna and

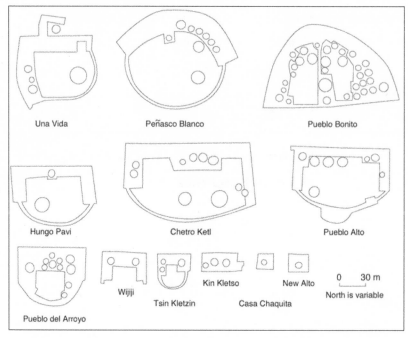

**FIGURE 3.1**

*Great House ground plans, Chaco Canyon. (After Lekson 1984a:figure 1.2)*

Truell 1986). Great Houses were certainly not the only architectural expression of whatever it was that Chaco was about. The Chacoan monumental landscape—we will say "cityscape"—extended beyond Great Houses in a complex architectural composition, discussed below. The Chaco cityscape was unprecedented in Pueblo prehistory and unexpected in modern understandings of ancient Southwestern architecture.

An important side issue in Pueblo II Great House architecture concerns the diverse range of form and construction techniques within the canyon (and its immediate environs, the "Chaco core," or "Chaco halo") (see figures 1.2a and 2.1). Construction techniques (that is, wall types) and ground plans vary considerably within Chacoan Great Houses. Great Houses were constructed mostly, but not entirely, with the well-crafted core and veneer masonry typical of Chacoan building. Pueblo Bonito displays every defined type of Chacoan masonry, as well as much stonework that we would not recognize as Chacoan if it

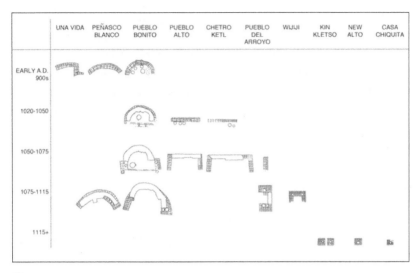

**FIGURE 3.2**

*Schematic Great House forms through time, Chaco Canyon. (After Lekson 1991:figure 3.2)*

occurred outside the canyon. Bis sa'ani, a putative "outlier" about 10 km from Una Vida, was built with massive, poured adobe walls (Breternitz, Doyel, and Marshall 1982). Yet, Bis sa'ani is certainly a Chacoan Great House. In form, too, there is notable variability both through time and among contemporary buildings (figure 3.2). (As noted below, many small sites at Chaco Canyon share Great House elements; if these were included in this discussion, the form and technique in Chaco Great Houses would vary even more.)

We note the architectural range observed within Chaco for two reasons. First, we have recognized the variability of Chacoan building primarily through contrasts between buildings (for example, classificatory distinctions between McElmo-phase buildings and Bonito-phase buildings; Vivian and Mathews 1965). Often, though, we have overlooked the remarkable variability within a single building, such as Pueblo Bonito. Large sections of Pueblo Bonito (the type site for the Bonito phase, narrowly construed) are built of McElmo-style masonry. Second, some have used architectural variability among outlier Great Houses to argue for those sites' independence and against a Chacoan regional system (Kantner and Mahoney 2000; Kantner and Kintigh, chapter 5 of this volume).

We note, however, that variability among the 150-plus outliers is not much greater than variability within the dozen Great Houses in Chaco Canyon or the halo. That is, architectural variability within the canyon equals or perhaps even exceeds architectural variability within Great Houses in the larger Chaco region. Therefore, we question architectural arguments against a larger regional expression of Chacoan building traditions (Lekson, chapter 1 of this volume). Of course, we could logically transfer arguments similar to those applied to architectural variability in outlier Great Houses to Chaco Canyon Great Houses, an intriguing possibility we leave to others.

## PUEBLO I GREAT HOUSES: THE ROOTS OF CHACO

If we are to understand Great Houses and their function and role in Chacoan society, then identifying the earliest sites that provide links to our classic mid–A.D. 1000s image is paramount. Wilshusen and Van Dyke (chapter 7 of this volume) discuss the regional history of early Great Houses; here, we focus on Chaco Canyon and its near vicinity.

It is hard to visualize earlier Chaco Great Houses without later, massive, multistoried architecture clouding the image. Even classic "downtown" Chaco Great Houses were formed from smaller units on sites that defy the normality of the times. Hayes (1981) interpreted these early beginnings (such as the early structures at Pueblo Bonito) as merely typical of their era, but they were anything but typical. If we choose to examine house architecture as one example of deviancy from the norm, then earlier events in Chaco and the region do show numerous examples of houses that defy the norm. Landscape modification in the form of prehistoric roads and the presence of public structures also add to the recognition model of early Great House stirrings.

Few would think that Basketmaker III in Chaco has much to offer for solutions. There are no ready architectural signs of budding Great Houses, although we must not overlook the importance of the Great House and its surrounding community. Two huge Basketmaker III villages (Shabik'eschee with 70-plus pit structures and 423/Peñasco Blanco with 100-plus pit structures) were settled in the late A.D. 400s and 500s at the east and west park canyon boundaries (figure 3.3; see figure 1.2b). They offer potential sources of the earliest experiments in aggregated community living, rarely seen again until the rise of the

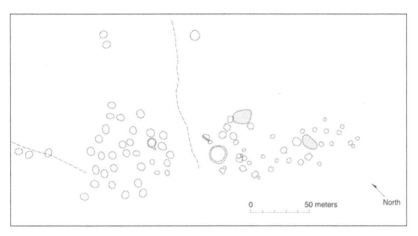

**FIGURE 3.3**

*Shabik'eschee, a large Basketmaker III site at Chaco Canyon. (After Wills and Windes 1989:figure 3)*

Great House communities in the late A.D. 800s and early 900s. Both had community structures (Great Kivas), imported much of their lithic material, and were aligned in a band across the local topography in defiance of normal settlement. Interestingly, we have tree-ring dates from the same year (A.D. 580/581) for their respective, latest Great Kivas, although it seems unlikely that their construction was exactly coeval. The search for prehistoric road connections to these two communities and of modified landscapes is presently ongoing.

Basketmaker III communities of the age and magnitude of Shabik'eschee and 423/Peñasco Blanco are rare or absent elsewhere in the Anasazi region (papers in Reed 2000). A few of the very largest Basketmaker III sites outside Chaco Canyon had approximately forty pit structures (and these date to the late seventh century). Most large Basketmaker III sites had twenty pit structures or fewer (Altschul and Huber 2000:table 7.1; Gilpin and Benallie 2000:table 8.1). The Chaco Canyon Basketmaker III sites are remarkably large and notably early. Our best ties to the developments in the A.D. 1000s, however, lie in communities established in the A.D. 775–850 period and afterwards, around but not in Chaco Canyon.

On the South Fork tributary of the Fajada Wash, 10 km south of Fajada Butte, lies the earliest Pueblo I community known in the canyon

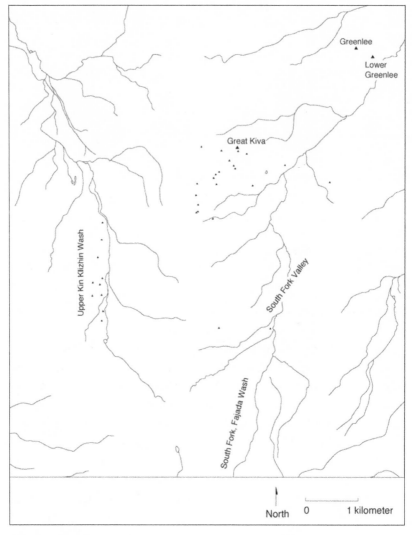

**FIGURE 3.4**

*Fajada Wash Pueblo I community.*

area (figure 3.4). This community contains about twenty-seven house sites concentrated in a relatively small area at the same elevation and distinct from other later occupations (primarily early Pueblo II) in the valley. It was short-lived, however, and no immediate successor is apparent within the local area.

Several aspects of this community are worth recognition:

- A cluster of many small habitation structures

- The probable location of public architecture (a Great Kiva) and associated prehistoric road(s)

- Two small houses that are much larger in elevation, by a magnitude of 10, than the normal houses, but still single story

- The use of Type I masonry construction for these two small houses (thereby causing the elevational magnitude uncommon to typical Pueblo I houses of the A.D. 800s, which exhibit almost no surface relief)

- The visibility of all other houses to these two unusual houses

- The visibility of all or nearly all houses to landmarks on the horizon (Fajada and Huerfano buttes) that might be considered sacred topographic features

- Visibility to the Una Vida and Kin Nahasbas early and possibly coeval Great House complex in Chaco

- The high percentage (15–45) of exotic lithic material in the form of yellow-spotted chert (for example, sourced in the Zuni Mountains) at many small houses

- The later addition in Pueblo II times of unusual sites within or near the settlement, which are connected with prehistoric roads, suggesting continued cultural use of the area

- The budding of an ornament industry in the form of tools, raw materials, and ornaments in various stages of manufacture

- The existence of a similar community—with all the preceding attributes, except for the known presence of a community structure—in the head of the Kin Klizhin Wash directly west a few kilometers

This community and a similar one just to the west in the head of upper Kin Klizhin Wash are short-lived and do not have successors in the immediate vicinity.

Between about A.D. 860/875 and 900, a wave of small-site intrusions into the Chaco area are evident, together with the rise of massive, Type I masonry–constructed Great Houses. This is a critical period in the rise of Chacoan society and provides our first true links with the downtown Chaco Great Houses. These Great House communities reveal lithic and ceramic ties with different areas of the San Juan Basin, depending on which side of the canyon area they are located. The western areas are Chuskan dominated, the south areas reveal ties to the south, the eastern areas reveal ties to the north and south, and the core/downtown areas seemingly link primarily to the west. Our poorest data come from the earliest Great Houses within the core of Chaco Canyon. The rise of these sites and communities and the coeval abandonment of the large Pueblo I house communities north of the San Juan River cannot be coincidental, especially with the evidence that one founding community at Pueblo Pintado has ceramic ties with the northern area, presumably bringing pottery vessels from their homeland.

Thus, late 800s Great Houses or those suspected under later constructions are centered at Pueblo Pintado, the East Community, Una Vida, Kin Nahasbas, Pueblo Bonito, Peñasco Blanco, the Padilla Well Great House, Kin Bineola, and Casa del Rio (see figure 1.2). Pueblo Pintado and Casa del Rio occupy the eastern and western approaches to the Chaco Canyon and are crucial nexuses for understanding the core grouping.

The most important site tying together the Pueblo I and Pueblo II periods rests at Casa del Rio (figure 3.5). Its importance cannot be underestimated as we examine the rise of the Bonito phase and links to the huge Pueblo I communities that once dominated community life north of the San Juan River. Just one other site carries this important link—Skunk Springs on the Chuskan slope. Both sites were initially settled as huge Pueblo I houses similar to those in the northern San Juan but rare in the San Juan Basin. Both have prehistoric roads in association, and both have large early Great Houses on them. Without excavation, we cannot temporally link the large Pueblo I houses with the Great Houses built on them. The Pueblo I house at Casa del Rio formed a house block 112 m long, with impressive amounts of trash. But the A.D. 900s, single-story, 38-m-long Great House built over it must have caused a break in occupation to allow it to eliminate much of the

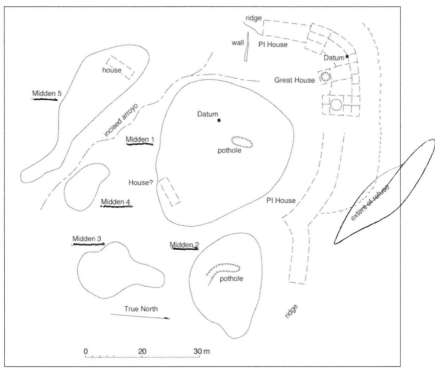

**FIGURE 3.5**
Casa del Rio. *Just Fin chap I*

Pueblo I housing. Still, the positioning of the two houses suggests some sort of cultural continuity.

Both Great Houses at Padilla Well (with a probably earlier A.D. late 800s/early 900s structure under it) and Casa del Rio are situated within clear sight of the communication shrine located at the top edge of the West Mesa cliffs overlooking the region. We do not know whether Chacoans established this communication system during the initial construction of these Great Houses, but the houses are in position to be part of any communications system.

Casa del Rio is in a startling, barren location just west of Padilla Well along the Chaco "River." Its name belies the huge amounts of groundstone found on it (more than five hundred pieces of *manos* and *metates* on the site), suggesting much food production. No other site in the Chaco area has produced so much groundstone on the surface; the amounts buried must be staggering. In addition, the small number of Great House rooms (about twenty) cannot justify a habitation group large enough (two–five households, at most) to account for the assumed food production and discard at this locality. The A.D. 900s trash midden rivals that of Pueblo Alto's in volume and height, but, unlike the A.D. 1000s Great House middens, this is filled with presumably domestic trash. It is darkened with charcoal and ash, like the predecessors from the underlying Pueblo I house, and is rich in bones, lithics, sherds, and probable vegetal material. The chemical makeup of the two refuse depositions, however, is not the same and mirrors the differences observed at the Pueblo Pintado community sites.

The location of Casa del Rio gives it a better advantage for horticultural production than any other location in and around Chaco, suggesting that the groundstone inventory is no fluke. The setting allows a multitude of crop production strategies, including runoff, dune, and wash bottom and bank/floor plain agriculture. Even in the driest of times, this area could have supported farmers. If ever there was a source for crop surplus in the region, it is here (followed by Pueblo Pintado) rather than anywhere in the canyon. For example, at the Chaco East Community, a locality well protected from treasure hunters, surface groundstone was so rare that the entire community of seventy sites would not begin to approach the numbers of groundstone found on Casa del Rio alone (differing by a magnitude of 10?).

Other early (A.D. 900s) Great House trash deposits at Pueblo Bonito and Peñasco Blanco mixed with charcoal and ash also suggest much household refuse until a shift in deposition in the A.D. 1000s, indicating a possible change in domestic residency. Between A.D. 875 and 925 the density of refuse at small houses and Great Houses alike dramatically alters. Aside from the two Basketmaker III communities mentioned above, the early Pueblo sites yield sparse refuse until about A.D. 875, when artifact density increases almost tenfold.

Within Chaco Canyon, it is clear that Pueblo Bonito and Una Vida started as "small" house sites similar to those in the South Fork community. They are built of stone (Type I) masonry rather than the favored adobe. Both have tree-ring dates in the late 800s. To make room for newer construction, the Chacoans did not demolish these early houses but incorporated them into it. At Una Vida, they completely reoriented the newer addition, leaving the older house sticking out asymmetrically but still attached. Despite newer modifications, the old houses retained considerable importance. At the East Community and Casa del Rio, the Chacoans maintained the Great Houses in their original Type I masonry plan well into the A.D. 1000s, without subsequent modifications and masonry work (both are single story). Both structures were important in the A.D. 900s, but they lack associated Great Kivas and differ in the refuse depositions (the East Community Great House has no evident, massive, A.D. 900s refuse mound). Also, a community of small house sites surrounds the East Community Great House, whereas few house sites exist around Casa del Rio.

At Pueblo Pintado at the eastern end of Chaco Canyon, settlement begins in the 875–925 period exactly when the Dolores region is abandoned. The earliest houses exhibit pottery from north of the San Juan River, and the largest house is reminiscent of the long-arcing Pueblo I houses found to the north. In a second new settlement about 2 km away, houses contain ceramic assemblages that appear to have been made in the Mount Taylor area. An early Great House under Pueblo Pintado may have completed the initial community. The Pintado area also provides a rich environment for farming but is limited by a short frost-free season. It has the highest rainfall of any locale in the canyon area.

Even among early Great Houses, the various distinctions defy an overall simplistic answer as to the role and function of Great Houses within the Chacoan area and associated community. There must be many more such early Great Houses and sites with linkages to the early beginnings that we have not yet recognized, however. We cannot safely say that these early beginnings started in or around Chaco Canyon.

Although Type I masonry, single-story roomblocks start to appear as early as A.D. 800 to 850 around Chaco, our limited tree-ring-dated sample suggests that single- and multi-story Great Houses began to appear somewhat later, with the arrival of new immigrants from the south, west, and north by about A.D. 860/875. Chacoans continued to build Great Houses in the A.D. 900s, but the canyon shows little evidence of this important era. It would be fruitful to investigate whether the abandonment of the large Pueblo I villages north of the San Juan River produced a revamped society that started anew in the Chaco region and elsewhere in the San Juan Basin.

## PUEBLO II GREAT HOUSES

The basis of this section is chapter 5, "Conclusions," from *Great Pueblo Architecture* (Lekson 1984a, reprinted by the University of New Mexico Press in 1986 and again by Elliot Werner Press in 2005), cited as GPA. Much of the information presented in GPA still seems valid today; some does not. There have been more recent, important projects on Chacoan architecture, and we refer to some of that work below. Paralleling GPA, this section addresses changes in chronology, the social ramifications of construction, and the social correlates of form.

Eleven Great Houses appear on most maps of Chaco Canyon. From west to east, they are Peñasco Blanco, Casa Chiquita, Kin Kletso, Pueblo del Arroyo, Pueblo Bonito, New Alto, Pueblo Alto, Tsin Kletzin, Chetro Ketl, Una Vida, and Wijiji (see figure 3.1; refer to figure 1.2). Additional in-canyon Great Houses have been proposed at Kin Nahasbas (Mathien and Windes 1989), Talus Unit (Lekson 1985), the Headquarters Site (Vivian and Mathews 1965:81), "Robert's Small House" (Roberts 1929:1), and, much farther up-canyon, at East Community (Windes et al. 2000) and, beyond that, Pueblo Pintado, bringing the total of in-canyon Great Houses to seventeen (refer to figure 1.2). Several "small sites" built with Great House masonry and formality may increase the number even more. Other candidate Great Houses are in the Chaco halo (the area immediately around Chaco Canyon), including Bis sa'ani (Breternitz, Doyel, and Marshall 1982). (The park also includes more distant, outlier Great Houses at Kin Bineola and Kin Ya'a.) GPA considered only the first eleven of these buildings; the inclusion of many more, albeit small, Great Houses would significantly affect GPA's conclusions.

### Chronology

In general, the site-by-site construction chronologies presented in GPA remain valid. Figure 3.2 presents these sequences schematically. Thomas Windes and Dabney Ford are sampling every exposed piece of wood in the park for dendrochronology, so there are hundreds of new dates, mostly unpublished (Windes and Ford 1996). From preliminary analysis of these dates, the construction chronologies in GPA appear to be, more or less, correct. The major changes will be

**FIGURE 3.6**

*Corner doors at Pueblo Bonito.*

- Pueblo Bonito (Windes and Ford 1996; Windes 2003) began earlier than presented in GPA (about 860), with major construction in 1045–1050 and 1075–1085.

- Pueblo del Arroyo's construction began ten years later than presented in GPA (compress the GPA dating to 1078–1105).

- Hungo Pavi's construction started ten years later and ended twenty years earlier than presented in GPA (shorten to 1006–1060).

### Construction

What were the social ramifications of construction? GPA concluded that Great Houses were exercises in labor, not advances in engineering. Most of the architectural technologies derived from earlier Chacoan and Anasazi traditions; we can trace most new technologies as evolving within the three-century history of Great House building. For example, to support substantially more height than previously attempted, builders developed core and veneer walls from earlier masonry techniques that failed at Pueblo Bonito (although they worked well at Una Vida, still standing three stories tall!). Chacoan builders considered the problem and solved it. Even features apparently unique at Great Houses, such as corner doorways (figure 3.6), represented the novel placement or redesign of existing forms. To be sure, there were innovations, but, in general, Great House building did not represent novel techniques or structural designs. Great Houses and other Chacoan architectural forms (roads, mounds, and so on) required much planning and labor.

Labor is key to understanding the social ramifications of construction. GPA summarized labor in a graph showing levels of labor for Great Houses from A.D. 900 to 1150 (reproduced here as figure 3.7). This chart, as well as the data it represents, has been central to many subsequent discussions of labor in Great House construction (for example, Durand 1992; Metcalf 2003; Wills 2000). New chronological data and new information on wood sources will change the shape of the chart and, presumably, our conclusions about the social ramifications of construction.

In light of the changes in chronology, the labor estimates in figure 3.7 will change. Because hundreds of new dates have not been analyzed, we refrain from recalculating the data used to generate figure 3.7. To present a new chart now would introduce a short-shelf-life schematic destined to be replaced by a more accurate representation. We are reasonably confident, however, that new chronological information will alter that chart in the following ways: It will flatten or displace negatively (earlier) the small peak at 930, possibly to 900. It will also flatten the curve from 1050 to 1100, possibly filling in the "valley" at 1070 and lowering the "peak" at 1100—still a slope up from 1050 to 1100, but perhaps a straighter and lower slope.

Additional new information affecting labor in figure 3.7 concerns the origins of the beams and wood. Wood procurement was, in total, the largest single class of labor for Chacoan construction events, and most of that labor cost came from transportation of the beams from distant forests to Chaco Canyon. GPA erroneously assumed the closest

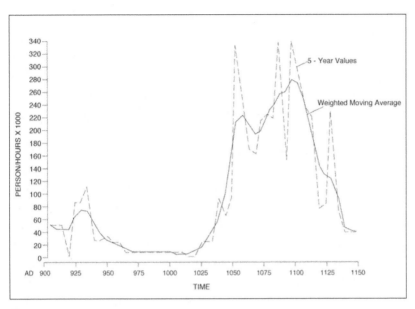

**FIGURE 3.7**

*The labor necessary to build Chaco Canyon Great Houses over time. (After Lekson
1984a:figure 5.2)*

forested source, Lobo Mesa, and a transport distance of 48 km (along
the South Road). Chemical "sourcing" has now determined that many
and perhaps most beams came from the Chuska Mountains or from
Mount Taylor (Durand et al. 1999; English et al. 2001). The airline distance from Pueblo Bonito to the Chuska Mountains (that is,
Washington Pass) is about 82 km, almost twice as far as the distances
used in GPA. We believe that these new data and new distances will
affect figure 3.7 in the following ways: relatively minor impacts on pre-
1000 construction, because many local species were used in early construction; significantly increased total labor requirements for the span
from 1050 to 1100, possibly by as much as 20 percent; and more mod-
estly increased (possibly by 5 percent) total labor requirements for
post-1100 construction, when room spans were smaller and timbering
less prodigal.

In combination, the new datings and new source studies should
have the effect of markedly increasing the magnitude of the labor
curve from 1050 to 1100, "flattening" that curve (that is, filling in

"valleys") and slightly decreasing its slope. The curve may look more like a histogram than a Dow-Jones average, with a solid block of high, sustained, and moderately increasing labor demands from 1050 to 1100. Tenth-century construction shifts slightly earlier to incorporate new ninth-century dates from Pueblo Bonito, and post-1100 construction plummets even more sharply than previously thought.

Fundamentally, the social ramifications of construction rest on the balance between available labor and labor demands. Does "1,000 person/days" mean one person working every day for two and three quarter years or fifty people for a fortnight? Unless somehow rooted in real experience, these kinds of calculations can devolve into numerology or worse. GPA offered a model of construction based on Richard Ford's data on San Juan Pueblo ditch clearing, arguing that a single, very large construction event could have been accomplished with social organization much like San Juan's, by a Chaco Canyon population of about five thousand (a figure very close to Hayes's [1981] population estimates from surveys). As noted in GPA, two obvious considerations should temper acceptance of the San Juan ditch-clearing model: typically, many construction events went on simultaneously at Chaco, and estimates of 5,000 people in the canyon are probably too high. Based on the number of kivas, Lekson (1984a) estimated between 2,100 and 2,700 people. Others estimate much lower permanent population at Chaco, as low as several hundred during 1050–1100 (Bernadini 1999; Windes 1984a). With resident population plummeting and labor requirements rising during the 1050–1100 span, the social ramifications of construction merit a new look. It seems likely that the labor force that built Chacoan Great Houses did not reside permanently in the canyon. Yet, Great Houses apparently had small but substantial numbers of permanent residents. Therefore, it is fair to say that the many built for the few.

The combination of fewer residents and significantly higher labor requirements suggests to us (at least) greater complexity in the organization of construction. Recent re-analyses, however, tend towards more simplicity, even communalism. Saitta (1997:19) rejects hierarchical complexity in Chacoan building, arguing instead for "collective appropriation of labor for Great House and road construction." How this might actually work is mysterious, and Saitta (1997:12) notes that "Chaco communalism...is of an unprecedented sort that lacks a good ethnographic analogue." Wills (2000:37) offers another argument for construction of Great Houses, by "patches," or largely independent work groups: "As long as patches share information with a few other patches and do not attempt to coordinate with all others, the overall system will converge on an optimal solution without direction from a centralized authority." In this model, the overarching motive for Great House building was ritual. Great House construction was a "collective ritual" (Wills 2000:37). Saitta and Wills eschew centralized hierarchies at Chaco, and they are not alone (for example, Mills 2002:77–80).

We believe that Great House construction required and reflected centralized, hierarchical decision making at Chaco. Increased labor requirements and decreased canyon population almost demand substantial external labor, its recruitment, and its coordination. "Patches" might optimize local construction activities, but those activities were in the service of architectural production of form. Patches and communalism might build the kind of haphazard villages (familiar all over the ancient Pueblo area) to which Great Houses stand in stark, formal contrast. We question "self-organization" of form: Great Houses, the city of Chaco, and the region itself were designed, and their creation coordinated, by planners and decision makers. As much or more than the labor required to create Chacoan architecture, its scale and formality strongly suggest centralized authority and hierarchy. We might wish that it were otherwise, but Chacoan construction very likely had bosses.

### Form

What *were* Great Houses? What were the *social correlates of form?* Originally, researchers assumed that Great Houses were pueblos, that is, agricultural villages with family residences (consisting of living rooms and storage rooms) and nondomestic spaces (such as kivas and plazas). In this model, the size of storage areas was, presumably, proportionate to family needs. Probable storage areas were much larger at Great Houses than in living pueblos. Moreover, far fewer people lived in Great Houses than we might expect from their total floor area (Bernadini 1999; Windes 1984a, 1987a, 1987b). This conundrum can be appreciated from both sides of the formula: first, by identifying small areas of residential space and, second, by identifying large areas of nonresidential space.

Several researchers have argued that, proportionately, only small areas of Great Houses were identifiably domestic. This conclusion primarily reflects the relative absence of floor features suggesting domestic or residential use (for example, fire pits). Might this absence be a problem of sampling or preservation? Architectural features such as fire pits might be underrepresented because Chaco Canyon Great House fire pits were, in fact, features usually recorded as "heating pits." Upper-story residential areas are underrepresented because floors with features did not survive. Upper-story residential space may be underrepresented in current reconstructions of Pueblo Bonito, Chetro Ketl, and other multistoried Great Houses. This problem, however, should not affect Windes's conclusions about single-story Pueblo Alto: only five households, Windes (1987a, 1987b) projects, for more than one hundred rooms. Pueblo Alto supports relatively low proportions of domestic or residential space at Great Houses.

*Kivas.* Another method for estimating population is the kiva (for example, Rohn 1983). Kivas avoid most problems of underrepresentation (very few upper-story kivas would be lost). Also, it should be noted, every kiva had a fine, formal fire pit (figure 3.8)—resolving, perhaps, the mystery of Chaco's missing fire pits? Rohn (1983) equated kivas with social units of twelve to fifteen people and considered kivas as dedicated ceremonial structures. Lekson estimated Chaco population directly from numbers of kivas, which he sees as primary residences. That is, each household had one kiva that was not a dedicated ceremonial chamber but, instead, the principal domestic structure. For Lekson, each Pueblo II kiva was the equivalent of a Pueblo I pit house, which is generally equated to a single household of five or six people (Lekson 1988a). This figure is half of Rohn's estimate. Rohn assumed that each kiva was associated with ten to twelve aboveground rooms, but that figure at large, recently excavated sites is much smaller, with one kiva per five to six rooms at the huge Yellow Jacket Site (Kuckelman 2003).

Kivas at Great Houses and other Pueblo II and III sites are conventionally interpreted as ceremonial structures, "underground chambers which may be compared to churches of later times" (according to the current Mesa Verde National Park brochure). Sites with many kivas are often interpreted as "ceremonial centers." Almost every large Pueblo III site in the Four Corners area has many kivas; consequently, the Mesa

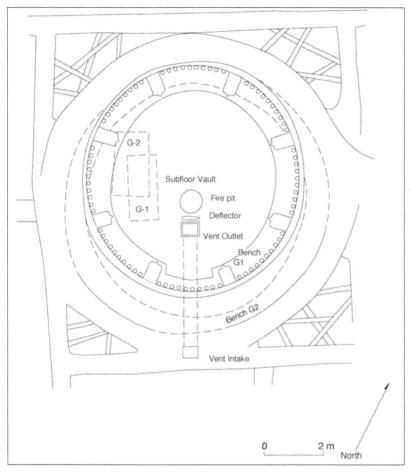

**FIGURE 3.8**

*A Chaco-style kiva: Kiva G at Chetro Ketl. (After Lekson, ed., 1983:figure 2.11)*

Verde region contains a surprising number of ceremonial centers (for example, Yellow Jacket: Lange et al. 1988)—all churches, no people. National Park Service (NPS) brochures once interpreted Chaco Great Houses with more kivas as more ceremonial than Great Houses with fewer kivas; therefore, Pueblo Bonito was godlier than Chetro Ketl. There is an element of absurdity here that was not lost on archaeologists, even as they perpetuated the idea that kivas were churches (for a good, brief review of the problem, reaching conclusions contrary to that presented here, see Crown and Wills 2003:518–519).

Lekson argues that kivas before 1300 were, in fact, pit houses (Lekson 1988a, 1988b, 1989a). In brief, what we have conventionally called "kivas" at Four Corners sites in the eleventh, twelfth, and thirteenth centuries are poor analogues for kivas at modern pueblos. Kivas at modern pueblos act (in part) as "integrative facilities" (Adler and Wilshusen 1990) and typically occur in ratios of one kiva per several scores or even hundreds of rooms. (Room-kiva ratios are assumed to indicate the approximate size of social groups "serviced" by the kiva [Lipe 1989; Plog 1974; Steward 1937].) Kivas before 1300 appear to be associated with families or households and (as noted above) appear in ratios of one kiva per six rooms, or less. Small kivas at Chaco and in the larger Four Corners region are better understood as the last, most elaborate stage in a long tradition of pit houses, which began in the Late Archaic and ended dramatically with the epochal depopulation of the Four Corners and massive population movements of the fourteenth century. Before 1300, Pueblo II and III kivas were as common as pit houses had been in Pueblo I, with scores and even hundreds of kivas at large sites. After 1300, small kivas all but disappear, at least in the Eastern Anasazi.

Kivas at these Chaco and Mesa Verde sites were one element (and maybe the most significant element) of a house or household. The house also encompassed a suite or apartment of a half-dozen, aboveground "Pueblo" rooms. At Pueblo Bonito, these suites were linear, running from plaza to exterior wall of the building. Plaza-facing rooms and the second room in were probably for daily activities; additional interior rooms may have been for domestic storage (figure 3.9). The kiva was the focus of the household and probably the main sleeping area during cold winters and hot summers. This is not to say that kivas were not also ritual; almost certainly, domestic and life-cycle ritual was a substantial aspect of kivas.

Thus, numbers of small kivas at Great Houses directly reflect the number of households. At Pueblo Bonito, this number was about thirty-seven (of which perhaps a half, at a guess, were used contemporaneously). At Wijiji, that number was only two. Population estimates based on the number of kivas at Great Houses are congruent with those of Bernadini and Windes (developed on other data) and support the notion of relatively few households at Great Houses. Again, only small portions of Great Houses were residential.

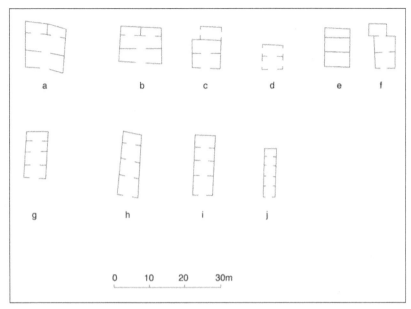

**FIGURE 3.9**

*Schematic room suites from Chaco Canyon Great Houses:* (a), *920–935;* (b), *1020–1040;* (c), (d), *and* (e), *1050–1060;* (f) *and* (g), *1065–1070;* (h), *1075–1085;* (i), *1095–1105;* (j), *after 1105. (After Lekson, 1984a:figure 3.8)*

Great Kivas are the most conspicuous ritual or ceremonial architecture at Chaco, although we are increasingly appreciating roads and mounds in this regard. Consider Great Kivas (figure 3.10). Archaeologists not anachronistically bound to historical Pueblo models have suggested that Great Kivas were administrative centers (albeit for Mexican administrators: Kelley and Kelley 1975) or redistribution facilities (Plog 1974:127).

We believe, with most archaeologists, that Great Kivas were indeed "community integrative structures" (Adler and Wilshusen 1990). The key for us is the term *community*. Great Kivas appear to be associated with Anasazi communities in general and are not specific to either Great Houses or Chaco Canyon. Of course, there were Great Kivas at Chaco, and a few were built into Chaco Great Houses, but the distribution of Great Kivas in time and space argues that they are not essential to the Chacoan architectural tradition. The Great Kiva form precedes and follows the era of Chaco Great Houses: there are Great Kivas at

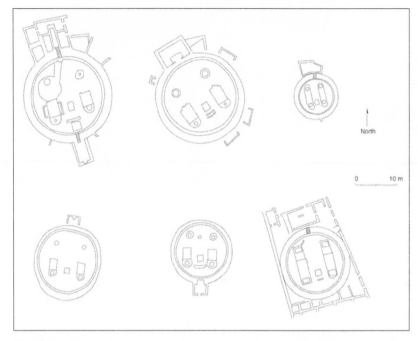

**Figure 3.10**

*Great Kivas at Chaco Canyon.* Top row, left to right: *Casa Rinconada, Chetro Ketl, and Chetro Ketl "Court Kiva."* Bottom row, left to right: *Kin Nahasbas, Pueblo Bonito II, and Pueblo Bonito I. (Redrawn from plans in Vivian and Reiter 1960)*

Basketmaker III sites and at Pueblo IV villages—and, perhaps, in the plazas of many modern Rio Grande pueblos. (Great Kivas of Chaco and Mesa Verde are more reasonably seen as "ancestral" versions of contemporary pueblo kivas, if we are looking for architectural precedents.) Details of construction and internal features vary with place and change with time—how should they not? But a large, "communal integrative structure" central to Anasazi communities defines the much larger Pueblo, and not Chaco, building tradition.

Some Chaco Great Houses have Great Kivas; some do not. Some Anasazi communities contemporary with Chaco Canyon have Great Kivas but not Great Houses (for example, Herr 2001). There are Great Kivas without communities (*isolated Great Kivas*). We do not entirely understand how Great Kivas worked or what they did. We do think that Great Kivas and Great Houses operated in different but intersecting contexts. Again, outliers may demonstrate this more clearly than the dense palimpsest of downtown Chaco. For example, a circular berm/earthwork surrounded the Bluff Great House; a Great Kiva, on the same terrace, lies outside the berm (Cameron 2002). That pattern is common to, and we believe typical of, Chacoan communities. Great Kivas and Great Houses are present, but often not in near proximity or direct association. Van Dyke (n.d.a) notes that Chaco Canyon may "capture" Great Kivas from the Chaco halo—and we see her argument as demonstrating that Great Houses were one thing and Great Kivas, another.

*Warehouses.* The reverse of the problem of residential/nonresidential space addresses large areas of apparently nonresidential space. If large segments of Great Houses were not residential, then what were they? Large, empty, featureless interior rooms (which constitute the vast majority of Great House spaces) are conventionally consigned to the general category of storage. In view of low proportions of residential space, many archaeologists conclude that the few residents of Great Houses enjoyed or administered disproportionate storage space (as discussed above). Featureless rooms, of course, represent generalized space, which might be used for almost anything. Motels? Slave pens? Architectural massing to create tall, impressive, empty monuments?

A positive argument for storage, instead of temporary quarters or empty massing, can be made for the southeast quarter of Pueblo Bonito (refer to figure 1.4 and plate 5). This part of Pueblo Bonito was added late in Chaco's history (1077–1082; Windes and Ford 1996). It consisted of three rows of rooms, three or four stories tall. These were large, (apparently) featureless, (mostly) interior rooms. Ground-level floors were featureless, and there is no information suggesting floor features on upper stories. When excavated, these rooms were empty, save for a few interesting artifacts (such as two axes in the middle of a floor) that may represent closing ceremonies instead of detritus or refuse. (It seems unlikely that two stone axes, carefully placed in the center of an otherwise empty floor, represent an ax storage room.)

The majority of these rooms would have been deeply enclosed, two or more rooms away from the exterior, horizontally, and one or more floors from the exterior, vertically. They would not conventionally be seen as residential spaces. The types of doors seen in these rooms support a storage function. Exterior doors in Chacoan buildings were often (typically?) T-shaped; interior residential doors were sometimes (often?) full-length and rectangular. Doors in storage rooms, at Chaco and elsewhere in the Anasazi region are often (typically?) small, window-like openings midway up the wall (see figure 3.6). Storage doors were small, to allow easy sealing with stone or wood slabs, mudded in place (as in many canyon granaries through the Four Corners region). Slabs were often accommodated by "secondary jambs," narrow, sloping, inset jambs against which the closing slab would fit tightly. These slabs give us evidence of access patterns: they slope out in the direction from which the room was "closed." Like a corked bottle, the small storage door was capable of very complete closure, protecting whatever was behind the sealed door.

Multiple, small "storage" doors penetrate the walls of southeastern Pueblo Bonito. Many walls have more than one such door; one wall has five, two in each corner and three along the length of the wall. Almost all of Pueblo Bonito's "corner doors" (storage doors running diagonally through corners) are found in this area, connecting rooms in all directions. Moreover, along the rear (exterior) wall of the southeast part of Pueblo Bonito (and, indeed, along Pueblo Bonito's rear wall around most of its circumference), there were very narrow continuous balconies along the second and perhaps third stories. The exterior walls, along the balconies, were pierced by a series of small storage doors at each room (now blocked with masonry). The balconies served (at least in part) for access from the exterior into storage rooms.

Some walls in this part of Pueblo Bonito look like Swiss cheese: (almost) more doors than masonry (see figure 3.6). This plethora—an embarrassment of doors—together with external "balconies," maximized movement around closed/sealed rooms (and, possibly, through subdivided, closed/sealed rooms). If an interior room was closed/sealed, access to rooms beyond it was still possible via corner doors or rear balconies. With so many potential routes of access, there is no way that "you can't get there from here." Vertical connections through the three levels of floors undoubtedly ramified communication routes. Like fire pits, hatchways are now gone beyond recovery, so we cannot accurately model their occurrence. The likelihood of internal hatchways and vertical connections in most rooms greatly increases access (and compromises horizontal models of connectivity based only on preserved doorways; for example, Bustard 2003, among others).

The southeastern part of Pueblo Bonito was designed (and subsequently much modified) to allow access and movement around, rather than through, "sealed" rooms. Presumably, if doors were sealed, something was stored inside. The architecture of this portion of Pueblo Bonito probably represents a long-term, warehouse-like storage technology and hints at the function of massed internal rooms at other Great Houses.

It should be noted that other units proposed in GPA as "warehouse" sections or buildings (such as Kin Kletso, of which more below) do not exhibit the remarkable redundancy of doorway and access patterns of this section of Pueblo Bonito. Conversely, walls at Kin Kletso are much shorter in horizontal dimension than Pueblo Bonito, not room for more than one door per wall.

Therefore, we believe that relatively few people lived in Great Houses, as indicated by the relatively small numbers of kivas per room compared with Chacoan small sites and Pueblo III sites. Great Houses had large areas designed for storage, and the architecture of those areas suggests something other than the domestic storage seen at non Great House sites.

Not all Great Houses, it seems, were functionally equivalent. Envisioning identical or even similar functions at Pueblo Bonito and a McElmo site such as Kin Kletso, for example, is difficult. Even though the resident population was relatively small at Pueblo Bonito, McElmo structures such as Kin Kletso, New Alto, or Wijiji may have had only one or two households (based on the number of kivas). The absence of middens or trash mounds at most late or McElmo-phase Great Houses (Vivian and Mathews 1965) also supports the idea of very small populations at these structures.

Gordon Vivian and T. W. Mathews (1965) and Gwinn Vivian (1990) interpret these differences as ethnic; that is, different ethnic groups built and occupied McElmo sites and sites like Pueblo Bonito. In our opinion, McElmo sites do not represent a separate ethnic group, but rather a different type of building, probably nondomestic, built late in the history of Chacoan architecture. Compare arguments in Lekson (1984a:267–269) and Gwinn Vivian (1990:375–376) and, for an intriguing new analysis of McElmo sites as monuments, Van Dyke (2004). After full, fair, and balanced deliberation, Lekson favors Lekson.

*Palaces.* Who were the relatively small numbers of people who lived in Great Houses? Many archaeologists refer to these small, permanent resident populations as "caretaker populations" of structures that were basically ceremonial (for example, Bernardini 1999; Crown and Wills 2003; Judge 1989; Wills 2000, 2001.). Great Houses were, in some undefined way, ritual structures. (Exactly how a Great House promoted or supported ritual is seldom, if ever, addressed. What ritual required construction of Pueblo Bonito?) The argument can also be made that the Great Houses were elite residences (Neitzel 2003a; Lipe, chapter 8, and Lekson, chapter 1, of this volume).

Elite habitation (and warehouse functions, suggested here) do not preclude large and perhaps preeminent ceremonial functions. In Pueblo society today, church and state are not structurally separate, nor should we expect them to be separate, architecturally, in ancient times.

Major Great Houses were something like palaces—if *palace* is taken to mean a residence of rulers that also incorporates other important functions, such as nondomestic storage, public ceremony, and offices (dedicated spaces) for community functions and secondary leadership. Elite residence was only one of several functions of the largest buildings: warehouse-like storage rooms, ritual architecture (Great Kivas, platform mounds, and so on), sharply defined public assembly areas (enclosed plazas), and a range of other functions.

We believe that the residents of Great Houses were social elites and rulers. As discussed elsewhere (Lekson, chapter 1 of this volume), this interpretation meets with considerable resistance. One line of argument counters that we cannot see the rulers—they built no monuments to themselves. There are no stelae at Chaco, at least, none that we recognize. Can we "see" these rulers? Yes, in burials (Akins 2001, 2003; Akins and Schelberg 1984) and—most important, if apparently circularly—in their architecture. The strongest substantiation of hierarchy at Chaco comes from the sites that *define* Chaco: Great Houses—not Great Temples, or Great Pilgrimage Destinations, or Great Community Halls, but *Great Houses*. The Great House form begins as oversized Anasazi residential architecture and then separates from Anasazi building in an architectural tradition that combines residence (kivas and room suites) with other forms and functions. But the residential "house" was never lost.

The very core of Chacoan archaeology is the difference between Great Houses and other Anasazi building, including (most important) contemporary small sites. At a guess, 95 percent of Anasazi people in Chaco's region resided in small "unit pueblos" or "Prudden units," whereas 5 percent lived in Great Houses. Chaco is Great Houses. The vast difference in housing seems such obvious, unmistakable evidence of hierarchy that I have trouble understanding why this, the central "fact" of Chaco archaeology, is questioned. But it is.

## SMALL SITES

Small sites are the other side of Chaco's architectural coin. National Park Service surveys of the canyon located more than three hundred "pueblos" of various sizes contemporaneous with Great Houses (Hayes 1981:26–30). Discussions of Chacoan architecture have long been tainted by the assumptions and lexicon of the 1930s, which heavily influenced subsequent work as analyses of dichotomy. With only marginal success, the Chaco Project tried to sidestep baggage-laden labels such as "village," "Hosta Butte," and "hamlet" applied to smaller pueblos, by calling them "small sites." Discussion of architecture in Chaco remained divided (Lekson 1984a versus McKenna and Truell 1986). As Truell recognized, our best approach to the architecture of Chaco is possibly from the standpoint of continuous variation rather than difference (Truell 1986:315; see also Lekson in McKenna and Truell 1986:1; Bustard 1996).

We believe, along with many other archaeologists, that before the late ninth century, the architectural sequence at Chaco paralleled and even lagged behind architectural developments in the larger Anasazi region (Wilshusen and Van Dyke, chapter 7, and Lipe, chapter 8, of this volume). Only in the late ninth century did Chaco's architecture diverge from larger regional traditions, and then, only in the emergent "Great House" form.

There was an exception: Chaco early experienced an exceptionally large pair of Basketmaker III sites, Shabik'eschee and 29SJ423 (discussed above; see also Wills and Windes 1989). Chaco Basketmaker III architecture, however, was very similar to its contemporaries within the larger region. Subsequent small-site architecture paralleled the larger region through at least the mid-eleventh century, when builders began using, in some small sites, attributes long employed in Great House construction. Before this, the architecture of Chaco's small buildings was modular and predictable. Earth and adobe were the principle elements. Ground plans for earlier small sites consisted of a unit pueblo, or Prudden unit, (Lipe, chapter 8 of this volume) with a pit structure backed by a single room suite or several contiguous suites. Each suite consisted of a large room backed with two smaller rooms (often with tub-like depressions in them, a common feature in Pueblo I) (figure 3.11; refer to figure 1.4). Walls were of puddled adobe or irregular, hand-formed adobe bricks ("turtlebacks," from their slightly ridged, loaf shape), with few, if any, stone elements.

This modular unit also provided the model for the early ninth-century Great House suites, only writ in stone (Type I masonry). During the eleventh century, many domestic features (mealing bins, storage pits/bins, hearths) previously found in pit structures began appearing in surface rooms. Pit structures changed form and shrank as Chacoans moved the domestic features to nearby rooms. Aboveground rooms increasingly became more uniform in size. After A.D. 1050, Chacoans moved pit structures, now circular and conventionally referred to as "kivas," closer to the aboveground house and often enclosed them within rectangular walls ("blocked-in," Truell 1986:174). Most small-site walls were now built of stone masonry. Other than this change in fabric and the repositioning of domestic features from pit structures to rooms, small site architecture remained unremarkable in its regional context. No novel forms, new construction techniques, or unique patterning of fixed features set Chaco small sites apart from the larger regional tradition.

Nonetheless, the history of small sites at Chaco is far more complex than the steady progression suggested by Hayes (1981), based largely on surface survey data. Variation within contemporary Chaco small sites, for example, in kiva construction and form (figure 3.12), is sufficient to warrant the suggestion that builders in Chaco operated under different traditions. That is, small sites suggest a multiethnic valley in the center of the San Juan Basin. The suggestion of disparate, contemporary cultural traditions is a strong thread in discussions of the "town-

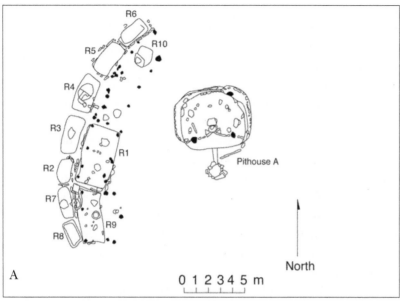

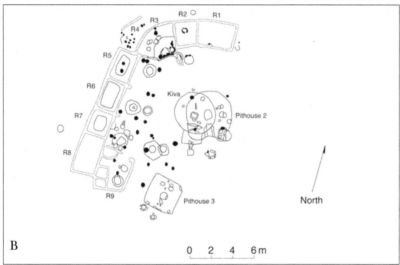

**FIGURE 3.11**

(a) *Pueblo I unit pueblo, site 29SJ724, Chaco Canyon (after McKenna and Truell 1986:figure 1.15)* and (b) *Pueblo II unit pueblo, site 29SJ629, Chaco Canyon (after McKenna and Truell 1986:figure 1.16).*

village" differences initiated by Kluckhohn (1939:158–159) and extended by Gordon Vivian (Vivian and Mathews 1965) and Gwinn Vivian (1990), who see one cultural tradition in small sites and another in Great Houses. As discussed above, Gordon Vivian also suggested two separate traditions within the Great House sites, the "Bonito Phase" and "McElmo Phase" (Vivian and Mathews 1965:108–111), extending the number of contemporary traditions to three.

Considerations of multiple ethnic or cultural traditions have never been applied *within* the set of residential small sites. Studies at the Pueblo Pintado community, however, suggested to Windes and others (2000) that two early small-house communities each showed ceramic evidence of origins from opposite sides of the basin. According to Windes, these two distinct communities later joined to construct the Great House of Pueblo Pintado, itself an architectural fusion of diverse small-site groups. We suggest, then, that small sites at Chaco may have represented more than one ethnic or cultural tradition, a matter of potential significance to the history of Chaco Canyon and the nature of the Bonito phase.

In the latter eleventh century, numerous architectural techniques and features characteristic of Great Houses existed at many small sites, elements of classic Chaco-style kivas (radial pilasters, floor vaults, and subfloor ventilators). Masonry, usually compound in form, became more massive and Great House–like, and several multistoried small sites were built. Marcia Truell (1986:figure 2.16 and appendix B) noted more than forty small sites with core and veneer masonry, a staple of Great House construction. Almost all these sites are late in the Chaco sequence, that is, after 1080. Several sites were more formal in plan than earlier unit pueblos and contain the Chaco-style kivas. These Great House–like sites concentrate around South Gap in downtown Chaco. Several of the largest small sites are comparable in size to named, smaller Great Houses such as Casa Chiquita. A few may not represent "Pueblos." Some of these Great House–like constructions may instead represent monumental architecture related to roads (for example, ramps) or other nondomestic structures (Stein, Friedman, and Blackhorse n.d.). It is our opinion that, if transported to other parts of the Anasazi region, many of the late South Gap small sites would receive serious consideration as outlying Great Houses. Is this a problem of semantics? of classification? Certainly. But increased massing extends to other small sites, particularly in the canyon's core area, suggesting a "Bonito effect" (if you will), techniques and traditions that subtly permeate the architecture of contemporary small sites.

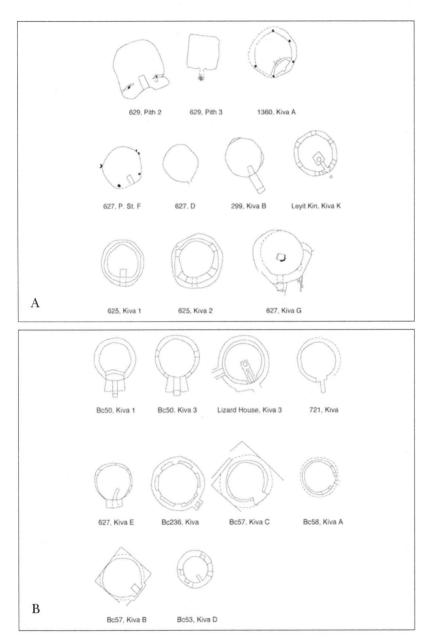

**FIGURE 3.12**

*Small house kivas from selected Chaco Canyon sites:* (a) *late 900s to mid-1000s (after McKenna and Truell 1986:figure 2.7) and* (b) *late 1000s to mid-1100s (after McKenna and Truell 1986:figure 2.8).*

Yet, before and during the Bonito phase, unit pueblo small sites were almost certainly family residences—albeit, in some cases, for large extended families. Some Chaco small sites consist of aggregations of several unit pueblos, notably the Bc sites in downtown Chaco (figure 3.13). Comparative space-syntax studies of spatial arrangements at small sites and Great Houses by Wendy Bustard (1996, 2003) show that Chacoans arranged and used the two classes of buildings (after the early Bonito phase) in very different ways. Although both show strong "tree" patterns of accessibility (versus "circularity" patterns), identification of households in Great Houses becomes difficult after the Early Bonito phase. In contrast, the residential patterns remain sufficiently strong for Bustard to find a persistent and consistent module, or "genotype," for small site room function and organization (Bustard 1995).

Whether the occupation of small sites is of consistent intensity through time is not clear. There is certainly good reason to suggest low late Basketmaker and Pueblo I period occupations (much lower than projected by Hayes 1981). For subsequent periods, multiple occupations (creating deep, often stratigraphically mixed, complex sites) pose challenges in interpreting occupational periods, particularly for the 1050–1100 period, when (convention holds) Chaco was most heavily occupied. Excavations at small sites by the Chaco Project (in the Una Vida cluster) and by the University of New Mexico (in the Bc sites of the Pueblo Bonito cluster) failed to recover strong evidence of the 1050–1100 horizon in ceramic assemblages. Reassessment by Windes (1993, 2001a) suggests that some movement occurred during this span, perhaps concentrating residents around Pueblo Bonito and the core downtown area at the expense of other communities in the canyon. Again, this points to the developing urbanization of the central canyon and the increasing interaction between Great Houses and small sites (in footprint if not in function) through time.

Three lines of evidence suggest a continuum of architectural design and construction style between the two site types in Chaco: (1) the commonality of suite design between early Great Houses and small sites of all periods, (2) Windes's case studies suggesting small site convergence into Great House forms, and (3) possible coalescence of small sites into the central canyon (downtown). Clearly, the timing and sequence of small sites makes a great difference in understanding Chaco's demographics and the Bonito-phase cityscape. There was far

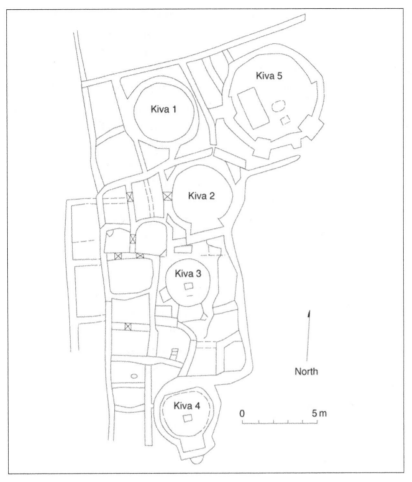

**FIGURE 3.13**

*Bc 59: note the conjoined, multiple "unit pueblos." (After McKenna and Truell 1986:figure A.111)*

more to Chaco than a dozen named Great Houses, but how much more and what small sites mean in the history and architecture of Chaco are matters still open to interpretive debate.

## AFTER CHACO

They ceased building Great Houses at Chaco Canyon about 1125. The elements might conspire to mask later building: uppermost stories or plaza-facing rooms (undoubtedly among the last built) would expose beams more directly to rain and snow than deeper, earlier interior rooms. For this reason, our tree-ring samples may be biased toward earlier construction and against later building. Even so, major construction likely stopped after the first quarter of the twelfth century.

How did Chaco end? Notably, large sections of Pueblo Bonito were apparently burnt. Large-scale conflagrations probably were not accidental. Chacoan masonry made very effective fire walls, so how could fire jump from one room to another over large areas of the site? Fire was common at kivas in many Great Houses, but less so in rooms. Large parts of Pueblo del Arroyo and Pueblo Bonito burned, but Pueblo Alto, Chetro Ketl, and Kin Kletso did not.

We have devoted far more time and energy to Chaco's origins than its end. A big drought from 1130 to 1180 pretty much explains everything, yes? Things were probably more complicated than that. The shift from Chaco to Salmon and Aztec predates that final drought by decades; that is, the move was on while the rain was still falling. For Pueblo history, the leaving of Chaco may be of more moment than its beginning. Many Pueblo people remember Chaco as a place where both wonderful and terrible things happened, and its end signaled the beginning of new ceremonial understandings, new social contracts, new ways of living.

What became of Great Houses after Chaco ended? In immediate and practical terms, people either reoccupied or continued to occupy them long after final dated construction (Lekson and Cameron 1995). They subdivided large Chacoan rooms, dismantled ceilings, and inserted small kivas into old square and rectangular chambers. It is worth noting that several Great Kivas were reroofed and refloored in the thirteenth century. That is, although people detrimentally modified or dismantled the Great Houses, they maintained the Great Kivas. Wilcox (1993) (and, at one time, Lekson—and he may yet again) believed that Chaco Canyon continued as a vital center through the twelfth century and into the thirteenth. According to this argument, the end of large-scale construction did not signal the end of Chaco Canyon. Wilcox could be right: the buildings were so well built (and the environment so dry) that sections remained standing, open, and usable seven centuries after they were built. Unless deliberately dismantled, Great Houses were probably in excellent condition through the late twelfth and thirteenth centuries.

And the *idea* of Chacoan building? What became of the architectural tradition? There are several possibilities. Great Houses, effectively identical to Pueblo Bonito and Chetro Ketl, continued to be built at Aztec and in the Totah district of the San Juan River (McKenna and Toll 1992). Salmon Ruins (directly on the San Juan River) was built in the mid to late 1080s, and the Great House complex at Aztec (on Rio Animas, a smaller tributary of the San Juan) began shortly thereafter, with most construction between 1100 and 1270. Lekson (1999) suggests Chaco as a political capital and ceremonial center moved north, physically relocating itself from Chaco Canyon to Aztec Ruins (a reconstruction earlier proposed by Judge 1989, among others). Wilcox, as noted above, sees Aztec and Chaco as contemporary, competing centers. However Aztec is interpreted, there can be no doubt that Aztec was the principal and perhaps unrivaled center in the northern San Juan region throughout the Pueblo III period, and it continued the canons and scales of downtown Chaco.

The Chacoan architectural tradition continued in other areas as well. Lipe (chapter 8 of this volume) and Duff and Lekson (chapter 9 of this volume) present more detailed treatments of post-Chacoan architecture in and beyond the old Chaco region. Here, we offer a few general observations on the larger legacy of Chaco's Great Houses. Fowler and Stein (1992) argue that Great House forms continued and evolved (without Chaco) well into Pueblo III, an idea supported by the subsequent work of Kintigh (1994, 1996; Kintigh, Howell, and Duff 1996). Lekson suggests that Chaco Great Houses were the first examples of architectural "pueblos"—large, massed, multistoried, terraced, plaza-oriented, village-size settlements (Lekson 1989b; Lekson and Cameron 1995). In art historian George Kubler's (1962) terms, Great Houses were the "prime objects" of Pueblo building, creations both profound and fundamental, which inspired and transformed the subsequent trajectory of regional architecture. The Bonito phase produced the first and possibly greatest "Pueblo-style" buildings, and we can trace that tradition through Pueblo III and Pueblo IV towns to the living Pueblo villages of today.

## CITYSCAPE

Chaco was a city. This controversial claim may strike archaeologists working with real civilizations as shameless social climbing.

Recognizing Chaco as urban is important, however, both particularly and generally. Particularly, the historical development of a city in the Pueblo past goes far in explaining the Pueblo present. Generally, Chaco offers a significant (and unusual) case for the larger understanding of urbanization. In this section, we discuss principles, elements, and Ciudad Chaco. The section "Principles" leaps past the details to make a case for an urban Chaco, briefly presenting remarkable new research that demonstrates architectural conceptions in Chaco Canyon far beyond the scale of individual buildings. "Elements" briefly recounts the wide range of monumental and nonmonumental forms that, combined with Great Houses, composed a large, complicated urban center. "Ciudad Chaco" evaluates Chaco in the larger world of cities and explores why urbanization at Chaco was and is important.

### Principles

Chaco architecture operated on scales much larger than individual buildings. The Chaco Project, following long-established Southwestern conventions, initially treated each Great House as a separate settlement (for example, Hayes 1981), but we soon recognized that the central core of Chaco Canyon (downtown) was a larger settlement of intriguing complexity, consisting of Great Houses, small sites, roads, platform mounds, earthworks, and many other landscape features (Lekson 1984a; Stein and Lekson 1992). Subsequent research has enormously expanded our understanding of downtown Chaco as a large architectural composition: a really big settlement or (as we argue here) a small city.

Most of the recent important work on the Chaco cityscape has been done by two groups: the Chaco Protection Sites group of John Stein, Taft Blackhorse, Rich Friedman, and allies and the Solstice Project of Anna Sofaer and her colleagues. (All participated in the Chaco Synthesis Project.) The work of both groups is unconventional and, to a degree, underpublished, but both groups have produced valuable conclusions and insights. Sofaer (1997) and a very useful video ("The Mystery of Chaco Canyon," 1999) have summarized the Solstice Project's remarkable work. The Chaco Protection Site group's work has been presented, most accessibly, by Stein, Ford, and Friedman (2003) and Stein, Friedman, and Blackhorse (n.d.). Their reconstructions of Chaco are, admittedly, "a balance of fact and reasoned fantasy" (Stein, Ford, and Friedman 2003:59), combining meticulous field observations and measurements with creative but (I feel) reasonable extrapolation and interpretation. All archaeology beyond simple measurements extrapolates and interprets, and the limits we impose on those actions reflect taste as much as method. "The observer should feel entirely free to disagree with the suggested restoration and to revise it to the satisfaction of his own judgment" (Proskouriakoff [1946] 1963:xv). Interpretively, we should err on the side of complication, elaboration ("The Sin of Ockham," Lekson, chapter 1 of this volume.) We may be certain that ancient life and all its material manifestations were far more complicated than the simplest account we could write, our closest reading of the data. Therefore, I credit these architectural reconstructions as being closer to the truth (and more responsible to the past) than are the bare facts (or our simplest account of them), the "data" so often invoked to keep Chaco simple.

A picture is worth a thousand words. The image in plate 8, produced by the Chaco Protection Site group (Stein, Friedman, and Blackhorse n.d.), may not be "correct" in every detail, but I believe that, in fact, Chaco looked something like this. Stein and his colleagues and Sofaer and her colleagues follow the pioneering and underappreciated work of John Fritz (1978), who perceived Chaco as a landscape or cityscape with important design canons that transcend functional requirements or precepts. For decades, archaeologists and architects have considered the cityscape of Chaco to be determined largely by local ecologies/hydrologies, or other functional or utilitarian criteria: An early, influential study interpreted the design of Pueblo Bonito as "solar efficient" (for example, Knowles 1974, one of the first, but not the last, solar analyses of Pueblo Bonito). The placement of larger Great Houses on the northern side of Chaco Wash has long been linked to the higher runoff rates of canyon rims on the north side, contrasted to the south side (Vivian 1990).

Without a doubt, pragmatic and practical considerations were influential in the Chaco cityscape (particularly in the earlier part of the Chaco era). But Fritz, Stein, Sofaer, and their colleagues make a strong case that Chaco was much more than villages built at environmentally favorable sites. Whether their interpretations of the cityscape are completely accurate, they are visionary in demonstrating that Chaco (like Mississippian and Mesoamerican cityscapes) was created *by design*; that is, Chacoans built according to cosmological, geomantic, aesthetic, and symbolic principles. Chaco design canons were, to a large degree, unconstrained by pragmatic factors such as solar efficiency and water control, except as forms inherited from earlier traditions, reinterpreted in Chaco's architectural grammar.

### Elements

We have discussed Great Houses and small houses; the other constructed elements of the cityscape included earthworks, roads, and waterworks (see also Lekson, chapter 1 of this volume). These elements were combined in a complex cityscape, which we have recognized only in the past decade and are only beginning to understand.

Small houses were a major element of the cityscape. Windes argues that many small houses were abandoned during the Bonito phase. Lekson thinks that most were occupied simultaneously with Great Houses. In either case, small houses were conspicuous landscape features, as living houses or as ruins. If occupied contemporaneously with the Great Houses, they might have brought life to the formal Chacoan landscape. The daily activities of the Anasazi world would be manifest in these homes and houses, in stark contrast to the huge, walled, enclosed Great Houses. Would elite residents of the Great Houses comport themselves conspicuously over Great House roofs and plazas, mending moccasins, weaving baskets, plucking turkeys, or performing any of the quotidian activities shown in conventional reconstructions of Pueblo Bonito?

Maybe not. All that daily business and practical bustle characterized small house life, but perhaps not Great Houses. Great Houses were scenes of action (constant construction, much pomp, and possibly circumstance) but not rustic village scenes. If, however, small houses were largely empty during the heyday of Great Houses (as Windes suggests), the decaying ruins of the smaller structures would create an altogether different architectural complement to the growing Great Houses, which were almost constantly under construction. In either case, forms of and actions around Great House and small sites could have been counterpart and, in some sense, counterpoint.

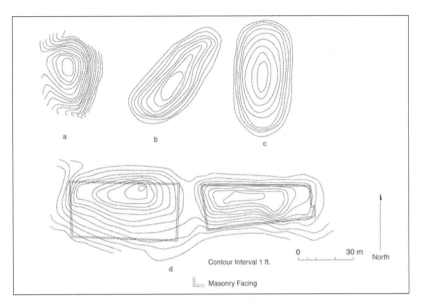

**FIGURE 3.14**

*Mounds, Chaco Canyon:* (a), *Peñasco Blanco;* (b), *Pueblo Alto;* (c), *Chetro Ketl; and* (d), *Pueblo Bonito. (After Lekson 1984a:figure 3.14)*

Earthworks were another major element of Chacoan building (Cameron 2002; Stein and Lekson 1992; for a skeptical analysis, see Wills 2001), and they probably have a deep history in Anasazi architectural traditions. Historically, low earthen mounds at Anasazi sites were conventionally seen as middens or trash mounds. That was because they contained the detritus of daily living—trash—but they also, and importantly, contained nontrash: burials of loved ones, caches of ritual objects, and architectural features such as fire pits. Trash mounds in early Anasazi building were more than middens.

The most obvious examples of earthen architecture were two rectangular, masonry-faced platform mounds in front of Pueblo Bonito (figure 3.14; see plate 8). These mounds stood almost 2 m tall, and they had thick, repeated adobe upper surfaces, with stairways to reach these surfaces from ground level. Other mounds, such as those at Chetro Ketl and Pueblo Alto, lacked the masonry facing, surfaces, and stairways, but they, too, can be seen as architecture instead of simple middens. Notably, several large Great Houses lack mounds altogether

(Hungo Pavi, Wijiji); some others have mounds wildly out of proportion to their size. Significant portions of the fill of these mounds were, indeed, trash, but often that trash was not the result of conventional daily living. Toll argues that much of the deposition at the Alto trash mound was ritual or ceremonial in nature (Toll 1985).

Wills (2001) says that both interpretations are wrong and that Chaco mounds are, in fact, middens. (Windes also believes that mounds are, at least in part, middens but fulfilled other architectural roles, much as they did at small sites.) Wills is probably wrong about Alto (Toll, chapter 4 of this volume), and he is almost certainly wrong about Pueblo Bonito. Its mounds are clearly architectural (although they incorporated midden deposits). We feel that the reconstructions of these mounds in GPA (Lekson 1984a:figure 3.14) survive Wills's critique. The mounds remain walled rectangular forms, with internal cells and access stairways; they are architecture. In Wills's critique of the reconstructed profile, he ignores excavation photographs that specifically show a thickly replastered adobe surface atop the mounds, published by Windes (1987a, 1987b:figure 8.10). We remain confident that the Pueblo Bonito trash middens were platform mounds comparable in form and size to later Hohokam examples.

Is there something wrong, untoward, about earthen architecture at Chaco? Mounds (that is, earthen architecture) were common among corn-growing societies in North America (Morgan 1994:44, 1999) and Mexican/Mesoamerican examples too numerous to cite. Mounds were a fixture of Chaco's near neighbor, the Hohokam (Crown and Judge 1991; Haury 1976). Given the nearly continental distribution of mounds and earthen architecture, we think that it would be remarkable if earthen features were absent at Chaco. We do not understand the reluctance of some archaeologists to acknowledge architectural mounds at Chaco Canyon. Why should this architectural tradition—modest in comparison with Hohokam, Hopewell, and Mississippian—strike us as outré, beyond the limits or possibilities of Anasazi building?

At Great House outliers, there is a clarity that makes this point more emphatically than in the crowded, complex, heavily impacted downtown Chaco. Stein and Lekson (1992) once looked to Chaco Canyon to validate earthen architecture posited at outliers; now we move away from the canyon to reestablish the reality of earthen building at the center. We briefly overstep the chapter's geographic boundaries to offer some strong (unarguable?) examples of earthen architecture: large (300–400 m diameter), almost perfectly circular berms surrounding several outliers. These are Holmes's Group, on the Rio La Plata near Farmington, New Mexico (Dykeman and Langenfeld 1987); Brewer Mesa Pueblo about 10 miles south of Dove Creek, Colorado (now protected by the Archaeological Conservancy); and Lee's Circle, a few miles southwest of Ganado, Arizona (Baker 2003). In size and geometric precision (but not in total fill), these circles rival earlier, more massive, and culturally unrelated Hopewell earthworks (Morgan 1999)—the Newark circle is 320 m in diameter. It cannot be argued that these circular earthworks were simple middens. (These berms may or may not parallel "roads," but that does not affect the argument.) Earthen circles confirm the reality and importance of Chacoan earthen architecture.

Mounds at Pueblo Bonito and other Great Houses were not the only earthen structures in the Chaco cityscape. Substantial berms lined several intracanyon roads (that is, the Poco site; Drager and Lyons 1985:20), and freestanding mounds, unassociated with any particular Great House, have been suggested for downtown Chaco (Stein, Friedman, and Blackhorse n.d.).

Roads themselves have a long, if discontinuous, history in Chacoan research (ably chronicled by Gwinn Vivian 1997a, 1997b; see also Lekson, chapter 1 of this volume). Roads are wide, linear, landscape constructions that connect sites and landscape features within and beyond the canyon. Linear features are familiar in world archaeology: cursus, dyke, *sacbe*—none functioned as do modern transportation corridors. What were they? It seems clear that people moved along Chacoan roads. Where a road meets a cliff or slope, people constructed an elaborate stairway that continued the road's alignment and (equally important) the road's width. Hand and toe holds sufficed for the vast majority of Anasazi trails; road ramps and stairs were broad, formal, and monumental. We do not believe, however, that roads within the canyon were primarily utilitarian. Rather, roads appear to have linked, physically and symbolically, different buildings; roads channeled or directed traffic to and from impressive view points (for example, the cliffs behind Pueblo Bonito and Chetro Ketl).

Chaco designed, built, and maintained roads (refer to plates 3 and 4). Chaco's structure (social, political, ceremonial) was probably formal and institutional. The width of the roads is a telling clue: we think it likely that Chaco roads were designed for groups of people in solemn (or not so solemn) procession. If religious, then priesthoods and formal processions of large groups directed by priests (pilgrimage groups?). If administrative, then entourages of administrators (tax collectors?) or even groups for enforcing the rules (inquisitors? troops?). Wide roads seem designed for groups, and narrow trails (as demonstrated by hand and toe holds), for individuals.

Like all public architecture, roads undoubtedly symbolized myriad, as well as several major, themes, such as alliance, pilgrimage, and projection of power. Each road may have answered a different design question. The Great North Road leaves Chaco and runs well beyond Kutz Canyon—we believe, as far as Salmon Ruins and probably as far as Aztec (Lekson 1999, chapter 1 of this volume). For all we know, the North Road may continue on to Hesperus Peak or some other holy mountain. The South Road runs through major communities, ending ultimately at Hosta Butte. Roads within Chaco Canyon combine alignments between buildings and linkages to important natural features. Windes (1987a, 1987b) documented the complex network of roads and road-related features in the northern half of downtown Chaco (figure 3.15), and the Chaco Protection Site group has greatly expanded the road network (Stein, Friedman, and Blackhorse n.d.). For example, a complex network of roads is now known from southeastern Utah (Till 2001; Till and Hurst 2002), which appeared as a blank area on early Chaco road maps (for example, Lekson et al. 1988).

A final element defining (perhaps uniquely, in its time) downtown Chaco was waterworks (Vivian 1974, 1990; Vivian and others, chapter 2 of this volume). Chaco was a dry desert, but gardens, ponds, and canals apparently filled much of the space between Great Houses, small sites, mounds, and roads (see figures 2.2 and 2.3). Indeed, a large artificial pond or lake apparently filled the lower canyon (Force et al. 2002; Vivian and others, chapter 2 of this volume). This water came from the heavens as rainfall. The wash itself was a trickle, at best. Chaco, when it rained, was a glittering water world, with rainfall spilling over cliffs and rushing through a maze of channels into ponds and reservoirs. (Today, that runoff roars, almost unseen, through deeply incised arroyos.)

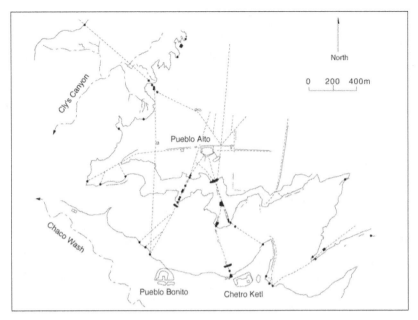

**FIGURE 3.15**

*"Downtown" Chaco Canyon (north half). Dashed lines represent road alignments. (After Windes 1987a:figure 5.2)*

Chaco was still a carefully managed water park, with stored water moving to gardens and other water-filled features. The picture conjured by the scale and extent of Vivian's waterworks is spectacularly different from the bleak, dry canyon of today (and the bleak, dry canyon of popular reconstructions).

Chacoan waterworks are conventionally interpreted as agricultural features, channeling precious water to individual corn plants, allowing a hard-pressed population to survive in Chaco's marginal environment. But Chaco's glory days were wet (Vivian and others, chapter 2 of this volume). Decades of good rainfall allowed the expenditure of huge quantities of water, not in farming, but in construction projects. Chacoans not only grew corn in the canyon but also imported it into the canyon (Benson and others 2003); we do not know proportions, but we favor import over local production. Certainly, much Chaco water went to corn and crops, but could Chacoan gardens also grow flowers? Flowers were of signal importance to Pueblo cosmology, in ancient times and now (Hays-Gilpin and Hill 2000). Was Chaco corn for eating, or did Chacoans nurture some plants to produce large and perfect "corn mothers," rich with symbolism and ritual import (and economic value)? Chacoans gardened, and their gardening had more than domestic or nutritional intent. The most striking example was a huge, solitary ponderosa pine that was watered and cared for in Pueblo Bonito's plaza, where it constituted a key natural/artificial element of that Great House (Stein, Suiter, and Ford 1997).

Were Chaco waterworks monumental? Some water went to crops and domestic use. We wonder, however, whether a significant *architectural* aspect of these waterworks has been overlooked: they would have been a major visual theme in the cityscape. Control and manipulation of water is an element of many public or ceremonial landscapes, from Machu Pichu, to Balinese Water Temples, to Versailles. Water was, of course, especially critical in the arid Southwest, and its manipulation must have been a major focus of Chacoan power and ceremony. Anasazi traditions (like later Pueblo traditions) probably encompassed ponds, streams, springs, and other water features as landscape architecture. For example, Mummy Lake, a reservoir or "Great Pond" (our term) at Mesa Verde that only periodically held water (Wright 2003), could have been a water monument, a landscape feature focused as much on the cultural manipulation of water as on water management. Sheathing (as we should) Ockham's razor, waterworks might become sparkling, dynamic, life-giving monuments, fringed with flowers. Was Chaco a place of water, reeds, and herons? Might Chaco be remembered as an island in a lake?

Chaco itself was monumental, a formally designed composition of many diverse architectural elements. At great cost of labor and material, Chaco was built to be seen, to be experienced, even to awe. By whom? For whom? Much of Chaco can be perceived from a "two-meter platform" of observation, that is, by human beings standing on the ground. Lines of sight and viewsheds were important elements of the cityscape (Kievit 1998). But much of Chaco's monumental composition would not have been obvious to people walking through the canyon (Fritz 1978; Sofaer 1997; Stein, Friedman, and Blackhorse n.d.). The formal, geometric layouts of Pueblo Bonito and Chetro Ketl could be appreciated (as they are today) by normal mortals from cliff-top viewing areas. But the oval of Peñasco Blanco and the half-rectangle of

Pueblo Alto disclose themselves to the clouds or to cloud people. Larger symmetries in the cityscape and landscape (Doxtater 2002; Fritz 1978; Lekson 1999; Stein, Friedman, and Blackhorse n.d.) were evident, in this world, only to those who originally planned them.

These larger compositions should not surprise us. Many early cities and ceremonial centers had geometrical or astronomical ground plans. Of interest at Chaco is why. Why create symmetries and cityscapes that would never be visible from the "two-meter platform"? We do not have an easy answer to that question, but it seems clear that Chaco's design principles, architectural elements, and cityscape were not driven by quotidian necessity.

### Ciudad Chaco

*Pueblo* means "small town" or "country village" in Spanish. Thus, Indians who lived in small towns or country villages received this name. Chaco was neither. As a formal tradition, Chacoan architecture appeared at hundreds of country villages throughout the larger region. Chaco itself was qualitatively different: much larger, far more diverse, unique in its time. Chaco was a city, the premier city of the eleventh-century Pueblo world.

Calling Chaco a "city" offends poetasters of urbanism—viscerally, visibly, volubly. We came, we claimed, we galled: Chaco was a city. We offer excuses for our ill manners at the conclusion of this section. First, however, we compound the offense by considering the nature of archaeological cities, perceived and real.

There are many archaeological definitions of *city*, and we assert (without citations) that, until lately, these definitions were generally consistent or produced consistent results in application, on the high end. Cities were big, crowded, and dense. That kind of urbanism is a closed and exclusive club. City has trait lists (enshrined since Childe, at least), size limits, requisite densities, fixed positions within states—a number of physical, social, structural, and functional requirements that exclude places like Chaco. Cities, by definition, should be civilized, so we seek our paragons from that ilk. Indeed, criteria for urbanism are often conflated with those for civilization (as in the otherwise estimable discussion of Childe in Smith, ed. 2003:9). Judgment becomes almost aesthetic. We know a real city, a good city, when we see it. Then we pool those shared excellences, defining good to exclude bad urbanism. Chaco, as it is conventionally understood, is bad urbanism: puny, poor, unlettered, living hand-to-mouth in hardscrabble peasant equality. All that Chaco has going for it, city-wise, are a few remarkably well preserved big buildings. And those, we (conventionally) know, were *pueblos*—that is, towns.

The Chaco we present here is not that Chaco, Chaco as it is conventionally understood. Chaco was not a valley with a half-dozen large pueblos. Chaco, we think, was a large, formal, designed settlement. Estimates of population vary; Lekson's (used here because Lekson is writing) is about 2,100 to 2,700 people within a core area of about 7 sq km and a total area of 15 sq km (Lekson 1984a). Chaco was monumental: a range of large, costly, permanent forms were employed to create a place unlike any other in its world. Chaco was multiethnic: conventional arguments for different cultural or ethnic groups within the canyon are buttressed by Chaco's place within its region (of which, more below), so large that many distinct groups and languages are implicated. Chaco was, for its time and place, cosmopolitan: both its defining architecture and the wide range of exotica imported and exported suggest worldliness far beyond the typical Anasazi unit pueblo. Chaco was formally hierarchical: architecturally, the gray area between Great House and small site (while interesting and meaningful) is small. If we are correct that Great Houses were elite residences, then Chaco was also socially and politically hierarchical, within itself and within its region. Different groups at Chaco labored at different tasks: ruling, priesting, building, crafting, and so forth. While almost all may have farmed, there was also (we think) a division of labor or, at least, of tasks. If we are correct about the function of empty rooms at Great Houses, there was at least the appearance of concentration of surplus. Chaco was central within a large region, a "primate center" (jargon suggesting a monkey farm). Its centrality may have been political and ceremonial (our position) or merely geographic and scalar, but few would deny that Chaco was flat-out bigger and flashier than anything else (thus, the park, the Chaco Project, the Chaco Synthesis). Chaco was conspicuous for its time and place in long-distance trade and exchange, both within its region and beyond. Calendrics, hydrology, and, above all, architecture speak to the early development of predictive systems and rudimentary engineering.

Attentive readers will have noticed many of V. Gordon Childe's antique but influential traits of civilization. Let us complete the run: Writing is not found, but we suggest elsewhere that Chacoans accomplished coded communication with smoke and mirrors, perhaps a precursor (Lekson, chapter 1 of this volume). Artwork was not standardized as Childe would like it, but the Dogoszhi style so typical of Chaco suggests conventionalized art (Neitzel 1995; Plog 2003; Toll, chapter 4 of this volume.) These are stretches, though, climbing above Chaco's station. Chaco was not a high civilization. It was a little city in a desert region.

Lekson has called Chaco a ceremonial city, extrapolating from Wheatley (1971) without perfect accuracy. While much of Wheatley's model transfers well to Chaco, there is no need to overlay Chinese patterns on Pueblo fabrics. The adjective *ceremonial* seemed to make *city* go down easier. Chaco stands as a city on its own merits, and on imposed criteria. Another definition of city, picked (almost) at random from my bookshelf, wants a large and diverse population, complexity and interdependence, formal and impersonal organization, nonagricultural activities, and centralized services for the city and its region (Redman 1978:216).

Amid many post-Childe prescriptions for urbanism, these characteristics still seem current: we want cities to be like that—and Chaco was. At about 2,500 people, it was as large as many small cities in the New and Old Worlds (see also Rohn 1983, for other Anasazi "budding urban centers" of this size). It was ethnically diverse. It was architecturally complex and interdependent in social, ritual, and probably economic asymmetries reflected in Great House–small site, center-region morphologies. It was formal to a fault, but we cannot judge its impersonality (we think of Chaco as severe, impersonal, even grim, but those are impressions only). It was rich with nonagricultural activities (economic, ritual, and political) and was a (preindustrial) "central place," with services (real and imagined, ritual or political) for core and region. Chaco meets most requirements, minimally in some cases, extravagantly in others.

Chaco's openness bothers pundits of the polis: cities should be dense. The space between Great House ruins, today, gives an impression of sparsity that is only partially false. In the eleventh century, the canyon was much more heavily built and landscaped than it appears today, but space was an important element or dimension of Chaco (as discussed further, below). Chaco was a spacious city, not unlike many Maya centers or Asian ceremonial cities. Indeed, this aspect of Chaco demonstrates its interest for larger studies of urbanism.

Was there too much space at Chaco, too little built area? Compared with what? Roland Fletcher, in his masterful 1995 study *The Limits of Settlement Growth*, defines two major dimensions of city settlement: an Interaction Limit of "tolerable residential density" and a Communication Limit of "distances over which a communication system can operate" (Fletcher 1995:xxiii). These limits vary with economy and technology, and Fletcher estimated empirical values for both, from an encyclopedic study of hunter-gatherer, horticultural, agricultural, preindustrial, and industrial settlements and cities. Chaco's maximum densities (3.6 persons per hectare, with 2,500 in the 7-sq-km core) are far below its projected interaction limit—all that space between buildings! With a core area of 700 ha and a total area of 1,500 ha, Chaco greatly exceeds the cross-culturally derived communication limit for preindustrial agricultural cities of about 100 ha. Fletcher (1995:117) calls Chaco a "bypass settlement" and notes: "Such settlements can reach an enormous size, well in excess of the size limits of their communication assemblage, but they attain these sizes only by following a trajectory to very low residential densities below the T-limit. Possible examples which bypassed the 100 ha limit are Cahokia...and Chaco Canyon. They are smaller scale equivalents...of Tikal and Angkor."

Fletcher assumes that "communication assemblage," including Chaco's, was primarily verbal. Therefore, "the effective limit for a given assemblage is...the size of the settlement across which verbal messages can spread out and overlap without losing their communication efficiency" (Fletcher 1995:83). Nonverbal, largely visual aspects of communication are more fully discussed by Amos Rapoport in *The Meaning of the Built Environment: A Nonverbal Communication Approach* (1982, especially chapter 6; note that Fletcher is well aware of nonverbal modalities). The Chaco cityscape communicated and extended communication through redundant, reinforcing layers and forms: Great Houses, earthen architecture, the dense network of intracanyon roads, and (critical for communication limits) a system of formal intervisibilities. Chaco was remarkable for its clear and prominent use of medium- and long-distance visual communication: intracanyon intervisibilities are famous, for example, between Pueblo Bonito and Peñasco Blanco, between Pueblo Alto and Tsin Kletzin. We believe that a dense network of visual communication nodes, actively used as a communication assemblage, linked Great Houses and other monumental features. The business of the canyon could be broadcast through nonverbal, visual means. Thus, Chaco reached remarkable size with low overall densities (but high spot densities) and still operated successfully as a city, integrated by nonverbal communications.

Interaction across space was probably the defining character of Chaco's cityscape. The remarkable vistas of the Four Corners, and their ineffable distances, shaped Chacoan zeitgeist within the canyon and throughout its region. Space became a fundamental principle of Chacoan city planning and a vehicle of Chacoan power (Lekson, chapter 1 of this volume). Chaco defined its own rules of urbanism, not unique but, at the very least, unusual. We happily deconstruct hierarchy, unpack complexity, complicate history, but *city* as a classification remains remarkably resistant to revision. Conventional thinking on cities seems, to us, if not blatantly Eurocentric then (at best) strongly biased to Great Civilizations. "There is no escape from the fact that our intellectual resources for analyzing and understanding cities are predominantly recent and Euro-American," notes Adrian Southall (1998:5) in his survey *The City in Time and Place*. Perhaps we should rethink *city*. Did all ancient cities prefigure the Big Apple? Probably not.

Monica Smith (2003:7–8), in her introductory chapter to *The Social Construction of Ancient Cities*, finds conventional approaches to archaeological urbanism, such as trait lists, insufficient. Cities, she notes, range widely in size and form. Moreover, they are inherently dynamic and changeable. A loose threshold of size, density, monumentality, and the like, seems necessary (or, at least, comforting), but beyond an ill-defined minimum (which Chaco meets), cities were richly variable. Her new definition of cities—less top-heavy, less bound to traits and qualities of high civilizations—is made with admirable clarity by Roderick McIntosh and Susan McIntosh, in Smith's volume: "Theories of urbanism [shift] emphasis from what a city *is* (widely agreed to be a futile pursuit in view of the tremendous range of urban forms) to what a city *does*....Whatever else a city may be, it is a unit of settlement that performs specialized functions in relation to a broader hinterland" (citing Trigger 1972; McIntosh and McIntosh 2003:106, original emphases). Trigger, revisiting demographic definitions of early cities (total population, density, and so forth), concludes that "definitions based on arbitrary quantitative divisions appear to bear little relation to concepts [of urbanism] used in early civilizations and rarely contribute to a better understanding of urban phenomena" (Trigger 2003:120–121; early cities, he notes, were as small as "a few thousand inhabitants"). Trigger (2003:120) returns to his 1972 insight: "The key defining feature of an urban center is that it performs specialized functions in relation to a broader hinterland." The reality and dynamics of the Chacoan region (Lekson, chapter 1, and Kantner and Kintigh, chapter 5, of this volume) have profound implications for understanding the canyon itself. Chaco controlled a region politically or serviced a region ritually; either way, it performed *specialized functions for a broader hinterland.* That is why Chaco was a city, and later, larger Pueblo IV towns were not.

Is it possible to call Chaco a city? Does that matter? We think so. A fundamental question for anthropological archaeology is, why did/do people live together in towns and cities? To answer this question, we need a broad sample of urban forms, familiar and exotic, from a wide range of times and places, not just the high-end slam dunks but the smaller, more intriguing cities-in-becoming. Big ones, small ones, short ones, tall ones. Chaco is minor and (on the global scale) historically inconsequential, but its unusual cityscape (and use of space) merits mention in Fletcher's study (and others) as an example of one very intriguing way *cities were done.* While there may be few direct applications for contemporary city planning to be gained from Chaco, we would be surprised if principles and lessons were not awaiting studies that move beyond conventions and recognize Ciudad Chaco.

Chaco's modest urbanism was not "pristine" or original. Chaco was not even a secondary or tertiary city; it was far, far down the line of urban dominos. Chaco was never more than a distant reflection of ancient and more important prime objects: Olmec centers, the unique megametropolis of Teotihuacan, countless Postclassic Mexican cities that Chaco never knew yet to which it owed debts. Chaco was far more than a rural village or congeries of pueblos. Chaco was a city.

# 4

## Organization of Production

### H. Wolcott Toll

Chaco buildings and landscapes are tremendously organized. When we euphemistically speak of the "organization of production," do we imply levels of organization similar to those we see in Great House architecture? Was manufacture and acquisition of artifacts and material planned and directed to the extent that Great House building was, or did the pieces fall together more organically and responsively? All the constituent actions were, of course, conscious choices, but only portions were consciously organized. As is true of architecture, there were surely different types of production and different levels of participation, and the participants and the relationships changed through time. Numerous people have studied aspects of production in many ways over many years. In March 1999 a diverse group of archaeologists met at the University of Colorado, Boulder, to integrate what is known about Chaco with production and exchange studies in comparable worldwide settings. This group put together a synthesis of past work and today's models of how materials and artifacts were acquired, made, processed, exchanged, and used during the Chaco era. The results of their effort appeared in *American Antiquity* (January 2001, vol. 66, no. 1).[1]

In addition to "organization," the concept of "production" has been adapted to a particular meaning. In the modern world, one of the first connotations of production has to do with agriculture and food, but food production is left to another block in the capstone (Vivian and others, chapter 2 of this volume). This chapter focuses on the production and acquisition of artifacts and building timbers. As an acquired, processed, and transported natural resource, timber was also "produced," under this definition.

Production in modern situations is often associated with factories and assembly lines. How things were made, and by whom, is central to this phase of the inquiry, but searches for mass production can lead to misguided assumptions and expectations. Because economy is focal, this material necessarily overlaps variously with chapter 2, "Ecology and Economy." The good news is that, although the division of labor may seem procrustean and at odds with some modern economic concepts, we are trying to bring all these aspects back together where they belong.

My aim here is to provide a temporal outline of important, known trends of artifact manufacture and movement, including mundane and exotic items. I also present means of producing and acquiring these materials and, more difficult but at least as important, thoughts about motivations for doing so. This synthesis builds on the 1999 conference and the 2001 *American Antiquity* papers and subsequent capstone meetings.

"Chaco" has become a nebulous concept that includes different extents and characteristics for different people. Our discussions of material culture heavily focused on Chaco Canyon because of the wealth of accessible data from that place, from both the Chaco Project and decades of other research. I try to restrict the use of *Chaco* to the broad sense, the big idea, the "Chaco Phenomenon," what the capstone is trying to capture. This is similar to *Chaco system*, although here that term indicates sites for which we have evidence of material exchange. *Chaco region* I take to mean the area in which sites conform to architectural patterns defined as Chacoan (see Lekson 1991:47). I use *Chaco Canyon* to indicate sites large and small within the main part of the national park (see figures 2.1 and 3.15). Of necessity, the canyon serves as a proxy for the grander picture, but its location at the peak of

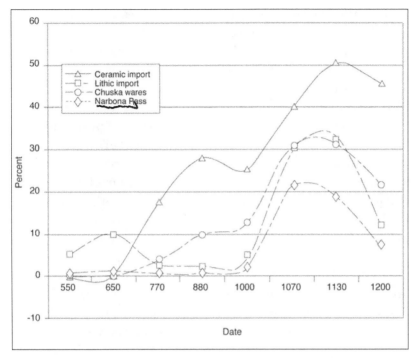

**FIGURE 4.1**

*Temporal distribution of percentages of ceramics and lithics imported to Chaco Project sites, showing overall import and quantity of Chuskan ceramics and Narbona Pass chert with all wares combined. Note that, although Chuskan materials form a large part of imported goods, materials from other areas are also abundant.*

the pyramid, in at least some aspects of the system, makes that a suspect accounting practice.

## A CHRONOLOGICAL OUTLINE OF IMPORT AND PRODUCTION

For this temporal outline, I have divided the Chaco Canyon sequence into epochs that seem to be useful, logical units (see figure 1.3; Chaco Timeline; figure 4.1). Within each epoch, I summarize salient points about timber, ceramics and lithics, and exotic materials. These are only summaries: vastly more information exists in the cited, and uncited, literature.

### 860–950: The Foundation of the Great Houses in Chaco

All Chaco Project materials from 860–950 are from small sites (McKenna and Truell 1986; Windes 1993). Tree-ring evidence of pre-900 activity at the earliest Great Houses has been burgeoning, but well-controlled samples from Great Houses are still scant. During this time, Wilshusen and Ortman (1999), Windes (n.d.), and Wilshusen and Van Dyke (chapter 7 of this volume) see a great influx of people into the San Juan Basin, a transition to the use of stone for building and multi-story construction, and the establishment of a number of Great Houses, with major mounds, beyond the traditional triad of Una Vida, Pueblo Bonito, and Peñasco Blanco. The period is clearly an important baseline for material use patterns to come, and Windes (n.d.) has greatly elucidated this period since the Chaco Project.

*Timber.* Windes and McKenna (2001) note an absence of clustered tree-ring dates, making timber acquisition patterns unclear. There was a distinct emphasis on piñon, *Populus* (aspen and cottonwood), and ponderosa (Windes and Ford 1996:303–305). Species from higher elevations than ponderosa, such as fir and spruce, are nearly absent. Through time in the canyon, non–Great House sites used primarily piñon and juniper in roof construction. These species were available closer to the canyon than longer, straighter taxa. Even these species became more difficult to get, so reuse of timber was standard practice. Although acquisition of smaller, locally available materials is obviously a related type of economic activity, I focus on major beams obtained away from the canyon. In addition to the major transport effort in these timbers, they were more often extensively processed.

*Ceramics and Lithics.* The ceramic assemblage from this particular period provides an important illustration of the dynamic nature of participation in the Chaco system. Sources for ceramics are already becoming complex, with materials from the San Juan area and the Chuska area present, but materials probably from the south, in the well-settled Red Mesa Valley (Kantner 2000; Van Dyke 1997a, 2000) are more abundant than from other sources (Toll and McKenna 1997:130). These sources are not as well reflected in the chipped stone material (Cameron 1997:546; 2001), but, for both ceramic supply and settlement early in the Chaco world, the importance of this area is evident. Also, ceramics from the Chuska area become a meaningful portion of the canyon assemblage. Windes (n.d.) has demonstrated a clinal distribution of trachyte-tempered ceramics across Great Houses, from the Chuskas to central Chaco and beyond, decreasing with distance from the Chuska Valley.

*Exotica.* We know of few turquoise workshops before A.D. 900. Shell objects are present throughout the Chaco sequence and in contexts dating to this period. In particular, we do not know of Mesoamerican goods, macaws, and copper from this period, although contextual control at Pueblo Bonito and, much worse, Peñasco Blanco is sufficiently weak that we cannot rule them out.

### 950–1020: Great House Consolidation and Slow Growth

Because moisture was favorable during 950–1020 and Great House construction less frenetic than in the latter 1000s, there is a tendency to think that not much happened. The paucity of data abets the tendency. It is, however, a period of relatively greater levels of exchange elsewhere, such as the La Plata Valley and the Dolores area (Blinman and Wilson 1993), and Chaco Canyon was a part of and probably a stimulus for that activity. Moreover, during this time, patterns followed for the next two hundred years were established. When opportunities to research this period arise, the discipline should wisely cultivate them.

*Timber.* Windes and Ford (1996:306–308) note that the correspondence of major building events with moist periods at the first canyon Great Houses is especially good during this interval. Pueblo Bonito beams dating to this period are ponderosa, with liberal use of more local species. Presumably, this wood was acquired from stands closer to the building than was possible later.

*Ceramics and Lithics.* Materials from the south of the canyon, particularly the Red Mesa Valley, were especially important in providing lithics and ceramics to the canyon. Contacts with the Chuska Valley are apparent in the artifacts, but at lower frequencies than later (see figure 4.1). This period, then, evidenced a more diverse set of contacts than

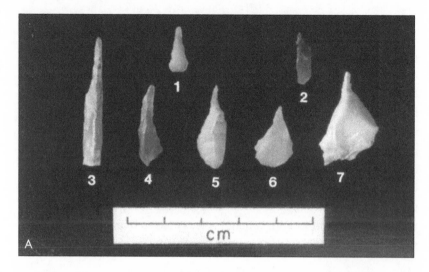

was true later. Substantial quantities of pottery from locations away from the canyon became a well-established pattern in this period. In part, fuel scarcity in the canyon and the fuel-consumptive nature of pottery firing are probably responsible for this pattern, which strengthens in subsequent periods. Combined with production difficulties in the central basin, however, is the presence of people from other communities in the canyon, either as visitors or part-time residents.

*Exotica.* Some of the best-documented turquoise workshops date from this period (for example, Mathien 1997:1162–1163, 1204; Windes 1993). The "industry" was well established by this time (figure 4.2), but we know little of where the products were used and deposited. Surface evidence from sites in the canyon suggests that turquoise working occurred at most sites (Windes 1992). The presence of turquoise artifacts in great numbers in Pueblo Bonito seems likely to be from the next period, although it is equally likely that deposition of turquoise and other exotic items at Pueblo Bonito became well established during this period.

### 1020–1040: Great House Construction and Scale Increase

Obviously, the 1020–1040 time slot is too narrow to be realistically separated for most materials and deposits. It is, however, an important time of transition that we can discuss for timber and ceramics.

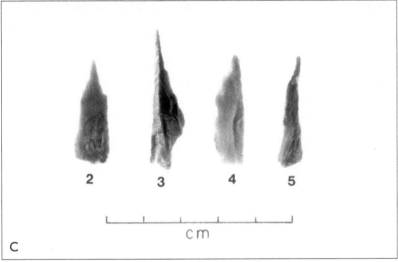

**FIGURE 4.2**

*Turquoise debris and drills from the Spadefoot Toad Site (29SJ629), a "small site" on the south side of Chaco Canyon. Drills (a, c), abraders, and turquoise working debris, including fragments and broken beads (b) were found in plaza and pithouse proveniences. All 1:1 scale. (Windes 1993:vol. II, 293 and 194, plate 3.3 [a], 5.1 [b], and 3.4 [c] [2–5] [NPS31425, 24526, 31426])*

*Timber.* Chacoans established and substantially built several Great Houses, including Chetro Ketl and Pueblo Alto (Lekson 1984a:259; Windes 1987a).[2] The added scale and intensity of building projects must have involved changes in timber acquisition. Windes and McKenna (2001:135–137) conclude that timber acquisition for the canyon Great Houses never required a very large workforce. The greatly increased demand for wood at around 1030, however, would have necessitated some elaboration, if not greater change, in the smaller groups formerly providing wood for construction in the canyon.

*Ceramics and Lithics.* An important design shift in the decoration of black-on-white ceramics took place. The Red Mesa style comprises mostly solid-painted elements laid out in band designs, as well as parallel framing lines and, less commonly, widely spaced hachured elements. Designs similar to Red Mesa persist, but the design style associated with Chaco, in which hachure lines fill almost all painted elements of the decoration (Gallup Black-on-white), become abundant during this time. Gallup Black-on-white uses a different design layout covering whole decorative fields and complex symmetries as opposed to band layouts (Plog 2003; Toll and McKenna 1987, 1997; Washburn 2004).

*Exotica.* Separating trade in long-distance items from this short period is impractical. During this and other construction phases, we do see one use of shell and turquoise—in the placement of offerings during kiva construction (see Windes 1987b:404).

### 1040–1105: Massive Building and Proliferation
From 1040 to 1105 many "mosts" were attained: the most building episodes (see figure 3.7), the most high-elevation species, the most imports, the most turquoise. This period, or perhaps even just a subset of it, produced the aspects of Chaco Canyon that have drawn attention to it from many directions in subsequent centuries. Preceding decades laid a necessary foundation to this period, and after 1105 Chaco Canyon remained an important place. This time of superlatives pushed Chaco to a new level.

*Timber.* Building activity was phenomenal (Lekson 1984a:259, 263; 1984b), and the amount of wood brought to the canyon from both the west and the southeast is staggering (Dean and Warren 1983; Durand et al. 1999). Although ponderosa remains the most abundant species, builders used significant amounts of higher elevation wood (Windes and Ford 1996:303–305). The use of species from higher elevations and longer distances, in combination with the pattern of large beams predating smaller materials such as lintels and closing material (*latillas*) by several years, shows that the level of organization of wood acquisition had increased. Higher levels of organization were necessary to meet increased consumption levels that depleted closer sources of beams. Dates of timbers from Pueblo del Arroyo, the latest "classic" Great House in the canyon, stop at 1103 (Lekson 1984a:221).

*Ceramics and Lithics.* Gallup Black-on-white and its elaboration, Chaco Black-on-white, become firmly established and prevalent in central San Juan Basin decorated ceramics between 1040 and 1105, with the finer hachure and broader framing lines of Chaco Black-on-white more abundant post-1090 (figure 4.3; Toll and McKenna 1997:286–335). Other modes of ceramic decoration persist within the San Juan Basin and in the general eastern Anasazi sphere (Toll, Blinman, and Wilson 1992). The popular and actual association of hachured decoration has tempted scholars to suggest a symbolic association with this type of decoration and the "Chaco Idea," or even the place (for example, Plog 1990, 2003; see Toll, Blinman, and Wilson 1992:151). Dominant hachure is a time marker, and in many ways the latter eleventh century is the time of Chaco, but hachure occurs throughout the Colorado Plateau.

Ceramic exchange is often thought of as involving principally decorated wares, but in this period participants in events in Chaco brought in large numbers of utility vessels from the Chuska slopes (figure 4.4), more than half of the corrugated vessels present in the central canyon are Chuskan (Shepard 1956, also in Judd 1954:234–238; King 2003; Toll and McKenna 1997). People were also moving less easily identified decorated and utility pottery from other areas. There is a steady, if low-level, flow of red wares and polished smudged brown wares into the canyon, as well as steady and more abundant import of white wares,

**FIGURE 4.3**

*Hachure is a design element that occurs in pottery in Chaco Canyon sites in the 900s through the 1100s. These photos show its change through time: (a) Red Mesa Black-on-white (975–1040) sherds from 29SJ629. Note the band layouts' use of ticked triangles and scrolls; widely spaced hachure is also seen in this type (Toll and McKenna 1993:35–36, negs 31956, 31952). (b) Five fragmented, apparently intentionally destroyed Gallup Black-on-white (1040–1100) bowls from the Pueblo Alto mound, showing the type of hachure and layout (Toll and McKenna 1987:54, figure 1.6B). (c) A Chaco Black-on-white (1075–1100) olla from 29SJ627. Note the heavy framing lines, extremely fine hachure, and complete vessel layout (Toll and McKenna 1997:335, figure 2A.17, Chaco negative 13987).*

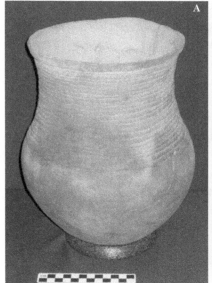

**FIGURE 4.4**

*Grayware vessels from the Chuska Valley.
By the late 1000s grayware vessels from the
Chuska Valley account for more than half
the utility pottery found in Chaco Canyon.
(a) Neckbanded (900s) jar from the Red
Rock post area, diameter 26.5 cm (Lister
and Lister 1969:25), (b) corrugated jar or
pitcher from Tohatchi, diameter 14.7 cm,
and (c) large corrugated olla (1000s to
early 1100s) from the Newcomb area,
diameter 27.6 cm, height 31.9 cm (b and
c, Lister and Lister 1969:43–44).
University of Colorado Museum nos.
9451, 9513, 9532.*

principally as bowls but also as closed forms. The pottery from the
Chuska area is especially noteworthy, dominated by large grayware jars,
probably the most difficult form to transport (see figure 4.1). Chuska
area potters were making the full repertoire of whiteware vessels, some

of which were brought to Chaco Canyon, but never in the quantities that gray wares were. This preference must have stemmed from recognition of the vessels' quality and durability, but it also seems to express a deep relationship between the two areas. The identity of the transporters and the importers is, of course, unknown but is likely complex. That is, some may be explained by families living in both the supply area and Chaco Canyon moving vessels between residences, some by exchange between residents of the canyon with residents of supply areas, taking place in either location, and some by supply area residents bringing vessels to the canyon for specific purposes.

Though rare, cylinder vessels date to this period, an icon for Chaco today and perhaps in the past as well. They have been recovered from only a few contexts, principally in Pueblo Bonito, where researchers discovered a cache of more than a hundred in an early room in the core of the building (see figure 10.3a; Pepper 1920:114–121; Toll 2001:color photo 6). Although no one has done a thorough study of the vessels' sources, their production shows sufficient variability to suggest that they come from many communities and that community members may have placed their community's vessel in special contexts as part of regional rituals (Toll 1990).

In addition to utility pottery, deposits contain high (more than 20 percent) quantities of Narbona Pass chert from the same area of the Chuskas as the pottery (see figure 4.1; Cameron 2001; Toll 2001:color photo 7). Much of this material remains in the form of debitage or expedient Anasazi tools, instead of formal tools such as projectile points or retouched blades, further evidence that large quantities of materials were transported from the west.

*Exotica.* The huge quantities of turquoise, the remarkable shell artifacts, copper bells, macaws, and unusual vessel forms reported by Judd (1954) and Pepper (1920) from Pueblo Bonito probably were deposited primarily during this period (Toll 2001:color photo 5). We base this chronological placement on associated ceramics and intensity of building effort at Bonito. The artifacts, placement, scale, and long-term maintenance of and additions to Pueblo Bonito, however, leave little doubt of its importance as a focus and repository for Chaco, in the big sense. The exotica there is likely to date to the multicentury span of the building; the bulk is probably from the eleventh century (Mathien 2003).

### 1105–1150: Reorientations

Many things changed after the frenetic late 1000s and turn of the twelfth century. These include reduced scale of building, masonry style at Great Houses, Great House layout, dispersion of Great Houses in the new style in the north, ceramic pigment, and even wall alignments (Van Dyke 2004).

*Timber.* Post-1100 dates from Pueblo Bonito are all small-scale renovations (Windes and Ford 1996:303). Construction dates at the new "McElmo" style of Great House are concentrated between 1105 and 1130, with marked cessation at 1130 (Lekson 1984a, 1984b:69; Van Dyke 2004). Just about the only species identified in these buildings from within the canyon is ponderosa (Bannister 1965:171, 195; Vivian and Mathews 1965:39), but the sample is small. The commencement of a serious, prolonged drought in 1130 is an unavoidable factor accounting for change during this period.

Large-scale building at other Great Houses, particularly in the north at Salmon and Aztec, takes off at this time (see figures 8.3 and 8.4). The need for long, straight, large timbers—in this case, ponderosa and aspen—again caused builders to acquire materials at great distance (Brown, Windes, and McKenna 2002).

*Ceramics and Lithics.* Another important and widespread change in ceramic decoration occurred during this period. Although organic-painted pottery existed during the 900s and 1000s in areas in contact with Chaco, including parts of the Chuskas, makers of the great majority of decorated pottery used mineral paints. Beginning around 1100, the use of organic paint on white wares became far more common, until, in short order, organic paint was the dominant type in most of the area formerly characterized by mineral paint (see Wilson 1996). Achieving the desired black design on a white ground is different for the two paint types, and greater use of organic paint may relate to larger groups cooperating to fire pottery in trench kilns, or at least to larger lots being fired (Bernardini 2000:373– 375; Fuller 1984; Purcell 1993). Because organic paint requires lower temperatures than mineral paint, fuel shortage is another likely stimulus to this change; developing the knowledge to match clay properties with paint retention (Stewart and Adams 1999:676–661) would have facilitated it.

Import of Narbona Pass chert and ceramics from the Chuska area continued at only slightly lower frequencies than in the preceding period. Somewhat increased in Chaco Canyon sites are ceramics from both the San Juan River and northeastern Arizona areas (see figure 4.1). That the San Juan area becomes a bastion of organic paint use and that organic paint has a long history in northeastern Arizona may relate to the paint shift noted above. Along with these ceramic shifts, the sites in Chaco Canyon show a marked increase in the presence of obsidian, primarily from the Jemez Mountains to the east. Obsidian is present in the earliest sites in the canyon, but during the main Great House phases it is present only in very small quantities. The reemphasis on this desirable material, concurrent with other changes in production and architecture, further indicates a change in regional organization.

*Exotica.* Chronologically well-placed exotica are, again, scarce. Subjectively, a decline in the occurrence of these materials similar to the decline in large timbers probably occurred. Given that prime obsidian and turquoise sources are in the same geographic sector, we might also expect a spike in turquoise acquisition, but there is little evidence for one.

### 1150–1250: The Move to the North

The apparent transfer of the location for high devotional expression from Chaco Canyon to Aztec (see, for example, Lekson 1999; Lipe, chapter 8 of this volume, figure 8.4) took place after some of the important shifts in resource use and manufacture methods noted above. With change underway at the time of the transfer and with a changed location, what continuities are there in the organization of production?

*Timber.* Tree-ring dates in Chaco Canyon are virtually absent and include no major building timbers. Building and beam acquisition continued apace at Aztec, however. Although Aztec and other Great Houses in the Totah (McKenna and Toll 1992; Lipe, chapter 8 of this volume) are located in areas with more available moisture than Chaco Canyon, large building timbers are not present near the Great Houses. Production of vigas, then, continued in some form. All the Totah Great

Houses are conveniently located by large streams, and some use of river transport for building timber seems inevitable. This impression, however, may well stem from today's ingrained aversion to physical labor and may have been contrary to eleventh- and twelfth-century standards of labor investment required for such constructions.

*Ceramics and Lithics.* Although materials from the Chuska area are never nearly as abundant in site assemblages north of the San Juan River as they are in Chaco Canyon, they are present. In this latest period, they are likely insignificant, in part, because of reduced occupation of the Chuska area and, in part, because of reorganized social relationships. The Totah has a long tradition of apparent self-sufficiency in both ceramics and lithics, with only trace occurrences of obsidian, Narbona chert, and nonlocal ceramics. At least at smaller sites, this pattern continues.

After the relocation of "Chaco's" focus, then, mobilization of labor for construction and concentration of activity continued, but movement of utilitarian goods seems to have scaled back. Turquoise, too, seems to have been moved in considerably smaller volume.

*Exotica.* The remarkable quantities of special goods from Pueblo Bonito have had a lasting effect on expectations for Chacoan Great House assemblages (see Mathien 2003; Toll 1991:86). The amounts of turquoise there point to an important association prehistorically between Chaco the Idea and turquoise (Plog 2003). The scarcity of turquoise in archaeological contexts outside Chaco Canyon strengthens this association. If Aztec was, in fact, the relocated hub of the organization, the huge reduction in amounts of turquoise shows that the organization or its symbolic content changed in the move. While assemblages at Aztec continue to have abundant shell, turquoise is much less common (see Mathien 1997:1193, 1197–1198).

## ORGANIZATIONAL TRENDS

Within the 270-year history of Great House use and construction in Chaco Canyon, each of the materials I have focused on shows trends of gradual increase culminating in rapid intensification during the latter 1000s, tailing off gradually in the early 1100s, and rather abruptly

declining after 1130. With the exception of timber acquisition, procurement and production of mundane and exotic materials continue
in the canyon, but on a much smaller scale.

## Timber

Looking strictly at nonlocal timber, new levels of sophistication and
organization became necessary in the face of increased demand and
more distant sources. Spreading the task over a sufficient amount of
time, however, means that a small labor force could still have effected
the process. Transport of large timbers for more than 50 km is inconceivable to us moderns, but, factoring in the carrying ability of human
porters (Malville 2001), modern Native American feats of running
(Nabokov 1981), and the motivating force of sacred events (DeBoer
2001; Renfrew 2001; Lipe, chapter 8 of this volume), we can begin to
see how Chacoans might have accomplished this.

## Ceramics and Lithics

From a viewpoint admittedly skewed toward ceramics, important
changes in scale (and, concomitantly, organization) are signaled by
changes in ceramics (see figure 4.3). Thus, concurrent with the commencement of the period during which builders expended the most
effort in canyon Great House construction, there was a notable shift in
both design layout and element filling. Layouts changed from bands
circling the field to covering all or most of the field. Design elements
changed from solid fill with ticking along the edges of some elements
to elements filled with hachure and no ticks. At the time when Great
House architectural changes occur and the scale of construction efforts
in the canyon decreases, there is a shift back to band layouts, but with
greater emphasis on rectilinearity, and a change in the paint medium
that would have required further modifications in firing procedures.

Like many stylistic changes in prehistoric Pueblo pottery, these
shifts are apparent over expanses far broader than Chaco Canyon or
the San Juan Basin. Why did such shifts occur, how were they effected,
and how did the changes at Chaco relate to them? Having concluded
that actual production was organized at the household or community
level rather than centrally directed (which would be much easier to
describe, but highly unlikely), how can we account for these broad

changes? Chaco was clearly important to much of the Pueblo world in the 1000s and 1100s, and the concept continued to be important for at least as long as heavy occupation of the Colorado Plateau lasted. The consistency with which pottery changed through time tells us that communication, awareness of other communities, and circulation of people were always features of Pueblo life. Pottery decoration was an important means of demonstrating subscription to the concepts and relationships of the ultra-community centered in Chaco in the late 1000s and Aztec in the late 1100s. Decisions to use designs would have been made by the community and, ultimately, household by household. The rationale probably included intricately interrelated economic concepts such as exchangeability, social concepts such as group membership and correctness, and religious symbolism. The process of creating new designs and then getting them accepted is far from our reach but likely started with the religious cognoscenti working from tradition and with potters. Contacts among communities and potters could then foster spread of design modes.

The timing of changes in ceramic decoration and architecture is intriguing. Possibly, periods of increased climatic stress anticipated or precipitated these changes. Thus, in the early 900s and the late 1000s ceramic change followed periods of reduced moisture. Perhaps dry spells catalyzed social changes, expressed by alterations in building and ceramic decoration techniques. These links could have several bases, including greater movement of people and consequent reorganization of social relationships and ways to express them, a search for new avenues to the supernatural to resolve climatic shortfalls, and adjustments in food and artifact production strategies. Such changes also symbolize the adaptability of Pueblo society to variations in their social and physical environments.

Both utilitarian goods and building timbers emphasize the major role the Chuska Mountains and piedmont played in the occupation and florescence of Chaco Canyon. Preliminary results also indicate that some maize in Chaco came from the Chuska area as well (Benson et al. 2003), although quantities are unknown. Truly remarkable volumes of goods were moved across an inhospitable 60 km or more from the Chuskas to the canyon (see plate 1). This supply was in effect throughout the 1000s, as well as before and after. Other areas were also providing material, but the Chuska area is the most important in socially and archaeologically identifiable goods. The nature of this strong relationship is crucial, but difficult to specify. It likely involved a complicated mix of mobility, kin relationships, ritual obligation, and direct acquisition. Some families with residences in Chaco Canyon may well have had houses in one of the Chuskan communities also (see also King 2003; McKenna and Truell 1986), moving between them seasonally or in response to farming conditions. This sort of multiple residence and visitation of the ritual center by families living more of the time in the Chuska area would have naturally resulted in kin and trading relationships that facilitated movement among communities.

Belief and participation in the ritual events in Chaco Canyon would have created obligation and desire to travel to the canyon, resulting in movement of materials. The rich resource base of the Chuskas and other important exchange areas, the ritual and social draw of the canyon, and a long tradition of mobility combined to allow the system to operate as it did. The Chuskan case is remarkably visible archaeologically, but I cannot emphasize enough that it was only one of the regional communities interacting in Chaco. The other half of the pottery and two-thirds of the lithics came from locations within the San Juan Basin and the Red Mesa Valley, and we know that timber was coming from the southeast, around Mount Taylor (see figure 1.2).

As remarkable as the accomplishments of the seemingly brief (1040–1105) period of peak activity are, many of the most striking accomplishments fit within an even shorter period, from sometime in the 1070s into the 1090s. This is best exemplified in the building history (Lekson 1984a:259–263), which serves as a concomitant for the other superlatives discussed. In addition to reinforcing the knowledge that change was continuous, the brevity of this period forces us to be open to more localized explanation. Clearly, this short period falls within a single "career" or, at most, two careers. The discipline has developed an increasingly detailed picture of the length and breadth of development in and around Chaco. We have come to think of this picture as what Chaco was: an organizational tradition that had deep temporal roots and encompassed an ever-increasing region, lasting for three to five hundred years, depending on which formulation one uses.

This same increased acuity, however, enables us to examine the stages more closely. After years of considering the grand sweep of

"Chaco," I was finally and repeatedly struck during the synthesis discussions by how short the period was when Chaco was really roaring (or, to quote Wilshusen, Sesler, and Hovezak [2000], from a different Pueblo era, "Things just went nuts"). It seems to me that the increasing complexity and scope created an opportunity for one or a few charismatic, forceful individuals to promote a new order of organization, especially in a period of heightened climatic and productive unpredictability and unease.

To fit this interpretation, it is easy—and perhaps not far-fetched— to envision a scenario involving the elaborately buried individuals in Pueblo Bonito. These leaders convinced participants in the in-place system to ratchet up participation and probably their personal importance. The short flurries of enhanced activity fit well with the influence of particular individuals. As Lekson argues, Pueblo groups then decided that they did not want to see this situation again and have developed—or, more likely, reinstituted—elaborate means of suppressing it.

This seems to be another lesson about casting our nets too broadly: we want to know what the organization of production or the social organization of Chaco was. That we can even think of arguing for the influence of one career in a sweep of three hundred years alerts us to how often and how much the conditions changed. Perhaps out of stubbornness, I continue to regard the corporate as paramount through much of the history we are studying, but, no doubt, there were many variations on that theme (Earle 2001:27–28).

Indeed, the reincarnation of the Chaco idea at Aztec may also have been brief (Cameron 2002:691). If flurries of increased influence and activity characterize Chacoan history, which seems to me to be the case, our difficult job is made more so. Not only does the context of productive activity undergo rapid change, but also references in artifacts and architecture to forms, symbols, and places with past importance present an ambiguous image to our already impaired vision.

### Exotica

In absolute quantities, weight, or volume, or even counts, the amounts of copper, turquoise, shell, and exotic birds (or perhaps, more important, their feathers) are minuscule compared with timbers and ceramics (see Akins 1985:327–328 for exotic bird counts). Distances are far greater, but, still, a few mobile and motivated people could have accomplished acquisition and transport, especially when the quantity is spread over a couple of centuries. These items "invoke" the idea of the larger and more complex societies of Mesoamerica (Nelson, chapter 10 of this volume) and situate Chaco within the larger continental world of which its residents were well aware (Lekson 1983a, 1999). With the strong evidence for turquoise processing in domestic structures away from the Great Houses, we have little reason to think that these materials were processed beyond the household level. Surely, rare goods held very important places in the symbolic structure of the society, but small groups can account for their "production." It is very likely that only people with societal permission could produce artifacts with high ritual significance (Lewis 2002; Spielmann 1998). In some cases, knowledge of or access to the materials, preparation, and manufacture may have been restricted. In other cases, such as ceramic forms, rules might have dictated who could make or who could use specific products. Good examples are the famous cylinder jars, a simple form made by using standard ceramic materials but highly restricted in distribution (see figure 10.3a; Toll 1990; Crown and Wills 2003:511–518).

Exotic goods such as shell and turquoise, as well as ornaments made of materials more locally available (see Mathien 1997), are the clearest examples of items with time investment in both transport and processing. Eventually, Chacoans removed these from circulation and placed them in invisible contexts (for example, sealed them into Great Kiva niches), with burials, or in ritual caches (see, for example, Akins 1986:112–124; Judd 1954; Neitzel 2003b; Pepper 1920:112–199; Toll 2001:color photo 4). We could consider production of some other items in the same way. Although beams create a visible building element, the careful shaping and the beautiful stonework were covered. Chert from long distances may have been used, but much of it wound up in the mounds. Chacoans ritually destroyed vessels. All these end states indicate a specific role of production: to signify places as important and, further, to demonstrate connections between places and their inhabitants.

If turquoise, copper, beads, staffs, painted items, and specialized vessels had such significance, would these not have been removed during relocations of ritual focus and important people or, at least, looted after the end of the social order? Some such loss may influence our view of the quantities of these special items produced and used, but more impressive to me is how much we *have* found in place after eight hundred years. The presence of these special items may be a testimony to the continued importance—power—of the locations where they were placed. Perhaps, as in the restricted production of an easily made but valued form such as a cylinder jar, people during and after the height of activity in Chaco Canyon believed strongly enough in the context of these items to leave them, signifying a continued understanding and acceptance of them into the present. As with a fence, these concepts work only with the honest people. This "fence" must have been strong, and inclusive.

## THE BIG PICTURE AND THE BIG IDEA

Within the approximate span of the Chacoan sphere are six known Pueblo languages in four families. Hopi oral history describes the formation of villages, with components drawn from all parts of this linguistic complexity (Foster 1996; Mindeleff 1891:16–41). Indications of genetic diversity support the idea that Chacoan society had an intricate composition (Schillachi and Stojanowski 2002:348–349). The formation process was fraught with tensions, conflicts, and relocations. We have little reason to think that the social situation was simpler during the eleventh century than during the nineteenth. How, then, were production and interaction organized over a large area with a diverse population? How do we account for the impressively large quantities of goods that were moved from all over this region to Chaco? Although some denigrate "vacant cities, festive pilgrims, and wholesale consumption of goods in brief but periodic events" (Vivian 1991:75), I continue to believe that an interacting region of this size and complexity had to operate on a primarily voluntary instead of coercive basis and that transport of goods was an important element of Chaco life and belief. Figures 4.5 and 4.6 show both symbolic and actual burden baskets recovered from Pueblo Bonito; similar baskets are shown in use on Hohokam pottery (Haury 1976:238-239, 345), indicating the pan-Southwestern importance of transport.

Today, people from many places and of various ethnicities come together for trade fairs, fiestas, and ritual gatherings, as they did in the past (Malville and Malville 2001). The reasons these systems exist are enormously involved (Smith 1977), and stripping away the colonial

**FIGURE 4.5**

*Burden baskets are iconic of goods and material movement. Excavations have recovered two forms of these bifurcated baskets, in miniature as ceramic effigies and as actual baskets (fig. 4.6). That they were created in effigy reinforces their importance. Burden basket effigies at the same scale: on the left is an effigy of a basket containing a ceramic olla (15.2 by 5.7 cm) from Pueblo Bonito, Room 329, a west-wing burial room (see also Judd 1954:plate 97 lower); on the right is the largest effigy (23.4 cm long by 10.1 cm wide), from Pueblo del Arroyo, Room 27, an interior room with an extraordinary ceramic assemblage (Judd 1959:23–24). Others were recovered from Room 27 as well as from Pueblo Bonito, Room 330 (west wing), Room 350 (a room inside the west plaza at the south edge), Room 347 (a deep deposit in the plaza in front of Room 324 in the west wing), and the east mound. The two above and many others have perforations or lugs on the back sides for affixing to some other object, and the tall loops on the righthand basket likely represent a tump line. (From Judd 1954:plate 88 and figure 100; drawn by Marjorie Leggitt)*

and market processes is perhaps impossible. Although there are instances of suggested status (Akins 2001), they are few even in central Chaco and almost unknown in communities outside Chaco, and I argue that these were brief. DeBoer (2001) describes cases in South

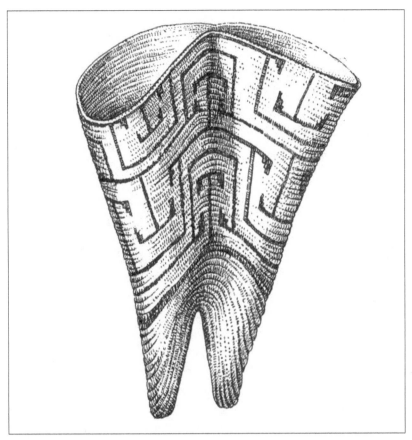

**FIGURE 4.6**

*A burden basket from Room 320, an early room within the west roomblock (39.6 by 30.4 by 20.3 cm). (Judd 1954:313; redrafted by Marjorie Leggitt).*

America in which social complexity is essentially dormant during much of the year but becomes much more apparent at times of regional ceremony. From a Chacoan perspective, one especially intriguing event in these communities is log racing. Groups carry large logs over long distances on straight, sometimes parallel paths in an expression of cohesion. "These races occur with some frequency during the period of village aggregation and would appear to be a classic instance of the integrative role of ritual" (DeBoer 2001:25). DeBoer describes societies in Brazil, Peru, and Ecuador that meet for major ceremonies at centers mostly deserted for much of the year. During these gatherings, leaders deal with disputes that have occurred during dispersed living and during the gatherings themselves. When the people disperse, these powers become dormant again (see also Malville and Malville 2001 for Asian examples). In more than one of the cases described, long straight paths lead to the center, and some serve as regional necropoleis (reminding me of the many burials placed in the Aztec West Ruin during the occupation of Aztec East—and making me wonder about Pueblo Bonito). DeBoer suggests that this form of situational complexity could be relevant in Chaco.

Gwinn Vivian has long argued for the presence of two differently organized groups in Chaco (for example, Vivian 1990:446–448), a model given credence by the presence of the Tewa on First Mesa at Hopi. Wilshusen and Ortman (1999) and Windes (n.d.) suggest that such multiethnicity existed in the Dolores area as early as Pueblo I. I have become increasingly convinced that there must have been different language groups and ethnicities within the Chaco sphere. I suggest, however, that the various major architectural forms present in Chaco communities are based on differences in structure function rather than ethnicity. Variation in smaller houses could signal part-time residents from other locations (McKenna and Truell 1986; Toll, Newren, and McKenna 2005), but Great House–small house variation is mostly functional (see figure 3.12). To identify ethnicities within the Chaco system, we must decipher the many subtle differences in site layout and ceramic decoration.

Mahoney (2000) has been using ethnographic and settlement data to define areal and population sizes of communities within the Chaco sphere. She has found that communities were probably dispersed enough to be sustainable in terms of subsistence production, granting sufficient moisture, but that many were too small in population to sustain mating pools. Therefore, even in years when subsistence production was sufficient to supply a community, a need for mates would have encouraged participation in intercommunity networks.

No doubt, gatherings of people from dispersed places for special events have their roots in at least the Archaic in the Southwest. Flexibility in location, leadership, and group constitution were critical to survival in the high plateau. With adjustments for greater population and increased reliance on agriculture, this time depth could give added credence to the importance of participating in events far from home. Construction of large public buildings possibly manifested this pattern of gathering for regional events, and requirements for renewal and periodic observation of ritual would have ensured continued participation of contributing populations (see Crown and Wills 2003). Great Kivas can accommodate many people, but the presence of formal plazas and buildings from which to view them is even more suited to large convocations of people.

In the 1970s and early 1980s the Chaco Project devoted much attention to the concept of Chaco as a system of redistribution. For suspect reasons, redistribution fell into interpretive disrepute toward the end of this time (see Toll 1991:100–102). Doubters of redistributive function based their objections on three main reasons: inefficiency of food transport (Lightfoot 1979), absence of materials from Chaco in outlying communities, and rejection of chiefly redistribution models. Especially because we are unable to see either the personnel and mechanism of exchange or the distribution of most perishable goods, we must modify our perception of "redistribution." Rather than conceive it as a chiefly personage doling out vessels, we should focus on goods movement. Gatherings of people from dispersed communities promote exchanges of all varieties: social, genetic (addressing the mating size quandary, Mahoney 2000), comestible, and material (Ford 1972). That is, clearly, the organization of community relationships facilitated the distribution of goods and food through gatherings, population movement, and exchange.

As Tom Windes has said many times, the jumble of structures and occupations and variable research in central Chaco Canyon is so confusing that we can hardly hope to understand it. There is a raging debate about who used the large structures for what purposes. Deciding the "answer" to these questions is, in turn, key to discussing for whom various producers were working. Reference to less architecturally complicated communities away from the canyon avoids the problems in the central canyon. Communities that are contemporary with the canyon developments and graphically linked to it with roads typically have a few differentiated structures in a prominent place (Great House, Great Kiva, landscape features) and many more residential structures of various sizes, mostly small. These are the much rehearsed "outliers," a few good examples of which are Bis sa'ani

(Breternitz 1982), Andrews (Marshall et al. 1979; Van Dyke 1997a), Kin Nizhoni (Sebastian and Toll 1987; Marshall et al. 1979), and Peach Springs (Powers, Gillespie, and Lekson 1983). For this discussion, the important thing about these locations is the scale of the "great" house.

Room size, siting, massive masonry, and earthworks all make Great Houses distinctive in clusters of structures (see plates 4–7). Other than a few exceptions, though, most of these structures do not have large numbers of rooms or huge "footprints" (Lekson 1991; Schelberg 1984, 1992). Few have been excavated, but it can be argued that designers and builders devoted little of the area in these structures to living space. If they built these structures as public spaces for communities rather than as high-status residences, this gives us an index of the communities' ability to perform major tasks. Using this community model as a baseline for organization of the larger interaction area manifested in the Chaco "community of communities," some of us (with avid dissent from others) could argue that large structures in Chaco were primarily public spaces (see also Saitta 1997). These huge projects were, doubtless, under the direction of leaders. Based on many historic models, including the modern Pueblos, however, these leaders endeavored to be heard but not seen. The relevance of this model to production is that it can provide insight into how people organized production and for whom. An ideal of simplicity and equality does not necessarily mean equality in practice (Feinman 1992). But if equality is the ideal, as historic Pueblo practice would suggest, inequality will be harder to see.

## CONCLUSION

In what sense was production organized? Many linguistic, ethnic, productive, and areal groups were interacting on multiple levels. The setting is large enough, unpredictable enough, and diffuse enough that no one could *control* it, although individuals could certainly manipulate it. When thinking about the economy, we should not confuse elements we identify, such as types of material exchange or construction events, as being separate systems. Rather, they are strands that make up the whole rope.

Much of what impresses us about Chaco is its increases in scale: the extent of contacts, size of buildings, amounts of staple goods movement, quantities of exotica. This increase in scale is coupled with great attention to detail and superimposition of formality. Leadership of some sort was in place to coordinate such outcomes. Our seminar produced several versions of organization whose common thread was that the individuals holding those positions of increased knowledge and power would have valued the group over the individual and would have striven to maintain a low profile (see Mills 2002:80).

Explanations from the Chaco Organization of Production Synthesis emphasized voluntaristic participation instead of violent or coercive leadership, corporate instead of networked organization, group instead of individually focused leadership (Earle 2001; Feinman, Lightfoot, and Upham 2000; Peregrine 2001; Renfrew 2001; ). Under these explanations, the leadership indeed organized production more than coerced it. In addition to providing a creditable belief structure, the leadership would have had to schedule meaningful events in which populations from diverse locations would have been ready to participate at considerable energy expense (see also Pauketat et al. 2002). In discussing the time depth and importance of communal feasting in Pueblo society, Potter (2000:480) argues that large-scale, community-focused (instead of competitive) feasting developed among the Pueblos at the time the Katsina Cult emerged, around 1275. But, I believe (Toll 2001:70–75; Toll and McKenna 1987), the evidence shows that very large gatherings surely involving feasts were already taking place in Chaco Canyon, especially during the late 1000s. I believe that both the stratigraphy and contents of the large mounds in front of numerous Great Houses (see figure 3.14 and plate 4) signify periodic events at these locations (Toll 1985, 1991, 2001; Toll and McKenna 1987).[3] In accordance with Renfrew's model and Earle's model, these gatherings could have effected large corporate efforts and financed the monuments that stand to the idea to this day.

The functions and populations of Great Houses must remain central questions to Chaco research, and more carefully collected data from mounds and all other Great House contexts would be of enormous use (see figure 3.14). The consistent locations, scale, and associated constructions (see Windes 1987b:616–667; Cameron 2002) leave little doubt that placement and use of mounds were "intentional" (little in Great Houses lacks intention). Even in the context of trash-phobic modern times, ash heaps retain sacred significance for today's

Pueblos, and the Chaco heaps must have had importance. Of course, we cannot say which rituals took place where and, for the most part, which of the broken vessels or pieces of chipped stone people used in ritual. The evidence is quite convincing: one of many things that happened during activities at Pueblo Alto was the intentional destruction of vessels (of which there are, again, ethnographic examples; see figure 4.3). This destruction would have increased the ceramic content of the mound, but cooking likely contributed more to the ceramic component than vessel sacrifice, contrary to some subsequent renditions of our interpretation that now claim that the entire mound is sacrificed vessels. Given small year-round populations in Great Houses, large quantities of used-up artifacts (there are many in those mounds, no matter how you count them), and ethnographic gatherings throughout the world, periodic use of Great Houses remains an eminently reasonable function for them. Initial gatherings were probably for large construction events, but in the Pueblo Alto mound, at least, construction debris clearly antecedes food and artifactual debris. If one chooses to downplay architectural metaphor as *constituted by the whole* (Wills 2001), from Great House complex to Chaco Canyon and beyond, explaining Chaco becomes far more difficult.

Almost certainly, individual households organized production of portable artifacts, whether pots or pendants. Scheduling of labor investment would have been critical at many levels in the Chacoan scheme. As discussed by Hagstrum (2001), the flexibility of household scheduling is important to providing for the household and performing tasks at appropriate times. Many households' strategy included production of some food or artifacts or available labor beyond the household's own needs. While it was important that the household be in charge of its own task scheduling (no micromanagement!), control of the annual calendar would be the most direct way to "organize production" or for "manipulation of collective ritual by corporate groups" (Earle 2001:33; Spielmann 1998:158). The timing of ritual events is focal to historic Pueblo ritual (for example, Ortiz 1969:116). So, too, are feasting and associated large gatherings, which are, in turn, scheduled by the same calendar.

Long-distance movement of quantities and volumes of products is inconceivable to our motor-bound minds, but designs and plans cover much more space, and more thoroughly, than physical objects. The origins of such concepts and the mechanism of instituting them over a region are fundamental blocks in understanding production (see Van Dyke 2000). The actual process of creating a design such as black-on-white hachure or notched bench kivas is probably the nexus of a skilled artisan, ritual leaders' approval, and good communication channels. Acceptance of the new style, in turn, would require ritual determination of correctness and processes for demonstrating membership in a community and in the community of communities. The Dogoszhi design style and McElmo Great House layouts are two excellent examples of this phenomenon (Van Dyke 2004, chapter 7 of this volume; Plog 2003). These also exemplify the hazards of geographic names to later interpretations.

Erecting monumental buildings and capturing rapid runoff must have required more overt direction and larger groups of people than increasing production of pots and pottage. Water control would have necessarily involved the local population because of the need for quick response, but major building projects could have drawn from a much larger area and would have relied heavily on scheduling by ritual leaders (Renfrew 2001). As envisioned by Earle (2001:32–34), "the types of goods mobilized within a staple-finance system include food and other goods used to support specialist personnel of institutions and to support the ceremonial, group-oriented activities of the institutions.... Most goods are expected to stay within the center to support activities closely associated with the institutions of the center."

Compared with contemporary related sites such as those in the Totah (McKenna and Toll 1992), the amount of materials from considerable distance found in sites in Chaco Canyon is large. The extent of sites following the Chaco pattern (Lekson 1991) and probably subscribing to many tenets of Chaco organization and interacting with other sites doing likewise is enormous. That scale and the level of goods movement strongly suggest that one of the Chaco system's accomplishments was to create sufficient security so that wide-ranging travel and exchange were feasible: the "Pax Chaco" (Lekson 2002). The scarcity of evidence for violent events during the 900s and 1000s (contra Turner and Turner 1999) further supports the existence of a period of relative calm.[4] By encouraging exchange and transport of goods, sharing and communication of designs and productive techniques would have increased, and production for exchange might have become more common.

Small societies can put enormous pressures on members to conform; at times, these pressures involve violence. Perceived economic, spiritual, and social benefit stimulate communities, and the households that compose them, to produce—be it food, ceramics, building material, building labor, timber transport, special chipped stone, or exotic materials. Maintaining that situation through good times and bad was the organizational challenge in all fields of endeavor at Chaco.

In summary, during the tenth and eleventh centuries, agriculturalists in the San Juan Basin, the Totah and its rivers, the Chuskas, and the Puerco rivers (east and west) lived in dispersed but interconnected settlements (see figure 1.1). Although we have only linguistic, spatial, biometric, and ceramic hints of it, this population was probably ethnically diverse. The subsistence pattern and the advantages of wide participation, acquaintance, and affiliation were such that architectural and artifactual remains look very similar and show the interconnectivity of communities. Subsistence and artifactual production took place in every community; the majority of households provided for most of their own needs, endeavoring to store sufficient food for ever-impending dry years. Based on deep historical patterns of mobility, there was more fluidity of location than the scale of structures might lead us to assume, as well as movement between aggregated and dispersed states (Wilshusen 1991). Effects of this mobility could be the appearance of goods at a considerable distance from their sources and the movement of labor or goods to places where they were required.

Based on local resources, some communities produced more or less of certain commodities than others. In some cases, communities produced sufficient quantities beyond their own needs to supply other communities; certainly, this would have occurred among household production units within the same community. If each household could satisfy basic needs, why do we see common items, such as culinary pots and barely modified chipped stone, that people clearly transported and/or exchanged? In addition to productive shortages, maintaining interaction with people in removed locations provides a fallback during times of subsistence or other stress. There are records of Hopis going to Zuni, and vice versa, as well as to Keres and Tiwa Pueblos, during droughts and epidemics (Adams 1981:325–328); it is significant for the multiethnic, mono-economic model that these interchanges involved multiple linguistic groups. Such community mobility and interaction among distinct linguistic groups have deep antiquity (Wilshusen and Ortman 1999:382–383).

The leaders, whatever their form, surely had the ability to call for increased production of votive goods. As suggested by the periodicity of gatherings in South America (DeBoer 2001) and among the modern Pueblos, as well as the stratigraphy of the Pueblo Alto mound (see plate 6; Toll 2001:70–74), some of this control probably stemmed from knowledge of and control over the ceremonial calendar. This control and knowledge could have been sufficient to effect increases of labor, whether for votive production of artifacts and food or for construction and ritual performance.

This ritually organized system of exchange and directed interaction would have enabled the linguistically diverse population of a large area to function cooperatively for perhaps two hundred years. Recent fixation upon prehistoric violence shows that operation of the system was not always pacific and without problems. We can as easily view the violence as ethnic conflict or witchcraft (for witches seem more likely to be from some ethnic group other than your own). A certain portion of increased production of precious goods served to acquire like goods from Mesoamerica (Nelson, chapter 10 of this volume), but we have no clear data on the volume of Chaco products in Mesoamerica.

Most organization took place at the household level, the primary unit of production for most tasks. Ecological and traditional circumstances changed the types of goods produced to small degrees, but not on the level of large-scale production of any commodity. Community and regional leaders, primarily in charge of scheduling, could induce these productive units to increase production for communitywide and regionwide events they directed. Although there was general knowledge of events and practices in other parts of the network, participation in production and exchanges involving the center in Chaco Canyon during the eleventh century varied on bases of proximity, barriers, and need. As described by Earle (2001:32), "much more distant Chaco constructions probably represented ceremonial[ly] linked, but economically separate, polities." This organization accomplished re-markable feats of construction and involvement for approximately a century but eventually could no longer function in the difficult setting of Chaco Canyon. The organization in modified form continued north of the San Juan River in the twelfth century and probably in the Rio Grande after that.

What was Chaco? Chaco was a community of communities. Sched-uling and planning were paramount features of life, or, at least, life as it related to Chaco. Within the confines of an agricultural calendar, the timing of communal events was crucial, and the sense of symmetry and order was on an order unfamiliar to us. These events included building and landscaping projects and religious observances. A society of many areal groups and social groups could be manipulated through control of scheduling. A profound subscription to the tenets of an encompass-ing ceremonial order was essential in motivating a dispersed popula-tion to provide large bursts of labor and material. The fundamentals of this belief system were deeply rooted, and their elaboration took place over time, by incorporation of groups and areas. This deep foundation was fertile ground for implementation of enormous effort, initiated by some combination of good or even bad conditions and, as pointed out by John Kantner, obviating questions such as "what was Chaco?" A lead-ership that wanted the place and organization to achieve even greater earthly and spiritual significance, a leadership that possessed the per-sonal prestige and charisma to make it happen, cultivated these fertile conditions. It was a short run, but it had a long epilogue and many iter-ations in subsequent centuries.

Chaco was a combined set of ideas that were similar enough to cre-ate observable patterns but held by enough different people to mani-fest variation. It created a landscape that promoted relationships between places and people and emphasized structuring experience: it was a focus of ritual activity and therefore belief. In the context of that focus, there were many allegiances and groups. The social context allowed and fostered interactions between similar groups and with more spatially and ethnically removed ones. Mobility and flexibility among locations, again within agricultural restraints, was a frequently employed option, and multiple residences are an eminent possibility.

Chaco was a place permeated with meaning, embellished and elaborated to remarkable degrees. It was a "Location of High Devotional Expression" (Renfrew 2001), a "Rituality" (Yoffee 2001), with the material and survival correlates that accompany them. Chaco was where diverse peoples from many places could make all sorts of connections, and one way to bring them together was through gatherings at the central and important place with the Great Houses—Chaco Canyon.

Part of what makes a place and time is joy, and our reconstructions are notably joyless. What made people happy in Chaco? Things done right and made well. The word *right* must be emphasized here: ceremonies, work, buildings, pots, jewelry. The beautiful setting with Fajada Butte, dramatic light on spectacular buildings, powerful rain and runoff, ever-changing inspirational views. Chaco was a social place providing helpful connections, full storerooms, an exciting game of chance, or a race. It embodied balance and symmetry.

Among all these things, even in good times, life at Chaco was never *easy*.

### Notes

Cathy Cameron did the majority of work in organizing the production portion of the synthesis effort. I included her as an author on early drafts of this chapter but then removed her name after repeated requests from her. There was a condition to this, however: she wanted to take all blame for problems with the chapter, a deal I happily accepted for the sake of an unusual acknowledgment. Any shortcomings in this chapter are not my fault. I repeat our thanks to all the participants in the session (see the introduction) and thank the people who have provided guidance since, including Peter McKenna, Tom Windes, Rich Wilshusen, Eric Blinman, Nancy Akins, Ben Nelson, John Kantner, Barbara Mills, Steve Plog, Mollie Toll, and, of course, Cathy Cameron. Although capping the capstone in May 2003 at the School of American Research appeared, at first, to be gilding the lily, it seems as though some of us can never get over talking about Chaco. People not already mentioned who provided helpful insights include Lynne Sebastian, Ruth Van Dyke, Tim Pauketat, Linda Cordell, Norm Yoffee, Jim Judge, Richard Leventhal, and the peripatetic Steve Lekson.

1. I have tried to bring the discussions of Renfrew, Earle, Hagstrum, Peregrine, Cameron, Mathien, and Windes and McKenna (all 2001) to bear on my own understanding of how the organization of production changed through

time. Each of these scholars contributed to particular aspects of this summary, and I encourage the reader to consult their papers and extensive documentation in the Chaco issue of *American Antiquity* (vol. 66, no. 1). Colin Renfrew and Timothy Earle discuss social organizations from several other contexts and describe similarities to and differences from the evidence at Chaco. Peter Peregrine continues this vein of discussion, including foci on kinship and turquoise production. Melissa Hagstrum discusses the household as the fundamental organizational unit within the system. Toll and Cameron present data on ceramics and lithics, respectively, and Joan Mathien describes ornaments, particularly turquoise, which she has studied over many years. Thomas Windes and Peter McKenna cover uses, sources, and processing of the large quantities of construction wood in Chaco Canyon. A full reference to each of these papers appears in the references section.

2. The great editorial urge today is to use the active voice wherever possible. This leads to frequent reference to the "Chacoans." The implications of this term concern me. I am increasingly convinced that the people building and, importantly, living only part-time in Chaco came from diverse locations and probably linguistic traditions. They were not the same as a single pueblo or even language group today. Saying that "the Chacoans built this or imported that" implies that a single group was acting. When we speak about New Yorkers or Santa Fesinos, we understand that either is a diverse, fluid group. If we hear "New Yorkers built the Empire State Building," we understand the figure of speech and know that a small segment of laborers, designers, and financiers made the project happen. In the interest of talking about people instead of buildings, artifacts, and time periods (the stuff of our analyses), I have consented to "Chacoans" with the proviso that it be understood as a conglomerate not as diverse as "New Yorkers," but less uniform than the members of a single modern pueblo or language group.

3. Wills (2001) has found fault with interpretations of mounds as meaningful parts of Great Houses in Chaco Canyon and around the system that contain evidence of the signification of those places and the occurrence of events there. In my view, the contention that builders intentionally created mounds as elements in an architectural metaphor for Chacoan society has yet to be substantiated (Wills 2001:448). This argument reiterates many points made in initial presentations of the data, en route to the conclusion that researchers have overinterpreted the mounds' significance, that they are merely results of construction and daily activity. In coming to the widely held conclusion that mound formation was complex, Wills does adduce additional factors that would have contributed to mound

formation. He does not, however, venture into the more treacherous ground of what Great Houses were for. He finds it remarkable that interpretations are still using data from the 1920s and 1930s and that, with little addition of further data, interpretations of mounds have changed. Like it or not, most central Chaco Great House excavation took place from 1890 to 1940; those data are all there are. With our currently expanded understanding of Chaco, the real marvel is that anyone should be bemused by our revisiting and revising mound significance. Those who have suggested significance for the mounds and whose interpretations are based on data they fully recognize are insufficient have never doubted the complexity of mound formation. They have not argued for anything else, nor did they say anywhere that mounds were formed purely through intentional destruction of vessels. You can find further discussion of this position in Windes (2003:3–4). Were the mounds the sole result of smashing pots? Of course not. Do their stratigraphy, location, and disproportionate size set them apart from other such features? Indeed they do.

4. Lekson (2002:621) shows many "extreme processing events" of human remains events during this time but does not specify them. In my limited experience, they are post-1100 or even 1150 (see also Lipe, chapter 8 of this volume).

Plate 1. Crest of the Chuska Mountains, looking east across the San Juan Basin toward Chaco Canyon, just below the horizon. Chaco Canyon is 75 km from the crest line. (Courtesy Adriel Heisey, NM14-5944-31)

*Plate 2. Chaco Canyon from Fajada Butte (lower right) to the confluence of Chaco Wash and Escavada Wash (upper right), looking west. The square structure (center bottom) is a modern water tank. (Courtesy Adriel Heisey, NM 14-52-01)*

*Plate 3. Kin Ya'a and Hosta Butte, looking southwest. <u>Hosta Butte</u> (the high point on the horizon) is 12 km from Kin Ya'a (foreground). Note the <u>prehistoric roads</u> running from bottom center into Kin Ya'a, and from Kin Ya'a towards a point just to the right of Hosta Butte. (Courtesy Adriel Heisey, NM14-1450-13)*

Plate 4. *"Downtown" Chaco, looking northwest down Chaco Wash. Chetro Ketl (lower right); Pueblo Bonito (left center); Pueblo Alto (right center). Note the segment of prehistoric road on the highest bench between Pueblo Alto and Chetro Ketl. (Courtesy Adriel Heisey, NM14-1860-10)*

*Plate 5. Pueblo Bonito. The top of the image is north-northeast. Note the two "trash mounds" between Pueblo Bonito and the lower-left corner of the image. (Courtesy Adriel Heisey, NM14-5717-24)*

*Plate 6. Pueblo Alto (lower left) looking south-southeast across Chaco Canyon towards Mount Taylor (upper right). <u>Mount Taylor</u> is 95 km from Pueblo Alto. Note the road segment running from Pueblo Alto down the ridge at "two o'clock," towards Pueblo Bonito (below the canyon rim, not visible). (Courtesy Adriel Heisey, NM14-5748-26)*

*Plate 7. Peñasco Blanco. The top of the image is west-northwest. Escavada Wash runs right to left across the top of the image; Chaco Wash runs up from bottom center to its confluence with Escavada Wash (right center). Note the remnants of the sand dune across Chaco Wash at the confluence. (Courtesy Adriel Heisey, NM14-5750-05)*

*Plate 8. A reconstruction of Pueblo Bonito (left center) and Hillside Ruin (right center) by John R. Stein, Richard Freeman, and Taft Blackhorse. Note the paired platform mounds in front of Pueblo Bonito, the platform behind Hillside Ruin, "Threatening Rock" (the detached slab of cliff to the right of Pueblo Bonito), and the roads (light green). (Courtesy Navajo Nation Chaco Sites Protection Program)*

# 5

# The Chaco World

## John W. Kantner and Keith W. Kintigh

A key issue in Chaco archaeology is the large number of Great House communities located outside Chaco Canyon—sites often referred to as "outliers." The geographic distribution of those sites (figure 5.1) delineates the "Chaco World," although the actual nature and dynamics of that world are matters for research, not assertion. For example, the commonly used term *outlier* has implications for the history of Chaco Canyon that may or may not be warranted (see Mills 2002 for an excellent overview of Chaco studies and recent studies on this theme). This chapter summarizes research on questions generated in the Chaco World conference and the Chaco Synthesis: How do we define Chacoan or Great House communities? What level of interaction occurred among these communities and between Chaco Canyon and them? What degree of symbolic and sociopolitical unity existed across the Chaco world?[1] At the end of this chapter, we assess the Chaco Timeline from the perspective of research outside Chaco Canyon.

## GREAT HOUSE COMMUNITIES

What was the Chaco world? Kintigh (2003) reviews the substantial confusion and disagreement that surrounds research on Chaco. Not

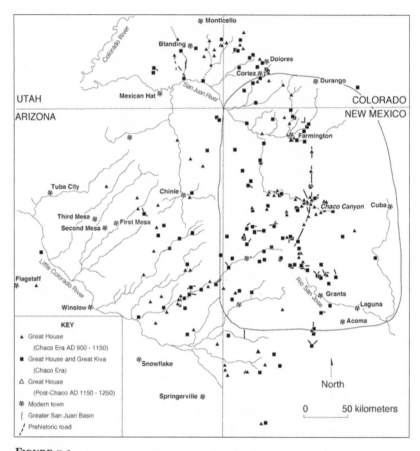

**FIGURE 5.1**

*Great House architecture in the Chaco World database (http://sipapu.gsu.edu/chacoworld. html). Great House names in italic are tentative additions to the database, pending further information.*

only do scholars disagree on archaeological interpretation, but also we do not agree on even the relevant corpus of data we are trying to interpret. Further compounding the problem is the apparent circularity in defining the Chaco world as that which includes Chacoan features. Also confusing are terms, such as *Chaco outlier*, that sometimes refer to specific architecture and other times refer to entire communities of people, while also implying the nature of the relationships structuring the Chaco world (Kantner and Mahoney 2000:6). In general, however, most scholars would concede that the Chaco world *minimally* comprised those areas outside Chaco Canyon where distinctively Chacoan architectural complexes were constructed between *at least* A.D. 1020 and 1150, the peak era of construction activity inside and outside the canyon (Kintigh 2003:96–97).

What is a *Chacoan architectural complex?* This term refers to a cluster of archaeological features that exhibit a strong affinity to those same features found in Chaco Canyon (Kintigh 2003:97–99). The central component of a complex is a Chacoan Great House, an unusually imposing structure ideally characterized by core-veneer masonry, multiple-story or exceptional single-story height, oversized rooms, and blocked-in or elevated kivas—characteristics found in Chaco Canyon's Great Houses. Chacoan architectural complexes also ideally include one or more formal Great Kivas (although, in most cases, we cannot distinguish these from their less formal predecessors because excavation is so rare), road segments, and earthworks such as berms that encircle the Great House itself. Because few places in the putative Chaco world appear to have fully realized Chacoan architectural complexes, scholars debate how many characteristics are necessary to label an architectural complex "Chacoan" (for example, Gilpin 2003; Kintigh 2003; Lekson 1991). Generally, participants in the Chaco World conference agreed that, to be Chacoan, a complex needed a reasonably distinctive Great House contemporaneous with comparable features found in Chaco Canyon.

Although defining Chacoan architectural complexes is important for bounding the Chaco world, most scholarship has focused on the community as the primary social building block because aggregations of Puebloan households predate the emergence of Chacoan patterns. As such, the development of the Chaco world needs to be understood in terms of evolving relationships *among* communities instead of transformative relationships *within* communities. This is not to say that substantial changes did not occur at the same time within communities— clearly, they did (for example, Durand and Durand 2000; Gilpin 2003; Van Dyke 1997a, 1999a). The point is that Chaco was primarily a regional development and not a set of internal changes that occurred independently in a similar fashion in every community (see Lekson 1999:37; Van Dyke 2003a).

What is a *community?* In Chaco scholarship, as Gilpin (2003) and

Kintigh (2003) describe, the definition is more often implicit than explicit. Scholars use the term *community* in many ways; it can refer to a distinct archaeological pattern or to a meaningful social setting, and the two are not necessarily the same (Yaeger and Canuto 2000). Mahoney has recently noted (2000; see also Kolb and Snead 1997; Varien 1999) that the traditional approach in archaeology is to identify household clusters separated by comparatively empty spaces as communities, relying on the ethnographic correlate that a community consists of those people engaged in regular, face-to-face interaction. She challenges this definition, pointing out that many prehistoric Puebloan communities identified in this way would not have been demographically stable, as defined by Wobst (1975). Mahoney proposes that an effective community would have needed multiple household aggregations to fulfill a minimal mating network. Gilpin (2003) pursues this idea, demonstrating that only fourteen Great House communities in the Chaco world had momentary populations above the 475-person threshold Mahoney identifies as sustainable. He therefore concludes that meaningful Chaco-era community boundaries must have transcended spatially discrete concentrations of households, often encompassing multiple clusters of Puebloan sites.

Although Mahoney and Gilpin highlight serious problems resulting from simply using habitation clusters to define analytically meaningful communities, we should consider three points when basing interpretations on arguments of demographic sustainability. First, Kintigh (2003) notes that the 475-person threshold was at the upper end of Wobst's (1975) simulated sustainable demographic networks. He points out that Wobst's lower estimates—ranging from seventy-five to two hundred people—would substantially impact Mahoney's interpretations; more household clusters, in fact, would have been demographically sustainable at these lower levels, increasing the number qualifying for community status as defined by Mahoney. Second, Kantner (2003a, 2003b) argues that household aggregations too small to be demographically self-sufficient would not necessarily have recognized that their long-term stability was endangered. Also, the implied consequences of small mating pools are likely to manifest very slowly, certainly more slowly than the 115-year average community lifespan identified by Gilpin (2003). Social expectations that define potential mates can serve as proximate mechanisms enforcing demographic sustainability (Kintigh 2003:103–105), but the ethnographic, historical, and osteological records reveal many times in human history when social rules were altered in ways contrary to bioevolutionary expectations (for example, Kantner 2003b).

A third point to consider when determining community boundaries in the Chaco world is that people must have had a reason for maintaining the space that often (but not always; see Gilpin 2003) exists between household aggregations. Undoubtedly, they also valued the identity likely associated with each cluster. Gilpin's discovery (2003) that Chaco-era settlement clusters are at least thirty times as densely packed as the surrounding area supports these conclusions (see also Lipe, chapter 8 of this volume). Even if these clusters were a consequence of environmental factors, such as the availability of water, arable land, or open habitation space in a given location, membership in a particular aggregation must have been meaningful to those people. They likely interacted more regularly with their immediate neighbors, even while maintaining social relationships at other scales. Van Dyke (2003b; Wilshusen and Van Dyke, chapter 7 of this volume) points out that individuals within communities may have "imagined" their social communities to be larger than the immediate landscape. She also discusses how public features within residential clusters focused attention and identity locally—a focus that may have been intentionally manipulated. For example, to simulate ancestral community connections to the landscape, people may have created earthworks to look like ancient middens accumulated over many years. For these reasons, we can regard the spatially distinct cluster of habitations, with public infrastructure including Chacoan architectural complexes, as the basic community unit.

## DEFINITION OF THE CHACO WORLD

Which communities were part of the Chaco world? We can minimally include all spatially defined communities containing the Chacoan architectural complexes discussed above—the Great House, with its inordinately large size, core-veneer masonry, and blocked-in kivas; formal Great Kivas; prehistoric road segments; and earthworks or berms. The Chaco World database includes these variables.[2] The

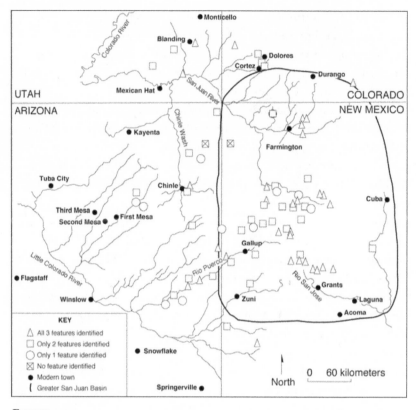

**FIGURE 5.2**

*The number of Chacoan features identified at Great Houses for which complete data are available in the Chaco World database. Only those three features most often associated with Chacoan architecture are considered: core-veneer masonry, multiple stories, and blocked-in kivas. Because of the intensity of research within the San Juan Basin and immediately surrounding areas, more complete data are available there than in the more distant parts of the Chaco world.*

majority of the communities in the database for which enough information is available contain architectural complexes with most of these features, and these are what we refer to as "Chacoan" or "Great House" communities.

As Van Dyke (2003a) identifies, however, these features do not occur together as a cohesive package of traits (figure 5.2), but rather in regional and temporal clusters in which a set of communities share some but not all of the features seen in Chaco Canyon. Most frequently, for example, we find core-veneer masonry and low kiva/room ratios at Great Houses in communities whose association with the central canyon is seemingly indisputable, such as those in the San Juan Basin. Roadways and enclosed plazas are also common in this area. Great Houses less similar to the Chaco Canyon archetypes and with varying suites of accompanying features usually characterize more distant communities. We defer the issue as to what this feature variability indicates about the integration and interdependence of Great House communities in the Chaco world until later (and see Van Dyke 2003a).

At this point, we have defined which units minimally compose the Chaco world communities with Chacoan architectural complexes—but we also note that none of the variables characterizing these complexes are perfectly correlated through time or space. As research on Chacoan patterns outside Chaco Canyon continues, another topic in need of investigation is the identification and description of communities without Great Houses (see Gilpin 2003). Does patterning in their locations and composition explain their lack of Chacoan features? Were they resisting whatever it was that Chaco was about, or were they intentionally excluded? Similarly, Great Houses without associated households also merit additional attention. Did they serve as community centers for nearby household aggregations, or are these explainable in some other way, such as the road-related Great Houses like Halfway House? Kantner (1997) notes that small Great Houses with no associated Great Kivas or berms were built along likely footpaths between some communities, perhaps to serve as boundary markers instead of central ceremonial complexes.

One example of the challenges in defining Great House communities—and therefore the boundaries of the Chaco world—is the Red Mesa Valley, some 40 km south of Chaco Canyon. On the valley's north side, more than a dozen spatially distinct communities feature likely Chacoan architectural complexes. In one intriguing area are three neighboring communities known as "Andrews," "Blue J," and "Casamero" (figure 5.3). In the Chaco World database, Andrews includes twenty-seven habitations and an architectural complex featuring a multistoried, core-veneer Great House with blocked-in kivas; road segments and at least one Great Kiva are associated with the Great House, but no earthworks are reported (also see Van Dyke 1999a,

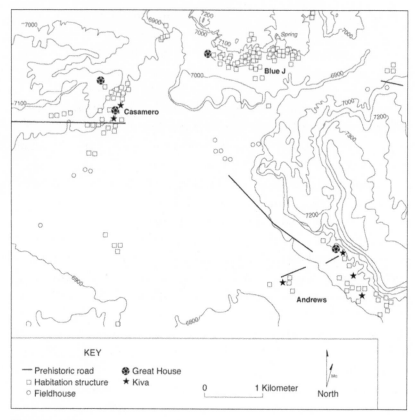

**FIGURE 5.3**

*In the Red Mesa Valley, the Chaco-era communities of Andrews, Blue J, and Casamero are situated within a few kilometers of one another. Andrews and Casamero include Chacoan architectural complexes with quite different features and layouts. Only a small structure with a single core-veneer wall is found in the large Blue J community.*

2000). The Great House has not been excavated to determine room sizes. Casamero's twenty-eight habitations are accompanied by perhaps two separate Great House complexes; one of these may, in fact, predate the Chaco era (also see Harper et al. 1988). The larger Great House is multistoried and features core-veneer masonry, but its association with a nearby Great Kiva and road segment is unclear. Excavations revealed rooms of only modest size (Sigleo 1981). The Blue J community is perhaps the most perplexing, for it is quite large, with more than sixty habitations, but the candidate Great House is a small, isolated, one-story structure with a single core-veneer wall (Kantner 2004)—and Blue J has no Great Kiva, no confirmed roadways, and no earthworks.

These three communities in the Red Mesa Valley illustrate the difficulties in defining the Chaco world. On the one hand, they form spatially distinctive habitation clusters, which affirms our approach for bounding Great House communities as both archaeological and social entities. On the other hand, the largest community—arguably the largest in the entire Red Mesa Valley—has no obvious Chacoan architectural complex. Was it therefore socially tied to Andrews or Casamero and their Great Houses, or was it an autonomous community that was simply not participating in the Chaco world?

## INTERACTION IN THE CHACO WORLD

All models describing the development of Chaco Canyon and the Chaco world implicitly rely on or explicitly propose an understanding of how outlying Great House communities interacted with one another and with Chaco Canyon (for example, Sebastian 1992a; Vivian 1990). Although defining the Chaco world is largely a matter of empirically identifying patterns shared with Chaco Canyon, we cannot easily interpret those patterns until we understand what kinds of interactions took place across the region. Chacoan scholarship has generally explored two major sources of data when considering interaction between communities exhibiting Chacoan characteristics: the remains of roadways and the evidence for exchange. Also, a few scholars have focused on archaeological features that may have been part of a communication system based in Chaco Canyon.

### Roadways

Roadways have served as an indication that communities were regularly interacting with one another. In fact, they are associated with the majority of Great Houses in the Chaco World database (refer to plate 3). Recent research by Roney (1992), Vivian (1997a, 1997b), and Kantner (1997), however, suggests that the roads found throughout the northern Southwest may not have formed a network connecting communities with one another and with Chaco Canyon (see discussion in Durand 2003; but see Lekson, chapter 1 of this volume).

Kantner (1997), for example, examined road segments identified on either side of Lobo Mesa—including those associated with the Red Mesa Valley communities described above. Using a geographic information system (GIS) that digitally modeled the landscape, Kantner found that prehistoric road segments did not even remotely correspond with the idealized, economical pathways connecting communities. Instead, the majority of roadways apparently served only to link communities with neighboring hamlets or to direct attention towards nearby landscape features with presumed cosmological meaning. Because roadways articulated with Great Houses, they were, effectively, extensions of Chacoan architectural complexes, further directing attention towards these centers by physically tying them to the landscape. In the Andrews Great House community, for example, archaeologists have identified two roadways. One clearly connects the community's Chacoan architectural complex with a nearby small cluster of habitations. The other road aligns both along a straight-line projection towards Hosta Butte and with an idealized pathway to this prominent geological feature (figure 5.4).

The evidence suggests that most road segments do not represent intense and consistent interaction at a regional level. Small local networks of roads, however, may have formed in some areas of the northern Southwest on the edge of the Chaco world. In southeastern Utah, for example, a series of road segments identified in Cottonwood and Comb washes may be the remains of lengthy roadways that snaked along the washes; importantly, the segments most clearly link Great Houses, not the communities of which they are a part. Although linear segments crossing the intervening mesa likely joined the two canyon roadways, possibly forming a small network, they do not articulate with any other Chacoan roads outside the area (Till 2001; Till and Hurst 2002; but see Lekson, chapter 1 of this volume).

Despite the absence of a Chaco world–wide road network, the fact remains that at least two and perhaps three major roadways with apparent continuity do emanate from Chaco Canyon and cross to edges of the San Juan Basin (see figure 5.1). Three characteristics of these features merit discussion. First, the intended destinations of these roads remain a mystery. These roads do pass through a number of large communities exhibiting Chacoan characteristics. But their ultimate destinations do not appear to be those communities; rather, they are directed towards prominent points on the landscape. For example, the

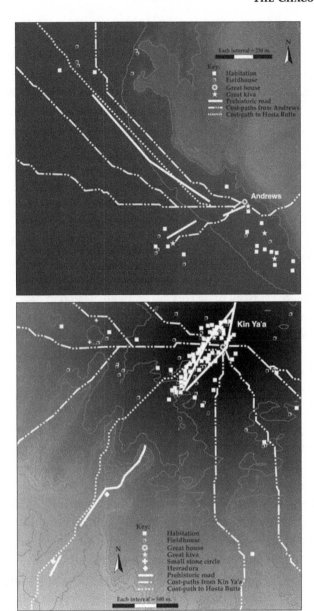

**FIGURE 5.4**

*Roadways associated with Great House communities along the edges of Lobo Mesa do not correspond with simulated economical pathways connecting neighboring communities. On the top, the Andrews road segments head towards the prominent Hosta Butte, as well as a nearby cluster of households "(the lighter the gray, the higher the elevation). On the bottom, the South Road passes through Kin Ya'a and follows an efficient route up the mesa and to Hosta Butte (the lighter gray, the greater the travel time).*

South Road, although passing through or near several Great House communities, including Kin Ya'a (see figure 5.4), almost certainly had the impressive Hosta Butte as its destination (Nials, Stein, and Roney 1987). It falls on the idealized pathway to this prominent landscape feature (Kantner 1997). The North Road's linearity and direction, as well as its termination at Kutz Canyon, seem more significant than any connections it might have provided with population centers (Kincaid 1983; Lekson 1999). Apparently, these lengthy roads—and the unconfirmed third road allegedly connecting Chaco Canyon with the Chuska Mountains—were built not to promote regular interaction between communities but rather to direct regional attention to meaningful points on the landscape (Sofaer, Marshall, and Sinclair 1989; but see Lekson, chapter 1 of this volume).

Were these roads built to access resource areas and funnel materials to Chaco Canyon or across an alleged Chacoan "system"? No continuous roadway extends to Narbona/Washington Pass, where distinctive chert lithic material and trachyte pottery found in large quantities in Chaco Canyon originated (Cameron 2001; Mills, Carpenter, and Grimm 1997). Similarly, no road reaches into the Red Mesa Valley, the likely origin of some of the chert, obsidian, and petrified wood found in the central canyon (for example, LeTourneau 1997).

Snygg and Windes (1998) suggest that the lengthier roads were used to move construction beams to the central canyon, for timbers are known to have been imported from considerable distances (Windes and McKenna 2001). This proposal is supported by recent compositional analyses comparing beams from Chaco Canyon buildings with the forests from which they possibly originated (Durand et al. 1999; English et al. 2001). It is interesting to note, however, that no confirmed roadways go to either the San Mateo or the Chuska mountains (refer to plate 1), the two tentatively identified sources for timbers (the compositional studies so far have not sampled the forests located at the end of the North or South roads). Similar compositional studies of prehistoric maize also fail to tie samples recovered from Chaco Canyon with potential sources at the end of the two major roadways, although these analyses are still in their preliminary stages (Benson et al. 2003).

The second interesting characteristic of the roads is that the quantities of ceramic and lithic material along roads or associated with roadway features suggest that little travel actually occurred on them. For example, Nials, Stein, and Roney (1987) reveal that *herraduras*—horseshoe-shaped masonry enclosures—and other architectural features associated with the roadways were mostly devoid of artifacts (see also Obenauf 1980b:146). If the roadways were conduits for regional interaction, one might expect that they would show more use than they do. Frequencies of artifact deposition along roadways outside Chaco Canyon proper (for example, Windes 1991) should be explored in more depth.

The third and final point regarding roadways concerns the labor needed to construct and maintain them. Surely, one might propose, the considerable labor required to build the roads is evidence for regular, regional interaction. Roadway labor deserves more attention, but a few facts might provide insight into this issue. First, even the longer roadways, such as the South Road, have their most substantial manifestations along those segments located in or near Great House communities; most roads disappear altogether in areas away from populations (Nials, Stein, and Roney 1987). Second, despite the impressive ramps and stairways emphasized in the popular literature (for example, Gabriel 1991), most identified roadways are barely recognizable linear segments with ephemeral or nonexistent berms. Third, the roadways do not appear to have been consistently maintained after they were built; only one of the road cross-sections reported in Nials (1983) shows evidence of maintenance, and this was apparently a one-time event.

These points suggest that the construction of the longer roadways does not necessarily evidence regular interaction among Chacoan people but, instead, is more consistent with sporadic interaction between those local villagers who formalized the routes closest to their communities and those who suggested that such lengthy roads to distant features of the cosmographic landscape be constructed. Smaller, localized roadways found farther from Chaco Canyon, such as those in the Haystack community (see figure 5.4), seem to be modeled after the lengthier roads emanating from the central canyon—outlying Chacoan architectural complexes, with their more diminutive roadways extending to local features of importance, are Chaco Canyon writ small and local.

### Exchange

The exchange of material goods between Chacoan communities is a research topic that has received substantial attention and could provide evidence for the regularity of regional interaction (Cameron and Toll 2001; Duff and Lekson, chapter 9, and Toll, chapter 4, of this volume). Toll's studies (1985, 1991, 2001, chapter 4 of this volume; Toll and McKenna 1997) of the movement of ceramics across the San Juan Basin shows that materials were flowing into the central canyon, with the areas of origin changing over time. Studies of lithic material (Cameron 1984, 2001) and even faunal remains (Akins 1985) substantiate this evidence. Certainly, these changing frequencies indicate interaction between Chaco Canyon Great Houses and specific outlying areas at different points in time. The mechanisms for this interaction and its regularity, however, have yet to be demonstrated. A common proposal is that the canyon hosted large, periodic ceremonial events during which materials were brought in by pilgrims and perhaps were even ritually destroyed (Judge 1993; Stoltman 1999; Toll 1985, 2001; Windes 1987a, 1987b). Recently, this interpretation has been challenged (Wills 2001). Many questions regarding material flow into Chaco Canyon remain unanswered, but it is informative to note the lower frequencies of imported materials and evidence for local production identified at the smaller habitations in Chaco Canyon (Toll and McKenna 1997; Windes et al. 2000)—materials imported into the canyon went to the Great Houses.

Almost all studies of the movement of material across the Chaco world demonstrate that little of the material flowing into Chaco Canyon ever flowed back out (for example, Betancourt, Dean, and Hull 1986; Van Dyke 1997b). Neither was material bypassing Chaco and moving directly between different areas of the Colorado Plateau. Although some areas of the Chaco world apparently engaged in interregional exchange more than others (Gilpin 2003; Neitzel et al. 2002; Windes et al. 2000), the vast majority of ceramics in most Great House communities are local (for example, Gilpin and Purcell 2000; Van Dyke 1997b). The preliminary compositional analysis of maize mentioned earlier supports these contentions. Samples of maize recovered in Pueblo Bonito were traced to the distant Chuska Mountain region, whereas maize consumed at the Aztec Great House was produced locally (Benson et al. 2003).

Compositional analyses of ceramics further demonstrate how restricted the flow of utilitarian material was across the Chaco world (for example, Duff 1994a; Glowacki et al. 2002; Huntley, Mahoney, and Kintigh 1998; King 2004; Neitzel and Bishop 1990; Neitzel et al. 2002; Sullivan and Malville 1993). One such study focused on the exchange of ceramics among Great House communities north and south of Lobo Mesa, an area that includes the Red Mesa Valley (Kantner et al. 2000). This study analyzed more than two hundred pottery samples from five Great House communities by using X-ray fluorescence (XRF), an analytical approach for characterizing the chemical content of the ceramics. To reconstruct patterns of exchange, this approach determines where each sample originated and then compares that with where it was recovered.

The study confirmed that the vast majority of ceramics were locally produced and consumed; it also demonstrated that patterns of exchange among neighboring Great House communities were quite variable (figure 5.5). In particular, the physical boundaries surrounding the San Juan Basin, such as Lobo Mesa and the Dutton Plateau, substantially limited interaction over a wider area. Less visible sociopolitical boundaries likely restricted material flow as well. In the Lobo Mesa study, immediately neighboring Great House communities traded pottery less than did communities somewhat more distant from one another, as illustrated in figure 5.5 (Kantner et al. 2000).

In general, the exchange of utilitarian materials in the Chaco world seems to have been heavily localized, with each community producing its own pottery and lithic tools and trading them relatively short distances as facilitated by topography. Only Chaco Canyon was unique in acquiring substantial quantities of materials from considerable distances. These studies of exchange suggest that regularity in exchange-based interaction was not systemic in the sense that all participating communities interacted with one another. Rather, the evidence demonstrates that Chacoan material interaction was one-way, directed almost exclusively towards Chaco Canyon, and perhaps not very frequent. Utilitarian material in Chaco originated along the inside edges of the San Juan Basin, further indicating that the central canyon imported these materials from a limited area.

Exotic items such as turquoise or copper bells ultimately came to Chaco Canyon from much farther away, although the mechanisms by

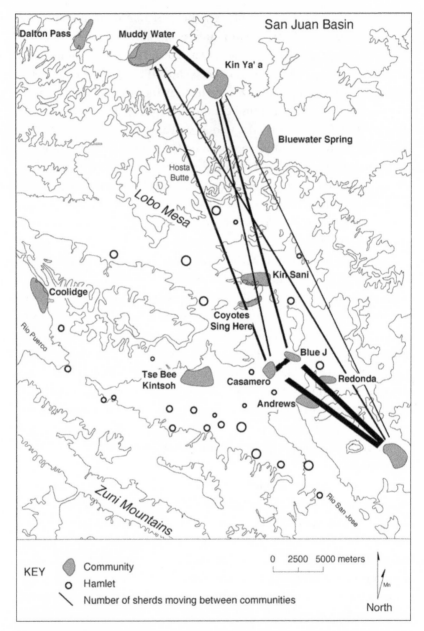

**FIGURE 5.5**

*The movement of ceramics among five Great House communities studied in the XRF compositional analysis. Line thickness represents relative amounts of pottery moving between the communities, with thicker lines indicating greater levels of interaction and/or exchange.*

which they were brought to the canyon are unknown. Lekson (1999, 2000) has recently emphasized the role of exotic items, especially copper bells and macaws from Mesoamerica, in stimulating sociopolitical developments in the Southwest. Lekson's interest is in relationships between Chaco and Paquimé, so he is not explicit in how these rare goods were used in the region, except to note that they contributed to a "political-prestige economy" (Lekson 1999:54–55). The proposal for a prestige-goods economy based on Mesoamerican items seems inconsistent with the fact that virtually all these items have been found in Chaco Canyon but not elsewhere. As with utilitarian goods, Chaco was a consumer, not a distributor. In contrast, other items often classified as valuables, such as shell and turquoise, were seemingly too common in the Chaco world to have fueled a prestige-goods economy centered in Chaco Canyon. Recent excavations in the Red Mesa Valley—an area closer than Chaco Canyon to all possible sources of valuables and exotics—have identified evidence of limited shell and turquoise ornament manufacture at a variety of households. For example, researchers recovered turquoise chips, shell debris, and completed ornaments of these materials from all five habitation sites recently tested in the Blue J community. This suggests that outlying Great House communities did not rely on the central canyon for obtaining or producing their valuables.

### Communication Systems

One final source of information can give us insight into the intensity of interaction across the Chaco world. In Chaco Canyon, researchers have identified unusual features such as stone circles containing few artifacts as components of a canyonwide communication system (Hayes and Windes 1975; Windes et al. 2000). Experiments using flares and fires suggest that people intentionally positioned these features to ensure intervisibility, although no one has methodically evaluated this proposition. Anecdotal accounts further suggest that people could have relayed signals beyond the canyon's borders (Lekson, chapter 1 of this volume). Architectural features identified as part of this alleged communication system include tower kivas, which are defined as elevated kivas that project one or more stories above the rest of a Great House structure. People may have used these kivas'

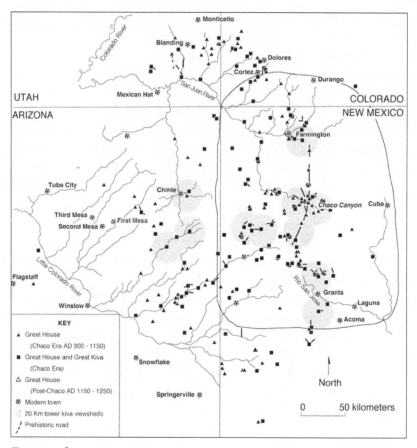

**FIGURE 5.6**

*The Chaco World database identifies twelve Great Houses with tower kivas. On average, they are approximately 40 km from one another, with surprisingly little overlap between their catchments.*

elevated positions, combined with still undiscovered "repeater" stations, to relay signals from community to community (Wilcox 1999:133–136).

The Chaco World database includes data on tower kivas, revealing that the twelve tower kivas are spaced, on average, approximately 40 km from one another, with surprisingly little overlap except near Chaco Canyon itself (figure 5.6). This pattern is indeed suggestive of their use as signaling stations, and the distances fall within the range of ethnographically documented signaling techniques (for example, Swanson

2003). This observation, however, does not take into account whether the Chaco world towers are actually intervisible.

To address the question of tower kiva intervisibility more methodically, researchers conducted a recent GIS-enhanced study to determine whether two of the tower kivas could have signaled each other using intermediate relay points (Kantner and Hobgood 2003). A computerized model of the now collapsed tower kivas at Kin Ya'a and Haystack and the surrounding landscape (figure 5.7) convinced researchers that, even if intermediate relaying stations existed, the tower kivas were not likely meant to communicate with each other. The computer analysis did identify potential relay points between the tower kivas, but no archaeological features can be found at these locations. Perhaps more important, these points already were visible from the ground—in other words, the towers were superfluous, for they did not achieve long-distance visibility. According to the analysis, though, their extra height did greatly improve visibility of the immediate community area (Kantner and Hobgood 2003). This is consistent with other sources of data discussed so far that indicate the local emphasis of Chacoan architectural complexes in outlying Great House communities. This study also parallels a recent analysis of post-Chaco towers in the Mesa Verde region, which found that people built these structures to oversee and lay claim to local farmlands (Johnson 2003).

The weight of the evidence on Chaco world interaction indicates that, with the exception of material flowing into Chaco Canyon from outlying areas, most economic interaction was local. In some outlying Great House communities, virtually no identifiable material came from more than a couple dozen kilometers away (for example, Kantner et al. 2000). In other parts of the Chaco world, economic interaction may have been more far-reaching but was still limited to exchange with neighboring regions (for example, Gilpin and Purcell 2000). Certainly, unlike Chaco Canyon, no outlying community received commodities from distant parts of the Chaco world. Roads and tower kivas suggest other forms of interaction, but they, too, appear to have their greatest relevance to local populations, rather than at a regional level. Only Chaco Canyon itself exhibits such a tremendous reach across the northern Southwest, and, apparently, what went into Chaco Canyon very rarely came back out.

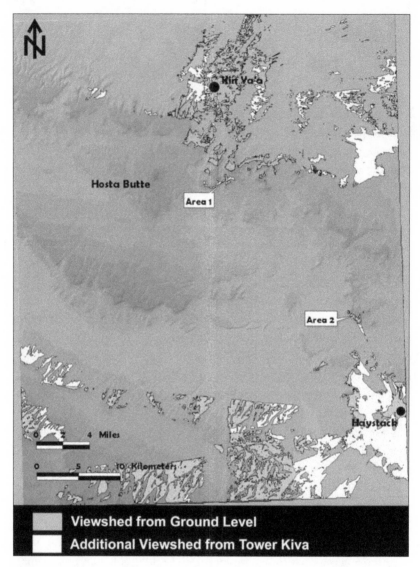

**FIGURE 5.7**

*The elevated positions of tower kivas in Kin Ya'a and Haystack did not facilitate intervisibility between the two communities. Although researchers identified areas on Lobo Mesa where the two viewsheds (labeled Area 1 and Area 2) overlapped, they could not identify "relay stations" at these points. In any case, those same areas were visible from the ground. The tower kivas were probably not part of a regional communication system, but their height did enhance the viewshed of the local area.*

## INTERDEPENDENCE IN THE CHACO WORLD

The issue of interdependence hearkens back to the redistribution models of the 1970s and 1980s (for example, Judge 1979; Schelberg 1984). These models, which generally propose that the regional relationships centered on Chaco Canyon were established to share highly variable food surpluses, continue to receive attention today. Lekson (1999:36–37), for example, proposes that redistribution still explains the developments within the San Juan Basin, especially during the initial stages. The classic model of redistribution is that materials flow into a center, where they are stored, and then are taken back out to the periphery as needed. Materials found in Great House communities along the edge of the basin, however, are not distributed in a way suggesting that redistribution took place (see also Durand 2003). As mentioned earlier, virtually all pottery and lithics found in each peripheral community were local products. Although Chacoan communities no doubt interacted with their immediate neighbors (for example, Kantner et al. 2000; Till 2001), they do not seem to have participated in a regional economy drawing upon Chaco Canyon (for example, Duff and Lekson, chapter 9 of this volume). And why should they? Chaco Canyon had no material resources needed by the outlying communities, almost all of which were situated in comparatively resource-rich areas.

One alternative proposed is that Chaco Canyon served as a regional exchange facilitator, with people from outlying areas bringing their food and perhaps other crafts for exchange in places such as Pueblo Alto's plaza (Stoltman 1999; Windes 1987a, 1987b). Such exchange, however, must have been delayed reciprocal or generalized exchange, for, as discussed earlier, there is no evidence of material moving among disparate outlying areas of the San Juan Basin. If one group was bringing in surplus maize, for example, it apparently got nothing in return except the hope that someday its generosity would be reciprocated. Presumably, those in need of food brought their own empty pots or baskets with them for transporting materials back out; there is no evidence for the movement of pottery from area to area within the Chaco world.

In general, all scenarios of redistribution seem to rely on highly improbable sociopolitical relationships, with no apparent parallel in the ethnographic literature. Why would a community such as Dalton Pass, situated near a number of springs and a major wash that drains Lobo Mesa, want to participate in a redistributive system whose members presumably included Greenlee and Grey Hill Springs, which were located in much more marginal environments? What economic advantages would Dalton Pass have received?

If Great House communities were not economically interdependent, could they have been demographically interdependent? Is it possible that Chaco Canyon emerged as a center where distant communities could establish social ties? As noted earlier, Mahoney (2000) proposes that most Great House communities, as they are traditionally defined, were not demographically sustainable, because their populations were too small for maintaining sufficient mating networks. Perhaps Chaco Canyon provided opportunities for forming long-distance demographic networks, a proposal supported by Schillaci's craniometric analyses (2003) tentatively indicating that *burial*—not necessarily residential—populations in Chaco Canyon were genetically diverse. Kantner (2003b), however, argues that it is improbable that communities exhibiting Chacoan characteristics intentionally interacted with one another and with Chaco Canyon to expand social and mating networks, especially because the consequences of inadequate mating networks, arguably, could not have been readily recognizable to people over the few generations represented by Chaco's rise and fall. Kintigh (2003), on the other hand, proposes that people living in small communities would have sought larger mating pools when they recognized that no one living around them was eligible for marriage. In either case, any demographic interdependence that may have developed in the region seems unlikely to be causally related to what the Chaco entity was and why it developed.

The archaeological record makes claims of economic or demographic interdependence difficult to support, suggesting that simple materialist explanations for the Chaco world's existence are inadequate. The appearance of Chacoan architectural features in so many areas, however, perhaps even among varying ethnic and linguistic groups (Toll, chapter 4 of this volume), shows how compelling Chaco Canyon and its materialized belief system were to people across the Puebloan landscape. At the community level, this implies a *two-way* dependence between outlying areas and the central canyon, instead of a regional, multiway interdependence among all Great House communities. Chaco saw outlying areas as a source of needed material, and inhabitants of these areas saw Chaco as the center of a powerful belief system.

Still unknown are the sociopolitical dynamics that made Chaco's ideological power important in local settings throughout the Chaco world. One possibility is that a kind of political interdependence developed between leading members of outlying communities and the leadership of Chaco Canyon, with the latter providing the materialized legitimacy for the former and the former mobilizing local populations to build, maintain, and supply the canyon's infrastructure. Such a scenario is compelling, but a thorough evaluation awaits more focused investigations of outlying Great House communities.

## UNITY IN THE CHACO WORLD

The discussions above suggest that the Chaco world was not well integrated; the communities exhibiting Chacoan characteristics do not appear to have formed a single, consolidated, socioeconomic unit, a conclusion also reached by other scholars (for example, Fish 1999:49–50; Wilcox 1993, 1999; the contributors to the *Kiva* volume [69(2)]; but see Lekson, chapter 1 of this volume). Some communities were firmly connected to Chaco Canyon via roadways. More distant communities vaguely emulated a few of the patterns seen within the San Juan Basin (see contributions in Kantner and Mahoney 2000; Durand 2003; Van Dyke 1999c, 2003a). Overall, the impression is decidedly not of a unified whole, but rather of a disconnected heterogeneity. It is still possible, however, that a significant level of cultural identity was shared throughout the Chaco world, an identity transcending the more fleeting social, political, and economic relationships that, no doubt, also characterized interactions among Great House communities.

### Great House Architectural Unity

When discussing the "wholeness" of Chacoan cultural patterning, scholars emphasize shared stylistic conventions such as the Chacoan architectural complex and the Dogoszhi-style ceramic decoration that appeared during the Chaco era. Debate on the former is perhaps the most problematic, for two scholars can look at the same architectural features and come to separate conclusions regarding the implications for the unity of Chacoan style. For example, Lekson (chapter 1 of this volume) argues that Great Houses everywhere are so similar that they must have been part of a regionwide polity. The majority of "outlier" scholars, however, emphasize diversity instead of similarity in funda-mental aspects of Great House architecture (for example, Duff and Lekson, chapter 9 of this volume; Durand 2003; Gilpin 2003; Hurst 2000; Kantner 1996; Van Dyke 2000).

Through most of the Chaco era, the most impressive Great Houses were located closer to Chaco Canyon than were the more diminutive structures whose identities as Great Houses are questionable (see fig-ure 5.2). Those situated on the edges of the San Juan Basin are particu-larly striking models of Chacoan architecture. A bit more than 40 km to the southwest of Chaco Canyon, for example, is Kin Ya'a. This large structure once included more than forty rooms built of massive core-veneer masonry walls rising three stories; one of the four original kivas built into the structure is a tower kiva that still stands nearly four stories tall (see figure 5.6). In contrast, 125 km to the northwest of Chaco Canyon, well beyond the boundaries of the San Juan Basin, is the Cove Great House. This small, single-story structure of eighteen rooms was built using a more modest style of compound masonry.

Van Dyke (2003a) recently used the Chaco World database to inves-tigate patterning in Chacoan architectural complexes more closely. Her results statistically confirm the variability apparent across the Chaco world. For example, distance from Chaco Canyon substantially affected the suite of features characterizing Chacoan architectural complexes. Great Houses in the San Juan Basin consistently exhibit core-veneer masonry and contain plaza areas enclosed on at least three sides by walls, mirroring the architecture of Chaco Canyon. Unlike the canyon, however, Great Houses in the San Juan Basin generally are not associated with Great Kivas, roadways, or earthworks. These contrasting patterns suggest that ties between the central canyon and its nearest neighbors were comparatively strong but also that Chaco's Great House complexes largely supplanted outlying Great Kivas, the tradi-tional ceremonial centers of Puebloan communities. Van Dyke found, however, that when you move beyond the boundaries of the San Juan Basin, Great Kivas become more prominent, as do earthworks and roadways, as if these communities and their Chacoan architectural complexes were independent of Chaco Canyon. The overall pattern suggests that, despite a superficial stylistic unity across the Chaco world, different regions maintained their own substyles, which varied through time and space according to the social, political, and economic fortunes of individual Great House communities (see also Herr 2001).

### Great House Functional Unity

Despite Great House architectural variability, Durand (2003) does identify a patterning in the material culture recovered from these structures that appears to be shared across the Chaco world. Her discussion indicates that items of likely ritual use—rare painted wooden artifacts, turquoise ornaments, the remains of unusual birds—are found in all excavated Great Houses, indicating that they universally served ceremonial functions, even if other activities also were associated with them (for example, Lipe, chapter 8 of this volume). Furthermore, she found that these ritual items exist more often in Great Houses than in the domestic structures surrounding them. Durand also discovered that, as with all material goods, the quantities of such items recovered from the handful of excavated outlying Great Houses pale next to the magnificent contents of Chaco Canyon's Great Houses.

Durand's research on avifauna (Durand 2003; Roler 1999) particularly illustrates this pattern. According to the Puebloan ethnographic record, birds of a wide variety of species were ritually important, with the Zuni alone reportedly using more than fifty species in ceremonial contexts. Durand therefore examined the number of bird taxa recovered from various Chaco-era sites, including Chaco Canyon Great Houses, Chaco Canyon "small house" residences, and the equivalent contexts in the Guadalupe Great House community located approximately 90 km southeast of the central canyon. Durand's statistical procedures found that bird remains are more diverse in canyon Great Houses than anywhere else. Interestingly, the small houses of Chaco Canyon have avifauna diversity similar to that of the Guadalupe Great House, but the latter, in turn, exhibits greater diversity than the domestic sites in the Guadalupe community.

Although more data from excavated Great Houses are needed, Durand reasonably interprets the artifactual and avifaunal record as evidence for the primarily ritual function of all Great Houses found in the Chaco world. She does note that those in Chaco Canyon—especially Pueblo Bonito—contain a substantially greater quantity of ritual artifacts than discovered anywhere else in the northern Southwest but that the frequencies of these items differ greatly in outlying communities. This suggests that Great Houses were part of a shared cultural pattern centered on Chaco Canyon, but the degree of unity represented by this pattern is questionable because of its highly variable expression.

### Ceramic Stylistic Unity

The Dogoszhi ceramic style is characterized by hachure-filled motifs, and its appearance in the A.D. 1030s and 1040s correlates with the ascendancy of Chaco Canyon—in fact, the finest examples are called "*Chaco* Black-on-white." A tendency for this style to appear in Chacoan architectural complexes in greater quantities than other contemporaneous styles further suggests an association with Chaco. Plog (2003) argues that the hachure design symbolically represents the color blue-green, to emulate the colors of turquoise, contrasting with the solid black design of other pottery styles, which, he proposes, symbolizes jet. Plog concludes that either Dogozhi served as an emblematic style representing direct participation in a Chacoan socioeconomic system or it was the by-product of a shared worldview and/or ceremonial tradition. Considering the lack of evidence for the former interpretation, the latter seems more likely to be true.

Studies of Dogoszhi ceramics can provide some insight into how the style related to the development of the Chaco world. From a microstylistic perspective, Dogoszhi is so standardized, compared with its predecessors and contemporaries, such as Red Mesa and Sosi Black-on-white styles, that it seems to reflect symbolic unity among Chacoan communities (for example, Neitzel 1995). Even in this case, however, sufficient variability exists in the Dogoszhi style to allow for the symboling of community-based identity. For example, a microstylistic study of ceramics in the Lobo Mesa area examined 2,275 sherds from five Great House communities; the analysis considered both Red Mesa and Gallup (the local version of Dogoszhi) Black-on-white styles. The results revealed that the earlier Red Mesa style was much more variable than the later Gallup hachure designs, an unsurprising result, considering how many motifs and attributes are possible for Red Mesa. The Gallup sherds are much less variable, as expected, but statistically significant differences in hachure spacing, line width, and framing-line thickness clearly distinguish some neighboring Great House communities from one another. Apparently, although the Dogoszhi style is more standardized and the hachure style makes it more difficult to create highly visible variability, people across the Chaco world produced different hachure designs. This is more consistent with the proposal that the style represented a shared worldview instead of explicit membership in a Chaco-centered socioeconomic system (Kantner 1999a).

Still unknown is whether distinctive "Chacoan" patterns and styles, such as Great House forms and Dogoszhi designs, emanated from Chaco Canyon. Although antecedent versions of Great House architecture may be found in the northern San Juan region (for example, Lipe, chapter 8, and Wilshusen and Van Dyke, chapter 7, of this volume), the classic Chacoan Great House tradition appears to have originated in the canyon (Windes and Ford 1996). The Chaco World database confirms this by showing that the earliest Chaco-era Great Houses outside Chaco Canyon were located close to the canyon (figure 5.8; Gilpin 2003; Windes n.d.; Lekson, Windes, and McKenna, chapter 3, and Wilshusen and Van Dyke, chapter 7, of this volume). Roadways are so difficult to date that documenting their origin is not yet possible, but their greater formality and size in areas within and near Chaco Canyon suggest their origin there as well (Vivian 1997a; Windes 1991). The origin of Dogoszhi-style hachure and the sequence of its spread are also unclear, even though its appearance in Chacoan contexts is abrupt (Plog 2003; Windes 1984b).

The most relevant issue here, however, is whether the stylistic similarities across a wide area indicate a high degree of sociopolitical unity. Most Chaco World conference participants agreed that they do not, concurring with scholars (for example, Toll and McKenna 1997:211–214) who emphasize that these patterns reflect no more than a low but important degree of shared cultural identity that different communities exhibited to varying degrees. This is similar in many ways to other religious traditions with powerful spiritual centers that experienced

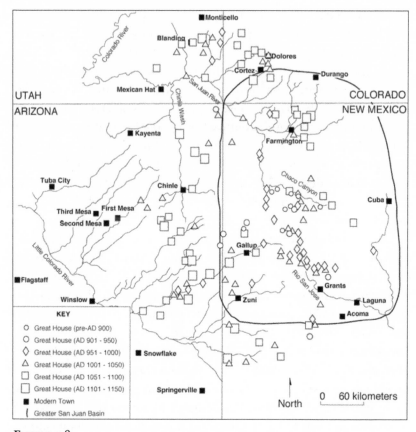

**FIGURE 5.8**

*Estimated construction dates for the Great House architecture in the Chaco World database. The figure includes only those Great Houses for which dates are available.*

a degradation in symbolic fidelity and sociopolitical allegiance as distance from the center increased and as time passed. Research in this area, however, is still too incomplete for drawing confident conclusions regarding the degree and kind of unity across the Chaco world.

## THE CHACO TIMELINE

Comparing developments inside Chaco Canyon with those elsewhere in the Chaco world is a difficult task, for research on outlying Great House communities is still in its infancy. A handful of Chacoan architectural complexes outside Chaco Canyon have been well investigated; a great many others are barely known at all. Reconstructing temporal trends across the entire region is especially challenging because dating unexcavated structures is more an art than a science. Most complexes are dated only very generally, which tends to lengthen occupation spans for the outlying Great Houses. Starting dates for many structures are probably too early, and, as Duff and Lekson (chapter 9 of this volume) discuss, this means that a few architectural complexes built after Chaco's demise are included in samples of Chaco-era Great Houses. On the other hand, later reuse of Great Houses during the late A.D. 1100s often obscures earlier dates. Despite these potential problems, in this section we attempt to compare spatiotemporal trends from the Chaco World database with events identified in the Chaco Timeline.

The origin of the Chacoan architectural style is difficult to determine, given how little archaeological investigation has been conducted on the topic (Windes n.d.; Wilshusen and Van Dyke, chapter 7, and Lekson, Windes, and McKenna, chapter 3, of this volume). A few patterns have been identified as potentially important. The evidence, tentative as it is, suggests that the first extracanyon public structures within the San Juan Basin appeared at places like Willow Canyon and Padilla Well in the late A.D. 700s, well before true "Chacoan" features emerged in the canyon itself. These are aboveground, open, public spaces with minimal architecture. They little resemble later Chacoan architectural complexes, so some scholars have looked elsewhere for sources of Great House architecture. Wilshusen and Van Dyke (chapter 7 of this volume; see also Lipe, chapter 8 of this volume) note that a precedent for U-shaped roomblocks with public architectural components is found north of the San Juan River during Pueblo I. For example, McPhee Pueblo exhibits masonry similar to the "Type 1" style of early Chaco Canyon Great Houses, and researchers identified an oversized pit structure in the U-shaped structure's plaza area (see also Wilshusen and Ortman 1999). Noting that this region was largely abandoned by the A.D. 900s, Wilshusen and Van Dyke (chapter 7 of this volume) suggest that immigrants to Chaco Canyon introduced a proto–Great House design that was elaborated in subsequent decades.

No matter what their genesis, by the late A.D. 800s distinctive Chacoan architectural traits emerged in and immediately around

Chaco Canyon in places such as Pueblo Bonito, Peñasco Blanco, Una Vida, Kin Nahasbas, Casa del Rio, and the East Community. At least in some cases, these complexes supplanted earlier public structures. At Padilla Well, core-veneer masonry and an enclosed plaza were eventually added to the Pueblo I complex, but when is unknown. The same process occurred at Casa del Rio, where an early Chaco-style Great House was built over a large U-shaped structure dating back to Pueblo I (Windes 2001a:42).

According to the Chaco World database, people in areas immediately surrounding Chaco Canyon elaborated Chacoan features sooner than in other regions. The features then appear to have spread to the southern San Juan Basin in the late A.D. 920s to the 940s (see figure 5.8). As Vivian has suggested (1990; see Wilshusen and Van Dyke, chapter 7 of this volume), the southern area probably had historical and social ties to Chaco Canyon, providing opportunities to share Chacoan patterns. Interestingly, although Chacoan influence extended towards the south during a brief downturn in climatic conditions, the appearance of these earliest outlying Great Houses is not correlated with a shift from low to high spatial variability in rainfall, which occurs a decade *later*. This is inconsistent with views that see the development of the Chaco world as an adaptive response to spatial climatic instability (for example, Dean 1992).

By the end of the early A.D. 900s, Chacoan features apparently spread quickly according to geography: through the Rio Puerco and Rio San Jose drainages in the late A.D. 940s, up the Chuska slope by the turn of the eleventh century and perhaps earlier, and into the San Juan River area mostly in the mid-1000s and later (Lipe, chapter 8 of this volume). Areas along the inner edge of the San Juan Basin exhibit Chacoan patterns first (figure 5.9); communities well outside the basin tended to build Great Houses much later and with less accurate replication of Chacoan features (see figures 5.2 and 5.8; see also Gilpin 2003; Van Dyke 2003a). In all areas, big bursts of Great House construction in outlying communities occurred in the latter half of the eleventh century. By the turn of the twelfth century, the greatest number were in active use. The Chaco Timeline shows that this expansion transpired during a period of relatively high rainfall, followed by a few decades of less favorable conditions.

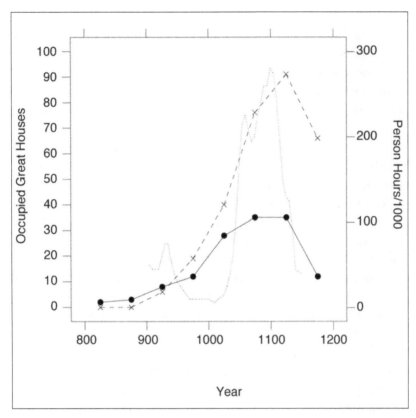

**FIGURE 5.9**

*The number of occupied Great Houses within (solid line) and outside (dashed line) the San Juan Basin. The dotted line shows Lekson's Chaco Canyon Great House construction labor estimates (1984a:263, values estimated from figure 5.2), read against the scale on the right.*

The frequency of goods imported into Chaco Canyon shows some rough correlations with the appearance of Great Houses in specific outlying areas. According to the Chaco Timeline, ornaments of nonlocal materials, especially shell and turquoise, seemed to increase in the same decades that Great Houses were built in areas south of Chaco Canyon. Whether this was accompanied by the import of basic commodities such as pottery from these areas is unclear, particularly because researchers cannot easily distinguish southern pottery from vessels produced elsewhere. Narbona Pass chert was imported in small quantities at about the same time that Great Houses appeared on the

Chuska slope; in the following decades, both the number of Great Houses in this area and the frequency of the chert in Chaco Canyon increased. Interestingly, the import of Chuskan pottery did not reach a height until much later, in the early A.D. 1100s, when people were just beginning to abandon many outlying Great Houses. Studies of the movement of materials into Chaco Canyon (for example, Kantner et al. 2000) suggest that Great House communities beyond the San Juan Basin were not as closely tied to the central canyon, a point confirmed by other Chaco World conference contributors and the Chaco Timeline (and see Duff and Lekson, chapter 9 of this volume).

The Chaco Timeline reveals that labor expenditures in canyon construction roughly correlate with the appearance and use of Great Houses in outlying communities (see figure 5.9). For example, the first Great Houses in the southern San Juan Basin and in the Red Mesa Valley appeared during the first peak in construction in Chaco Canyon in the A.D. 900s. The height of Great House use in these areas further correlates with the A.D. 1050s labor expenditures in the canyon—this is also when Chacoan features are most frequently seen in new Great Houses built in all outlying areas (and it correlates with the transition from Red Mesa to Dogoszhi ceramic styles). The final frenzy of canyon construction at the turn of the twelfth century occurred when the greatest number of outlying Great Houses across the Chaco world was in use.

Great House abandonment began as early as the tenth century (figure 5.10). As in all discussions of outlying Great Houses, however, the lack of fine temporal control makes these conclusions tentative, particularly because people reoccupied many Great Houses at the turn of the thirteenth century. Nevertheless, the frequency of abandonment was clearly greatest in the first half of the twelfth century, perhaps as a result of the sustained dry conditions at the turn of the A.D. 1100s. Brief as this drought was, it was worse than earlier ones and hit during the time that Chaco Canyon required the most resources and labor from the Chaco world—when Chacoans were constructing the North Road, investing the greatest amount of labor in Great House architecture, and bringing the largest quantities of pottery into the canyon. The regional sequence of Great House abandonments occurred roughly in the reverse order of Great House construction, with use of most southern

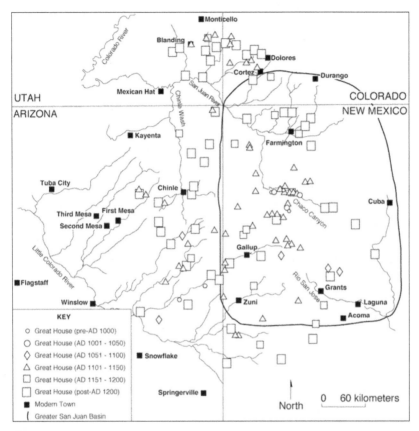

**FIGURE 5.10**

*Estimated abandonment dates for the Great House architecture in the Chaco World database. This figure includes only those Great Houses for which dates are available.*

Great Houses ending early in the twelfth century and use of northern Great Houses persevering longer. Great Houses most distant from Chaco Canyon remained in use for longer, such as in the Cibola region to the south, Puebloan areas west of the Chuska Mountains, and the region around the middle San Juan River.

Ultimately, Chaco's influence continued into the post-Chaco era, the decades after Chaco Canyon was mostly abandoned. Herr (2001) suggests that areas as distant as the Silver Creek–Mogollon Rim region received disenfranchised immigrants from the Chaco world, who then re-created modified elements of Chacoan architectural complexes, especially large, open Great Kivas. Similar trends occurred in the Cibola region, where elaborate ceremonial complexes with modified Chacoan features were built (for example, Kintigh 1996; Kintigh, Howell, and Duff 1996). In the San Juan River area, perhaps six Great Houses and a sizeable community persisted at Aztec well into the late A.D. 1100s (see Toll, chapter 4 of this volume). This center's influence appears to have waned as Chacoan architectural complexes faded in importance (for example, Lipe, chapter 8 of this volume; but see Lekson 1999). As Toll (chapter 4 of this volume) describes, the quantities of imported commodities and exotic items at Aztec were miniscule compared with the flow of goods into Chaco Canyon at its height in the eleventh century. By the middle of the twelfth century, the Great House and Great Kiva forms persevered, but their use and meaning were purely local. The Chaco world, such as it was, no longer existed.

## CONCLUSION

The patterns in imports and labor in Chaco Canyon revealed in the Chaco Timeline are consistent with views that see the canyon as becoming increasingly powerful as a religious center (for example, Judge 1989, 1993; Malville and Malville 2001). It seems unlikely, though, that Chaco ever became strongly hegemonic in the sense that it was able to control activity in the distant Great House communities. Instead, the canyon seems to have been occasionally visited by members of some outlying communities bearing gifts or offering services such as labor. Of course, outlying Great House communities must have engaged with Chaco Canyon in ways that also helped them. Participating communities might have reaped the benefits of occasional large-scale social occasions, extended social networks, and perhaps even enhanced observations of seasonal changes or farming schedules (Malville 1994; Sofaer and Sinclair 1987).

Judging by the patterns discussed above, the extent of these mutual relationships and shared ideology was apparently strongest between Chaco Canyon and communities within the San Juan Basin proper, especially those to the south and west. Durand's (2003) discussion of competitive emulation and symbolic entrainment is consistent with this view of different areas in the Chaco world linking to Chaco Canyon in various ways to achieve a number of ends, both for canyon leaders and their counterparts in outlying communities.

The assessments offered in this contribution are, of course, preliminary and are not completely elaborated here. The primary conclusion is that the communities exhibiting Chacoan features outside Chaco Canyon were interacting with the canyon in multiple ways. One could propose that at least those communities within the San Juan Basin and surrounding highlands were somewhat regularly interacting with one another and with Chaco Canyon, thereby forming an interdependent socioeconomic entity. Although the literature on Chaco Canyon always emphasizes the movement of basic commodities such as pottery and timber, this flow of goods does not correlate well with activities in outlying areas. Substantial quantities of Chuskan pottery were not imported into Chaco Canyon, for example, until well after the establishment of Great Houses on the Chuska slope. Instead, the trend in the construction of outlying Great Houses is that their appearance most closely correlates with the movement of prestige goods, perhaps including valuable cherts such as Narbona Pass. Bursts of interaction seem to appear consistently during periods of relatively good rainfall that follow several years of unstable conditions.

All these patterns are more consistent with models that see the Chaco "phenomenon" as emerging not so much to contend with the marginal environment but rather as part of a more socially and politically dynamic era. A working model might consider how aspiring leaders in the canyon and in the outlying communities depended on each other for continued legitimization of their local activities. The sustainability of the outlying communities themselves, arguably, was not dependent on Chaco world interactions—on the other hand, the sustainability of Chaco Canyon as a prominent religious center likely was.

### Notes

We would like to thank the participants in the 1999 Chaco World conference and the contributors to the Chaco World database: David Anderson, Roger Anyon, David Doyel, Kathy Roler Durand, Dennis Gilpin, Sarah Herr, Winston Hurst, Jim Kendrick, Nancy Mahoney, Joan Mathien, Tim Pauketat, Bob Powers, Sara Schlanger, Tom Windes, Ruth Van Dyke, and, of course, Steve Lekson. We would especially like to thank our fellow contributors to the 2003 issue of the journal *Kiva* (69[2]), from which much of this chapter was derived: Kathy Roler Durand, Dennis Gilpin, and Ruth Van Dyke. Thanks also to the National Center for Preservation Training and Technology, which provided funding to build the Chaco World database. Finally, we are most grateful for the valuable comments from the two reviewers of this chapter and the effective guidance of Steve Lekson. Of course, we take full responsibility for any errors of fact, unintended omissions, or flaws in the chapter's arguments.

1. From September 25 to 27, 1999, a dozen archaeologists met at Arizona State University for the Chaco World conference, one of the topic seminars in the NPS Chaco Synthesis series. Organized by Keith Kintigh, Nancy Mahoney, and John Kantner, the conference brought together many of the archaeologists currently investigating Chacoan Great House communities located outside Chaco Canyon. The event was moderated by Keith Kintigh, and two scholars from outside the Southwest, Tim Pauketat and David Anderson, served as discussants. Many of the participants had participated in a symposium at the 1998 Society for American Archaeology Annual Meeting, the proceedings of which were published as Kantner and Mahoney (2000).

A subset of the participants in the Chaco World conference reworked the original position papers and updated them, using the expanded Chaco World database (see note 2). These new papers recently appeared in a special issue of the journal *Kiva* (69[2]), in which Ruth Van Dyke (2003a) discusses Great House architecture, Kathy Roler Durand (2003) addresses the function of Great Houses, Dennis Gilpin (2003) considers the Great House communities, John Kantner (2003a) brings these together to discuss the nature of a Chaco "system," and Keith Kintigh (2003) assesses the state of knowledge on the Chaco world.

2. Before the Chaco World conference, many of the participants contributed to a database representing the state of knowledge on outlying Great Houses and the communities in which they are found. Each scholar was assigned a relevant geographical region, and each alleged Great House in the region was assessed using a standardized set of variables. Many participants also provided detailed annotated information for each Great House community. The resulting data were assembled in a preliminary database that was available to participants preparing position papers for the Chaco World conference. Since then, the database has evolved into an online spatial database. In 2001 John Kantner received a grant from the National Center for Preservation Training and Technology (NCPTT) to finish data entry and improve the online interface for the database. The working version is available at http://sipapu.gsu.edu/chacoworld.html.

# 6

## Society and Polity

### W. James Judge and Linda S. Cordell

We examine Chaco society and polity as inferred primarily from the archaeology of Chaco Canyon.[1] We focus spatially on the "Chaco Core," that is, Chaco Canyon and its immediate environs (refer to figure 1.2 and plate 4), and on the canyon area from Peñasco Blanco on the west to Shabik'eschee on the east, which we refer to as *central Chaco* or simply, *the canyon*.

We view *society* and *polity*, respectively, as referring to the ways in which the people of Chaco organized and governed themselves. Because our points of reference are tangible archaeological features, such as architecture, roadways, water control features, and artifacts, our discussion is more conjectural than some others in this volume. Abundant anthropological theory is devoted to the development of society and polity in human culture. Far less middle-range theory links concrete archaeological remains to forms of organization, leadership, and control. A substantial recent literature explores the nature of Chaco society and polity from the perspective of general anthropological models of sociopolitical development (Mills 2002; Sebastian 1992a; Wills 2000) and writing that is informed by knowledge of other ancient societies far removed from Chaco Canyon (Earle 2001; Peregrine 2001; Renfrew 2001; Yoffee 2001, 2005).

Although all of these are useful and will reward time spent pursuing them, we draw much of our interpretive inspiration from ethnographic discussions of modern Pueblo organization. In this, we gratefully acknowledge the leadership of R. Gwinn Vivian (1990; Vivian et al., chapter 2 of this volume) and John Ware (2001). In what follows, we make inferences from discussions of modern Pueblo society and polity. We also use modern Pueblo society as a benchmark to indicate how the organization of Chacoan society differs from that of its descendant peoples. Finally, we do not categorize Chaco society and polity as a particular type, kind, or category of organization (that is, tribe, chiefdom, corporate/network, or rituality). We are concerned that these labels may obscure unique aspects of the society we want to understand.

To begin, we discuss the unique features of Chaco Canyon's local environment because we suspect that ancient Chacoan use of that environment encouraged development of organizational features that set Chaco society and polity on a path different from other Ancestral Pueblo populations. Following this is a coarse-grained chronology of events in Chaco. Contributors to this volume were asked to trace the trajectories of their topics (in our case, society and polity) over time so that timelines in the volume can be compared. We acknowledge that Chaco society and polity changed over the hundreds of years of Ancestral Pueblo occupation of the canyon. It is not possible for us to do more than broadly sketch some of what we think are important organizational characteristics over that time. We use episodes of building and apparent population growth as indices of features and strategies of social organization. By suggesting some Chacoan legacies in more recent Pueblo history, we follow our broad chronology of major developments in Chaco society and polity. To conclude, we comment on Chaco's uniqueness for its time and its role as a source for core features of historic and modern Pueblo society.[2]

## THE ENVIRONMENTAL PARAMETERS

The San Juan Basin is not and was not a generous environment for agriculture. As Vivian and others (chapter 2 of this volume) point out, successful farming in the San Juan Basin requires water and suitable soils, and no permanent watercourses existed in the basin interior.

Locations on the southern and western basin margins and on the slopes of the Chuska and Lukachukai mountains offered better hydrological conditions (refer to plate 1). Farmers colonized these areas before establishing settlements in Chaco Canyon. Within the central San Juan Basin, however, Chaco Canyon is hydrologically unique in collecting water from the specific configuration of drainages flowing into it, for the paths of summer storms moving through it, and for being close to the springs and higher elevation resources of bordering Chacra Mesa, which provided wild plant food, game, and wood (Vivian et al., chapter 2 of this volume).

In addition to the canyon's access to diverse sources of moisture, land in the canyon bottom has a southern exposure, which extends the growing season. There is more agricultural land on the south than on the north side of the canyon, and fields on the south side can be watered through a series of check-dams and terraces that do not require a large or well-organized labor force to build or maintain. On the canyon's north side, *rincons* are precipitous and drain large areas of slickrock. Chacoans' elaborately engineered water-control systems tapped runoff from summer storms pouring off the slickrock, slowed it through the rincons, and diverted it to fields. We agree with Vivian (1970, 1974, 1990) that an organized labor force was needed in order to construct and maintain the north-side slickrock water diversion systems. We also think that the leadership organization reflected in the north-side slick rock runoff water-control systems—leadership with the ability to marshal, direct, and support a substantial labor force—established an organizational pattern that was used in the construction of the Great Houses in Chaco Canyon and in the coordination of people and goods being transported into the canyon, episodically, from substantial distances (Vivian et al. chapter 2 of this volume; Wills and Windes 1989:365).

Because of the San Juan Basin's marginal agricultural potential today, much research has examined paleoenvironments in Chaco Canyon to understand how these settings could have supported the growth and development of the Chaco system (see Vivian et al., chapter 2 of this volume; Lagasse, Gillespie, and Eggert 1984; Loose and Lyons 1976; Vivian 1970, 1974; 1990, 1992). In addition to chapter 2 of this volume, we have found discussions by Jeffrey Dean (1992), Lynne Sebastian (1992a), Vivian (1990), and Thomas Windes (1993) especially useful and the study by Force and others (2002) intriguing. According to that study, channel cutting took place in Chaco in the A.D. 900s, and channel filling from A.D. 1025 to 1090, coincident with the period of the most intensive architectural construction in Chaco. The authors note that "Anasazi activity seems to have been tuned to changes in the Bonito channel with regard to construction of Pueblos and roads, and most notably of water control features" (Force et al. 2002:37). For a more detailed review of their argument, see chapter 2 of this volume. For the purposes of this chapter, it is noteworthy that the research by Force and others supports Sebastian's (1992a) findings that link Great House construction with times that were good for agriculture, when precipitation was relatively abundant and the Bonito channel was aggrading.

## A CHRONOLOGICAL OVERVIEW OF THE CHACOAN SYSTEM

In the fifth and sixth centuries, Basketmaker III settlements were dispersed from the Red Mesa Valley in the south to the Great Sage Plain in the north. In the canyon, two large Basketmaker III settlements— Shabik'eschee in the east and 29SJ423 in the west near Peñasco Blanco—were located on benches of Chacra Mesa (Windes 2001a, chapter 3 of this volume). Although these sites cover sizeable areas and each has more than seventy pit structures, they represent periodic seasonal aggregations (Wills and Windes 1989), rather than large, long-term population centers. The size of these sites, we suggest, indicates that from Basketmaker III times Chaco Canyon was a place of seasonal resource abundance in the central basin that periodically could support large numbers of people on a temporary basis. As suggested by Vivian (1990:436–437, following Eggan, Chang, and Fox), egalitarian lineage segments may have composed these Basketmaker III settlements. We do not know the specific origins of the late Basketmaker III groups that episodically congregated in the canyon, nor do we know whether they were linguistically or culturally homogeneous.

Elsewhere, we (Cordell and Judge 2001:figure 1) suggest that a specific motif of dancing figures—found on Basketmaker III bowls from sites extending from north of the San Juan River to the middle Rio Puerco (West) Valley—indicates that by A.D. 600, early in Ancestral Pueblo times, some symbols and rituals were shared over very great dis-

tances. The rituals may have been important means of integrating linguistically or culturally diverse groups when they came together, establishing a pattern that would eventually unite culturally heterogeneous
groups both within the canyon and throughout the region. Wilshusen
and Van Dyke (chapter 7 of this volume), Lipe (2002a), and Vivian
(1990) argue for an incursion of colonists into Chaco Canyon from the
northern San Juan in the eighth and ninth centuries, during Pueblo I.
The existence of widely shared symbols and participation in common
rituals could have facilitated the integration of these newcomers into
the societies already established on the south side of the canyon (Vivian
et al., chapter 2 of this volume).

### Ninth- and Tenth-Century Developments

The first major building episode in the canyon—one that corresponds to an influx of new residents—took place in the late ninth and
early tenth centuries. At that time, "Chaco Canyon...may have been the
best place to farm in the interior San Juan Basin" (Vivian et al., chapter
2 of this volume). People moving into the canyon might have
attempted to displace those already established there, yet there is no
evidence indicating this. Rather, there is an increase in the number of
sites on the south side of the canyon (Windes 2001a), suggesting that
Chacoans accepted new residents and developed food production to
support them, probably by intensifying an array of diverse water-collec-
tion systems, including elaboration of the south-side floodwater collection features.

Canyon residents also may have experimented with the design and
development of slickrock collection systems in several north-side locations. This is suggested by construction in the late 800s of the early
Great Houses at Peñasco Blanco, Pueblo Bonito, and Una Vida. Plans
of these buildings in their early stages (see Lekson 1984a:65 and
Windes and Ford 1992) resemble those of Pueblo I–style unit pueblos.
Windes, in chapter 3 of this volume, links these sites specifically to communities on the South Fork of Fajada Wash and at the head of Upper
Kin Klizhin Wash, but the Chacoan structures are multistoried and
have larger rooms. Windes and Ford (1992) suggest that people
used the early Great House structures primarily for storing surplus
agricultural yields.

The function of Great Houses, whether as residences, storage, sacred spaces, or symbols of power, continues to be contested. Sebastian (1992a) views them as evidence of aggrandizing behavior. Alternatively, Wills (2000) sees them as communal efforts. Mahoney (2001:22) agrees with Windes and Ford that they more likely functioned as storage for large agricultural surpluses. We agree with the authors mentioned above that functions of Great Houses likely changed over time. In the absence of extensive testing, it is difficult to estimate the size and configuration of settlements in the canyon in the A.D. 800s and 900s. We note that Pueblo Bonito and Una Vida are located opposite, and Peñasco Blanco adjacent to, broad arable rincons on the south side of the canyon, suggesting that they were situated near existing farmland that was being cultivated (Vivian et al., chapter 2 of this volume). Because we have no evidence that the earliest Great House residents forcibly displaced people, we suspect that these Great Houses were constructed, perhaps by the newcomers, near both poor land and less agricultural land and that the additional labor was used to intensify agricultural production on both sides of the canyon. Because of the unusual convergence of adequate sources of moisture, Chacoans could reliably produce agricultural crops to feed the growing population.

We see the initial aggregation of population in Chaco as reflecting people's attraction to potential agricultural surpluses, and we see construction of the early Great Houses as providing more rooms in which to store crops. In addition, we suggest that in the 900s Chacoans consolidated features of social organization dating from Basketmaker III to facilitate episodic use of the canyon, uniting people from diverse settings in and around the margins of the San Juan Basin at least periodically for weeks or seasons. Scheduled ritual activities such as ceremonies, dances, and feasts, we suggest, embodied these characteristics. We emphasize scheduling because an important characteristic of Chacoan society is its highly developed astronomical observations (Judge and Malville 2004), which far exceed those needed for successful agriculture or for anticipating the availability of wild foods. It seems much more likely to us that using refined calendars enabled dispersed populations to come together—at a known and specific time—for important social and ritual activities.

In the 900s Chacoans developed new features of organization that encouraged, or at least permitted, groups from different areas, who may have been linguistically or culturally diverse, to live and work together in the relatively small confines of Chaco Canyon. We follow Ware (2001) in believing that non-kin sodalities were crucial in this endeavor. We follow Vivian (1990, chapter 2 of this volume) in proposing that a moiety structure similar to that followed among today's Eastern Pueblos may have been an important addition to those sodalities. Because the terms *ritual, ritual leaders, priests,* and *sodalities* are essential to the rest of our discussion, we digress here to clarify our perspective and use of terms.

Ritual is instrumental action (Asad 1993:126; Judge 1991, 1993; Kendrick and Judge 2000; Renfrew 2001; Walker 1995; Yoffee 2001; Yoffee, Fish, and Milner 1999), not a system of belief or ideas. The archaeological study of ritual does not focus on belief systems. Rather, archaeological study of ritual involves finding, analyzing, and interpreting past ritual activities and the contexts of paraphernalia. Religion and its associated rituals may permeate social action, are manipulated by social actors, and often involve (and potentially inform archaeologists about) political and economic behaviors. For example, ritual may require feasting and specific foods that must be obtained through geographically dispersed social networks and then be redistributed according to political rules (Spielmann 2004; Wills and Crown 2004; Vivian et al., chapter 2 of this volume). For us, ritual can reflect both society and polity.

In this chapter, we use the term *priest* to refer to leaders whose authority derives primarily from their control of esoteric knowledge but who may wield that authority over much of everyday life (see Ware 2001). It should be noted that the distinction between priests exercising sacred and ritual authority and chiefs exerting political and economic authority is effectively a false dichotomy peculiar to a Western European perspective that isolates religion and marginalizes it as epiphenomenal. In modern Pueblo society (see Fox 1967), political, economic, sacred, and ritual authorities are not necessarily separate roles. When we use the term *priest* here, we acknowledge the primarily sacred source of the authority, but we do not deny that authority in economic or political affairs.

As we note above, some scholars have described Basketmaker III settlements as lineage based (Vivian 1990:436–437; Ware 2001), signify-ing that kinship was the basis of defining social relations. The Basketmaker III populations in the canyon may have originated from several sources. We cited data suggesting that likely sources were the south and extreme western portions of the canyon, especially along Chacra Mesa and the eastern slopes of the Chuska and Lukachukai mountains. New observations (Wilshusen and Van Dyke, chapter 7, and Vivian and others, chapter 2, of this volume) link the influx of Pueblo I inhabitants to the northern San Juan.

People who come from different directions and do not share his-torical/cultural traditions may develop ties through fictive kinship and intermarriage, as well as participation in non-kin sodalities. One of the most effective means of integrating heterogeneous populations, differ-ent sodalities, and different hierarchical aspects of sodalities is the dual division organization that is most visible today in the Eastern Tewa Pueblos and, arguably, has considerable time depth in the northern San Juan (Ortiz 1965; Rohn 1971; Vivian 1990, chapter 2 of this vol-ume; Ware 2001). Although Tewa dual divisions are called "moieties" in the literature, they are, in fact, pseudomoieties because they do not reg-ulate marriage and do not base recruitment strictly on descent. As described by Ortiz (1965), Dozier (1960), and Vivian and others (chap-ter 2 of this volume), Tewa moiety associations are responsible for all governmental and ceremonial affairs, with each moiety assuming gov-erning responsibilities alternately during the year (*Winter/Summer*, or *Turquoise/Squash*). The dual divisions are at the core of economic activi-ties, including planning and coordinating planting, harvesting, and construction and maintenance of irrigation canals. Notably, Gwinn Vivian (personal communication 1999) emphasizes the integration of ritual and economic functions of moieties; ritual is organized around the economic cycles and includes a parallel series of subsistence-related activities, including food redistribution.

If, as has been suggested, the initial year-round residents of the canyon were joined in Pueblo I, rather quickly, by an influx of people from the northern San Juan who participated in similar calendrical rit-uals, an existing organization that integrated both sodality and lineage would facilitate regular interaction, cooperation, and sharing between the groups. We think that dual divisions incorporating non-kin sodalities provided this integrating structure and, as Vivian (1990:298–300) suggested, are manifest in the canyon architecture's variability. We are mindful of the fact that the earliest Great Houses on the north side of the canyon were built close to existing settlements on both the north and south sides of the canyon. Farming in the canyon, especially on the north side, requires cooperative labor to construct and maintain slick-rock diversion irrigation features. We do not see burning and destruction that would suggest hostile competition among these communities, and we do not believe that the Chaco environment was productive enough to support competitive aggrandizing behavior among them.

Rather, we think that the successful integration of people from heterogeneous cultural backgrounds through a governing structure that was not based on kinship but did promote broad participation in rituals was the Chacoan solution. Our notion of Chacoan polity is similar to Wills's (2000) cooperative model, in which he advocates a noncompetitive, inclusive ritual that benefits entire communities. Priests who were sodality leaders had authority by virtue of their knowledge and had power to control not only esoteric ritual but also economic and political matters (see Fox 1967).

### Eleventh-Century Developments

Estimates of labor investment in building construction in the canyon are based on tree-ring dates from the early Great Houses. Interpreting the tree-ring date clusters, researchers have assumed that construction was significantly reduced during A.D. 960–1020 (Lekson 1984a:66; Sebastian 1992a:figure 16). Although Great House construction might well have diminished significantly during those years, we suggest that building and expanding irrigation canals, gridded fields, and slickrock catchment devices may have taken place at that time. The tree-ring dates would not reflect these activities.

It was in the A.D. 1000s that central Chaco emerged as a "rituality" (Yoffee 2001; Yoffee, Fish, and Milner 1999), a "sacred economy" (Renfrew 2001), or an "integrated ritual polity" (Judge 1991, 1993; Kendrick and Judge 2000), with both the ritual itself and the component economic networks firmly solidified. The first half of the 1000s witnessed a burst of new construction in Chaco Canyon, new kinds of structures, alterations in the configuration of buildings, and perhaps changes in building function. By the mid-1000s the canyon's natural habitat had undergone significant cultural enhancement, artificially inflating the carrying capacity and rendering Chaco an even more attractive setting for visitors.

In the eleventh century, the scale of imports into the canyon increased dramatically. During this century, outlying Great Houses and roads were built throughout much of the San Juan Basin (Kantner and Kintigh, chapter 5 of this volume; see plate 3). We would argue that this activity signals important changes in the nature of Chacoan society. At the same time, we acknowledge that there is little consensus about the nature of Chaco society and polity for this time period and that many differences in interpretation depend on the perspective of the archaeologists. Because it was our assigned task, we focus on the central canyon in what follows, recognizing that this provides only one view, and probably a biased one, of Chaco as a regional system.

In A.D. 1010–1065, Chacoans initiated construction at Pueblo Alto, Chetro Ketl, Pueblo del Arroyo, and Hungo Pavi (Lekson 1984a; Vivian 1990; Windes 1993). These new structures have a similar layout (sometimes referred to as rectilinear or D-shaped) that deviates from that of the three earlier Great Houses. Great Kiva construction in the canyon dates to this time period, A.D. 1040, if not earlier (Mahoney and Kantner 2000:8; Windes and Ford 1996:308). One of the most basic, and most contested, interpretations of Chaco society and polity involves whether the Great Houses served primarily as residences and whether those that may have been residences in the 800s and 900s remained residential in the eleventh century. National Park Service Chaco Project archaeologists, who worked primarily at Pueblo Alto, where there was little domestic debris, tend to see the new construction as nonresidential. Those who focus on older excavations at Pueblo Bonito and Chetro Ketl, which yielded abundant artifacts, generally view Great Houses as domiciles. The difference in interpretation is critical, influencing greatly divergent estimates of resident population in the canyon, opinions about whether the canyon could have provided adequate food for those who lived there, and whether the number of residents could support either aggrandizing behavior or political hierarchy.

Resolution of these issues is thwarted by the lack of modern excavation at canyon Great Houses and a paucity of dates from the small house sites. Here we note that the new Great House construction in the canyon, extensive canal-irrigation networks, formal roads and stairways, and abundance of imported items such as timber, trachyte-tempered pottery, turquoise, and at least some corn (Toll, chapter 4 of this volume; Benson et al. 2003) signal a new and different role for central Chaco in the San Juan Basin.

Even if the year-round resident population of the central canyon was relatively small, large numbers of people brought timbers from great distances for construction and may have served as laborers for building and remodeling Great Houses and other public structures. Sebastian (1992a) discusses the labor investment per building event for tree-ring-dated construction in the canyon and makes a strong case for the need to import food to support this labor despite relatively good conditions for agriculture during building episodes. Recently, strontium isotope studies of high-elevation trees used as building timbers in Chaco (English et al. 2001) have demonstrated that these timbers were brought in from distances of 90 km. Importing timber was not a rare event. An estimated two hundred thousand imported timbers were used in Chaco Canyon (Dean and Warren 1983; English et al. 2001). In addition to new buildings, some ritual activities required construction effort. For example, Crown and Wills (2003) note that many kivas were substantially razed and rebuilt several times in place.

In addition to timbers, Toll (chapter 4 of this volume; see Toll and McKenna 1997) notes that trachyte-tempered utility vessels from the Chuska slopes, 50 km from Chaco Canyon, account for more than half the corrugated vessels present in the central canyon. Significantly, Toll (chapter 4 of this volume) underscores that Chuskan pottery in Chaco is dominated by large grayware jars that are difficult to transport. Other imports into the canyon include red ware, white ware, brown and smudged ware, and cylinder vessels, from a variety of sources; Narbona Pass chert from the Chuskas (Toll, chapter 4 of this volume); corn from the Eastern Chuska slope and the San Juan River valley (Benson et al. 2003); and possibly large mammals as well, which appear in increased numbers compared with rabbits (Vivian et al., chapter 2 of this volume). Quantities of turquoise and unusual shell artifacts, macaws, and copper bells reported from Pueblo Bonito likely date to the mid- to late-eleventh century (see Toll, chapter 4, and Nelson, chapter 10, of this volume).

A tremendous amount of human energy was vested in Chaco in the eleventh century. Construction of buildings required the procurement and preparation of masonry stone in the canyon and the procurement and transport of wooden beams from distant sources. Much planning, continuing over at least two generations of workers, was involved in the design and construction of the massive Great House structures, roads, and stairways. The slickrock runoff collection system, the masonry ter-races, and the canal network and gridded garden plots also required a large amount of labor, both to construct and maintain. Planting, tend-ing, harvesting, and storing crops demanded intensive effort. One perennial question is whether the labor for these efforts was recruited solely from among the permanent residents of Chaco Canyon.

Our charge was to examine Chaco society and polity from within the canyon. Consideration of the exotic materials (for example, tim-bers, turquoise, chert, copper, and corn) naturally leads us to wonder about relationships between Chaco and its outlying Great Houses and their regions. Rather than stray from our course, however, we note that the direction of interactions changed over time and that the scale of interactions clearly differed at various times within the eleventh cen-tury. These dimensions intersect with observations we can make based on the contexts of exotic materials within the central canyon confines. For example, construction of Great Houses elsewhere in the San Juan Basin had been initiated by the early 1000s. Van Dyke (2000:93–94) reports that at least seven Great Houses in the Red Mesa Valley are dated (by ceramic cross-dating) to the late tenth and middle eleventh centuries. Windes and Ford (1992) identify early Great Houses to the south and on the Chuskan slopes to the west as well. There is little evi-dence of Great Houses in the northern San Juan at this time (Varien 2001:54). We agree with Neitzel's (1994) contention that the Chaco sys-tem boundary shifted from south, to west, to north as it developed.

With respect to differences in scale of intensity at any one time, we note that the amount of material from the Chuska-Lukachukai region (timber, utility vessels, Narbona Pass chert, possibly corn) suggests an especially close or intense relationship with Chaco, compared with that reflected in the lesser amounts of obsidian and turquoise, from the

Jemez and Cerrillos areas, respectively, or the even more exotic copper bells and macaws (Toll, chapter 4 of this volume). Scale, of course, intersects with time. The Chaco-Chuskan connection appears strong before and after the eleventh century but diminishes toward the end of the eleventh century as interaction with the Jemez increases (Cameron 2001; Toll 2001, chapter 4 of this volume). Further, even though notions of redistribution at one time figured in discussions of Chaco economy, Chaco Canyon appears to have been a sink for exotics. Little that made its way into the canyon seems to have been dispersed. This, of course, suggests that the exchanges were primarily not "economic" in modern Western terms.

If we then focus on the locations in which imports occur within the canyon, we see that most of them suggest participation in ritual events and that the events may be interpreted as signaling a variety of inter-personal relationships between and among individuals and communities (see Toll, chapter 4 of this volume). In this regard, the burials found in Pueblo Bonito, with the wealth of grave goods accompanying them, are distinctive compared with others found in the canyon, reflecting better nutritional status and accumulation of sumptuary goods. We suggest that these represent concomitants of power based on ritual, where people who served their knowledgeable priests also constructed Great Houses, irrigation systems, and other public architecture.

Turquoise provides a good example of material functioning within a symbolic context. Imported into the canyon from a number of distant sources (Mathien 2001:115–116), turquoise was modified by individuals living in canyon small-house sites and eventually deposited in finished form in concealed locations in Great Houses (Judge 1989:237–238; Mathien 2001; Neitzel 1995:409–410). Stephen Plog (2003:690) suggests the symbolic extension of the idea of turquoise in specific hachured designs on Gallup Black-on-white pottery. Plog is careful in not concluding that the distribution of hachure necessarily coincides with participation in the Chacoan system. Rather, he suggests that it may be a "product of a broad social network in which people share at least some elements of a common worldview or ritual framework" (Plog 2003:690). We agree and also add that different sets of social relationships are reflected among those who obtained turquoise, worked turquoise into beads and pendants, deposited finished turquoise items in sealed niches, and shared an understanding of turquoise represented in a different medium.

The ceremonial network that developed would have facilitated the exchange of resources through ritual ties, serving to integrate the outlying polities economically and politically and to reduce competition for a stressed resource base. Perhaps members of groups residing outside the canyon provided much of the labor involved in constructing buildings, Great Kivas, canal systems, and other public works, such as roads and stairs, during the mid to late 1000s. Participation in the ritual system may have included periodic pilgrimages to Chaco to carry out ceremonies there (Crown and Judge 1991b:295) and perform service in the form of building and public works construction. These visitors would augment the population of the canyon periodically, reminiscent of, but on a much larger scale than, the seasonal aggregations earlier in Basketmaker III times.

We suggest that the placement and architecture of the Great Houses constructed in the mid-eleventh century, as well as the objects cached within them, may reflect diverse social relationships between the canyon and outlying settlements. In contrast to the three early Great Houses, which may have been built by groups claiming separate sections of the canyon, the placement and architecture of the eleventh-century Great Houses suggest that they were not built by the same canyon residents. The eleventh-century Great Houses have similar floor plans, quite distinct from the earlier sites. The new Great Houses of Chetro Ketl and Pueblo del Arroyo are almost within a stone's throw of Pueblo Bonito; Hungo Pavi and Pueblo Alto are in relatively isolated locales to the east and north, respectively.

Scholars have offered several interpretations of the relationship between the eleventh-century Great Houses and others in the canyon. One interpretation is that groups from geographical sectors outside the canyon built the later structures to facilitate and legitimize their participation in canyon ceremonies, to serve as residences for pilgrims, and to store ritual paraphernalia. For example, Toll (1990:296) notes that cylinder jars might have been made by outside communities who cached them, for ceremonial use, in Pueblo Bonito. This could have been the case for other sites and other types of ceremonial artifacts, for example, the wooden artifacts discovered in a back room at Chetro Ketl (Vivian, Dogden, and Hartman 1978).

It is possible, too, that construction of these Great Houses in the canyon was a means by which people from outlying communities could participate in the common cultural identity of Chaco, offsetting any tendency to diverge along linguistic or ethnic lines and promoting, if not ensuring, peaceful interactions. We agree with Toll (chapter 4 of this volume) that the apparent movement in and out of Chaco and the large-scale transport of ritual items into Chaco argue for sufficient security for a "Pax Chaco" (Lekson 2002) across the San Juan Basin. Some might argue that, if there was a Pax Chaco, it was created through brutality and fear (Turner and Turner 1999). We point out that the few instances of apparent violence at Chaco postdate the eleventh century, the period during which the Chaco regional system flourished (Bustard 2000).

External groups may have constructed, owned, and maintained some Great House architecture of central Chaco, but components such as roads, ramps, and stairs were truly communal and public. Both canyon residents and nonresidents may have constructed communal Great Kivas such as Casa Rinconada and Kin Nahasbas. Pueblo Alto on the north mesa and Tsin Kletzin on the south, both Great Houses with cardinal direction layouts, may have been built communally to serve as primary ritual structures for the canyon as a whole. Each has access from the canyon floor by very formal road and stair configurations, and each has commanding views of the surrounding terrain. These would have been tremendously impressive to people coming into the canyon.

The extensive system of roads found outside Chaco Canyon probably served ritual and symbolic purposes, although it is doubtful that they were ignored by those carrying wooden beams into Chaco or those engaged in pilgrimages (see Morenon 1977; Toll, chapter 4 of this volume; Vivian 1997b). As in the outlying areas, road segments in Chaco are associated with Great Houses and Great Kivas and tend to become increasingly formal as they approach these structures. The formal roads may have been built by communal workforces from the outlying sectors served by the roads.

Much of the rhetoric and speculation about Chaco concerns the nature of leadership during this period of intense labor investment.

For example, were leaders vying with one another for power? How much control did leaders have over labor? How did leaders come by their authority? Unfortunately, we lack basic data that would help resolve these questions. As we noted elsewhere (Cordell and Judge 2001:6–9), the size of the population resident in Chaco Canyon has important implications for understanding the nature of leadership; however, we do not know the size of the canyon population during this time. We must do much more work in the Great Houses to assess the degree to which they functioned as permanent residences and whether individual Great Houses served the same functions, primarily as residences, storage, places to enact ceremonies, or various combinations of these. Further, we lack information from the small houses to begin to estimate how many were occupied simultaneously and whether they were inhabited seasonally or throughout the year.

To account for the amount of construction that took place in the eleventh century, we think that outside labor considerably augmented the resident workforce in the canyon. Given the absence of firearms, we believe that these laborers were voluntarily engaged in their tasks and that they were provided with food and water throughout construction episodes. Construction by an outside labor force garnered from a diverse basin population suggests a potential for architectural diversity. Similarity of design in the eleventh-century construction contradicts this, however, and points to leadership by a common authority in the canyon.

In some models explaining the rise of chiefdoms, chiefs competitively display wealth and power to aggrandize their status. Although Chaco Canyon's resources were adequate to support the emergence of ritual elaboration based on communal and voluntary labor, they were probably insufficient to support long-term, competitive aggrandizement among chiefs. Some individuals were better nourished than others, but there is little evidence of the accumulation of riches in Chaco. It is also possible that the kinds of dual organizations we suggested for the tenth century might have coordinated labor in the eleventh, as well as serving to minimize competitive aggrandizement. Dual organization leadership, if it were like that in Eastern Pueblos today, would have provided leaders from among a group of knowledgeable individuals in which no one individual served in one office for life. The challenges of leadership in the eleventh century would have been to maintain adequate subsistence levels for the permanent residents, direct activities of the temporary workers who came in to construct new buildings (as well as support them with housing and food), schedule and direct ritual activities, and accommodate pilgrimages to the ceremonial center. However authority was accomplished, it seemed to suppress whatever potential conflicts might have emerged among the diverse human components of the San Juan Basin, as well as between permanent and temporary canyon residents.

## THE DECLINE OF CHACOAN SOCIETY

During the construction frenzy of the middle and late A.D. 1000s, those resources in Chaco Canyon that were devoted to supporting the construction workforce would have become increasingly taxed, a condition exacerbated by the continuation of periodic pilgrimages requiring considerable local support. Because of the escalating construction and continued provisioning of visitors, the demand for agricultural yield, faunal resources, and water would have intensified dramatically toward the end of the eleventh century. As the canyon's popularity grew, its carrying capacity, even though artificially augmented by runoff irrigation systems, was approached with equal rapidity.

A dry interval in A.D. 1080–1100 interrupted the positive climatic regime in the canyon during A.D. 1060–1130. As noted by Vivian (1990:483), "the onset of a two-decade decrease in precipitation at approximately 1080 combined with continuing long-term deterioration of irrigated fields in Chaco Canyon forced more serious consideration of alternatives." We would add that, in addition to a deteriorating environment, both construction and the number of visitors were probably increasing, with the result that the canyon was simply unable to provide adequate support for its population. Even though the eleventh-century environment had been quite favorable, the canyon was not without limitations as to the size and character of human population it could sustain. Canyon residents probably did import food occasionally, and visitors may also have brought provisions with them. Yet, it is not likely that enough food was imported to support residents and visitors alike on a regular, quotidian basis. Nor is it likely that abundant water was imported.

Given the dry interval, we suggest that by A.D. 1090–1100 canyon residents, and perhaps individuals moving into the canyon seeking relief, would have seriously questioned the effectiveness of the dominant ritual and its leadership. This observed failure of the canyon could have led to a decision to reestablish the center in a location near the Animas and San Juan rivers to the north (Lekson 1999:159). In Chaco Canyon, after reorganization in the early A.D. 1100s, the remaining population probably consisted solely of its long-term, permanent residents. The twelfth-century shift from large mammals to turkeys (Vivian 2000) would tend to confirm the notion of diminishing traffic into Chaco. In fact, central Chaco itself may have become politically ancillary to the Aztec-Salmon center (Judge 1991:26). The canyon's post-1100 buildings seem to reflect domestic or residential use rather than ritual or ceremonial use. This may explain the distinctive "McElmo" configuration of the architectural construction (that is, New Alto, Casa Chiquita, Kin Kletso, Wijiji). One might ask why people constructed new buildings at all, rather than simply occupy existing Great Houses. If, as suggested here, the canyon's eleventh-century Great Houses exemplified and legitimized ritual authority that significantly diminished in the early 1100s, then people might have avoided its architectural manifestations and constructed new houses, in a novel style, for domestic and residential needs.

## LEGACIES FROM CHACO

Surely the most important legacies from Chaco are modern Pueblo Indians whose vibrant traditions retain tremendous continuity with the past, as reflected in agriculture, architecture, ritual, symbolism, iconography, and features of social organization. Chacoans were Pueblo Indians. That having been said, it is also true that seven hundred years separate the last Pueblo occupants of Chaco Canyon from their modern descendents and those years witnessed depopulation of most Ancestral Pueblo territory, the traumas of European conquest and colonization, and the introduction of cash economies and various institutions of modern industrial America. Nevertheless, we think that some aspects of Chacoan society and polity remained and were modified over the centuries.

A salient aspect of Pueblo polity today is that individual villages are politically autonomous and economically independent. Yet, legacies from Chaco suggest economic ties among villages, the persistence of which has been underappreciated in the study of fourteenth- and fifteenth-century Pueblos. The classic case is Pecos Pueblo (1300–1838), where Anna O. Shepard (Kidder and Shepard 1936) demonstrated petrographically that, far from pottery making being a household craft, the earliest decorated types excavated at Pecos had been imported. As Kidder (1936:xxxiii) wrote, "It has always been assumed that potting was one of the regular household tasks of every Pueblo woman; that each town was in this regard self-sufficient. But if whole classes of pottery, such as Glaze I and Biscuit, were imported, we must postulate an extraordinary volume of trade and allow for a compensating outward flow of other commodities. Furthermore, we must believe that the production of vessels at the source of supply was much greater than was needed for home consumption, in other words, that rudimentary commercial manufacturing was practiced."

Shepard's findings, especially the implications of her findings at Pecos, were ignored. Had archaeologists worked with a Chacoan model of production, again, first suggested by Shepard (1939) but this time supported by others (Toll 1991, chapter 4 of this volume), they might have developed a better understanding of the social economies of Pecos and other Pueblos.

The recent work showing that some corn found at Pueblo Bonito was grown on or near the Chuskan pediment (Benson et al. 2003) suggests another tie between Chaco and the Eastern Chuskas. We do not know the composition or home villages of the groups who cut the timber and made the pottery that was transported into Chaco Canyon. What we do know of Chuskan pottery production and its transport into Chaco does not, however, assume that there was commercial trade between communities in the Chuskas and those in Chaco Canyon, nor does it presume that individual families or households did these tasks independently, as Kidder assumed for pottery production at Pecos. It is entirely possible that these activities, and their timing, were part of a ritual cycle of obligations involving large segments of Chacoan society but coordinated by much smaller groups of ritual specialists (Hensler and Blinman 2002:369). The same may well have been true for the production and import of pottery to thirteenth- and fourteenth-century Pecos.

We have agreed with Vivian's (1990) assessment that Chacoan society was able to maintain peace among, if not integrate, communities with diverse cultural and historical backgrounds. Chaco sustained multiple, large, potentially divided and divisive populations in close proximity. We believe that Chacoans accomplished this through cultural means, through participation in shared rituals and ceremonies. Interactions among Pueblos through ritual sodalities and ritual specialists continue today and may be an important Chacoan legacy. In modern times, such interaction is reflected in some shared terminology even among Pueblos speaking different languages. For example, the pan-Pueblo word *kiva* is derived from a Keresan word, as is *Katsina* or *Kachina* (Fox 1967:12).

As Ware (2001:84) notes, referencing several sources, "Ceremonialists throughout the Eastern Pueblo region are connected by complex networks built upon the reciprocal exchange of esoteric knowledge and ritual paraphernalia." When prospective members of an esoteric society that was borrowed are trained for initiation, they may be sent to the pueblo where the society originated. Ware (2001:84) gives the example of Tewa Bear Medicine men receiving training at Keresan-speaking Cochiti or Towa-speaking Jemez. A. Ortiz (1994, cited in Ware 2001) discusses instances in which a priesthood that is about to become extinct may be "replanted" by priests from other villages who provide training and initiation. Bunzel (1973:901) gives an example of San Felipe (Keresan) and Hopi (Hopi) priests sharing esoteric information in English. It is important to note, as Ware does, that Eastern Pueblo ritual leaders protect their political power, by layers of secrecy, from noninitiated insiders, as well as outsiders, yet share this power with ritual leaders from other pueblos. Ties among ritual leaders and ritual societies seem to be a Chacoan legacy that may have permitted Chacoan ceremonialists to reestablish themselves along the San Juan River in the twelfth century. Ties among villages that involved sharing personnel for ceremonies could have been a factor in the regional depopulations of the late thirteenth century in that no villages may have been able to stay behind because they were united through rituals that needed to be performed. Ties among villages through ritual leaders may also have provided the pathways along which migrations occurred.

Chacoan ability to allow peaceful interactions, through ritual lead-ers, among people with different culture histories may provide a model for historic situations that are otherwise seen as highly unusual. These include examples of enclaves within Pueblo villages and unified action among several Pueblos. The enclave example most commonly cited is Hopi-Tewa Village on the Hopi First Mesa, which is culturally Hopi and linguistically Tewa and was established by Tanoan refugees from the Galisteo Basin. Also, a colony of Laguna (Keresan) at Isleta (Tiwa) maintains its own ceremonies, not performed by the Isleta (Fox 1967:17). Another well-known example is the surviving population from Pecos Pueblo and their descendants, who reside at Jemez. Pecos and Jemez spoke a common language (Towa). The Pecos Eagle Hunt Society introduced and maintained the Pecos bull dance at Jemez (Schroeder 1979:434), where today many families retain *Pecos* as a sur-name. What is less well-known is that Santo Domingo (Keresan) and Isleta (Tiwa) also took in Pecos refugees (Levine 1999). Finally, Blinman and Ware (1999) and Ware (2001) remind us of the role that ritual societies and ceremonial networks played in the Pueblo Revolt of 1680, directed from the kivas of Taos by a ceremonialist from San Juan Pueblo.

## CONCLUSION

Central Chaco Canyon exhibits natural habitat diversity unique to the San Juan Basin, with which it shares an unpredictable precipitation pattern. Underwritten by a productive environment, the cultural processes and adaptations that took place in the canyon were excep-tional among Ancestral Pueblo peoples. Peoples of diverse culture-his-torical backgrounds came to inhabit the canyon. Three early Great Houses shaped the emergence of a common, ritual practice, which served to integrate residents of the canyon and those of outlying settle-ments. We have suggested that leadership authority was derived from control over ritual and esoteric information and that it may have been imbedded in a dual organization that could integrate hierarchies already in place among diverse segments of the canyon population. The dual organization leaders would have come from a knowledgeable segment of the population but would not have sustained aggrandizing behavior over long periods of time. The qualities of leadership at

Chaco encouraged the elaboration of architecture in the canyon while minimizing potential conflict among diverse cultural entities. Construction of a complex of Great Houses, Great Kivas, roads, and stairways led to the elaboration of the canyon as the basin's ceremonial center, a center supported by an enhanced agricultural system and a relatively favorable climate. The system thrived until it fell victim to a deteriorating environment at the turn of the twelfth century.

Under the unifying principles that emerged in central Chaco, the diverse polities of the San Juan Basin chose to cooperate rather than compete for its scarce resources. This highly successful strategy sustained them for two centuries. As such, they provided an enduring foundation for the cooperative social processes that characterize and sustain an equally diverse Pueblo world today.

### Notes

1. In May 1999 we convened a working conference, "Chaco Society and Polity," at Fort Lewis College in Durango, Colorado. Participating in the conference were Linda S. Cordell (convener), W. James Judge (convener), Stephen H. Lekson, Nancy Mahoney, F. Joan Mathien, Mark Varien, John Ware, Thomas Windes, Henry Wright, and Norman Yoffee. Papers from that meeting were addressed to an audience of professional Southwestern archaeologists and were subsequently published (Cordell, Judge, and Piper 2001). We thank all the participants in the 1999 workshop for their thoughtful discussions, and we thank Steve Lekson, Karin Burd Larken, and Sujan Bryan for bringing us together. In fall 2002 the Chaco Synthesis Project convened a capstone conference in Albuquerque and in May 2003 a small working conference at the School of American Research (Lekson, chapter 1 of this volume). We are grateful to Steve Lekson for convening these opportunities for further exchange of ideas. The goal of these last two meetings was to develop a series of papers, derived from NPS Chaco Project research and the working conferences, for a broader audience of anthropologists, archaeologists, historians, and others interested in Chaco Canyon and its Ancestral Pueblo peoples.

2. Our focus on the environment, agriculture, and the cultural and historical backgrounds of Chacoan populations owes a tremendous debt to the insights of R. Gwinn Vivian (1990), for whose dedication to and knowledge of things Chacoan we, and other Chaco researchers, are thankful.

# 7

# Chaco's Beginnings

## Richard H. Wilshusen and Ruth M. Van Dyke

The origins of the Chaco system have been difficult to find and to understand. The massive constructions of A.D. 1020–1120 draw so much attention that scholars rarely have focused on the beginnings of Chaco in late Pueblo I and early Pueblo II. The Chaco Project of the 1970s and early 1980s attempted to overcome this deficit, but the reports of small-site excavations and discussions of early tenth-century Chaco (for example, Judge et al. 1981; McKenna and Truell 1986; Windes, ed., 1993) are still not nearly as well-known in Southwestern archaeology as the investigations of the Basketmaker III site Shabik'eshchee (refer to figure 3.3) (Roberts 1929; Wills and Windes 1989) that precede it or the Classic Bonito-phase Chaco Great Houses that follow it (for example, Judd 1964; Lekson 1984a; Sebastian 1992a).

## THE MAZE OF CHACO CANYON'S BEGINNINGS

Early Great House sites within the canyon were, no doubt, the beginnings of what became the center of the Chaco system. Archaeologists, however, have offered few satisfying explanations to account for how and why the system came to be. One explanation suggests a shift from a basic reciprocal exchange system to an emergent redistributive exchange system (for example, Judge et al. 1981:79–81), but archaeological data have yet to substantiate this scenario. These late Pueblo I/early Pueblo II sites show little indication of being the center of an emergent system that would have influence over a region of 50,000–100,000 sq km within two centuries.

Part of the reason many archaeologists have given little attention to the Pueblo I evidence at Chaco Canyon may be that the evidence from the relatively modest Pueblo I occupation in Chaco does not comport with the dramatic development of incipient Great Houses in the same locale by the late ninth and early tenth centuries. Gwinn Vivian (1990) turned us in a promising direction with his attempt to raise the analysis of the origins of Chaco to a regional level. Only in the past decade have we found compelling evidence regarding regionwide population movements in Pueblo I that influenced Chaco's early development. To discover the origins of the Chaco system, scholars must look at the whole San Juan River watershed (figure 7.1) and examine the significant differences between the Northern (Mesa Verdean) and Southern (Chacoan) San Juan areas in Pueblo I. Understanding the emergence of the Chaco system may be like mapping a maze; we may have to look for its beginnings on the outside to understand how to get to its center.

An increasing number of investigators—especially those whose last names begin in *V* or *W* (Schachner 2001:186; Varien et al. 1996:93; Vivian 1990:184; Ware and Blinman 2000; Wills 2000:38–39; Wilshusen 2002:105–107; Wilshusen and Ortman 1999; Wilshusen and Wilson 1995:76–80; Windes, ed., 1993:1; Windes et al. 2000:56)—point out that Chaco's beginnings may be bound up in regionwide changes in late Pueblo I (A.D. 850–900). To find the origins of the Chaco system, it is necessary to look at not only Pueblo I in Chaco Canyon proper but also the centers of social and economic power throughout the San Juan River drainage basin between A.D. 850 and 950. In the mid-ninth century, the primary centers of social power were largely around the periphery of the San Juan geologic basin, not in its center. Only after A.D. 950 or 1000 does the preeminence of the Great Houses in Chaco Canyon become evident. Here we discuss the events that either triggered or foreshadowed this change.

This chapter covers three main points. First, we summarize and

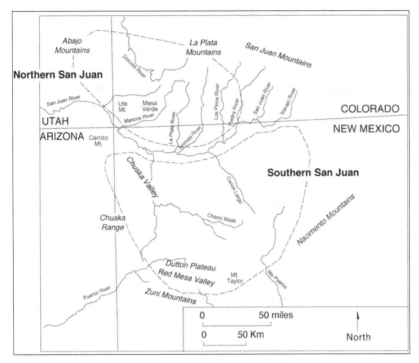

**FIGURE 7.1**

*Major physiographic features of the Northern and Southern San Juan regions.*

compare the settlement histories and cultural landscapes of the northern and southern halves of the San Juan River basin (see figure 7.1) for
the Pueblo I period (A.D. 750–900). We argue that the collapse and
abandonment of large Pueblo I centers to the north of the San Juan
River by A.D. 890 have to figure into *any* explanation of the nearly contemporaneous beginnings of the Chaco Great Houses and their rapidly
expanding communities to the south of the San Juan. Only by comparing the record of the Southern San Juan (what Kidder originally
labeled the "Chaco subculture" [1924:figure 6]) with that of the
Northern San Juan (Kidder's "Mesa Verde subculture") can we understand both the beginning and the end of Chaco.

Second, by examining how the centers of social organization and
power shifted within the San Juan watershed between A.D. 850 and 950,
we can better explain the origins of Chaco and the regional system of
Great Houses associated with it. The early large communities around

its periphery reveal Chaco's origins as much as the incipient, "candidate" Great Houses at its center. Finally, we suggest how the origins of the Chaco system in the late ninth and early tenth century bear upon Chaco at its height at A.D. 1050–1125 (refer to figure 5.1) and its collapse soon after.

## PUEBLO I DEVELOPMENTS IN THE SAN JUAN AREA: REGIONAL SETTLEMENT HISTORIES AND CULTURAL DIFFERENCES

Early in the history of Southwestern archaeology, A. V. Kidder considered the San Juan a single "cultural area," with a Mesa Verdean sub-area primarily to the north of the San Juan and a Chacoan sub-area to the south (Kidder 1924:figure 6). Over the past eighty years, archaeological research has elaborated the culture histories of Mesa Verde and Chaco and has made them appear very distinct from each other. Although a few archaeologists have tried to link the histories of the two areas (for example, Vivian 1990), most archaeologists working in this area consider themselves to be expert in one region or the other, but not both. Consequently, one can almost discuss summaries of research in the two regions separately. We first discuss the Pueblo I archaeology of the Northern San Juan, or Mesa Verde, region and then follow with the Southern San Juan, or Chaco, region. At the end, we demonstrate that certain discontinuities or contradictions in the data from both regions necessitate considering how the two may be tied together, especially during the late Pueblo I and early Pueblo II periods (ca. A.D. 850–950).

### Pueblo I Developments in the Northern San Juan, or Mesa Verde, Region

Research on Pueblo I communities in the Northern San Juan has primarily focused on refining our understanding of regional variations in Pueblo I settlement and organization across the region. The general Pecos Classification characterization of Pueblo I, first formulated by Kidder (1927) and then amended by the investigations of Brew (1946) and Morris (1939), served as a fine overarching framework for archaeologists through the 1980s. The work done on Pueblo I sites north of the San Juan is well-known in the Southwestern literature and is regarded as prime data for illustrating the initial shift from smaller pit-house settlements to larger, pueblo-based settlements. Investigations at Navajo Reservoir (Eddy 1966, 1972) and Mesa Verde (Gillespie 1976; Hayes 1964; Hayes and Lancaster 1975; Reed 1958; Rohn 1977) dominated the phase-based fine-tuning of Pueblo I in the northern half of the San Juan watershed through the 1980s.

The considerable research into Pueblo I communities at Dolores in the 1980s originally contributed to our understanding of ninth-century developments in a particular Northern San Juan locality (for example, Blinman 1994; Kane 1984, 1986). The large scale of the project and the intensity of the investigations ultimately permitted a much better picture of the development of Pueblo I throughout the whole region (for example, Kohler 1993; Schlanger 1988; Wilshusen 1999; Wilson and Blinman 1993). Three significant conclusions derived from the Dolores synthesis. First, large Pueblo I villages, which are defined here as sites with at least fifteen households or thirty-five surface rooms, were more prevalent on the local landscape than had been previously thought. Although early researchers had recognized the large size of some Pueblo I villages (Brew 1946), they little understood the large number and size of Pueblo I villages before the research done in the 1980s. Experienced researchers of Basketmaker III and Pueblo I admitted in the 1970s that "the evidence from excavated sites of the period is diverse and disparate if not contradictory" (Plog 1979:115). It took the large research projects of the 1970s and 1980s to sort out many of the contradictions.

Second, local and regional population movement was a much more important aspect in Pueblo I than had previously been understood. Both these conclusions deserve elaboration because they bear on the following discussion of Pueblo I at Chaco. A third set of conclusions, which was a major point of contention in the 1980s, had to do with the social organization of Pueblo I villages (Kane 1989; Lipe 1986; Wilshusen 1991). This topic deserves renewed attention (for example, Schachner 2002; Ware 2002a) with special focus on the corporate or ritual leadership within villages, as opposed to the 1980s concentration on individual leadership. We discuss issues of social power and organization in a later section of this chapter.

Pueblo I village formation in the Northern San Juan region is particularly striking because no other areas in the northern Southwest had comparable villages at this time. In addition, the villages created a totally new set of environmental problems and social demands for their inhabitants. The contradictory nature of Pueblo I suggested by Fred Plog above has to do partially with its different manifestations in various regions of the northern Southwest. Within the San Juan Basin, large villages are primarily evident in the northern half of the watershed and not nearly as common or large in the southern half (figure 7.2).

Even in the Northern San Juan, trends in settlement patterns between A.D. 750 and 900 are potentially contradictory. Villages occurred in different areas at different times throughout this period. The focus of village formation moved from one locale to another over almost a century's time. The first Pueblo I villages are found in Utah or along the Utah-Colorado border (A.D. 770–830); thereafter, villages are evident on Mesa Verde, along the Mancos River, and in the Durango area (A.D. 810–860). Only at the end of this period do we find villages stretching from the northern part of Montezuma Valley to Mesa Verde (A.D. 840–880). Although the "center" of village clusters shifted, both population and villages continually increased in the Four Corners from A.D. 750 on. By A.D. 860 at least one-third to one-half of the known population in the Anasazi world was in the Northern San Juan region (Wilshusen and Ortman 1999:figures 2 and 3).

Pueblo I villages typically have at least one large roomblock of ten to thirty households, with a number of smaller, surrounding roomblocks. Although hamlet-size habitations of two to six households exist within these villages, these smaller roomblocks are typically within 50 m of the next roomblock. A whole village of three to eighteen roomblocks typically covers no more than 10–15 ha. McPhee Pueblo, one of the larger roomblocks within McPhee Village, illustrates the sizeable scale of some roomblocks in Pueblo I villages (figure 7.3a). The individual U-shaped roomblock units in McPhee Pueblo are not unusual in some Pueblo I villages, but to have two of the roomblocks joined, as at McPhee, is unusual. McPhee Village is illustrated because it is one of the few villages in which more than a couple of individual roomblocks have been excavated. Archaeologists have long recognized the presence of large Pueblo I roomblocks (Morris 1919), but only in the past two decades have they regularly understood that villages are usually

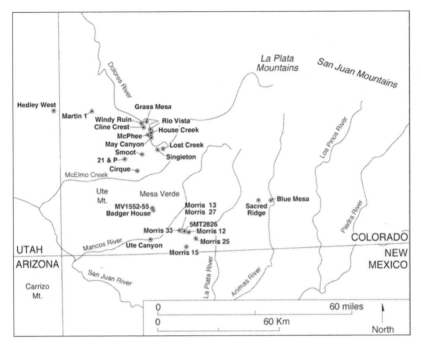

FIGURE 7.2
*Documented Northern San Juan Pueblo I villages with occupations dating to A.D. 775–875. A village is defined as a site having a minimum of fifteen households or thirty-five surface rooms.*

made up of linked or multiple roomblocks. Brew (1946) documented such a roomblock early in the research history of Pueblo I, Alkali Ridge Site 13 (in southeastern Utah), which archaeologists generally regarded as an exceptionally large, instead of a normal, habitation site. As Pueblo I sites documented in the 1930s have been relocated and remapped in the past decades, it has become clear that they are much larger than originally conceived; Morris sites 33 and 13 (in the La Plata River district) are good examples (figure 7.3b). In addition, whereas early archaeologists proposed that these sites represented a sequential occupation of one roomblock after another over hundreds of years, it now appears that the roomblocks, in most cases, were occupied contemporaneously and that the village occupation lasted only thirty to forty years.

Average village population between A.D. 840 and 880 is estimated to be forty-eight households, based on twenty-one villages from this period (Wilshusen and Ortman 1999:table 1). Although these sites are unremarkable in overall construction, their large population size and their apparent dominance over certain landscapes are impressive. Certainly, no other areas in the northern Southwest are known to have had comparable-size sites or population densities during the ninth century. It must be emphasized that we are using the word *village* to mean a very specific settlement phenomenon, rather than in the broader sense that many archaeologists use the term (for example, Flannery 2002).

The high local-population densities of these villages placed new demands on the landscape for good agricultural land (Kohler 1992; Kohler et al. 1986), wood for housing and heating (Kohler and Matthews 1988), wild food resources (Floyd and Kohler 1990; Potter 2000), and clean water. In addition, the disparate cultural groups (Wilshusen and Ortman 1999), the differences in socioreligious organization between villages (Wilshusen 1989, 1991; Wilshusen and Ortman 1999), and the relative lack of well-defined, decision-making hierarchies (Wilshusen 1991; see Kane 1989 for an alternative view) made for a volatile combination.

One of the themes that emerged from the Pueblo I research in the Northern San Juan was the short life of most villages and the need to understand local movements of people around the landscape (Schlanger 1988). Certain places were reused through time (Schlanger 1992), but the typical life of a village clearly was only a generation or two. To truly estimate the population of the area through Pueblo I, we had to devise methods to estimate site occupations at temporal scales comparable in precision to site use-life estimates (Schlanger and Wilshusen 1993; Varien 1999). As other archaeological surveys added to our understanding of the settlement patterns and chronological developments in particular Northern San Juan locales, several striking observations came into focus for the period between A.D. 750 and 950.

To begin with, there was an incredible increase in population in the general area, beginning by late in Basketmaker III and continuing through Pueblo I (Wilshusen and Ortman 1999:377–382). This demographic growth was not just an archaeological phenomenon whereby a basically stable population utilized different areas at different times, thereby creating lots of sites over the course of a century. Instead, the scale of expansion suggests that immigrants were joining a local

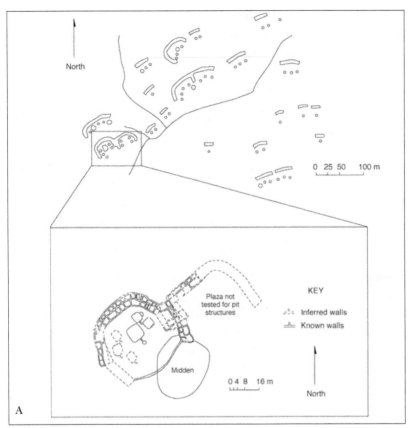

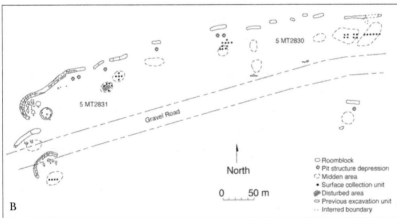

**FIGURE 7.3**

(a) *McPhee Village (A.D. 875) and McPhee Pueblo, one roomblock within the village, and*
(b) *Morris sites 33 (5MT2831) and 13 (5MT2830), both occupied ca. A.D. 825.*

populace that was, itself, increasing. In many cases, it is clear that these immigrants were from the south or west of the area and were coming from 50 to 100 km away. Many settlements originally labeled in the literature as late Basketmaker III (for example, Carlson 1963; Gooding 1980) were actually early to mid-Pueblo I settlements of newly arrived immigrants. Researchers labeled these sites in this manner because aspects of the settlement types and subsistence strategies "look" Basketmaker III yet the tree-ring dates are between A.D. 760 and 820. As groups arrived at the periphery of the area, they may have lived in hamlet apartment complexes of two to four households. By A.D. 825–850, however, the vast majority of the regional population had been drawn into villages, each with a minimum of fifteen households, more typically with thirty to fifty households.

Additionally, the evidence from ceramic and tree-ring chronologies and regional site databases demonstrates that only a handful of sites in the main area of Pueblo I villages can be clearly dated to A.D. 880–950. A significant population lived in the area at approximately A.D. 860–875, but very few sites immediately postdate this occupation (Varien et al. 1996:92–93; Wilshusen and Ortman 1999:377–382; Wilshusen and Wilson 1995:73–80). Varien's (1999:figure 7.16) plot of all the Mesa Verde region cutting dates between A.D. 400 and 1300 shows a dramatic dip in the archaeological tree-ring record between A.D. 880 and 1020. Archaeologists have intensively excavated many hundreds of sites in this region, so it is unlikely that they inadvertently missed sites of this period. Even if that were the case, we might still expect that trees dating to this period would show up as reused timber—if they were being cut down. A large number of Pueblo II habitations exist in the region, but the vast majority of these sites date between A.D. 1000 and 1150 (Lipe and Varien 1999a:253–256). Consequently, many archaeologists in the Northern San Juan increasingly have accepted the interpretation that the area was significantly depopulated in the tenth century.

All these archaeological interpretations are reasonably consistent with the available ethnographic, historic cross-cultural data on non-state villages (Wilshusen 1991). Ethnographically documented villages outside the influence of modern states typically have use-lives averaging twenty-five years, with the smallest villages having at least 75 people (or approximately 15 households) and the largest villages rarely having more than 650 people (130 households). There are two levels of decision making in most agricultural villages (at the corporate group and village levels), yet this authority and integration is insufficient to hold a village together when subsistence resources or social structures are put under stress and the population knows of better circumstances in other areas.

The northern Pueblo I villages, with their large size and volatility, stand in stark contrast to the contemporary settlements in the south. Yet, connections between the two regions clearly exist, and the San Juan River is only an approximate line of demarcation for this discussion. Before discussing the relationship between north and south, we must review the Pueblo I background for the Southern San Juan, or the region with Chaco Canyon at its eastern center.

### Pueblo I Developments in the Southern San Juan, or Chaco, Region

For many decades, the place of the late Pueblo I/early Pueblo II period within the Southern San Juan watershed was poorly documented. Some of the best-known, early excavations of Pueblo I sites were at the southern edge of the San Juan drainage in the West Puerco and Red Mesa valleys (Gladwin 1945; Roberts 1931, 1939) or on the eastern slope of the Chuska Mountains (Morris 1959). Before the mid-1970s little research had been reported on Pueblo I and early Pueblo II in Chaco Canyon proper, with only limited views of buried early construction at a few small sites south of the wash (Bc 50 and 51) or deep within Pueblo Bonito (Judd 1964; Kluckhohn 1939). One of the best-known early sites was actually a small early Pueblo II site, the Three-C Site (refer to figure 1.4a) (Vivian 1965). The Chaco Project of the 1970s and many energy-related archaeological projects in the 1980s and 1990s have considerably extended our understanding of Pueblo I in the south. We now have at least a basic knowledge of representative Pueblo I to early Pueblo II sites distributed throughout the Southern San Juan watershed (figure 7.4).

*Pueblo I in the Chaco Core.* The Chaco Project of the 1970s dramatically increased the data about the early Pueblo occupation in Chaco

Canyon. We probably know more about Pueblo I and early Pueblo II in this area than anywhere else in the Southern San Juan watershed. The project included a monumentwide survey, excavation of several smaller Pueblo I/Pueblo II sites, and reexamination of the early architecture within the foundations of the later Great Houses as part of an overall scheme to understand early developments in the Chaco core, the area encompassing both the canyon and nearby secondary drainage areas (see Vivian and Hilpert 2002:67 for a more precise definition of this core area). As with many big projects, it has taken several decades to publish, understand, and reconcile the various data.

The general inventory of the Chaco Canyon National Monument (Hayes 1981:figure 15) originally estimated a high house count in Pueblo I and early Pueblo II and found a surprisingly high density of sites dating to this period (twelve to fifteen sites per square kilometer). Researchers such as Hayes (1981) and Vivian (1990:463–472) placed Pueblo I and early Pueblo II developments at Chaco in a context of intrinsic local population growth. Judge and others (1981:76) recognized that mobility is an option in times of stress but suggested that large-scale regional population movement was increasingly unlikely by the tenth century. Given recent analysis of excavated Pueblo I sites, as well as additional surveys just outside the monument, Windes (ed., 1993) suggested that the 1970s site inventory almost certainly overrepresented the Pueblo I sites and that Pueblo I may primarily be a very late phenomenon in the Chaco Canyon area. If Windes's analysis is correct, then one must consider large-scale population movement to account for indisputably higher populations by late Pueblo I/early Pueblo II (ca. A.D. 875–950). Trends in regionwide data on the emergence of early Great Houses between A.D. 860 and 940 reinforce his arguments (Windes n.d., chapter 3 of this volume). These new data have significantly improved our ability to interpret the previous survey and excavation data for Pueblo I and Pueblo II sites (Hayes 1981; McKenna and Truell 1986).

Several small sites excavated in Marcia and Werito's rincons, to the south of Chaco Wash, are the best examples of habitations in the canyon dating to A.D. 750–900. Site 29SJ627 is a multicomponent site, with its earliest component dating to sometime between A.D. 780 and 910. It consists of approximately ten to fourteen small storage rooms

APP TYPE: SALE
APP Label: CHASE VISA
AID: 0333D
Auth: 05333
TVR: 0010000000000A
0008000000
TSI: E080

---

Check Closed
08/30/2024 03:01 PM

---

Sign up for our loyalty program
Starbucks Rewards
Join our Rewards
Visit starbucks.com/rewards
or download our app
At participating stores
Some restrictions apply

Type: SALE
App Label: CHASE VISA
Auth: 03993D
AID: A000000031010
TVR: 0000008000
TSI: E800

------ Check Closed ------
06/30/2024 03:01 PM

Join our loyalty program
Starbucks Rewards®
Sign up for promotional emails
Visit Starbucks.com/rewards
Or download our app
At participating stores
Some restrictions apply

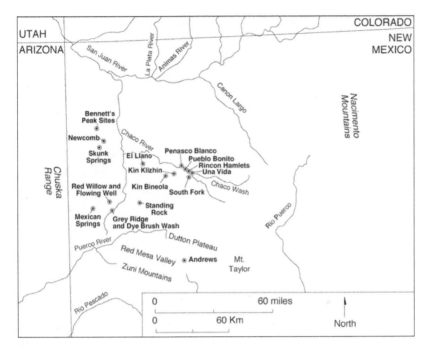

**FIGURE 7.4**

*Southern San Juan Pueblo I communities and large hamlets.*

and ramada areas in a small roomblock and one to three contemporary pit structures (McKenna and Truell 1986). As with almost all the Pueblo I components at Chaco, the occupation can only be generally dated by associated ceramics. Based on other, comparable, well-analyzed, well-dated sites, the actual occupation of the site likely lasted no more than a total of ten to thirty years at one or more times between A.D. 780 and 910 (for example, Ahlstrom 1985; Lightfoot 1992, 1994; Varien 1999). Site 29SJ724 dates to approximately A.D. 760–820 and is the most well-preserved example of a Pueblo I site in the Chaco region (figure 7.5; refer to figure 3.11a). It has a single component of occupation and consists of eleven surface rooms or associated ramadas and a single pit structure (McKenna and Truell 1986). Both 29SJ724 and 29SJ627 are the largest of the excavated Pueblo I hamlets in Chaco Canyon, besides the early Great Houses that date to late in the ninth century. In contrast to the Northern San Juan, these smaller Pueblo I hamlets—instead of villages—are the norm to the south of the San Juan River.

A third nearby excavated hamlet, 29SJ629, the Spadefoot Toad site, taught Chaco excavators much about the difficulties of identifying mid- to late- Pueblo I and early Pueblo II sites (refer to figure 3.11b). Based on the original surface survey of the architecture and ceramics, Spadefoot Toad appeared to be a Pueblo I/early Pueblo II site (Windes, ed., 1993:7). After extensive excavation and analysis, it was evident that the primary occupation of the site dated within the range of A.D. 950–1050. Windes concluded that some key diagnostic markers of Pueblo I in the Northern San Juan, especially neck-banded pottery, became predominant in the Chaco area only in early Pueblo II (Windes, ed., 1993:339–340). The excavation results of the various small Pueblo I and Pueblo II sites by the Chaco Project demonstrate that early surveys overestimated the number of Pueblo I habitations in the Chaco core. Early Pueblo II houses were far more numerous than previously estimated (Windes, ed., 1993:340; Windes n.d.).

Within the Chaco core are several Pueblo I communities, but, interestingly, the largest and best-documented community is not directly within the canyon, but 12 km south of the monument (Windes, chapter 3 of this volume, n.d.). Between 1991 and 2000 Windes extensively mapped and recorded the Fajada Wash, South Fork community (see figure 3.4) (Windes n.d.). The approximately twenty-five to twenty-seven small hamlets within this community may date close to A.D. 800. The hamlets have an average of two households, with relatively modest middens and residential architecture. Most are located in line-of-sight of two unusual, adjacent masonry Pueblo I houses within a small part of the valley. A probable Pueblo I Great Kiva lies just below the two masonry houses and connects with them via a short prehistoric road. Another cluster of Pueblo I sites is present in the next drainage to the west (Kin Klizhin Wash). Windes estimates that these sites represent fifty to seventy Pueblo I households. A subsequent, separate early Pueblo II community is also present in this area (Tom Windes, personal communication with Van Dyke, 2003).

Excavation data from the 1920s and 1930s (for example, Judd 1964) and the analysis of early construction patterns in the Great Houses (Gillespie 1984:figure 4.4a; Lekson 1984a:figures 4.12a, 4.20a)

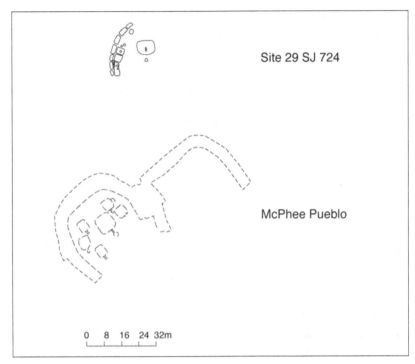

Site 29 SJ 724

McPhee Pueblo

0   8   16   24 32m

**FIGURE 7.5**

*An example of a Pueblo I Chaco-area hamlet: site 29SJ724 (at the same scale as the McPhee Pueblo in figure 7.3a).*

remain fundamental to understanding Pueblo I and Pueblo II in the Chaco core. Among scholars of Chaco (Judge et al. 1981; Lekson 1999:51; Sebastian 1992a; Vivian 1990:158), there is a general consensus that the earliest defining features of the Chaco phenomenon date between the late ninth century and the early tenth. The first Great Houses in Chaco Canyon—Peñasco Blanco, Pueblo Bonito, and Una Vida—were built at the confluences of major lateral tributaries with the Chaco River (refer to plate 7, vertical of Peñasco Blanco). Around these sites was some of the best-watered agricultural land in the area. In some explanations, this, coupled with favorable climatic conditions, offered the possibility of "greatness."

Precise dating of the construction of these early Great Houses is difficult because almost all the earliest structural material has been either remodeled or covered by the much more massive later Great

House buildings. Although there are early tree-ring dates from all three early Great Houses in Chaco Canyon, only Pueblo Bonito has more than a handful of dates between A.D. 820 and 950. We interpret the dates in a later section of this chapter, so here we offer only a basic summary. It appears that one segment of the early construction of Pueblo Bonito dates to the A.D. 860s but the main constructions at all three early Great Houses appear to date to the first decades of the tenth century. Two additional possible Great Houses, Kin Nahasbas and the East Community Great House, are also in the canyon, but they are only generally dated to late Pueblo I/early Pueblo II, based on their early architecture and ceramic assemblages. Another possible early Great House just to the west of the canyon, Casa del Rio, dates to the late ninth century, based on the associated ceramic types. Casa del Rio is a very impressive site in both the extent of the pueblo and its immense midden deposits (refer to figure 3.5) (Windes 2001a, chapter 3 of this volume).

Other nearby Great House sites with potentially significant late Pueblo I/early Pueblo II occupations include Pueblo Pintado, Kin Klizhin, and Kin Bineola. In the area immediately adjacent to Pueblo Pintado, Windes documented five Pueblo I small-house sites; interestingly, all five also had Pueblo III components (Marshall et al. 1979:86). At Kin Klizhin, the Chaco Additions survey recorded fourteen Pueblo I or early Pueblo II habitation components, ranging in size from three to ten rooms. At Kin Bineola, the Chaco Additions survey recorded twenty-two Pueblo I or early Pueblo II habitation components, ranging in size from three to fifteen rooms. Here, most of the Pueblo I roomblocks form a tight cluster surrounding a Great Kiva situated approximately 3 km south of the later Kin Bineola Great House. Several of the early Pueblo II roomblocks surround a nearby early Great House ceramically dated between A.D. 890 and 1130 and exhibiting Type 1 masonry (Van Dyke, ed., n.d.).

*Outside the Chaco Core: Pueblo I Elsewhere in the Southern San Juan Drainage.* Surprisingly, researchers have investigated few Pueblo I sites in the Southern San Juan drainage outside the Chaco core. As we have searched through state site records, published reports, and available Cultural Resource Management (CRM) reports and asked about the relative lack of sites, researchers have offered various reasons for the relative lack of Pueblo I sites, compared with the Northern San Juan. Some have noted that Pueblo I sites are difficult to find in this area because they are often buried by eolian deposits or covered by later site components. Others have suggested that the large block surveys in the Southern San Juan have been in areas with low probability of Pueblo I settlements (for example, the Navajo Irrigation Project survey blocks just south of Bloomfield) and that areas with higher potential for Pueblo I sites (that is, the Chuska slope) have not been adequately surveyed. Although both these arguments have some merit, the healthy representation of Basketmaker III and Pueblo II sites in this area reinforces the view that the relatively low number of Pueblo I sites is a real phenomenon. Also supporting this proposition is the evidence at the few relatively large Pueblo I sites that have been investigated in the Southern San Juan watershed.

One of the earliest investigations of a relatively large Pueblo I site was Earl Morris's 1932 Carnegie excavation of the Bennett's Peak Site (Morris 1959) on the Chuska slope approximately 50 km south of Shiprock. A number of tree-ring date clusters suggest possible construction episodes between A.D. 799 and 850. Because the samples are only generally provenienced to the site, however, dating the construction of specific structures is difficult. The site consists of a single roomblock of twenty-two contiguous rooms arranged in a double row. Earl Morris found numerous Pueblo I hamlets and villages in the Northern San Juan, yet we can attribute only three Pueblo I hamlets to Morris's various investigations south of the San Juan. The other two hamlets, Bennett's Peak Site 2 and the Mitten Rock Site (Bannister, Robinson, and Warren 1970:13, 19), are 5–16 km away from the site he did excavate, and they appear to be smaller early Pueblo I sites. None of these sites begins to approach the size of the smallest contemporary villages north of the San Juan.

On Tohatchi Flats, the El Paso pipeline project investigated several hamlets of approximately the same size as the Bennett's Peak Site. Red Willow Hamlet consisted of an arc of thirteen jacal rooms fronted by two deep pit structures. Ceramics and radiocarbon and archaeomagnetic dating suggest a range of A.D. 750–800/840 for this site. An earlier, underlying arc of six rooms dates to A.D. 725–775 (Loebig 2000).

Less than 1 km to the northeast, Flowing Well Hamlet contained a single pit structure dated by the same means to A.D. 750–830 (Loebig, Yost, and Van Dyke 2000). This pit structure was likely part of a larger settlement. At both sites, researchers did not identify Pueblo I structures before subsurface investigations. Also, because of the project's nature, they did not extend these investigations beyond the pipeline right-of-way to better define the Pueblo I components.

The Zuni Archaeological Program excavated another possible Pueblo I hamlet near Mexican Springs, 10 km southwest of Tohatchi. Here, at three multicomponent sites, researchers dated a total of six pit structures by means of ceramics and archaeomagnetism to periods between the early 700s and the late 800s (Damp 1999). It is entirely possible that larger Pueblo I settlements are present in the area of Tohatchi.

At Kin Ya'a (see plate 3, Kin Ya'a and Hosta Butte), just north of the Dutton Plateau, a single Pueblo I arc of six to ten rooms is present within a much larger and later Chacoan community (Tom Windes, personal communication with Van Dyke, 2003). Beyond the southwestern edge of the Red Mesa Valley is White Mound Village, which is in the West Puerco drainage close to the Arizona–New Mexico border (Gladwin 1945). White Mound Village may have had an approximate total of twenty-five rooms arranged in three roomblocks and as many as six pit structures. Tree-ring dates place its construction between A.D. 780 and the early 800s.

Although researchers have reported additional Pueblo I communities from the Southern San Juan, upon closer examination, many of these sites are dated between the late A.D. 800s and the mid-900s. The date of A.D. 950 is sometimes used as the end of Pueblo I in the Southern San Juan, which further conflates the issue. The overall pattern of an increase in Southern San Juan sites in the late 800s and early 900s fits our argument for a rapid and dramatic population growth after A.D. 880.

Marshall and Sofaer (1988:37–41) report that the Dye Brush community, in the area of Coyote Canyon, contains "many...early slab houses." No one has undertaken a complete inventory of this community, but Marshall and Sofaer assign it to A.D. 500–1050 on the basis of ceramics and architecture. Marshall and Sofaer speculate that this community may be associated with the Los Rayos Great Kiva, 4.5 km to the east and ceramically dated to the early A.D. 900s (Van Dyke 2003b). Just up Dye Brush Wash, a site in the Grey Ridge community contains seven pit structures ceramically dated between the late A.D. 700s and early A.D. 900s (Dennis Gilpin, personal communication with Van Dyke, 2003).

Along the Chuskan slope, the closest parallels to the large Pueblo I communities of the north are the Newcomb and Skunk Springs site clusters. Substantial multiroomblock Pueblo I/early Pueblo II occupations exist at both sites. In addition, at least one early Great Kiva exists at Skunk Springs, and up to three early Great Kivas at Newcomb (Gilpin, Dykeman, and Reed 1996; also, Marshall et al. 1979). The largest early rubble mound at Skunk Springs is an arc-shaped roomblock area 40 m long by 6 m wide (Marshall et al. 1979; compare with Powers, Gillespie, and Lekson 1983 for a more conservative evaluation). At both sites, considerable construction associated with late Pueblo II/early Pueblo III Great House communities limits the definition of the Pueblo I/early Pueblo II components. The dating of these early components is also confounded by relatively few well-dated late Pueblo I/early Pueblo II site assemblages from this area. As noted above, some scholars use the date A.D. 950 as the end of Pueblo I in this area (for example, Gilpin, Dykeman, and Reed 1996:figure 33), in contrast to the end date of A.D. 900. A best guess of these communities' early occupation date is between A.D. 875 and 950.

The only other significant, large Pueblo I communities west of Chaco are two late Pueblo I/early Pueblo II communities—Standing Rock and El Llano—along Indian Creek between Chaco Canyon and the Chuskas. Marshall and Bradley (1994) characterize these sites as Pueblo I, but the pottery-type frequencies listed in the site survey data are what we would expect in very late Pueblo I/early Pueblo II sites (A.D. 875–950). They also end Pueblo I at A.D. 950, later than the A.D. 900 end date used in the Northern San Juan. Windes's reinvestigation of these sites in 2003 confirms the dating of the main occupation to approximately A.D. 875–925. The Standing Rock community could have been quite large at approximately A.D. 900, with about twenty habitation sites containing three hundred to four hundred surface units. One roomblock has an estimated fifty rooms, and one complex of eight roomblocks within a 200×300 m area is reminiscent of the slightly earlier villages of the Northern San Juan. Most of these settlements, however, are dispersed over a 1-sq-km area, which is much too scattered for them to have functioned in the same manner as villages. Nonetheless, they are impressive communities for the early 900s.

In the Red Mesa Valley, far to the south of the Southern San Juan watershed on the south side of the Dutton Plateau, a number of small communities date from the late ninth and early tenth centuries (refer to figure 5.3). At the Andrews community, eleven roomblocks and two Great Kivas are ceramically dated between A.D. 880 and A.D. 940. These roomblocks average three to six rooms in size and appear to represent individual households dispersed across a 370-acre area (Van Dyke 1999a). The Fort Wingate community reportedly contains a substantial but undefined late Pueblo I/early Pueblo II component (Marshall et al. 1979:155). The Red Mesa Valley also contains several well-excavated, late ninth- and early tenth-century sites tested by Gladwin. Just beyond the southeastern edge of the San Juan watershed and with the East Puerco drainage, the El Rito community includes approximately ten Pueblo I/early Pueblo II habitations in a square kilometer (Powers, Gillespie, and Lekson 1983).

Between A.D. 800 and 875 the Southern San Juan had significantly less total population than the Northern San Juan. Not only are site sizes much smaller, but also the overall number of sites. With a few exceptions, the average site size in the south is a hamlet of two to three households. In the north, the majority of habitations are villages of at least fifteen households and often as many as forty or more. Yet, by the early A.D. 900s a clear population shift was underway, and people began the initial Great House communities in the Southern San Juan. We can understand these events only by comparing the settlement histories both north and south of the San Juan River for the ninth and early tenth centuries.

### Patterns of Population Density and Migration

The settlement histories of the Northern and Southern San Juan between Pueblo I (A.D. 750–900) and early Pueblo II (A.D. 900–950) exhibit several remarkable correspondences within the San Juan watershed. In early Pueblo I, both areas had dispersed distributions of hamlet-size settlements consisting of one to seven households. By the early ninth century, population increased significantly in the Northern San Juan. For this same period in the Southern San Juan, population was either stéady or declining. By at least A.D. 850 the estimated population of the central portion of the Northern San Juan (the Mesa Verde region) was approximately eight thousand people, whereas the Southern San Juan contained, at most, two to four thousand (Wilshusen and Ortman 1999:figure 2). The majority of the northern population is associated with villages having typical populations of approximately two hundred people. To the south of the San Juan, the largest hamlets of this time had approximately thirty people, and the typical site housed no more than five to ten individuals. No known comparable villages existed in the Southern San Juan in A.D. 850. Yet, the northern area appears to have been significantly depopulated by A.D. 900–925, at the very time that the earliest Great House communities were on the rise not only in the Chaco core but also along the Chuska slope and elsewhere in the Southern San Juan.

In interpreting the prehistory of the San Juan watershed, we want to emphasize three revisionist aspects: (1) the previous overestimation of Pueblo I population in the Chaco core, (2) the depopulation of much of the Northern San Juan in the late ninth and early tenth centuries, and (3) the growth of early communities around candidate Great Houses.

*Pueblo I in the Chaco Core.* The original site survey work in and around Chaco Canyon suggested that Pueblo I habitation site numbers were relatively high (Hayes 1981:75). Windes (ed., 1993:339–340), who was involved in the original survey, has argued that several factors may have biased the placement of sites in the Pueblo I category and overinflated the Pueblo I site count. He suggests that most sites dating to A.D. 875–950 could not be distinguished from earlier Pueblo I sites in the 1970s because of limited excavation experience with Pueblo I and early Pueblo II sites in the Chaco locale. These late Pueblo I/early Pueblo II sites (that is, the sites dating to A.D. 875–950) appear to represent an essential part of the total Pueblo I count, thereby creating the impression of a larger and more stable Pueblo I population in Chaco Canyon than was the case.

In addition, excavation data from the 1980s demonstrated that the presence of Red Mesa Black-on-white and neck-banded grayware pottery was more consistently associated with Chaco Canyon sites dated in the A.D. 900s. These pottery types, however, were previously taken as indicators of a Pueblo I occupation (Hayes 1981:19). It appears that the advent of neck-banded pottery was particularly late in Chaco Canyon and may postdate A.D. 875 (Windes, ed., 1993:tables 9.1 and 9.2). This date is surprisingly late when compared with other tree-ring-dated sites with this style of pottery in the Northern San Juan (Blinman 1988), where wide neck-banding appears as early as A.D. 775. Windes's suggestion that neck-banded gray ware may be a later introduction in the Southern San Juan is consistent with lower-than-expected frequencies of neck-banded and clapboarded sherds at Pueblo I sites dating to A.D. 890 just north of the San Juan River (Wilshusen and Wilson 1995:49–52).

Although notable Pueblo I communities of dispersed hamlets within the Chaco core may date to A.D. 800–850, their total populations cannot have comprised more than five hundred to a thousand. Outside the Chaco core, Pueblo I communities are less obvious but clearly present, especially at the edge of the Chuska slope and to the south of the Dutton Plateau. A comparison with the Northern San Juan is striking. There are thousands of known Pueblo I hamlets and almost forty documented villages, with the construction dates of at least forty-five of these hamlets and villages substantiated by clustered tree-ring dates (Wilshusen 1999). Some have argued that the relatively low numbers of southern Pueblo I residential sites are due to visibility problems, such as overlying eolian deposits, or to a lack of sufficient archaeological survey. These potential problems, however, cannot account for the lack of large communities in the south at A.D. 850, at the same time that there were more than twenty known, and many estimated, large village-based communities in the north.

*Tracing Population Movement in the Northern San Juan.* As archaeologists achieved greater temporal control over the history of the growth and decline of the Northern San Juan villages in Pueblo I, they increasingly had to look outside a particular locale to account for initial village population growth and migration destinations as the whole region lost population in the late ninth century. The place where several of us began the search was the area with the most significant cluster of late A.D. 890s tree-ring dates in the Northern San Juan, the area of the San Juan River now covered by Navajo Reservoir (Eddy 1966:table 7). Researchers in this area had already proposed an environmentally driven sequence of upstream migration along a single drainage over hundreds of years to deal with a proposed sequence of arroyo cutting (Eddy 1972, 1974). Using the large-scale, intensive archaeological surveys associated with the massive Fruitland Project and limited excavation of Pueblo I sites in areas to the west and south of Navajo Reservoir, we have been able to propose an alternative model of population movement to that proposed by Eddy.

Instead of population movements of tens of kilometers within a single drainage, we propose, the formation of villages in the Northern San Juan partially drew upon the influx of southern populations from as far as 100 km away. Migrants came with knowledge of the ceramics, architecture, and site organization typical of the Southern San Juan and the western periphery close to the Abajo Mountains (Wilshusen 1999; Wilshusen and Ortman 1999; Wilshusen, Sesler, and Hovezak 2000; Wilshusen and Wilson 1995). By examining population changes throughout the whole Northern San Juan, as well as considering that people from different cultural backgrounds may have immigrated to the region, we have been able to account for patterns seen at a much larger spatial scale (that is, the Northern San Juan) with much finer temporal precision (twenty to fifty years). With a database of more than 4,500 Pueblo I (A.D. 750–900) sites in southwestern Colorado (Wilshusen 1999) and more than 2,300 Pueblo I sites in northwestern New Mexico (ARMS file generated April 8, 1999), we have been able to place local changes into a regional context.

When people began to abandon the large villages of the Northern San Juan in the A.D. 880s and 890s, it should not surprise us that new communities with many traits of the northern villages began to appear close to the San Juan River (Eddy 1966; Wilshusen, Sesler, and Hovezak 2000; Wilshusen and Wilson 1995). Based on the small size of their middens and relative simplicity of their site plans and architecture, these late Pueblo I/early Pueblo II communities appear to be settlements that lasted no more than five to fifteen years. By the early A.D. 910s these late Piedra-phase communities of fifteen to forty habitations typically were burned down, with no signs of continuing habitation in the area. They appear to have served as halfway stations between the villages 40–50 km to the north that were abandoned in the A.D. 880s and locales throughout the Southern San Juan that show increased population in the early tenth century. A similar influx of population is also evident in southeastern Utah (Hurst and Till 2002:22).

*Early Candidate Great House Communities.* The interpretation that the Southern San Juan provided some of the burgeoning village populations of the early to mid ninth century and served as the ultimate destination for the tenth-century migrants is consistent with the proposal that migrants typically move to places about which they have detailed knowledge (Cameron 1995; Cordell 1995; Duff 1998). Several intensive block surveys in the Chaco core in the past fifteen years suggest that the number of sites dating to early Pueblo II is probably much higher than previously thought. Windes (n.d., chapter 3 of this volume) details the late Pueblo I/early Pueblo II Great Houses that came into being at Pueblo Bonito, Peñasco Blanco, Una Vida, Kin Nahasbas, and the East Community, as well as the nearby pueblo of Casa del Rio. He has documented the long-lived Fajada Gap community, which is associated with the beginnings of the Great Houses Una Vida and Kin Nahasbas. We have already mentioned the large sites and associated communities in the South Gap/Pueblo Bonito and Peñasco Blanco areas. All these Great Houses began between late Pueblo I and early Pueblo II, consistent with Windes's argument that habitations may have proliferated by the early A.D. 900s. Further reinforcing this suggestion is the presence of substantial late Pueblo I communities documented to the south of Chaco along the South Fork of Fajada Wash (Windes n.d., chapter 3 of this volume) and along the Kim-me-ni-oli and Kin Klizhin washes (Van Dyke, ed., n.d.).

For the sake of argument, if we associate thirty households with at least nine late Pueblo I/early Pueblo II (A.D. 875–950) communities in the wider Chaco Canyon area, a population of at least 1,350 inhabitants is reasonable. Although Chaco Canyon was not the center of early Pueblo II population, it clearly was a very prominent collection of communities. But the late Pueblo I/early Pueblo II communities in and around Chaco Canyon were not alone, as we will suggest later. Similar-size early Pueblo II clusters of communities were present along parts of the Chuska slope (Skunk Springs, Newcomb), along Indian Creek (Standing Rock, El Llano), in the Red Mesa Valley (Andrews, El Rito), close to the San Juan River, and possibly in the western part of the Northern San Juan in present-day Utah (Nancy Patterson, Red Bowl Ruin, Edge of the Cedars).

Many Southern San Juan communities exhibited significant growth in the early 900s. In both the Kin Bineola and Kin Klizhin communities, populations increased dramatically between the A.D. 700–880 and the A.D. 890–1025 periods (Sebastian and Altschul n.d.). At the Andrews community in the Red Mesa Valley, Van Dyke (2001) found that a population increase between the A.D. 880–920 and 920–960 periods strongly suggests that immigrants were joining the community.

What is striking about the present limited picture of the early tenth-century population distribution is that it resembles the distribution of later Great House communities (see Kantner and Mahoney 2000) as Chaco's influence was beginning to wane. Later in the chapter, we revisit these early Great Houses and examine their place in the landscape of A.D. 925.

### Why the San Juan River Divides Two Cultural Areas

When considering river drainage basins, we commonly think of them as a unified whole. Yet, in the case of the San Juan, the northern and southern aspects of the watershed have distinctly different characteristics. We must at least mention them here to place the disparate developments in the Northern and Southern San Juan areas into economic and ecological contexts. This may enable others to begin analyzing why populations may have been attracted to the possibilities of, or been pushed from, the north or the south at different times and in different circumstances.

The Northern San Juan has the southern Rocky Mountains along its northern and eastern edges and the Abajo Mountains and Elk Ridge to its west. These higher elevations typically receive more rainfall in the summer and more snowfall in the winter. The vast majority of Pueblo I sites in the north are in an elevational band between 1,829 and 2,134 m (6,000 and 7,000 ft), which typically receives 330–457 mm (13–18 in) of annual precipitation. This precipitation is almost equally divided between winter and summer, and a summer drought is quite possible even after a winter with plentiful snowfall. While average precipitation is adequate for growing corn at this elevational band, the average corn-growing-degree days are at the minimum of what is needed to mature maize (Adams and Petersen 1999:23–28). Agricultural lands with a favorable southern aspect or tilt, however, have a significantly higher chance of maturing a crop. Early and late summer frosts and cold air drainage further limit where horticulture can be practiced. In compensation, the region has excellent forests and wild plant and game resources.

The Southern San Juan, as we are defining it here, is circumscribed by the Chuska Mountains to the west, the San Juan River to the north, the Nacimiento and San Pedro mountains to the east, and the Red Mesa Valley to the south. The landscape and climate vary considerably across the south, so we will use the Chaco core as a locale to illustrate some of the differences from the north. It should be noted that the Chaco core has a very low annual precipitation (230 mm, or 9 in) but is favored with a late spring and summer-dominant precipitation pattern. Especially in wet years, 60–70 percent of the annual precipitation occurs between late spring and early fall. The majority of the Southern San Juan watershed is similarly in a summer-dominant rainfall pattern, whereas the Northern San Juan is almost entirely in a bimodal annual precipitation pattern. As a result, even though the annual precipitation in the Chaco area is about 60 percent of that in the uplands of the Dolores area, the effective summer precipitation may not differ, especially in wet summer years.

Cold air drainage and late spring or early fall frosts are a threat at Chaco, but the presence of large cliff faces appears to create microenvironments that are significantly warmer than the canyon bottom. These same cliffs and the mesas above them are well-known in the Chaco literature as potential sources of rainfall runoff that could be used in flood-water farming (for example, Vivian 1974). Although horticulture is certainly viable in the canyon, many other resources, such as wood, large game, and some wild plants, are not as plentiful as in parts of the Northern San Juan. Whereas visible mountains frame the boundaries of the Northern San Juan, more variable topography, including mountain ranges, mesas, and distant buttes, borders the Southern San Juan.

People would have regarded the landscapes of the Northern and Southern San Juan in discrete economic and historical terms. Even though maize horticulture is possible in both areas, success in the north is critically dependent on both winter and summer weather. In the south, the summer weather is critical. A series of difficult droughts in the A.D. 880s through the 890s (Schlanger and Wilshusen 1993:figure 7.3), with increasingly shortened growing seasons (Petersen 1994), appear to have contributed to the contraction of the potentially productive arable land in the north in the late ninth century. Alternative locales in the Northern San Juan were available for horticulture in this time of stress, but the areas favored for villages in the mid-800s were particularly vulnerable. These events must have contributed to the collapse of the Pueblo I florescence in this area. In contrast, above-average precipitation characterized the early 900s in Chaco Canyon, as well as much of the tenth century. During this same wet period, researchers conclude, people accumulated food surpluses and constructed the first true Great Houses (Sebastian 1992a).

## THE MATERIAL CORRELATES OF SOCIAL ORGANIZATION AND POWER: CHANGES IN NORTH AND SOUTH A.D. 875–925

Thus far, we have discussed Pueblo I/early Pueblo II developments to the north and south of the San Juan largely in settlement terms. Next, we summarize these comparisons and examine changes pertaining to social organization and power, focusing on the dramatic shifts in both population and power that occurred between A.D. 875 and A.D. 925. Scholars have regarded the Northern and Southern San Juan as representing separate phenomena, with little sense of significant interaction or the need for comparison—except during the mid-twelfth century. We argue that the interactions between north and south may have been quite substantial in the early tenth century.

### Site and Settlement Patterns

Changes in sites and settlements in the San Juan drainage basin progress very rapidly in the late ninth and early tenth centuries. We have focused on A.D. 875 and 925 in the Northern and Southern San Juan to illustrate how the fundamental shifts in site distribution and settlement organization compare and contrast in these regions over a fifty-year period.

*North and South in A.D. 875.* The Pueblo villages of the Northern San Juan were at their height in A.D. 875. The size of a village varied considerably; twenty-one villages in the Northern San Juan averaged forty-eight households, with a standard deviation of 32 (Wilshusen and Ortman 1999:table 1). The smallest may have had only twelve to eighteen households, and the largest more than eighty households (more than four hundred people). The large Pueblo I villages are surprisingly short-lived, typically lasting only thirty to forty years. In spite of this, some roomblocks in these villages are remarkably substantial. For example, the full masonry wall construction associated with McPhee Pueblo, one of the largest roomblocks at McPhee Village (Brisbin, Kane, and Morris 1988), reveals clear Type 1 Chaco masonry in its central arc. The architecture at many of these early northern villages must have been quite substantial during its use-life, but the heavy dependence on wooden roof supports, as opposed to load-bearing masonry walls, creates a more perishable and short-lived architecture than that found in slightly later Great House Chaco constructions (Wilshusen 1988a). The increased winter moisture in the Northern San Juan, combined with winter temperature fluctuations, probably created more havoc with exposed architecture than is the case in much of the Southern San Juan, such as at Chaco Canyon, with its much lower average winter precipitation. Finally, ethnographic examples suggest that social and economic issues make it difficult to maintain non-state villages for more than several decades.

Within the northern villages are usually one or two very large roomblocks 100–200 m long, with multiple pit structures. Much smaller roomblocks flank or surround them. The large roomblocks—especially those shaped like horseshoes and with well-defined plazas (see McPhee Village in figure 7.3a)—have distinctly larger pit structures associated with them, and these buildings have feature and artifact assemblages that suggest a central role in the performance of community rituals (Blinman 1988; Wilshusen 1986, 1988b, 1989). When people abandoned these villages in the last decades of the ninth century, they vacated these buildings in a very patterned manner, deliberately burning down the main ceremonial pit structures with ritual paraphernalia in place and with paired human burials entombed in nearby pit structures. A second type of Pueblo I village has long, relatively straight roomblocks (see Morris sites 33 and 13 in figure 7.3b) in place of the horseshoe-shaped roomblocks. These villages often have associated Great Kivas and histories that are distinct from villages such as McPhee. Instead of the relatively rapid abandonment at McPhee, we see a gradual abandonment of this second type of village, with the roomblocks falling into disrepair and many small "pocket" pit houses built throughout the village in the last decade of its occupation. These distinctive differences in village layout and abandonment constitute two of five lines of evidence that Wilshusen and Ortman (1999) used to argue that at least two cultural traditions were present in the large late Pueblo I villages of the Northern San Juan.

If we use settlement data for the Chaco core as a proxy for the Southern San Juan in A.D. 875, it is striking how much smaller all residential hamlets were than the contemporary Northern San Juan villages. Representative Chaco Canyon sites that date to the ninth century, such as 29SJ724 (see figures 7.5 and 3.11a) or 29SJ627 (McKenna and Truell 1986), contained approximately ten to fourteen surface rooms and one to two pit structures. The estimated number of households at these sites ranges from two to four. Hamlets such as these were a common settlement type in various locales of the Northern San Juan, especially between A.D. 750 and 850. More than twenty-five excavated hamlets with tree-ring clusters date their construction to this period (Wilshusen 1999:213–219), and more than forty other excavated hamlets clearly date to the Pueblo I period. Hamlets were present throughout all of Pueblo I, but villages with 15–130 households were increasingly predominant between A.D. 820 and 880 north of the San Juan. In contrast, small residential hamlets were the norm in Chaco throughout all of Pueblo I and into Pueblo II.

In Chaco at A.D. 875, only Pueblo Bonito or Una Vida could compare with some of the smaller contemporary villages to the north. Yet, construction was just beginning at these sites in the A.D. 860s, whereas the northern villages were established in the 840s. Later construction heavily altered the early components at both Pueblo Bonito and Una Vida, so reconstruction of the earliest components is a real challenge.

Many researchers agree that the earliest building segment at Bonito was the central portion of the three building segments (figure 7.6a) that make up Old Bonito (Judd 1964:58), but Windes and Ford (1996:300–301) emphasize that some of the earliest tree-ring dates come from the western wing of rooms. We propose that the A.D. 850s and 860s tree-ring dates are best tied to the construction of the central element and that the mid-ninth-century timbers in the west wing (Windes and Ford 1996:table 2) probably represent reused timbers from the remodeling of the pueblo's central portion and the west addition in approximately A.D. 920. The smaller size of the central arc of rooms mirrors what is typical of other Pueblo I hamlets in this area in the mid-ninth century. Chacoans used the rooms in this central area as burial crypts for very high-status individuals 150–200 years later, which suggests their fundamental importance in the Pueblo's history (Akins 1986; Stein, Ford, and Friedman 2003). Finally, over the course of many major remodelings of the Bonito roomblock, this central complex of rooms remains firmly set in the middle, almost perfectly bisected by the spine wall that divided the plaza into two halves by A.D. 1050–1070 (Stein, Ford, and Friedman 2003:figure 4.17).

We propose that at approximately A.D. 875 Pueblo Bonito had one large pit structure and a pueblo of approximately five to six household suites. While this site was much larger than nearby hamlets, it was much smaller than contemporary villages to the north of the San Juan. Not until approximately A.D. 925 did the "Old Bonito" construction become as large as one of the larger roomblocks within a large village such as McPhee. The hamlets in Chaco Canyon were clearly much less extensive than contemporary structures in the villages to the north.

*North and South in A.D. 925.* Between A.D. 875 and 925 site and settlement patterns for the Northern and Southern San Juan contrast markedly. Whereas a very large northern population was evident in A.D. 875, only a handful of Northern San Juan sites appear to date to A.D. 925. None of these later sites are anywhere near the size of a village such as McPhee. Archaeological researchers are always aware of sampling bias and difficult-to-date periods, but it seems increasingly evident that population decreased in many locales of the Northern San Juan between A.D. 900 and 940. For the A.D. 940–980 period, only five

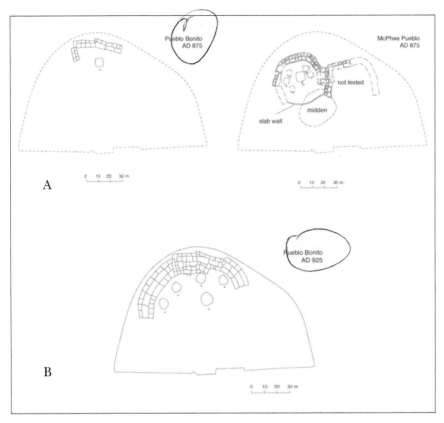

**FIGURE 7.6**

(a) *Plans of Pueblo Bonito and McPhee Pueblo, both around* A.D. *875. For size comparison, the dashed line shows the extent of Pueblo Bonito by* A.D. *1115 in both plans.* (b) *A plan of Pueblo Bonito around* A.D. *925. For size comparison, the solid enclosing line shows the extent of Pueblo Bonito by* A.D. *1115.*

well-dated sites exist in all of southwestern Colorado (Scott Ortman, personal communication with Wilshusen, 2003). Some settlements and sites in southeastern Utah and northwestern New Mexico and a few locales in southwestern Colorado may date to nearly A.D. 925, but most of these sites are documented by only relative chronological measures from survey records or limited excavations. By contrast, Chaco Canyon and many other areas of the Southern San Juan were booming in A.D. 925.

As documented in the preceding section, there appears to have been a major migration of northern population out of the arc of late Pueblo I villages and into an area close to the San Juan River by A.D. 890, as well as a migration, presumably southward, from these temporary communities by A.D. 920. This does not mean that the Northern San Juan was totally abandoned (see Coffey 2004 for documentation of tenth-century population in one northern locale), but it certainly played a much less powerful role in the Anasazi world during the tenth century. In fact, its role was so diminished that, at this point, archaeologists have difficulty defining what was occurring within the Northern San Juan. The exact opposite is the case for the Southern San Juan, especially the Chaco core.

By A.D. 920 Chaco had begun to emerge as one of the potential central places in the Southern San Juan. The eastern and western wings of Old Bonito were added in approximately A.D. 920–935 (see figure 7.6b and plate 5, vertical of Pueblo Bonito); the A.D. 850–860s dates in the western wing probably represent salvaged timbers from the original building. Plotting the distribution of all early cut dates for Old Bonito (Wills 2000:figure 2.9), it appears that the bulk of Old Bonito was built about A.D. 920–935, as originally proposed by Lekson (1984a:127–132). Well-dated and well-understood Pueblo I sites like Duckfoot demonstrate that, even in wood-rich areas such as the Northern San Juan, people incorporated a tremendous amount of salvaged or old wood into pueblos that may predate an actual construction date by ten to seventy years (Lightfoot 1994:figure 2.2). The A.D. 920–935 construction at Old Bonito clearly is at least two, some have argued three, stories high (Lekson 1984a:132; Stein, Ford, and Friedman 2003:44; Windes and Ford 1996:figure 4). This multistory construction may have begun as early as the A.D. 860s but is evident by the early tenth century with the remodeling of the central roomblock area and addition of the western and eastern sections. Possibly, the extremely small size of certain original rooms in the center may represent later subdivisions of rooms to place additional load-bearing walls within that portion of the building originally designed primarily as a one-story structure.

If we are correct, then not until about A.D. 920 did small, village-size sites appear on the Chaco landscape. Not until the Classic Bonito phase (A.D. 1040–1100) did these sites become as sizeable as the earlier Pueblo I villages to the north, even though some researchers still question whether a significant number of households ever occupied so many rooms (Bernardini 1999).

In contrast to the Chaco hamlets, the early tenth-century, multi-story construction projects in Chaco were quite impressive (Judge et al. 1981:81–84). The high degree of craftsmanship and the massive character of wall construction at the later Great Houses surpassed all other contemporaneous examples. The scale of Peñasco Blanco and Pueblo Bonito in the early tenth century was at least nine times larger than nearby canyon hamlets. As extensive as these sites were, they were still many times smaller in numbers of rooms and population than the largest five Northern San Juan villages in A.D. 860. Even if we add in the potential room areas represented by upper stories at early Great Houses, these structures remain smaller than the large northern villages. Yet, in other ways, these early candidate Great Houses were more imposing than the slightly earlier and larger villages of the north.

### Control of Local and Regional Resources

Discussions about the acquisition of social power by individuals or corporate groups have often focused on the control of resources. These can include developed resources such as parcels of arable land; natural resources such as timber, game, or potable water; and social resources such as human labor. Even though this issue is not at the core of our present investigations, we briefly examine the topic to understand how developments in the Chaco core in A.D. 925 are informed by events in the north, fifty years earlier.

The northern villages of the mid-ninth century represent a significant population, but nothing in the archaeological record suggests more than local control of local resources. It is evident that particular Pueblo I villages differed significantly in the resources they reasonably controlled. Villages were spaced to maximize their control of local resources, but not so distant or so distinct in size or construction to suggest fundamental differences in access to regional resources. If we look at particular resources such as the amount of potentially arable land, the degree of agricultural risk, and predicted agricultural surpluses for specific periods of time (based on our best models of prehistoric climate), we can see significant local resource differences among villages. These potential economic disparities may explain some of the variation evident in the villages' organization and architecture and even their abandonment sequences (Wilshusen 1991:156–199), but cultural and historical reasons may also account for the disparities (Wilshusen and Ortman 1999). Resource control was, at best, local; the largest Pueblo I villages do not appear to have assumed material or organizational leadership over other villages.

By contrast, past Chaco research has suggested that the beginnings of a regionally differentiated system might have emerged at Chaco by the tenth century (Judge et al. 1981:90–91). The construction of massive buildings in the Chaco core between A.D. 1025 and 1125 would have required access to imported timber, foodstuffs, and labor. Judge and others (1981) have argued that early Pueblo II Chaco construction and leadership were based on control of regional trade or redistribution networks.

Yet, the distinctive nature of the early Chaco Great House construction is not necessarily mirrored in the presence of excessive exotic materials such as turquoise or nonlocal shell in early contexts at Chaco. Some researchers have proposed that the exchange and trade of items such as turquoise and other exotic materials partially fueled the Chaco system at its height (Neitzel 1989; Schelberg 1984; Windes 1992). Others, such as Toll (1985, 1991), have pointed out that a huge number of nonlocal utilitarian items found in the canyon Great Houses eclipses the quantity of exotics. Whether trade was a cause or a consequence of Chaco's regional prominence by A.D. 1050, the manufacture and use of exotic materials does not appear to have been a prominent aspect of society before A.D. 925 (Mathien 1993:312, 2001; Windes, ed., 1993:387). Exotics may be as common or more common in the Dolores Pueblo I villages as they are at contemporaneous Chaco sites. In the Dolores Archaeological Program's database are at least 243 occurrences of ornaments, most of which are manufactured from rare stones or shell, with both a cache of beads or a single pendant fragment in a single provenience being equally considered an "occurrence" (Newland 1999:97).

One difference between Chaco in A.D. 925 and the Northern San Juan in A.D. 875 may be the Chaco core's potential to produce or manage food surpluses. Long ago, Grebinger (1973) suggested that water diversion and managed garden agriculture would have allowed significant surpluses as early as the Bonito phase. Judge and others (1981:79) doubted that this was the case, arguing that at the heart of Chaco's early success was a moister climate regime after A.D. 910, as well as reduced risk through pooling of resources. Gwinn Vivian (1990:308–313; Vivian 1974) has long argued that water management was an important aspect of developments at Chaco. For Sebastian (1992a), water control technology led to the creation of agricultural surplus, a critical factor in the emergence of leaders at Chaco. Recently, the importance of impounded water in Chaco's early development has gained a new dimension. Force and others (2002) have argued that until A.D. 900 or 920 a large area of ponded water extended from Escavada Wash up the Chaco Wash toward the area of "downtown" Chaco. The importance of water diversion and the possibility for agricultural surpluses call for much more intensive debate, but marked differences between the agricultural economies of the north and south may prove important to understanding Chaco's emergence as a regional power by the early eleventh century.

### Evidence of Ranked or Ritual Leadership and Changes in Social Organization

Although the general assessment is that the Dolores villages were basically egalitarian in their organization, it does appear that particular individuals or groups of individuals must have increasingly controlled political and ritual power (Kane 1989; Schachner 2001; Wilshusen 1991). These individuals may have occupied some of the largest and earliest-constructed horseshoe-shaped roomblocks within villages such as McPhee. These village societies probably had only two levels of organization, and evidence of this leadership may be identifiable archaeologically only when these leaders were associated with a village's failure instead of its success. For example, with the failure and abandonment of one of the most hierarchically organized villages, adult couples (male and female) were deliberately killed and buried in ritual contexts (Wilshusen 1986). We have consistently found these adult burials in pit structures that may have been controlled by particular corporate groups (Wilshusen 1989:103). These pit structures are identifiable by their special placement within the plaza and by the presence of particular ritual features within the structures.

Wilshusen and Ortman (1999) have detailed how ritual organization, abandonment, and other aspects of material culture differ between two contemporary, neighboring sets of Pueblo I villages. Among architectural distinctions is the presence or absence of Great Kivas, as well as striking differences in the layout of villages. Some have long, relatively straight roomblocks with poorly defined plazas; others have horseshoe-shaped roomblocks with clearly defined plazas. These and other material attributes led Wilshusen and Ortman (1999:391) to conclude that two distinct cultural groups were represented in the Dolores villages and to further suggest that the "ancestors of both Chacoans and Mesa Verdeans lived together and interacted intensively in the Dolores–Mesa Verde area in the late ninth century." It is possible that Chacoan-style Great House organization and later Mesa Verdean–style villages originated in different classes of Northern San Juan Pueblo I villages. If this is the case, then aspects of leadership evident in some of these Pueblo I villages should be present in the early Great Houses in Chaco Canyon. For example, the large horseshoe-shaped roomblocks in some villages almost always have a single over-sized pit structure with special ritual features such as a vaulted *sipapu* (sometimes called a "floor drum"). Substantial middens and other evidence suggest that these particular roomblocks hosted community feasts (Blinman 1989; Potter 1997).

By A.D. 925 people had completely abandoned the villages of the north, and the early Great Houses of the Chaco were approaching the size of the largest roomblocks within the abandoned northern villages. Early Great Houses at Chaco were much more dramatic in appearance than the earlier, northern village roomblocks. Two and possibly three stories in height, these early Great Houses must have presented an impressive sight, especially when compared with other residential structures in the canyon present by that time. Early Great House rooms were significantly larger than comparable rooms at other sites. These construction differences and the labor mobilization required to produce them hint at what later may have distinguished the rank or entitlement of particular individuals (Akins 1986; Akins and Schelberg 1984; Neitzel 1989; Wills 2000) or the households associated with them (Windes 1984a). The corporate or religious power materialized in these early Great Houses, however, is simply a more obvious expression of the social power evident in the principal roomblocks of some slightly earlier Pueblo I villages (Schachner 2002; Windes and Ford 1992). We argue that the remarkable Great Houses of Chaco, as well as the social dynamics that produced them, had historical precedent in the villages of the Northern San Juan.

The Great Houses of Chaco were not alone in A.D. 925, however. Other, similar structures were built during this era in Southern San Juan locales such as the Chuskan slope, Indian Creek, the Dutton Plateau, and the Red Mesa Valley. Therefore, the origins of Chaco must be tied to regional, not necessarily local, developments. Even though Great Houses were a dramatic new development on the Chacoan landscape, Great Kivas also appear to have been an important focus for many early tenth-century site communities outside the Chaco core, such as Andrews, Kin Bineola South, Red Willow, Skunk Springs, and Willow Canyon. By contrast, Great Kivas were of minimal importance in Chaco Canyon during this period; only three of the eighteen Great Kivas in Chaco Canyon (at Kin Nahasbas, Una Vida, and Pueblo Bonito) are dated to the 900s (Van Dyke 2003b). Social developments across the Southern San Juan during this period were varied, not uniform.

## THE RISE OF GREAT HOUSES: EARLY CANDIDATES AND LATER EVENTS

Scholars have offered several points of evidence to connect the Pueblo I and early Pueblo II histories of the Southern and Northern San Juan. First, 1970s and 1980s investigations of Basketmaker III and Pueblo I sites in Chaco demonstrated that, although Basketmaker III sites such as Shabik'eshchee Village were clearly important, the subsequent and sparse Pueblo I occupation in Chaco offered little hint of the large Pueblo II communities that would follow. Several researchers now suggest that the original site estimates for Pueblo I in the canyon were too high and that not until after A.D. 875 did habitation site numbers begin to increase dramatically in the Chaco area. Second, whereas Pueblo I habitations in Chaco Canyon were typically hamlets with one to four households, villages with average populations of forty-eight households were the norm in the Northern San Juan between A.D. 840 and 880. Although these villages are not impressive in some aspects, they are much larger than even the very large, early constructions at Pueblo Bonito or Peñasco Blanco. Third, an immense population lived in the Northern San Juan in A.D. 860, but much of this population moved south of the San Juan River or west of Montezuma Creek between A.D. 875 and 925.

All these points lead to the final proposal that the beginnings of Chaco had as much to do with its periphery as its core. As stated at the outset, understanding the origins of the Chaco regional system may be analogous to walking a maze. To reach the center, one must navigate the twists, turns, and cul-de-sacs of the perimeter. In late Pueblo I/early Pueblo II, there were early candidate Great Houses inside Chaco Canyon, in the uplands just north of the San Juan River, to the west along the Chuska slope and Indian Creek, and in the Red Mesa Valley. Some of these early candidates later became Chacoan Great Houses; others were never again reoccupied. We have traditionally viewed Chaco in the early 900s as the center for Great House development because we knew that Chaco would ultimately become the center of the maze. In the early A.D. 900s, however, this was not yet evident.

### The Definition of Early Great Houses

Early Great Houses date between A.D. 850 and A.D. 1000. An early Great House is typically associated with a Great Kiva at least 10 m in diameter, a large habitation site of six to twelve households, and a substantial midden. Such a site is not quite as large as a Northern San Juan village but is much larger than a typical hamlet. A Great House is the public center of a much larger community that—although clustered around the Great House—comprises many residences of one to three households dispersed over 1–2 km around the community center.

Whereas later Chacoan Great Houses are identified by specific formal architectural elements (for example, large rooms with high ceilings, blocked-in kivas, and core and veneer masonry) and associated monumental elements such as Great Kivas and "roads," pre-A.D. 1000 Great Houses do not necessarily have all these attributes (Mills 2002:81). Early Great Houses, however, may have some of the key functional attributes ascribed to later Chacoan Great Houses. Various scholars (Judge 1989; Sebastian 1992a; Varien 2000:155; Vivian and Hilpert 2002:111–113) have suggested that Chacoan Great Houses served as larger-than-average residences for small social groups and also as settings for ritual events. We propose that early Great Houses had the same functions, with a slightly different set of settlement and site characteristics. Early Great Houses served as a means for people to reimagine what "community" should look like after the large villages to the north failed. Instead of the aggregated setting of a village, a Great House was a center for rituals and feasting, where leaders sought alternative ways of organizing communities of one hundred to one thousand people. Certain sites persisted to become Chacoan Great Houses, and others lasted only one to two generations.

We have chosen to call these community centers "early" or "candidate" Great Houses to emphasize that no site or area in the late ninth through the mid-tenth century was yet part of a Chacoan regional system. If we acknowledge the large size, multifaceted organization, and substantial architectural features of the earlier Pueblo I villages of the Northern San Juan, it is difficult to conceive of these early tenth-century sites, even Old Bonito, as being "greater" than the villages that preceded them, even though they represent a different kind of community center than is evident in villages. Also, we want to emphasize that it was not evident until much later in the tenth century or possibly the early eleventh century that the early Great Houses in Chaco were more than *primus inter pares* among the other Great Houses in the Southern San Juan. This may seem a heretical view, but it makes perfectly good sense for someone looking forward from the ninth century, rather than looking back with the knowledge of what happened later in the eleventh century.

### Early Cases of Candidate Great Houses (other than Chaco Canyon)

Any Great House that potentially dates to the tenth century is noteworthy, but we focus on those sites that may date to A.D. 900–950. In two cases (Skunk Springs and Newcomb), the Great Houses are in locales that became some of the largest communities of the eleventh and twelfth centuries. In the two other cases (Cedar Hill), the sites are in late Pueblo I communities that people in the classic Chaco period did not reuse. We include the two sites that did not become Chacoan Great Houses, because later construction did not obscure their architecture. Although not as impressive as sites that later developed into Chacoan Great Houses, they have some essential features we expect at candidate

Great Houses dating to the late Pueblo I/early Pueblo II period. They also illustrate that the settlement organization and public architecture we expect at Great Houses predate the Chaco system.

At least ten to twenty Great Houses have significant late Pueblo I or early Pueblo II components, either under the Great Houses or closely associated with them (figure 7.7). Both the Skunk Springs and Newcomb communities have large Pueblo I occupations and are located on the eastern slope of the Chuska Mountains. This general area is about 75 km west of Chaco Canyon, and the sites are more than 50 km south of the San Juan River. We focus on the Chuskan sites because we see a clear tie between the Chaco and Chuska areas by the Classic Bonito phase. Some scholars have suggested that these later ties may extend to a common population in both areas (Toll 1991).

Skunk Springs has a late Pueblo I/early Pueblo II Great House that consisted of at least one large, arc-shaped roomblock, a Great Kiva, and a plaza that likely was enclosed (figure 7.8). This area was largely altered by the construction of a Chacoan Great House, which was built over it (Gilpin, Dykeman, and Reed 1996; Marshall et al. 1979). Numerous Pueblo I or early Pueblo II middens and a number of possible contemporary roomblocks are scattered across an area that may cover more than 2 km. The later Chaco-era community has numerous nearby residential sites, with a total of approximately 1,000 rooms and 160 kiva depressions within the settlement cluster. This large community overlooks one of the main drainages on the east side of the Chuska Mountains. It should be reemphasized that in the Chuska area some researchers divide Pueblo I and Pueblo II at A.D. 950 (Gilpin, Dykeman, and Reed 1996:figure 33) and that occupations a Northern San Juan investigator would term early Pueblo II (A.D. 900–950) are sometimes characterized as being late Pueblo I in this area.

The Newcomb community also has evidence of a substantial Pueblo I occupation, with at least two and possibly three Pueblo I-era Great Kivas (Gilpin, Dykeman, and Reed 1996). Earl Morris informally excavated in this area in the 1920s and 1930s. Later, Elizabeth Morris (1959) reported on at least one of the Pueblo I sites he dug a few kilometers north of the area. The later Chaco-era occupation of Newcomb appears to have been a slightly smaller community than Skunk Springs but is still one of the largest, documented, late Pueblo II communities

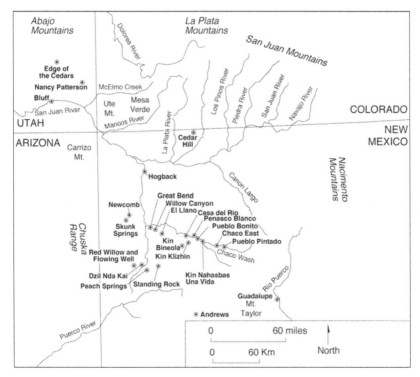

**FIGURE 7.7**

*Candidate Great Houses dating to A.D. 900–950.*

with a Chacoan Great House in the Southern San Juan.

A number of other sites with late Pueblo II Great Houses also have either late Pueblo I or early Pueblo II components. Houses or locales with more detailed recent studies include Andrews (Van Dyke 1999a, 2000), the Bluff Great House (Cameron 2002; Till 2001:59–60), Casa Abajo (Marshall et al. 1979:45–49; Windes n.d.), Cove (Reed and Hensler 2000), Edge of the Cedars (Hurst 2000), El Llano, or House of the Giant Midden (Marshall and Bradley 1994; Windes n.d.), Guadalupe Ruin (Durand and Durand 2000), Kin Bineola (Van Dyke, ed., n.d.), Peach Springs (Gilpin and Purcell 2000), and Standing Rock (Marshall and Bradley 1994). In addition, a number of Great House sites reported by Marshall and others (1979) have probable early Pueblo II components (for example, Dzil Nda Kai, Great Bend, and Hogback). Willow Canyon (Marshall et al. 1979:91–93; Windes n.d.) is

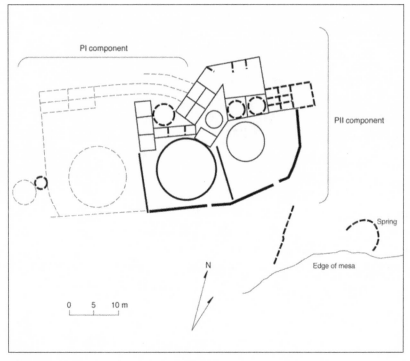

**FIGURE 7.8**

*Skunk Springs Great House, illustrating the Pueblo I and II components at the site.*

a late Pueblo I/early Pueblo II community with several odd slab and jacal structures, including at least one late Pueblo I/early Pueblo II candidate Great House, but this community was apparently abandoned by A.D. 950. Most of the Great House sites with earlier components have evidence of several large Pueblo I or early Pueblo II middens, one or more substantial early roomblocks, and potentially contemporaneous early Great Kivas. Few of these sites, however, have been extensively excavated, and investigations have rarely focused on the early components.

Documented near Cedar Hill in northwestern New Mexico are two potential early Great Houses in two late Pueblo I communities (Wilshusen and Wilson 1995). The sites were documented by intensive reconnaissance and limited excavation and dating of nearby sites within the largest community. Both sites have associated late Pueblo I Great Kivas, large associated trash deposits, and three to five roomblock areas. One candidate Great House is in the area of the confluence of the three major drainages in this valley and close to an important spring. The second is on a key prominence overlooking another major spring, as well as the upper portion of the valley. Even though both these sites are at the lower end of village size, the presence of monumental features—such as Great Kivas that appear to have been roofed—distinguishes them from other settlements in the community. To construct a workable roof on a Great Kiva with an estimated roof area of 270 sq m is no simple task; it requires massive-size timber and a very different architectural design than a conventional pit structure roof (Lightfoot 1988). In addition, although not villages, both these sites have four to five associated roomblocks and more substantial midden deposits than is common at other nearby sites.

More than thirty roomblocks are associated with each Cedar Hill community. In many ways, these early tenth-century settlement patterns are remarkably similar to later Chacoan Great House communities (figure 7.9). Based on roomblock size and assuming 80 percent occupancy of the sites, maximum community population for each community is estimated to have been 210 and 290 individuals. The residences and special use sites for each community were within areas of approximately 4 sq km. More than 70 percent of the residential structures in both communities had been burned down at the time of abandonment, and various lines of evidence reinforced an estimated primary occupation date between A.D. 885 and 915. In the largest community, two residential sites that were excavated because they were in pipeline right-of-ways had tree-ring date clusters that placed their construction to the A.D. 890s.

### The Need for Additional Documentation

Before the 1992 work in the Cedar Hill area, researchers had documented very few late Pueblo I sites in this area, and almost all the previously recorded sites had been dated only to the A.D. 700–1050 period. In other areas, the local temporal nomenclature assigns these early Great Houses to the Pueblo I period, so the fact that they are probably early Pueblo II Great Houses is unknown to the general researcher. Archaeologists are only beginning to have sufficient experience to recognize and interpret these late Pueblo I/early Pueblo II sites (for

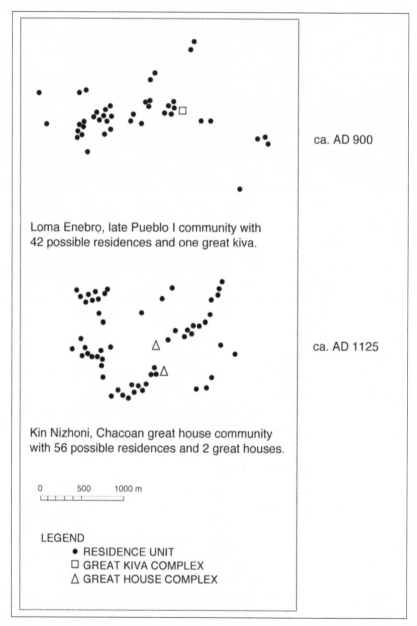

ca. AD 900

Loma Enebro, late Pueblo I community with 42 possible residences and one great kiva.

ca. AD 1125

Kin Nizhoni, Chacoan great house community with 56 possible residences and 2 great houses.

0       500     1000 m

LEGEND
● RESIDENCE UNIT
□ GREAT KIVA COMPLEX
△ GREAT HOUSE COMPLEX

**FIGURE 7.9**

*Cedar Hill (Loma Enebro) early Great House and its associated residential community, ca. A.D. 900, compared with Kin Nizhoni Chacoan Great Houses and their associated residential community, ca. A.D. 1125.*

example, Wilshusen 1995:119; Windes n.d.). Only ten to fifteen years ago, many of us would have misrecorded these communities as early- to mid-Pueblo I sites. The large-scale survey, excavation data, tree-ring results, and regional syntheses of the 1990s have revealed errors in our previous conceptions of what sites dating to A.D. 880–940 should look like. Unfortunately, the majority of our present examples of early Great Houses are at very complicated sites with later Chacoan Great Houses such as Skunk Springs and Pueblo Bonito. In northwestern New Mexico are a number of other potential early Great House sites, as well as some anomalous late Pueblo I/early Pueblo II villages, but information on these sites and the potential communities associated with them is still limited.

If we look at the locations of the presently known early Great House communities outside Chaco Canyon, they are either associated with or very near the locations of Chacoan Great Houses (Aztec, Skunk Springs, Andrews) that date approximately 150–200 years later. These Great House communities are in the sometimes better watered, more wooded uplands and mountain slope areas on the eastern, northern, and southern edges of the San Juan geologic basin. These same areas supplied much of the timber, lithic materials, pottery, animals, and other resources that were not so readily available in Chaco Canyon as its growth depleted its more limited resources. Many scholars have traced the beginnings of the later Chaco system to the Great Houses at Chaco Canyon. What if its beginnings were equally in the uplands above present-day Aztec, on the eastern slopes of the Chuska Mountains, and in the Red Mesa Valley? What if early Great Houses were competing in the A.D. 890s and early 900s for the immigrants from the villages that dissolved in the north? What if people revised rituals, formed different social organizations, and developed new settlement and subsistence patterns to address some of what had failed in the north of the San Juan?

If we accept almost any aspect of these scenarios, then early Pueblo II becomes a much less stable, much less composed, and much more interesting phenomenon. If the minimal population estimates offered for the clusters of late Pueblo I villages are even close and if the late Pueblo I migration from the Northern San Juan is as important as we and others have argued, then many Great House communities likely had inhabitants or first-generation descendants of inhabitants who, only a decade or two before, had lived in relatively close proximity to one another. They probably shared common rituals; at least several generations had a shared history. Given that many of the northern villages drew in population from the south and west of the central Mesa Verde region, is it surprising that many of these northern villagers were aware of a much larger Southern San Juan landscape? The last question, then, is why did many of these early Great House communities flourish when the earlier villages failed? Why was the Southern San Juan, and ultimately Chaco, so attractive?

As stated in the opening sections of this chapter, the Southern San Juan was a likely source for migrants who moved into the Northern San Juan during the late Basketmaker III and early Pueblo I periods. A century or more later, when migrants began to move back in the opposite direction, the Southern San Juan landscape was not merely an area of attractive resources. It was also a landscape of social memory, where ancestors had lived and died, where perhaps mythic events had taken place (Van Dyke 2003b). Peoples on the move are "pulled" to areas they know, to regions that hold significance for them in terms of kin ties or in terms of meaning and memory. Ancestral Basketmaker III sites such as Shabik'eshchee Village and 29SJ423 in Chaco Canyon dotted the landscape of the Southern San Juan. It is little wonder that early Pueblo II sites such as Chaco East and Peñasco Blanco were initiated literally in the shadows of those ancestral communities. But late Pueblo I migrants returned to many places throughout the Southern San Juan, not just to Chaco Canyon. Social memory alone cannot account for the unique developments that followed at Chaco.

At Chaco Canyon, early Pueblo II populations found a landscape that not only reverberated with memory but also resonated with aspects of a Pueblo worldview that seemed to be very ancient, including notions of center place, dualism, and balance. Situated between two geologic zones, at the center of the San Juan Basin, with prominent topographic features and far-reaching vistas, Chaco Canyon was a sound choice for an *axis mundi*. A unique and powerful combination of resources, rituals, and beliefs at Chaco led to the rise of truly Great Houses during the eleventh century (Van Dyke n.d.b).

## CONCLUSION

Why did Great House communities succeed and formative villages fail? This question is too big to answer here, but it is important to ask. Early Great House communities contain the historical answer to the question of why formative villages failed. Wilshusen and Wilson (1995) suggested that early southern Great House communities "reformatted" the social landscape from what had been typical in the northern villages. By "reformatting," we meant that the ways in which people organized their society, performed their rituals, and made their living from the land in the Southern San Juan differed sufficiently from those of the Northern San Juan that this represented a fundamental cultural change. Comparing the north and south is all it takes to understand the extent of these changes.

As we have noted, the northern A.D. 875 and southern A.D. 925 communities had tantalizing differences, even though many people who lived in the later southern communities may have been direct descendants of the slightly earlier northern villages. For example, settlement strategy shifted from the northern aggregated villages of fifteen to eighty households in three to twelve closely aligned roomblocks covering, at most, 0.2 sq km (ca. A.D. 860) to more dispersed southern communities of twenty to forty small habitations across a landscape of 4–6 sq km. In many cases, these southern communities were centered around a Great House consisting of a larger-than-average roomblock with an associated Great Kiva (ca. A.D. 910). The locus of community ritual performance changed from an oversized (35–75 sq m) pit structure and associated plaza in some northern villages to a Great Kiva (80–250 sq m) in some of the early Great House communities. Great Kivas appear to have been important centers of early 900s southern communities such as Andrews, Kin Bineola, and Red Willow but did not become popular in the Chaco core until the mid-eleventh century. Other changes in subsistence practices (such as increasing dependence on controlling the delivery of summer rainfall runoff to agricultural plots) and possibly interhousehold economic organization occurred, suggesting widespread changes from A.D. 875 to 925. These kinds of changes are not uncommon in migrant groups and often result in new and pluralistic social identities in communities with significant migrant populations (Stanfield 1996; Waters 1995).

What must be emphasized here is that the way in which communities operated, the scale at which people imagined their potential communities, and the possibilities for power all functioned increasingly at a regional, as well as local, scale. To survive and succeed, communities required knowledge of what was occurring 30–60 km away. There were simply too many people with too many historical ties after Pueblo I to expect that any single cultural group could live in isolation. Early forms of Great Houses are potentially much more widespread than previously thought and are the likely centers of community cooperation and contest. Yet, the individuals in communities probably "imagined" their communities (Isbell 2000) as being much larger than the landscape immediately surrounding their residences. How Chaco became the symbolic center of this larger landscape is a question for eleventh-century data. We hope that this chapter offers a better understanding of the forces at play during Chaco's beginning in the tenth century.

The experience in manipulating corporate power (Schachner 2002), the potential for progressively more networked, regional ritual leadership (Ware and Blinman 2000; Ware 2001, 2002a, 2002b), the selective use of violence (LeBlanc 1999), and potential variations in agricultural strategy and labor organization (Peregrine 2001; Vivian 1990) are evident in village settings but are not sufficient to hold villages together in hard times (Dean 1996). These very changes also suggest reasons for the ultimate transformation of early Great Houses into Chacoan Great Houses as they competed on this increasingly connected regional landscape. Moreover, the changes suggest that many more "candidate Great Houses" existed than we might have expected and that the emergence of Chaco Canyon as a regional power center must have a much more interesting history than we have recognized.

### Notes

Tom Windes kindly offered some seed money to Wilshusen to fund initial work on the research in this chapter more than three years ago. We are glad to reward him, finally, with a paper. Go get 'em Tom! Let us know where we are wrong. Wilshusen's colleagues at La Plata Archaeological Consultants, the University of Colorado, and Crow Canyon Archaeological Center influenced elements of the work included in this chapter. Van Dyke is indebted to Jonathan

Damp, Dennis Gilpin, Bob Powers, Tom Windes, and the Farmington WCRM office for some of the data discussed here. Cathy Cameron, Grant Coffey, Steve Lekson, Bill Lipe, Joan Mathien, Curtis Nepstad-Thornberry, Scott Ortman, Greg Schachner, Jonathan Till, Wolky Toll, Gwinn Vivian, and Tom Windes commented on an earlier draft of this chapter. These comments were incredibly thoughtful and made revision of that original draft much more straightforward. We thank these friends for their aid, while not implying that they necessarily agree with the interpretations in this chapter.

# 8

# Notes from the North

## William D. Lipe

As I understand it, my role in the Chaco capstone effort is to serve as a "synthetic scholar" (presumably as opposed to the authentic ones who really know something about Chaco) who can comment on the Chaco phenomenon from the vantage point of an adjacent area, in this case, the Northern San Juan or Mesa Verde region (figure 8.1).[1] I address four topics here. First, I discuss how the developments centered at Chaco Canyon employed architectural symbolism derived from some basic cultural patterns widely present in both the northern and southern portions of the San Juan drainage.[2] Wilshusen and Van Dyke (chapter 7 of this volume) develop aspects of this theme in greater detail. Second, I provide some archaeological context for the expansion of the Chacoan Great House system north of the San Juan, including what succeeded it there. Third, because I have been given an opening, I add my two cents worth on how the Chaco system might have worked during its florescent period, from about A.D. 1040 to 1135. This is the period in which Great House building projects grew in scale, Great House architecture became much more formalized and elaborate, Chacoans imported large quantities of construction timbers and

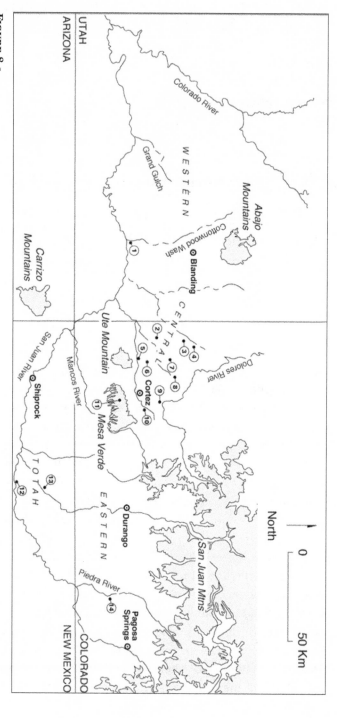

**FIGURE 8.1**

The Northern San Juan or Mesa Verde area, showing the Western, Central, Eastern, and Totah regions. The central Mesa Verde region extends approximately from the Mesa Verde proper in Colorado to Cottonwood Wash in Utah. Locations are indicated for selected sites mentioned in the text: (1) Bluff, (2) Seven Towers, (3) Lowry, (4) Ansel Hall, (5) Castle Rock, (6) Sand Canyon Pueblo, (7) Albert Porter, (8) Yellow Jacket, (9) Escalante, (10) Lakeview Group (Wallace, Ida Jean, Haney), (11) Far View, (12) Salmon Ruin, (13) Aztec Group (Aztec West, East, and North; Hubbard Site), and (14) Chimney Rock.

other materials into Chaco Canyon and Aztec, and numerous communities occurring over a very large area of the upland Southwest built Chaco-style Great Houses. Fourth, I comment on whether the Chacoan sociocultural system or something like it continued to be important in the Northern San Juan after the early A.D. 1100s.

## CHACO ARCHITECTURAL SYMBOLISM AND THE SAN JUAN CULTURAL PATTERN

What I am calling the "San Juan pattern" is a complex of architectural and settlement layout characteristics that developed in the San Juan drainage in the A.D. 600s and 700s and lasted until the late 1200s. The pattern extended into adjacent portions of the Little Colorado drainage before the Chacoan expansion but does not appear to have persisted in those areas after the middle or late A.D. 1100s. Several characteristics of Chacoan Great House architecture and settlement layout appear to be elaborations on the San Juan pattern. In the period of Chacoan florescence, these elaborated versions helped provide symbolic support for a new, more complex social order by connecting it to historically well-established and widespread architectural and cultural traditions.

The basic, widespread version of the San Juan pattern includes the following: Prudden units, north-south orientation at several scales, and kivas great and small.

### Prudden Units

From the A.D. 700s through the 1200s, most people in the San Juan drainage lived in relentlessly modular habitation units (Bullard 1962), each of which was occupied by a nuclear or small extended family-based household. Architecturally, the habitation unit includes (a) a single domestic pit structure (usually called a "protokiva" in the Pueblo I period and a "kiva" in Pueblo II and III), (b) a small (five to ten rooms, on average) block of usually contiguous surface rooms of jacal or masonry located just north or northwest of the pit structure, and (c) a midden area located south or southeast of the pit structure. Sometimes the surface rooms are divided into larger, general-purpose "living" rooms and smaller, more tightly built storage rooms. Associated with the habitation unit are burials located in the midden area and/or within abandoned structures. In multi-unit roomblocks, middens usually extend the length of the roomblock, indicating that individual households continued to deposit trash directly in front of their own habitation unit. Lacking are cemeteries that serve whole communities or particular groups of households within communities.

Scholars sometimes refer to San Juan–pattern habitation units as "Prudden units," after T. Mitchell Prudden, who recognized them early in the twentieth century. He called them "unit type pueblos" (figure 8.2; see figures 1.4 and 3.11) and noted that they could occur as individual small sites but also as the basic residential modules within roomblocks or house clusters in larger sites (Prudden 1903, 1914, 1918). Household-based habitation units composed of a pit structure and a few surface rooms occurred with some frequency in other parts of the upland Southwest before the A.D. 1000s or early 1100s. Outside the San Juan drainage, pit structures/kivas tended to decrease in frequency after that time and to be associated with multihousehold roomblocks or whole settlements rather than with specific habitation units. By contrast, in the San Juan drainage the kiva remained a central structure at the household level and evidently had domestic, as well as ritual, functions until the end of Puebloan occupation in the late 1200s (Cater and Chenault 1988; Lekson 1988b; Lipe 1989; Lipe and Varien 1999b). Gilman's (1987) ideas about a "pithouse to pueblo" transition are therefore more applicable outside the San Juan region than within it.

### North-South Orientation at Several Scales

Architectural and settlement layouts exhibit a strong north-south or northwest-southeast orientation. The habitation unit faces south, more or less. The pit structure (that is, protokiva or kiva) is bilaterally symmetrical relative to an approximate south-to-north axis extending through the ventilator, deflector, fire pit, and *sipapu* (if present). Occasionally, a niche in the pit structure's north wall also lies on this axis, although there may be niches that do not. Often, though not always, an extension of the axis that is grounded in the pit structure approximately bisects the block of associated surface rooms. The midden area usually lies south or southeast of the pit structure, also (more or less) on the axis established by the pit structure's floor features. When habitation units are strung together into larger roomblocks and

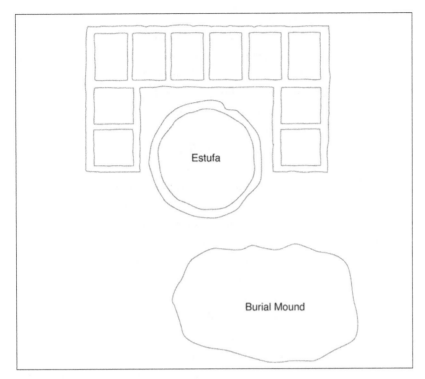

**FIGURE 8.2**

*Prudden's "unit type" pueblo. The feature labeled* estufa *is now called a "kiva." (After*
*Prudden 1903:235)*

when habitation units and/or roomblocks are clustered into villages,
all these larger entities remain "front-oriented," to use Erik Reed's
(1956) term. That is, they face approximately south. Trash and evidence of outdoor use areas are very sparse just north of the surface
architecture, whether the settlement consists of a single habitation, a
roomblock of multiple habitation units, or a large aggregated village.

The directional orientation of San Juan sites, therefore, is expressed at the scale of the habitation unit, the roomblock, and the settlement. I believe that it has a strong symbolic referent, although I do
not know the specific meanings associated with it. In any case, the layout and orientation of San Juan habitation units and settlements in the
period A.D. 700 to 1300 are distinctive relative to the patterns found
at other times and places in the Puebloan Southwest.

### Kivas Great and Small

In the San Juan pattern, structures and features having probable symbolic/ideological importance are present at both household and suprahousehold levels. At the household level, Pueblo II and III kivas (and, to some extent, earlier Pueblo I protokivas) show a greater degree of architectural investment and formality than do associated surface rooms, in addition to establishing the habitation unit's north-south axis of bilateral symmetry (for Chaco examples, refer to figure 3.12). The fully or partially subterranean character of these structures, their roof entries, and the frequent occurrence of a sipapu north of the fireplace likely symbolize the universal Puebloan belief in the emergence of humans and other forms of life from a series of worlds lying below the present one. Wilshusen (1989) demonstrates that vault features, which occasionally occur either flanking or north of the fireplace in these pit structures, are related to sipapus and are likely to have similar symbolic/ritual associations. Functionally (no historical connection is implied), San Juan household protokivas and kivas resemble historic Navajo hogans: they are built to a mythologically grounded prescription and therefore express particular religious concepts, they are the core structure in a set of residential facilities used by a household, and they are the appropriate facilities for certain kinds of religious ceremonies. Kidder (1917) was so impressed with the frequency of small kivas at sites in the San Juan drainage that he used the term *kiva culture* to refer to the Pueblo II/Pueblo III period sites of that area. It is arguable, though not demonstrated, that a few of the small, San Juan–pattern kivas at some large sites (such as the late Pueblo III village Sand Canyon Pueblo) were nonresidential and had more specialized, probably ritual, functions (Bradley 1993; Lipe and Ortman 2000).

In the San Juan drainage, several types of public (or better, civic) architecture also occur.[3] Through time, Great Kivas were the most common such structures, but, as noted below, other types of civic architecture eclipsed them in frequency in the A.D. 1200s. San Juan–pattern Great Kivas clearly repeat the symbolic-ideological references of household kivas, including extending below the ground surface, having bilateral symmetry around an approximate north-south axis, and containing lateral vaults or other pit features related to sipapus (for Chaco examples, refer to figure 3.10). Like household kivas, they are fully enclosed and therefore not "public"—that is, activities taking place there would not have been visible to people unless they had been permitted to enter the structure. Spatially, Great Kivas are usually associated with particular communities (whether or not these communities are more dispersed or more aggregated). Not all communities have one, and they are rare or nonexistent in areas of low population density. The spatial patterning of their occurrence suggests that people from individual communities or clusters of small communities built and maintained them. Great Kivas are not closely associated with particular household-habitation units or roomblocks and are ordinarily located apart from other structures (with notable exceptions at some Chacoan Great Houses).

Lightfoot (1988) estimates that a 22-m-diameter, Pueblo I period Great Kiva located at the Grass Mesa Site in southwestern Colorado could have been built in five to six weeks by forty adult laborers working forty to fifty hours a week. This amount of effort is much greater than a single household could have supplied but is quite feasible for a community of twenty or more households. Alternatively, sodalities or other nonresidential groups possibly participated in the construction or use of Great Kivas.

Great Kivas appeared in the San Juan area as early as the A.D. 600s and occurred through the late 1200s, although with decreasing frequency after the mid-1100s (Churchill, Kuckelman, and Varien 1998). Great Kivas also occurred widely in the upland Southwest outside the San Juan drainage, but it is my impression that these examples generally lack San Juan–type floor features and orientations. Great Kivas persisted in the Northern San Juan until the area was depopulated in the late 1200s.

After about A.D. 1300 this long-lived architectural form apparently survived only in the northern Rio Grande area. In the Classic period (A.D. 1325–1600), there are a few occurrences of large kivas, generally in association with plaza-oriented pueblos. Both circular and rectangular plans are present, and all appear to fall near the lower end of the 10–25-m size range of the Great Kivas surveyed by Vivian and Reiter (1960:84). For example, Creamer (1993:104) reports that Kiva J at Arroyo Hondo dates to the early A.D. 1300s and has a diameter of 10.5 m. Vivian and Reiter (1960:105–106) mention several Classic-period Rio Grande kivas with diameters of 10–14 m (also see Wendorf and Reed 1955:152). Floor features and orientations are variable and do not clearly replicate earlier San Juan patterns. For the historic period, Ellis (1950) notes that many Rio Grande pueblos had one or two "big kivas" used for communitywide events. Examination of the 1948 aerial photos and maps published by Stubbs (1950) indicates that a number of twentieth-century Rio Grande Pueblo "big kivas" exceed 10 m in diameter.

For other areas of the Southwest, E. C. Adams (1989, 1991) argues that, during the A.D. 1200s, central plazas replaced Great Kivas in aggregated settlements located in the Little Colorado drainage. He also shows how plaza-oriented villages became the norm in both the Rio Grande and the Western Pueblo area in the late 1200s and early 1300s. Kintigh, Howell, and Duff (1996) report that circular, unroofed Great Kivas occurred in the Zuni area in the A.D. 1200s but note that they did not persist after 1300, when large, plaza-oriented villages became standard. Overall, the decline of the Great Kiva as an element of civic architecture appears related to the emergence and spread of the plaza-oriented village pattern.

### Chacoan Architectural Symbolism

The main point here is that, for at least five or six centuries, San Juan households and communities employed in their architecture and manner of spatial arrangement a set of powerful symbols, at least some of which referred to widespread emergence/creation beliefs. The architectural patterning of habitation units indicates that individual households had substantial control over the use of these symbols and probably the religious rituals connected with them. This "spiritual independence" may have facilitated settlement pattern flexibility and mobility at the household level and may have also made communities fragile and prone to fission. Over most of the period involved, the typical settlement pattern was one of dispersed households living individually or in small hamlets of several households located near agricultural fields. Communities are recognizable as loose clusters of these dispersed habitations; some have an identifiable "center" consisting of a Great Kiva, a Great House, a denser concentration of habitation units, or combinations of the above. Only episodically in the Northern San Juan (that is, in late Pueblo I and late Pueblo III) do we see communities that are coterminous with a densely settled village (Lipe 2002b;

Lipe and Ortman 2000; Lipe and Varien 1999b; Varien 1999; Varien et al. 1996).

What does this have to do with Chaco? It appears to me that the builders of the Chacoan Great Houses took widely used and long-held San Juan conventions of architecture and layout and made them much more formal and much larger-scale. This process of formal elaboration characterizes Great House architecture throughout but is significantly amplified in what I am calling the period of "Chacoan florescence," from about A.D. 1040 to 1135. It is also most pronounced at the major Great Houses in Chaco Canyon and at the Aztec and Salmon sites in the Totah region. Even in this period, Great Houses remained clearly connected to both contemporary and earlier architectural and symbolic conventions that occurred widely in the San Juan drainage. Thus, the occupants of the Great Houses were symbolically linking themselves to the widespread belief system and mode of social organization represented by the San Juan pattern.

If we see Chacoan Great Houses as greatly enlarged and elaborated San Juan–type roomblocks, the number of "regular"-size kivas becomes a better measure of the number of households present in a Great House than is the number of surface rooms. That is, the large size of Great Houses results primarily from a big increase in the number of aboveground rooms associated with each household and, generally, in the size of these rooms. A Great House having multiple, regular-size kivas is equivalent to a roomblock formed by multiple (undoubtedly, related) households in a "regular" San Juan site. The Great Houses, however, have many more surface rooms per kiva (Lipe 1989; Van Dyke 1999c).

In addition to an overall increase in the scale, formality, and elaboration of architecture, as well as in the abundance of surface rooms relative to kivas, Great Houses depart from the San Juan pattern in several other ways. First, although kivas are generally located south of the main mass of surface rooms and the house itself is oriented toward the south, the south-to-north patterning of pit structure versus rooms is not as clear or regular. Second, individual Prudden units, consisting of a pit structure and a distinguishable block of spatially associated surface rooms, are often harder to identify. Third, middens are placed relative to the Great House as a whole (rather than to specific habitation units), are more formally bounded, are generally located at a greater distance from the architectural elements than is the case in the San Juan pattern, and are often part of a system of constructed earthworks or berms surrounding the Great House (Cameron 2002). Fourth, Great Kivas are sometimes included within the larger Great Houses, making access to them more restricted. Overall, Great House architecture and layout suggest both greater functional differentiation and integration than is the case for the structurally simple and relentlessly modular "ordinary" San Juan roomblocks.

The architectural symbolism associated with Chacoan polities is likely to have been rooted in beliefs and symbolic systems that were widely held through most of the San Juan drainage and that long preceded the Chacoan florescence of ca. A.D. 1040–1135 (compare with Wilshusen and Van Dyke, chapter 7 of this volume). Evidently, people began to build Chacoan-style Great Houses in areas south of Chaco Canyon before A.D. 1040 (Kantner and Kintigh, chapter 5, and Duff and Lekson, chapter 9, of this volume), but the distribution of Great Houses reached its maximum extent during the florescent period. Although the Great House system flourished primarily in areas where the San Juan pattern was already established, Chacoan Great Houses and whatever religious ideology they represented also appeared in some communities that did not share that pattern.

The principal example in the Northern San Juan is at Chimney Rock, near the Piedra River in southwestern Colorado (Eddy 1977, 1993). The Chimney Rock Great House is very Chacoan in architectural details and layout, but the surrounding community is represented by "crater houses" (Eddy 1977; Kane 1993). These are large, more or less circular, aboveground masonry structures with walls that are often more than a meter thick. They lack standard kiva features and often have one or two small, adjoined, surface masonry rooms with thin walls. Also, there is a thick-walled Great Kiva that lacks San Juan–style floor features. The architecture and associated pottery of these structures suggest possible relationships to the Largo-Gallina cultural tradition of northern New Mexico (Breternitz 1993a; Kane 1993).

The notion that the builders of the Great Houses at the major Chacoan centers appropriated older and widely held architectural symbols does not imply that the social transformations of the Chacoan florescent period were minor or gradual—nor that the occupants of the small, outlying Great House communities had social prerogatives and interests identical to those of the major Great House centers. The use of familiar symbols representing widely held beliefs may have facilitated development of the labor-intensive institutions and practices from which a new, more hierarchical, and more differentiated social order emerged (practices such as the long-distance transport of timbers, pottery, and maize; construction of Great Houses and roads; development of new ceremonies; and hosting of pilgrims). In the process, new "memories" of what the Great Houses represented could have been constructed to facilitate both the inclusion of people from different communities and the delegation of ritual/political authority to certain kin groups. As Pauketat (2001:6) notes with respect to recognized cultural patterns, "the 'deep' thematic qualities that lend an appearance of cultural persistence also [make] the myths, icons, or cosmological themes especially effective political symbols to be displayed, manipulated, and co-opted by social movements or astute politicians" (also see Pauketat and Alt 2003; Van Dyke and Alcock 2003).

## THE ARCHAEOLOGICAL CONTEXT OF CHACOAN GREAT HOUSES IN THE NORTHERN SAN JUAN

The expansion of Chacoan Great House architecture into the Northern San Juan was rather late relative to other regions of the Southwest and also included the construction—at Salmon and Aztec—of the largest Great Houses outside Chaco Canyon proper. In the post-Chacoan period, the architectural and community patterns of the Northern San Juan diverged in some ways from those developing elsewhere. These topics are briefly explored below.

### Patterns in the Northern San Juan

As noted, Chaco-related Great Houses appeared earlier south and southwest of Chaco Canyon than north of the San Juan. Some southern Great Houses predate the period of Chacoan florescence. The expansion of Chaco influence into the Northern San Juan (Mesa Verde) region appears to be primarily and perhaps entirely in the latter part of the florescent period, after about 1075. Given the cultural and historical similarities between Chaco and the communities of the Northern San Juan, why this area lagged as a focus of Chaco attention is unclear. Demographic factors may have been involved. Recent population estimates indicate that the Northern San Juan regional population dramatically declined in the A.D. 900s and did not start growing rapidly again until the mid to late A.D. 1000s (Kohler et al. 2005; Ortman, Varien, and Spitzer 2003).

Accompanying the expansion of the Great House system to the north is the construction of several large Great Houses (Salmon Ruin and Aztec West) in the Totah region that rival those of Chaco Canyon in size and elaboration (figures 8.3 and 8.4). (The Totah is the part of the Northern San Juan that includes the lower Animas and La Plata River valleys and the adjoining San Juan River valley in northwestern New Mexico [McKenna and Toll 1992]). Salmon Ruin, a pueblo of 275–325 rooms (see figure 8.3), was largely built in several construction events well dated by tree rings to between A.D. 1090 and 1094 (Paul Reed, personal communication 2004). Aztec West (see figure 8.4) was constructed in two bursts of activity between A.D. 1112 and 1125. It is the largest building in a complex of contemporaneous sites that stretches for two miles along the terrace above the Animas Valley and that includes several Great Kivas and at least one other, unexcavated, massive Great House of the florescent-period Aztec North (Brown, Windes, and McKenna 2002; McKenna and Toll 2001). Brown, Windes, and McKenna (2002) interpret the ceramic associations of the site complex on the Animas terrace near Aztec West to indicate that construction of Aztec North and other terrace sites probably pre-date Aztec West by a generation, making them approximately contemporaneous with the Primary building phase at Salmon Ruin. The construction of Salmon Ruin and the Aztec complex arguably represents a shift in the main seat of Chacoan ceremonial and political power from Chaco Canyon to the Totah (Judge 1989; Lekson 1999).

Lekson (1999) argues that the location of the Aztec complex was approximately due north of central Chaco Canyon intentionally, to fall on the "Chaco Meridian," which he sees as having formed the symbolic axis of the Pueblo world for several centuries. The "great north road" out of Chaco traces this connection partway. The construction of the Aztec complex thus makes this a "road through time" that physically symbolizes a historical connection between the two major centers. John Fritz (1973) pioneered the idea that the Chacoans located settle-

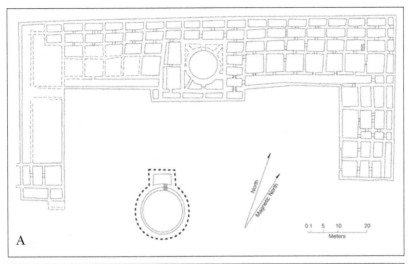

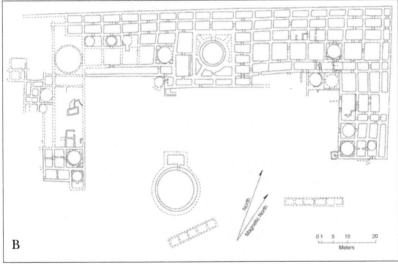

**FIGURE 8.3**

(a) *Salmon Ruin, Primary Construction Phase III, early* A.D. *1100s (after R. Adams 1980:210), and* (b) *Salmon Ruin, Secondary Construction Phase II,* A.D. *1260s. Note the subdivision and/or construction of small kivas in some rooms (after R. Adams 1980:218).*

ments to conform to a kind of large-scale, sacred geometry. Fritz noted that, in the central part of Chaco Canyon, the complex of Great Houses and Great Kivas displays bilateral symmetry around a north-south axis—in effect, a larger version of the old San Juan layout pattern seen

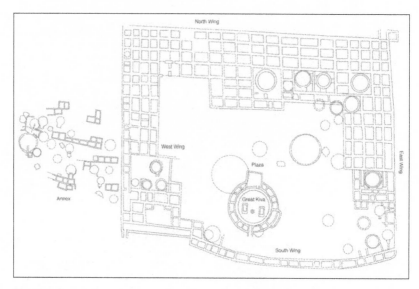

**FIGURE 8.4**

*Aztec West: Primary construction in the early A.D. 1100s, but with additions in the late 1100s and 1200s (for example, the "Annex"). (Compiled from Lister and Lister 1990:31, 201)*

in kivas, habitation units, and individual settlements. Lekson (1999) thinks that, when the seat of Chacoan power moved from Chaco Canyon to the Aztec complex, the leadership of the Chacoan polity found it symbolically important to locate the new center on the same north-south axis that had structured the arrangement of buildings in central Chaco Canyon. This argument seems to me consistent with the way the florescent-period Chacoans used architecture and the landscape to represent both ideology and political power. The remaining part of Lekson's Chaco Meridian hypothesis—that a politically powerful Chacoan elite flourished at Aztec until the late A.D. 1200s, then moved hundreds of kilometers south down the meridian to build a major center at Paquimé—seems much more problematical.

Undoubtedly, the construction of major Chacoan Great Houses in the Totah between about A.D. 1090 and 1125 contributed to the surge of Great House building throughout the Northern San Juan in the very late 1000s and early 1100s. At Lowry Ruin, the Great Kiva and the nucleus of the Great House were built in A.D. 1089–1090, with additional construction and probably remodeling in the period A.D. 1106–1120 (Ahlstrom 1985:337–340). The Bluff Great House, located in southeastern Utah, has a noncutting date of A.D. 1111 associated with Chaco-era construction, and pottery assemblages are consistent with a late A.D. 1000s/early 1100s date (Cameron 2002). The Ida Jean Site (an excavated but largely unreported site near Wallace Ruin in the Lakeview Group near Cortez) yielded a cluster of cutting dates indicating kiva construction at A.D. 1124 (Chaco World Database 2004). At the Escalante Site, a small Great House near Dolores, Colorado, the tree-ring, ceramic, and stratigraphic evidence is not entirely consistent (Hallasi 1979), but tree-ring dates from Room 20 cluster at A.D. 1129 and there is a weak cluster of dates from Kiva A in the late 1130s.

Also, there is evidence that some of the region's Chaco-style Great Houses were built before A.D. 1090 and therefore may pre-date the large Totah centers. At Chimney Rock in the Piedra River drainage of southwestern Colorado, there is a single cutting date of A.D. 1076 from the ventilator tunnel of the East Kiva. Room 8 has a strong date cluster at A.D. 1093, and the East Kiva also yielded a cutting date of A.D. 1093, which Eddy (1977) interprets as indicating remodeling (Ahlstrom 1985). Far View House on Chapin Mesa in Mesa Verde National Park may have been a Chacoan-style Great House when it was constructed in the Pueblo II period, but it was extensively rebuilt in the A.D. 1200s and the excavation reports (Fewkes 1917, 1922) are too sketchy to provide an understanding of construction sequences. Cutting dates from the site range from A.D. 1018 to 1243 (Robinson and Harrill 1974; Chaco World Database 2004).

Bradley (1988) argues that the Wallace Great House (located in the Lakeview Group near Cortez, Colorado) began in A.D. 1045 as a very small, two-storied complex of rooms. Four groundfloor rooms with a second and, in one case, a third story are assigned to this early stage of construction. Bradley (1988) infers that the total groundfloor footprint at this stage was five to ten rooms and a kiva. The bulk of construction at the Wallace Great House appears to have been in the very late 1000s or early 1100s (Bradley 1988) when the site grew rapidly to approximately seventy rooms. The tree-ring dates from the initial stage of construction at Wallace include one date of A.D. 1071; the dates from the 1040s possibly represent beams recycled from an earlier building in the locality. That people built a tiny "Great House" in 1045 and then did not expand it for another fifty or sixty years seems unlikely.

In general, both the ceramic and tree-ring evidence indicates that the burst of construction of Chacoan-style Great Houses in the Northern San Juan falls between about A.D. 1075 and the A.D. 1130s. Additional research will be necessary to determine whether most of this construction occurred after A.D. 1090 (that is, after major centers were initiated in the Totah) or whether Northern San Juan Great Houses began to be established even before A.D. 1075.

In the middle 1100s, after construction of classic Chaco-style Great Houses apparently ceased in the Northern San Juan, the regional population may have declined or at least stabilized in response to severe and prolonged drought (Dean and Van West 2002; Lipe and Varien 1999b). The archaeological tree-ring record from the central Mesa Verde region shows a lull in construction, with harvesting of beams declining and then staying at a low level from about A.D. 1150 to 1200 (Lipe and Varien 1999b; Varien 1999). Ceramic-based dating of a broad-based sample of sites (Ortman, Varien, and Spitzer 2003:figure 10) indicates, however, only a slight drop in regional population between about A.D. 1140 and 1180, followed by renewed population growth. More recent work in the central Mesa Verde region (Kohler et al. 2005) indicates that population continued to increase during this period. Both the beam-harvesting and the ceramic data indicate that regional population reached an all-time peak in the early to middle 1200s, with a rapid final depopulation in the late 1200s, probably in the late 1270s and early 1280s (Lipe 1995; Lipe and Varien 1999b). The San Juan architectural and layout pattern continued to flourish in the region until the end of occupation, although the size of community centers and the kinds of civic architecture changed during the last several generations (Lipe and Ortman 2000; also see discussion in this chapter).

During the late A.D. 1100s and 1200s, people continued to use Chaco-style Great Houses built during the 1075–1135 period, but many of these became spatially peripheral to the community settlement pattern as the community centers relocated to canyons and canyon rims. In the Totah region, however, the large Great Houses at Salmon and Aztec evidently continued to function as community centers in both a population and a ceremonial sense (Brown, Windes, and McKenna 2002). Many of the smaller, outlying, Chaco-era Great Houses also appear to have had residential use during the late A.D. 1100s and 1200s (for example, Cameron 2002; Ryan 2003, 2004), but whether the occupants had special status or the houses were also used for important rituals is not clear.

### Patterns in the Greater Southwest

As these post-Chacoan developments unfolded in the San Juan drainage in the A.D. 1200s, population was growing rapidly in the Rio Grande, the Little Colorado drainage, and the Mogollon Highlands. In the latter two areas, patterns of domestic and civic architecture and of site layout contrast strongly with those of the San Juan region. Lacking are small "household" kivas and the highly modular habitation units formed around such kivas, as well as strong north-south orientations. The ratio of kivas to surface rooms is much lower, and kivas are usually larger and more variable in form and formality. They also are not closely associated with specific small blocks of surface habitation and storage rooms. Habitation sites increased in size, and plaza-oriented layouts became common. An example is Broken K Pueblo, which dates between approximately A.D. 1150 and 1280 (Hill 1970:8) and is located in the Upper Little Colorado drainage (figure 8.5).

In the northern Rio Grande, the same shifts were taking place, but the timing was more variable. Unit-type habitations, each with a kiva and a small block of associated surface rooms, continued to be built in some locations through the Early Coalition period (A.D. 1200–1250). Kohler and Root (2004:213) note that on the Pajarito Plateau kiva-to-room ratios in the Early Coalition ranged from 1:8 (typical of the San Juan pattern) to 1:24. The layout, directional orientation, and kiva features of most of these habitations do not conform very closely to San Juan formats, but there are some exceptions. In the Late Coalition (A.D. 1250–1325), plaza-oriented pueblos (for example, the late component at Burnt Mesa Pueblo [Kohler and Root 2004]) became common on the Pajarito Plateau and elsewhere in the northern Rio Grande. These sites typically have very low ratios of kivas to rooms, and the kivas are frequently located in the plaza. Smith's (1998) survey of northern Rio Grande kivas indicates, however, that a few Late Coalition sites

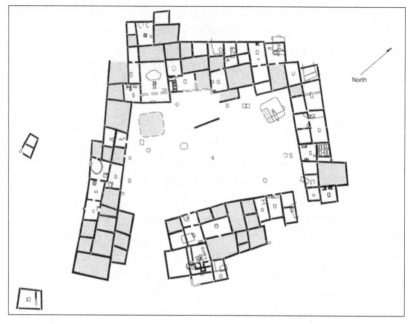

**FIGURE 8.5**

*Broken K Pueblo, Upper Little Colorado drainage. Estimated date is A.D. 1150–1280.*
*Shaded structures were not excavated. (After Hill 1970:9)*

continued to have high kiva-to-room ratios.

The widespread trend during the A.D. 1200s was for settlements outside the San Juan, including the Rio Grande area, to become increasingly "plaza-oriented," instead of "front-oriented" (E. C. Adams 1989, 1991; Reed 1956). That is, the roomblocks appear to be oriented to the plaza rather than to the south or southeast (Lipe 1989). The shift away from the San Juan type of layout seems to be complete by the early 1300s.

The distinctive architectural complex that characterized central Mesa Verde–area villages in the late A.D. 1200s did not "make the trip" to the Rio Grande or Western Pueblo areas when the Northern San Juan was depopulated (Lipe and Lekson 2001). This complex included not only San Juan–pattern habitation units and front-oriented settlements facing south or southeast but also D-shaped, multiwalled civic structures, enclosing walls, towers, blocks of storage rooms, and bilateral layouts.[4] Instead, the architectural and site layout patterns that had initially appeared outside the San Juan drainage in the late 1100s and 1200s became the norm for the Pueblo world. These settlements look much more like those of the historic-period Pueblos than like San Juan settlements, including the ones we call "Chacoan." By the early 1300s, aggregation into village-size Pueblos had also become standard. Dispersed community patterns of the sort that had characterized San Juan (including Chacoan) communities became increasingly rare, and individual households appear to have become more dependent on their "pueblo" for physical security and spiritual welfare. Early on, Steward (1937) recognized the social implications of these architectural and community pattern changes.

I think that these shifts in the character of household facilities and community settlement patterns represent the spread and development of a mode of community organization that de-emphasized household political and religious (though perhaps not economic) autonomy and that could organize large groups of people without concentrating power in the hands of particular individuals and small groups. Rather, what knit the community together were multiple sodalities and the parceling out of ceremonial and political authority to multiple individuals and groups with resulting checks and balances. The religious ideology associated with this shift undoubtedly incorporated elements of earlier belief and symbol systems from the San Juan and other (for example, Mimbres?) areas in a new configuration that also included innovative elements.[5]

The demographic and social upheavals of the A.D. 1200s and 1300s provided fertile ground for the spread of the katsina cult (E. C. Adams 1991). Crown (1994) also discusses the appearance and spread of a more generalized "Southwestern regional cult" in areas outside the San Juan drainage. The organizational and ideological changes of the late 1200s and early 1300s therefore resulted in a substantial transformation of Puebloan society that had not been accomplished by the elaboration and expansion of the Chacoan system in the late A.D. 1000s and early 1100s. In this sense, the Chacoan florescence can be seen as a brief flirtation with sociopolitical hierarchy, one that incorporated many existing cultural patterns and probably did not result in the restructuring of social relations in most of the smaller communities outside the major Chacoan centers. The San Juan architectural and settlement pattern appears to reflect an emphasis on the sociopolitical autonomy of households and of groups of closely related households. This type of community organization may have provided a context in which some families or kin groups transformed themselves into local and perhaps regional elites with considerable social power. By contrast, the social, religious, and settlement systems that developed south of the San Juan in the 1200s and spread throughout the Pueblo world in the late 1200s and 1300s appear designed to emphasize community integration at the expense of household political autonomy and to prevent individuals or kin groups from gaining control of multiple reins of power.

## CHACO FLORESCENCE: A.D. 1040 TO 1135

I do not think that we would have a Chaco Synthesis volume if the "Chaco florescence" had not occurred. What I mean by this label is the approximate century in which (1) large-scale, planned construction of very large, highly formal Great Houses took place, first at Chaco Canyon and then in the Totah area to the north; (2) large quantities of construction beams, pottery, exotic goods, and probably maize were imported into Chaco Canyon (the Totah centers also appear to have imported quantities of construction beams and exotic goods); (3) the distribution of Chacoan-style Great Houses reached its maximum geographic extent; and (4) there was maximum differentiation in formality, elaboration, and scale between Great House architecture and ordinary residential architecture in all areas, that is, in the main Chaco Canyon and Totah centers, as well as in the various far-flung communities with smaller Great Houses that referenced Chacoan architectural models.

I pick the bracketing dates of 1040 to 1135 because these include the major Great House building programs at the two major centers—earlier, Chaco Canyon, and later, the Aztec and Salmon complex in the Totah. Great House building started much earlier than 1040 at Chaco Canyon and, to some extent, in areas south of Chaco, but these efforts do not come close to the scale and organization of construction characteristic of the period of florescence. I concur with Sebastian (1991, 1992a) in thinking that the Chacoan sociopolitical system rapidly and substantially "ramped up" in scale and complexity concurrent with the onset of major building programs at Chaco Canyon about 1040.

The end of the florescent period followed, by a few years, the end of large-scale Great House construction in the Totah (it had declined earlier in Chaco Canyon). In the outlying areas of the Northern San Juan, there was a concurrent end of construction of Great Houses that clearly reference the architecture of the central Great Houses and that contrast markedly with the residential architecture of their surrounding dispersed communities. The latest dates for construction of an outlying Great House come from the Escalante Ruin near Dolores, Colorado, which has a strong cluster of cutting dates from A.D. 1129 and a weak cluster in the 1130s (Ahlstrom 1985). The end of Chaco-style Great House construction and of the florescent period is more clear-cut in the Northern San Juan than in the southern part of the old Chacoan domain, where Great Houses incorporating classic Chacoan features continued to be built into the 1200s (Kintigh, Howell, and Duff 1996).

The following questions have occupied the most recent couple of generations of Chaco scholars: How complex was Chacoan society during its florescent period? How did it work? What was the relationship between the major centers and the many outlying Great House communities? What, if any, was the role of coercive violence in the expansion or maintenance of the extended regional system? From the perspective of a Northern San Juan specialist looking south, I will make a few comments about these questions.

### How Complex Was Chaco?

By "complexity" I mean the development of vertical (hierarchical) differentiation, as well as horizontal (division-of-labor) differentiation (Blanton et al. 1981; Mann 1986). Chaco comes across as relatively complex, at least if we are talking about "downtown" Chaco Canyon and Aztec and at least if we are comparing florescent-period Chaco with Puebloan culture and society both before and after that period.

The size and distinctive architecture of the major Great Houses of Chaco Canyon and the Totah offer the best evidence for vertical differentiation. These clearly are "houses" in the sense that they are constructed of elements and conventions with deep time depth in the domestic architecture of the San Juan drainage. Although arguments remain about whether they actually were residences throughout the period of Chacoan florescence (compare with Bustard 2003), my bet is that they housed (as well as symbolized) an elite segment of the population. We also can argue about just how much the lives of these people differed from those of the rest of the population and about the sources of the social power that sustained them as an elite, but I cannot imagine that archaeology could offer us any clearer evidence of at least two levels of vertical social differentiation. These Great Houses are aptly named. They ostentatiously communicate that the people who lived there were special and were different from the rest of the population—what Mahoney (2001) calls "conspicuous display." In other words, they were bigger-than-life people living in bigger-than-life houses. That is the message we receive today, and I think that it is the message communicated to people who viewed these structures 950 years ago. These are houses raised to the level of monumental architecture.

The spaces in and around these buildings, undoubtedly, were used for various kinds of gatherings, some of which were exterior and public and some of which were in spaces where entry could be controlled (Cooper 1997). They also were large storehouses, probably primarily for food that the elite used to sustain themselves and, more importantly, for food that enabled them to be generous hosts at various gatherings. These buildings may also have provided space for honored guests and relatives from "out of town," as well as for other elite social and ceremonial activities.

At Chaco Canyon, mortuary studies provide evidence of differences in status and living standards between those buried at Pueblo Bonito and those at small sites in the canyon. The Great House burials had greater stature, lower levels of infant mortality, and lower frequencies of porotic osteoporosis (Akins 1986:35–137, 2003). Significantly larger amounts of ornaments and exotic materials such as turquoise accompanied Great House burials than small site burials. A group of burials in the northern portion of Pueblo Bonito had the largest amounts of valuable associations, and the subfloor burials of two mature males in this area would measure up to any in the Southwest for quantity and elaboration of burial goods (Akins 1986:116–118, 131–132, 2003).

The much smaller Great Houses outside Chaco Canyon and Aztec seem designed to send the message that the local leaders of these communities were important too. San Juan communities both before and after the florescent period often had distinguishable centers marked by civic architecture of some type and sometimes by the presence of a larger-than-ordinary residential roomblock as the nucleus of a dispersed settlement pattern. Before, during, and after the Chacoan florescence, community religious/political leaders must have controlled the construction of and access to important structures and spaces at the centers of their communities. Having some moderately distinctive architecture at the center of one's community was nothing particularly unusual for the Puebloans of the San Juan drainage (Wilshusen and Van Dyke, chapter 7 of this volume)—nor, by implication, was the presence of some households and kin groups that exercised considerable influence and authority in certain spheres of community life.

During the heyday of the Great House system, however, the leaders of the outlying Great House communities were evidently more willing to display their status ostentatiously than were the leaders of earlier or later communities in the Northern San Juan. Even the smaller Great Houses contrast strongly with surrounding residences in size, number of stories, and formality of construction. Also, they often have specific features, such as banded masonry, elevated kivas, or associated berms, that reference models at the Chaco Canyon or Totah centers (Cameron 2002; Van Dyke 1999c) and that usually lack local antecedents. On the other hand, the outlying Great Houses are quite variable in size, layout, architectural characteristics, and patterns of access (Van Dyke 1999c), indicating that overseers from the major Chacoan centers probably did not supervise their construction.

Although Chacoan Great Houses publicly display evidence of status differences, and a few "high status burials" have been found, the political/religious elites of both the main and the outlying Chacoan Great Houses remain largely invisible. I believe that this has tended to confuse discussions of Chacoan complexity because many of us, implicitly or explicitly, expect "big men" or "aggrandizing" leaders to drive increases in sociopolitical complexity (compare with Hayden 1995; Mahoney 2001). To use Feinman's (2000) terminology, such societies exhibit a "network" mode of sociopolitical organization. He proposes a second mode, "corporate" organization, in which leaders represent themselves as acting on behalf of the community or of a kin group and are therefore much less likely to advertise their status through ostentatious personal display. The Chacoan use of house architecture, instead of individual tombs or monuments, to represent the holders of social power is consistent with this second mode, as is the lack of iconography designed to glorify individual leaders.

Being on the corporate side of this organizational continuum is no impediment to the development of hierarchy and social power; for example, Harappa is high on both the hierarchical and the corporate mode axes in Feinman's model. The major centers (at Chaco Canyon and in the Totah) must have been considerably farther along on the "hierarchical" axis of Feinman's scheme than were most or all of the Chaco-related outlier communities.

At the main centers in Chaco Canyon and the Totah, Chacoan leaders clearly were able to organize large work forces and to hold them to a quite high standard of performance. This is a significant accomplishment because, even if workers are willing to volunteer their time on a complex project, not much gets done without clear direction. Good managerial control is most evident in the construction of large, planned architectural components at the Great Houses. This involved organizing the transport of timbers, stone, water, and mud from various locations, some quite far away, and overseeing their use in the construction of large buildings, often many tens and even hundreds of rooms at a time. Managing these efforts implies the exercise of substantial social power—that is, the ability of individuals or groups to control or direct the actions of other individuals and groups (Lipe 2002b:169; Mann 1986). This is not a claim that the people doing the work were under constant or even frequent threat of physical coercion, although the occasional use of force (actual or threatened) was probably part of the equation. Leaders can also exercise social power by tapping religious motivations, by controlling productive resources, and/or by establishing debt obligations (Mann 1986; Sebastian 1992a).

It must have taken a reasonably hierarchical and efficient political organization, at least at Chaco Canyon and later at Aztec, to make this system work. Organizing large ceremonies, feasts, and work parties requires significant skill and the effective use of authority within established systems of social control. The leaders at Chaco Canyon and in the Totah must have exercised institutionalized social power, not only to construct the major Great Houses but also to conduct the activities that were associated with these Great Houses and that made them influential over a very large area.

One distinctive characteristic of florescent Chacoan complexity was an increase in the number and kinds of materials imported into Chaco Canyon and, to a lesser extent, into the centers at Salmon and Aztec. Chaco Canyon had been a significant importer of pottery and some other goods for more than a century before the florescent period. It continued to be an importer even after 1130, but the scale of importation of most items ramped up in the years between 1020–1040 and 1105 (Toll, chapter 4 of this volume). Many thousands of construction beams were brought in from highlands many tens of kilometers away (Betancourt, Dean, and Hull 1986; Windes and McKenna 2001); there were massive imports of pottery into Chaco Canyon from settlements 60 or 70 km away on the Chuska slope (Toll 2001, chapter 4 of this volume); maize was imported into Chaco Canyon from the Chuska slope and probably from the Totah region as well (Benson et al. 2003); occurrences of distinctive pink chert from Narbona Pass in the Chuskas increased dramatically in frequency after about A.D. 1020 (Cameron 2001); and there were large (relative to the rest of the Pueblo world at the time) imports of turquoise, shell, and other exotic items (Mathien 1997, 2001). The scale of the imports of pottery and probably of maize from the Chuska slope suggests that this area was likely to have been part of a single political and economic system centered in Chaco Canyon. If so, it implies a polity consisting of many communities in an area of more than 1,000 sq km, with a population probably numbering more than ten thousand.

In any case, nothing elsewhere in the Pueblo archaeological record compares to the display of organized social power evident in the construction and operation of the main florescent-period Chacoan centers and in the importation of both mundane and prestige goods. Acquiring parrots, turquoise, copper bells, and the like would have demonstrated the elite's ability to obtain items not available to the general population and also would have displayed connections with other powerful elites far to the south. As we move away from the main centers, my impression is that the Great House outlier communities—at least those in the Northern San Juan outside the Totah—exhibit far less evidence of social differentiation and exercise of social power. Some of the outlying Great Houses do show evidence that large numbers of rooms were constructed during single building episodes, as opposed to the incremental growth of "ordinary" residences. The scale of even the largest of these building projects, however, is much less than at the central Great Houses in Chaco Canyon and the Totah, and there is little evidence that quantities of building materials were brought in from a distance. The variety and quantity of exotics such as turquoise are also considerably lower (relative to total artifact discard) than at the main centers during the florescent period.

### How Did Chaco Work?

I take this to be a question about how leaders in Chacoan society mobilized and employed social power. Leaders can control or direct the actions of other individuals or groups by using or threatening to use physical coercion, by providing or withholding things of value, or by simple persuasion. The "things of value" can include economic goods and services, access to mates, ideological approval, religious benefaction, and protection in wartime. Secular or religious rituals often legitimate social power differentials; the display and manipulation of potent, generally accepted symbols and rituals are regular aspects of the exercise of power (Kertzer 1988). In all but the most despotic of societies, the use of power requires some compliance on the part of those affected by it. In state-level societies, control of an effective bureaucracy is another source of power for the political leadership (Mann 1986), but this would not apply to the Chacoan case.

Sebastian's (1992a) model for the establishment and subsequent florescence of Chacoan sociopolitical power remains a good one. My personal elaboration of her ideas is as follows: Families or kin groups that controlled the most productive lands in Chaco Canyon were able to become creditors to the less fortunate during occasional environmental downturns. The latter repaid their obligations with labor, some of which helped to enhance water control systems and to expand early Great Houses. Patrons could use both the Great Houses and the water control systems to maintain and promote their own status and political influence. R. Gwinn Vivian (1990, 2001, chapter 2 of this volume) documents elaborate runoff control and water management systems at several locations in

Chaco Canyon. The ownership and management of these systems could well have been a context in which social power was regularly practiced and eventually institutionalized. The construction of these systems would have required the mobilization and supervision of a labor force, and an organized labor force may also have been necessary to ensure the proper distribution of water during and after heavy rainstorms.

These developments set the stage for the start of the florescent period, which marks the formation of an integrated polity based in Chaco Canyon that probably included some communities outside the canyon. One strategy employed by the existing political-religious leadership or by an ambitious faction must have been to assert control over major (and, undoubtedly, newly elaborated) ceremonies. Aspiring leaders could assert their ties to supernatural forces and their ability to provide access to spiritual benefits by organizing elaborate ceremonies and feasts, staged in the impressive settings provided by the Great Houses and the constructed landscapes surrounding them. By contributing the labor needed to construct such facilities and by participating in the ceremonies, ordinary people were able to gain religious benefaction (Renfrew 2001). This reaffirmed the elite as gatekeepers for important kinds of religious participation, and the facilities themselves stood as constant public reminders of the elite's special status and powers and its ability to acquire and organize labor (Wilson 1988). This does not imply that control of productive lands within Chaco Canyon ceased to be important or that physical coercion, or the threat of physical coercion, was never available to the leadership. The northern Southwest is a big place, however, and its archaeological record is replete with evidence of household and community mobility. Surely, regular physical repression could not have been the principal way to induce people to support the leaders and the institutions that were central to this political-religious system, even at the main centers, and certainly not in relationship to the far-flung outlier communities.

### How Were the Main Centers Related to the Outlying Great House Communities?

The kind of system described above—at Chaco and elsewhere in the world of early complex societies—had the capability to expand its influence geographically to incorporate the leaders of communities located at a distance. Competition among such leaders to acquire status by demonstrating links to the powerful Chaco Canyon centers would have amplified the spread. The evidence that Chaco Canyon was a pilgrimage center (Judge 1989; Renfrew 2001) is consistent with this intepretation. That is, leaders of outlying communities could improve their status and influence in their own communities by traveling to Chaco Canyon to participate in special ceremonies, thereby receiving special benefaction. They may have been expected to bring groups large enough to form work parties and/or to contribute food or other materials.

The point is that this was seen as a reciprocal relationship—the pilgrims obtained benefaction and status, and the Chacoans received labor, materials, and participants in the activities they staged at their Great Houses. This reaffirmed and reinforced the standing of both the central and the peripheral players who, together, made up the "system." Contemporary pilgrimage centers, such as the Vatican and Mecca, are likewise supported economically by a large body of the faithful, only some of whom directly take part in pilgrimages. In the Chaco case, the larger populace of the region provided support for the pilgrims and work parties, as well as food and other materials to be carried to Chaco, even if not everyone was an actual pilgrim. It also seems likely that the Chacoan elite would have forged alliances with some outlying Great House communities through arranged marriages, in part to forestall the rise of competitive centers close to Chaco Canyon.

The geographic extent of an actual Chacoan polity remains an open question. The system could have worked even if the polity, as such, was limited to Chaco Canyon and later to the Aztec-Salmon locality. Inclusion of the nearby settlements in the "Chacoan halo" (Marshall, Doyel, and Breternitz 1982), however, seems very likely. Also, as noted, the evidence that extensive quantities of pottery, Narbona chert, and probably maize were imported from communities on the Chuska slope (Benson et al. 2003; Cameron 2001; Toll, chapter 4 of this volume) may indicate that the leadership at Chaco Canyon controlled or, at least, formed strong alliances with these communities.

Outside these core areas, however, the distances involved and the substantial variability in outlying Great House construction and layout (Van Dyke 1999c) indicate that the main centers exercised little actual political control over outlying Great House communities, including those of the Northern San Juan. The A.D. 1000s and early 1100s appear to have been a time of generally good summer rainfall, when most people in the Northern San Juan and elsewhere in the northern Southwest were living in small settlements of one or a few households, which commonly were occupied for only a few years or a generation. It would have been difficult for an elite at Chaco Canyon, or later at Aztec, to manage the political affairs of such scattered, mobile populations, and the difficulties would have increased with distance from the main centers.

The power of the political-religious elite at the main Chacoan centers to exert influence over a huge area would have therefore resided largely in its ability to provide (and also to control) special religious ceremonies and events such as feasts and work parties—activities that would enhance the participants' religious and political status. In addition, gatherings at the main centers would have enabled those attending to exchange information and goods and to find mates. In the Northern San Juan, A.D. 1040–1135 is a time when greater quantities of materials from outside the region are present in site assemblages than in the succeeding 150 years (Lipe 2002b). This indicates effective networks for the interregional movement of goods. Even so, the amounts of long-distance and exotic goods are quite small at most sites outside the main centers.

The successful operation of this geographically extensive system must have required that thousands of people living in many communities over a wide area accept the efficacy of a broadly defined core set of religious ideas, rituals, and symbols. There must have been widespread acceptance of a small set of "ultimate sacred propositions" (Rappaport 1971) that, in turn, were manifested in ritual practice and also supported aspects of the social order. In this view, people may have regarded rituals held at the main centers as the most highly sanctified, but widely held beliefs tied these to local ritual systems as well. Leaders great and small could enhance their own social power by conducting and probably by developing rituals that promised spiritual and, no doubt, material benefaction for those who participated and that also reinforced the nature of the social order within which they played important roles. In some cases, leaders might have aggressively promoted the spread of the ritual-ideological complex or, more likely, of particular rituals with which they were identified.

If the Chacoan ritual-ideological complex was built on the same widespread beliefs that underlay the San Juan architectural pattern, a great deal of "missionary" work would not have been necessary to build relationships between outlying communities and the main Chacoan centers. Furthermore, nothing in this conception of "how things work" would have required centralized theocratic control in order to spread this kind of system, any more than the spread of the katsina cult in the A.D. 1300s implies centralized control (E. C. Adams 1991). This view also does not imply that the ritual and ideological system was separate from the political system and was merely manipulated by an elite leadership that had largely material goals. As Yoffee (2001) argues, accumulating social power at Chaco was probably a means to an end—the end being the successful conduct of widely supported rituals and other events that drew people from near and far and the means being the ability to organize these events successfully.

Moving to a different type of evidence, it seems unlikely that control over scarce productive farmlands or over elaborate runoff distribution systems could have been the basis for extension of a Chacoan polity to higher areas on the peripheries of the central San Juan (geologic) Basin, including most of the Northern San Juan area. In the Northern San Juan, dry farming is possible over large tracts of land, and potential floodwater/runoff farming locations are numerous as well. For the central Mesa Verde region, Van West (1994) has shown that the supply of arable land amply exceeded potential demands, even in dry years. Varien (1999) provides evidence that, in this same area, households frequently shifted their primary fields, indicating that dry-farming locations, though variable in quality, were not confined to just a few situations. Also, outside Chaco Canyon, runoff control devices were ordinarily not very elaborate and could have been constructed and managed by households or other small groups (Rohn 1963; Wilshusen, Churchill, and Potter 1997; Winter 1978).

The presence of perennial streams (the Animas, La Plata, and San Juan) in the Totah region suggests the possibility that irrigation systems were constructed there. At Aztec, Morgan ([1881]1965:210) refers obliquely to the presence of a canal, and Moorehead (1908) states that, in the lower La Plata valley, ancient irrigation ditches could be traced for several miles. At Aztec, management of an irrigation system could have bolstered the leadership's social power, much as the management of elaborate runoff distribution systems may have promoted the development of power differentials at Chaco Canyon. The social order represented by the Totah Great Houses, however, did not develop gradually in place, as at Chaco, but appears to have arrived fully formed, probably the result of colonization from Chaco Canyon proper. In any case, control of irrigation does not seem likely to have provided a way for the Chacoan leadership at Aztec to extend political control throughout the Totah valleys, let alone to the nearby uplands. R. Gwinn Vivian (1990:313, referencing Morris 1939) notes that water tables in the lower Animas and La Plata floodplains were high enough to support crops in these valleys without irrigation and that good river-bottom farmlands extended for more than 30 km from Morris's Site 41 to the San Juan River. This suggests that, in the Totah region, productive farming areas were not highly circumscribed or dependent on irrigation and that it would have been difficult for an elite based at Aztec to gain a monopoly on good farmland.

Systems of land tenure and land dispute resolution appear to have developed in areas of the Northern San Juan where population density became high (Adler 1996; Varien 1999), but there is no evidence that these systems were instituted at a supracommunity level or that they were associated with the development of powerful elites of the sort that can be recognized at the main Chacoan centers (Lipe 2002b; Ware 2002b). The types of politico-religious leadership and the institutions responsible for resolving land disputes probably were present both before and after the brief period of Great House construction in the Northern San Juan. In this perspective, local community leaders might have seen a "Chaco connection" as a way of enhancing what they were already doing. It also implies that they had the ability to "opt out" if the relationship turned sour or the perceived benefits diminished.

### Did Chacoans Use Coercive Violence to Control the Northern San Juan?

Turner and Turner (1999) and Lekson (2002) have argued that the political hierarchy at Chaco Canyon (and, according to Lekson, thereafter at Aztec) exercised control over distant communities by occasionally using extreme brutality as an instrument of intimidation. Kantner (1999b) takes a more generalized view, correlating these events to the greater instance of social and political inequality in the Pueblo II period. Turner and Turner (1999) focus on the evidence for cannibalism. Kantner (1999b) and Lekson (2002) discuss what Kuckelman, Lightfoot, and Martin (2000) call "EP" (extreme processing) incidents. These refer to cases in which human bodies have been severely mutilated, whether or not cannibalism was involved.

Both Lekson and the Turners assert that the time-space distribution of these incidents indicates that they may have been occasional "lesson-teaching" acts centrally directed by the leaders of a Chacoan polity. I think that this interpretation goes well beyond what the evidence will bear. The underlying assumptions are (1) that there was a strong Chacoan polity from sometime in the A.D. 900s to sometime in the 1200s, (2) that, throughout this period, a centralized political leadership was able to exert substantial control over a large area of the Southwest—essentially, the entire area where Chacoan Great Houses ever occurred, and (3) that violence and especially cannibalism are most likely to be associated with hierarchical political systems. Although I do not doubt that the Chacoan leadership at the major centers had the ability to use some degree of physical coercion, I think that there are serious flaws in the three assumptions used to suggest that this ability extended very widely in both time and space.

It seems to me that the time-space distribution of Chaco-style Great Houses is the best indicator of when and where Chacoan influence was being exercised outside Chaco Canyon and the Aztec locality and, therefore, of the times and places when one might expect to see evidence of physical coercion, if it was being used as a technique of political domination. In the Northern San Juan, small outlying Chacoan Great Houses occur widely, from the Totah region north of Aztec to many locations in southwestern Colorado and southeastern Utah. Their construction, however, appears to be confined to a narrow time band, from about A.D. 1075 to 1135. If occasional executions or massacres were an instrument of Chacoan political control, one would expect that the evidence of these events would cluster in this time period.

Many of the best documented and best dated of the Southwestern EP incidents are, in fact, from the Northern San Juan (Billman, Lambert, and Leonard 2000; Kuckelman, Lightfoot, and Martin 2000, 2002; LeBlanc 1999). But nearly all of these fall outside the brief period of Great House construction in the Northern San Juan, and many fall well outside this period. For example, Turner and Turner (1999:383) include Salmon Ruin in a list of Chacoan Great Houses where researchers have found evidence of cannibalism or other violence. Of course, Salmon is a major Great House, but the evidence in question refers to a set of adult and infant remains placed on the roof of the tower kiva when it was intentionally burned sometime after A.D. 1260 (R. Adams 1980; Turner and Turner 1999:326–331). This is at the end of the Secondary period occupation of Salmon by people using Mesa Verde–tradition pottery and at a time when evidence of an effective political hierarchy at Salmon is quite weak. Also, Kuckelman, Lightfoot, and Martin (2002) have recently published evidence that EP, and probably cannibalism, took place in the very late A.D. 1200s after attackers massacred the entire small village of Castle Rock Pueblo I. They also report several cases in which extreme violence was inflicted on a few individuals at the contemporary but much larger Sand Canyon Pueblo.

These episodes are consistent with other evidence that intercommunity warfare was common in the middle and late A.D. 1200s in the central Mesa Verde region. Therefore, incidents of extreme violence in the Northern San Juan are not temporally correlated with the brief period when Chacoan Great Houses were being built in the area, or even with the longer period of Chacoan florescence.

Of the EP incidents in the Northern San Juan that could possibly overlap in time with the dates of Chacoan Great House construction, most are at the very end rather than the beginning of this period. They could not have been part of the expansion and consolidation of the system, although some could have been involved in its end or collapse. A well-dated and well-documented group of EP cases from the central Mesa Verde region falls in a narrow time range from about A.D. 1130 to 1160, dates that cover the early part of the severe drought of the middle 1100s.[6] It is also a time when Great House construction had largely ceased. By the 1130s or, at the latest, by the 1140s the Chacoan system as it was during the florescent period appears to have fallen apart. This is likely to have been a time of general social disruption and economic hardship, when perhaps people had scores to settle or when some families or communities were facing crop failure (Billman, Lambert, and Leonard 2000).

Some of the incidents that fall in this A.D. 1130–1160 cluster, for example, the Cowboy Wash case (Billman, Lambert, and Leonard 2000), involved large numbers of individuals. This case, like the later one at Castle Rock Pueblo, could have been the result of intercommunity warfare instead of "state terrorism" organized by a centralized regional hierarchy.

The Southwestern and cross-cultural evidence for extreme violence is abundant, including mutilation of bodies and/or cannibalism. This came about for a variety of reasons and was not strongly associated with hierarchical social formations. Keeley (1996) summarizes cross-cultural evidence showing that massacres of large percentages of defeated groups, as well as incidents of "extreme processing" and cannibalism, often occur as part of tribal-level warfare (also see Bullock 1991, 1998). Extreme violence and, in some cases, cannibalism may also take place during the execution of witches as a mechanism of intra-community social control, again, in a nonhierarchical context (Darling 1998). Sanday's (1986) cross-cultural study showed that institutionalized, non-famine-related cannibalism occurred in about a third of her sample of world cultures, indicating that it is neither rare nor confined to a particular type of sociopolitical system. She found cannibalism most often in the context of warfare. The frequency of archaeological cases of extreme violence in the northern Southwest likely is due to the high quality of the evidence obtained and analyses conducted in that area in recent years. Researchers will probably find similar archaeological evidence of extreme violence, including cannibalism, in many other parts of the world when they apply the careful analytical techniques described by Turner and Turner (1999) and Kuckelman, Lightfoot, and Martin (2002).

Kohler and Kramer (2003), however, have recently presented evidence that potentially could support Lekson's "Aztec hegemony" model for the post-florescent period. They investigated burial data to estimate sex ratios across time and space in the northern Southwest. They find that, in the period A.D. 1000–1100, the central San Juan Basin (where Chaco Canyon is located) has a female-biased sex ratio, consistent with raiding for women. The central Mesa Verde area at this time does not show a significant departure from a sex ratio of 0.5, or equal numbers of males and females. In the A.D. 1200s, however, the Totah region (where Aztec and Salmon are located) shows a strongly female-biased sex ratio, and the central Mesa Verde area is male biased, suggesting that raids for women might have focused on the latter area. The sample sizes are small, but, even though other possible explanations account for the results, the suggestion of interregional raiding from the Totah into the central Mesa Verde region is intriguing. These data are consistent with the Turners' and Lekson's hypothesis that "Chaco-sponsored terrorism" continued to emanate from Aztec in the A.D. 1200s, but they do not unequivocally support it either. As noted, cross-cultural surveys of tribal warfare (Keeley 1996; Kohler and Kramer 2003; Sanday 1986) indicate that interregional raiding occurs in the absence of hierarchical social formations. It may have been one facet of the widespread violence that plagued the Four Corners area in the A.D. 1200s (Lipe 1995).

## THE NORTHERN SAN JUAN AFTER THE CHACOAN FLORESCENCE

The tree-ring record indicates that the period A.D. 1130–1180 was a time of severe drought in the Four Corners area (Dean and Van West 2002). Brown, Windes, and McKenna (2002) argue that the last, large-scale construction event at Aztec West took place between A.D. 1118 and 1125 or 1130. As noted above, the latest outlying Great House—Escalante Ruin—has tree-ring dates in the late A.D. 1120s and 1130s. The onset of the severe mid-1100s drought coincides almost perfectly with the end of large, planned construction events in the major centers of the Totah and with the end of construction of smaller, Chaco-pattern Great Houses in outlying areas of the Northern San Juan. By *Chaco-pattern* I mean architecturally formal buildings that clearly reference the major Chacoan Great Houses and are spatially separate from and architecturally contrastive with the standard residential architecture of the communities in which they occur.

A reasonable hypothesis is that construction of both large and small Great Houses stopped because drought-related crop failures undercut belief in the benefits of the religious ceremonies and pilgrimages that were vital to the operation of the late florescent Chacoan system. Crop failures would also have undercut the prestige and authority of leaders at both the major centers and the outlying communities.

A histogram of cutting dates from southwestern Colorado and southeastern Utah, assembled by Varien (1999:190), indicates that the mid-1100s drought seriously diminished building activities in the Northern San Juan. Substantial numbers of dates are present from the decade centered on A.D. 1110 to the one centered on 1150. In the decade centered on 1160, however, fewer than ten dates are recorded, a level nearly as low as those recorded for the A.D. 900s, when the area was significantly depopulated. Cutting dates increase in the decades centered on 1170 through 1190 and then show a large increase around A.D. 1200. For the Totah portion of the Northern San Juan, McKenna and Toll (2001:140) assess both ceramic and tree-ring dates as indicating a lull in construction activity during the last half of the 1100s.

This pattern indicates that building activity declined markedly after the onset of the severe and prolonged mid-1100s drought. Whether this also indicates an actual regional population decline is less clear. Increased mortality may have caused some in-place shrinkage of population, but there is no evidence of population increase in adjacent regions, as would be the case with sizable emigration. Furthermore, population estimates based on ceramic dating of a large sample of sites from the central Mesa Verde region indicate either a slight decline in the period A.D. 1140–1180 (Ortman, Varien, and Spitzer 2003) or continued population growth (Kohler et al. 2005). My guess is that the middle 1100s was a time of hardship and "hunkering down" throughout the Northern San Juan, resulting in reduced building activity. Apparently, this also diminished the population's willingness to invest the time, energy, and resources required to maintain the Chacoan regional system.

### What Role Did Aztec Play in the A.D. 1200s?

Lekson (1999) has argued that, until the middle A.D. 1200s, a Chacoan elite continued to reside at Aztec, with Aztec functioning as the political and sociocultural center of the Northern San Juan region. Evidence from both Salmon and Aztec, however, indicates that no large-scale building events were organized at these centers after the early 1100s, that long-distance importation of construction timbers ceased, and that imports of nonlocal pottery and Narbona Pass chert declined dramatically. Therefore, many indicators of centralized and hierarchical social power that made the Chaco florescent period distinctive appear to have been absent at Aztec and Salmon after about A.D. 1130. Furthermore, we cannot rule out the possibility that people abandoned the major Totah Great Houses for a time in the middle A.D. 1100s. It is difficult to conclude that the sociopolitical system of a Chacoan elite remained intact after that date. I will briefly review the evidence of these changes.

Earl Morris, the excavator of Aztec West, thought that the structure was abandoned following the "primary" (Chacoan) occupation and before the "secondary" (Mesa Verde) occupation. He writes, "The building must have remained vacant for a long time to have permitted the elements to have brought about the advanced degree of destruction in various places to be observed beneath the lowest levels at which the second pottery occurs" (Morris 1928:419).

Brown, Windes, and McKenna (2002) argue, however, that surface ceramics at sites in the Aztec complex indicate dates in the middle or late A.D. 1100s and that construction continued on the massive East Ruin through the late 1100s and 1200s. Aztec East has two adjacent, compact, multistoried buildings containing several hundred rooms and a walled-in plaza with a Great Kiva (figure 8.6).

Although researchers have excavated only small portions of Aztec East, they have obtained about three hundred tree-ring dates. Brown, Windes, and McKenna (2002:6) infer that the core portion of Aztec East was built "about the same time that construction was completed at Aztec West" (presumably in the A.D. 1120s). It is clear that subsequent construction was incremental, with a few dates falling between the A.D. 1120s and 1200 (though none between the late 1140s and the early 1160s), followed by several substantial date clusters in the first half of the 1200s.

Brown, Windes, and McKenna (2002:6) state that, in its finished version in the A.D. 1200s, Aztec East's basic layout and complementary symmetry with Aztec West and other components in the Aztec Ruins Group indicate that the original footprint of the building involved considerable planning and formal conceptual elements, even if construction did not always follow the original plan.

Brown, Windes, and McKenna (2002) conclude that building activity at Aztec East in the A.D. 1200s resulted in completion of a structure

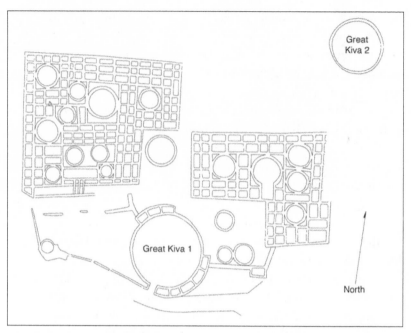

**FIGURE 8.6**

*Aztec East. The majority of the rooms are multistoried. (After Lister and Lister 1990:159)*

that Chacoans had designed in the early 1100s. They argue that Aztec East is also part of a larger "landscape" plan that includes Aztec West, East, and North and several tri-wall structures. The completion of Aztec East as the last element in this plan was done cumulatively, however, over several decades, rather than in one or a few well-organized, major building episodes, as had been the practice in the florescent period. Elsewhere in the Northern San Juan, Great Houses that had been built in the A.D. 1000s and early 1100s also underwent some remodeling and/or additions coincident with renewed or increased occupation in the A.D. 1200s. At most of these, though, the work resulted in blurring rather than completing the original florescent-period plans, so Aztec East is unusual in this regard. At Aztec West and Salmon Ruin, remodeling in the A.D. 1200s resulted in the subdivision of some large Chacoan rooms and the addition of small Mesa Verde–style kivas, so even the major buildings of the Totah were not immune to this kind of change (see figures 8.3 and 8.4).

Wood use at Aztec East contrasts strongly with that at Aztec West (Brown, Windes, and McKenna 2002). Aztec West shows a pattern typical of the largest, florescent-period Chacoan Great Houses—heavy reliance on large conifers brought from a considerable distance to furnish primary roof construction beams. Even the secondary roof beams are often of aspen brought from distant mountains rather than the closely related cottonwood, which would have been very common in the local floodplain (Tennessen, Blanchette, and Windes 2002). By contrast, at Aztec East, beams dating after A.D. 1140 are almost exclusively juniper, showing a clear shift to local wood sources (Brown, Windes, and McKenna 2002:7). Although Aztec East is as large as some of the major Great Houses of the florescent period, its manner of construction—incremental additions and the use of local building timbers—was much more like the "regular" Northern San Juan pattern than that of the Chaco florescent period.

From Salmon Ruin, R. Adams (1980) reports on 253 cutting dates and probable cutting dates. The majority of these dates represent several large-scale beam-cutting and building episodes from the Primary (Chacoan) occupation—A.D. 1088–1090, A.D. 1093–1094, and A.D. 1105–1106. There is a hiatus in tree-ring dates of any sort between A.D. 1116 and 1186, and a hiatus of cutting dates between A.D. 1116 and 1242 (R. Adams 1980). Researchers also collected archaeomagnetic samples from various contexts at Salmon Ruin, and these show a hiatus of fifty-five years, between about A.D. 1130 and 1185 (R. Adams 1980:223). Examination of data from stratigraphy and ceramics led Adams (1980:230) to question, however, whether abandonment during this period was complete: "The site may, in fact, have been abandoned for the entire 55 years. However, the depositional sequence in several rooms seems to refute the possibility of total site abandonment for such an extended period of time. A more likely possibility, which the deposition and ceramic data seem to support, is that after Chacoan abandonment but prior to the advent of the Mesa Verdean reoccupation, a local San Juan population moved into the Pueblo or were moving in as the Chacoans were moving out."

On the basis of stylistic continuity in San Juan Whitewares, Franklin (1980:94) also questions whether the site was ever completely abandoned in the A.D. 1100s. Adams's reference to a "local San Juan population" apparently is based on Franklin's identification of a ceramic complex dominated by McElmo Black-on-white instead of Mesa Verde Black-on-white in contexts thought to date to the late A.D. 1100s (Franklin 1980:95). Overall, the evidence from Salmon suggests that occupation in the middle and late A.D. 1100s was light but that a period of complete abandonment cannot be ruled out.

Examination of the tree-ring analysis records from Salmon Ruin (courtesy of Jeffrey Dean at the Laboratory of Tree-Ring Research, University of Arizona) shows shifts in construction wood similar to those noted at the Aztec complex. Wood species used for beams in initial construction in the late A.D. 1000s and early 1100s contrast strongly with post-A.D. 1200 construction wood (with most but not all of the latter dates coming from the reroofing of the Great Kiva in the A.D. 1260s). In the Primary or florescent Chacoan occupation, 308 wood samples having non-vv dates were tabulated. Of these, 25 percent were juniper, 65 percent ponderosa pine, 9 percent fir or Douglas fir, and 1 percent white fir and piñon pine. For the later or Secondary occupation, 83 wood samples yielded post-A.D. 1200 dates (including a few vv dates). Of these, 81 percent were juniper, and 19 percent were fir or Douglas fir. In both building periods, the juniper could have been obtained nearby, because it "grows vigorously and abundantly within a 10 km radius" of Salmon Ruin (K. Adams 1980:494). Douglas fir can grow on sheltered, north-facing canyon walls at quite low elevations, so it could also have come from nearby canyons, although the nearest dense stands are some 80 km away (K. Adams 1980:501). The biggest contrast between the two periods of construction is the predominance of ponderosa pine in the earlier period and its complete absence in the later period. K. Adams (1980:490) notes that ponderosa has been observed 34 km southwest of Salmon but that abundant stands are not available until "one travels over 80 km north and east and reaches the mountains of southwestern Colorado."

Because reroofing the Great Kiva in the A.D. 1260s would have required large, straight timbers, builders would have preferred beams of either Douglas fir or ponderosa pine. What is striking, however, is that they did not use ponderosa pine at all, despite heavy dependence on it during initial construction of the Salmon Great House more than 150 years earlier. The small number of fir beams recorded for the

A.D. 1200s construction could have been acquired close to the site—occasional use of Douglas fir is not uncommon in Pueblo III sites from the Northern San Juan. At Salmon Ruin, systems for organizing and motivating work parties, either from Salmon or from communities located closer to the supply of ponderosa pine, evidently were no longer viable in the 1200s, even though builders had relied upon them during the initial construction phase in the late A.D. 1000s and early 1100s.

Turning to another characteristic of the major, florescent-period Chacoan Great Houses—imports of materials from outside the locality—we see a dramatic reduction in scale and variety of imports at Salmon Ruin after the early A.D. 1100s. The excavators of Salmon Ruin recognized three periods of occupation: Primary, representing initial Chacoan construction and occupation; Intermediate, representing a light occupation in the late 1100s and perhaps early 1200s, dominated by McElmo Black-on-white pottery; and a heavy Secondary occupation in the 1200s, dominated by Mesa Verde Black-on-white. Franklin (1980:186–187) characterizes the changes in ceramics through the Salmon Ruin sequence:

> The most obvious trend observed in the qualitative assignments of types and varieties to occupation lies in the difference between the Primary and later periods. Although containing fewer ceramics than the Secondary, the Primary assemblage contains a representation of many more series and types than do the later periods.... By contrast, the Intermediate and Secondary occupations are dominated by vast quantities of San Juan ceramics (over 90% of the decorated assemblage). There are very few intrusives in the post-Primary periods...and those are almost entirely from the White Mountain Redware series.... The utility wares also become exclusively San Juan graywares by the Secondary. The considerable amounts of intrusive utility ware from the Chuska and Chaco areas decline, along with the whiteware imports from those regions.

Franklin (1980:187–188) attributed the decline in nonlocal pottery after the Primary occupation to a collapse of the Chacoan trading network. Comparable quantitative data from Morris's excavations at Aztec West are not available.

Shelley's (1980) analysis of lithic materials from Salmon also shows that frequencies of Narbona Pass chert (previously called "Washington Pass chert") decline dramatically after the Primary occupation. Of the 3,022 Primary-occupation lithic items identified as to source, 279, or 10.8 percent, were of the distinctive Narbona chert that also figures prominently as an import into Chaco Canyon during the florescent period (Cameron 2001). In the Secondary occupation at Salmon, Narbona chert fell to 181 out of 11,486 items, or 1.6 percent. Shelley (1980:53–54) reports that the Secondary occupation occurrences of Narbona chert were concentrated in fallen roof deposits from rooms that also had Primary occupation refuse with high frequencies of Washington Pass (Narbona) chert. This implies that much and perhaps most of the Secondary occupation occurrences of Narbona chert were initially deposited during the Primary occupation.

Shelley (1980:149) also reports thirty-four pieces of turquoise from Mesa Verde (presumably Secondary) contexts at Salmon. It does not appear that the sample includes items left with burials. Surprisingly, the Primary occupation yielded only nine pieces of turquoise (Shelley 1980:52). Numbers of source-identified lithics can provide a rough basis for standardizing these numbers for the purpose of comparison. Turquoise occurrences are equal to about 0.3 percent of the number of lithics in both the Primary and Secondary occupations, indicating no change in relative frequencies. Morris's (1924) report on burials from Aztec West does show that, during the Mesa Verde period (equivalent to the Secondary occupation at Salmon), several burials had associated items of turquoise, olivella, and abalone shell, as well as ornaments likely made of local materials. The quantities of turquoise and shell from Mesa Verde–period burials reported by Morris (1924) appear lower, on average, than at florescent-period burials from Chaco Canyon Great Houses.

In summary, if a Chacoan elite survived in the Totah region after the end of the Chacoan florescent period, its social power appears to have been much diminished and little, if at all, different from that of leaders at other contemporary and equally large communities in the Northern San Juan. After the A.D. 1130s none of the Northern San Juan

Great House communities, including Aztec, displayed the indicators of social complexity that were present at the major Chacoan centers during the florescent period. For example, there were no large-scale, planned construction events involving large numbers of rooms at the Aztec complex or at Salmon after the early 1100s. The leaders at the major Totah Great Houses could no longer motivate and organize work parties to bring in large construction beams from a distance. Furthermore, the data from Salmon indicate that the scale of long-distance import of both utilitarian and exotic materials decreased dramatically after the early A.D. 1100s.

### Were There Outlying Chacoan Great Houses in the Northern San Juan after the A.D. 1130s?

Most of the Northern San Juan Chaco-style Great Houses built in the late A.D. 1000s and early 1100s continued to be occupied or were reoccupied during the 1200s, and they may well have retained considerable importance in the ceremonial and social life of their associated communities. A tree-ring cutting date of A.D. 1172 indicates that people repaired the Great Kiva at the Lowry Site and evidently used it several generations after its construction (Ahlstrom 1985). On the other hand, the kind of remodeling done at most of these Great Houses is consistent with their conversion to ordinary residential use by multiple households. Although some Great Houses were incorporated into new types of community centers in the 1200s, most became spatially peripheral to these new centers.

It is also important to remember that all Southwestern "Great Houses" are not Chacoan Great Houses. Nucleated settlement patterns with larger-than-ordinary buildings or roomblocks at their center occurred in the San Juan area well before and well after the period of Chacoan florescence.[7] What distinguishes outlying Chacoan Great Houses from other San Juan central structures is that they reference specifically Chacoan architectural styles and layouts, as established at the major centers. Also, Chacoan Great Houses and associated Great Kivas are distinguished by construction that is more formal and that required substantially more investment of labor, compared with surrounding "ordinary" residences. Chacoan Great Houses contrast strongly with surrounding residences, which were usually dispersed over a radius of several kilometers during the florescent period.

Neither Aztec West nor Aztec East appears to have served as an architectural model for the community centers constructed in the Northern San Juan area in the late A.D. 1100s through the early 1200s (early Pueblo III period), implying that building a house that ostentatiously referenced one of the major Chacoan centers was no longer a useful strategy for displaying prestige. At this time, Northern San Juan communities consisted predominantly of dispersed small habitations, but some communities had nuclei of multiple residential roomblocks, each containing several contiguous Prudden units. Varying numbers of smaller roomblocks or individual habitation units are widely scattered around the nucleus. Great Kivas are sometimes associated, but civic architecture in general is rare (Lipe and Ortman 2000; Lipe and Varien 1999b; Varien 1999). At some communities, one can dimly perceive a "Great House" section within one of the nuclear roomblocks—that is, a multiple-story section, perhaps with blocked-in kivas but with room sizes and kiva-to-room ratios little if any different from the surrounding architecture.

A good example is the Bass Site complex (figure 8.7) in the Woods Canyon locality of southwestern Colorado (Lipe 1999b; Lipe and Ortman 2000). Here, a residential roomblock with nine kivas includes a two-story section that has three blocked-in kivas and four towers on its periphery. Associated pottery indicates an occupation in the late A.D. 1100s or early 1200s (Lipe and Ortman 2000). Several additional single-story, multiple-habitation roomblocks are nearby. Outside this central complex is a dispersed pattern of one- and two-unit habitations.

In any case, the subtle level of architectural differentiation of the Bass complex "Great House" differs greatly from that displayed by Great Houses of the Chaco florescent period, not only at the main centers but also at the outliers. Overall, the early Pueblo III period community patterns in the central Mesa Verde region contrast with those of the Chaco florescent period. They also do not mimic the architectural pattern of Aztec East, which was constructed largely in Pueblo III but appears to retain the essential characteristics of a Chaco florescent-period Great House. West of the central Mesa Verde area, however, the Chacoan pattern may have continued to prevail. In the San Juan River valley in southeastern Utah, the Bluff Great House, which displays sev-

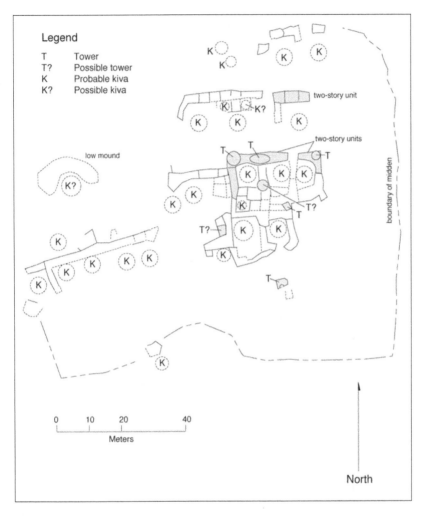

**FIGURE 8.7**

*The Bass Site complex. The roomblock with a two-story section dates to the early A.D. 1200s, based on seriation of associated pottery. (After Lipe 1999b; also see Lipe and Ortman 2000)*

eral classic Chaco features, including constructed berms (Cameron 2002), appears to have been built in the late A.D. 1000s or early 1100s but evidently continued to be the central structure in a widely dispersed settlement pattern well into the A.D. 1200s.

In the late Pueblo III period (A.D. 1225–1290), a different type of

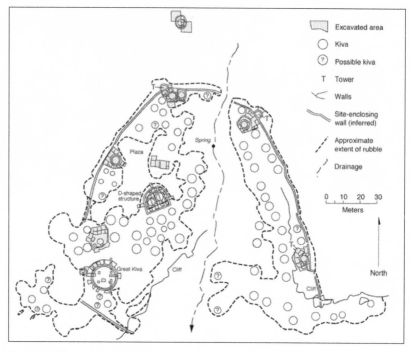

**FIGURE 8.8**

*Sand Canyon Pueblo, a late Pueblo III canyon-rim village in southwestern Colorado. Architectural details are shown only in excavated areas. (After Ortman and Bradley 2002:42)*

community center developed in the Northern San Juan, coincident with a settlement shift to canyon-oriented locations and, evidently, with the intensification of warfare throughout the region (Lipe 1995; Lipe and Ortman 2000; Ortman et al. 2000). Examples include Sand Canyon Pueblo (figure 8.8) and Seven Towers Pueblo (figure 8.9). Most Chaco-style Great Houses built in the early 1100s became more marginal to the centers of their communities at this time, although many have evidence of continued use. The increasingly aggregated, canyon-oriented villages of the middle and late 1200s display the usual San Juan–pattern habitation units organized around small household kivas. Often, these units are built to conform to irregular canyon topography and/or to adjacent units, so they are not as uniform in layout as earlier examples. In the more tightly aggregated villages, habitation units are adjacent to one another, forming large roomblocks; in others, the

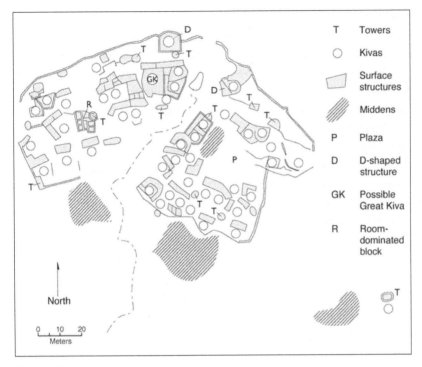

**FIGURE 8.9**

*Seven Towers Pueblo, an unexcavated late Pueblo III canyon-rim village in southwestern Colorado. (After Lipe and Ortman 2000:99)*

habitations are merely clustered. These villages typically have a precinct with distinctive civic architecture, including a D-shaped, multiwalled building, an informal plaza, a tower complex, and occasionally a Great Kiva and/or a complex of storage rooms not associated with a particular habitation. In addition to defensible locations, the late Pueblo III villages usually have a masonry wall enclosing all or part of the settlement.

These late villages do not appear to have been modeled on the Great Houses at Aztec, including Aztec East, which evidently was completed in the A.D. 1200s (Brown, Windes, and McKenna 2002). The central Mesa Verde villages consist of multiple, single-story masonry roomblocks, rather than one or two massive, multiple-story structures (as at Aztec). Although sites such as Sand Canyon Pueblo (Bradley 1993; Ortman and Bradley 2002) may have followed a very general plan, they grew by small additions, not as a result of rapidly executed building projects simultaneously involving numerous structures. Furthermore, surface rooms are typically small and low-ceilinged, only locally available building timbers were used, and the masonry construction and architectural details are more variable and much less formal than in the major florescent-period Chacoan Great Houses.

Despite the differences noted above, there are some points of similarity. One can see bilateral spatial organization both at Aztec East (where two massive buildings are set side-by-side fronting a plaza) and in the late Pueblo III canyon-rim villages, which are usually bisected by a drainage or, in a few cases, by a wall (Lipe and Ortman 2000). The circular tri-wall structures associated with some Chacoan Great Houses (for example, the Hubbard Site at Aztec West and a similar structure at Pueblo del Arroyo at Chaco Canyon) could have provided models for the multiwalled, nonresidential structures present at most of the late Pueblo III villages in the central Mesa Verde region. On the basis of associated pottery, Vivian (1959) interpreted the Hubbard tri-wall as dating to the A.D. 1200s, but Lekson (1983b) makes a case that this structure, like the one at Pueblo del Arroyo, was built in the middle or even early A.D. 1100s. The great tower at Yellow Jacket Pueblo (Kuckelman 2003) bears some resemblance to the Hubbard tri-wall and dates to the middle or late A.D. 1200s. The great majority of the late Pueblo III multiple-walled structures in the central Mesa Verde area, however, are not circular tri-walls but are D-shaped bi-walls (Sun Temple at Mesa Verde National Park is probably the best-known example). If these emulate a Chacoan prototype, they do so only in a remote way. To my knowledge, D-shaped bi-walls are not part of the Aztec or Chaco Canyon architectural repertoires.

Pueblo III in the central Mesa Verde region is also characterized by a marked drop (relative to the late Pueblo II period) in the number and relative frequency of artifacts originating outside the region. High-value exotic items such as shell and turquoise disappear almost entirely from assemblages. For example, ten years of excavations by the Crow Canyon Archaeological Center at Pueblo III sites in southwestern Colorado yielded nearly 135,000 corrugated cooking pot sherds, but only 3 items of turquoise, 9 of obsidian, 18 of shell, and 10 of jet. There was little difference in the frequency of these items between the four-hundred-room Sand Canyon Pueblo and the much smaller, nearby sites that were tested (Lipe 2002b). By contrast, in excavations by the Chaco Archaeological Project in Pueblo II contexts at Chaco Canyon, turquoise was more than one hundred times as common relative to sherds than in the southwestern Colorado Pueblo III sites (Lipe 2002b; Phillips 1993). Ceramic wares originating outside the Northern San Juan are also quite rare at sites dating to the A.D. 1200s in the central Mesa Verde region. That this is also true for the post-florescent occupation at Salmon Ruin in the Totah has already been discussed.

The decline in long-distance circulation of both utilitarian and exotic goods in the Northern San Juan is consistent with the inference that regional and interregional exchange networks had broken down. As argued above and elsewhere (Judge 1989), a pilgrimage system tying distant communities to the major centers at Chaco Canyon and Aztec probably facilitated such exchanges during the Chacoan florescent period. The implication is that neither Aztec nor other sites in the Northern San Juan functioned in this way after the early A.D. 1100s.

One other piece of evidence indicates that Aztec is unlikely to have been a primate political center for the Northern San Juan after the period of Chacoan florescence. Between the early A.D. 1100s and the 1200s, the settlement gap between Aztec and the rest of the Northern San Juan greatly widened (Lipe and Varien 1999b). Continuing a trend evident in the Pueblo II period, the Pueblo III Northern San Juan population concentrated in two areas—the Totah region of New Mexico and the central Mesa Verde region (the Mesa Verde/Mancos, Ute, and Monument/McElmo subregions, to use the terminology of Lipe and Varien 1999b). After A.D. 1150 few habitation sites remained in the Piedra drainage, the Colorado portion of the La Plata and Animas drainages, or the easternmost headwaters of the Mancos and McElmo, that is, in the areas north of Aztec. What this means is unclear, but it could indicate that a hostile relationship between the communities of the Totah and those of the central Mesa Verde region led to the formation of a "no-man's land" north of Aztec. This would be consistent with Kohler and Kramer's (2003) inference that raiding parties from the Totah might have been capturing women in the central Mesa Verde area in the 1200s (also see Martin 1997).

Overall, the regional structure of Northern San Juan settlement and community patterns in the late A.D. 1100s through 1200s implies that numerous, politically independent, and probably competitive communities and community clusters existed (Lipe 2002b). This also is consistent with evidence that raiding was regionally endemic at that time. We cannot rule out the formation of large, multicommunity alliances, but there is no evidence that such alliances were strong enough and long-lasting enough to be reflected in architectural and settlement patterns.

In general, the data from the post-florescent period indicate a return to "normal" in the Four Corners region, with relatively low levels of political hierarchy and low levels of regional political and economic integration. This is not to say that people did not remember the Chacoan florescence or that it had no effect on what happened subsequently (Bradley 1996). These effects, however, appear to be primarily the result of Chaco's role in the region's cultural history, rather than due to the continuation of a political and ceremonial system that had flourished for nearly a century between A.D. 1040 and 1135.

## CONCLUSION

The San Juan pattern of architecture and settlement layout must have symbolized several long-lasting, widely held beliefs about cosmology and the social order. By incorporating elaborated versions of these existing symbols into Great House architecture and community patterns, Chacoan leaders were able to link newly hierarchical and large-scale social formations to beliefs already widely accepted by San Juan populations. Elements of the basic San Juan pattern were maintained in Northern San Juan communities after the collapse of the hierarchical Chacoan system. This pattern—and probably some aspects of community organization linked to it—did not survive the depopulation of the Northern San Juan in the late A.D. 1200s and the widespread rise of plaza-oriented pueblos in northern Rio Grande and Western Pueblo areas in the A.D. 1200s and 1300s.

During the time of Chacoan florescence—from about A.D. 1040 to 1135—the main Chaco Canyon and Totah centers supported an elite ceremonial/political leadership that exercised greater social power than any that preceded or succeeded it in the Pueblo tradition. Evidence includes the organization of large-scale building projects, the importation of quantities of construction beams, pottery, turquoise, maize, and certain lithic materials, and the ostentation of the architectural contrasts between the Great Houses and ordinary residences.

The expansion of Chacoan-style Great Houses into the Northern San Juan was relatively late and short-lived—from about A.D. 1075 to 1130 or 1135. Construction of major Great Houses at Salmon and in the Aztec group probably represents a relocation northward of the major locus of Chacoan power and influence. Smaller Great Houses that clearly referenced Chacoan architectural models were built in many communities in the Northern San Juan during this period.

Outlying Great House communities in the Northern San Juan do not appear to have been politically or economically controlled by the major centers. Rather, the leaders of the outlying communities probably used pilgrimages to Chaco or later to Aztec to acquire status and influence in their own communities. In turn, they mobilized contributions of labor and materials that helped support the social and ceremonial systems operative at the major Great Houses. In the Northern San Juan, the period of Chacoan florescence was a time when pottery and some other goods circulated more widely than both before and later. Most people lived in small habitation units, or clusters of such units, that composed dispersed communities centered on a small Great House and/or other elements of civic architecture. Residential mobility appears to have been high on a local, and perhaps regional, level.

There is little evidence that Chacoan leaders at the major centers used coercive violence to extend their political control or influence into the Northern San Juan hinterland. Several well-documented cases of cannibalism and/or extreme violence from the Northern San Juan occurred in the period A.D. 1130–1160, when the severe mid-1100s drought was setting in and when the regional influence of the main Chacoan centers seems to have dissipated or to have been in steep decline.

After the middle A.D. 1100s most outlying Northern San Juan communities no longer referenced Chacoan models when constructing civic architecture, even though the massive Chacoan-period buildings at Aztec and Salmon continued to be occupied. There, large-scale organized building projects no longer took place, local instead of distantly acquired building timbers were used, and imports of nonlocal pottery and lithic materials declined substantially. Thus, evidence of social hierarchy and control diminished, even at the major Great Houses that continued to be occupied in the Totah region.

In the A.D. 1200s new forms of public architecture and settlement layout spread through the Northern San Juan, making the increasingly aggregated villages of this period even more different from preceding Chacoan models. Although construction of the Aztec East Great House dates largely to the 1200s, it did not serve as a model for the construction of central buildings at outlying communities, as had the earlier major Great Houses. Warfare—probably among multiple communities—also intensified during the A.D. 1200s. The evidence indicates that, during the A.D. 1200s, the Northern San Juan had a multitude of small independent polities, with no primate center of political, ceremonial, or economic influence.

### Notes

1. Northern San Juan region and Mesa Verde region refer to the same area and are used interchangeably. Within the Northern San Juan, I refer to the central Mesa Verde region as the area from the Mesa Verde proper to Cottonwood Wash in southeastern Utah. Totah refers to the area that includes the lower Animas and La Plata River valleys and adjacent portions of the San Juan River valley in northwestern New Mexico.

2. Throughout the chapter, San Juan drainage, Northern San Juan, and Southern San Juan refer to hydrologic basins, that is, the areas drained by the San Juan River or by its northern and southern tributaries. In the regional literature, the term *San Juan Basin* often applies to the San Juan geologic basin, a large area centered in northwestern New Mexico that is defined on the basis of a structural depression in the underlying geologic formations. The San Juan geologic basin is bordered on the north by the San Juan and La Plata mountains of southwestern Colorado, on the west by the Defiance uplifts and the Chuska Mountains, on the south by the Zuni Mountains, and on the east by the Nacimiento Uplift. The southwestern portion of the San Juan geologic basin extends into the Upper Little Colorado drainage, and the southeastern portion extends into the headwaters of the Rio Puerco, which drains into the Rio Grande. Chaco Canyon is located in the central San Juan geologic basin, which is often what is meant by references in the Chacoan literature to "the San Juan Basin."

3. Flannery and Marcus (1976) introduced the term *public architecture* in reference to facilities associated with public rituals or other activities that promote the social integration of communities or segments of communities. In the Pueblo Southwest, this label often applies to Great Kivas, Great Houses, multiwalled struc-

tures, plazas, and so on. Bradley (1996) has suggested that a more appropriate label for such structures would be *civic architecture*, because some of the structures referenced were probably not public in the sense of having unrestricted access. In addition, Bradley's term is general enough to include the houses of community leaders, which cross-culturally are often larger or more elaborate than ordinary residences.

4. In addition to the architectural and settlement layout features noted in the text, traits that did not accompany Mesa Verde–region migrants to their new locations include pecked-block "McElmo style" masonry, Mesa Verde mugs and kiva jars, and deer humerus scrapers (Lipe and Lekson 2001).

5. I read the architectural and settlement data to indicate a considerable disjunction between Pueblo III San Juan community organization and that represented by both contemporary and later plaza-oriented pueblos. Ware (2002b) has recently used similar data to argue that deep-rooted continuities linked some aspects of San Juan social organization to Pueblo IV and historic Pueblo forms.

6. The sites that fall into a mid-A.D. 1100s group (as listed in Kuckelman, Lightfoot, and Martin 2000) include 5MT10207 in Aztec Wash, the Cowboy Wash sites, the Grinnell Site, Hanson Pueblo, La Plata 41, Mancos Canyon, Marshview Hamlet, Mesa Verde 499, Rattlesnake Ruin, Yellow Jacket 5MT3, and the Seed Jar Site (5MT3892).

7. In my opinion, many Northern San Juan sites listed as Chaco-era (A.D. 900–1150) Great Houses in the Chaco World database (2004) and in Kantner (2003c) probably postdate A.D. 1150, and some lack clear evidence of Chacoan architectural influences. They may be Great Houses, but are they Chacoan Great Houses?

# 9

# Notes from the South

Andrew I. Duff and Stephen H. Lekson

This chapter explores Chaco's external relationships and lasting influences by looking to its southern neighbors. South stands in contrast to North (Lipe, chapter 8 of this volume) in that there is no clear southern boundary of societies with the potential for interaction with Chaco: potential peer, near-peer, and superior societies that could have affected Chaco's history are plentiful. North of Chaco, fully agricultural Pueblo societies reach their limit in southern Utah and Colorado, about latitude 35 degrees. To the south, Pueblo-like sites extend well into Chihuahua, Mexico. Agricultural societies, of varying degrees of complexity, extend to southern Chile. Where to stop?

Faraway places were not irrelevant (see Nelson, chapter 10 of this volume). The remarkable, discontinuous distribution of metallurgy from Ecuador to western Mexico to the greater Southwest (Hosler 1994) may someday prove useful for understanding Chaco. Here, however, we confine ourselves to the "Greater Southwest." We believe that Chaco's near southern neighbors were neither full participants in whatever Chaco was nor bystanders unaware of developments to the north (and south). Ideas, apparently more so than materials, from both directions shaped Chaco and subsequent Pueblo history in important and

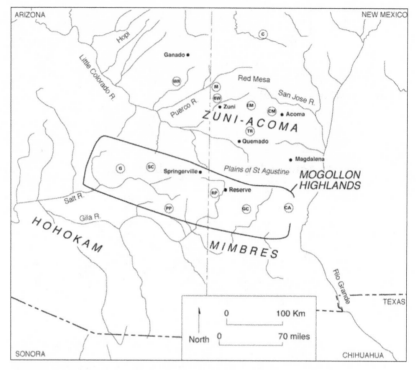

**FIGURE 9.1**

*Selected sites and places mentioned in this chapter:* BW, *Bosson Wash;* C, *Chaco;* CA, *Cañada Alamosa;* CM, *Cebolleta Mesa;* EM, *El Morro;* G, *Grasshopper;* GC, *Gila Cliff Dwellings;* M, *Manuelito Canyon;* PP, *Point of Pines;* RP, *Reserve-Pine Lawn;* SC, *Silver Creek;* TR, *Tom's Rock;* and WR, *Wide Ruins.*

enduring ways. Chaco's waves reached the southernmost margins of the Colorado Plateau, while north-moving ripples crossed the "Chichimec Sea" (Mathien and McGuire 1986). They met in the southern Southwest, creating a complex moiré of historically unique, interconnected patterns. Here, we address Chaco's relations with areas to the south, using the three heuristic spatial zones. From near to far these are (1) Zuni-Acoma, (2) the Mogollon Highlands, and (3) the Mimbres and Hohokam deserts (figure 9.1).

## ZUNI AND ACOMA

We use *Zuni-Acoma* to refer to a large and diverse area encompassing the Acoma (Dittert 1959) and Zuni (Ferguson and Hart 1985) regions, as most would recognize them, but extending these west and south to the apparent periphery of the Great House distribution. The heart of this region encompasses "Cibola" (LeBlanc 1989a; Vivian 1990:figure 9.1), but the patterning discussed here exceeds Cibola as it is traditionally conceived. In every respect, this area exhibits more diversity than homogeneity, except when viewed in relation to Chaco. These regions were touched by Chaco and possess Great Houses, but— as we argue below—they appear to have been less directly implicated during Chacoan times than might be expected. Importantly, and in contrast to the North, Pueblo peoples still make their home in this area. Many Pueblo groups have historical interests and ties to Chaco and the southern area. We use *Zuni-Acoma* as an archaeological convention, not as a cultural affiliation.

On the north, the region's boundary approximates the route of Interstate 40, following the courses of the Rio San Jose and Rio Puerco of the West. On the south, the boundary corresponds approximately with the northern reaches of the Sitgreaves, Apache, Gila, and Cibola national forests or with a curving line from west of Springerville, Arizona, to Magdalena, New Mexico.

The northern boundary is the most problematic (see Kantner and Kintigh, chapter 5 of this volume). Between Chaco and the Zuni-Acoma region, the Red Mesa Valley clearly defines a transitional zone in both physiography and patterning. Vivian (1990) has argued that the Hosta Butte small-house pattern at Chaco Canyon represents a southern tradition from the Red Mesa Valley and southern San Juan Basin, but he also sees strong ties to the north in the Great House–occupying populations of Chaco Canyon. Others, including contributors to this volume such as Lipe, Wilshusen, and Van Dyke, also argue for a strong northern connection for Chaco and its early peers. Most researchers, from Gladwin to Vivian, include the Red Mesa Valley within the larger Chacoan region. Therefore, we consider the cultural dynamics of Chaco and the Red Mesa/Southern San Juan area to be an internal affair. Included in our discussion is the Puerco of the West Valley, in many ways the western extension of the Red Mesa Valley (see Vivian 1990). Although it most closely resembles Chacoan patterning during Chaco's heyday, patterning along the river and northward (annexing turf usually considered "Tusayan") parallels the larger, post-Chacoan developments of the Zuni-Acoma region.

For many researchers, the northern and central portions of the

Zuni-Acoma district were a part of the Chacoan region—whatever *Chacoan region* might mean. This is both true and misleading. We argue that Chaco was an enduring and influential force in the district, but even more so after it was gone. Residents of areas on Chaco's immediate and more distant fringes shared organizational strategies and selectively incorporated elements of Chacoan materiality, but in the context of local histories and traditions that differed from the larger San Juan Basin. Departing from much of the recent scholarship on peripheral Great House communities, what strike us as most significant about Chaco in the Zuni-Acoma region are its uses and relevance during the post-Chacoan period. To make this case, we will briefly reevaluate the developmental sequence and the distribution of Chacoan Great Houses in the region.

Pre-Chaco-era archaeology for this area is surprisingly poorly known, best represented from its western and southern flanks. We know of large Pueblo I sites from the Ganado area (Gilpin and Benallie 2000), south of the Puerco in Arizona (Roberts 1931, 1939), and the Quemado region (Bullard 1962; Smith 1973) and from wide-ranging surveys (Beeson 1966; Danson 1957; Whalen 1984; Peter McKenna, personal communication 2003). Although research agendas and issues of visibility contribute to the apparent dearth of Chacoan precursors, the patchy Pueblo I settlement across this area suggests a lower density phenomenon than its northern counterpart—even lower than the southern reaches of the San Juan Basin discussed by Wilshusen and Van Dyke (chapter 7 of this volume).

Additionally, known Pueblo I sites suggest that mobility remained a larger component of the adaptation in the South than for its more northern and San Juan Basin counterparts. For example, pit structures from Kiatuthlanna, namesake site for the diagnostic pottery type of the later A.D. 800s and early 900s, are quite variable, relatively small, and unaccompanied by substantial aboveground constructions (Roberts 1931:figures 1, 5, 7). Comparable nearby sites exhibit more analogous surface structures, with jacal rooms and granaries (Roberts 1939:figures 1, 25), but nothing on the scale or with the formality of northern Pueblo I constructions. Early Chaco Canyon construction patterning has more direct parallels with populations to the north (Vivian 1990; Wilshusen and Ortman 1999; Wilshusen and Van Dyke, chapter 7, and Lipe, chapter 8, of this volume).

There are few pre-1000 Great House candidates in the region and the southern San Juan Basin (Vivian 1990:figure 7.6; Wilshusen and Van Dyke, chapter 7 of this volume, figure 7.7). Bosson Wash (Fowler, Stein, and Anyon 1987:139) on the Zuni Reservation and some settlements along the Rio Puerco (Kantner and Kintigh, chapter 5 of this volume, figure 5.8; Van Dyke 2000) seem to us to be the strongest candidates. Additional possibilities exist along the northern boundary (Wilshusen and Van Dyke, chapter 7 of this volume).

By the mid-1000s, communities organized around Great Houses became widespread throughout the Colorado Plateau (Lekson 1991; Vivian 1990) (refer to figure 5.1). Great Houses are documented from Acoma (Dittert 1959), all along the Rio Puerco of the West (Fowler and Stein 1992; Warburton and Graves 1992), from the Zuni Reservation (Fowler, Stein, and Anyon 1987; Roberts 1932), and as far south as the Quemado area (Duff and Schachner n.d.; Fowler, Stein, and Anyon 1987). The Great House pattern extends along the west side of the Chuskas and Chinle Wash (Kantner and Kintigh, chapter 5 of this volume; Stein and Fowler 1996:124), into the Northern San Juan (Lipe, chapter 8 of this volume), and east to Guadalupe (Durand and Durand 2000). The clarity of the Chacoan pattern dissipates or disappears as one moves beyond these areas.

Chaco-era Great Houses and communities are present and recognizable throughout the region, but the nature and extent of their interactions with Chaco, if any, are as much matters of inquiry for the Zuni-Acoma region as for other non-core Chacoan Great Houses (Duff and Schachner n.d.). Some settlements, especially those in the Puerco of the West drainage, clearly indicate Chaco's touch, at least, relative to earlier structures in the immediate area (Roberts 1931:175–176). Yet, Zuni-Acoma settlements and Great Houses appear not to have participated in the same spheres of interaction as did Chaco. Material goods were neither derived from nor funneled toward Chaco Canyon (Duff and Schachner n.d.; Toll, chapter 4 of this volume).

Pottery characteristic of the era includes hachure-painted types (Chaco/Gallup Black-on-white), but similar designs executed in solids and the development of interacting designs (Wingate-Reserve style, Carlson 1970) are more common at both Great House and community sites. Several Great Houses and associated communities appear in areas lacking previous settlement. These contain decorated ceramic assemblages and architectural patterning consistent with northern roots, but also plainware assemblages dominated by brown ware, frequently with smudging, characteristics reminiscent of more southern mountain origins (Duff 2002).

Great Houses known from the region satisfy the "big bump–little bump" distinction (Lekson 1991) with recognizable Chacoan elements, yet the structures are small, internally variable, and not always associated with Great Kivas (Kantner and Kintigh, chapter 5 of this volume). Great Houses from the Zuni-Acoma, though variable, fall within the bounds of variation, given the larger population of outliers. Many architectural details of these buildings appear to be consistent with local technological traditions emulating Chaco Canyon construction patterns; detailed evaluations of construction knowledge and technique await further excavations (Van Dyke 1999c). Great House architectural variability within the canyon is extensive but seems to elaborate on a more formal theme than is the case among outlying Great Houses.

Bordering the heartland of the Zuni-Acoma region with Great Houses are areas that did not participate directly in Chacoan developments, at least, as expressed by Great Houses. If we use Great Houses as the hallmark of Chacoan influence, the peripheries of the Zuni-Acoma region away from the San Juan Basin mark the system's edge. The edge calls for careful consideration, however. Because maps showing the distribution of Chacoan Great Houses have proliferated in the past two decades, researchers need to scrutinize their contents more carefully now. We would like to introduce a note of caution regarding the interpretation of the Great House patterning for the Zuni-Acoma region, an illustration that has potential implications for other areas.

Kintigh (1994:131) noted that, once we developed the conceptual understanding of Great Houses and outliers, we began to see them everywhere. Frequently, we reinterpreted previously recorded sites in a new light. Kintigh (1994) went on to detail a second conceptual model, that of Stein and Fowler (Fowler and Stein 1992; Fowler, Stein, and Anyon 1987; Kintigh, Howell, and Duff 1996). The new model recognized that elements of the Chaco pattern—Great Houses, Great Kivas, berms, paths, and roads—were carried forward, in modified form, to sites that postdate Chaco. Even though scholars have widely acknowledged post-Chacoan Great House patterning and aggregated communities, they have not projected this recognition back to understand the distribution of Great Houses within the Zuni-Acoma region. A brief consideration of Great House distribution maps and reference to a few particular sites will highlight our point.

Perspectives on Chaco, its extent, and organization range widely from conservative to more liberal or expansive constructions. Judge's (1989:figure 24, 1991:figure 2.1) maps of the Great House distribution show only Village of the Great Kivas (Roberts 1932) south of the Rio Puerco. We use this simply as an example, not to characterize Judge's present position. In the same volume, Lekson (1991:figure 3.10) attributes approximately twenty additional sites to the pattern of Great Houses and/or Great Kivas for the area south of the Puerco, several of which are indicated as "documented" (as opposed to reported). Similarly, there is an expansion of sites west of the Chuskas. Comparable distribution maps are widely reproduced (for example, Lekson et al. 1988; Kantner and Kintigh, chapter 5 of this volume, figure 5.1).

What is sometimes conflated in these maps is the difference between Chaco and post-Chacoan Great Houses. While some differentiate temporal patterning in overall distributions (Fowler and Stein 1992:figure 9.1; Mahoney and Kantner 2000:figure 1.2; Stein and Lekson 1992:figure 8.1; Wilcox 1993:figure 4), many do not. Inspection of the cases just noted reveals a substantial difference in the construal of pattern and temporal association. We would expect this to be the case, given the state of data available (or unavailable) for many sites, with limited recording and a lack of recent visitation. Several sites frequently plotted as Chacoan, however, may well postdate Chaco. Some of this derives from the long-term hangover of the Pecos Classification in site records—where *Pueblo II–Pueblo III* means time to some and pattern to others—but it also reflects thoughts about the meaning of Chaco.

Examples familiar to the authors for the southern extent of the Zuni-Acoma region include Tom's Rock (Fowler, Stein, and Anyon 1987:175–177), recently revisited by Duff and others. Here, the ceramics and patterning suggest a Tularosa Black-on-white and St. Johns Polychrome ceramic association dating to the later 1100s into the 1200s. Similarly, LA 4030 (Fowler, Stein, and Anyon 1987:186–187), revisited by Duff and Schachner in 2002, is also characterized by Tularosa–St. Johns types. Although an impressive rubble mound, LA 4030 has few characteristics of a Great House other than height. It is visible and near Goesling, a post-Chacoan Great House. Bean Patch Ruin, just inside the Arizona border and often plotted as Chacoan, is also a post-Chacoan Great House community (Kintigh 1996:appendix entry 24).

Other sites in the vicinity, known only from site cards with limited information, have become Chacoan Great Houses to many researchers. One example is LA 31808: "Although the details of this structure are not available, the size and height of the rubble suggests a possible two-story building. This could be a great house, and is certainly worth rein-vestigating" (Fowler, Stein, and Anyon 1987:187). Another example is Largo Gap: "Unfortunately no ceramic information is available, but Hammack and Marshall place the site in the Tularosa Phase around A.D. 1150" (Fowler, Stein, and Anyon 1987:164). Some of these may well be Chacoan Great Houses, but many appear to postdate Chaco.

Now that we have a greater conceptual appreciation for post-Chacoan Great Houses and commonly acknowledge the ceramic asso-ciations of particular, absolute, temporal intervals, we need to revisit these sites. For example, Manuelito Canyon exemplified the post-Chacoan Great House pattern (Fowler, Stein, and Anyon 1987; Fowler and Stein 1992; Stein and Fowler 1996), and it may be worth reexamin-ing areas north of the Puerco where Great Houses are noted. Similarly, at least some sites in the Rio Puerco, such as Fenced-Up-Horse Canyon, oft indicated as a Chacoan Great House site, are also post-Chacoan (Schutt 1997; Vivian 1990:344). First indicated as a possibility by Marshall and others (1979), it seems to have become a fixture despite considerations suggesting otherwise (Vivian 1990:344). As many as half the sites conventionally plotted as Chacoan in the Zuni-Acoma region may well have had their primary occupations after the A.D. 1130s. We suspect that this extends to other areas.

Without diminishing the fact that Chacoan Great Houses were pre-sent within the Zuni-Acoma region, we must strive to better understand our data to better appreciate what Chaco meant and was. This makes a difference. It matters because models of the scale, configuration, and workings of the "system" depend on these data. What we hope to accomplish with these limited examples is to suggest that Chaco-era Great House patterning is weaker—but no less important or interesting—than scholars conventionally assume.

The post-Chaco archaeology of this region is much better known: following A.D. 1150 the region first sees strong continuities with Chaco in the development of aggregated, post-Chacoan Great House communities (Kintigh 1994; Kintigh, Howell, and Duff 1996), followed by the development of a remarkable number of nucleated pueblos (Duff 2002; Fowler and Stein 1992; Fowler, Stein, and Anyon 1987; Kintigh 1985, 1996).

If the preceding review is marginally accurate, the prevalence of the post-Chacoan community pattern may be even more important than we have heretofore acknowledged, because many sites thought to be Chacoan date to the post-Chacoan period. In the later 1100s the Zuni-Acoma region is characterized by marked population aggregations organized around a Great House that was not occupied during the Chacoan period (Kintigh 1994, 1996; Roney 1996). A notable element of transformed continuity is the presence of large, unroofed, circular kivas at several post-Chacoan Great House communities (Kintigh 1996; Kintigh, Howell, and Duff 1996). These unroofed kivas can, and may have been designed to, accommodate larger groups associated with aggregated communities (Kintigh 1994:137). That they were open, with whatever activities occurred in them visible to all, marks an important and conscious contrast to the Great Kivas of the Chacoan era. As Lekson notes (chapter 1 of this volume), developments after Chaco were, in part, a reaction to Chaco. Unroofed ritual and political architecture—Great Kivas—appear to be a visible reaction evident in the southern Zuni-Acoma region.

Although some sites may have been previously occupied, aggregation focused around Great House structures included many more households than appear to have been part of most Chacoan communities. Possibly, Chacoan communities did not have the demographic capacity to be self-sustaining (Mahoney 2000; Kantner and Kintigh, chapter 5 of this volume), but post-Chacoan communities probably exceeded the demographic threshold for potential community endogamy. Social considerations and connections may still have dictated preference to exogamous ties between communities; ceramic circulation data show some indications of this (Duff 1994b; Stone 1999). The pattern of post-Chacoan, Great House–oriented communities appears to persist within the region through the mid-1200s.

In the early 1200s near modern Zuni emerged a new community form. Nucleated communities with as many as 1,400 rooms developed (Duff 2000; Kintigh 1985), among the largest prehistoric pueblos in the Southwest. Interestingly, the largest of these sites emerged within an area that lacks Chacoan Great Houses—the El Morro Valley. Many ideas from that era, however, were clearly referenced in architecture, if not in ritual and action. These sites were very formal in layout, with circular or rectangular ground plans (figure 9.2), and were contemporaneous with continued occupation of Great House–oriented, aggregated communities. Is this formality a continuity with earlier Chacoan canons simply transformed for the world after Chaco? Yes, clearly, but also no.

Cibola nucleated towns differ remarkably from earlier Chaco and post-Chaco communities and from contemporary Mesa Verde towns in that the architectural signature of individual households as visible entities is lost, submerged in the massive constructions emblematic of community. Unlike the manically modular dwellers of the North (Lipe, chapter 8 of this volume), the numerous small kivas seen at Mesa Verde and Chacoan sites are conspicuously absent, replaced by formal plazas. Compulsion to conformity in pit structure form appears never to have afflicted the South to the same degree as the North, but what is notable, if not completely novel, is the shift to relatively few "household" or "sodality" kivas and the emergence of a new public form— defined, open, and community-focal space completely surrounded by household construction, with entry and orientation to this space.

Gone is the architectural visibility of household, something that had persisted for roughly a thousand years in the northern Southwest. Chaco and post-Chaco public structures make the house a metaphor for whatever it is these structures come to represent—they are "Great Houses," after all. Nucleated structures represent a new metaphor for community organization, a reconceptualization of the constituent parts of social life. This, too, may have been a reaction to the power gained by some houses and their occupants during Chacoan times. Scholars have suggested meanings for the new metaphors, usually

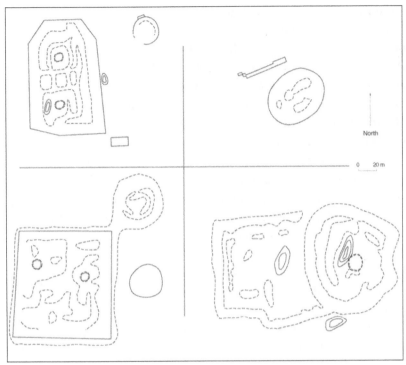

**FIGURE 9.2**

*Pueblo IV ground plans from Zuni area sites. (Redrawn from plans in Kintigh 1985)*

related to plan-view shape. This is and is not wholesale transformation, at least, not immediately. A few of the earliest nucleated structures (Kluckhohn 1939:Box S) have an unroofed Great Kiva of the post-Chacoan form, as well as constructions within the plaza (Duff and Schachner n.d.). One transformed continuity was the mobilization of labor—towns were constructed in well-organized, large-scale construction events. Patterning organized on the template of Chaco characterizes most of the region; reconceptualization appears to have developed in the portion of the region that lacked Chaco-era occupation.

The spread of this development did not take long. By about A.D. 1275 it became the nearly exclusive architectural form for the Western Pueblo area (Duff 2000, 2002; Kintigh 1990). Undoubtedly, the reconfiguration of communities in the minds of their memberships varied extensively, but many elements of Puebloan social structure for

Western Pueblos crystallized during this period (Adams 1991; Crown 1994; Duff 2002). This nucleated settlement pattern extends to all portions of the region that had Chacoan Great Houses (including the Rio Puerco of the West, Wide Ruins, Cebolleta Mesa, and Mariana Mesa) and to neighboring areas that did not (including the Arizona Mountains, the Middle Little Colorado, Anderson Mesa, and the Hopi Mesas). With these developments, Chaco apparently began to decline in referential importance, but it did not disappear.

Consolidations throughout the Western Pueblo area resulted in greater interactions among regional populations. By about A.D. 1400 another series of reconfigurations resulted in settlement contraction to the areas occupied at the time of initial Spanish contact: the Hopi Mesas, near modern Zuni, and Acoma.

## THE MOGOLLON HIGHLANDS

The Mogollon Highlands constitute a broad band of forested mountains along the Mogollon Rim. Of particular interest here are the sites of the Silver Creek region (Mills, Herr, and Van Keuren 1999), the area around the Plains of St. Agustine, and the highlands of the Mogollon Mountains in New Mexico. Within this region, Chaco's influence was variable and variably problematic. On the west, Sarah Herr (2001) argues, residents from within the reaches of the Chaco region immigrated to the Silver Creek area, organizing themselves in communities centered on Great Kivas, while consciously electing to leave behind Great Houses and Chaco itself. The Arizona highlands, according to Herr, were literally "beyond Chaco." To the east, in hills around the Plains of St. Augustine, are old and cryptic reports of Great House–like structures near the town of Reserve (Aragon; Hough 1907) and, perhaps, Magdalena ("Camelot-on-the-San-Augustine," LA 5975, notes on file at the Laboratory of Anthropology). Neither has been confirmed, but they appear on many outlier maps (published or personal).

In the past few decades, Chaco seldom appeared in archaeological thinking about the Mogollon Highlands of southwestern New Mexico and southeastern Arizona, and then, mainly in negation (for a cogent, late 1980s argument for Chaco in the Mogollon Highlands, see LeBlanc 1989a). Chaco, Cibola, and Anasazi peoples, however, are slipping back into the picture of the Mogollon Highlands, in both New Mexico and Arizona.

Emil Haury (1985) was a strong proponent of Anasazi movements after A.D. 1000 into the Mogollon Highlands (and beyond, into the Mimbres region, discussed below). Haury's position was echoed by his student, Joe Ben Wheat (1955), in Mogollon's "organic act": *Mogollon Culture prior to A.D. 1000.* Wheat (1955:229) saw increased "cultural blending" with Anasazi through time, especially after A.D. 900. In recent decades, the spectre of "Anasazi swamping" or "Anasazification" (Haury's playful terms) was anathema in Mogollon archaeology (LeBlanc 1983), but perhaps the time is right to revive Haury's (and other early archaeologists') notions of Mogollon after A.D. 1000. Recent work in the Silver Creek region of central Arizona reaches a conclusion congruent with Haury's: significant in-migration by Chaco Anasazi populations from 1000 to the early 1100s (Herr 2001; Mills 1998; Mills, Herr, and Van Keuren 1999). *Chaco Anasazi* does not literally mean people from Chaco Canyon, but rather populations from the densely settled, southern Chaco region, perhaps the Puerco of the West area.

Herr does not see the Chaco Great House community pattern in the Mogollon Highlands. Rather, she concludes that people "beyond Chaco" created small communities around circular (that is, Chaco-style) Great Kivas. She notes that "the great kivas of the region were similar to those of the Chacoan region, but comparatively lacked the same kind of labor investment.... The settlers built a structure that would house their rituals, but because the value of labor was so high in this sparsely populated region, they could not or would not replicate the labor-intensive structures of the Chacoan region" (Herr 2001:93).

In New Mexico, much earlier work by Martin and his colleagues identified significant migration and/or trait diffusion into the Reserve–Pine Lawn Valley at about A.D. 1000, potentially from the Zuni-Quemado region (Martin et al. 1956:201–202), with additional suggestive evidence in the vicinity (for example, Bluhm 1957:76–80). Reserve-phase sites in the New Mexico mountains do contain circular, large (great?) kivas, a pattern that does not persist and may be indicative of ideas, if not people, from above the rim (Bluhm 1957). Several of Hough's (1907) sites along the Blue and Tularosa rivers and Luna Valley, visited so long ago, have large circular depressions. Hough's sites appear to be primarily Reserve- and Tularosa-phase complexes. Additionally, the total number of Reserve-phase sites increases dramatically in the highlands in the vicinity of Luna and Reserve, and they are distributed throughout the region (Oakes 1999a). Farther west in the Forestdale Valley, Haury (1985:416, figure 1) noted that circular Great Kivas were the norm until the Pueblo IV period. Recent major research in the Mogollon Highlands of southwestern New Mexico echoes many of Haury's conclusions: "Based on site and room counts, and radical changes in adaptations that were occurring at this time in the Mogollon Highlands, we suggest that an actual migration of new peoples may have taken place. And given the location of most of the Reserve and Tularosa phase sites, we believe that the influx came from the Cibola area to the north" (Oakes 1999b:35).

They note that this migration occurred "earlier in the A.D. 1000s" (Oakes 1999b:36). We should also note that, in the area immediately north of Reserve and Luna, the southern portion of the Zuni-Acoma area just above the rim, settlements organized around Great Houses were also founded at about this time (for example, Cox Ranch Pueblo). Further west in the Grasshopper/Q-Ranch area, populations from both above and below the rim were using the mountain zones on an intermittent basis, based on pottery recovered from surface scatters (Reid et al. 1996:76).

Therefore, it appears that significant migrations or expansions from the Zuni-Acoma areas into the Mogollon Highlands probably occurred during the Chaco era. The connection between Chaco and these population movements remains an unstudied but potentially interesting matter. If not under the thumb or aegis of Chaco itself, these movements seem likely related to events in the central Chaco core. The Cibola expansion in the eleventh century is, arguably, part of a larger "Pueblo II expansion" during environmentally favorable times (Dean 2000:101–102). We set *Pueblo II expansion* in quotes because it was a phrase current in Southwestern archaeology in the mid-twentieth century, referring to the general perception, codified in textbooks (for example, McGregor 1941:figure 129). It seems as if the Pueblo world expanded greatly during the late Pueblo II period (A.D. 1000–1150). While limited earlier (and, in a few cases, later) occupations are known in some of the areas subsumed in the expansion, the Pueblo II period was remarkable for the appearance of stone pueblos, black-on-white or black-on-gray pottery, and other Puebloan features over a huge area. Pueblo II, in some form, extended west to Las Vegas, Nevada (Lyneis 1996), north to Wyoming (Madsen 1989), and south into and perhaps beyond the Mogollon Highlands.

The expansion was also internal: the Four Corners area, long considered the Anasazi hearth, was reoccupied during Pueblo II after near total depopulation at the end of Pueblo I (Duff and Wilshusen 2000; Varien 1999; Wilshusen 2002; Wilshusen and Van Dyke, chapter 7, and Lipe, chapter 8, of this volume). There was, apparently, no comparable Pueblo II expansion to the east. The Developmental period in the Rio Grande was sparse and demographically stagnant during Chaco's era (Crown, Orcutt, and Kohler 1996) and, beyond the Rio Grande, Pueblo-like remains on the southern Plains date to the much later Pueblo IV period (Habicht-Mauche 2000; Spielmann 1989, 1991).

After the Chaco era, the Mogollon Highlands region sees a number of large sites with Tularosa Black-on-white conspicuous in their assemblages (Lekson 1996). Tularosa-phase sites in New Mexico (Martin et al. 1956; Martin, Rinaldo, and Barter 1957; Rinaldo 1959), roughly contemporaneous with post-Chacoan Great House aggregated settlements in the Zuni-Acoma area, were structured quite differently. Aggregated in plan, these settlements tend towards an upper limit of roughly fifty rooms, with an attached or nearby, rectangular or square Great Kiva. In the early 1200s this pattern begins to occur above the rim in the headwaters of the Little Colorado River in the vicinity of Springerville at such sites as Casa Malpais, Rudd Creek, Hooper Ranch, and Sherwood Ranch (Duff 2002). By the later 1200s some Tularosa sites continued to grow. Similar structures reach as far south as about latitude 33° 30'—from Turkey Creek on the west (at Point of Pines, Arizona; Lowell 1991), through the Delgar Ruin near Reserve, New Mexico (Hough 1907:73, 1914), through the Gila Cliff Dwellings, to Cañada Alamosa, New Mexico (Lekson 1996). Notably, earlier sites, such as the Victorio Site at Cañada Alamosa (ca. A.D. 1100–1200), are communities with small units tightly clustered around a possible Great House (Laumbach and Wakeman 1999:188). Later towns are more aggregated and even walled, defensively, but neither as formal nor as large as the nucleated towns of the Zuni-Acoma district.

Migration into the region below the rim picked up steam in the later 1200s (Haury 1958; Zedeño 1994). Populations came to include some from above the rim, but reorganization of residents from within the region below the rim was also prevalent (Ezzo, Johnson, and Price 1997), potentially including folks from the Mimbres region (Duff 1998). Nucleated communities of the late 1200s and 1300s appear to be an architectural blend of the Tularosa-pattern constructions and the plaza-oriented pattern of the Zuni-Acoma area. Many grew into the plaza-oriented form, rather than being constructed this way from the outset (for example, Grasshopper; Riggs 2001). By the later 1200s many areas below the rim in New Mexico ceased to be occupied, with populations moving to join other communities to the west in Arizona or above the rim in New Mexico. By the 1300s many western settlements in the mountains, composed of migrants from various sources, began to wane. In patterning that parallels adjacent areas, populations left the mountains by 1400, moving northward to the areas occupied at contact.

## THE HOHOKAM AND THE MIMBRES

Far to the south of Chaco were two major Southwestern cultures contemporary with and usefully comparable to Chaco: the Hohokam of southern Arizona and the Mimbres Mogollon of southwestern New Mexico.

Hohokam was certainly Chaco's equal. In many spectacular ways, it was also Chaco's superior. For example, Chaco's efforts at water control pale in comparison with the immense system of Hohokam canals (Abbott 2000; Doolittle 1990; Howard 1993, 1996). Hohokam shell jewelry production (Crown 1991a; Doyel 1991; Nelson 1991) was impressively large in geographic scale and much more complex in organization than Chaco's turquoise trade (the reality of which is still a matter of debate). Hohokam's connections to the south (West Mexico) suggest a more cosmopolitan sphere of action than Chaco's.

*Hohokam*, as an archaeological term, refers to a pattern of material culture that included red-on-buff pottery, ball courts, a mortuary complex involving cremations, palettes and censers, and (more often than not) major canal irrigation (Crown 1991b; Doyel, Fish, and Fish 2000; Gumerman 1991). Hohokam, in this sense, started about 700–750 in

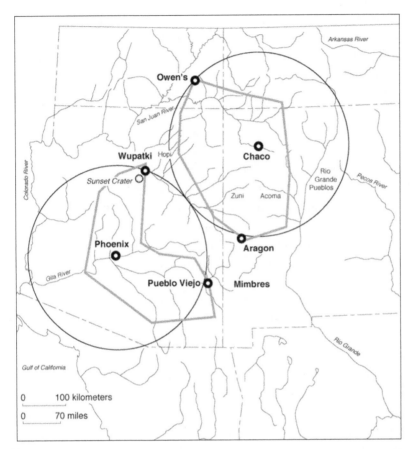

**FIGURE 9.3**

*Distances, Chaco and Hohokam.*

the Phoenix Basin (that is, along the middle Gila and lower Salt rivers). During the Colonial period (about 750–950), Hohokam exploded outward, up river valleys north, east, and south—and, a shorter distance, west to Gila Bend (figure 9.3). Things fell apart about 1100, when the Hohokam region contracted back into the Phoenix Basin, ball courts ceased to be built, and the mortuary complex ceased to operate (the apparently misnamed "Classic period," 1150–1450; Abbott 2003).

Ball courts were the architectural sine qua non of Hohokam. Ball courts are large, earth-bermed ovals in which people played some form of Mexican ball. There are 238 ball courts known at 194 sites (Marshall

2001; Wilcox 1991)—numbers intriguingly close to 200 possible Chaco outlier Great Houses in the Chaco World database. (More ball courts were, undoubtedly, lost to agricultural leveling.) In this dimension, at least, we are comparing apples and apples with Chaco and Hohokam.

Scholars have long viewed ball courts as a "regional system" comparable to Chaco's (Crown 1991b; Wilcox 1991). In the Hohokam case, *regional system* has economic teeth. Ball courts are thought to have established or marked a market system for circulation of goods within the Hohokam core (Abbott 2000; Abbott, ed. 2003). No one postulates bulk materials circulating from the farthest-flung ball courts (Wupatki and Pueblo Viejo [near Safford, Arizona], for example) back into Phoenix, but there is the notion that these distant courts were integrated into a large regional system, which consisted of several subregional subsystems with economic dimensions (Crown 1991a; Doyel 1991; Wilcox 1991).

How big was Hohokam? The modern city of Phoenix forms an arbitrary (but archaeologically reasonable) center of the Hohokam world. From Phoenix, the most distant, well-documented ball courts are near Wupatki, to the north, and at the Pueblo Viejo Site near Safford, to the east. These are about 240 km distant from Phoenix (see figure 9.3). Compare with Chaco and its region: Aragon, the southernmost candidate Great House, about 240 km from Chaco Canyon, as is Owen's Great House (42 SA 24584), the northwesternmost, definite Great House of which we are aware (see figure 9.3).

Hohokam distances offer insights for Chacoan archaeology. To many Chaco specialists, 240 km between Chaco and Aragon (or Chaco and Owen's) seems excessive, immoderate, perhaps impossible (see Kantner and Kintigh, chapter 5 of this volume). Hohokam archaeologists have no difficulty thinking about regional systems on this scale (a 240-km radius around the Phoenix Basin). Indeed, Hohokam archaeologists seem to think that those distances are interesting, not alarming.

Chaco and Hohokam, at their peaks, were contemporaries in the eleventh and early twelfth centuries. These two sprawling "strong patterns" were separated by the Mogollon Rim, a formidable barrier to automotive radiators and archaeological proprieties (recall heated reviews of Berry 1982, which dared to suggest trans-rim dynamics).

Studies of Chaco and Hohokam conclude that there was little recognizable interaction between the two (Crown and Judge 1991a). Researchers have found almost no Hohokam pottery at Chaco (Toll 1991:90; Toll and McKenna 1997) and only small quantities of Cibola ceramics at major Hohokam sites (Doyel 1991:table 10.3). Of course, pottery may not be the most useful or relevant artifact class with which to monitor international relations. Shell jewelry, a major Hohokam industry, reached Chaco from Arizona sources, and pyrite mirrors at Chaco probably came from the Hohokam area, where they occur in larger numbers (Bradley 2000; Crown 1991a; Doyel 1991; Mathien 1997; Toll, chapter 4, and Nelson, chapter 10, of this volume). During the Chaco era, cotton may have been produced in the Arizona deserts and traded or exchanged in the Chacoan region (Teague 1998). Intriguingly, one key Hohokam architectural form, the rectangular platform mound, may actually appear at Chaco before its important appearance in the Hohokam area (Elson and Abbott 2000; Gregory 1991; Stein and Lekson 1992; Stein, Ford, and Friedman 2003). In the main, however, archaeologists seem to believe that the two biggest kids on the block ignored each other.

The affairs of Chaco and Hohokam intrigue us. Either the two engaged in very little commerce, or archaeology is not recognizing appropriate evidence. If the former, Chaco and Hohokam present a remarkable example of adjacent, complex societies that did not interact. Chaco (on the Colorado Plateau) and Hohokam (in the Sonoran Desert) were in two different ecological worlds, and the potential for useful exchange seems high. Did it not happen? Or did it happen in media or modalities that archaeology does not see, for example, textiles or perhaps *glycymeris* shell bracelets, which some archaeologists suggest were a "badge" of Hohokam identity (Bayman 2002)?

Elsewhere, Lekson has written at length about Chaco and Mimbres (Lekson 1992, 1993, 1999). In the Mimbres area, the piñon-juniper life zones (characteristic of the Chaco Anasazi region, where rainfall farming was possible) interfinger into the Chihuahuan Desert—adjacent to and arid as the Hohokam's Sonoran Desert (where canal irrigation is required). There is no need for more than a brief summary of Lekson's Mimbres here: before A.D. 1000, Mimbres was deeply engaged with Hohokam; thereafter, Mimbres became part of the Anasazi (read

"Chaco") world. Mimbres and Chaco (according to Lekson) knew each other and acted on that knowledge. The "pit house to pueblo" shift in Mimbres at about A.D. 1000 was part of the larger "Pueblo II expansion" discussed above. Mimbres masonry pueblos, kivas, and black-on-white and corrugated pottery certainly suggest Anasazi; Mimbres canal irrigation (required in the desert, all but absent in the Anasazi area) owes much to Hohokam. After A.D. 1000 Mimbres was an Anasazi lifestyle supported by Hohokam infrastructure: pueblos strung along canals.

This view of Mimbres reflects earlier conclusions of Emil Haury (1986:452–453) and Joe Ben Wheat (1955), who saw Mogollon after A.D. 1000 as profoundly Anasazi. In contrast, more recent scholarship vigorously denies any Anasazi influence or authority over Mimbres (LeBlanc 1989b; Shafer 1995, 1999). Today's orthodoxy sees Mimbres as separate and equal to Anasazi and Hohokam (Hegmon 2002), but recent research hints that Mimbres might reconnect with Hohokam, if not Anasazi (Creel and Anyon 2003). Given the recent recognition of major population movements from the north into the Mogollon Highlands around A.D. 1000 (discussed above), Haury and Wheat's Anasazi may someday move farther south and reappear in the Mimbres Valley. If so, can Chaco be far behind?

In any event, the parallels between Chaco and Mimbres in the distribution of exotic goods, particularly macaws, copper artifacts, and turquoise, are intriguing. Mimbres sites contain almost as many macaws as Chaco sites do (Creel and McKusick 1994) and as many copper artifacts as Chaco (Vargas 1995). Moreover, the ancient Old Hachita turquoise mines rivaled Cerrillos in size (Weigand and Harbottle 1993), and they were much closer to the Mimbres than were the Cerrillos mines to Chaco. It seems unreasonable to consider Mimbres involvement in West Mexican exotica during the eleventh century and possible turquoise mining without thinking also about Chaco doing the same things at the same time. Perhaps Mimbres was entrained in Chaco's world; perhaps Chaco was getting its exotica from the Mimbres Valley. Either way, the two are worth considering together.

Chaco and Hohokam may have stayed at arm's distance. More likely, they interacted in ways we have not yet learned to see. Lekson suggests that Chaco and Hohokam met and mingled in Mimbres, with concrete and visible consequences. But his is a minority view.

## CONCLUSION

Puebloan influences during Chaco's era reach far beyond the conventional Pueblo region to the north, west, and south in the "Pueblo II expansion": as far west as Las Vegas, Nevada, in the short-lived Virgin Anasazi (Lyneis 1996) and as far north, perhaps, as Wyoming in the extreme reaches of Fremont. In these cases, the maximum expansion of stone Pueblo-style architecture, painted pottery, and corn coincided with Chaco—that is, Pueblo II. We have noted, above, the emerging consensus that substantial Pueblo II populations moved south into the Mogollon Highlands, as well as a minority view that extends this into the Mimbres region. Surely these population movements were part of the larger "Pueblo II expansion," which, itself, must relate in some as yet undefined way to the remarkable developments at Chaco Canyon.

From where did all these people come? Some of the Pueblo penumbra around Chaco may represent shifts in local lifestyles (some or all of Fremont, for example). Taken together, though, archaeological appeals to migration north, west, and south, as well as the reestablishment of populations in the Four Corners, implicate a great many people. Happily, our focus here is the South alone.

Lipe (chapter 8 of this volume), Wilshusen and Van Dyke (chapter 7 of this volume), Windes (n.d.), Vivian (1990), and others argue that the Great House tradition began during Pueblo I in the North. We agree: the origins of Great House architecture were northern. We also agree that there were fundamental historical differences between plateau, mountain, and desert populations, some of which may extend as far back as the Archaic—as Shafer (1995) has suggested and Crown (1994) hints at for the Mimbres. But we also see long-term, historically important connections, interactions, and even commonalities.

We are of two minds on some of these questions, literally and figuratively. Lekson sees *Great Houses* and *Chaco*, and *Chaco* and *piñon-juniper*, as synonymous. Duff sees distinctly Chacoan Great Houses stopping at the Mogollon Rim's edge and believes that they were already a blend of histories at that point. Lekson (chapter 1 of this volume) sees more complexity and management. Duff sees it for Chaco Canyon but would argue that Great Houses were different things inside and outside the canyon. What transcends these differences is a belief that similarities in organizational patterning—not details of hachure or

Type II masonry—were widely shared, were easily transferable to different settings, and *were shared and transferred* through migrant populations. The underlying structure had roots in direct history, perhaps simultaneously shared by peoples moving back and forth between Highland Mimbres and the southern Colorado Plateau, within the northern and southern Zuni-Acoma region, and between the Totah and central Mesa Verde regions. We need neither marathon runners nor sprinters; overlapping webs of movement within ancestral territories can produce similarity within diversity. Details differ, of course.

The severe formality of Chacoan Great House architecture may have originated in the North, as did the need for Great Houses. The Northern San Juan and Four Corners country were grim places, the extreme limits of agricultural life during ninth and tenth centuries. Neighbors to the north, west, and east were not farmers, did not live in villages, did not lead similar lives. Agricultural life in the North was not easy. Northern villages were sometimes large, but they were short-lived (Lipe 2002b; Varien 1999, 2002; Varien et al. 1996). They had Great Houses, or proto–Great Houses, which we suggest represent village leadership (there are, of course, other interpretations.)

In contrast, Hohokam and Mimbres towns of pre-Chaco times were large, permanent, and cosmopolitan. Their size and permanence manifest reliance on canal irrigation—far more productive and dependable than Anasazi "dry farming." Irrigation systems require community-level decision making. Preclassic Hohokam and Late Pit House Mimbres must have developed social mechanisms for the ordering of life and economy, but Great Houses (and implied, socially marked leadership) are conspicuous by their absence. Without reviewing the large literatures, it seems safe to say that consensus sees no kings at Snaketown or Galaz. Yet, Chaco had rulers, according to some accounts (Lekson, chapter 1 of this volume).

Chaco was more politically complex but less cosmopolitan than its neighbors to the South. Both Hohokam and Mimbres had strong connections to Mexico; so, too, did Chaco (Nelson, chapter 10 of this volume). Lekson, with Nelson, has argued that Chaco's rulers used their distance from Mexican centers as a tactic for legitimizing their rule (Lekson 1999; Lekson and Peregrine 2004; both citing Helms 1988). A fair index: ball courts. A large ballcourt system integrated Hohokam society (Wilcox 1991), architecturally reflecting Hohokam's profound connections with Mesoamerican civilization. Chaco (insofar as we know) had no ball courts. Certainly, these Mesoamerican features and the cultural principles they represent did not link Chacoan communities of the North and South. Chaco must have known about ball courts but chose not to play: it kept Mesoamerica at a safe distance, using bits and pieces of Mexico to build a new society. Preclassic Hohokam peoples were not shy about trade and exchange (Doyel 1991); lack of commerce between Hohokam and Chaco suggests isolation on the part of the latter, perhaps as a matter of policy.

# 10

## Mesoamerican Objects and Symbols in Chaco Canyon Contexts

### Ben A. Nelson

A goal of this volume is to identify important inflections in the course of Chaco Canyon's history and relate them to one another. Such an effort would be incomplete without consideration of Chacoans' interaction with Mesoamerica. Many scholars have argued that Chacoans had links to Mesoamerica or even that Mesoamerican agents founded Chaco Canyon's occupation. Native American legends also mark the importance of the southern regions, referring to them as the "Red Land." My interest is in relating Chacoans' adoption of Meso-american artifacts, symbols, and practices to the history of the canyon's development, thereby to learn something about the nature of interaction between urbanized regions and distant places they may affect. This general question has interested scholars in other regions, such as the Southern Levant, with respect to Mesopotamia (Algaze 1989); the Aegean, with respect to Egypt (Cherry 1986; Watrous 1987); or southern Europe, with respect to the Etruscan and Greek states (Dietler 2001).

More specific questions that I hope to help answer are (1) whether Chaco Canyon's growth as a ritual center was part of a macroregional cycle originating in Mesoamerica, (2) when evidence of Mesoamerican interaction is greatest in Chaco Canyon's own developmental cycle, (3) whether Chacoans were frequently in direct contact with Meso-american peoples or if Mesoamerican cultures mainly provided background material from which to borrow symbols, (4) why people in Chaco Canyon may have used Mesoamerican-derived practices and symbols, and (5) what kinds of social themes they may have encoded in their Mesoamerican-derived symbols and practices. I approach these questions by observing the timing, contexts, and symbolic content of Mesoamerican interaction markers in the Chacoan context.

Synchronicities suggest that the growth of the Chaco Canyon center was indeed stimulated by a cycle originating in Mesoamerica. A pronounced expansion of the frontier in Mexico occurred by A.D. 500. By A.D. 750 southern Southwestern peoples (especially in the Hohokam region and, to some extent, the Mimbres) had connected themselves to these cycles; by around A.D. 900 northerners were also engaged. In Chaco's own history, the major inflection point of Mesoamerican interaction may have come as the building boom began ca. A.D. 1040. This change was not a wholesale one, however; each object and practice that constitutes evidence of such interaction (architectural features, copper bells, and so forth) has its own fascinating history. Chacoans employed Mesoamerican-style symbolism mostly during what I am calling here the "consolidation phase," ca. A.D. 1040–1120 (see below for discussion of dating). Perhaps significantly, there is evidence for abandonment or suppression of one practice near the end of the occupation.

The evidence concerning directness is varied; some of the most noted practices and symbols actually were not imports or quotations of Mesoamerican concepts but were only stylistic references to them, which is consistent with thematic borrowing instead of direct involvement. Other patterns, however, are consistent with direct interaction, perhaps in the form of exchange with distant partners. The evidence does not imply that these partnerships were central to Chacoan power, nor frequent, but the contexts in which Mesoamerican objects and symbols occur suggest that they were socially important.

I propose that local religious specialists made use of Mesoamerican materials and symbols late in Chaco's own cycle. I reject the idea of domination by intruders, for several specific reasons given below. A close look shows that most of the objects, symbols, and practices adopted by the Chacoans were not from the cities of Mesoamerica, but from the outer regions that we know as the Northern Frontier and West Mexico. This difference is important because it reveals a layering of connections. In a process similar to symbolic entrainment (Renfrew 1986) but with a hierarchical dimension, societies were arranged along scales of sociopolitical complexity and geographic distance. Elites in smaller-scale, less hierarchical societies used symbols that were essentially quotations about a cosmological and social order established in a distant, idealized world. Their adoption of distant elements shows that the urbanized Mesoamerican world and its frontier provided a store of symbolism that could foster selected social principles. Although the principles per se are not accessible to us, evidence discussed below suggests that they had to do with the religious sanctification of social power, or the social sanctification of religious power. I label this adoption and recasting of objects and symbols as "invoking distant ideals."

Local people outside urban Mesoamerica, including Chacoans, probably used these distantly derived practices and symbols to legitimize and consolidate their emerging positions during periods of increasing societal hierarchy and scale. The process of shaping elite identities and the attachment of followers to them drew the trappings of civilization ever outward. Symbolic invocations of distant, mystified places of great power (ultimately in actual cities) could have been useful to those attempting to establish and consolidate new principles of social relations in places such as Chaco Canyon, growing ritual centers whose sacred significance had the potential of being transformed into political power. Closer to the Mesoamerican core—for example, in Nayarit and Zacatecas—such florescences, alternating with collapse and reorganization, began by at least A.D. 200. There, as in the Southwest, newly formed centers exhibiting stylistic continuities with old collapsed ones sometimes appeared in new locations and brought new symbolic themes to the hinterlands. Through iterations of these cycles, Mesoamerican-derived notions of cosmology and political-religious authority gradually spread northward, simultaneously establishing a basis for long-distance material exchanges.

That people had distantly derived practices and symbols does not necessarily mean that their social relations were fully fashioned on a distant social model. To interpret the social themes encoded in borrowed Mesoamerican practices, I place as much weight on missing Mesoamerican elements as on the ones adopted. The absence of certain themes, coupled with the apparent suppression of others alluded to above, may have expressed people's resistance to an attempted legitimization of supracommunity social power. The social themes encoded in the rejected symbols may have been incompatible with prevailing notions of equality and morality. Nonetheless, I consider the *accepted* symbols and practices as invocations of Mesoamerican elements of social power because of their ultimate derivation from Mesoamerican elite and ceremonial contexts.

## MACROREGIONAL CHANGE

Chaco Canyon was a large development yet was part of something even larger. I refer not to the web of Great Houses that spanned the San Juan Basin and beyond, but to an even larger array of about ten centers of intensive sociopolitical development, A.D. 500–1400, in what is now northwestern Mexico and the southwestern United States (figure 10.1). Each instance may be described as a "florescence," defined by the emergence of a regional ceremonial center (or centers) and the apparent self-identification with that center by minion-settlements or outliers. These developments happened in semichaotic series; however, the timing was nonrandom.

I can only sketch the northern Mexican chronological developments here and suggest how they were relevant to the appearance of Chaco Canyon. The pattern consists of large regional systems jointly inscribing a halting northward expansion; the pattern's discontinuities, great geographic extent, and long time span make it difficult to observe. One can easily miss the underlying pattern by focusing on too small a region or too short a span of time.

As some centers collapsed, nearby centers absorbed their populations; others decomposed into smaller communities that never regained their former dimensions. Chaco was the northernmost yet fell in the middle of the time range; rebounds and retractions periodically reversed the underlying expansion of affected territory. At any given time, there were also "holes" in the territory, some consisting of areas that had been or were to be incorporated into a large regional system, others (for example, southern Chihuahua) that never came under the domain of a large regional polity.

Such discontinuities are disturbing only if one tries to think of the

FIGURE 10.1

*A map of northern Mexico and the American Southwest showing major regional centers.*

affected territory as a nation-state. It is more productive to think of polities that were autonomous (which is not to say without relation) and driving developmental forces that weakened or varied in strength with distance from the highly urbanized core. Indeed, the Aztec dominion, which was far more organized than the territory referred to here, had such "internal frontiers" (Berdan et al. 1996).

Teotihuacan is an important beginning point because it was a huge urban formation and a cosmological center as well, containing perhaps one hundred thousand people. Processes connected with its apogee (ca. A.D. 150–600) and collapse may have triggered the formation of distant polities, that is, within Mesoamerica. By A.D. 500 Teotihuacan's presence abroad had reached a maximum (Berlo 1989; Coggins 1993; R. Millon 1981). By ca. 600–700 the urban center collapsed and lost population (Cowgill 2000).

Most relevant to present concerns is the growth of centers after A.D.

500 at increasing distances northward from core Mesoamerica (B. Nelson 2000). It is important to realize, however, that this frontier growth occurred simultaneously with the development of new central Mexican centers that filled the power vacuum left by Teotihuacan's demise (García 1991; Gaxiola 1999; González et al. 1995; Nagao 1989). Northern Mesoamerican regional centers flourished outside the old core, inland at first, A.D. 500–900, through the Bajío of Guanajuato and the Altos of Jalisco, along the foot of the Sierra Madre Occidental in Zacatecas and Durango.[1] The centers in the Northern Frontier (Zacatecas and Durango) had definite stylistic links with the American Southwest, though not directly with Chaco Canyon. Potters at La Quemada and Alta Vista made red-on-buff vessels that bore clear resemblances to Hohokam red-on-buff pottery (Braniff and Areti-Hers 1998; Braniff 1995; Carot 2001; B. Nelson and Crider 2001). Stylistic connections continued later, affecting other polities even after Chaco Canyon's abandonment, through the Aztatlan Horizon of West Mexico (Michoacan, Jalisco, Colima, Nayarit, and Sinaloa), especially along the coast (Ekholm 1942; Kelley 1986; Kelley and Winters 1960; Kelly 1938; Sauer and Brand 1932). Through the above-mentioned periods, there were differences in the timing of florescence and geographic shifts in the conduits created by chains of centers. Yet, the collective existence of these centers effectively shortened the distance that Ancestral Puebloan people had to travel to experience Mesoamerican material culture and models of social reproduction.

The Toltecs, whose capital arose ca. A.D. 800–900 (Cobean 1990), have been linked with Southwestern developments (Turner and Turner 1999; Weigand, Harbottle, and Sayre 1977). The Toltecs created new economic networks and stylistic connections within Mesoamerica proper. Their obsidian exchange shifted away from dependence on the sources Teotihuacanos had dominated and emphasized alternative ones in West Mexico (Healan, Kerley, and Bey 1983; Pollard and Vogel 1994). Toltec-style figurines were especially recognizable and far-flung. Tula probably controlled the importation of Maya Tohil Plumbate in central Mexico (Mastache, Cobean, and Healan 2002:48). There are no clear Toltec objects or styles in Chaco Canyon (see below under "Direct and Indirect Interactions"). Yet, the arguments suggesting Toltecs as likely agents of Southwestern change are not without merit in the sense that history records widespread disturbances and population shifts contemporary with the formation of their capital (Davies 1977). Aztec history glorified the artistic and bellicose achievements of the Toltecs, and many rulers from central Mexico to the Maya Highlands sought to legitimize themselves by claiming Toltec ancestry (Carmack 1981; Fox 1981, 1987).

## INTERACTION MARKERS IN CHACO'S OWN CYCLE

In the following discussion, I use *Mesoamerican interaction marker* to encompass a variety of archaeological patterns that are reminiscent of Mesoamerican counterparts. I employ such a term reluctantly because one must consider objects, practices, and styles individually and contextually to make sense of the interactions they represent. The concept of the interaction marker glosses over several classes of thought and action (for example, religious and political) and ignores the important behavioral distinction between interaction and exchange (Plog 1980). It also has the liability of implying that the users self-identified as Mesoamerican related, which I am not sure was the case. Yet, the loss of precision is necessary to identify the phenomenological set of interest.

By Chaco's *developmental cycle*, I mean the generalized phases of growth and decline that Chaco Canyon shares with many other regional centers. This notion of cycle is related to what Anderson (1990) and Steponaitis (1991) discuss as cycling for Mississippian centers. Their notion of cycling shows how, as individual centers rise and fall, one may replace another in regional prominence over time. Marcus points out a similar phenomenon for the polities of central Mexico. Lekson (1999) proposes such a process for the relationship between Chaco Canyon and Aztec. Yet, this notion of cycling does not enter into the local development of the individual center.

I want to examine the occurrence of interaction markers in the context of the individual polity's cycle. For Moundville, Knight and Steponaitis (1998) model such a cycle as consisting of intensification, centralization, consolidation, entrenchment, and collapse and reorganization. Pauketat (1998) describes the cycle at Cahokia in somewhat similar terms, and Vivian (1990) suggests emergence, growth, and decline at Chaco Canyon. Redman and Kinzig (2003) suggest that human systems in their landscapes may be characterized, like many other kinds of systems, as having cycles that include growth, conservation, release, and reorganization. All these cycles have the general properties of growth, consolidation, and decline, followed by reorganization; I use these terms in describing Chaco Canyon's cycle. Chaco Canyon, like any other complex systemic phenomenon, may have its own particular properties and deviations from such a generalized model.

We might expect that Chacoans' interest in and receptivity to interaction markers would vary in relation to such a cycle, because the cycle's phases would mark differing local sociopolitical conditions. Such variation might result from the acceptance of ideational principles, the need to legitimize social roles, the desire to signal affiliation with allies, or the need to express a Chacoan identity. Following Bawden's (1995) ideas about Moche iconography, we might also expect that changes in "high culture" (Baines and Yoffee 1998) would mark the creation of ideology that accounts for, legitimizes, and naturalizes elite authority (setting aside, for the moment, the nature of that authority).[2] Further, we might expect that the kinds of items that would be effective at various stages in the establishment versus maintenance of authority might differ (Hastorf 1990). These expectations, while not specifying what kinds of interaction markers to expect at which times, predict that Chacoans adopted such markers dynamically.

Scholars are still in the process of defining Chaco Canyon's cycle. Windes and Ford (1996) date the founding of Pueblo Bonito to ca. A.D. 830; this construction may mark the beginning of the center's monumental history. Although other, less easily distinguished patterns of use may have preceded this construction, it will serve as the founding event for purposes of this discussion. Only very recently have archaeologists realized that the intensification of building, landscape transformation, and ritual activity in the canyon, instead of occurring steadily from ca. A.D. 900 to 1150, was concentrated between 1040 and 1140.[3] This realization frames the consolidation phase; I cannot review here all the evidence for dating. The growth and consolidation phases, however, are particularly important to the information discussed below. I take the relatively shabby construction at the end of Chetro Ketl's occupation to mark the beginning of a quick decline and estimate it to have been done at 1120 (further discussion below). This assumption gives periods of A.D. 830–1020 for the growth phase, 1040–1120 for consolidation, 1120–1140 for decline, and 1140 and beyond for reorganization.

When in Chaco Canyon's cycle do markers of interaction appear? Did the architects, craftspeople, and exchange partners of Chaco use the Mesoamerican styles, objects, and iconography throughout the history of the canyon's growth or at particular times? How do the periods of use relate to the growth, consolidation, release, and reorganization of the Chacoan system of ritual or political power? Do the timing or the uses of such objects and symbols help us to understand Chacoan concepts of power itself?

The timing varies; each class of practice, symbol, or object has an independent history. Considered either individually or in their aggregate, they offer intriguing evidence of social, political, and religious change. I consider five examples: colonnades, roads, copper bells, shell bracelets, and unusual ceramic vessels. I return to these same interaction markers below to consider the kinds of interactions implied and why people might have chosen to adopt them. For the moment, this issue is timing alone.

### Colonnades

A colonnade, according to the *Oxford English Dictionary*, is "a series of columns placed at regular intervals." Lekson (1983c:78) describes the colonnade at Chetro Ketl (refer to plate 4) as a "series of square piers"; it may have supported an entablature or an upper span of masonry. Architectural historians describe colonnades as "magnificent" and "pompous," terms that may or may not be relevant to the Ancestral Pueblo sense of their meaning. In some Mesoamerican monumental architecture, colonnades are an important feature, as discussed below in "Direct and Indirect Interactions."

Both context and timing are important to understanding the ideological significance of the colonnade. If meant to monumentalize enduring principles of social relations, the columns should have been placed in a position of visibility and should have existed throughout the period when those principles were in force. For example, if the columns were part of the original construction, efforts should have been made to include or preserve them in building-renewal episodes, even to the point of building around the original features rather than replacing them.

In keeping with the expectations about context, the Chetro Ketl colonnade occupied a prominent place in the site's layout. It was placed in the Central North Block, a series of rooms, including kivas, which began to grow soon after the general plan of the site had taken shape. The colonnade was not an original feature of the configuration, however. One of the early steps in the construction of the Central North Block was the placement of rooms around Kiva G, one of two original kivas that had been located in outdoor or plaza space (Lekson 1983c:264). The architects made regular additions to this central block, increasing its height by adding stories, its footprint by adding rows of rooms, and its complexity by adding various special features. The colonnade was apparently the last of these additions (Lekson 1983c:287–288) and would have been a dramatic, plaza-facing embellishment of a principal set of ritual facilities.

In contrast to the expectations about timing, the colonnade of Chetro Ketl was late and short-lived; deliberate concealment soon followed its construction. Tree-ring analysis provides good evidence for the timing of construction. Lekson (1983c:267) places the construction after A.D. 1105 and presumably before 1140, when all construction ceased. No datable wood was obtained in direct association with the columns; they are dated by stratigraphic relationship to other, well-dated features. Some time after construction, the spaces between the columns were filled, presumably also sometime between A.D. 1105 and 1140. Subsequently, but within that same period, the builders erected more walls. The result was that they completely obscured the colonnade.

Considering colonnades as markers of Mesoamerica interaction, then, one would conclude that the architects made use of Mesoamerican symbolism only at the end of the consolidation phase of the occupation. Their interest in this symbolism does not seem to have come as the monumentality of the Great Houses was being established, but rather afterward. Perhaps most significantly, the social messages sent by the colonnades were quickly quashed.

### Roads

We do not often think of roads as Mesoamerican artifacts, but, as Turner and Turner (1999) suggest, they could be so conceived. Dating of roads is problematic because there are no tree-ring dates and few detailed studies of artifacts along them. Roads, in general, may be quite long-lived and yet possibly did not all function at the same time. Roney's (1992) work suggests that many roads were contemporary with one settlement and led back to another, abandoned one. Could some sense of this relationship also have existed at a larger scale, between outlying sites and the canyon in the larger Chacoan world? Alternatively, might construction of roads to and from parts of the San Juan Basin coincide with the south-east-north swing of relations with the larger Chaco world, as identified in Sebastian's summary of the Chaco Capstone Conference? These are questions we simply cannot answer at present, but, with more dating evidence from the roads, it should be possible to learn about the timing of their construction relative to that of Great Houses in the canyon and elsewhere.

Given the sheer volume of work involved in constructing roads, as well as the amount of use-wear necessary to make them visible archaeologically, it appears unlikely that they belonged to any single moment in time. One can imagine that the buildup began as early as when monuments appeared in Chaco Canyon. Our best assumption at present is that they date throughout the canyon's occupation.

### Copper Bells

Bells appear in Chaco Canyon's developmental cycle on a different schedule from that of columns and possibly of roads. Instead of showing up near the end of the occupation like the colonnade or being of ambiguous dating, they seem to have been deposited mainly during the canyon's consolidation phase, A.D. 1040–1120. According to Judd (1954:109), the excavators of Pueblo Bonito (refer to plate 5) recovered two of the twenty-one copper bells in "dwellings of the Old Bonitians," thirteen from "third-period rooms and kivas," and three from "fourth-period houses." The building periods to which Judd refers are tied to the four masonry styles that he and other early investigators defined (Judd 1954:plate 5). On this basis, Judd suggests that bells may have tended not to reach Pueblo Bonito until A.D. 1050.

The bells' stylistic properties (figure 10.2) are consistent with Judd's spatially based inference. They are undoubtedly of West Mexican origin (Vargas 1995) and can be dated according to chronology there (Hosler 1994). Most of the bells depicted by Judd (1954: figure 28) could have been obtained as early as A.D. 900, when bells were made thick-walled and small.[4] One bell, however, the smelted wirework specimen in Judd's figure 28g, must have been obtained nearer A.D. 1200, when false wirework technology and style developed in West Mexico and the bells tended to be much larger (Hosler 1994:83, 129, 135). A confusing aspect of this evidence is that Judd depicts fewer than half of the recovered bells. Specimens of the later style, being thinner (Hosler 1994:129), were possibly less often preserved in a state worthy of depiction. A valuable laboratory exercise would be to examine the undepicted bells for stylistic and chronological information.

A further chronological complication is that people are likely to have curated these rare, symbolically charged objects, creating an heirloom effect that biases the dating. A rigorous examination of formation processes, were it possible, would lead to further insights about the chronological contexts of the bells. Keeping these unresolved issues in mind, the weight of the evidence is consistent with the use of copper bells primarily in the consolidation phase.

### Shell Bracelets

*Glycymeris* shell bracelets are not usually considered Mesoamerican artifacts because they abound in the Hohokam region and evidence of their production is found within the region also (McGuire and Howard 1987; R. Nelson 1991). As is widely recognized, though, the Hohokam obtained the raw materials from the west coast of Mexico. A fact less well-known, the significance of which is unclear, is that bracelets very similar to those of the Hohokam are found as far south as the Rio Balsas at the boundary between Michoacan and Guerrero (Beltrán 2001; Maldonado 1980). Moreover, the Hohokam bracelets are decorated with Mesoamerican motifs (Haury 1976:figure 15.28) and tend to occur in contexts that contain other Mesoamerican objects (R. Nelson 1991:77, 95–96).

Chacoans probably would have obtained shell objects through the Hohokam region; people there were geographically situated to serve as manufacturers and intermediaries. If so, the dating of Hohokam exportation of shell products, in general, might be helpful in pinpointing the place of shell acquisition in Chaco's development. Nelson (1991) indicates that the greatest abundance of decorated bracelets is

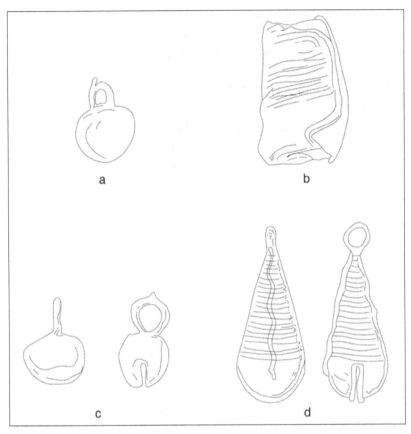

**FIGURE 10.2**

*Copper bells: (a) and (b) cast copper and wire-worked bronze from Pueblo Bonito (after Judd 1954:109), (c) an example of a Period 1 bell from West Mexico (after Hosler 1994:55), and (d) an example of Period 2 from West Mexico (after Hosler 1994:133; drawn by Jean Baker).*

in Late Colonial and Sedentary periods, that is, ca. 900–1150, and that Hohokam products appear elsewhere most frequently during this time, particularly in the Mogollon region. This information confirms that the Hohokam region is a likely source, but it does not help us understand the place of shell goods acquisition within Chaco's cycle of development. A closer examination of the proveniences of the shell objects (most of which Judd does not give) might reveal changes in contacts through time. The most defensible assumption is that the contacts were open throughout the cycle.

### Unusual Ceramic Vessels

I include two kinds of vessels here, the often mentioned cylindrical vessels and the completely overlooked thong-foot pots. Researchers have put forward more than two hundred cylindrical vessels (figure 10.3), mostly from Pueblo Bonito (Toll 2001), as evidence of Mesoamerican contact (Kelley and Kelley 1975; Washburn 1980). This suggestion deserves to be explored; the cylindrical vase is unknown elsewhere in the American Southwest yet is an important ceremonial form among many Mesoamerican peoples, from the Lowland Maya (Reents-Budet 1994) to Teotihuacan (Conides 1997; C. Millon 1973). Although one should not just assume Mesoamerican inspiration, for purposes of this discussion I ask what the timing of deposition of such pots might imply about Chaco Canyon's Mesoamerican contacts.

Chacoan cylindrical jar forms have a significant relationship to Mesoamerica vase chronology. They are distinct from the Classic period (A.D. 200–900) forms of central Mexico and similar to those predominant in the Early Postclassic (A.D. 900–1200) from the Maya region and West Mexico, except that they lack feet. The resemblance to the latter forms is in the slightly tapering cylindrical profile, as opposed to the concave profiles of central Mexican Classic-period vases. According to Brainerd (1955:117), this "churn" form was found in the Maya area from the Early Preclassic (800 B.C.) onward. We can add that it does not occur in central, West, or northern Mexico until much later, ca. A.D. 900, except in the enigmatic Chupicuaro tradition of Guanajuato ca. A.D. 100–400 (Braniff 1998). At present, the Mexican chronologies do not permit finer-grained chronological alignment, but, with further progress in West Mexican research, we may get better resolution.

The cylindrical jars in the Chacoan context appear to date post-1040 and possibly nearer to 1100 on the basis of the decorated Chaco and Gallup Black-on-white designs (Toll 1990:289–290). Toll points out that, although one-third are undecorated, all the undecorated pots are associated with Chaco and Gallup Black-on-white examples. Crown and Wills (2003) observe that some of the vessels have secondary applications of designs, which they believe to be evidence of the ritual renewal of the vessels. They convincingly infer that occasions for renewal came up periodically and do not represent erasures of unsatisfactory work upon original manufacture. The stylistic and renewal evidence is

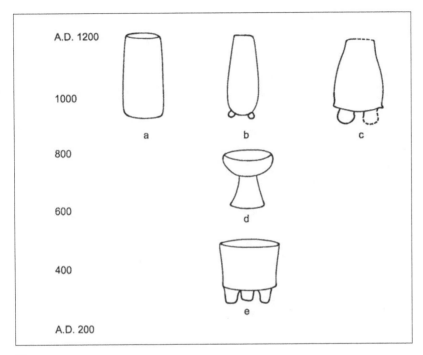

**FIGURE 10.3**

*Cylindrical vases and related vessels: (a) a cylindrical jar from Chaco Canyon (after color plate 4, American Antiquity 66[1]:1), (b) a cylindrical vase from Amapa (after Meighan 1976:476), (c) a "churn"-shaped vase from Yucatan (after Brainerd 1955:figure 86d), (d) a copa from Alta Vista, Chalchihuites (after Noguera 1930:100), and (e) a cylindrical vase from Teotihuacan (after Séjourné 1966:117). All are drawn to approximately the same scale. Heights range from 25 to 30 cm. Drawn by Jean Baker.*

important because it differs from what depositional history alone suggests. The rooms in which the famous cache of Chacoan cylindrical vessels was found appear to have been in use early in Pueblo Bonito's construction history. Judd (1954:plate 6) pictures a large cache consisting exclusively of these pots being left "in the middle of the floor of Room 28." Toll (2001:63) reports that there were 111 vessels. This room existed in Judd's Old Bonitian phase (Judd 1964:figure 3), though it appears to be a late addition. Later fill covered the deposit, and additional rooms were built above (Judd 1954:plate 6, lower). Judging from the large numbers of them, the fact that they seem to have been found in a variety of other contexts (Toll 2001), and the fact that they were renewed and probably cached for reuse over time, I infer that the form could have been used throughout the later parts of the occupation.

Thong-foot pots (Judd 1954:figure 61) were rare, but important because they constituted a connection to specific place within Mesoamerica (figure 10.4). I discuss that geographic connection below under "Direct and Indirect Interactions." Here we consider dating within the Chacoan cycle. The chronological evidence, though limited, suggests that these pots could have been in use through much of the Great House's lifespan. Of the three thong-foot vessels that Judd pictures (1954:225), two are from identified proveniences; 61f came from Room 316, and 61g from Room 329 (Judd 1954:382). Room 316 was built during additions and modifications made during Judd's third building episode (the consolidation phase). Room 329, on the other hand, was part of Old Bonito (Judd 1964:72, 75). It was built in the late 800s or early 900s, a single-story room with a brush roof and post-and-mud and wall-wide stone walls. Exactly when Room 329 went out of use is difficult to tell. While making the late additions to this part of the site, builders added a "second story," which seems impossible unless the lower rooms were filled in. Infilling seems likely, given the approximately 2.5-m-thick trash deposits that accumulated between construction phases in the area of Room 87 before the initiation of late construction. Apparently, many rooms went into disuse and were, intentionally or unintentionally, filled as the base level of the construction rose through time, penetrated by kivas. If I am correct in assuming that Room 329 was filled by the beginning of Pepper's Late Bonitian phase, then the two provenienced, thong-foot vessels probably came from quite different parts of the Chacoan cycle.

Of the contexts for the two provenienced examples of thong-foot pots, the most significant aspect is that they were located in symmetrically opposite, small rooms (316 and 329) on the main plaza of Pueblo Bonito. Judd (1964:74) suggests that these banks of rooms may have been of "ceremonial significance" as "adjuncts to circular subterranean kivas." Room 316 mirrored Room 328, which was next to 329, in its unusual floor and ventilator features. These rooms may have been "backstage" areas where people prepared for performances presented in the kivas. That the rooms were built at very different times suggests

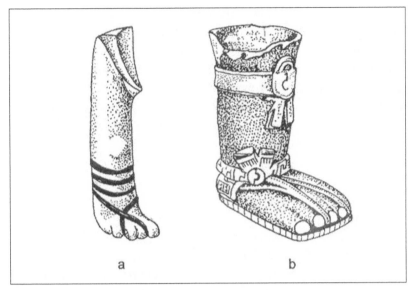

a                 b

**FIGURE 10.4**

*Thong-foot vessels from* (a) *Amapa (after Meighan 1976:457) and* (b) *Pueblo Bonito (after Judd 1954:225; drawn by Jean Baker).*

that the ritual practices in which they were used, if not the vessels themselves, spanned an appreciable part of the occupation.

Imperfect as the chronological information is, it does permit the elimination of a model in which Mesoamerican contact is only part of founding events. The timing of the different interaction markers varies substantially. Cylindrical vessels appear to date to 1040–1100 or later, that is, during consolidation. Copper bells coincide primarily with consolidation. Thong-foot pots, roads, and shell bracelets may have been used throughout. The colonnade, a prominent architectural marker, appears very late in the consolidation phase and is covered up during decline. Most of this information indicates late appearance and prolonged interaction—and no clear associations with Chaco's beginnings.

## DIRECT AND INDIRECT INTERACTIONS

Several distinguished scholars have raised the possibility of Mesoamerican origins for Southwestern sedentary peoples. Haury

(1945, 1976) postulates migration outside the space-time framework of Chaco Canyon. Kelley and Kelley's (1975) idea of Mesoamerican imperialists' direct control of Chaco, like DiPeso's (DiPeso, Rinaldo, and Fenner 1974) similar scenario for Paquimé, poses Toltecs as the likely agents. Many scholars—for example, Lekson (1983a), Mathien (1986), McGuire (1980), and McGuire and others (1994)—have dismissed the Toltec connection. Biological anthropologists Turner and Turner (1999), however, have proposed it again. In recent decades, most archaeologists have disavowed or been reluctant to address this connection, concentrating instead on local and regional developments. Yet, the problem remains, how to situate Mesoamerican influence in explanations of Chacoan development.

The inference that Mesoamerican agents, instead of local actors, were responsible for introducing Mesoamerican practices rests partly on the assumption that Chaco Canyon is so different in scale and hierarchy that some external stimulus is necessary to explain this. Also, Chacoan architects built Mesoamerican-style elements (columns, platform mounds, and roads), and people used reputedly Mesoamerican-style artifacts (for example, cylindrical vessels) in certain contexts. To some scholars, these circumstances have made migrants, merchants, and conquerors plausible agents of change. I see these arguments as parallel to the now rejected assumption that Mesoamerican invaders, instead of native Southeastern peoples, must have built Mississippian mounds, because the native populations were incapable of it (Trigger 1989:119). This argument, in fact, is vaguely racist, suggesting incompetence of the local populations.

Another widely accepted explanation for Mesoamerican objects in Chaco Canyon, as well as elsewhere in the Southwest, such as in Paquimé, is that Mesoamerican empires engaged these areas in trade and managed them at a distance, primarily for the purpose of obtaining turquoise (DiPeso, Rinaldo, and Fenner 1974; Kelley and Kelley 1975; Weigand 1982; Weigand, Harbottle, and Sayre 1977). Some archaeologists consider Chaco Canyon a production center or mercantile entrepot in which the mineral trade was a driving economic force (Weigand 1978). If such mercantile operations were economically important, one would expect large-scale facilities to support them. Some archaeologists (Mathien 1986; Renfrew 2001) find the quantities of turquoise and other traded objects to be too small to represent economically significant production or trade volume. Renfrew (2001) summarizes these objections by alluding to a sacred economy, instead of a commercial one, and labeling Chaco Canyon a "location of high devotional expression," not a center of production and commerce. It is also possible that traders operated on smaller scales than the preceding scenarios suggest or that trade was embedded in other social processes.

Invasion and long-distance mercantilism, however, are logical possibilities we cannot exclude without examining evidence. Dominance by a distant power should be reflected in architecture and personal adornment, on which the state would impose its ideology of control. If any imperial agents dominated Chaco Canyon, the Toltecs are the most likely suspects. They were the strongest political agents in western Mesoamerica during the time Chaco arose. If the Toltecs were the founders, then we could expect their presence to be registered iconographically, in legend, architecture, and the contents of elite burials.

I reject the assertion that the Toltecs founded or dominated Chaco Canyon, for five reasons: (1) Native American legends do not record the presence of any such people; (2) the styles of objects and architecture that might be Toltec related are diluted forms, not direct copies or imports; (3) other than one Mesoamerican-style disc encrusted with turquoise tessarae (Cobean Transeue and Estrada 1994:78), there is no evidence of Southwestern contact in the artifactual assemblage of Tula, the Toltec capital; (4) the distance between Tula and Chaco Canyon is too great for logistical security, four times that from the Aztec capital of Tenochtitlan to its most distant colony; and (5) the timing of columns is wrong (too late for founding, consolidation, or any other strong role).

Toltec imagery should be detectable in legend, in the iconographic repertoire, or in specific artifact forms. The absence of such imagery seems significant because Toltec identity was strongly materialized in public architecture (figure 10.5) and in portable objects. If Ancestral Pueblo peoples interacted directly with the ferocious Toltec warriors whom Mesoamerican peoples remember and whom the Tula columns depict, would they have forgotten these characters? Turner and Turner (1999:470–471) dismiss such an expectation as simplistic, suggesting that the Toltecs could have constituted a "small but powerful influence" without leaving much of an archaeological signature. They cite many fascinating details of resemblance between mythological characters of the Pueblos and Mesoamerica in general. It is difficult to imagine foreigners achieving much effect without replicating the facilities, emblems, and other markers of power from which they derived their authority at home. The Tarascans, for example, upon conquering a new area, took pains to burn temples and substitute their deity images for local ones (Pollard 1991). The resemblances cited by Turner and Turner, on the other hand, are understandable as products of long-term, mostly indirect contacts during which ritual performances communicated the concepts of cosmology and social control.

*Colonnades.* The Chetro Ketl colonnade could, conceivably, indicate the identity of interaction partners in Mesoamerica. That the closest architectural analogies are Mesoamerican suggests Mesoamerican-derived, urban principles of rulership. Yet, there are no architectural features in Mexico to which the Chetro Ketl feature directly corresponds. Because colonnades are characteristic of public architecture in the Maya area and central Mexico from ca. A.D. 900 onward, for example, at Tula and Chichen Itza, they are widely thought to be markers of Postclassic, that is, post-900 dating, and some archaeologists assume that sites with colonnaded halls are attributable to the Toltecs. Yet, the Chacoans probably did not get the idea of colonnades from these Mesoamerican heartland populations, who were secondary users of columns (Braniff and Areti-Hers 1998). The idea of a colonnaded hall was developed in northern Mexico by ca. A.D. 550 at Alta Vista (Holien and Pickering 1978) and probably not long afterward in La Quemada (B. Nelson 1997). These latter sites in Zacatecas are considerably closer to the American Southwest than the more widely known examples, such as Tula and Chichen Itza. Their regions, and not those dominated by the Toltec capital, are likely sources of interaction partners for Chacoans.

*Roads.* Evidence suggests that the idea of roads probably represents indirect forms of interaction. Roads, or causeways, as they are known in the Maya area, were built by 800 B.C. Mayanists distinguish intrasite causeways, linking sectors within a site, from intersite roads (Folan et al. 2001). The Maya built intrasite causeways by the Middle Preclassic (ca.

**FIGURE 10.5**

*Columns of Tula, Hidalgo, the capital of the Toltecs. (Photograph courtesy of James Q. Jacobs)*

800–300 B.C.) and intersite roads at least as early as the Late Preclassic (300 B.C.–A.D. 200) (Folan, Marcus, and Miller 1995; Marcus 2003). If one takes Lekson's (chapter 3 of this volume) view of Chaco Canyon as one urban settlement, then the Chacoans had both varieties of roads. In any event, the nearest relative of the Chacoan road system is found around La Quemada, Zacatecas (Medina González 2000; Trombold 1991). Elsewhere (B. Nelson 1995), I discuss the similarities and dissimilarities between Chaco's road system and that of La Quemada, the nearest documented example. The two are quite similar in radiating from multiple centers and in the individual roads being especially robust and elaborate as they approach major sites. They are very different, however, in overall geographic scale; the Chacoan system is an order of magnitude larger.

An important difference between the Chacoan and most Mesoamerican road systems is that the latter usually are features of cities, converging at a central plaza surrounded by palaces and temples. The Chacoan system, on the other hand, converges on an empty, architecturally undefined space between two towns, Pueblo Bonito and Chetro Ketl. The connection that it celebrates is about the towns, the land-

359

scape, and the celestial bodies, not an urban plaza. A recent study by Medina (2000) pins down some of the cosmological concepts in the La Quemada road system by relating it to Huichol and Mexican cosmology. Clearly, one principal attribute of the La Quemada road system is the quincunx, or rhombus with center point, which depicts a central point of origin and connected cardinal points. Unless I am missing something about the Chacoan road system, it lacks this property or any attributes that symbolically tie it to a specific Mesoamerican model.

*Copper Bells.* In contrast to the markers discussed thus far, the copper bells found in Chaco Canyon have a very different significance for directness of interaction. Without question, these objects were obtained from distant sources. The raw materials for copper bells may have existed in the American Southwest, but there is no evidence that native groups obtained ore and cast it into these forms.

The Toltecs are not the source of the bells; Hosler and MacFarlane (1996) document that copper objects made from A.D. 900 to 1300 were manufactured in West Mexico. Not until the Late Postclassic, well after the fall of the Toltecs, did metallurgy pass to the interior of Mexico and to the eastern regions. Hosler now believes that scholars have misinterpreted many places thought to have evidence of copper manufacture and that the only documented metallurgical site in Mesoamerica is in highland Guerrero (Hosler, personal communication 2001).

Because copper bells are more common in the Hohokam and Mimbres regions than in Chaco Canyon (Vargas 1995, 2001), Chacoans likely obtained the West Mexican bells through some form of indirect interaction, with people in the southern Southwest serving as intermediaries. Copper bells are sometimes considered evidence of mercantile exchange, but, as Renfrew (2001) points out, they are too infrequent in Chaco Canyon to be considered commodities there. Bells and bracelets might have been acquired through interactions with distant partners in a *kula*-like trading system (Godelier 1999; Mauss 1966). Such exchange could account for the appearance of precise replicas of technologically sophisticated, distantly manufactured items in low, noncommercial frequencies. Participants in the kula system benefited not from "owning" the objects, in a Western sense, but rather from being engaged in the objects' circulation and therefore, by association, gaining "name" from being in contact with very high-status individuals who were at the ends of the circulation pattern (Godelier 1999)

A further implication of this kind of system is a deliberate circulation route with specific termini; Chaco Canyon itself is a plausible terminus. Yet, the kula was a distinctly elite-to-elite pattern of interaction, whereas copper bells and shell bracelets, as well as turquoise, are found in a range of social settings in Chaco Canyon (Judd 1954; Windes et al. 2000:58). Another way of accounting for the portable items might be a *murina*-like system. Murina partners marked their loyalties on feast days by ritual presents, the values of which usually were carefully gauged so as not to offend. Sometimes, however, the givers intentionally offended their partners by giving too much or too little, marking troubled relationships. Murina exchanges occurred not only among elite but also among any number of households, because each was expected to link with another (Davenport 1986).

*Shell Bracelets.* The sources and manufacturers of the Chacoans' shell ornaments are unknown, but use of these ornaments connected Chaco Canyon to a network that reached well into Mesoamerica. The bracelets appear to have been uncommon in Pueblo Bonito; Judd illustrates only one (Judd 1954:figure 15t) and does not give its provenience. He mentions two *glycymeris* shell fragments, whose hinges were carved into pendants and which were recovered from Rooms 241 and 227-I (Judd 1954:26). Judd suggests that these and numerous other shell objects, especially beads, may have been obtained from Sonora. Beltrán (2001) describes shell manufacturing based in what he calls "port sites" because they are typically located on small, natural bays from Colima to Nayarit.

We might solve the question of whether these imported objects were manufactured in West Mexico or in the Hohokam region by giving close attention to raw material species and technological styles. Beltrán's port sites, which I have visited with him, contain what can legitimately be called industrial quantities of shell-manufacturing debris. The practiced eye can divide the masses of shell into categories of by-products from the making of rings, hooks, trumpets, and so forth. Judd provides a list of more than twenty species, in addition to the *glycymeris* that made up the overall shell assemblage, and mentions several objects other than bracelets. A closer matching of the various species listed by Judd (1954), coupled with analysis of the technological styles of shell objects, may produce more precise identification of potential trading partners.

*Unusual Ceramic Vessels.* As noted above, cylindrical vases were widespread and ritually important in Mesoamerica. The form goes back to perhaps 800 B.C. and has many variants. The Chupicuaro form pictured in Frierman (1969:74) is similar to those found at Chaco Canyon but must have been made before A.D. 400 (Braniff 1998). As noted above, there is also little formal similarity with Classic period Teotihuacan cylindrical vases, which is not surprising because potters there ceased making them after about A.D. 600. The cylindrical vase is not included in the Epiclassic (A.D. 600–900) Coyotlatelco assemblage at Teotihuacan. The Epiclassic pseudo-cloisonné *copas* (goblet-shaped jars) of Alta Vista and La Quemada, which are potential contemporaries on the early end of the Chaco occupation, also bear little resemblance in form to the Chacoan jars. In Toltec ceramics, the nearest equivalents are ring-based jars tending toward hourglass shape; Cobean (1990:399– 416) calls them "*braseros*" and suggests that they were probably used to heat rooms, cook food, or burn incense. These vessels are huge and crude, 60 cm in diameter and 1 m in height, and cannot be classified together with the cylindrical jars of Chaco Canyon. As described above, the greatest formal similarities are with Amapa, Nayarit, and the Yucatec Maya. The formal similarity there is important in that it manifests a general synchronization with Mesoamerican change, but vague enough to suggest only indirect contact.

Decorative designs and techniques are also inconsistent with direct-intrusion or direct-exchange models of interaction. The Teotihuacan, Alta Vista, La Quemada, and Amapa examples are decorated with polychrome paints and stuccoes or textured with incising or engraving. The Chacoan examples, on the other hand, are decorated in black-on-white designs native to the San Juan Basin or else are plain and red wares (Toll 2001:63). The imagery on the Epiclassic and Early Postclassic vessels depicts dancers, priests, or rulers in ornate costumes and headdresses; that of Chaco is abstract and geometric. The decorative styles and iconographies of cylindrical vessels in Chaco Canyon and Mesoamerica are distinctly different.

Thong-foot vessels, previously unrecognized as interaction markers, strongly suggest a direct connection with coastal Nayarit. Meighan (1976:457) pictures one of these vessels, to which the Chaco examples have an uncanny resemblance, especially in the way the thongs wrap about the foot and leg. An important difference is that the Nayarit cases are whole foot–shaped vessels, whereas the Chacoan ones are vessel supports. The contextual evidence discussed above definitively places these vessels in the ritual realm. Conceivably, the connection with coastal Nayarit figured into ritual that, among other things, evoked the exotic and the distant.

I do not believe that the evidence described above rules out interaction with the Toltecs; on the other hand, I see no particular evidence of their being among Chacoans' interaction partners. I also see no evidence for direct interaction with any central Mexican partners. The partnerships most in evidence are in West Mexico.

## ACCEPTED AND REJECTED THEMES

We can partially decode the content of the communications by comparing the design and use of specific items in Chaco Canyon with those in Mesoamerica and intervening regions. Up to this point, I have examined presence; equally important are absence and contrast. In this section, I note contrasts associated with columns, copper bells, and cylindrical vessels. To identify what seems to be absent, I briefly contrast the Mesoamerican practices and objects found in Chaco with those found in other regions. The absences may mark exclusivity among Southwestern groups; they may also suggest certain social messages— about inequality, for example—that were or were not being emitted in particular contexts.

Mesoamerican-style themes were probably crucial to a regional system of ritual communication that reiterated and justified Chacoan social practice. Messages in durable media such as buildings, ceramics, and personal adornment likely expressed and shaped intercommunity, interhousehold, and gender relations. The communications, in other words, were essential to social reproduction. Because the stylistic references, even some specific objects, were also symbolic pointers toward urban contexts in Mesoamerica, the relations being reproduced were, conceivably, similar in some ways to those in distant urban contexts. It might even follow that Mesoamerican styles were introduced right along with the institution of tribute relations, the establishment of political inequalities, or the otherwise increasing complexity of the political economy.

One indication of distinctions between Chacoan and Mesoamerican practices is that several items just mentioned are missing at Chaco Canyon, such as ball courts, pallets, plaques, and mirrors. Obviously, Chaco Canyon also lacks a number of more quintessential urban Mesoamerican traits, such as writing and such as temples dedicated to specific deities (Quetzalcoatl, Tezcatlipoca, Huitzilopochtli, Tlaloc). More subtle and perhaps more interesting are some of the partially missing or hidden elements.

*Colonnades.* The cover-up of the Chetro Ketl colonnade shortly after its construction suggests a rejected message. If the colonnade was a reference to the same principles of social power with which columns are associated in Mesoamerica, that invocation apparently did not take root in the Chacoan case. The principle itself may have been rejected, or constituencies may not have been comfortable with openly expressing the principle. In places such as Tula and La Quemada, where colonnades were incorporated into public architecture, the columns possibly stood for social units, such as lineages who subordinated themselves to a larger whole. Be that as it may, the late appearance and low endurance of the colonnade seem to be important contextual clues to its significance. Whatever symbolism it embodied was not accepted.

*Copper Bells.* The bells are an example of complete acceptance of a Mesoamerican object, although this does not mean that their meaning was the same as in the original context. Tarascan figures wear copper bells in "bunches" on the legs, arms, or neck in the *Relación de Michoacán* (Hosler 1994:53). From the elaborate clothing and postures of the depicted individuals, bells seem to be markers of religious or civil authority. Hosler (1994) infers that those bells evoked the divine through their perfect attributes of sound and color. These themes would seem usable in the Chaco Canyon or any Southwestern context, and, to that extent, copper bells probably are indicators of the acceptance of Mesoamerican themes. At the same time, it may be significant that several kinds of copper implements often found together with copper bells in West Mexico are absent in Chaco Canyon. These include macrotweezers, earspools, axes, needles, rings, plaques or slugs of unknown function, fishhooks, awls, wire, beads, and chains, found at places such as Amapa (Meighan 1976), Tomatlan (Mountjoy and Torres 1985), and Cañon del Molino (Ganot and Peschard 1995). Macrotweezers are depicted in the *Relación de Michoacán* as pendants worn on the chests of priests (Hosler 1994:67). Their purpose is unclear, but their association with the elite appears to be exclusive. I do not know any depictions of earspools that are definitively copper, but I assume that these items also were not available to commoners. Most of the other items not depicted in the codices seem prosaic. An explanation for the absence of the large tweezers and earspools, which is not completely satisfactory because it ignores these utilitarian items, is social rejection of the messages associated with sumptuary goods. Whereas bells could have unquestionable religious connotations, macrotweezers and earspools may have been more suggestive of purely political power and, as such, unacceptable in the Chacoan ethos. Bells, on the other hand, may have been acceptable because they related to eliteness cast as religiosity, or even to religion itself.

*Shell Bracelets.* Like copper bells, the bracelets seem to exemplify complete acceptance or sharing of material, technique, and symbol. These objects are sufficiently uncommon at Chaco Canyon to make it difficult to infer much else about their significance.

*Unusual Ceramic Vessels.* The cylindrical vessels might be designed for feasting, burning special substances, or ritual ablutions. If Chacoan feasts and ritual events were organized like Mesoamerican ones, participants might have used similar principles in the vessels' design, use, and ultimate deposition. We actually know very little about Mesoamerican feasting. From the codices—for example, Sahagún (1950)—we can see that feasting was associated with public ritual that may have been, in some senses, the equivalent of law. Feasts offered opportunities to negotiate social positions, affirm agreements, and mark political and life-cycle events. Every part of foodways is potentially symbolic (Dietler 2001), including production, selection, preparation, presentation, and the spatial ordering of individuals within the commensal group.

Painted murals depict Maya cylindrical vases as ritual drinking vessels (Reents-Budet 1994). Sherds of Teotihuacan cylinder jars occur in unusually high frequencies along the avenue of the dead (Cowgill, Altschul, and Sload 1994), and the vessels are depicted, in painted images on some of the vessels themselves, as smokers or incense burners being carried by priest figures (Conides 1997). At La Quemada (Lelgemann 2000; B. Nelson, Millhauser, and To 1998) and Alta Vista (Holien and Pickering 1978), the copa, which appears to be related to the hourglass-shaped version of the Tula cylinders, is found in sacrificial burials and a multiple, disarticulated burial pit.

None of these ritual connotations seems directly applicable to the Chacoan cylindrical jars. They do seem to have been ritually deposited; it is difficult to imagine a quotidian practice that would lead to the piling of 111 specially made jars in the middle of a room. No contextual evidence of violence exists. The interpretation that Toll (2001:63) proposes, that the jars were deposited together to commemorate an agreement among representatives of several parts of the Chaco world, seems plausible against the backdrop of Mesoamerican analogies.

The thong-foot pots are an example of sharing a motif. Someone— such as a prophet, widely known merchant, or deified leader—must have been associated with this symbolism, but it is lost to us. What we can reliably infer is that the object and its referents were important in religious contexts, as evidenced by their recovery from opposing sets of rooms auxiliary to kivas at Pueblo Bonito.

## CONCLUSION

The dynamics of Chacoan development were synchronous in broad outline with northern Mesoamerican cycles of change. By taking a wide chronological and spatial view, one can see the Chacoan development in a context in which many regional centers came and went. In the background was the Mesoamerican core, where large-scale social disturbances such as urban collapse and shifting macroeconomic networks generated systemic effects that may have propagated far and wide. Nearer to Chaco Canyon, but still within Mesoamerica, were the Northern Frontier and West Mexican regions. No Mesoamerican group founded or took over Chaco; we cannot link Chacoan development directly with any core or frontier event, person, deity, or population.

Yet, northern Mexican and American Southwestern developments were clearly related; the changing sociopolitical landscape progressively encouraged the formation of polities on a scale beyond the local valley.

Mesoamerican people did not found Chaco Canyon; most interaction markers occur in the consolidation phase, A.D. 1040–1120, long after the Chaco phenomenon began. Moreover, the interaction markers do not refer to a particular empire or capital. People in Chaco Canyon adopted Mesoamerican techniques, designs, symbols, and practices from temporally and geographically scattered sources, which were less cities than regions where other peoples had drawn strands from the urban core and reinterpreted them in local contexts. These nonurbanized people invented some very important elements, such as colonnades and metallurgy, that were taken up by urban societies in the post-Chaco era. There might not have been a single urban or ideological model that co-opted the Chacoans, but, instead, an array of societal transformations ultimately involving yet not directly emanating from the urban core. With access to some of these interactions, Chacoans selected scattered ideological elements that were significant in Mesoamerican contexts. Many also had some prior importance in the American Southwest, especially the Hohokam region. The Chaco leaders may not have drawn from a particular core urban site, but from several areas that were "secondary," that had, themselves, drawn from the core.

Along with others (Lekson 1983a, 1999; Mathien 1986; McGuire 1980; McGuire and others 1994), I conclude that the Chacoans knew about Mesoamerican societies and interacted with them but were not their minions in any sense. Chaco had its own kind of complexity and was not a copy of any Mesoamerican center. This conclusion complements Lipe's (chapter 8 of this volume) revelations about the northern San Juan origins of Chacoan architecture. Lipe shows that the architectural layouts of Pueblo Bonito and other Great Houses in Chaco Canyon were enlarged, elaborated, and evolved versions of northern San Juan Basin Pueblo I village architecture, basically compressing the separate elements of northern villages into single buildings. By comparison with the few highly transformed Mesoamerican characteristics of Chacoan architecture mentioned below, these attributes state strongly that the population that came to inhabit the canyon ca.

A.D. 900–1150 had a northern origin. The interesting question is, why were these northern peoples so interested in adopting southern artifacts and practices?

The importance of Mesoamerican themes in Chaco Canyon probably lies not so much in origins as in communications about Chacoan social order and cultural identity. Whether the messages were ideological, in the Marxist sense of promoting factional or class interests (McGuire 1992; Pauketat 1998), or more broadly ideational, we do not know. Following out the themes Chacoans accepted and rejected, using Mesoamerican ideology as a backdrop, may be a fruitful line of investigation.

The identities of communities with emergent leadership roles may have formed around the leaders themselves (Hill and Clark 2001). The social needs of the emergent leadership for symbols to mark and legitimize the new social order may have constituted one force that drew strands of Mesoamerican culture outward from the urban core. Whalen and Minnis (2001:327) propose that typical of Casas Grandes (Paquimé) may have been "the building and maintenance of outside contacts, through which local aspirants to power import the goods and ideologies that strengthen and legitimize their positions." I would add that some of the social strategies inherent in urbanism may have had practical use in these far northern contexts but that others may have been threatening.

Helms (1988, 1993) shows how acquisition serves to naturalize the role of the elite. She defines *acquisition* as obtaining objects that are special in their physical properties or come from great distances. Acquisition of objects from a distance is powerful in that the possession of acquired items implies a potential to connect with world-sustaining forces. If the objects are made from technological principles that are locally unknown, all the better. Besides being technologically sophisticated, the Mesoamerican-style objects found in Chaco Canyon represent active invocations of concepts of social and cosmological order that were ultimately derived from urban Mesoamerica. Such distant urban places could easily be mystified and sanctified as sources of power for those knowledgeable of their workings.

Was the population at Chaco frequently in direct contact with Mesoamerican peoples, or did Mesoamerican cultures mainly provide background material from which Chacoans borrowed? The answers to this question may be almost as diverse as the interaction markers. For reasons that Renfrew (2001) points out, mercantile exchange was not likely important in operationalizing these urban concepts. Whatever the mechanisms of exchange, I conclude that some form of interaction with distant partners and adoption of their material symbols was useful in establishing the elite's responsibility for and effectiveness in ritual. This legitimization was probably accomplished by importing and transforming "ultimate sacred propositions" (Rappaport 1974) or "doxa" (Bourdieu 1994), that is, unquestionable truths about the social and natural order, which were continually invoked, reinforced, and reiterated by sacred objects. The linking of these propositions with distant cities would have been an effective means of legitimization, the increased Mesoamerican flavor being a consequence instead of a cause of change. Yet, in some significant measure, these acquisitions entrained the polity as a whole, connecting it to a larger political-economic world.

The idea of distant partners, proposed by Mauss (1966) and used by other sociocultural anthropologists, such as Weiner (1992) and Godelier (1999), appears to accommodate some of the patterns of exchange and adoption better than any commercial, military, or other extant political-economic models. It suggests that, quite to the contrary of being a macroregional subordinate, the Chacoan elite may have used interaction with distant partners to further its own interests. One strategy of interaction may have constituted a chain of exchange similar to the Melanesian kula, in which goods were continually passed between distant trading partners through intermediaries, who, in turn, shared some of the status gains afforded by temporary possession of valued objects. In such an exchange process, one might expect the very long distances observed, the gradual, selective adoption of distant practices, and the absence of commoditization of exchanged objects. These patterns appear relevant to copper bells and shell bracelets, yet one must note that there is no obvious export of a high-value, finished product from Chaco Canyon. Possibly, raw or partially shaped turquoise pieces were the nearest equivalent, and these were shaped to local religious specifications at destinations in Mesoamerica (Weigand and García de Weigand 2001).

Notions of power at Chaco Canyon may have been carefully

cloaked in references to distant places, landscapes, and celestial phenomena. The elite probably were not kings, but people highly knowledgeable about the constructed supernatural and natural order. As such, they may have been entrusted with directorial instead of dictatorial powers by the population. If one must attach a universal label to the central actors, *priest* or *chief* is probably most appropriate. Renfrew's (2001) notion of a sacred economy and Yoffee's notion of "rituality" seem to capture the imagined social arrangement well. Within such contexts, in Mesoamerican objects, symbols, and practices, leaders probably found a convenient repertoire for glorifying themselves and the social principles they sought to establish.

As Vivian (1990) notes, sociopolitical complexity is not necessarily a permanent state. Keating (2000) shows how contrasting assumptions of hierarchy and equality may play into the smallest social interactions, resulting in moments when social hierarchy is expressed alternating with moments that reflect more egalitarian assumptions about the social order. Some Chaco Canyon inhabitants may have promoted hierarchy while others resisted it; the balance of these forces may have tipped periodically. The construction of the colonnade at Chetro Ketl and the events canonized in the legend of the Gambler Noqoìlpi may represent one such moment. It is not unlikely, as legend suggests (Gabriel 1996:88), that power got out of hand at some point, possibly by abuse, leading to disruption of regional accords as to Chaco's centrality. The social impossibility of institutionalizing hierarchical relations seems to be expressed materially in the quick concealment of the colonnade, followed not long afterward by collapse of the Chacoan center.

### Notes

The fieldwork at La Quemada was conducted with permission of the Consejo Nacional de Arqueología of the Instituto Nacional de Antropología e Historia. Joaquín García Bárcena, Alejandro Martínez Muriel, Peter Jiménez Betts, and Baudelina García Uranga of that institution have provided guidance and intellectual stimulation. I am indebted to Steve Lekson and Lynn Sebastian for including me in the Chaco conference series and for their courage, thoroughness, and originality in constructing and running the meeting series. Michelle

Hegmon, Joyce Marcus, Paul Minnis, Michael Ohnersorgen, and Wolcott Toll provided very useful information and comments. Funding sources that have contributed to my fieldwork in Mexico include the National Science Foundation, the National Endowment for the Humanities, the Wenner-Gren Foundation for Anthropological Research, the Foundation for the Advancement of Mesoamerican Studies, Deans Ross MacKinnon of Social Sciences at SUNY-Buffalo, Gary Krahenbuhl and David Young of Liberal Arts and Sciences at Arizona State University, and an anonymous private donor.

1. This was the process that Kelley (1956) referred to as the expansion of the Northern Frontier, although the dating of it was understood differently at the time that he wrote.

2. Baines and Yoffee (1998:235) define *high culture* as "the production and consumption of aesthetic items under the control, and for the benefit, of the inner elite of a civilization, including the ruler and the gods." They consider high culture to be an exclusive characteristic of civilizations. It is unclear to me why archaeologists should restrict the concept of high culture to civilizations, because "aesthetic items" are produced in less complex social formations for the same purposes. The idea seems equally applicable in the Chacoan context, in which the degree of aesthetic development differs so much from that of settlements in the surrounding areas.

3. A result of the Chaco Synthesis conference.

4. Mountjoy and Torres's (1985) finds at Tomatlán and Hers's (1989) at Cerro del Huistle persuaded Hosler (1994) that copper bells may have circulated as early as A.D. 600. In both cases, A.D. 600 is the earliest conceivable date for the strata from which researchers recovered the bells, and we cannot eliminate dates closer to 900. The absence of copper bells in the phases pre-dating 900 at La Quemada and Alta Vista leads me to believe that bells began to circulate no earlier than 900.

**Environmental Variables**

| DATA CATEGORY | 500 | 525 | 550 | 575 | 600 | 625 | 650 | 675 | 700 | 725 | 750 | 775 | 800 | 825 |

**Rainfall**

Schematic representation of lower-frequency trends in rainfall

Long term mean is 8.9 ± 1.42 inches

11 —
10 —
9 —
8 —
7 —

Inches

**Channel dynamics**

Aggradation

Degradation

**Temporal variability**

High
Low

**Spatial variability**

High
Low

| 500 | 525 | 550 | 575 | 600 | 625 | 650 | 675 | 700 | 725 | 750 | 775 | 800 | 825 |

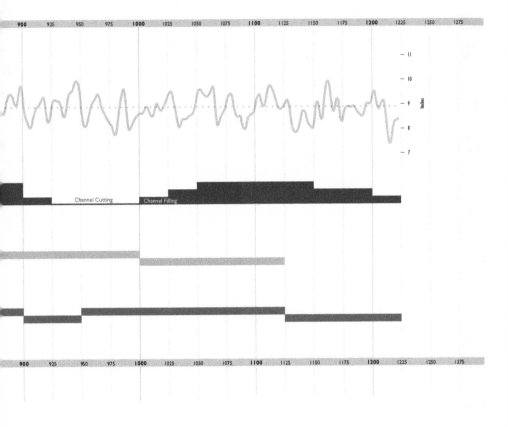

Channel Cutting    Channel Filling

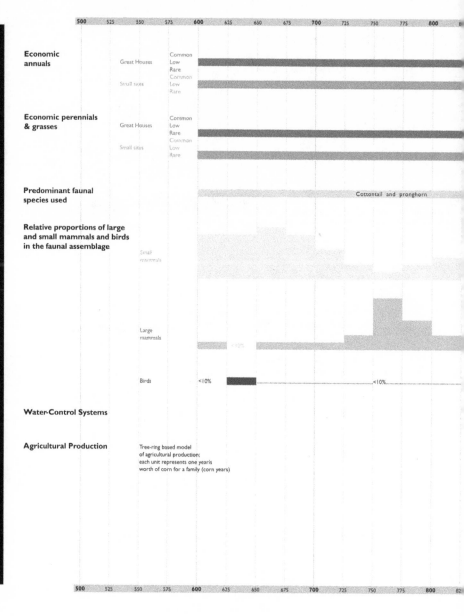

**Subsistence Resources**

| 500 | 525 | 550 | 575 | 600 | 625 | 650 | 675 | 700 | 725 | 750 | 775 | 800 | 8 |

**Economic annuals**

Great Houses — Common / Low / Rare

Small sites — Common / Low / Rare

**Economic perennials & grasses**

Great Houses — Common / Low / Rare

Small sites — Common / Low / Rare

**Predominant faunal species used**

Cottontail and pronghorn

**Relative proportions of large and small mammals and birds in the faunal assemblage**

Small mammals

Large mammals — <10%

Birds — <10% ......................................................<10%....................

**Water-Control Systems**

**Agricultural Production**

Tree-ring based model of agricultural production; each unit represents one year's worth of corn for a family (corn years)

| 500 | 525 | 550 | 575 | 600 | 625 | 650 | 675 | 700 | 725 | 750 | 775 | 800 | 82 |

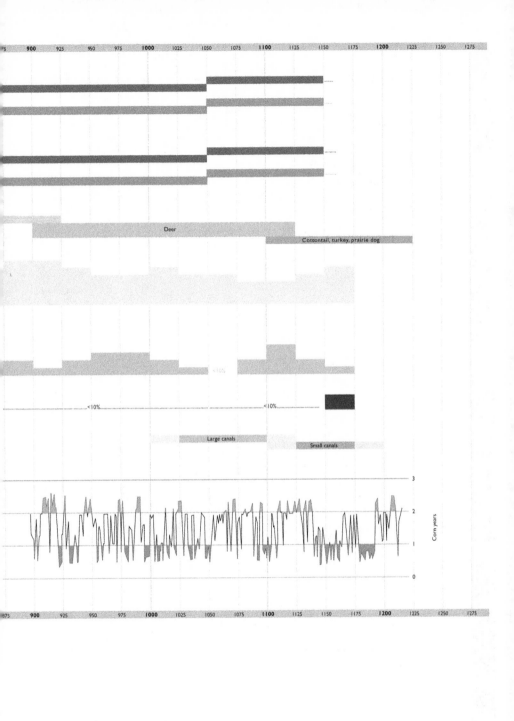

| | 900 | 925 | 950 | 975 | 1000 | 1025 | 1050 | 1075 | 1100 | 1125 | 1150 | 1175 | 1200 | 1225 | 1250 | 1275 |

Deer

Cottontail, turkey, prairie dog

<10%

<10%                <10%

Large canals

Small canals

Corn years

3

2

1

0

| 875 | 900 | 925 | 950 | 975 | 1000 | 1025 | 1050 | 1075 | 1100 | 1125 | 1150 | 1175 | 1200 | 1225 | 1250 | 1275 |

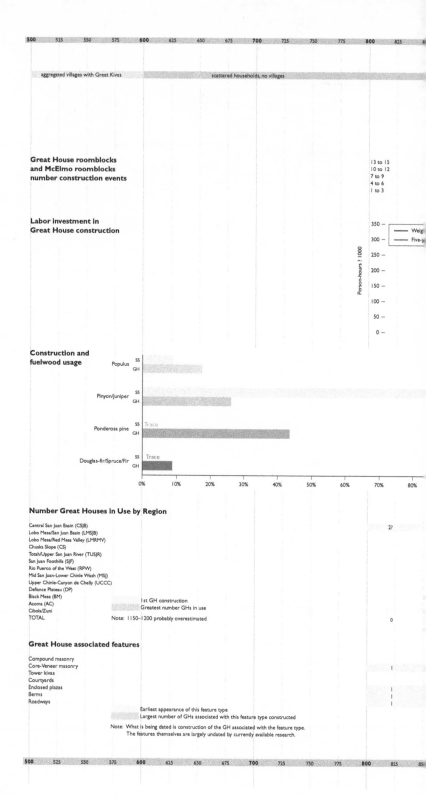

500 525 550 575 600 625 650 675 700 725 750 775 800 825

aggregated villages with Great Kivas   scattered households, no villages

**Great House roomblocks
and McElmo roomblocks
number construction events**

13 to 15
10 to 12
7 to 9
4 to 6
1 to 3

**Labor investment in
Great House construction**

350 —   ▬ Weig
300 —   ▬ Five-y
250 —
200 —
150 —
100 —
50 —
0 —

Person-hours ? 1000

**Construction and
fuelwood usage**

Populus   SS
GH

Pinyon/Juniper   SS
GH

Ponderosa pine   SS   Trace
GH

Douglas-fir/Spruce/Fir   SS   Trace
GH

0%   10%   20%   30%   40%   50%   60%   70%   80%

**Number Great Houses in Use by Region**

Central San Juan Basin (CSJB)
Lobo Mesa/San Juan Basin (LMSJB)
Lobo Mesa/Red Mesa Valley (LMRMV)
Chuska Slope (CS)
Totah/Upper San Juan River (TUSJR)
San Juan Foothills (SJF)
Rio Puerco of the West (RPW)
Mid San Juan-Lower Chinle Wash (MSJ)
Upper Chinle-Canyon de Chelly (UCCC)
Defiance Plateau (DP)
Black Mesa (BM)
Acoma (AC)   1st GH construction
Cibola/Zuni   Greatest number GHs in use
TOTAL   Note: 1150–1200 probably overestimated

2?

0

**Great House associated features**

Compound masonry
Core-Veneer masonry
Tower kivas
Courtyards
Enclosed plazas
Berms
Roadways

Earliest appearance of this feature type
Largest number of GHs associated with this feature type constructed

Note: What is being dated is construction of the GH associated with the feature type.
The features themselves are largely undated by currently available research.

500 525 550 575 600 625 650 675 700 725 750 775 800 825 85

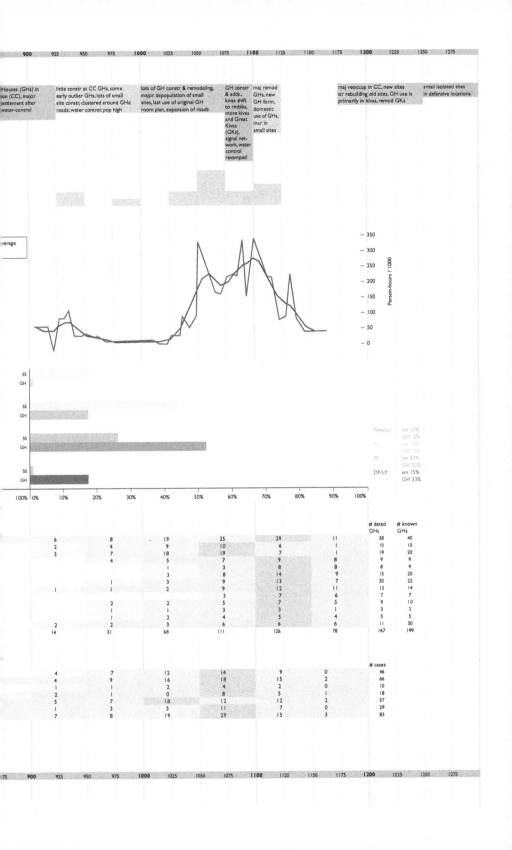

Houses (GHs) in
ion (CC), major
ettlement after
water-control

little constr at CC GHs, some
early outlier GHs; lots of small
site constr, clustered around GHs;
roads; water control; pop high

lots of GH constr & remodeling,
major depopulation of small
sites, last use of original GH
room plan, expansion of roads

GH constr
& adds.,
kivas shift
to rmblks,
more kivas
and Great
Kivas
(GKs),
signal net-
work, water
control
revamped

maj remod
GHs, new
GH form,
domestic
use of GHs,
incr in
small sites

maj reoccup in CC, new sites
or rebuilding old sites, GH use is
primarily in kivas, remod GKs

small isolated sites
in defensive locations

verage

— 350
— 300
— 250
— 200
— 150
— 100
— 50
— 0

Person-hours ? 1000

| | SS | | |
|---|---|---|---|
| | GH | | |

SS
GH

SS
GH

SS
GH

| Populus | sm 17% |
| | GH 2% |
| P? | sm 57% |
| | GH 2% |
| PP | sm 37% |
| | GH 52% |
| DF/s/f | sm 15% |
| | GH 33% |

100% | 0% · 10% · 20% · 30% · 40% · 50% · 60% · 70% · 80% · 90% · 100%

| | | | | | | | # dated GHs | # known GHs |
|---|---|---|---|---|---|---|---|---|
| 6 | 8 | 19 | 25 | 29 | 11 | | 38 | 40 |
| 2 | 4 | 9 | 10 | 6 | 1 | | 10 | 10 |
| 3 | 7 | 18 | 19 | 7 | 1 | | 19 | 20 |
| | 4 | 5 | 7 | 9 | 8 | | 9 | 9 |
| | | 1 | 3 | 8 | 8 | | 8 | 9 |
| | | 3 | 8 | 14 | 9 | | 15 | 20 |
| | 1 | 3 | 9 | 13 | 7 | | 20 | 22 |
| 1 | 1 | 2 | 9 | 12 | 11 | | 13 | 14 |
| | | | 3 | 7 | 6 | | 7 | 7 |
| | 2 | 2 | 5 | 7 | 5 | | 9 | 10 |
| | 1 | 1 | 3 | 3 | 1 | | 3 | 3 |
| | 1 | 2 | 4 | 5 | 4 | | 5 | 5 |
| 2 | 2 | 3 | 6 | 6 | 6 | | 11 | 30 |
| 14 | 31 | 68 | 111 | 126 | 78 | | 167 | 199 |

| | | | | | | | # cases |
|---|---|---|---|---|---|---|---|
| 4 | 7 | 12 | 14 | 9 | 0 | | 46 |
| 4 | 9 | 16 | 18 | 15 | 2 | | 66 |
| 1 | 1 | 2 | 4 | 2 | 0 | | 10 |
| 2 | 1 | 0 | 8 | 5 | 1 | | 18 |
| 5 | 7 | 18 | 12 | 12 | 2 | | 57 |
| 1 | 3 | 5 | 11 | 7 | 0 | | 29 |
| 7 | 8 | 19 | 29 | 15 | 3 | | 83 |

**Material Culture**

| | 500 | 525 | 550 | 575 | 600 | 625 | 650 | 675 | 700 | 725 | 750 | 775 | 800 | 8 |
|---|---|---|---|---|---|---|---|---|---|---|---|---|---|---|

**Chipped Stone**

low frequencies nonlocal material: obsidian 3.6% of assemblage, mostly as tools (proj. pts.)

Grants obsidian 8% of assemblage, mostly as finished tools (proj. pts.)

trace amounts nonlocal materials: obsidian 1.5% of assemblage, mostly as finished tools (proj. pts.)

**Ornaments/ Minerals**

few items, few forms (esp. beads & pendants, little inlay); local minerals (calcite, gypsum, jet, hematite) used, but not for ornaments; bone and nonlocal turquoise and shell from Gulf of California (*Olivella* & *Glycymeris*)

more items, few forms; nonlocal minerals (malachite, azurite, serpentine) from periphery of San Juan Basin; new shell from Pacific Ocean (*Haliotis*) and freshwater clams (unknown source); no known workshops in Chaco Canyon, but mfg. debris found at Shabik'eshchee; turquoise & shell recovered in site outside of San Juan Basin, including Rio Grande Valley

**Ceramic Wares**

Gray ware — Plain gray

White ware

Red ware

Brown ware — Earliest pottery

**Ceramic Import Percentage**

40–50%
30–40%
20–30%
10–20%
0–10%

3.6%
Chuskan

16.6%
Total

| DATA CATEGORY | 500 | 525 | 550 | 575 | 600 | 625 | 650 | 675 | 700 | 725 | 750 | 775 | 800 | 825 |
|---|---|---|---|---|---|---|---|---|---|---|---|---|---|---|

**materials**

| low frequencies of nonlocal materials: NPC (Narbona Pass chert) 2.1% of assemblage | key period for increase in nonlocal, esp. late 1000s: NPC 21.1%, Morrison Fm. 4.3%, Zuni silicified wood 2.8%; obsidian rare; local silic. woods increase in frequency | some nonlocal materials decrease: NPC 18.9%, Morrison Fm. 2.6%, & Zuni silic. wood 1.1%; some increase: obsidian, mostly debitage 7.3%, & yellow-brown spotted chert 3% | all nonlocal materials decrease: NPC 7%, Morrison Fm. 0.9%, Zuni silic. wood 0%, yellow-brown spotted 2.4%, & obsidian 2% |

| many items, many forms (more inlay, effigies, rings); new shell in small sites and GHs likely from G of C: *Argopectin, Spondylus, Chama, Trachycardium, Episcynia, Strombus, Oliva,* and *Conus*; one small site burial with shale bead necklace, at least one GH burial with turquoise; workshops known; turquoise in offerings | many items, many forms (inlay, copper bells); new minerals: argillite, selenite, gypsite, green quartz, geothite; new shell from G of C: *Choromytilus*; workshop known; offerings in shrines, kivas, and burials; Pueblo Bonito contains store rooms for minerals, shell, & turquoise | fewer items, fewer forms; new G of C shell: *Nassarius*; possible workshops at small sites and GHs | fewer items, few forms; continued use of ornaments and minerals beyond Chaco at Aztec and Guadalupe; little material imported from north of the San Juan River (Mesa Verde) area |

Neck-banded

Neck corrugation

Overall corrugation

period of peak Chuska import

Red Mesa

Gallup-Chaco Hatchure

Chaco McElmo

mineral to organic paint shift, 1095–1105

specialized forms: cylinder jars, pitchers, human effigies, 1040–1110

White Mountain

Tusayan

Polished smudged

| | | | | | | | | 39.8% | | 31.3% | | 50.4% | | 45.7% | |
| .1% | | | 25.2% | | | 30.7% | | | | | | | | 21.6% | |
| | 12.3% | | | | | | | | | | | | | | |

| tal | | Chuskan | Total | | | Chuskan | Total | | | Chuskan | Total | Chuskan | Total | | |

# 11

## The Chaco Project in Historical Context

### Richard H. Wilshusen and W. Derek Hamilton

The immense scale and architectural magnificence of the Great Houses at Chaco Canyon immediately impress any visitor. For archaeologists, the Chaco phenomenon is equally imposing in its historical scope and effect on Southwestern cultures. If you are an archaeologist in the northern Southwest, you can avoid neither sagebrush nor Chaco. The Chaco Project of the 1970s and 1980s was intended by its originators to be equally as big and impressive as the ruins it was to study. No matter what any investigator may think about its results, the Chaco Project also cannot be avoided. Since 1990 approximately two hundred *primary* references on Chaco have been published (Mills 2002:101–114), and almost every one of these works draws significantly on Chaco Project references or research. Yet, in spite of the huge output on Chaco and the many spin-offs from the Chaco Project, there has been practically no discussion of the Chaco Project's place within the recent history of American archaeology (compare with Maruca 1982). We contend that the Chaco Project was a fundamental turning point in the modern revitalization of American public archaeology.

The historical sequence of events leading up to and during the

Chaco Project mark a shift in the United States from small-scale salvage archaeology to the cultural resource management (CRM) archaeology at the state and national levels, which we take for granted today. First envisioned in the late 1960s, the Chaco Project began in the 1970s and lasted into the mid-1980s. It exemplifies the shift to government-mandated, "big" archaeology projects (Rogge 1983), with the substantial money and scientific where-with-all—as well as the administrative, bureaucratic, and publishing headaches—that accompany modern CRM projects.

Both the scale and intensity of the project's research dwarfed previous large reservoir salvage projects such as Navajo Reservoir (Eddy 1966) and Glen Canyon (Jennings 1966), as well as National Park Service (NPS) development projects such as Wetherill Mesa (Hayes 1964). In the beginning, the project centered its work within the confines of what was then the Chaco Canyon National Monument. By the end, parts of the survey extended to Chacoan-style Great House outliers more than 50 km away from the Chaco core. It was a very unique project in its regional focus. Ultimately, the Chaco Project influenced the context of archaeology in the Southwest more than similarly large public archaeology projects such as the Dolores Project or Black Mesa. Unlike previous big projects, it had a direct effect on decisions to expand the area of protection around Chaco Canyon (ultimately becoming the Chaco Culture National Historical Park) and to expand the compass of research to a truly regional level.

In retrospect, the project's shift in focus was monumental but not altogether unexpected when we place the project within a larger historical framework. Unlike many large projects that seem to take on a life of their own or to be shaped primarily by the principal investigators, the Chaco Project was a product of many people's efforts and the time during which they worked. The originators and initial organizers had actively participated in the River Basin Survey salvage work of the 1950s and 1960s. They were tried-and-true researchers with the good sense, or audacity, to hire the best young professionals available in the Southwest. Many of the most innovative Southwestern researchers of the 1970s identified with the "New" archaeology; as these individuals took increasing control of the project, its focus changed. By the end, the theoretical perspectives of the Chaco Project exhibited a healthy eclecticism.

This chapter focuses on how American archaeology transformed at both national and regional scales and how this transformation played out in the Chaco Project. By the 1960s the practice of archaeology faced many national challenges (for example, Brew 1961; Johnson 1966), and the NPS leadership attempted to address those challenges squarely with the Chaco Project (Ernest Connally, quoted in Maruca 1982:12). After setting the historical stage in the 1960s and remarking on the fast pace of change in archaeology in the 1970s, we will focus on how important the individuals were in shaping the way the Chaco Project was run. By looking at the variety of individuals who had a hand in the project, we will also show how archaeological research evolved, from the maturing of the New Archaeology to the "historic turn" in the social sciences. This shift figured in the project's physical bounds, the questions it tried to answer, the way it conveyed the initial results to researchers and the larger public, and how scholars understand the Chaco phenomenon today.

## FACING THE 1960s CRISIS IN PUBLIC ARCHAEOLOGY AND CREATING THE CHACO PROJECT

The Chaco Project began when what was left of the national River Basin Survey (RBS) merged into NPS (in 1969) and when public archaeology as we presently know it was being created (Snyder et al. 2000). After World War II, a flurry of dam, highway, and other construction projects seriously threatened American archaeology. Although the NPS External Program (Interagency Archeological Salvage Program) and the River Basin Salvage Act (1960) had funded immense archaeological efforts in the 1950s and 1960s, these monies were woefully short to finance the tasks that needed to be accomplished (Rogge 1983). Over a twenty-five-year period, approximately five hundred reservoir surveys performed in forty-three states led to the discovery of approximately twenty thousand sites. RBS archaeologists (Brew 1968) conducted nearly five hundred major excavations for less than ten million dollars (1980 dollars), a sum that would soon characterize the cost of a single large project in the late 1970s and 1980s (for example, Breternitz 1993b). Even though RBS produced many classic reports, Lehmer (1971) estimated that it reported only 25 percent of all the research. Also, an enormous amount of critical archaeological information went missing because vast numbers of sites had been lost in the process.

By the late 1960s NPS and many archaeologists, historians, and urban planners recognized the need for a new approach to historic preservation and public archaeology. Passage of the National Historic Preservation Act (1966), the National Environmental Policy Act (1969), and the Moss-Bennett amendments to the original Reservoir Salvage Act (1974) laid the legal foundation for modern CRM archaeology (NPS 2002). In addition, calls for more responsive yet conservation-minded models of resource management (Lipe1974; McGimsey and Davis 1977) and the emergence of New Archaeology in the 1960s (for example, Binford 1964; Struever 1968) set the stage for a more regionally based, research-driven archaeology. NPS Chief Archeologist John Corbett was in the middle of many national discussions. Beginning in 1966 he pushed forward the idea of the Chaco Project. Ernest Connally, then NPS Chief of the Office of Archeology and Historic Preservation, remembered that they had hoped to raise the Chaco Project "to an undisputed place on the cutting edge of scientific inquiry." Connally (cited in Maruca 1982:12) noted: "If the USA could not support archaeological investigation carried out by the most sophisticated means, then who could?"

In 1969 Corbett and Doug Schwartz of the School of American Research (SAR) in Santa Fe gathered together an intriguing mix of NPS administrators, New Archaeologists, established scholars, and ex-RBS archaeologists to discuss the studies a Chaco Project might include.[1] Later that year, Wilfred Logan and Zorro Bradley (1969) summarized these discussions in a prospectus, which was used to sell the project to administrators and Congress (Maruca 1982:26). As a result, the Chaco Project was primarily funded by in-house NPS monies instead of "outhouse" (that is, External Program) monies. National Science Foundation (NSF) monies for archaeology fell dramatically between 1966 and 1975 as the Vietnam War drained the national budget, but Corbett and others effectively defended the NPS archaeology program monies. By 1970 NPS's External Program budget was almost double the NSF archaeological budget (Rogge 1983:figure 2.4), the other main source of government funds for archaeological research at that time.

The Chaco investigations began after the completion of the fieldwork and write-up of NPS's Wetherill Mesa Project (1958–1965), which was associated with the expansion of the facilities at Mesa Verde National Park (MVNP). For the Wetherill Mesa work, there appears to have been only a limited general-research design and implicit theoretical orientation. The Wetherill Mesa Project employed a variety of investigators and lacked an overarching methodology or design to unify site investigations as we would expect since the 1980s. Although several notable reports resulted (Cattanach 1980; Hayes 1964; Hayes and Lancaster 1975; Rohn 1971), publication usually followed fieldwork by a decade or more. The project was explicitly interdisciplinary, drawing on soil science, ecology, and cultural anthropology to interpret the area's prehistory (Osborne 1965). Yet, at its core, the Mesa Verde work focused on developing more sites for display on Wetherill Mesa and alleviating traffic congestion on Chapin Mesa. The MVNP work was performed just before the New Archaeology debates of the 1960s. With a few exceptions in the archaeology (for example, Hayes 1964; Rohn 1971), it was still site-specific, concentrating on site and artifact description and sorting out the sequence and dates of occupation.

The Chaco Project, however, would be distinctly different from Wetherill Mesa, even though some of the original key personnel for Chaco were recruited because of their Wetherill Mesa experience. The Mesa Verde project conducted some of its research in cooperation with the University of Colorado, but the Chaco Project would be based at the University of New Mexico (UNM), an institution with extensive research and historical interest in Chaco. This was much more in keeping with the RBS projects in the 1950s and 1960s, when researchers set up field offices at major universities and employed university associates to direct the projects. The Chaco research prospectus emphasized that the "concentrated, long-term inquiries" should serve NPS management and interpretive needs but also research outside conventional interpretative needs. Throughout the decade-long series of investigations, the stated goals of the project changed noticeably.

## PUTTING THE CHACO PROJECT AND ITS OBJECTIVES WITHIN A HISTORICAL CONTEXT

The first serious discussion of the Chaco Project objectives took place at the School of American Research in January 1969. Twelve key scholars and NPS administrators reviewed important questions about the local archaeology and ecology of Chaco Canyon and the regional influences that might have shaped its history. With this background, they then discussed projects that might contribute to answering the questions and sketched out the necessary facilities and personnel for such an endeavor. The program was much more ambitious than typical RBS salvage projects or even NPS projects in the past. Not only did the prospectus (Logan and Bradley 1969) establish the nature of the relationship between the project and the park, but it also detailed the project's investigative scope, suggested methods for accomplishing its goals, and divided research into two broad categories.

The investigative scope was four-fold: (1) to clarify the events in prehistory within the park, (2) to explain their occurrence, (3) to supplement existing "exhibits-in-place" with representative pre-Bonito-phase examples, and (4) to develop more extensive museum collections from each time period. The broad research categories entailed (1) investigations into the processes of cultural development and (2) analysis of human and environmental interaction during historic times within the canyon. The second category led to the implementation of a broad-based, ecological research design that examined rainfall, vegetation, faunal distribution, and mineral resources. The project would map the results spatially and temporally with a focus on archaeological sites and their sequences. All of this became an effort to understand the nature of human and environmental interaction in the past.

The heavy emphasis on human ecology was a characteristic means of integrating the improved chronological and settlement pattern information of the 1950s and 1960s with Leslie White's ideas about cultural adaptation to the environment and the evolution of social organization (Lipe 1999b:73). By wrapping this updated structural-functionalist view of anthropology into an ecologically framed "systems" approach, researchers could look for sources of change within the "closed" environment of a particular region or in technological innovation within a particular culture. During the 1970s answers to questions in these spheres were certainly more achievable than in the more difficult social system spheres such as human agency, interregional migration, or large-scale conflict. This "processual" approach was part of the larger revitalization of American archaeology, which was equally, if not more significantly, shaped by the massive shift in how archaeology was funded.

By 1970 the combined NPS External Program and NSF archaeology budgets were about four million dollars (Rogge 1983:figure 2.4, 1980 dollars). This represented the majority of federal archaeological spending in 1970. By the late 1970s to mid-1980s, however, federal spending on archaeology escalated to 100–300 million dollars annually (see Rogge 1983 for estimates). The vast majority of archaeologists, as well as Congress, had not understood the importance of the NHPA when it was passed in 1966 (Mitchell n.d.), but by the early 1970s archaeologists were awakening to the needs and possibilities of CRM archaeology for funding a more scientifically rigorous, multidisciplinary approach to archaeology. When tied to the potent rhetoric of processualism, it is understandable why some even claimed that a scientific revolution was afoot. In hindsight, though, the transformation had more in common with a revitalization movement (Wallace 1966:158–166).

The conception and initial years of the Chaco Project occurred exactly in the middle of this major shift in archaeology, in the late 1960s–early 1970s. In a sense, the Chaco Project was the first of the big CRM archaeology projects. Certainly, Black Mesa is an equal contender for this honor in the Southwest, with its beginnings in 1967, but the humble beginnings of that project and the problems created by the collapse of its original sponsoring institution (Prescott College) in the early 1970s make it difficult to compare Black Mesa's origins (Powell et al. 1983; Powell, Gumerman, and Smiley 2002) with those of the Chaco Project. From its initial stages, the Chaco Project looked like "big archaeology" and was clearly intended as NPS's response to the question of how to incorporate the potential advances of processualism and the challenges of historic preservation into the practice of American archaeology.

In many ways, NPS was logically at the center of this revitalization. It had taken over RBS's Midwest offices in 1969 and controlled the lion's share of archaeological research monies in the United States in 1970. The NPS already had a strong interdisciplinary staff in *natural* resource management (Sellars 1997). That the NPS should blaze the path to practice *cultural* resource management seemed reasonable.

Certainly, no one in the early 1970s knew the path that CRM archaeology would take, even though it was increasingly a topic of discussion. For the NPS to turn over so much control of a big project to what appeared, in some ways, to be a contract operation was revolutionary at the time. The NPS bureaucracy was not set up to allow the flexibility required to create a nonpermanent research staff. Bob Lister (and later, Jim Judge) struggled to find ways to hire staff for more than a year. Negotiating a relatively minor change to the Memorandum of Agreement in 1973 between the NPS and UNM proved to be a challenge even for a seasoned project manager such as Bob Lister. At the time, he noted: "I had thought it would be a simple task, but it is turning out to be almost like negotiating a peace in Viet Nam" (cited in Maruca 1982:18). Yet, eventually, peace was negotiated in both Vietnam and Chaco. By 1973 investigations at Chaco were well underway.

## PRACTICING GOOD ARCHAEOLOGY AND NEW ARCHAEOLOGY

The Chaco Project's choice of its first director hints at how much this project differed from previous salvage archaeology projects. In 1969 Tom Lyons, an anthropologist and geologist with a background in remote-sensing techniques, was appointed the acting director of the Chaco Project. For two years, he oversaw a range of initial research projects that focused on natural resource studies (see Mathien 2005 for details). The projects also included archaeological investigations of water control features and roads (Vivian 1974; Ware and Gumerman 1977) and an initial sample survey of the park (Hayes, Brugge, and Judge 1981). The variety of research projects in the initial stages of the work, with at least four departments at UNM and at least seven institutions formally involved in either contracts or cooperative agreements, was unusual for archaeology at this time. In addition, the appointment of a remote-sensing specialist to be director, even acting director, was unusual. Yet, this initial stage of work was also very reminiscent of the multidisciplinary approach employed in the Wetherill Mesa Project; many of the initial studies aimed to help park management anticipate increases in future visitation that would place new demands on the facility (Maruca 1982:27).

Between 1971 and 1976 the Chaco Project was a strange and wonderful archaeological brew. Bob Lister, chief archaeologist, and Alden Hayes, supervisory archaeologist, were dyed-in-the-wool Southwestern archaeologists with pedigrees that went back to the 1930s. Both were instrumental in the early success of the Chaco Project but were very different researchers from Jim Judge, a UNM professor in charge of the Chaco contracts handled by the university's Office of Contract Archeology, or Tom Lyons, focused on the project's remote-sensing work. Whereas Judge would design and implement a single-season survey of a representative sample of all the sites in the park (Judge 1981), Hayes (1981) would pursue a four-season, 100 percent survey of the whole park. Lister was interested in substantially excavating another of the Great Houses, such as Una Vida or Hungo Pavi, for research and display. Judge was much more attracted to sampling a site such as Pueblo Alto, to tie together the unexplained phenomena of Chaco-era roads, possible outlying Great Houses, and the Great Houses of the Chaco core. It was a curious, yet workable, mix of old and New archaeology.

In the first five years of fieldwork, the major effort went into a complete survey of the park and excavation or testing of more than thirty smaller sites. Most of the excavated sites dated to the early occupations of the park area and ranged in age from Archaic to early Pueblo II. Of the ten small sites intensively excavated, six dated to Basketmaker III or Pueblo I, three dated to Pueblo II, and one to Pueblo III (McKenna 1986). Researchers tested a few later road segments and Great House sites such as Pueblo Alto but mainly concentrated on building an early chronology for the park. In many ways, the strategy was not unlike that pursued by NPS in developing the Ruins Road sites for display on MVNP's Chapin Mesa or the mini-train route on Wetherill Mesa in the 1950s and 1960s. For potential research and later display, Hayes sought sites that were "pure" examples of a particular period. The small site investigations offered wonderfully detailed information on the persistence of habitations in particular locales of the canyon through time and challenged some previous distinctions between the "small" sites and nearby Great Houses (Truell 1986). In addition, this work proved of tremendous value by significantly amending certain key, early interpretations of Basketmaker III (Roberts 1929), Pueblo I (Hayes 1981), and Pueblo II (Vivian 1965). These small sites were analyzed and recognized to have different occupation histories than originally thought (for example, Wills and Windes 1989; Windes 1993).

Yet, only after 1976 did the Chaco Project begin to take shape as a very different type of project from any archaeological project before. Excavations at a major site finally began, seven years after the initial studies for the Chaco Project in 1969. Unlike what the original prospectus outlined, the site was Pueblo Alto and not Una Vida. The initial remote-sensing studies of the roads (Lyons and Hitchcock 1977), along with the recognition that Pueblo Alto was the node for several major roads connecting it to the larger region (Windes 1987a), made it imperative for researchers to look at the Pueblo Alto site in more detail. It was increasingly clear to the New Archaeologists that Chaco was the center of a regional phenomenon that stitched together outlying Great Houses with a system of straight-as-arrow roads. Initial outlier surveys were begun as early as 1976 (Powers, Gillespie, and Lekson 1983), soon complemented by other agencies' surveys (Marshall et al. 1979).

More than twenty-five years later, we find it difficult to remember how heady a time 1976 was in American archaeology. The recognition that Chaco Canyon was the center of a potentially immense regional phenomenon made it the epitome of what the New Archaeology had to offer. New, relatively well-funded, large, multidisciplinary projects such as the Chaco Project became all the more attractive because they used what was then cutting-edge technology. To address questions about how such an immense system as Chaco thrived in this arid to semiarid region, researchers initiated studies of pollen and flotation samples (M. Toll 1987), tree-ring paleoclimate and dating (Dean and Warren 1983; Rose, Robinson, and Dean 1982), paleoecology (Hall 1977), mineral sourcing (Mathien 1981), and ceramic materials sourcing (Warren 1980). This was a far cry from the early days of site and artifact description and sorting out the sequence and dates of occupation. In the hands of New Archaeologists, the Chaco Project was going to ask important questions, collect the necessary samples, analyze the data, and give us fresh answers. The 1970s were, indeed, heady days in archaeology, and the Chaco Project team had enough young "Turks" on its staff to ensure that it had a good crack at making valuable statements about what happened at Chaco.

## TRACING CHACO'S ROLE IN REGIONAL HISTORY

Although we now regard many of the Chaco young Turks as practitioners of the New Archaeology, they pushed well beyond this by the end of the project. Typically focused on reconstructing settlement-subsistence systems and getting good population estimates, New Archaeologists also tried to infer the nature of the "social system" and how it changed over time. One heard plenty of New Archaeology "systems speak" on the Chaco Project. Unlike some other New Archaeology endeavors, which left regional histories relatively untouched, Chaco Project archaeological research ventured well outside the canyon by the mid-1970s. This work foreshadowed a larger "turn to regional social history" in archaeology by the 1980s and 1990s (Gupta and Ferguson 1997:1). The Chaco Project dealt primarily with Chacoan outliers, Chaco-era sites with the distinctive Bonito-style architecture first characterized in Chaco Canyon. Yet, it also attempted to associate these outliers with the canyon's core through arguments that related roads, feasting, trade, and possible elites.

Whereas the project's initial goal was straightforward, to understand the interaction between Chacoan Anasazi and their environs better, by 1976 aspects of the project were actually trying to relate the construction and maintenance of the main Great Houses to a sociopolitical network spanning an area of more than 100,000 sq km. It began innocently enough with an initial reconnaissance of outlying sites by Bob Powers, Bill Gillespie, and Steve Lekson, as well as a companion study a year later funded by the State Historic Preservation Office (SHPO) and the Public Service Company of New Mexico (Marshall and others 1979). At the beginning, Chaco Project researchers barely understood or even accepted the phenomenon of outliers (Logan and Bradley 1969); by the early 1980s they had identified more than seventy possible Chacoan outliers (Cordell 1984:261; Powers, Gillespie, and Lekson 1983). In addition, the road systems that had been originally part of the remote-sensing research appeared to link the Great Houses of the Chaco core area with outliers (Obenauf 1980a, 1983).

The recognition of a possible Chacoan system of roads and outliers had the effect of shifting the emphasis in the second half of the project. Rather than test a large site such as Hungo Pavi or Una Vida, as the prospectus had suggested, it was much more important to understand the chronology and function of Pueblo Alto, a Great House on top of the north mesa that appeared to be the nexus of several key roadways. In 1975 researchers tested Pueblo Alto and, during the next three field seasons, excavated approximately 10 percent of the site. They also profiled and tested the immense midden at Pueblo Alto, testing various outside features and structures as well. Windes (1984a, 1987a) suggested that year-round population at this site of more than 120 rooms was remarkably low, possibly no more than twenty-five people, based on his interpretation of the midden and a surprising lack of fire pits inside structures. Windes (1987a:411) concluded that the site's "primary advantage is its view of the surrounding Chaco world" and that the site functioned more as an intermittent or a seasonal meeting place than as a residential site.

Wolky Toll's ceramic analyses of materials from the excavated sites reinforced the sense that Chaco Canyon was tied to a much larger system of sites and resources. Toll (1985; also, Toll, Windes, and McKenna 1980) demonstrated that a startlingly high percentage of the Chacoan ceramics were from the Chuskan slope of western New Mexico, as well as other nonlocal sources. His findings were consistent with Anna Shepard's (1939) early discovery of the tie between the Chuskas and Chaco Canyon and with researchers' heightened awareness of nonlocal goods in Chaco's regional role. Multiple reasons for the link between the timber-rich Chuskas and timber-poor Chaco became obvious as researchers began to consider how much wood was needed for firing pots (Toll 1985) and constructing Great House roofs (Betancourt, Dean, and Hull 1986).

Toll's (1985) interpretations of trash at Pueblo Alto also contributed to rethinking Chaco's role in the region. He offered evidence of large-scale feasting, based partially on unusually high ceramic-vessel accumulation rates and a number of discrete trash layers in the midden that might be interpreted as distinct deposition units associated with feasting events. Toll's interpretations were reinforced somewhat by Nancy Akin's (1984) findings that higher percentages of higher quality faunal remains were recovered from the Alto midden than from contemporary small sites. Akins (1984), however, interpreted this as signifying differences in social ranking rather than feasting. Whatever one's interpretation of middens (compare with Wills 2001), the original contributions of Toll, of Windes, and of Akins have emerged as central points in many discussions about how Chaco was organized, how many people lived in the locale at any particular time, and how Chaco functioned as a regional center.

Nancy Akins and John Schelberg (1984) added the final ingredient to the new interpretation of Chaco, with their analyses of the distribution and nature of grave goods from both the Chaco Project and previous excavations. They argued that the mortuary data supported the existence of a stratified society in Chaco's heyday and that the Great Houses and nonlocal goods were best understood within the context of a local elite. Akins (1986) furthered this argument in her bioarchaeological analysis of the burials and suggested that two distinct burial populations were represented in the oldest portions of Pueblo Bonito.

Probably the best-known publication from the Chaco Project is Lekson's (1984a) *Great Pueblo Architecture of Chaco Canyon, New Mexico.* Using tree-ring dates, construction styles, and other chronological information, Lekson framed building histories for each of twelve Great Houses in the Chaco core. He then estimated the scale and timing of key construction events within the canyon Great Houses. Based on these data, he broke Chaco occupation into three periods between A.D. 900 and 1140 and traced this society's increasing sociopolitical complexity. Lekson's synthesis of the Great House architecture was a highwater mark for integrating sixty years of varied, underpublished research with the new ways of looking at architecture as artifact. Amazingly, his was the first modern attempt to place the great architecture into a canyonwide frame of analysis.

At least 155 archaeologists, laborers, surveyors, technicians, secretaries, editorial staff, and lab workers participated in the Chaco Project between 1969 and 1985 (Mathien 2005:xvii–xix). The individual contributions and aspects of the Chaco Project illustrated above are intended to show how individuals were the key agents of change, possibly more so on this project than on some other contract or government projects. Many other stories involve names whose contributions are not as easily recounted almost twenty years later. Our emphasis here is that a variety of unusual contributions shaped this project. The Chaco Project was distinguished by a surprisingly high quality of work by many professionals in spite of many, many challenges.

## RUNNING OUT OF STEAM AND KEEPERS
## OF THE FLAME

Between 1982 and 1984 it became increasingly clear that the Chaco Project could not get sufficient funds to finish necessary analyses and report write-ups and that Judge was fighting an uphill battle to keep personnel. In hindsight, it is easy to blame the NPS, but problems in completing archaeological publications were not endemic only to the NPS. Publication of independent work at Bonito, such as that by Neil Judd in the 1920s, had taken more than thirty years (Judd 1954, 1964). Yet, some of the later RBS projects, such as Glen Canyon (1956–1963) and Navajo Reservoir (1956–1964), had published most of their reports within several years of completing their fieldwork. These RBS projects, however, had much smaller budgets and staffs, so they engaged in much less analysis and had much more manageable, though still diffi-cult, publication schedules.

One primary objective of the Chaco Project had been the early publication and dissemination of results (Logan and Bradley 1969:25); in 1982 it was just gearing up for its first important publications. The original prospectus called for project completion by 1982 (that is, ten years after the first year of major fieldwork) with most of its publica-tions in press. In many ways, the archaeologists, as well as the NPS, were unprepared for the sheer volume of analytical studies, write-ups, and publications resulting from an immense project such as Chaco. By 1997 there were nineteen government-published reports of Chaco Project work, many of these being multivolume reports (listed chronologically: Lyons 1976; Lyons and Hitchcock 1977; Windes 1978; Brugge 1980; Hayes, Brugge, and Judge 1981; Lekson, ed., 1983; Powers, Gillespie, and Lekson 1983; Brugge 1984; Judge and Schelberg 1984; Lekson 1984a; McKenna 1984; Mathien 1985; Akins 1986; Mathien and Windes 1987; McKenna and Truell 1986; Windes 1987a, 1987b; Mathien 1991, 1992; Truell 1992; Windes 1993; Mathien, ed., 1997). By 1985 a remark-able group of reports had been published, but many reports still awaited completion.

After 1985 Joan Mathien, Tom Windes, and a scientific illustrator, Jerry Livingston, formed the core of the Chaco Project, which was no longer called by that name. Mathien's presence ensured the final pub-lication of the remaining reports, even as monies for publication became scarce. She also worked on a synthetic summary of the Chaco research in the 1970s and 1980s. Windes had a hand in publications but primarily continued to explore aspects of Chacoan prehistory through his studies of architectural wood and outlying Pueblo I and early Pueblo II communities (for example, Windes and Ford 1992, 1996). In a sense, Mathien and Windes were keepers of the old research flame at Chaco. Their continued presence, along with administrative support from Larry Nordby and Bob Powers, facilitated new student research in the canyon and ensured that interest in Chaco would not wane. It is a testament to the importance and depth of the Chaco Project research that, more than twenty-five years after the last major excavations, vigorous debate continues about many issues originally framed by the project's investigations (Mills 2002).

Even though Steve Lekson has not been formally with NPS since 1985, he has been so active in promoting Chaco research that we must mention his contributions in this context. Beginning in the late 1990s he coordinated a major NPS effort—to summarize and synthesize the Chaco Project results since the 1980s—that would complement the synthesis being prepared by Mathien. The Chaco Synthesis project was initiated by Bob Powers, Dabney Ford, and other NPS staff and resulted in five topical working conferences and a capstone synthetic conference. Lekson, a provocative scholar who has always pushed the envelope (for example, Lekson 1999), was among the first to turn the project back to a more historical focus. He might agree, we think, with Jacquetta Hawkes (1968) that the aim of archaeology remains historical, or the description of individual events in time. But, being Lekson, he would probably reframe our statement to address some larger issue in a way that would leave us shaking our heads in astonishment.

Interestingly, a final contributor to the Chaco Project and its synthesis, Gwinn Vivian, never actually worked for the project. He grew up in the canyon and was a key contributor to the 1969 SAR planning conference but was already at the University of Arizona when the Chaco Project began. He contributed to the thinking about Chaco roads and agriculture during the project and later produced a major synthesis of Chacoan prehistory (Vivian 1990). His scholarship is fundamental in that it spans the gap from pre–Chaco Project to current research and public dissemination of this research (for example, Vivian and Hilpert 2002).

So far, we have attempted to place the Chaco Project into its own historical framework by outlining the archaeological and general social-scientific climate surrounding it. In archaeology, everything to do with public funding was changing over the course of the project. The NPS, one of the most powerful financial and research forces in American archaeology in the 1960s, became a minor player by the 1980s. The practice of social science shifted from "description" on the Wetherill Mesa Project (1958–1965) to "environment" at the outset of the Chaco Project (1969–1977) and finally to "regional history" at the project's close (1977–1985). Many "problems" associated with the project resulted from the NPS's inability to be sufficiently flexible in its hiring and contracting procedures to manage a project of such scope efficiently. Despite these problems, the project made some of the most notable contributions of any "big" archaeology project in the past thirty years. We suggest that the people on the Chaco Project were a remarkable collection of professionals and that they actively helped to mold not only that project but also modern American archaeology in the public domain.

## BRINGING THE LESSONS OF THE CHACO PROJECT TO THE PUBLIC

The research contributions of the Chaco Project are foremost in the minds of most archaeologists, but it is important to remember that the project was equally justified by the NPS for its own management and interpretive needs (Logan and Bradley 1969:2) and that two of the project's four main objectives had to do with interpretation. It is clear from the original prospectus that NPS could not have anticipated the many secondary benefits derived from the Chaco Project in the almost twenty years since its conclusion. The findings have been incorporated into visitor signage, park planning, videos, television programs, popular and scholarly books, and national legislation. Yet, only a small part of this was obvious during the course of the project. How did all of this come to be?

In park signage, visitor brochures, visitor trails, and museum exhibits, the Chaco Project had an immense effect on how the park has presented itself to the visitor in the past decades. In the late 1960s the park had relatively little signage and limited facilities. Annual visitation averaged about thirty-one thousand people in the mid-1960s, compared with approximately eighty-eight thousand in the late 1990s (http://www.aqd.nps.gov/npstats/select_report.cfm?by=year). In the late 1960s very little interpretation placed the sites at Chaco into a regional context, and the park presented very little archaeological research to the visitor.

The benefit of having directors such as Bob Lister and Jim Judge at the Chaco Center was that both came to the task with great respect for the presentation of archaeology to the public. Bob Lister and his wife, Florence, had written one popular book on Southwestern archaeology (F. Lister and R. Lister 1968) before joining the Chaco Project, and they went on to write several more on Chaco and Chaco outliers (R. Lister and F. Lister 1981, 1987; F. Lister 1993). At the very end of the Chaco Project, Jim Judge and others worked closely with author Kendrick Frazier, who produced a popular book that incorporated many of the project's initial results. The book was first published in 1986 and was sufficiently popular to be revised and reissued in paperback in 1999. A smaller but equally popular book on Chaco Canyon, by David Grant Noble (1984), also incorporated many of the new data from the Chaco Project. At least two summary articles appeared in popular science journals (for example, Lekson and others 1988), and at least one major museum exhibit presenting research findings was mounted at the Maxwell Museum, with Bob Lister's support.

Yet, the project produced more than books, articles, and museum exhibits. Jim Judge had grown up in a National Park Service family and was an early advocate of conservation archaeology. He was instrumental in the passage of Public Law 96-550, which recognized the importance of the Chaco phenomenon and called for a San Juan Basin database for the preservation, management, and development of resources in the basin. Quick recognition of the significance of the larger Chaco system and its outliers brought early acknowledgment of the need to protect not only Chaco Canyon but also the larger cultural phenomenon of which it was considered the center. This kind of advocacy was, and still remains, rare in public archaeology and really did distinguish the Chaco Project from most other projects. Its presentation of the ruins in the park to the public was unique among most other major national historical parks. The Chaco Great Houses are a remarkable part of the

Pueblo past and create a link for the public not only to the archaeology of the region but also to the modern Pueblos in New Mexico and Arizona.

In spite of a limited budget for public education, the staff was good at attracting outside interest in the project's research. They actively worked with the producers of a major Odyssey television program on Chaco, titled "The Chaco Legacy." This show aired for many years on the Public Broadcasting System, beginning in 1980, and has been available since 1988 as a video. Since the 1990s there have been several additional videos on Chaco, but with less attention to the results of the Chaco Project and more focus on the cosmological aspects of Great House alignment and the solstice marker on Fajada Butte (Sofaer 1997).

Compared with several other large projects of the 1960s–1980s, the Chaco Project did not reserve much of its own budget for educational objectives but, instead, depended on the park's budget. For example, the Dolores Project (1978–1985) made a substantial commitment to local preservation and education through the creation of the Anasazi Heritage Center and engaged in an active, local education program for the duration of the project. An earlier research project at Casas Grandes (1958–1961) in northern Mexico produced a series of striking volumes that combined research and public presentation of project results (Di Peso 1974). Nonetheless, the cachet of the Chaco Great House architecture, as well as the remarkable results of the Chaco Project, inspired books, television programs, and public presentation of the sites that were unusual for American archaeology. Facilitating these opportunities were several key personnel committed to bringing the project's findings to the public's attention.

## CONCLUSION

Few Southwestern archaeologists would argue with the Chaco Project's role in setting the stage for many of the most important debates of the past twenty-five years. Very few archaeologists, however, think of the Chaco Project as being a significant transition between the "little" RBS archaeological projects of the 1950s and 1960s and the "big" CRM projects of the 1980s and 1990s. Yet, the Chaco Project and the Black Mesa Archaeological Project (BMAP) span the crucial gap of the late 1960s and 1970s, during which key federal legislation reshaped the financial and legal frameworks for conducting American archaeology. Without denying the importance of BMAP, we were surprised at how many aspects of the Chaco Project foreshadowed developments in CRM archaeology in the decades that followed. Before 1970 the National Park Service had been the foremost practitioner and funder of American archaeology. With the Chaco Project, the NPS encountered inherent administrative and financial limitations that would ultimately deny it a major role in the emerging "big" archaeological projects after 1975. NPS increasingly positioned itself in an administrative and advisory role after the Chaco Project.

The picture of Chaco presented to the public has dramatically altered as a consequence of the Chaco Project. Based on the Chaco research, Chaco Canyon is no longer seen just as a locale with big sites, but as the center of a much larger cultural phenomenon. The demarcation of the "Chaco Region" has been contentious in archaeological research and varies, based on which class of material culture one chooses to use (Crown and Judge 1991a:2). But the idea that an archaeological phenomenon is larger than a single site is probably no better represented to the American public than at Chaco Culture National Historical Park. To understand Chaco, we must understand the links between sites at a regional level; to protect Chaco, we must likewise protect outlying sites. These remarkable concepts derive from the innovative research of the Chaco Project.

The Chaco Project was one of the largest archaeological projects ever conducted by the National Park Service. Approximately twenty-five thousand people-days over a fifteen-year period were devoted to the fieldwork, analysis, and publication of the project's results (see Maruca 1982:50 for fieldwork estimate, with a 1.5 factor added in for analysis and write-up). It is difficult to understand the magnitude of this labor investment until one realizes its remarkable similarity to the amount of time and labor, estimated by Lekson (1984a:220–223, 257–262), that it took to build much of Pueblo del Arroyo. To evaluate how several key investigators of the Chaco Project perceived the role of their contributions, almost twenty years after the close of the main project's work, we posed a simple question to them. If they were given the choice to pursue the Chaco Project again or to rebuild Pueblo del

Arroyo, which would they do? Each of them agreed that the National Park Service would be better served by an interpretive replica of Pueblo del Arroyo. We humbly beg to differ with them.

### Notes

This chapter could not have been written without the support of Steve Lekson, who first suggested that we write the chapter and then found financial support to enable us to visit Chaco and meet with key researchers. Joan Mathien and Steve Lekson provided critical background documents that substantially aided our understanding of the project. Jim Judge, Dabney Ford, Steve Lekson, Joan Mathien, and Tom Windes were patient through multiple interviews and read and commented on drafts of the chapter. Nancy Akins, Bill Gillespie, Marcia Truell Newren, and Wolky Toll also read the chapter and provided helpful critiques. Finally, Barbara Mills's excellent summary of Chaco research in the *Journal of Archaeological Research* (2002) and the research of the students in the Public Archaeology seminar at the University of Colorado at Boulder in spring 2003 motivated us to dig deeper. All are absolved of any blame for this article, yet all share in any credit.

1. Zorro Bradley (NPS), John Campbell (UNM), John Corbett (NPS), Richard Daugherty (WSU), Florence H. Ellis (UNM), William Haag (LSU), George Ewing (MNM), William Longacre (UofA), Loren Potter (UNM), Erik Reed (NPS), Gwinn Vivian (UofA), and Douglas Schwartz (SAR).

# 12

## The Chaco Synthesis

### Lynne Sebastian

When archaeologists use the term *synthesis*, they mean an examination of a broad body of research that has been carried out by many individuals. The end result is a summary of the data and of the various interpretations of those data offered by previous researchers. This is a daunting task in the best of circumstances, but, in the case of Chaco Canyon and the broader Chaco world, it goes way beyond daunting. Research on things Chacoan has continued unabated for more than one hundred years, and the resultant literature is voluminous. The recent references cited in a survey article on Chacoan archaeology (Mills 2002) run to sixteen single-spaced pages.

The other chapters in this volume present the results of an unprecedented series of team efforts to compile and synthesize Chacoan research on multiple topics—architecture, material culture, environment, ecology. One principal product of these discussions was the Chaco Timeline (after page 392), to which I refer throughout the following discussion.

As Lekson notes in chapter 1, many chapters in this volume are based on the papers that constituted the Chaco Capstone Conference in October 2002 and on the discussions that resulted from those papers at the following School of American Research advanced seminar in 2003. The conferees felt that, in addition to these topical syntheses, there should be a final chapter reflecting the points of agreement reached at the conference and expounding upon the Big Picture. Somehow, that task fell to me—a shining example of the dangers of being out of the room when a vote is taken.

The capstone conferees spent a long afternoon trying to identify points of agreement and points of disagreement about the nature of the Chacoan archaeological record and what that record tells us about life in the Chaco world. Given the often contentious nature of Chacoan archaeology, I think that everyone was surprised to discover just how much agreement there was.

We structured the capstone conference discussions around four topics. Under the rubric "Chaco in Temporal and Spatial Context," we covered what came before Chaco, what came after, and what was going on in the rest of the Southwest during the Chaco florescence. The topic "Intersection of Culture and Environment" helped us to place events in Chaco Canyon and, to a lesser extent, in the broader Chaco world in their environmental context. In "The Canyon and the Chaco World" discussions, we reached numerous points of agreement about Chacoan outliers and the nature of the relationship between Chaco Canyon and the outliers. The fourth topic, "Organizing Principles: Power, Ritual, Production/Consumption, Labor, and Management," yielded the fewest agreements and the most fundamental disagreements of all the discussions.

In the section below titled "What Do We Know?" I have attempted to combine the points of agreement reached at the capstone conference into a coherent picture of the Chacoan archaeological record. In the following section, titled "What Does It Mean?" I address the lack of consensus among the conferees, and among Chaco scholars in general, about what the Chacoan archaeological record *means*, and I offer some ideas about how we might go about seeking greater levels of agreement.

In the final section of this chapter, "Chacoan Research in the Twenty-First Century," I outline the critical future research directions proposed by the capstone conferees. This section identifies critical questions and the kinds of data and analyses needed to resolve some of the many unresolved issues.

Before launching into these discussions, however, I will provide some spatial definitions for terms used throughout the chapter. The conferees discussed Chaco in terms of three spheres of decreasingly intense interaction: "Downtown" Chaco, the Chaco core, and the San Juan Basin and beyond (refer to figures 1.1, 1.2, and 5.1 and plate 4). *Downtown Chaco* refers to the densely built and modified landscape of the central precinct of Chaco Canyon surrounding Pueblo Bonito, Chetro Ketl, Pueblo Alto, and Pueblo del Arroyo and their associated roads, mounds, Great Kivas, and residential sites. *Chaco core* means the area stretching from Lake Valley on the west to Pueblo Pintado on the east and from Kin Klizhin on the south to the Escavada Wash and Bis sa'ani on the north. *San Juan Basin* refers to a cultural rather than a geological phenomenon, bounded by the San Juan River on the north, the Dutton Plateau on the south, the Chuska Mountains on the west, and the Jemez Mountains on the east.

## WHAT DO WE KNOW?

The results of the capstone conference made it clear to us that we "know"—that is, have interpretable, empirical data upon which most Chaco scholars can agree—quite a lot about what life was like at Chaco. In the following sections, I summarize what we know about the environment in which the Chacoans lived, the origins of many of the cultural patterns we identify as Chacoan, the relationship between the canyon and the larger Chacoan world, and the patterns of the post-Chacoan Southwest.

### The Chacoan Environment

Without question, the Chaco core and the entire San Juan Basin are difficult environments for agriculture, requiring great skill on the part of precontact farmers. Yet, the conferees felt that previous research has overstated the harshness of the canyon environment, in part because several physiographic features increased the chances of agricultural success in the canyon during the Chacoan era, despite the technological limitations of the time.

Because Chacra Mesa (see figure 2.1) is a *questa* sloping from south to north, the geological layers exposed at the surface are different on the north and south sides of the canyon. Rainfall is absorbed by the talus slopes on the south side but runs off the harder sandstones exposed on the north side. The Chacoan people were thus able to capture runoff through a substantial array of water control features in many of the north-side *rincons* and direct this water onto farm fields.

Scholars have made much of the agricultural potential created by numerous side drainages that debouch into the Chaco Wash over the relatively small distance within the Chaco core (refer to plate 2). Some of these, such as the Escavada and Kin Bineola washes, drain large areas of the San Juan Basin. Within the central canyon, topography magnifies this potential: the abrupt south/southwest-facing uplift of the Chacra Mesa questa tends to catch storms coming in with the prevailing winds and to funnel them through the small number of openings in the mesa, concentrating the rainfall in these areas.

One of the most intriguing possibilities raised during the capstone discussions was the evidence for a natural sand-dune dam across the Chaco at the mouth of the Escavada early in the Chacoan era. It was argued that breeching of this dam at approximately A.D. 900 ended a 250-year period of aggradation in the Chaco Wash (see the Chaco Timeline) and that the resultant downcutting of the Chaco triggered development of the numerous water-control features designed to capture runoff from the north side of the canyon. Even more intriguing to the conferees was the possibility that in the early 1000s the Chacoans, recognizing the relationship between the breech in the dam and the downcutting of the Chaco, patched or rebuilt the dam using masonry, causing a second period of aggradation.

### Chaco Origins

Beginning about A.D. 750 and continuing through the 800s, in the area north of the San Juan River a settlement pattern developed that included large, relatively short-lived (thirty to forty years) villages. This was a time of substantial and frequent population movement, but by A.D. 825–850 most of the population lived in large residential communities of as many as thirty to fifty households. In many cases, the rapid growth of these villages clearly indicates in-migration. After a population peak between A.D. 860 and 875, the entire northern San Juan experienced a swift and substantial depopulation by the end of the ninth century.

The capstone conferees tended to accept proposals by Wilshusen and others (Wilshusen, Sesler, and Hovezak 2000; Wilshusen and Wilson 1995; Windes n.d.; Wilshusen and Van Dyke, chapter 7 of this volume) that the ninth-century growth of villages in the northern San Juan and the early tenth-century depopulation of the area represent movement of people from the San Juan Basin into and then back out of the area north of the river. During the mid to late 800s, when villages flourished in the north, most sites in the San Juan Basin, including those in the Chaco core, were much smaller—eleven to twelve households, compared with thirty to fifty in the north.

One aspect of northern San Juan villages that particularly interests Chaco scholars is the presence within many villages of large, community-oriented structures that are called "Great Kivas," even though they were far less formally designed and substantial in construction than the later (mid-1000s) Chacoan structures called by the same name. A second feature of interest in the northern villages, in otherwise residential communities, is clear archaeological evidence of "big houses"—larger-than-average roomblocks where we find indications of feasting and other villagewide activities. This pattern appears to have developed first in the northern San Juan but by the 860s appears to have been widespread in the San Juan Basin, particularly in the south.

Big houses, or what are half jokingly called "good houses," actually appear slightly later in the Chaco core than in the southernmost San Juan Basin, but by the late 800s a number of these structures appear in the core, with more being built in the early 900s. Some of these structures were long abandoned by the time of the Chacoan florescence, but others persisted for one hundred years or more and subsequently were submerged within the numerous massive additions built at the classic Chacoan Great Houses. It is important to note that the Great House phenomenon, which is so central to the definition of "Chaco," was an elaboration on a pattern that appeared first on the Colorado Plateau and then spread throughout the San Juan Basin.

The early good houses were generally built within existing communities of small residential sites. The initial structures looked very much like the type of residential structure that had been common for more than a century throughout the basin and the northern San Juan—a south-facing, double-rowed arc of rooms, with larger rooms in the front and pairs of smaller rooms in the back. The good houses, however, were much larger in scale and constructed more substantially and on a more formal plan than the contemporary domiciles. Although the 800s Great Houses are not unique to Chaco Canyon, they do occur there in greater concentrations than in the rest of the southern San Juan Basin.

We have no evidence for construction of Great Kivas during this early period (although structures dating to this time could have been obscured by the construction of later ones). Both Great Houses and small residential sites include small kivas—round subterranean rooms that have formalized features, at least some of which seem to have ceremonial significance.

### The Canyon and the Chaco World

This basic pattern of Great Houses constructed within communities of small sites continued in Chaco Canyon and in the region to the south of the canyon through the early 1000s. Around A.D. 1000, however, the scale of the canyon Great Houses began to outstrip architectural developments elsewhere in the basin. Also, beginning about A.D. 1020–1040, Chaco Canyon experienced a remarkable florescence, what Judge elsewhere refers to as the "Golden Century" (Judge 2004). This florescence was marked first by massive construction episodes beginning about A.D. 1020 at both existing and new Great Houses. Slightly later, beginning in the 1040s or 1050s, there was heavy investment in construction and formalization of ritual-related infrastructure and landscape features, including Great Kivas with formal sets of standard features, mounds and earthworks, and engineered roads. Although most mounds appear to be simply accumulations of materials, the ones in front of Pueblo Bonito (and perhaps others at unexcavated Great House sites) were masonry walled and included stairs. There is evidence that the entire landscape of the central canyon was designed and ordered by ritual and astronomically aligned features.

There is also evidence that this greater investment in ritual-associated construction was associated with large "consumptive events," possibly ritual-associated feasts involving large influxes of people into the canyon Great Houses. The large mounds associated with the canyon

Great Houses contain not only layers of building debris but also layers of trash from these "consumptive events" and, in at least two cases, prepared surfaces indicating that the mounds may have served as stages or locations for special activities. Excavations at Pueblo Alto revealed the presence of special milling rooms and large earth ovens suitable for preparing large quantities of food.

As the Chaco Timeline (after page 392 of this volume) shows, distinct changes also occurred at this time (A.D. 1020–1040) in many categories of material culture: ceramics, chipped stone, and minerals and ornaments, both locally produced and imported. Chaco Canyon clearly had a very strong relationship with communities along the Chuska slope, from which large amounts of pottery, chipped stone, and wood were being imported. The nature of this relationship, however, remains unclear. Some evidence suggests other relationships between specific parts of the Chaco core and specific outlying areas, but we need more data to confirm this. By the mid-1040s there is also clear evidence of inequitable distribution of exotic materials among sites in the canyon, with Great Houses having more exotics than small sites and Pueblo Bonito having more than the other Great Houses.

As the canyon's Golden Century began, Great Houses continued to be built in outlying communities in the southern basin and then in communities to the west and finally the north; outlying Great Houses are virtually unknown to the east of the Chaco core. By the A.D. 1020–1040 period, these outlier Great Houses began to exhibit Chacoan architectural traits and often had associated Great Kivas, roads, and other canyon-like trappings. Except for this overlay of Chacoan architectural features, however, these outlier communities are marked by local material goods and technology and a local focus of interaction. In addition, a substantial population appears to have been living outside the Great House communities in many parts of the basin. Not surprisingly, the outlier communities closest to the canyon exhibit the strongest relationship with the canyon sites; many of the closest-in outliers, for example, do not have Great Kivas, implying that they joined the central canyon population for activities involving these structures.

Although defined routes of travel were undoubtedly common throughout the Southwest from very early times, formal roads first appear as part of the landscape in the Chaco world between A.D. 1050 and 1070. The earliest substantial labor investment in road construction may have been in the canyon itself. Roads often formalize egress from and ingress to Great Houses; sometimes they control access and routes of approach. Some roads formalize directional symbolism; some articulate with important features of the physical or cultural landscape, including linking Great Houses with one another. Roads would have facilitated travel and transport, but that does not appear to have been their primary function. Most likely, the roads were used for processions and other formal ritual activities. Although the roads provide the best-known evidence for symbolic connection and connectivity within the Chaco world, by the late 1000s an extensive line-of-sight signaling network had also been established within the San Juan Basin and, most likely, beyond the basin as well.

The area encompassed by communities with Chaco-style Great Houses and related features continued to expand until the end of the eleventh century, eventually extending from the Rio Puerco on the east to Polacca Wash on the west and from Dove Creek on the north to the Plains of San Augustin on the south (refer to figure 5.1). Lekson suggests in chapter 1 that "the geographic distribution of Great Houses, Great House communities, road segments, and signaling stations extends over 80,000 sq km." Anecdotal evidence suggests that the maximal extent of Great Houses reflects a boundary that is also discernible in the distribution of other kinds of material culture. Beyond this boundary, the general Puebloan adaptation also reached its maximum extent at this time, at least to the north and west, as did the Mimbres and Hohokam societies to the south and southwest. As Duff and Lekson discuss in chapter 9, despite substantial contemporaneity among Chaco, Mimbres, and Colonial- and Sedentary-period Hohokam, it currently appears that there is remarkably little evidence for interaction (in the form of preserved imported materials) between Chaco and the other two great agriculturally based societies of the American Southwest, although there are indications of population migrations from the Chaco world to the south and southwest.

Beginning about A.D. 1080, well before the distribution of Chaco-style Great Houses reached maximal extent, dramatic changes began to occur, both in the canyon and within the larger Chaco world. Within the San Juan Basin, Great House construction substantially decreased. At the same time, massive investment in Great House construction occurred along and north of the San Juan River, as well as an associated northward shift in population. The suggestion has been made that, by A.D. 1080, intensification of agriculture in the canyon through water control technology had reached its limits and that additional development could only take place elsewhere. After 1080 the site of Aztec on the Animas River became a primate center, and Chaco Canyon began to decline. Additions to the canyon Great Houses in the A.D. 1080s and 1090s differed in style and magnitude from those of previous decades. Additions to the mounds ceased, and plazas at the Great Houses were enclosed, becoming controlled spaces rather than open, public spaces. By A.D. 1100 construction at both canyon Great Houses and San Juan Basin Great Houses had virtually ended.

From the end of the eleventh century through A.D. 1130, the amount of construction in the canyon continued to decrease, and the construction that did take place consisted largely of McElmo-style structures—buildings with a myriad of small grid-patterned rooms, few kivas, few features, and few artifacts. The centuries-old canyon Great Houses were still in use but show greater evidence of domestic activities during this period. The outliers in the southern basin were no longer in use, connections with the Chuskas declined dramatically, and much of the energy and focus of the Chaco world appears to have shifted to the San Juan River and beyond.

Beginning at A.D. 1130, an intense, long-term, and widespread drought struck the Colorado Plateau. In Chaco Canyon, the heavy investment in a single agricultural strategy—capture of runoff—would have been especially disastrous under these conditions. During the period from A.D. 1130 to 1180, construction ceased in the canyon, and the Chaco core was largely depopulated, although some occupation continued until approximately A.D. 1300.

During the A.D. 1130–1180 period, many outliers were abandoned briefly or permanently, and there is evidence of population dislocations and conflict. Great House architecture continued to be built outside the San Juan Basin through the late 1100s and into the 1200s. In the north, Chacoan architectural features appeared in new construction, and the older Great Houses continued to be used or were reused after a mid-1100s hiatus. In the south, new architecture with some Chacoan features replaced the older Great Houses.

### The Post-Chaco World

Some parts of the old Chaco world reorganized and rebuilt during the late twelfth century, but the focus of population and development had again shifted north of the San Juan River. A major question for the capstone conferees was the nature of the relationships among the remnants of the Chaco world and, particularly, the place of Aztec as a primate center. Most of the group felt that, after the mid-1100s, Aztec was still a large and important place but not central to the remnants of the Chaco world in the way that Chaco Canyon had been in the preceding century, a position articulated clearly and with good analytical support in Lipe's chapter 8 of this volume. Everyone agreed that large communities in the northern San Juan built after 1200 exhibit a very different architectural vocabulary and structure than the Chaco-era Great Houses. Even though some of the Chaco-era Great Houses continued to be occupied, many large thirteenth-century communities did not include a Great House. Some in the group argued, however, that Aztec continued to function as a primate center, integrating the settlements of the northern San Juan until the 1270s.

### WHAT DOES IT MEAN?

One fundamental assumption of archaeology is that patterns in the archaeological record reflect the organization of the human activities that produced that record; archaeological explanation is the art of using the former to infer the latter. Many patterns described throughout this book speak to the issue of the structure and organization of Chacoan society, and any reconstruction or interpretation of that society must account for the most salient of these patterns:

- The contemporaneous presence of massive, formally designed, out-of-scale, overbuilt Great Houses and more diminutive, informally constructed small houses

- The settlement pattern of the central canyon, which begins with separate communities and independently constructed Great Houses in the 800s and 900s but appears to have been a single, intensely ordered, designed, ritually organized landscape by the late 1000s

- The evidence for connection between the central canyon and the outlier communities, both the physical connections of road and line-of-sight signaling networks and the implied connection provided by construction of Chaco-style Great Houses and Great Kivas within outlying communities

- Change through time in the relationship among the canyon, the outliers, and the Aztec primate center

- The ability of canyon leaders to organize and mobilize labor for construction and water management

- The large quantities of material being imported into the canyon, especially from the Chuska slope

- The limited evidence for domestic use of the Great Houses

- The inequitable distribution of exotic materials among canyon sites

- The presence of a small number of burials accompanied by huge amounts of exotic materials

- The evidence for periodic aggregations and "consumptive events" at the canyon Great Houses

When attempting to identify points of agreement that would lead to a reconstruction or interpretation of the organization of Chacoan society, we could reach only a very few general agreements. We agreed that, if there was ever hierarchical organization within this society, the best evidence is in the Chaco/Aztec axis between A.D. 1040 and 1130. Certainly, the degree of centralization of authority at this time was beyond anything known before or after in Pueblo culture, but we could not agree on the extent to which authority was vested in individuals. At least part of the power base for this hypothesized hierarchy was ritual knowledge, performance, and events. We agreed that physical coercion did not play a role in Chacoan power/authority before A.D. 1080, but we could not agree on whether physical coercion contributed to power/authority after that time. There is evidence, however, of violence in the 1100s and 1200s, especially in the region north of the San Juan.

### Explanation and Chaco

As this book demonstrates, during the past one hundred years and especially in the past thirty, we have gained much descriptive knowledge about what Chaco was. We have recorded vast amounts of data and identified important patterns in the archaeological record left by the people of Chaco Canyon and the outliers. We know much about their challenging environment, their means of making and acquiring the goods they needed, their agricultural techniques, and their construction projects and even something about the extent to which they aligned their physical world with the celestial and cosmological world as they perceived it.

But when it comes to explaining how and why all of this came about, how Chacoan society was organized and functioned, sometimes we seem no farther along now than when the Chaco Project started more than thirty years ago. Every effort to explain what was going on at Chaco, as Judge and Cordell (chapter 6 of this volume) and Mills (2002) have pointed out, becomes bogged down in a whole variety of dichotomies—hierarchical versus nonhierarchical, competitive versus communal, egalitarian versus nonegalitarian, and, most recently, ritual versus political control (Lekson, chapter 1 of this volume).

Developing interpretations of social, political, and economic organization on the basis of archaeological data is always difficult. Unlike various aspects of material culture or technology, organizational principles cannot be directly observed or interpreted from empirical data. We can only infer the organizational aspects of a society from patterns we identify within the data. Because organizational interpretations may be based on several levels of inference, they are generally subject to considerable debate. Sometimes the exact same patterns in the archaeological record can be—and, in the Chaco case, are—offered as supporting evidence for diametrically opposed interpretations.

Lekson, in chapter 1 of this volume, for example, looks at the archaeological fact of two burials with a very large number of accompanying grave goods, and he sees kings: "We have seen Chaco's rulers, archaeologically, in the high-status burials from Pueblo Bonito and, particularly, the very rich crypt burials of two middle-aged men....I interpret scores of additional bodies piled above these burials as 'retainers.'"

Judge and Cordell in chapter 6 look at this same archaeological phenomenon: "The burials found in Pueblo Bonito, with the wealth of grave goods accompanying them, are distinctive compared with others found in the canyon, reflecting better nutritional status and accumulation of sumptuary goods." They see "knowledgeable priests" who administered a system of "noncompetitive, inclusive ritual that benefit[ed] entire communities."

The difficulty of drawing sound inferences from empirical data is common to all attempts to reconstruct the organization of past societies from archaeological data, but it seems to be far more virulent in the Chaco case. In other parts of the country, in other parts of the world, even in other parts of the Southwest, archaeologists have been able to make progress toward a consensus about the social organization of the Maya or the Mississippian towns or Neolithic Britain or the Hohokam. But in Chacoan archaeology we seem to exhaust ourselves arguing first about one dichotomy (simultaneous hierarchy versus sequential hierarchy, egalitarian versus elites and commoners, competitive versus communal) and then moving on to another. It is as if we keep hoping that, by finding some key pair of concepts around which we can build a level of agreement, we will finally progress toward refining a model of Chacoan organization instead of constantly creating brand new pairs of concepts to argue about. Judging from the discussions at the capstone conference, we are still doomed to be disappointed in that hope.

Why is this? Some would argue that this results from the contrariness of Southwestern archaeologists in general and Chaco specialists in particular. As I find my colleagues and myself to be perfectly charming and agreeable people, I am sure that this cannot be the problem. To me, the underlying difficulty seems to be that, no matter which dichotomy we happen to be arguing about at the time, it is really always the same argument: Was Chacoan society marked by institutionalized differences in social, economic, and political power? If so, what were the basis and structure of those inequalities? Until we can resolve these basic questions, we will continue having the same argument again and again, couched in different terms of different dyadic pairs. The changing terminology creates the illusion of research progress, but it is only that—an illusion.

For much of the 1970s and 1980s, researchers focusing on the organization of Chacoan society struggled with the question, was it complex or not? This was not because they were unaware of the complex appearance of the monumental architecture, road networks, signaling networks, runoff irrigation systems, and other things Chacoan that would have required managerial intervention and specialized knowledge. Rather, the problem was that Chaco did not fit neatly into any of the more complex, neo-evolutionary organizational categories that were popular in anthropological theory at the time. It did not have the properties of a "state," and efforts to fit Chaco into the "chiefdom" category ran squarely into that unresolved issue underlying all arguments about Chacoan organization—were there institutional differences in social, political, and economic power?

This issue proved difficult to resolve, in part because modern and historical Pueblo societies minimize and even suppress such power differences. Because of this and the close historical relationship, many people were uncomfortable with models that posited such differences among Ancestral Puebloan people. As Lekson points out in chapter 1, however, some Pueblo oral traditions indicate that the suppression of power differences observed among historical Pueblo people was a response to "bad things" that happened at Chaco. There were, of course, those willing to accept organizational principles for Chaco that differed substantially from what we see in modern Pueblo societies. Most of these individuals, however, based their concepts of what an inegalitarian, hierarchical, complex society should look like on classic neo-evolutionary "chiefdoms." Generally, they did not feel that Chaco was a good fit.

In the late 1980s and 1990s researchers began moving away from typological questions (band, tribe, chiefdom, or state?) and examining, instead, the evidence for particular organizing principles. Their efforts focused on competitive-versus-cooperative leadership models (Kantner 1996, 1999a; Saitta 1997; Schelberg 1984; Sebastian 1991, 1992a, 1992b; Toll 1985; Van Dyke 1999b; Wills 2000); evidence of warfare, coercive power, and violence (LeBlanc 1999; Lekson 2002; Turner and Turner 1999; Wilcox and Haas 1994); or characterizations of the cosmological structure of the Chacoan landscape and architecture (Marshall 1997; Sofaer 1997; Stein and Lekson 1992). The arguments, however, still turned on the presence or absence of differential power, on what such differences would look like archaeologically, and on what the basis and structure of any power differences would have been.

### Political or Ritual

By the early years of the twenty-first century, the central issue in studies of Chacoan organization was no longer *whether* it was complex, but rather *how* it was complex (Nelson 1995). Specifically, was the organization of Chacoan society politically based or ritually based (Lekson, chapter 1, and Judge and Cordell, chapter 6, of this volume; Malville and Malville 2001; Renfrew 2001; Yoffee 2001; Yoffee, Fish, and Milner 1999)? This question, like its predecessors, simply recasts the same old argument about the presence, basis, and structure of differential access to social, political, and economic power in different terms. As with the other dichotomous arguments, the political-versus-ritual argument reflects the continuing fundamental skepticism of many Southwestern archaeologists about attributing organizational principles involving differential power to precontact Puebloan societies.

The political-versus-ritual argument also continues to base interpretations of what differential power would *look* like in the archaeological record on ethnographic descriptions of classic neo-evolutionary chiefdoms. The term *political*, like its predecessor, *complex*, is taken to mean hierarchical, self-aggrandizing, coercive personal leadership—the stereotype of a Polynesian chiefdom. *Ritual*, in this dichotomy, is viewed as the antithesis of such a chiefdom—cooperative, egalitarian, and marked by situational, segmentary leadership.

Judge, in the conference draft of chapter 6 of this volume, summed up the dichotomy between ritual-based and politically based organization when he asked, "Did the Chacoan polity arise from chiefly power gained by, or based on, the accumulation of wealth, tending toward more coercive leadership, or did it arise from priestly authority acquired through, or based on, the effectiveness of esoteric ritual, tending toward more cooperative leadership?" Judge and Cordell

407

define *ritual* in chapter 6 simply as "instrumental action" and note that the "archaeological study of ritual involves finding, analyzing, and interpreting past ritual activities." Many (most?) scholars who view Chaco as a ritual-based society, however, assume that *political* means secular, personal authority, accumulation of material wealth, and coercive mobilization of labor and goods. Even Lekson (chapter 1 of this volume), who believes that, in fact, Chaco was a political phenomenon, subscribes to this view of the differences between ritual-based and politically based societies.

Increasingly, those who make these assumptions about the nature of politically based and ritual-based organization describe Chaco as a "rituality," a term that is generally attributed to Yoffee (Yoffee 2001; Yoffee, Fish, and Milner 1999), although it seems to have first been used by Drennan (1999). If one traces the term *rituality* back to its Drennan/Yoffee roots, one can see that this term was simply an alternative to *polity*, an alternative intended to emphasize that, in Chacoan society, ritual was a central component rather than being epiphenomenal. As Yoffee, Fish, and Milner (1999:266) note, "While we cannot forget that there were important aspects of economic and political behavior at Chaco and its outliers, the ritual nature of Chaco cannot be reduced to its being the handmaiden of economic and/or political institutions."

Yoffee (2001:67) cautions, however, that the "term 'rituality' is not intended to substitute a mode of cultural integration in place of what others have seen as a political integration." In my view, many of those who speak of Chaco as a "rituality" or "location of high devotional expression" have done exactly that. They have reified rituality as if it were a specific, known form of societal organization with analogues in the ethnographic record. They have merely dressed their authority figures in priest's robes instead of chiefly raiment and have directly substituted ritual-based authority for secular authority.

If Yoffee did not intend the Chacoan "rituality" to be simply Chaco integrated by ritual instead of Chaco integrated by politics, what did he mean? Interestingly, what he suggests is that we "not assume that Chaco society is 'integrated' in any functional, systemic way. Rather, various *groups and social identities* seem to have coexisted in Chaco within the context of the *relations* that called them into being" (Yoffee 2001:67, emphasis added). I would suggest that political and ritual are not alternative principles of organization or integration; rather, in Yoffee's terms, *ritual* refers to one category of *groups and social identities*, whereas *political* describes an important set of *relations* among groups and social identities.

The dictionary definition of *political* is simply "related to governance," and *governance* is defined as "providing direction and control and formulating policies." The opposite of political is not ritual or egalitarian or nonhierarchical. The opposite of political is anarchy. The political relationships within a society involve power, authority, and prestige (Anderson 1976:237–239). They may involve multiple levels of hierarchy or be simple and segmentary; they may be largely egalitarian or involve extremes of rank and class. Political power, authority, or prestige may be based on control of sacred knowledge and rituals, control of the means of production, coercive force, or access to valued resources. No matter what the structure of the relationships or the source of the power, authority, and prestige, the relationships are political and result in direction, control, and the formulation of policy.

Clearly, ritual activities and events were an extremely important component of Chacoan life; even the physical space Chacoans inhabited was transformed by them into a highly designed, almost certainly symbolic landscape. If the rituals and tenants of their belief system ordered their physical world, it is likely that the social identities and rituals of that belief system were central to much of the human experience. The pervasiveness of ritual behaviors and identities in the Chacoan world does not, however, mean that the web of power relationships we call "politics" was somehow nonexistent. One need only examine the history of medieval Europe or nineteenth-century Utah or the modern Middle East to find societies overtly ordered by the sacred and yet intensely political.

The organization of physical space in the Chacoan world tells us something else as well. As Lipe points out in chapter 8, we *know* what distributed power looks like; it looks like the Pueblo world of the late 1200s and later. It is reflected in a settlement system "designed to emphasize community integration at the expense of household political autonomy and to prevent individuals or kin groups from gaining control of multiple reins of power." The organization of space in the Chaco world looks nothing like that of the later precontact and contact-era Pueblos.

One of the central arguments against Chaco's having been a political enterprise rests on the absence of evidence for accumulation of personal wealth, as well as the absence of identifiable rulers (for example, Johnson 1989; Mills 2002; Renfrew 2001; Saitta 1997; Wills 2000). The argument is that political power is equated with individual, self-aggrandizing leadership and the accumulation of personal wealth. The conclusion drawn is that, because the Chacoan archaeological record manifests very little evidence for differences in personal wealth and therefore little evidence for the presence of powerful individuals, Chaco was not politically organized or controlled. In the absence of this, we can suggest various, and more nuanced, social formations.

One could, in the first instance, dispute the substance of this argument that little evidence exists for differences in personal wealth, as Lekson does in the first chapter of this volume. After all, there are a few extremely rich burials and a much larger number of "poor" ones in Chaco Canyon, and a few people lived in enormous, expensive buildings constructed through the labor of many people, while the great majority of Chacoan people did not. As Lekson puts the argument in chapter 1, Chaco "had rulers. Not only have we exhumed their bodies, but also we have turned their stately homes into a national park."

I agree with Lekson that the Chacoan archaeological record shows clear evidence of major differences in access to material goods. In the larger scheme of things, however, this may be beside the point. What is even more important is the validity of the underlying assumption. Is it true that evidence of personal wealth accumulation means that a society is organized politically and that the absence of such evidence means that the society is *not* organized politically? However one may feel about the presence or absence of evidence for powerful individuals or differential distribution of wealth in the Chacoan archaeological record, the problem is that this underlying assumption about the nature of political leadership brings us right back to the central unresolved issue: Was Chacoan society marked by institutionalized differences in social, economic, and political power? If so, what were the basis and structure of those inequalities?

### An Alternative Approach

So why do we keep restating and repeating this argument, and what can we do to get past it? I would suggest that we keep struggling with this issue because our models of what institutionalized differences in power should look like are too narrow. Arguments that Chacoan organization was not "complex" or "hierarchical" or "political" are based on the assumption that such power differentials require powerful individuals. In actuality, power in many societies is vested in corporate groups such as clans, lineages, fraternities, or councils. Chiefs and kings are not the only route to organizational complexity and differential power.

Some take the position that, if Chaco cannot be shown to have been the stereotypical chiefdom, with a repressive, self-aggrandizing, paramount ruler, it perforce must have been an egalitarian, communal, cooperative phenomenon. This has led to tortuous scenarios attempting to account for the highly differentiated *physical* remains of Chaco without violating an assumption that Chacoan society was egalitarian and socially undifferentiated. Scholars describe the large, highly planned additions to the Great Houses, which involved mobilization of huge amounts of various materials and substantial labor investments, as happening cooperatively without centralized planning or administration. Descriptions of great ritual events are posited in which large numbers of pilgrims appear simultaneously in Chaco Canyon and organize themselves cooperatively to carry out communal activities. I think that Lipe's comments in chapter 8 about the organizational requirements of "volunteer" efforts are particularly cogent in this regard: "Even if workers are willing to volunteer their time on a complex project, not much gets done without clear direction."

I have argued elsewhere: "If Chaco fit neatly into some straight-forward organizational 'box' based on common patterns that we see in the modern or historical world, we would have found that box by now. This doesn't mean that it was some unique specimen never seen before or since in the world; that is theoretically possible, but statistically unlikely. What is *more* likely...is that we haven't looked at enough boxes yet" (Sebastian 2004:99).

We need to move beyond direct analogy with historical and modern Pueblo societies, and we need to expand our concept of complex societies beyond the classic neo-evolutionary categories of chiefdom and state. Most especially, we need to examine the broad range of societies that exhibit institutional differences in social, political, and economic power but bear little resemblance to the stereotypical chiefdom (or kingdom, if I may beg our volume editor's pardon).

As one example of the many fruitful sources of potential analogues for Chacoan organization that exist in the ethnographic literature, I would suggest that we consider sub-Saharan Africa. Not only were large numbers of mid-level societies observed and recorded ethnographically in Africa, but also these societies exhibited a great wealth of organizational variability (for example, Vansina 1999). We have clear evidence from these studies that political power, economic control, and hierarchical structure can be linked, totally separate, or missing all together in these societies.

In a fascinating and very readable edited volume titled *Beyond Chiefdoms: Pathways to Complexity in Africa*, Susan Keech McIntosh (1999:4) asks, "To what extent can diverse pathways to complexity be discerned? Rather than taking centralization as a given in discussing complexity and then concentrating on how leaders maintain control through economic leverage or coercion, it is useful to ask what constitutes complexity and consider how social and ritual resources are mobilized and collective action made possible in the absence of significant economic control."

McIntosh goes on to suggest (following Bargatsky 1987:27) that capitalist societies have reduced the multidimensional, highly complex status systems of preindustrial societies to the overarching, unidimensional status symbol of material wealth. She argues that "this can blind us to the importance of status distinctions that lack a material, economic foundation, or even to the possibility that significant status differences can be thus constructed" (McIntosh 1999:6).

In this same volume, Kopytoff (1999) argues that western cultural values have not only caused us to view material wealth narrowly as the only "true" indicator of political status but have also limited our understanding of political status itself. He notes that African societies value the political status of the office holder as much for its own sake as for the ability to use political power to achieve other goals: "Being a chief means such things as being a visibly important man, one who can claim precedence in seating at public functions, who can wear exclusive insignia, who has a title. These are not merely 'symbols' of something more 'concrete,' such as power; they are valued goals in their own right, a part of 'power' rather than a representation of it.... Contemporary Westerners (unlike, say, their medieval ancestors) have little experience of or respect for an ethos that values hierarchical display for its own sake. This may make it difficult to conceive of impalpable preroga-tives as being more than merely means toward some tangible ends" (Kopytoff 1999:93).

In many African societies, control over people, not control over material wealth, marks and supports political power. Indeed, because polygamy is an important means of increasing the number of people controlled and bride prices may be substantial, the greater the political competition, the more wealth is distributed rather than amassed. As McIntosh (1999:7) explains, "The constant cycle of amassing then redistributing goods to expand one's prestige by enlarging the house-hold unit (adding wives or slaves) or by purchasing titles and society memberships, meant that many (but by no means all) African hierar-chical societies did not manifest the elements of economic stratifica-tion that archaeologists most often seek."

Thus, the absence of wealth in things does not negate the possibil-ity that wealth in people is a central feature of political power in a soci-ety. The obvious assumption, however, might be that wealth in people simply equates with control over labor and therefore does represent an amassing of economic resources, albeit of a nonmaterial sort. As many Africanists have noted, though, control over people is more often about gaining desired knowledge (Guyer and Belinga 1995) or access to specialized goods or skills (Kopytoff and Miers 1977) or ensuring vital trade (Northrup 1978). McIntosh (1999:16) suggests that "leader-ship in many African societies involves the composition of networks of social and ritual power. This permits us to expand our conceptual arena beyond the notions of control and competition that have tended to dominate discussions in the archaeological literature."

Contact-period Africa encompassed some large, stratified hierar-chical societies in which there was relatively modest differentiation in wealth, as well as some tiny societies with rich prestige economies and intense competition for titles and offices. Africa also provides us with models of societies (Kongo, for example, Ekholm 1972) in which pres-tige goods were acquired, owned, and circulated in a competitive, hier-archical system while subsistence resources and basic necessities were secured and consumed in the context of an egalitarian, locally based economy. Contrary to the network-versus-corporate power strategy model developed by Blanton and others (1996), many African prestige-goods economies involved knowledge-based components of social and political power, as well as material-based components. As Lipe points out in chapter 8, "being on the corporate side [of the Blanton and others model] is no impediment to the development of hierarchy and social power; for example, Harappa is high on both the hierarchical and the corporate mode axes."

In addition to societies in which substantial differences in social and political power exist in the absence of substantial differences in wealth, Africa also provides numerous examples of societies in which complex relations of political and social power take a variety of non-hierarchical forms. More than thirty years ago, Horton (1971) described two of these horizontally complex forms. The first consisted of dispersed, territorially defined communities comprising confederations of unrelated lineages (generally the result of in-migrations from varied donor locations). These communities were integrated through cult organizations that built upon existing, widespread, shared belief systems in the region. The second complex but nonhierarchical form consisted of large aggregated villages with substantial populations (sometimes in the thousands) integrated through associations, cults, and secret societies. In these cases, it was generally a council of title-holders in the societies or priests of the cult who exercised political and judicial, as well as moral and ritual, authority. McIntosh (1999:16) notes that "multiple hierarchies—political, administrative, and ritual—each with certain political tasks, are a regularly observed feature of African complex societies. The result is a range of societies with relatively weak vertical political control and extremely complex horizontal integration."

To bring this back to Chaco, let us consider some specific issues that have been raised. For example, what do the African cases suggest about the relationship between ritual and political organization? McIntosh (1999:12) argues:

> Ritual reduces "scalar stress" (i.e., social strains engendered by increasing numbers of people) in large sequential hierarchies, not primarily because of the opportunities that it provides for "passive stylistic signaling"—as Johnson [1982:405] suggested—but because the combination of fear, belief,

supernatural sanctions, and fines that typically accompany ritual is effective in securing compliant behavior and resolving disputes.... Cult associations and secret societies are, after all, ritual corporations that own property and control socially recognized resources....Through their control of ritual technology and ritual knowledge, which allows members to harness ritual power and direct it to specific ends, they have potent political roles. They also mobilize labor and wealth through payment of membership and initiation fees, payments for ritual services, and fines for infractions.

In many African societies, the leader's ability to use the appropriate specialized knowledge and ritual power makes him capable of effective political action.

Peter Robertshaw (1999) observes that established settlements constantly attempted to attract migrants in order to create a larger labor force, support part-time craft specialists, and provide increased security in times of conflict. He notes that, because it was so important for communities to retain population despite the ease with which individuals and families could relocate, the dominant lineages would often "legitimize their leadership and power through the assumption or co-option of ritual authority" (Robertshaw 1999:126).

Another important issue in the Chaco case is the nature of the relationship between the central canyon and the larger world of "outliers." In writing of the Alur, Aidan Southall (1999:31) concludes that "the segmentary state is one in which the spheres of ritual suzerainty and political sovereignty do not coincide. The former extends widely toward a flexible, changing periphery. The latter is confined to the central, core domain." Even though Southall is writing about a state-level society with a much greater population size and density, the concept of variable scales of ritual, social, and political integration can potentially assist our efforts to model the relationship between the canyon and the larger Chaco world.

As a final example to show the broad range of potentially applicable concepts from African ethnography, a number of the authors in the *Beyond Chiefdoms* volume discuss the problems of integrating immigrant populations into an existing society. This is especially germane to the Chaco case because we know from both archaeology and Native

American oral traditions that group migrations were a frequent and significant pattern of precontact Puebloan life. More specifically, Wilshusen and Van Dyke (chapter 7 of this volume) and Lipe (chapter 8 of this volume) demonstrate that Chaco and the rest of the central and southern San Juan Basin saw substantial in-migration from the northern San Juan in the tenth century.

Vansina (1999) traces the development of widely varying political structures out of a single pattern common to ancestral Bantu speakers. He notes that a widespread, shared belief system enabled ambitious leaders to legitimize their growing authority by creating or taking control of rituals tied to key beliefs. At the same time, this shared belief system made it easy for families and lineages to move from one settlement to another or even from one polity to another by demonstrating their place in and knowledge of the belief system.

Kopytoff (1999) examines the Aghem chiefdoms of western Cameroon, a situation not unlike the Chaco world in scale, in ethnic and linguistic heterogeneity, and in residential instability. The Grassfields region of Cameroon covers an area roughly 100 by 130 miles; the ethnographic population consisted of a number of closely interacting cultural and linguistic groups and was marked by frequent movement of families, lineages, and individuals among a series of settlement clusters and small polities.

The Aghem polity formed within a context of frequent segmentation of settlements and population movement and recombination, exemplifying principles of political formation that were widespread in west Africa and beyond. One of these principles was "primacy of the firstcomer: the earliest occupants establish a ritual relationship to the land to which later settlers must defer" (Kopytoff 1999:89). One result of this principle among the Aghem was a corporate form of leadership. As Kopytoff (1999:90) explains, "The Aghem chieftaincies were not created *ex nihilo* by enterprising or ambitious individuals who then conferred their achievements on their successors. Rather, each of the village headships existed from the beginning of settlement, vested in the corporate kin group of first settlers. An individual chief's position derived from his membership in his kin group; he held the chieftaincy in its name and in trust for it, the chieftaincy being part of its estate."

Another result of the primacy of the first comer was increasing differentiation in social status and political power over time. "Recent newcomers…were placed at the bottom of the chiefdom hierarchy—in effect on probation. The longer they stayed, the more weighty became their claim to Aghemhood, with its right to participate in local affairs. But their Aghemhood continued to be a matter of hierarchical gradation. At the top stood, unchallenged, the 'true' Aghem—the chiefly lineages and just below them their long-standing adherents who claimed to have been there at the founding of the settlement…passively, the founding lineage head finds himself to be a 'chief' by simply remaining at the top of a pyramid that grows at the bottom" (Kopytoff 1999:91).

A second widespread political principle exemplified by the Aghem is a marked tension between despotism and populism as these affect the relationship between chiefly and subject lineages. On the one hand, the Aghem chiefly lineage had the ability to assign or withhold land use rights and other critical economic and social resources, which can potentially produce despotic behavior. On the other hand, the chiefly lineage was part of a broader society in which relocation was a constant and frequent option. Society members who felt aggrieved or insufficiently compensated for their loyalty could easily vote with their feet, and the pyramid of which the chiefly lineage formed the apex could quickly collapse. As Kopytoff (1999:92) says, "Aghem chiefs could be harsh and arbitrary. But the harshness was systemically mitigated by the chiefs' need to have subjects, the more the better. There is a saying common in African societies, that one cannot be a chief and be alone; and so Aghem chiefs had magical devices to help them attract and retain subjects."

The third (and related) political principle clearly seen among the Aghem is the common African political power base of "wealth in people." As Kopytoff (1999:93) says, "The main ingredient in the rise of an Aghem chiefdom was the acquisition by the chief of control over more and more people—people being simultaneously the origin, the substance, the goal, and the currency of chiefly authority." The way that Aghem chiefly lineages gained control over people was by granting permission (or threatening to withhold permission) to reside in a community and by applying magico-religious knowledge and skills when necessary. Kopytoff (1999:93) argues that "provision of shelter and safety, of sociability, of psychic satisfactions in their various cultural guises" are benefits valued by potential subjects at least as highly as some of the material benefits proposed in classic studies of chiefdoms (for example, redistribution of goods).

We have seen the effects of frequent movement of families, lineages, and individuals on the political structure of the resultant communities and polities, but what about the problems of community integration that arise in this situation? John Ware has argued (2001 and elsewhere) that, in the American Southwest, the need to incorporate unrelated groups into formerly kin-based communities was met through the development of ritual sodalities that operated independently of and simultaneously with kinship structures.

McIntosh (1999) provides examples of African cases in which crosscutting associations enabled a society to achieve a substantial degree of complexity (defined as internal differentiation and intricacy of relations) and integrate activities over a broad area without vertical control hierarchies. In most cases, these associations operated simultaneously with and parallel to the existing local political structures.

By offering these examples of insights to be gained from the ethnographic record of sub-Saharan Africa, I am by no means recommending that we abandon Southwestern analogues and embrace African ones. As John Ware would say, the problem is not that most of us know too much about Pueblo ethnography but that we know too little. What I *am* suggesting is that, if we are ever to resolve some basic questions about the nature of Chacoan society, we must broaden our ideas about the range of possible organizational types beyond classic neo-evolutionary categories and beyond what the historical Pueblo world offered us—especially if, as Lekson suggests in chapter 1, the structure of that world was, to some degree, a reaction *against* the structure of the Chacoan world.

As David and Sterner (1999:98) suggest in their article in the *Beyond Chiefdoms* volume, "When we find seemingly anomalous forms of organization, perhaps we should consider that they may be the latest— and last—representatives of societal types once common in the past, and thus in the archaeological record. Rather than attempting to insert societies known through archaeology into the straightjacket of Friedian or derivative evolutionary sequences, we should be actively looking for evidence that might indicate that they belong to separate evolutionary lines...we may expect the bulk of Holocene archaeological cultures to represent societal types either extinct or existing only as relicts in the historical record and ethnographic present."

Interestingly, the last sentence in the paragraph quoted above (from a book about Africa) concludes, "Surely this is a more liberating approach than to expend great efforts on forcing recalcitrant archaeological entities—the Harappan is a prime example, the Chacoan phenomenon another—into the 'statejackets,' state-trajectory moulds that must be strained to bursting to contain them" (David and Sterner 1999:98–99).

## CHACOAN RESEARCH IN THE TWENTY-FIRST CENTURY

The final task that the capstone conferees set for themselves was identification of critical directions for future research. Most of these needs have been touched on in one or more of the chapters in this volume, but the full list of research needs specifically identified during the capstone conference appears below. Some of these directions for future research involve collection of specific types of needed data; others address specific functional or technological questions. What is perhaps most remarkable about this list, however, given the long history and intensity of Chacoan research, is the number of basic issues identified as *still* requiring substantive research and resolution.

*Empirical Data:*

- What kinds of features and artifacts are to be found in the upper stories of Great Houses?

- What is underneath the Great Houses?

- What was on top of the Pueblo Bonito mounds?

- What are the dates and distribution of the roads?

- What is the extent of the line-of-sight communications network?

*Functional Questions:*

- What was happening in the early canyon Great Houses for the first one hundred years after they were constructed?

- What was the function of McElmo structures? What is in them, and how were they used?

- What was the function of small kivas in the Great Houses? What is in them, and how were they used?

- What was the function of Great Kivas? What is in them, and how were they used?

*Interpretive Questions:*

- Did Aztec continue to be a primate center after the A.D. 1140s?

- What was the nature of the relationship between the canyon and the Chuska slope—trade, tribute, pilgrimage offerings, dual residence, other?

- What was the function of outlier Great Houses, and what is the relationship between these structures and the surrounding community of small sites?

- What was the population of the canyon at specific points in time?

- Was it necessary to import labor and/or food into the canyon?

*Specific Research Needs:*

- Intensive sampling effort to compare Great House and small site trash mounds both inside and outside the canyon

- Additional modeling of potential agricultural production

- Collection and evaluation of evidence for periodic "consumptive events" (such as feasts and pilgrimages)

One other aspect of this list is noteworthy: ten of the seventeen research topics outlined above would require new excavation-based data. A great deal of excavation has taken place at Chaco, the majority of it in the late 1800s and early 1900s—half a century before modern standards of excavation and research were developed. The excavation techniques were crude, documentation was cursory, and curation—both the decisions about what to keep and the accessioning and record keeping for retained materials—was often abysmal. We cannot use most of the pre–World War II data to answer many of these twenty-first-century questions.

Yet, as Lekson points out in chapter 1, major excavation projects are almost certainly a thing of the past at Chaco, for both fiscal and political reasons, at least during the lifetime of those of us who have acquired gray hair and bifocals in the course of our Chacoan research. What to do? As Lekson also notes, many younger scholars are focusing on the outlier communities, and this is a Good Thing. The more we know about what was going on at the other end of the (actual or metaphorical) road, the more we will understand about the canyon and the Chaco world.

Speaking of roads, the road network, the signaling network, the sources of imports into the canyon, and many questions about agricultural carrying capacity and other issues can be addressed through a variety of technological and largely noninvasive approaches. Other questions can be addressed through archaeological survey and in-field analysis of surface artifacts. Through years of sheer dogged determination, Tom Windes has used this approach to radically change our knowledge and understanding of early Great Houses along the Chaco.

We can do all these things, and we can redouble our efforts to coax every bit of possible data out of the limited records and large collections from the early years of Chacoan archaeology. As I have suggested above, we can also strengthen our interpretive frameworks by adopting a broader cross-cultural view and examining the patterned material remains of a wider variety of non-state societies. Ultimately, however, we are going to have to move more dirt in order to answer many of the questions above.

In the interim, I would suggest that we have had so much fun that we should all do this again sometime. That thundering noise you hear is my colleagues stampeding for the nearest exit. But wait, hear me out! Steve Lekson's pyramidal vision for how to achieve the impossible synthesis of more than one hundred years of Chacoan research—small topical conferences followed by a conference of the conference organizers—has yielded remarkable results, both expected and unexpected. If I might be allowed to point this out to my "Chaco as egalitarian enterprise" colleagues, there is a lot to be said for hierarchy and authority figures when you are trying to build a pyramid or a Great House.

Taking smart, knowledgeable people, feeding them good food, and locking them in a room for several days generally yields remarkable results, the Chaco Timeline being only a small example. There is so much existing data about Chaco and so much ongoing work, all the time, that my final recommendation for the future is this: we should remember that synthesis is not a product—it is a process. We need to be constantly on the lookout for ways to continue this synthesis process into the next century of Chacoan research.

# APPENDIX A

## Chaco Synthesis Meetings

### Compiled by Stephen H. Lekson
### with the assistance of F. Joan Mathien

**ORGANIZATION OF PRODUCTION**
University of Colorado, Boulder, Colorado
March 21–23, 1999

### Participants

Organizers: Catherine M. Cameron, H. Wolcott Toll

Panelists: Timothy Earle, Melissa Hagstrum, Peter Peregrine, Lord Colin Renfrew

NPS representatives: Peter J. McKenna, Frances Joan Mathien, Thomas C. Windes

Other attendees: Karin Burd, Michael Larkin, Stephen H. Lekson

### Publications

Cameron, Catherine M., and H. Wolcott Toll (guest editors)

2001 Special issue of *American Antiquity* 66(1):

Cameron, Catherine M., and H. Wolcott Toll
"Deciphering the Organization of Production in Chaco Canyon," pp. 5–13.

Renfrew, Colin
"Production and Consumption in a Sacred Economy: The Material Correlates of High Devotional Expression at Chaco Canyon," pp. 14–25.

Earle, Timothy
"Economic Support of Chaco Canyon Society," pp. 26–35.

Peregrine, Peter N.
"Matrilocality, Corporate Strategy, and the Organization of Production in the Chacoan World," pp. 36–46.

Hagstrum, Melissa
"Household Production in Chaco Canyon Society," pp. 47–55.

Toll, H. Wolcott
"Making and Breaking Pots in the Chaco World," pp. 56–78.

Cameron, Catherine M.
"Pink Chert, Projectile Points, and the Chacoan Regional System," pp. 79–102.

Mathien, Frances Joan
"The Organization of Turquoise Production and Consumption by the Prehistoric Chacoans," pp. 103–118.

Windes, Thomas C., and Peter J. McKenna
"Going Against the Grain: Wood Production in Chacoan Society," pp. 119–140.

## SOCIETY AND POLITY

Fort Lewis College, Durango, Colorado, and Chaco Culture National Historical Park, New Mexico

May 3–7, 1999

## Participants

Organizers: Linda S. Cordell, W. James Judge

Panelists: Nancy Mahoney, Mark Varien, John Ware, Henry T. Wright, Norman Yoffee

NPS representatives: Frances Joan Mathien, Thomas C. Windes

Other attendees: Susan Bryan, Karin Burd, Michael Larkin, Stephen H. Lekson

## Publications

Cordell, Linda S., W. James Judge, and June-el Piper (editors)
2001   *Chaco Society and Polity: Papers from the 1999 Conference.* New Mexico Archeological Council Special Publication No. 4. New Mexico Archeological Council, Albuquerque.

Lekson, Stephen H., and Karin Burd
"Foreword," pp. vii–ix.

Cordell, Linda S., and W. James Judge
"Perspectives on Chaco Society and Polity," pp. 1–12.

Mahoney, Nancy
"Monumental Architecture as Conspicuous Display in Chaco Canyon," pp. 13–29.

Windes, Thomas C.
"House Location Patterns in the Chaco Canyon Area: A Short Description," pp. 31–45.

Varien, Mark D.
"We Have Learned a Lot, But We Still Have More to Learn," pp. 47–61.

Yoffee, Norman
"The Chaco 'Rituality' Revisited," pp. 63–78.

Ware, John A.
"Chaco Social Organization: A Peripheral View," pp. 79–93.

## CHACO WORLD

Arizona State University, Tempe, Arizona

September 25–27, 1999

## Participants

Organizers: John Kantner, Keith Kintigh, Nancy Mahoney

Panelists: David Anderson, Roger Anyon, David Doyel, Dennis Gilpin, Sarah Herr, Winston Hurst, James Kendrick, Timothy Pauketat, Kathy Roler Durand, Sarah Schlanger, Ruth Van Dyke

NPS representatives: Dabney Ford, Frances Joan Mathien, Robert P. Powers, Charles Wilson, Thomas C. Windes

Other attendees: Karin Burd, Michael Larkin, Stephen H. Lekson

## Publications

Kantner, John (guest editor)
2003  Special issue of *Kiva* 69(2):

Kantner, John
"The Chaco World," pp. 83–92.

Kintigh, Keith
"Coming to Terms with the Chaco World," pp. 93–116.

Van Dyke, Ruth M.
"Bounding Chaco: Great House Architectural Variability across Time and Space," pp. 117–139.

Durand, Kathy Roler
"Function of Chaco-Era Great Houses," pp. 141–169.

Gilpin, Dennis
"Chaco-Era Site Clustering and the Concept of Communities," pp. 171–205.

Kantner, John
"Rethinking Chaco as a System," pp. 207–227.

Database: http://sipapu.gsu.edu/Chacoworld.html

## ECONOMY AND ECOLOGY
University of Arizona Desert Laboratory, Tucson, Arizona
October 28–30, 1999

### Participants
Organizers: Julio Betancourt, Jeffrey S. Dean, Carla Van West, R. Gwinn Vivian
Panelists: Nancy J. Akins, William Doolittle, Brian Fagan, Enrique Salmon,
   Mollie S. Toll
NPS representatives: Dabney Ford, Frances Joan Mathien, Charles Wilson,
   Thomas C. Windes
Other attendees: Karin Burd, Michael Larkin, Stephen H. Lekson

### Publications
Chapter 2 and Appendix B of this volume

## CHACO, MESA VERDE, AND THE CONFRONTATION WITH TIME
University of Colorado, Boulder, Colorado
February 24–26, 2000

### Participants
Organizers: Stephen H. Lekson, Patricia Limerick
Panelists: Vine Deloria Jr., Leah Dilworth, Ann Fabian, Peter Goin,
   Robert Greenlee, Roger Kennedy, Tessie Naranjo, Simon Ortiz,
   Enrique Salmon, Reg Saner, Charles Scoggin
NPS representatives: Russell Bodnar, Frances Joan Mathien

# CHACO ARCHITECTURE

University of New Mexico, Albuquerque, and Chaco Culture National Historical
Park, New Mexico
September 28–October 3, 2000

## Participants

Organizers: Stephen H. Lekson, Thomas C. Windes
Panelists: Nancy Akins, Wendy Ashmore, Taft Blackhorse, Patricia Fournier,
  Richard Friedman, Ben Nelson, John D. Schelberg, Anna Sofaer, David Stuart,
  John Stein, Philip Tuwaleststiwa, Ruth M. Van Dyke, Jay Williams
NPS representatives: Russ Bodnar, G. B. Cornucopia, Dabney Ford,
  Frances Joan Mathien, Charles Wilson
Other attendees: Elizabeth Bagwell, Karin Burd, Gretchen Jordan,
  Michael Larkin, Marianne Tyndell, Chris Ward, Devin White

## Publications

Lekson, Stephen H. (editor)
n.d. *Architecture of Chaco Canyon, New Mexico.* University of Utah Press, Salt Lake
City. In press.

> Lekson, Stephen H.
> "Foreword" and "Introduction to Chaco Architecture"

> Windes, Thomas C.
> "Gearing Up and Piling On: Early Greathouses in the Chaco Basin"

> Van Dyke, Ruth M.
> "Great Kivas in Time, Space, & Society"

> Neitzel, Jill E.
> "Interpreting Pueblo Bonito's Architecture"

> Lekson, Stephen H., Thomas C. Windes, and Patricia Fournier
> "The Changing Faces of Chetro Ketl"

> Ashmore, Wendy
> "Building Social History at Pueblo Bonito"

> Stein, John, Rich Friedman, and Taft Blackhorse
> "Revisiting Downtown Chaco"

> Sofaer, Anna
> "The Primary Architecture of the Chacoan Culture"

STEPHEN H. LEKSON

## CAPSTONE CONFERENCE
University of New Mexico, Albuquerque, New Mexico
October 16–19, 2002

### Participants
Organizer: Lynne Sebastian

Panelists: Catherine M. Cameron, W. James Judge, John Kantner, Keith Kintigh, Stephen H. Lekson, William Lipe, Ben Nelson, H. Wolcott Toll, R. Gwinn Vivian, Carla Van West

NPS representatives: Russell Bodnar, Stephanie Dubois, Dabney Ford, Frances Joan Mathien, Robert P. Powers, Thomas C. Windes

Other attendees: Brian Fagan, David Grant Noble

### Publications
This volume

## CHACO SYNTHESIS
School of American Research, Santa Fe, New Mexico
May 5–6, 2004

### Participants
Organizer: Stephen H. Lekson

Panelists: Linda Cordell, W. James Judge, John Kantner, Richard M. Leventhal, Ben Nelson, Timothy Pauketat, Lynne Sebastian, H. Wolcott Toll, Ruth M. Van Dyke, Norman Yoffee

NPS representatives: Frances Joan Mathien, Thomas C. Windes

Other attendees: David Grant Noble

### Publications
This volume

# APPENDIX B

Chacoan Ecology and Economy

R. Gwinn Vivian, Carla R. Van West,

Jeffrey S. Dean, Nancy Akins, Mollie Toll,

Tom Windes

The period between A.D. 600 and A.D. 1150 brackets the rise, existence, and decline of the Chaco regional system, as described in this volume. In the following pages, we partition this 550-year period into four geomorphic-stratigraphic periods following research published by Force et al. (2002). The Early Aggradation period likely began about 200 B.C. and continued through about A.D. 900. The Channel Cutting period began about A.D. 900 and ended about A.D. 1025. The Channel Filling period began about A.D. 1025 and ended by A.D. 1090. The Late Aggradation period began about 1090 and continued into the mid-1100s.

## EARLY AGGRADATION, A.D. 600–900 (LATE BASKETMAKER III–PUEBLO I; LA PLATA AND WHITE MOUND PHASES)

This geomorphic-stratigraphic period was characterized by a sediment deposit known as the "Chaco unit." It includes the water-laid deposits in the playa-lake behind the sand dune dam. Late Basketmaker III and Pueblo I occupations are known to have occurred in the

Chaco core and adjacent areas when these sediments were being deposited.

### Paleoclimate

Regionally, low temporal variability characterized this period until approximately A.D. 750, when the intervals between precipitation maxima and minima decreased. Spatial variability from A.D. 600 to 900 was low, and climatic conditions across the northern Southwest were generally uniform. Climate in the Chaco core was also relatively uniform but was punctuated in the mid-eighth century by one "unusually wet" period (A.D. 728–736) immediately followed by a notable dry interval from A.D. 738 to 757.

Rainfall in the final three years of the ninth century was great enough (> 10 in per year) to produce stream flow sufficient to breach a large eolian dune dam at the mouth of Chaco Canyon. At this point, the Chaco Wash is joined by the Escavada Wash and makes an abrupt southwesterly turn through a break in the Chacra Mesa. This long gap in the mesa forms a funnel into Chaco Canyon for storms moving north and carrying moisture and also sand from the wide, braided Chaco-Escavada drainage. Aerial photographs of the mouth of Chaco Canyon show the present dune extending from the Chaco Wash to and over low cliffs on the canyon's north side.

The dune dam that was breached around A.D. 899 may have been the most recent (200 B.C.–A.D. 900) of reoccurring dune dams in this location. Force and others (2002) have documented probable lake-playa deposits overlain by floodplain (delta) deposits in exposures in the banks of the Chaco Wash upstream from the present dune. These deposits are associated with Hall's (1977, 1983) late Holocene "Chaco unit" (a soil unit), which was present during most Ancestral Puebloan use of the canyon. Stratigraphic analysis strongly suggests that the dune barrier to canyon drainage served as a base-level control that affected the formation of canyon-floor sedimentary units. An apparent direct result of this process was the present perching of the canyon 4–5 m above the floor of the Escavada Wash. Arroyo formation (channel cutting) is thought to be linked to the breaching of the dune dam. Slow infiltration into the dune may have delayed breaching by preventing water levels from reaching a point that could lead to spillway erosion.

Regional temperatures for the latter part of this period have been estimated on the basis of San Francisco Peak (Flagstaff) bristlecone pine analysis (Salzer 2000a). Salzer (2000b:301) concluded that, "although probably most accurate locally, the reconstruction is applicable on a regional scale." In fact, the assumption that San Francisco Peak trends are similar for much of the northern Southwest has not been empirically tested. If the trends are regionally accurate, Chaco experienced warm periods during several decades in the mid and late ninth century, whereas the early and mid ninth century was cooler. Extremely cold years and years with possible killing frosts occurred during the mid- and late-ninth century.

### Agricultural Strategies and Techniques

Macrobotanical remains and pollen found in Chacoan sites occupied between A.D. 600 and 1150 in the Chaco core undisputedly confirm the production and consumption of domesticated plants, particularly maize. Physical evidence for agricultural fields and water control devices is limited to the eleventh and twelfth centuries.

Average annual precipitation in the interior San Juan Basin is not sufficient for dry farming under most conditions, and fields were placed in locales that received runoff or that could be watered with runoff distributed by water control facilities. Although available moisture was the primary criterion for field selection, soil type, exposure affecting ground temperature, and labor for field preparation conditioned the selection process. Given the erratic nature of Colorado Plateau climate, no agricultural strategy could remain static. Changes in effective moisture, aggradation, and degradation of Chaco Wash and its tributary drainages, groundwater levels, and temporal and spatial variability in seasonal moisture and temperature conditions stimulated adaptive social and technological adjustments to reduce the risk of crop failure.

A number of local environmental factors further conditioned Chacoan strategies. These included average annual precipitation of only 8.5 in and the San Juan Basin's transitional position with respect to the tracking of winter and summer storm systems. Specifically, the basin is near the southern limits of the winter storm path and on the northern periphery of the summer circulation route. This produces not only annual precipitation differences if seasonal circulation routes shift slightly to the north or south, but also north-south seasonal distribution differences. On a more local scale (the Chaco core), Chaco Canyon was a "water collector" created by drainage patterns and storm funneling into the canyon through four breaks in the Chacra Mesa. Offsetting this benefit was the absence of any suitable, adjacent, cooler, and wetter "highlands" that would have provided alternative field locations during warmer and drier climate regimes. Within Chaco Canyon, farming strategies were influenced by the presence or absence of the sand dune dam, which affected channel dynamics (Force et al. 2002), and by contrasting patterns of runoff on the north and south sides of the canyon.

There are no detailed studies of field areas and crop watering systems in Chaco Canyon or the Chaco core for the Early Aggradation period. Implications for farming from A.D. 800 to 900 are drawn from analyses of pollen (Cully 1985) and macrobotanical remains from small house sites 29SJ627 and 629 (Toll 1985). Climatic and geomorphological data suggest that Chaco Canyon may have been the best place to farm in the interior basin from A.D. 600 to 900. The period was characterized by the unusual persistence of hydrologic and aggradation/ degradation conditions in Chaco Canyon that had changed elsewhere in the southern Colorado Plateau at ca. A.D. 750. The presence of the eolian dam at the western end of Chaco Canyon throughout this period (or until at least A.D. 898) apparently prevented the onset in the mid-eighth century of arroyo cutting and degradation in the canyon. Declining effective moisture throughout the region after A.D. 750 may have lowered the water table, but the absence of arroyo cutting within the canyon probably slowed the loss rate and may have even "favored the accumulation of sediments in the Canyon" (Dean and Funkhouser 2002:40).

The simultaneous negative impacts of high temporal variability could have been somewhat ameliorated by spring and summer storms funneling into the canyon through four breaks in the Chacra Mesa. These gaps in the mesa extend from the Chaco Wash break at the western end of the canyon to Pueblo Pintado Pass on the east, with South Gap and Fajada Gap near mid-canyon. Windes and others (2000:42) point out that the Chacra Mesa forms a barrier to summer storms originating from the southwest and redirects them into the mesa, where these openings keep them "localized for extended periods." Rain gauges monitored by Windes show consistently higher annual precipitation in some of these locations. Warmer temperatures are also recorded for these zones.

Low spatial variability apparently reduced the option of moving to other areas in the interior San Juan Basin, including the top of Chacra Mesa west of Pueblo Pintado, where most localities lacked good farmland other than dune fields. In effect, the established populations of Chaco Canyon were "trapped"—they had no better place to go, and the hydrologic effects of the eolian dam provided a good reason for staying.

Within the canyon, hydrologic patterns and suitable soils conditioned field locations. These were well established by at least A.D. 550, if not earlier. Between A.D. 600 and 750 lower population permitted some settlement clustering in the canyon, such as the massive community at Peñasco Blanco, and downstream to Padilla Well. This community lay within one of the "funnel zones" located at breaks in the Chacra Mesa, but proximity to the wide Chaco Wash may have been an equally important determinant for community location. During periods of aggradation and rising water tables, canyon bottomlands received moisture from both overbank flooding of the Chaco Wash and runoff from side drainages. The combination of both sources had the additional benefit of producing a good soil balance of sand and clay or a sand layer underlain by more impermeable clay. There is no good evidence for water control systems during this period. Low, earthen diversion dams, small canals, and simple gates may have been employed to channel and spread floodwater to fields in some locations, but all were probably impermanent and subject to frequent destruction by flooding.

Floodplain farming along the Chaco Wash was feasible, but the potential for large center-canyon floods would represent a continual hazard, especially during years of high summer moisture. Side drainages had the advantage of more limited amounts of runoff, but the topography and large expanses of slickrock on the canyon's north side made these sources consistently more difficult to control. Drainages on the canyon's south side are especially well suited for shallow floodwater fan farming (*akchin*) that benefits from periods of increased effective moisture. A form of akchin probably was practiced as well on the canyon's north side, although measures to curb velocity of flow may have been necessary and could have been the precursors of later water-control facilities. Use of sand dunes for fields was almost certainly a practiced strategy.

The eolian dam at the western end of Chaco Canyon could have modified the negative impacts of erosion, channel cutting, and a lowered water table after A.D. 750, but it could not influence the amount or frequency of rainfall. When both decreased, one viable option for improving farming strategies was to move out of the canyon proper. Three small, widely spaced communities that appear after A.D. 800 in the Kin Klizhin and Kin Bineola drainages (Van Dyke, ed., n.d.) may have been established by segments of the canyon population relocating in better-watered zones. The South Fork of the Chaco Wash south of the Fajada Butte Gap also saw a major influx of population at this time. The period ends with the postulated breaching of the dune dam and the initiation of channel cutting sometime early in the tenth century.

### Macrobotanical Resources

Domesticated and wild plant use during the Early Aggradation period differs sufficiently from the succeeding period to suggest that problems of sampling and preservation may influence the spectrum of plant use. Macrobotanical remains from this time period carry indicators of farming and little else (Toll 1993). The broad spectrum of economic annuals, grasses, and perennials so common in later Great Houses and small house sites is represented in only a scanty and patchy fashion. Plant remains recovered include goosefoot, winged pigweed, pigweed, purslane, cocklebur, stickseed, and tobacco. Unburned seeds of groundcherry, stickleaf, and beeweed may represent other economic plants. Despite the early apparent scarcity of economic wild plants, the most salient aspect of their use in Chaco is its consistency from one era to the next. An array of weedy annuals utilized from Basketmaker times onward is present, including taxa with both edible greens and tiny seeds that typically grow in and around disturbed areas such as habitations and fields, suggesting that their growth was encouraged.

Sebastian's (1992a) simulated maize yields begin at A.D. 900, so data from her simulation are not available for this period. Based on recovered remains from late Basketmaker and early Pueblo sites for this period, Toll (1993) and others have determined that corn constitutes the highest percentage (53 percent) of all economic occurrences at this time. It then drops to a much lower 26 percent across other time and site types. Twelve-rowed cobs dominate Chacoan maize in this period, whereas cobs from contemporary sites to the west and south are primarily eight-rowed (Winter 1993). Cob diameters do not vary much across the San Juan Basin, but it is noteworthy that the largest-diameter cobs of any period occur at small sites in Chaco in the late Basketmaker and early Pueblo I periods. This patterning may tell us something about where farming was more successful. Other crop plants have a far patchier record. Cucurbit seeds (*C. mixta*) have been recovered from one small-house site (29SJ724), and these can be identified as the cushaw type (Toll 1985).

### Faunal Resources

Data for faunal use extends back to ca. A.D. 500 and is relatively comprehensive until about A.D. 850 (Akins 1985), but the sample is extremely small (n = 293) from 850 to 950. For comparative purposes, faunal use in the canyon during the A.D. 500s is briefly noted, even though the sample predates the Early Aggradation period. The sixth century was marked by heavy dependence on small mammals (86 percent), particularly cottontail, whereas large mammal use was notably limited (6 percent) and there was no significant difference in species taken. There is no recorded use of turkey for this period.

The first half of the Early Aggradation period showed continued dependence on small mammals (83 percent), and, while jackrabbit consumption increased, cottontails were the dominant species taken. Large mammal use increased only minimally (8.64 percent), with pronghorn occurring in substantial amounts. Turkey bone was recovered in trace amounts (.38 percent). This early strong focus in Chaco on small mammals, particularly cottontail, very likely reflects a horticultural strategy of hunting in gardens and cultivated fields. Increased horticultural activity provides habitats that support higher densities of small mammals, making them more available for human procurement (Speth and Scott 1989:74). Garden hunting has an economic advantage because little travel is involved and it is a defensive measure against small mammals that cause considerable damage to crops, field areas, and water control devices.

The small sample for the latter portion of this period is probably not a reliable indicator of faunal use. It shows continued dependence on small mammals (66 percent), with more jackrabbit than cottontail, and a decline in the minimal use of large mammals (6.48 percent). The shift to greater use of jackrabbit may represent a move towards communal instead of individual hunting, created by possible changes in habitat and larger human populations. Values between Great Houses and small house sites display no obvious distinctions. Studies of faunal assemblages from southern Arizona (Szuter and Bayham 1989) have shown that clearing land for agriculture or collecting wood and depleting brush cover should favor jackrabbits, which prefer open spaces with high visibility; cottontails prefer dense brush cover where they can hide. Lagomorph indices therefore may be used as an index of ground cover in a particular environment. Late in this period, turkey bone increased slightly (1.71 percent of the sample), a spike that did not occur again until the twelfth century. It should be noted that none of the faunal percentages for this period probably reflect canyonwide use patterns.

### Wood Use

Differences in Windes's and Toll's percentages of wood fuel and construction use in the Early Aggradation period probably reflect Toll's inclusion of shrubby plants as fuel and her more limited database: Pueblo Alto and two small-house sites (29SJ627 and 629). Windes considers only tree species and cites additional Great Houses and other structures. Wood use during this period reflects greater consumption of coniferous wood for both construction and fuel at early Great Houses, compared with small house sites, and some of this wood may have been derived from nonlocal sources. The limited data on fuel use for this period indicate that local conifers from side canyons and adjoining mesa tops formed a substantial percentage of fuel used.

Early Great House construction wood is a mix of nonconifers and both local and nonlocal conifers. More than half (52 percent) of the timbers used were conifers, including ponderosa pine (39 percent), Douglas fir (10 percent), and spruce/fir (3 percent). Many of the ponderosa timbers may have been from small scattered stands on the Chacra Mesa, particularly near the eastern end of Chaco Canyon. These beams are far more variable in age and include a substantial percentage of trees more than fifty years old, as would be expected of trees growing in moist pockets of the central Chaco Basin. As these trees were harvested and construction needs increased, Chacoan builders apparently shifted to more distant mountain forest stands, where growth is faster and more uniform. Local juniper (10 percent) and piñon (15 percent), as well as *Populus sp.*, and likely cottonwood (23 percent) constituted the remaining wood species. Far greater use of local juniper (45 percent) and piñon (42 percent) was documented for contemporaneous small-house sites, whereas *Populus* and other non-coniferous trees accounted for 11 percent of the wood used. Ponderosa pine occurred in only trace amounts.

## CHANNEL CUTTING, A.D. 900–1025 (EARLY BONITO PHASE)

This geomorphic-stratigraphic period is named for a depositional hiatus between the Chaco unit of the Early Aggradation period (200 B.C.–A.D. 900) and the Channel Filling period (A.D. 1025–1090). Early Pueblo II occupations of the Chaco core took place when erosion to the drainage system was underway.

### Paleoclimate

"The Channel Cutting period as a whole is characterized by high regional temporal variability, when conditions oscillated rapidly between maxima and minima, and low spatial variability, when uniform conditions prevailed across the northern Southwest" (Dean and Funkhouser 2002:40). A brief spike of high spatial variability, which may have favored arroyo cutting, apparently initiated the period. While arroyo cutting is often correlated with high temporal variability, channel entrenchment is not generally associated with low spatial variability. With a few exceptions, weather amplitudes in the Chaco core during this period were not marked by abrupt and steep changes. The period opened with a decade of unusually dry conditions following the three extremely wet years between A.D. 897 and 899. A decade of wet weather occurred in the 940s, and a period of "reduced variability around the mean and three successive intervals characterized by positive trends in precipitation" (Dean and Funkhouser 2002:40) began around A.D. 990. Salzer's (2000a) estimated regional temperatures indicate that this period was initiated by a regional warming trend, and warm periods were also plotted for A.D. 965–975 and A.D. 1005–1010. A regional cool period was charted from A.D. 1020 to 1030. Three extremely cold years occurred during this period, with multiple years marked by possible killing frosts.

### Agricultural Strategies and Techniques

The breaching of the eolian dam at the western end of Chaco Canyon in the late tenth or early eleventh century once again put geomorphological and hydrological processes in the canyon out of sync with the regional regime. These processes included initiation of a new cycle of aggradation and a rise in groundwater. A regionwide gradual increase in effective moisture may have offset somewhat the deleterious effects of new channel cutting and a lowering water table in Chaco Canyon. High temporal variability continued to the end of the period, but the canyon's position relative to seasonal circulation systems and storm paths from the south presumably continued to make it one of the best-watered locales in the interior San Juan Basin. Similarly, the continued pattern of low spatial variability reduced options for moving beyond the Chaco core.

Entrenchment of the Chaco Wash would have placed floodwater fields on the canyon's north side in jeopardy because side tributaries would have eroded to the base of the main channel, thereby flushing water directly into the wash. Presumably, the hydrologic and geomorphic conditions on the canyon's south side "resisted entrenchment and...would have been far better than the northern margins for agriculture based on *akchin* methods" (Force et al. 2002:36). Sand dunes, though limited, are primarily restricted to the canyon's south side, where they served as an additional farming microniche.

Deeply buried (up to 1 m below present ground surface) masonry headgates and associated canals at the Rinconada system may date to this period. Dating of these gates is based primarily on the superposition of later gates and less conclusively on associated ceramics. The morphology of these gates differs in several respects from later gates and has been used to establish the presence of other early gates elsewhere in the canyon. They are large, well constructed, and designed to handle major discharges of runoff. Despite these precautions, there is good evidence for their destruction by floods. Water control probably became a significant aspect of farming during this period.

With channel entrenchment, the hydrologic benefits of the canyon were reduced, perhaps significantly, and out-migration presumably assumed greater importance. Yet, the evidence for increased use of the South Fork, Kin Klizhin, and Kin Bineola valleys is slim, although Windes (n.d.) believes that the postulated tenth-century unit at the Kin Bineola Great House is much larger than previously thought. If this is true, then it may represent the first attempt to establish Great House communities in this drainage. Overall, however, these southern valleys do not appear to have been a refuge for canyon farmers seeking better agricultural land. Farming the Escavada floodplain remained an option, and the distance was not so great as to require establishing new settlements. This period ends with a series of wet years (A.D. 1022–1027) that highlighted the coming trend toward increased effective moisture and other conditions more conducive to simple farming.

**Macrobotanical Resources**

Before A.D. 900 maize dominated the macrobotanical collections from most sites in Chaco Canyon. After A.D. 900 the use of economic wild plant taxa is much more common in both small sites and Great Houses (Toll 1985, 1993). This period is marked by particularly high occurrences of some important wild perennials (piñon, pricklypear, hedgehog cactus) and some weedy annuals such as sunflower (Toll 1987). The lowest percent of samples with maize occurs at this time when all categories of wild plants are used widely, after which the ubiquity of maize rises steadily.

The frequency of maize in collections from all sites in Chaco Canyon dropped to 26 percent of all economic plant occurrences. Sebastian's (1992) simulation shows several decade-long, or longer, periods of high corn yields separated by usually longer periods with diminished returns. In general, there were fewer good times than stressful times from A.D. 900 to 1025. Short-term spikes lasting for less than a decade broke two particularly long periods of decreased yields, from A.D. 920 to 945 and from 995 to 1015. Cob length and diameter provide useful and simple measures of moisture, temperature, and mineral stress and reflect the degree of agricultural success within sub-areas of the San Juan Basin.

Sites in Chaco Canyon during this period share very similar

row-number configurations (only slightly more ten-rowed cobs than twelve-rowed cobs) with several other basin areas (Bis sa'ani [Donaldson and Toll 1982], ENRON and Navajo Mines [Toll 1983]). These same areas share the smallest cob diameters in the basin, ranging from an average of 9.14 mm in the Navajo Mines area to 12.4 mm in Chaco. Sites in better-watered zones such as the La Plata Valley (Toll 1993) are predominantly twelve-rowed and have average cob diameters ranging from 13.9 to 16.9 mm. Evidence of other domesticates is limited to *Cucurbita sp.* and the widespread and highly diversified common bean (*Phaseolus vulgaris*).

### Faunal Resources

Data on faunal use during this period are derived from sites with occupation spans from A.D. 920 to 1050 (Akins 1985). The small mammal/large mammal consumption pattern characterizing the preceding period continued until about A.D. 990 and was marked by heavy dependence on small mammals (75 percent) and relatively minor use of large mammals (8 percent) representing near equal amounts of pronghorn, deer, and bighorn. If the shift to greater use of jackrabbit sometime after A.D. 850 is correct, that trend was reversed after A.D. 920, when cottontail again became the dominant species. This could be interpreted as a shift from communal hunting to individual hunting in fields and gardens as agriculture increased and more time was spent in fields. Small mammals were not limited to lagomorphs but included field mice, pocket gophers, kangaroo rats, and prairie dogs. Although hunting of wild birds such as horned larks and ravens did not diminish, turkey use dropped to about one half of a percent (0.5) of all faunal use.

Changes in faunal assemblages occurred at or about A.D. 990 and continued to A.D. 1050. Small mammal use began to decrease (66.5 percent of recovered animal bone). Large mammals, representing fairly equal quantities of pronghorn, deer, and bighorn, increased significantly to 16.6 percent of animal bone collected. Turkey use declined by about half (.26 percent) during this time.

### Wood Use

Data on wood construction and fuel use for this period were derived from sites with occupation spans that cover both the Channel

Cutting and Channel Filling periods. Therefore, this summary may not reflect fluctuations in use during and after the Channel Cutting period. Wood use shows an increasing reliance on ponderosa pine for construction at both Great Houses and small house sites. There is a 20 percent increase in ponderosa pine (59 percent) for construction at Great Houses, and much of this wood probably was imported into the canyon because local stands were harvested during the preceding period. Nonlocal sources for Great House construction timber are also reflected in the notable increase in spruce/fir (14 percent); Douglas fir declined (6 percent), as did local juniper (5 percent) and piñon (10 percent). *Populus* accounted for only 5 percent of wood used in Great House building. Small house sites show a significant drop (almost 50 percent) in use of both juniper (24 percent) and piñon (19 percent), matched by a surge in ponderosa pine (28 percent). Smaller amounts (3 percent) of Douglas fir were recovered from these sites. *Populus* and other nonconiferous wood accounted for 26 percent of construction wood in these sites.

Most Great Houses and small house sites continued to depend predominantly on shrubby plants for firewood, although fuel at Pueblo Alto showed a 2 percent increase (to 17 percent) in juniper and piñon and a slightly lower (76 percent) use of shrubby plants. Saltbush and greasewood were the primary fuel sources for small house sites (82 percent), with local conifers and cottonwood/willow each contributing about 3 percent of the total.

## CHANNEL FILLING, A.D. 1025–1090 (CLASSIC BONITO PHASE)

This geomorphic-stratigraphic period is equivalent to the Bonito channel fill. These sediments accumulated in arroyo channels that formed during the tenth and early eleventh centuries at the height of the Chaco regional system.

### Paleoclimate

Regionally, the Channel Filling period was characterized by low temporal variability, with longer periods between notable increases and decreases in moisture. Spatial variability throughout the region increased during this period. Locally, the period was one of reduced variance of precipitation values around the mean, with three periods of increasing precipitation (A.D. 1020–1030, 1040–1060, and 1070–1080) separated by dry spells. Dean and Funkhouser (2002:41) point out, "While high regional spatial variability probably did not promote aggradation, low regional temporal variability and the locally reduced variance and upward trending rainfall undoubtedly contributed to the environmental stability that allowed deposition to occur."

Estimated regional temperatures (Salzer 2000a) indicate that the period began with a short cool episode that soon shifted into a long (A.D. 1035–1050) warm period. A second warm period was charted from A.D. 1070 to 1090. No extremely cold years occurred during the Channel Filling period, but several years were marked by possible killing frosts.

### Agricultural Strategies and Techniques

A period of vigorous cultural development and agricultural intensification roughly brackets the Classic Bonito phase (A.D. 1040–1100). Geomorphological and hydrological processes in Chaco Canyon "caught up" with regional trends in the early eleventh century, following the "out of sync" channel-cutting episode initiated in the early tenth century. The cessation of entrenchment at approximately A.D. 1025 may have been hastened and possibly even initiated by the construction of a masonry dam at the southern end of the breached eolian dam below Peñasco Blanco. The dune field at the western end of Chaco Canyon is currently breached where the Chaco Wash passes between the dune and the cliff face on the south side of the canyon. This was the location of a "rock dam and ditch" reported by Judd (1954:58) in August 1920. Earlier, Samuel Holsinger (1901:10) described a reservoir "built in a great bed of sand" and "lined with slabs of stone and clay" in this location. He also noted that "a weir by which the flood waters were diverted from the main channel and conducted to the reservoir was similarly flagged and cemented" (Holsinger 1901:10). This slab-and-clay lining probably served as a surfacing of the dune to reduce infiltration, and the same stone surfacing apparently extended across the front of the masonry dam to ensure greater impermeability at the point of initial contact with water flowing down the canyon. Marietta Wetherill, in an August 1948 interview with Gordon

Vivian, corroborated the presence of a masonry dam built of massive sandstone blocks. She remembered that the dam, or portions of it, had been covered with small dunes and was exposed around 1900 or slightly later by floods in the Escavada Wash that joined the Chaco Wash at this point.

The work by Force and others (2002) suggests that the efforts to re-create a dam at the western end of the canyon may not have been as successful as the earlier eolian dam. Buried deposits exposed in the current walls of the Chaco Wash about 1.5 km upstream from the dam location show floodplain or delta deposits overlying lake-playa deposits. Composition of the lower deposits, which date to the period before the tenth century, strongly suggests standing water over a long period of time. The upper (post-A.D. 1025) deposits may represent a temporary, though frequently replenished, shallower lake that might be attributed to a less efficient masonry dam. The presence of the masonry dam in the eleventh century raises the intriguing possibility that memory of an earlier lake, fostered through repetitive storytelling, may have led to the construction of a new dam and creation of another lake during the heyday of Chaco society.

Scale is a consideration if, as suspected, a dam was constructed across the Chaco Wash. Lagasse, Gillespie, and Eggert's (1984) analysis of water control systems in Chaco Canyon concluded that Vivian (1974) correctly identified systems capable of handling small water-sheds between major tributary drainages. But, they argued, he erred in proposing that Chacoans also harnessed floods in major drainages. The identification of a massive dam in Cly's Canyon and a canal system draining Gallo Canyon, however, clearly indicate that control struc-tures tapped large drainages for runoff. The masonry and earthen dam in the Kin Klizhin Valley and two similar dams on the Kin Bineola drainage are further proof of attempts to control large quantities of runoff. Volume of water carried in the Chaco and Kin Bineola drainages at peak floods has not been computed, but the Chaco drainage probably does not exceed the Kin Bineola drainage. Chacoans may well have assumed that they could dam the Chaco Wash.

Construction of this dam may or may not have enhanced or accel-erated the effects of regional processes conducive to increased agricul-tural production. Agricultural intensification in the canyon and core during this period reflects the regional shift to low temporal variability around A.D. 1000, aggradation, rising water tables, and several periods of notably increased precipitation. These relatively salubrious conditions may have triggered the establishment of several new canyon Great Houses outside the better-watered "funnel zones" through the Chacra Mesa.

The best archaeological evidence for agricultural field location, patterning, and watering in the canyon comes from this period. These systems were designed to collect and distribute runoff primarily in the lower 15 km of Chaco Canyon, from Gallo Canyon at the east end to the confluence of the Chaco and Escavada washes at the western terminus of the canyon. A dam and canal system was constructed near the Kin Klizhin Great House at the end of this period, but similar systems in the Kin Bineola Valley probably date to the early twelfth century.

Chaco Canyon collects water from the east via the Chaco Wash and from northern and southern tributaries that drain into the canyon. The importance of water in the Chaco Wash for farming is not known. As Loose and Lyons (1976:142) note, David Love "calculated that a typical modern 10 year rain event could flood the entire canyon floor if the Chaco were not entrenched." Runoff from drainages on the canyon's north and south sides was more critical for watering fields, although runoff patterns differ significantly on the two sides as a result of local geomorphology. The north mesa top is characterized by large expanses of bedrock and shallow soil that contribute to enhanced flow and reduced absorption, so large quantities of water reach the central canyon floor, often with considerable velocity. The mesa on the south is broken and terraced and has more soil cover, so surface flow tends to be absorbed in the floodplains of side canyons and little water reaches the main canyon. The south side of the canyon is relatively ideal for akchin-type farming, but some form of water control is necessary on the north to collect fast-flowing surface water. Within the lower 15 km of Chaco Canyon are approximately 400 ha of cultivatable land on the canyon's north side and 500 ha on the south side.

Water control features that probably date to this period are known in seventeen of the twenty-eight side canyons on the north side, between Wijiji and the western end of the canyon. Two of these systems were found in major tributaries—Cly's Canyon and Gallo Canyon—

and, almost certainly, water in Mockingbird Canyon also was collected and channeled to fields.

Similar water-control features were found at two locales on the canyon's south side, one opposite Pueblo Bonito and close by Casa Rinconada and the other below the mesa-top Great House of Peñasco Blanco. No other masonry and earthen features were located on the south, but the National Park Service has recorded some features in the Fajada Gap area.

The method for collecting, diverting, and spreading runoff was consistent throughout the canyon. Water flowing down side tributaries (*rincons*) was channeled into a canal near the mouth of the rincon by an earthen or masonry diversion dam. Masonry headgates designed to slow and further channel runoff were constructed at the ends of and possibly on the sides of the canals. Water leaving headgates flowed into smaller canals that distributed water to gridded fields. Variation in canal and headgate morphology can be traced over time, and these changes are repeated throughout the canyon. Morphological variation, in some cases, is documented stratigraphically because canal, gate, and field levels rose over time as sediments in runoff were deposited on the canyon floor. Three phases of variation—early, middle, and late—have been tentatively identified for canyon systems.

Early-phase canals averaged 4.5 m wide and 1.5 m deep and were faced with packed earth or stone slabs or were masonry walled. The headgates associated with these canals are well built of dressed sandstone and have the appearance of core and veneer walls in Chacoan Great Houses. The walls on either side of the channel opening (wing walls) are up to 2 m long, and channel length (equaling headgate depth) averages 2 m but may be twice this length. During the middle phase, the orientation of some canals and gates shifted. Only a slight change can be detected in canals; narrowing can be documented in at least one case (Rinconada system). This narrowing is better reflected in gates that become more compact, resulting in shorter wing walls and channel length. Gate capstones, which represent a design change to handle larger quantities of water, may have been added at this time, although they could also have been present in the early phase.

Sometime during the Channel Filling period, severe flooding damaged or destroyed a number of middle-phase gates and canals

445

throughout the canyon; most were repaired or remodeled. Late in the period, gate and canal morphology changed again. Late-phase canals become narrower and shallower, and gates are characterized by reduced size, cruder masonry, and the use of wood poles in place of masonry in some instances.

Similar changes have not been documented for gridded fields, although small field-type gates in fields do show some variation over time. Kirkby's (1973) analysis of agricultural water use and crop yields in the Oaxaca Valley demonstrated the critical importance of wisely spreading water evenly over fields, and gridding fields ensures more equal distribution of floodwater. The best information on gridded fields comes from the Chetro Ketl field documented in aerial photography and field tests. A 3-ha field visible in aerial photographs is divided into two rectangular, bordered plots separated by a feeder canal. Each plot was gridded into individual gardens averaging 22.5 by 13.5 m, for a total of about one hundred gardens per hectare. Much of the area is covered by recent alluvium, and the original field area is estimated at 9 ha.

Runoff also was used on the canyon's north side to water two small areas of masonry-terraced gardens near Pueblo Alto on the mesa top. Terracing is not known from other areas of the canyon, but wall-bordered mesa-top gardens may be present near Tsin Kletzin.

Morphologically similar water-control features were employed for farming in the Kin Klizhin Valley, but they were modified to suit the local runoff conditions. The Kin Klizhin Wash was the primary source of water that was collected behind a large earthen and masonry diversion dam built below the Great House. Water was channeled through a "spillway" into a canal that was routed towards a wide, flat portion of the valley. Investigation of this area for possible gridded fields has been limited.

Two similar dams near Kin Bineola may be contemporaneous. The watersheds in the Kin Klizhin and Kin Bineola valleys were considerably greater than any side drainages in Chaco Canyon, but large dams are known from Cly's Canyon and near Tsin Kletzin in the canyon. They also were probably present in Mockingbird and Gallo canyons, and there are historic references to a large masonry dam at the western end of the canyon. With the exception of the Tsin Kletzin dam, all appear to have been built to control large amounts of water temporarily. Well-developed canals are associated with dams in the Kin Bineola Valley. Canals and headgates in the Kin Klizhin and Kin Bineola systems have not been well studied but appear to resemble middle-phase facilities in Chaco Canyon.

During this period, the canyon again became an attractive farming oasis in the interior San Juan Basin as positive changes occurred in effective moisture, water tables, and temporal variability. The intense human manipulation of water in the canyon sometime after A.D. 1020 is a good measure of the degree of commitment to and investment in farming, despite occasional risks as manifested in the destruction of headgates and canals by flooding. Agricultural success may also be reflected in the growth of the East Community near the eastern head of Chaco Canyon after A.D. 1050, as well as the establishment of the Pueblo Pintado Great House in the 1060s farther to the east but within the Chaco core. If good farmland was becoming scarce in the lower canyon, establishing settlements in agriculturally favorable locations in the Chaco core was an option. Small settlements in the Kin Klizhin and Kin Bineola valleys increased markedly during this period. The establishment of the Kin Klizhin Great House in the late 1080s, however, may have been a response to local decreased moisture in the last two decades of the eleventh century.

**Macrobotanical Resources**

Maize was even more present during this period, although a wide variety of wild economic plants were consistently recovered at Great Houses and small house sites. Annuals, including goosefoot, pigweed, purslane, stickseed, and tobacco, were common. Grasses and perennials remained important but occurred in lower frequencies. Wild plant usage also showed an inverse relationship with maize late in the period at the Salmon Chacoan outlier on the San Juan River (Doebley 1981).

A trend toward a heavy reliance on maize cultivation is evident in the Chaco core and much of the San Juan Basin. Sebastian's (1992) simulated corn yields data show a surplus beginning at around A.D. 1015 and continuing to 1030, after which surpluses declined and lasted to about A.D. 1038. There was a brief surplus between 1038 and 1042, after which time corn in storage dropped until A.D. 1050. The period from 1050 to 1080 was marked by high yields, broken only by brief occasional dips; this was an extremely consistent period, comparable to those from A.D. 960 to 980 and from A.D. 1098 to 1130. The Channel Filling period ended with a decline in production between 1080 and 1098, with a brief spike in the late 1080s (ca. 1087–1088).

Maize assemblages in Chaco Canyon appear to sort out into two major patterns at this time. Pueblo Alto and small house sites have smaller, predominantly ten-rowed cobs, whereas two canyon-floor Great Houses, Pueblo Bonito and the Talus Unit at Chetro Ketl, have very large cobs, the majority of which are twelve-rowed. A possible third pattern was found in a small sample of measured corn from Pueblo del Arroyo, another canyon-bottom Great House, where cobs were large but were about equally divided between ten and twelve rows. Variability in cob size between Pueblo Alto and canyon-bottom Great Houses might result from different watering systems. Fields for Pueblo Alto may have been in the Escavada Wash floodplain to the north of the Great House, not in gridded fields on the canyon bottom. There is no similar explanation, however, for cob differences between Pueblo del Arroyo, Pueblo Bonito, and the Talus Unit. Tom Windes (personal communication 2003) points out that there are no temporal controls for maize from excavations at Pueblo Bonito and the Talus Unit and that the reported cobs may date from reoccupation of these buildings in the late 1100s or even the 1200s, thereby explaining the observed differences. Small house sites are presumed to have depended primarily on akchin floodwater fields and microniche farming such as dunes—factors that might account for smaller maize.

A decrease in cob size also was reported for the Salmon outlier Great House, where cob size was smaller and the majority was ten-rowed (Bohrer, Doebley, and Adams 1980). Likewise, undeveloped and irregular rows increased through time in the La Plata Valley, from 22 percent of cobs early in the period to 39 percent late in the period (Toll 1986, 1993). These observations suggest the likelihood that not just Chaco but many areas of the San Juan Basin and its peripheries may have experienced difficulties producing maize at this time.

Few changes were noted in other crop plants, the remains of which were far less common than corn. Squash (*Cucurbita sp.*) was reported from most sites, including Pueblo Alto and Pueblo Bonito. Similarly, common beans (*Phaseolus vulgaris*), in some cases up to seven varieties, were recovered from a number of small house sites and from Pueblo Bonito (Toll 1985).

### Faunal Resources

Information on faunal use is based on records from sites that generally span the beginning and ending of the Channel Filling period (A.D. 1025–1090), although some sites have earlier or later occupation dates. The 4:1 ratio of small mammal to large mammal use characterizing earlier periods continued, but large mammal use increased significantly at the close of this period. There was little change in use of turkey from previous periods.

Small mammal use fluctuated slightly during this period, beginning at about 66 percent, increasing to approximately 73 percent between A.D. 1050 and 1080, and dropping to roughly 68 percent by A.D. 1090. Cottontail and jackrabbit ratios varied minimally during the period, with more cottontail as the period began, jackrabbits exceeding cottontail slightly in mid-period, and a return to higher cottontail use after A.D. 1080.

Exploitation of large mammals showed continual growth, moving from about 17 percent at the beginning of the period to slightly more than 30 percent between A.D. 1050 and 1080. By A.D. 1090 large mammal use had dropped to about 23 percent. The preceding pattern of essentially equal use of pronghorn, deer, and bighorn changed after A.D. 1050, when deer bone increased substantially relative to pronghorn and bighorn sheep. A general pattern of greater use of artiodactyls by increasing human populations has been observed by Speth and Scott (1989:78). They consider it a socioeconomic response by aggregations of horticulturists who turn to scheduling hunting activities in order to provide high-quality protein. After depleting much of the locally available game, hunters travel greater distance to more productive areas and may increase their reliance on communal techniques.

Turning to the mix of artiodactyls, there are several implications in the data. Early deposits indicate that the preferred artiodactyl was pronghorn, a species that could have occurred in large numbers close to Chaco Canyon. The switch to deer could have several causes. A growing population forcing hunters to travel farther and to take deer and mountain sheep already could have depleted pronghorn. It could also signal a change in basic organization in which communal hunts were abandoned in favor of small group or individual hunts. Along those same lines, access to pronghorn habitats could have been denied while areas with deer and mountain sheep remained open or opened up. The time of the switch, around A.D. 1050, should provide some clues. Dog remains decrease at about the same time, another indication of a major shift in hunting strategy. Turkey use remained minimal and accounted for less than 1 percent of total recovered bone.

### Wood Use

Data on wood construction and fuel use for this period were derived from sites with occupation spans that cover both the Channel Cutting and Channel Filling periods. Percentages of consumption and use trends for this period are, therefore, essentially those reported for the preceding period.

Toll does have data on fuel use at Pueblo Alto that approximates this period. Conifer use increased to 41 percent, with ponderosa pine accounting for 1 percent (juniper = 25 percent, piñon = 15 percent). Given this shift, shrub fuel dropped to 53 percent, with saltbush and greasewood again constituting the major species (40 percent). *Populus* fuel was negligible (1 percent).

## LATE AGGRADATION, A.D. 1090–1125 (CHACO CENTER = LATE BONITO PHASE)

This geomorphic-stratigraphic period is named for the final interval of sediment deposition during the terminal years of the Chaco regional system. It is reflected as point-bar deposits within the Bonito channel of Chaco Wash and its tributaries, as well as the uppermost floodplain soil on the valley floor.

### Paleoclimate

Regional and local climatic conditions during the Late Aggradation period were almost identical to the preceding Channel Filling episode. The period ended with a shift back to low spatial variability and a significant drought that lasted from A.D. 1130 to 1180, although a short period of increased moisture occurred in the mid-twelfth century.

Dean and Funkhouser (2002:41) point out that a drought that may have been particularly severe in the summer "would have been especially destructive to the Canyon food production system, which depended on summer rainfall and surface runoff." Climatic improvement after A.D. 1180 came too late to benefit the Chacoan system, and the Chaco core was largely abandoned before the next severe drought in the 1210s and 1220s.

According to Salzer (2000a), the two decades of warm temperatures characterizing the end of the preceding period (A.D. 1070–1090) ended in 1095, when a regional cold period set in and persisted until A.D. 1125. A second cool period late in the century (A.D. 1190–1220) was preceded by a short warm period from A.D. 1140 to 1180. Extremely cold years were charted for A.D. 1102, 1112, and 1120. Possible killing frosts occurred in A.D. 1092 and 1109.

### Agricultural Strategies and Techniques

Force and others' (2002) end date for this period (A.D. 1125) has been extended to mid-century because continued Chacoan occupation of the canyon and Chaco core to at least this time is generally acknowledged. The period broadly brackets the Late Bonito phase (A.D. 1100–1140). Published materials on agricultural strategies and resources include those listed for the preceding period. In addition, Cully and others (1982) provide an excellent analysis of agricultural potential and practices at the Bis sa'ani Great House on the Escavada Wash north of Chaco Canyon but within the Chaco core.

A two-decade dry period that started around A.D. 1080 not only signaled the harsh realities of dependency on rainfall but also initiated a series of marked oscillations in effective moisture that ultimately proved too taxing for Chacoan farmers and triggered the eventual abandonment of the canyon and core. Continued aggradation, rising or stable water tables, and low temporal variability between A.D. 1080 and 1100 lessened the impact of reduced effective moisture. A significant increase in precipitation between A.D. 1100 and 1130, coupled with the preceding hydrological and geomorphological conditions, may have lulled Chacoan farmers into some degree of complacency. A surge in Great House construction in the canyon suggests this. Yet, at the same time, numerous outlier Great Houses were being established in the core and well beyond, including large settlements on the San Juan, Animas, and La Plata rivers. If these outliers were founded by population segments from the canyon (and there is some agreement that the Salmon and Aztec Great Houses were), not all farmers in Chaco Canyon may have read the weather the same way.

The relatively long-term wet period from A.D. 1100 to 1130 ended with a major drought that, except for a short midway break, lasted from A.D. 1130 to 1180. The concomitant shift to low spatial variability around A.D. 1130 could have radically altered a regional exchange system that may have developed in the preceding period. Dean and Funkhouser (2002:41) concluded that "this drought, which may have been particularly severe in the summer (Dean 1992:37–38), would have been especially destructive to the Canyon food production system, which depended on summer rainfall and surface runoff." As total effective moisture decreased, there was a break in the aggrading process and water tables stabilized or dropped. Continued establishment of outlier Great Houses beyond the core suggests that out-migration was the ultimate option for many Chacoan farmers.

For those who stayed in the canyon, commitment to certain agricultural strategies may have provided little leeway for adapting to changing climatic conditions in the twelfth century. The heavy social, technological, and labor investment in water control systems on the canyon's north side was compounded by the dedication of large tracts of land to a single method of crop watering. These systems probably worked well between A.D. 1100 and 1130, when precipitation increased, but dry spells from A.D. 1080 to 1100 and from 1130 to 1180 could have resulted in no runoff or far fewer gridded fields being watered. The last structural changes in canals and headgates (late phase) are believed to represent late system adjustments to changing rainfall patterns, and remodeled and repaired gates reported for the preceding period may date partially or entirely in this period. The latest canal in the Rinconada system very likely postdates the repaired gates and is presumed to date from the early to mid twelfth century. This ditch, the last in a series of superimposed canals, is 120 cm wide. One fully defined lower canal in this series is 7.5 m in width, and others may have been wider. A short, extremely simple gate located near Kin Kletso in the Cly Canyon system was of a size capable of handling water from a 120-cm-

wide ditch. Both features may postdate this period and late-phase morphology, however, and may represent mid to late twelfth-century water
control. The implication is that far less water was being collected and
channeled to fields.

Precise dating of changes in canals and gates is difficult. Ceramics
found in these features cannot necessarily be associated with construction, but they do establish that the canal or gate was in use during or
after the production of certain ceramic types. The date ranges for the
latest types found are approximately A.D. 1050–1150. Some sherds may
have been deposited after the systems were abandoned, but others are
clearly associated with use. It is assumed that the latest small canals and
gates (late phase) were in use sometime after A.D. 1130 and possibly as
late as A.D. 1150, when precipitation dropped. Destruction of middle-
phase gates may have occurred during the exceptionally wet years
between A.D. 1100 and 1130. The earliest gates and associated canals
(early phase) are believed to have been constructed in the mid-
eleventh century.

Adjustments to fluctuating precipitation levels were easier on the
canyon's south side, where, with the apparent exception of only two
zones of probable gridded fields, farming strategies remained multidimensional and responsive to changing moisture sources. Fields were
less rigidly confined to particular locales, and farmers could take advantage of dunes and several floodplain niches. This method of farming was
practiced at the Bis sa'ani Great House on the Escavada Wash north of
the canyon, where local geomorphology and runoff in the wash and
from slopes bordering the wash created multiple, diverse crop zones.

Farmers may have practiced similar methods in other areas of the
Chaco core, including the Kin Bineola, Kin Klizhin, and South Fork,
Fajada Wash valleys. The best evidence for farming strategies in these
valleys comes from the Kin Bineola and Kin Klizhin drainages, where
large-scale water control systems utilize many of the same features characterizing water control in the canyon. It is assumed that the two (and
possibly three) earthen and masonry dams with associated canals
located in the Kin Bineola Valley south of the Great House are contemporaneous with the major expansion of the Kin Bineola Great House
in the early twelfth century. Like the Kin Klizhin system inaugurated
possibly two decades earlier, water was drawn from the primary valley

drainage and distributed to fields situated farther down the valley. The size and extent of the Kin Bineola system reflect a major commitment to this type of farming, but the facilities may have been in use for fewer than fifty years. Though water control systems have not been verified in the South Valley, the presence of the Greenlee and Upper Greenlee Great House structures denotes probable agricultural use of this drainage.

### Macrobotanical Resources

The long period of continued wet weather in the first three decades of the twelfth century almost certainly contributed significantly to continued emphasis on corn agriculture for subsistence in the Chaco area. At the same time, climatic conditions resulting in stress on maize growth and maturation resulted in smaller and less well-developed cobs in some Chaco sites, including Bis sa'ani, as well as other areas of the basin. Continued reliance on wild plants, including annuals, perennials, and grasses, helped to offset shortages when they occurred. Essentially the same economic plant taxa that had been collected and widely used for centuries were found in late Chacoan sites. This pattern characterized both Great Houses and small house sites. Where detailed macrobotanical studies have been conducted, slight variations are apparent. At Pueblo Alto, for example, species of weedy annuals, grasses, and perennials were all reported as low occurrences.

Corn yields in Sebastian's (1992) simulation show an approximate decade (ca. A.D. 1088–1098) of decreased yields before resumption of more than three decades (ca. A.D. 1099–1130) of consistently high yields—an expected result of high and continuing precipitation. There were only brief, minor downward blips throughout this period, and the longest consistently high production episode in Sebastian's Chacoan record runs from ca. A.D. 1101 to 1120. Production becomes irregular between 1120 and 1130, and at 1130 a precipitous drop begins that results in the longest (ca. A.D. 1135–1155) and most severe reduction of crop yields in the simulation model for the Chacoan era.

### Faunal Resources

Data on faunal use is relatively comprehensive for this time period and extends to about A.D. 1150, with an apparent absence of data from the period between A.D. 1150 and 1200. The pattern characterizing the preceding Channel Filling period remained relatively unchanged through the Late Aggradation period but was significantly altered in the latest-dated deposits at Pueblo Alto. These deposits were tentatively dated between about A.D. 1120 and 1150 and were characterized by a major decline in small mammal use and a remarkable increase in turkey exploitation.

Use of small mammals rose slightly in the last decade of the eleventh century (68 percent to 71 percent) and continued to increase to about 75 percent in the next fifty years. Small mammal consumption, however, dropped to almost 36 percent sometime in the early A.D. 1100s. Species use varied as before, and prairie dogs became an additional source of food. In general, cottontails were dominant up to A.D. 1100 and became dominant again after A.D. 1200. Prairie dogs and jackrabbits were more heavily used between 1100 and 1150, with prairie dog use declining in the next fifty years.

The use of large mammals grew steadily from A.D. 1080 to 1150. They accounted for almost 14 percent of all bone between A.D. 1080 and 1100, 19 percent of bone between 1100 and 1150, and slightly more than 25 percent in the latest deposits from Pueblo Alto, where deer decreased slightly and pronghorn and bighorn increased considerably.

Changes in turkey use may be the most striking of all faunal exploitation patterns. A mere trace of turkey bone is reported from 1080 to 1100, but this pattern changes significantly sometime in the next fifty years. Slightly earlier deposits at Pueblo Alto and those from two small-house sites have a mean of only 3 percent of turkey bone recovered. In the latest-dated deposits from Pueblo Alto, however, turkey counts increased to almost 24 percent. Post-1200 records indicate only a modest decline to approximately 21 percent.

Turkeys were present from at least the late A.D. 700s but were relatively uncommon. Few of the early birds are burned or have indications of dismembering or other processing. Yet, evidence for raising turkeys is more common before A.D. 1100, with poults ranging from a few days to yearling found at a number of sites. In the later sites and components, numbers are greater, but almost all the birds are mature (Akins 1985:373–381). Therefore, in the later sites, turkeys were probably

imported as a food source and a substitute for artiodactyls. It is probably no coincidence that trade goods for this period indicate close ties
with areas to the north where turkeys would have access to more natural foods and a greater abundance of agricultural crops.

### Wood Use

Windes and Toll report slightly different percentages of wood construction and fuel use for sites with occupation spans that approximate
the Late Aggradation period. These differences reflect Toll's inclusion
of shrubby plants as fuel and her more limited database: Pueblo Alto,
Bis sa'ani, and two small-house sites (29SJ627, 629). Windes considers
only tree species and uses an expanded Great House and other structures database.

There is a slight decrease (51 percent) in ponderosa pine for construction at Great Houses during this period. Windes (personal communication 2003) believes that the decrease in ponderosa pine reflects
the increase in use of spruce/fir and aspen. In his view, this clearly
shows the significantly greater harvesting of trees from higher elevations late in Chacoan prehistory. Presumably, all this wood, as well as
the Douglas fir (15 percent), was transported into the canyon. The
spruce/fir (18 percent) definitely is not local. Great House use of
juniper (3 percent) and piñon (6 percent) continued to decline, but
there was a very slight increase (7 percent) in *Populus*. Windes (personal communication 2003) notes that the *Populus* reported from
Hungo Pavi has now been identified as aspen, which, he points out, logically correlates with the substantial jump in spruce/fir use. He
observes that "our late proxy, Pueblo del Arroyo, is loaded with
spruce/fir, and the roof in Room 44 and beam stubs in Room 43 are all
aspen. I suspect that the *Populus* at Pueblo Pintado, however, is cottonwood" (Windes, personal communication 2003).

Ponderosa pine actually increased slightly (37 percent) at small
house sites, whereas juniper (15 percent) and piñon (12 percent) continued to decline. Interestingly, spruce/fir accounted for 14 percent of
construction wood at small house sites. *Populus* and other nonconiferous wood made up 20 percent of building timbers.

Conifer use for fuel continued to increase at Pueblo Alto, where
local juniper (36 percent) and piñon (21 percent) accounted for more

than half of the fuel species consumed. Even greater use of conifers for fuel (53 percent) was reported from the late Great House, Bis sa'ani. Windes notes that the greater use of conifers at this time can be attributed primarily to scavenged roof wood and harvesting of local piñon rather than procurement outside the canyon. Shrub use dropped remarkably to 37 percent, with saltbush and greasewood again constituting the primary species selected. *Populus* and other woods were minimally used. Shrubs, including a notable quantity of sagebrush (21 percent), made up only 28 percent of the fuel base. Unknown or minor wood species accounted for the remaining 15 percent.

Percentages of fuel species used at contemporaneous small-house sites were remarkably similar to Great Houses. Conifers provided 48 percent of the fuel base, shrubs 28 percent, and cottonwood/willow and other species 15 percent.

# References

**Abbott, D. R.**

2000    *Ceramics and Community Organization among the Hohokam.* Tucson: University of Arizona Press.

**Abbott, D. R., ed.**

2003    *Centuries of Decline during the Hohokam Classic Period at Pueblo Grande.* Tucson: University of Arizona Press.

**Adams, E. C.**

1981    A View from the Hopi Mesas. In *The Protohistoric Period in the North American Southwest,* A.D. *1450–1700,* edited by D. R. Wilcox and W. B. Masse, pp. 321–335. Anthropological Research Papers no. 24. Tempe: Arizona State University.

1989    Changing Form and Function in Western Pueblo Ceremonial Architecture from A.D. 1000 to 1500. In *The Architecture of Social Integration in Prehistoric Pueblos,* edited by W. D. Lipe and M. Hegmon, pp. 155–160. Occasional Paper no. 1. Cortez, CO: Crow Canyon Archaeological Center.

1991    *The Origin and Development of the Pueblo Katsina Cult.* Tucson: University of Arizona Press.

**Adams, K. R.**

1980    Conifers: Part II, Interpretation of Prehistoric Conifers. In *Investigations at the Salmon Site: The Structure of Chacoan Society in the Northern Southwest,* vol. III, edited by C. Irwin-Williams and P. H. Shelley, pp. 417–562. Final Report to Funding Agencies. Portales: Eastern New Mexico University.

**Adams, K. R., and K. L. Petersen**

1999    Environment. In *Colorado Prehistory: A Context for the Southern Colorado Drainage Basin,* edited by W. D. Lipe, M. D. Varien, and R. H. Wilshusen, pp. 14–50. Denver: Colorado Council of Professional Archaeologists.

**Adams, R. K.**

1980    Salmon Ruin: Site Chronology and Formation Processes. In *Investigations at the Salmon Site: The Structure of Chacoan Society in the Northern Southwest,* vol. I, edited by C. Irwin-Williams and P. H. Shelley, pp. 187–313. Final Report to Funding Agencies. Portales: Eastern New Mexico University.

REFERENCES

**Adler, M. A.**
1996      Land Tenure, Archaeology, and the Ancestral Pueblo Landscape. *Journal of Anthropological Archaeology* 15(4):337–371.

**Adler, M. A., and R. H. Wilshusen**
1990      Large-Scale Integrative Facilities in Tribal Societies: Cross-cultural and Southwestern US Examples. *World Archaeology* 22(2):133–146.

**Ahlstrom, R. V. N.**
1985      The Interpretation of Archaeological Tree-Ring Dates. Ph.D. diss., University of Arizona, Tucson.

**Akins, N. J.**
1984      Temporal Variability in Faunal Assemblages from Chaco Canyon. In *Recent Research on Chaco Prehistory*, edited by W. J. Judge and J. D. Schelberg, pp. 225–240. Reports of the Chaco Center no. 8. Santa Fe, NM: Division of Cultural Research, National Park Service.

1985      Prehistoric Faunal Utilization in Chaco Canyon: Basketmaker III through Pueblo III. In *Environment and Subsistence of Chaco Canyon, New Mexico*, edited by F. J. Mathien, pp. 305–445. Publications in Archeology 18E, Chaco Canyon Studies. Albuquerque, NM: National Park Service, US Department of the Interior.

1986      *A Biocultural Approach to Human Burials from Chaco Canyon, New Mexico.* Reports of the Chaco Center no. 9. Santa Fe, NM: Division of Cultural Research, National Park Service.

2001      Chaco Canyon Mortuary Practices. Archeological Correlates of Complexity. In *Ancient Burial Practices in the American Southwest: Archaeology, Physical Anthropology, and Native American Perspectives*, edited by D. R. Mitchell and J. L. Brunson-Hadley, pp. 167–190. Albuquerque: University of New Mexico Press.

2003      The Burials of Pueblo Bonito. In *Pueblo Bonito: Center of the Chacoan World*, edited by J. E. Neitzel, pp. 94–106. Washington, DC: Smithsonian Institution Press.

**Akins, N. J., and J. D. Schelberg**
1984      Evidence of Organizational Complexity as Seen from the Mortuary Practices in Chaco Canyon. In *Recent Research on Chaco Prehistory*, edited by W. J. Judge and J. D. Schelberg, pp. 89–102. Reports of the Chaco Center no. 8. Albuquerque, NM: Division of Cultural Research, National Park Service.

**Algaze, G.**
1989      The Uruk Expansion. *Current Anthropology* 30(5):571–608.

**Altschul, J. H., and E. K. Huber**
2000      Economics, Site Structure, and Social Organization during the Basketmaker III Period. In *Foundations of Anasazi Culture: The Basketmaker-Pueblo Transition*, edited by P. F. Reed, pp. 145–160. Salt Lake City: University of Utah Press.

**Anderson, D. G.**

1990 Stability and Change in Chiefdom-Level Societies: An Examination of Mississippian Political Evolution on the South Atlantic Slope. In *Lamar Archaeology: Mississippian Chiefdoms in the Deep South,* edited by M. Williams and G. Shapiro, pp. 187–213. Tuscaloosa: University of Alabama Press.

1999 Examining Chiefdoms in the Southeast: An Application of Multi-scalar Analysis. In *Great Towns and Regional Polities in the Prehistoric American Southwest and Southeast,* edited by J. E. Neitzel, pp. 215–241. Albuquerque: University of New Mexico Press.

**Anderson, R.**

1976 *The Cultural Context.* Minneapolis, MN: Burgess Publishing.

**Asad, T.**

1993 *Genealogies of Religion: Discipline and Reasons of Power in Christianity and Islam.* Baltimore, MD: Johns Hopkins University Press.

**Baines, J., and N. Yoffee**

1998 Order, Legitimacy, and Wealth in Ancient Egypt and Mesopotamia. In *Archaic States,* edited by G. M. Feinman and J. Marcus, pp. 199–260. School of American Research Advanced Seminar Series. Santa Fe, NM: SAR Press.

**Baker, T.**

2003 Aerial Archaeology Newsletter. http://www.nmia.com/~jaybird/AANews letter/ChacoPage2.html#anchor93088 (accessed May 5, 2004).

**Bannister, B.**

1965 *Tree-Ring Dating of the Archeological Sites in the Chaco Canyon Region, New Mexico.* Technical Series 6, part 2. Globe, AZ: Southwest Parks and Monuments Association.

**Bannister, B., W. J. Robinson, and R. L. Warren**

1970 *Tree-Ring Dates from New Mexico A, G–H: Shiprock-Zuni-Mt. Taylor Area.* Laboratory of Tree-Ring Research. Tucson: University of Arizona Press.

**Bargatsky, T.**

1987 Upward Evolution, Suprasystem Dominance, and the Mature State. In *Early State Dynamics,* edited by H. J. M. Claessen and P. van de Velde, pp. 24–38. Leiden: E.J. Brill.

**Bawden, G.**

1995 The Structural Paradox: Moche Culture as Political Ideology. *Latin American Antiquity* 6(3):255–273.

**Bayman, J. M.**

2002 Hohokam Craft Economies and the Materialization of Power. *Journal of Archaeological Method and Theory* 9(1):69–95.

**Beeson, W. J.**

1966 Archaeological Survey near St. Johns, Arizona: A Methodological Study. Ph.D. diss., University of Arizona, Tucson.

## References

**Beltrán Medina, J. C.**

2001   *La Explotación de la Costa del Pacífico en el Occidente de Mesoamérica y los Contactos con Sudamérica y con otras Regiones Culturales.* Tepic, Nayarit, México: Universidad Autónoma de Nayarit.

**Benson, L., L. S. Cordell, K. Vincent, H. E. Taylor, J. R. Stein, G. L. Farmer, and K. Futa**

2003   Ancient Maize from Chacoan Great Houses: Where Was It Grown? *Proceedings of the National Academy of Sciences (PNAS)* 100(22):13111–13115.

**Berdan, F. F., R. E. Blanton, E. H. Boone, M. G. Hodge, M. Smith, and E. Umberger**

1996   *Aztec Imperial Strategies.* Washington, DC: Dumbarton Oaks Research Library and Collection.

**Berlo, J. C.**

1989   The Concept of the Epiclassic: A Critique. In *Mesoamerica after the Decline of Teotihuacan, AD 700–900,* edited by J. C. Berlo and R. A. Diehl, pp. 209–210. Washington, DC: Dumbarton Oaks Research Library and Collection.

**Bernardini, W.**

1999   Reassessing the Scale of Social Action at Pueblo Bonito, Chaco Canyon, New Mexico. *Kiva* 64(4):447–470.

2000   Kiln Firing Groups: Inter-household Economic Collaboration and Social Organization in the Northern American Southwest. *American Antiquity* 65(2):365–377.

**Berry, M. S.**

1982   *Time, Space, and Transition in Anasazi Prehistory.* Salt Lake City: University of Utah Press.

**Betancourt, J. L., J. S. Dean, and H. M. Hull**

1986   Prehistoric Long-Distance Transport of Construction Beams, Chaco Canyon, New Mexico. *American Antiquity* 51(2):370–375.

**Billman, B. R., P. M. Lambert, and B. L. Leonard**

2000   Cannibalism, Warfare, and Drought in the Mesa Verde Region during the Twelfth Century AD. *American Antiquity* 65(1):145–178.

**Binford, L. R.**

1964   A Consideration of Archaeological Research Design. *American Antiquity* 29(4):425–441.

**Blanton, R., G. Feinman, S. Kowalewski, and P. Peregrine**

1996   A Dual-Processual Theory for the Evolution of Mesoamerican Civilizations. *Current Anthropology* 37(1):1–14.

**Blanton, R. E., S. A. Kowalewski, G. Feinman, and J. Appel**

1981   *Ancient Mesoamerica: A Comparison of Change in Three Regions.* Cambridge: Cambridge University Press.

**Blinman, E.**

1988  Justification and Procedures for Ceramic Dating. In *Dolores Archaeological Program: Supporting Studies: Additive and Reductive Technologies*, compiled by E. Blinman, C. J. Phagan, and R. Wilshusen, pp. 501–544. Denver, CO: Bureau of Reclamation, US Department of the Interior.

1989  Potluck in the Protokiva: Ceramics and Ceremonialism in Pueblo I Villages. In *The Architecture of Social Integration in Prehistoric Pueblos*, edited by W. D. Lipe and M. Hegmon, pp. 113–124. Occasional Paper no. 1. Cortez, CO: Crow Canyon Archaeological Center.

1994  Adjusting the Pueblo I Chronology: Implications for Culture Change at Dolores and in the Mesa Verde Region at Large. In *Proceedings of the Anasazi Symposium 1991*, compiled by A. Hutchinson and J. E. Smith, pp. 51–60. Mesa Verde, CO: Mesa Verde Museum Association.

**Blinman, E., and J. A. Ware**

1999  Questioning Pueblo Political Autonomy: Ritual Exchange and Political Integration on the Rio Grande. Paper presented at the 64th annual meeting of the Society for American Archaeology, Chicago.

**Blinman, E., and C. D. Wilson**

1993  Ceramic Prespectives on Northern Anasazi Exchange. In *The American Southwest and Mesoamerica*, edited by J. E. Ericson and T. G. Baugh, pp. 65–94. New York: Plenum Press.

**Bloch, M.**

1983  *Marxism and Anthropology: The History of a Relationship.* Oxford: Clarendon Press.

**Bluhm, E.**

1957  The Sawmill Site: A Reserve Phase Village, Pine Lawn Valley, Western New Mexico. *Fieldiana: Anthropology*, vol. 47, no. 1. Chicago Natural History Museum Publication 813.

**Bohrer, V. L., with J. F. Doebley and K. R. Adams**

1980  Salmon Ruin Ethnobotanical Report, Part 7. In *Investigations at the Salmon Site: The Structure of Chacoan Society in the Northern Southwest*, vol. 3, edited by C. Irwin-Williams and P. H. Shelley, pp. 163–535. Portales: Eastern New Mexico University.

**Bourdieu, P.**

1994  Structures, Habitus, Power: Basis for a Theory of Symbolic Power. In *Culture/Power/History: A Reader in Contemporary Social Theory*, edited by N. B. Dirks, G. Eley, and S. B. Ortner, pp. 155–199. Princeton, NJ: Princeton University Press.

**Bradley, B. A.**

1988  Wallace Ruin Interim Report. *Southwestern Lore* 54(2):8–33.

1993  Planning, Growth, and Functional Differentiation at a Prehistoric Pueblo: A Case Study from SW Colorado. *Journal of Field Archaeology* 20(1):23–42.

1996      Pitchers to Mugs: Chacoan Revival at Sand Canyon Pueblo. *Kiva* 61(3):241–255.

**Bradley, R. J.**

2000      Networks of Shell and Ornament Exchange: A Critical Assessment of Prestige Economies in the North American Southwest. In *The Archaeology of Regional Interaction: Religion, Warfare, and Exchange across the American Southwest and Beyond*, edited by M. Hegmon, pp. 167–187. Boulder: University Press of Colorado.

**Brainerd, G. W.**

1955      *The Archaeological Ceramics of Yucatan.* Anthropological Records, vol. 19. Berkeley: University of California Press.

**Braniff, B.**

1998      *Morelos, Guanajuato, y la Tradición Chupícuaro.* Serie Arqueología. México, DF: Instituto Nacional de Antropología e Historia.

**Braniff, B., and M. Areti-Hers**

1998      Herencias Chichimecas. *Arqueología* 19:55–80.

**Braniff, B. C.**

1995      Diseños tradicionales mesoamericanos y norteños: ensayo de interpretación. In *Arqueología del norte y del Occidente de México: homenaje al Doctor J. Charles Kelley*, edited by B. Dahlgren and M. d. l. D. Soto, pp. 181–209. Mexico City: Instituto de Investigaciones Antropológicas, Universidad Nacional Autónoma de México.

**Breternitz, C. D.**

1982      Chronology: Dating the Bis sa'ani Community. In *Bis sa'ani: A Late Bonito Phase Community on Escavada Wash, Northwest New Mexico*, vol. 1, edited by C. D. Breternitz, D. E. Doyel, and M. P. Marshall, pp. 61–70. Navaho Nation Papers in Anthropology no. 14. Window Rock, AZ: Navajo Nation Cultural Resource Management Program.

**Breternitz, C. D., D. E. Doyel, and M. P. Marshall, eds.**

1982      *Bis sa'ani: A Late Bonito Phase Community on Escavada Wash, Northwest New Mexico.* Navaho Nation Papers in Anthropology no. 14. 3 vols. Window Rock, AZ: Navajo Nation Cultural Resource Management Program.

**Breternitz, D. A.**

1993a      Some Thoughts on Chimney Rock. In *The Chimney Rock Archaeological Symposium*, edited by J. M. Malville and G. Matlock, p. 7. General Technical Report RM-227. Fort Collins, CO: Rocky Mountain Forest and Range Experiment Station, US Department of Agriculture.

1993b      The Dolores Archaeological Program: In Memoriam. *American Antiquity* 58(1):118–125.

**Brew, J. O.**

1946      *Archaeology of Alkali Ridge, Southeastern Utah, with a Review of the Prehistory of the Mesa Verde Division of the San Juan and Some Observations on Archaeological*

*Systematics.* Papers of the Peabody Museum of American Archaeology and Ethnology no. 21. Cambridge, MA: Harvard University.

1961    Emergency Archaeology: Salvage in Advance of Technological Progress. *American Philosophical Society Proceedings* 105(1):1–10.

1968    Foreword. In *Bibliography of Salvage Archeology in the United States*, edited by J. E. Petsche, pp. 1–11. River Basin Surveys Publications in Salvage Archeology, vol.10. Washington, DC: Smithsonian Institution Press.

**Brisbin, J. M., A. E. Kane, and J. N. Morris**

1988    Excavations at Mcphee Pueblo (Site 5MT4475), a Pueblo I and Early Pueblo II Multicomponent Village. In *Dolores Archaeological Program: Anasazi Communities at Dolores: McPhee Village*, compiled by A. E. Kane and C. K. Robinson, pp. 61–401. Denver, CO: Bureau of Reclamation, US Department of the Interior.

**Brody, J. J.**

1977    *Mimbres Painted Pottery.* Albuquerque: School of American Research and University of New Mexico Press.

**Brown, G. M., T. C. Windes, and P. J. McKenna**

2002    Animas Anamnesis: Aztec Ruins or Anasazi Capital? Paper presented at the 67th annual meeting of the Society for American Archaeology, Denver.

**Brugge, D. M.**

1980    *A History of the Chaco Navajos.* Reports of the Chaco Center no. 4. Washington, DC: US Government Printing Office.

1984    *Tsegai: An Archeological Ethnohistory of the Chaco Region.* Washington, DC: National Park Service, US Department of the Interior.

**Bullard, W. R. Jr.**

1962    *The Cerro Colorado Site and Pithouse Architecture in the Southwestern United States prior to AD 900.* Papers of the Peabody Museum of Archaeology and Ethnology, vol. 44, no. 2. Cambridge, MA: Harvard University.

**Bullock, P. Y.**

1991    A Reappraisal of Anasazi Cannibalism. *Kiva* 57(1):5–16.

**Bullock, P. Y., ed.**

1998    *Deciphering Anasazi Violence.* Santa Fe, NM: HRM Books.

**Bunzel, R.**

1973    *Zuni Katcinas; An Analytical Study.* Glorieta, NM: Rio Grande Press.

**Bustard, W.**

1995    Genotype of Space: A Spatial Analysis of Domestic Structures in Chaco Canyon. Paper presented at the 60th annual meeting of the Society for American Archaeology, Minneapolis, MN.

1996    Space as Place: Small and Great House Spatial Organization in Chaco Canyon, New Mexico, AD 1000–1150. Ph.D. diss., University of New Mexico, Albuquerque.

2000 Chaco at the New Millennium: Nasty and Brutish? Paper presented at the 65th annual meeting of the Society for American Archaeology, Philadelphia.

2003 Pueblo Bonito: When a House Is Not a Home. In *Pueblo Bonito: Center of the Chacoan World*, edited by J. E. Neitzel, pp. 80–93. Washington, DC: Smithsonian Institution Press.

**Cameron, C. M.**

1984 A Regional View of Chipped Stone Raw Material Use in Chaco Canyon. In *Recent Research on Chaco Prehistory*, edited by W. J. Judge and J. D. Schelberg, pp. 137–152. Reports of the Chaco Center no. 8. Albuquerque, NM: Division of Cultural Research, National Park Service.

1995 Migration and the Movement of Southwestern Peoples. *Journal of Anthropological Archaeology* 14(2):104–124.

1997 The Chipped Stone of Chaco Canyon, New Mexico. In *Ceramics, Lithics, and Ornaments of Chaco Canyon*, vol. II, edited by F. J. Mathien, pp. 531–658. Publications in Archeology 18G, Chaco Canyon Studies. Santa Fe, NM: National Park Service, US Department of the Interior.

2001 Pink Chert, Projectile Points, and the Chacoan Regional System. *American Antiquity* 66(1):79–102.

2002 Sacred Earthen Architecture in the Northern Southwest: The Bluff Great House Berm. *American Antiquity* 67(4):677–695.

**Cameron, C. M., and H. W. Toll**

2001 Deciphering the Organization of Production in Chaco Canyon. *American Antiquity* 66(1):5–13.

**Carlson, R. A.**

1970 *White Mountain Redware.* Anthropological Papers no. 19. Tucson: University of Arizona Press.

**Carlson, R. L.**

1963 Basketmaker III Sites near Durango. University of Colorado Studies, Series in Anthropology 8. Boulder: University Press of Colorado.

**Carmack, R. M.**

1981 *The Quiché Mayas of Utatlán: The Evolution of a Highland Guatemala Kingdom.* Norman: University of Oklahoma Press.

**Carot, P.**

2001 *Le site de Loma Alta, Lac de Zacapu, Michoacan, Mexique.* Paris Monographs in American Archaeology 9, BAR International Series 920. Oxford: Archaeopress.

**Cater, J. D., and M. L. Chenault**

1988 Kiva Use Reinterpreted. *Southwestern Lore* 54(3):19–32.

**Cattanach, G. S. Jr.**

1980 *Long House, Mesa Verde National Park, Colorado.* Publications in Archeology 7H, Chaco Canyon Studies. Washington, DC: National Park Service, US Department of the Interior.

**Chaco World Database**
2004      http://sipapu.gsu.edu/html/chacoworld.html (accessed June 10, 2004).

**Cherry, J. F.**
1986      Polities and Palaces: Some Problems in Minoan State Formation. In
          *Peer Polity Interaction and Socio-Political Change*, edited by C. Renfrew and
          J. F. Cherry, pp. 19–45. Cambridge: Cambridge University Press.

**Churchill, M. J., K. Kuckelman, and M. D. Varien**
1998      Public Architecture in the Mesa Verde Region, AD 900 to 1300. Paper pre-
          sented at the 63rd annual meeting of the Society for American
          Archaeology, Seattle, WA.

**Cobean, R. H.**
1990      *La Cerámica de Tula, Hidalgo*. Mexico City: Instituto Nacional de
          Antropología e Historia.

**Cobean Transue, R. H., and E. Estrada Hernández**
1994      Ofrendas Toltecas en el Palacio Quemado de Tula. *Arqueología Mexicana*
          1(6):77–78.

**Coffey, G. D.**
2004      Regional Migration and Local Adaptation: A Study of Late Pueblo I and
          Early Pueblo I and Early Pueblo II Sites in the East Dove Creek Area. M.A.
          thesis, Northern Arizona University, Flagstaff.

**Coggins, C. C.**
1993      The Age of Teotihuacan and Its Mission Abroad. In *Teotihuacan: Art from
          the City of the Gods*, edited by K. Berrin and E. Pasztory, pp. 140–155. New
          York: Hudson.

**Conides, C. A.**
1997      Social Relations among Potters in Teotihuacan, Mexico. *Museum
          Anthropology* 21(3):39–54.

**Cooper, L. M.**
1997      Comparative Analysis of Chacoan Great Houses. In *Proceedings of the Space
          Syntax First International Symposium*, vol. II, pp. 22.1–22.11. London.

**Cordell, L. S.**
1984      *Prehistory of the Southwest*. San Diego: Academic Press.
1995      Tracing Migration Pathways from the Receiving End. *Journal of
          Anthropological Archaeology* 14(2):203–211.

**Cordell, L. S., and W. J. Judge**
2001      Perspectives on Chaco Society and Polity. In *Chaco Society and Polity: Papers
          from the 1999 Conference*, edited by L. S. Cordell, W. J. Judge, and J. Piper,
          pp. 1–12. NMAC Special Publication no. 4. Albuquerque: New Mexico
          Archeological Council.

**Cordell, L. S., W. J. Judge, and J. Piper, eds.**
2001      *Chaco Society and Polity: Papers from the 1999 Conference*. NMAC Special
          Publication no. 4. Albuquerque: New Mexico Archeological Council.

**Cowgill, G. L.**

2000    The Central Mexican Highlands from the Rise of Teotihuacan to the
Decline of Tula. In *The Cambridge History of the Native Peoples of the Americas*,
vol. II, Mesoamerica, part 1, edited by R. E. W. Adams and M. J. Macleod,
pp. 250–317. Cambridge: Cambridge University Press.

**Cowgill, G. L., J. H. Altschul, and R. S. Sload**

1994    Spatial Analysis of Teotihuacan: A Mesoamerican Metropolis. In *Intrasite
Spatial Analysis in Archaeology*, edited by H. J. Hietala, pp. 154–195.
Cambridge: Cambridge University Press.

**Creamer, W.**

1993    *The Architecture of Arroyo Hondo Pueblo, New Mexico*. Arroyo Hondo
Archaeological Series 7. School of American Research. Santa Fe, NM: SAR
Press.

**Creel, D., and R. Anyon**

2003    New Interpretations of Mimbres Public Architecture and Space:
Implications for Cultural Change. *American Antiquity* 68(1):67–92.

**Creel, D., and C. McKusick**

1994    Prehistoric Macaws and Parrots in the Mimbres Area, New Mexico.
*American Antiquity* 59(3):510–524.

**Crown, P. L.**

1991a   The Role of Exchange and Interaction in Salt-Gila Basin Hohokam
Prehistory. In *Exploring the Hohokam: Prehistoric Desert Peoples of the American
Southwest*, edited by G. J. Gumerman, pp. 383–415. Dragoon, AZ: Amerind
Foundation; Albuquerque: University of New Mexico Press.

1991b   The Hohokam: Current Views of Prehistory and the Regional System. In
*Chaco and Hohokam: Prehistoric Regional Systems in the American Southwest*,
edited by P. Crown and W. J. Judge, pp. 135–157. School of American
Research Advanced Seminar Series. Santa Fe, NM: SAR Press.

1994    *Ceramics and Ideology: Salado Polychrome Pottery*. Albuquerque: University of
New Mexico Press.

**Crown, P. L., and W. J. Judge**

1991a   Introduction. In *Chaco and Hohokam: Prehistoric Regional Systems in the
American Southwest*, edited by P. L. Crown and W. J. Judge, pp. 1–9. School
of American Research Advanced Seminar Series. Santa Fe, NM: SAR Press.

1991b   Synthesis and Conclusions. In *Chaco and Hohokam: Prehistoric Regional
Systems in the American Southwest*, edited by P. L. Crown and W. J. Judge, pp.
293–308. School of American Research Advanced Seminar Series. Santa
Fe, NM: SAR Press.

**Crown, P. L., and W. J. Judge, eds.**

1991    *Chaco and Hohokam: Prehistoric Regional Systems in the American Southwest*.
School of American Research Advanced Seminar Series. Santa Fe, NM:
SAR Press.

**Crown, P. L., J. D. Orcutt, and T. A. Kohler**

1996    Pueblo Cultures in Transition: The Northern Rio Grande. In *The Prehistoric Pueblo World, AD 1100–1300*, edited by M. A. Adler, pp. 188–204. Tucson: University of Arizona Press.

**Crown, P. L., and W. H. Wills**

2003    Modifying Pottery and Kivas at Chaco: Pentimento, Restoration, or Renewal? *American Antiquity* 68(3):511–532.

**Cully, A. C.**

1985    Pollen Evidence of Past Subsistence and Environment at Chaco Canyon, New Mexico. In *Environment and Subsistence of Chaco Canyon*, edited by F. J. Mathien, pp. 135–245. Publications in Archeology 18E, Chaco Canyon Studies. Albuquerque, NM: National Park Service, US Department of the Interior.

**Cully, A. C., M. L. Donaldson, M. S. Toll, and K. B. Kelley**

1982    Agriculture in the Bis sa'ani Community. In *Bis sa'ani: A Late Bonito Phase Community on Escavada Wash, Northwest New Mexico*, vol. 1, edited by C. D. Breternitz, D. E. Doyel, and M. P. Marshall, pp. 115–166. Navajo Nation Papers in Anthropology no. 14. Window Rock, AZ: Navajo Nation Cultural Resource Management Program.

**Damp, J. E.**

1999    *Chuska Chronologies, Houses, and Hogans: Archaeological and Ethnographic Inquiry along N30-31 between Mexican Springs and Navajo, McKinley County, New Mexico*. Zuni Cultural Resource Enterprise Research Series 10. Zuni, NM: Pueblo of Zuni.

**Danson, E. B.**

1957    *An Archaeological Survey of West Central New Mexico and East Central Arizona*. Papers of the Peabody Museum of Archaeology and Ethnology, vol. XLIV, no. 1. Cambridge, MA: Harvard University.

**Darling, J. A.**

1998    Mass Inhumation and the Execution of Witches in the American Southwest. *American Anthropologist* 100(3):732–752.

**Davenport, W. H.**

1986    Two Kinds of Value in the Eastern Solomon Islands. In *The Social Life of Things: Commodities in Cultural Perspective*, edited by A. Appadurai, pp. 95–109. Cambridge: Cambridge University Press.

**David, N., and J. Sterner**

1999    Wonderful Society: The Burgess Shale Creatures, Mandara Polities, and the Nature of Prehistory. In *Beyond Chiefdoms: Pathways to Complexity in Africa*, edited by S. K. McIntosh, pp. 97–109. Cambridge: Cambridge University Press.

**Davies, N.**

1977    *The Toltecs until the Fall of Tula*. Norman: University of Oklahoma Press.

REFERENCES

**Dean, J. S.**

1992    Environmental Factors in the Evolution of the Chacoan Sociopolitical System. In *Anasazi Regional Organization and the Chaco System*, edited by D. E. Doyel, pp. 35–43. Anthropological Papers no. 5. Albuquerque: Maxwell Museum of Anthropology, University of New Mexico.

1996    Demography, Environment, and Subsistence Stress. In *Evolving Complexity and Environmental Risk in the Prehistoric Southwest*, edited by J. A. Tainter and B. B. Tainter, pp. 25–56. Santa Fe Institute Studies in the Sciences of Complexity Proceedings, vol. 24. Reading, MA: Addison-Wesley.

2000    Complexity Theory and Sociocultural Change in the American Southwest. In *The Way the Wind Blows: Climate, History, and Human Action*, edited by R. McIntosh, J. Tainter, and S. McIntosh, pp. 89–118. New York: Columbia University Press.

**Dean, J. S., and G. Funkhouser**

2002    Dendroclimatology and Fluvial Chronology in Chaco Canyon. Appendix A in *Relation of "Bonito" Paleo-channels and Base-Level Variations to Anasazi Occupation, Chaco Canyon, New Mexico*, edited by E. R. Force, R. G. Vivian, T. C. Windes, and J. S. Dean, pp. 39–41. Archaeological Series 194. Tucson: Arizona State Museum, University of Arizona Press.

**Dean, J. S., and C. Van West**

2002    Environment-Behavior Relationships in Southwestern Colorado. In *Seeking the Center Place: Archaeology and Ancient Communities in the Mesa Verde Region*, edited by M. D. Varien and R. H. Wilshusen, pp. 81–99. Salt Lake City: University of Utah Press.

**Dean, J. S., and R. L. Warren**

1983    Dendrochronology. In *The Architecture and Dendrochronology of Chetro Ketl, Chaco Canyon, New Mexico*, edited by S. H. Lekson, pp. 105–240. Reports of the Chaco Center no. 6. Albuquerque, NM: Division of Cultural Research, National Park Service.

**DeBoer, W. R.**

2001    On-and-Off-Again Complexity from South America to the Southwest. In *Examining the Course of Southwestern Archaeology: The Durango Conference, September, 1995*, edited by D. A. Phillips and L. Sebastian, pp. 19–31. NMAC Special Publication no. 3. Albuquerque: New Mexico Archeological Council.

**Di Peso, C. C.**

1974    *Casas Grandes: A Fallen Trading Center of the Gran Chichimeca*. Vols. 1–3, series 9. Dragoon, AZ: Amerind Foundation.

**Di Peso, C. C., J. B. Rinaldo, and G. J. Fenner**

1974    *Casas Grandes: A Fallen Trading Center of the Gran Chichimeca*. Vol. 4. Dragoon, AZ: The Amerind Foundation.

**Diamond, J.**
1992    *The Third Chimpanzee: The Evolution and Future of the Human Animal.* New
        York: Harper Collins.

**Dietler, M.**
2001    Feasts and Commensal Politics in the Political Economy: Food, Power, and
        Status in Prehistoric Europe. In *Feasts: Archaeological and Ethnographic
        Perspectives,* edited by M. Dietler and B. Hayden, pp. 87–125. Washington,
        DC: Smithsonian Institution Press.

**Dittert, A. E.**
1959    Culture Change in the Cebolleta Mesa Region, Central Western New
        Mexico. Ph.D. diss., University of Arizona, Tucson.

**Doebley, J. F.**
1981    Plant Remains Recovered by Flotation from Trash at Salmon Ruin, New
        Mexico. *Kiva* 46(3):169–187.

**Donaldson, M. L., and M. S. Toll**
1982    Prehistoric Subsistence in the Bis sa'ani Community Area: Evidence from
        Flotation, Macrobotanical Remains, and Wood Identification. In *Bis sa'ani:
        A Late Bonito Phase Community on Escavada Wash, Northwest New Mexico,*
        vol. 3, edited by C. D. Breternitz, D. E. Doyel, and M. P. Marshall, pp.
        1099–1180. Navajo Nation Papers in Anthropology no. 14. Window Rock,
        AZ: Navajo Nation Cultural Resource Management Program.

**Doolittle, W. E.**
1990    *Canal Irrigation in Prehistoric Mexico: The Sequence of Technological Change.*
        Austin: University of Texas Press.

**Doxtater, D.**
2002    A Hypothetical Layout of Chaco Canyon Structures via Large-Scale
        Alignments between Significant Natural Features. *Kiva* 68(1):23–47.

**Doyel, D. E.**
1991    Hohokam Exchange and Interaction. In *Chaco and Hohokam: Prehistoric
        Regional Systems in the American Southwest,* edited by P. L. Crown and W. J.
        Judge, pp. 225–252. School of American Research Advanced Seminar
        Series. Santa Fe, NM: SAR Press.

**Doyel, D. E., C. D. Breternitz, and M. P. Marshall**
1984    Chacoan Community Structure: Bis sa'ani Pueblo and the Chaco Halo. In
        *Recent Research on Chaco Prehistory,* edited by W. J. Judge and J. D.
        Schelberg, pp. 37–54. Reports of the Chaco Center no. 8. Albuquerque,
        NM: Division of Cultural Research, National Park Service.

**Doyel, D. E., S. K. Fish, and P. R. Fish, eds.**
2000    *The Hohokam Village Revisited.* Fort Collins, CO: Southwestern and Rocky
        Mountain Division of the American Association for the Advancement of
        Science.

REFERENCES

**Dozier, E. P.**
1960    The Pueblos of the Southwestern United States. *Journal of the Royal Anthropological Institute of Great Britain and Ireland* 90(I-II):146–160.

**Drager, D. L., and T. R. Lyons**
1985    Remote Sensing: Photogrammetry in Archeology: The Chaco Mapping Project. In *Remote Sensing: A Handbook for Archeologists and Cultural Resource Managers*, edited by T. R. Lyons and T. E. Avery, supp. no. 10. Washington, DC: Division of Cultural Resource Management, National Park Service.

**Drennan, R. D.**
1999    Analytical Scales, Building Blocks, and Comparisons. In *Towns and Regional Polities in the Prehistoric American Southwest and Southeast*, edited by J. E. Neitzel, pp. 255–259. Albuquerque: University of New Mexico Press.

**Duff, A. I.**
1994a    Post-Chacoan Community Dynamics as Revealed by Household Interaction. Paper presented at the 59th annual meeting of the Society for American Archaeology, Anaheim, CA.

1994b    The Scope of Post-Chacoan Community Organization in the Lower Zuni River Region. In *Exploring Social, Political, and Economic Organization in the Zuni Region*, edited by T. L. Howell and T. Stone, pp. 25–45. Anthropological Research Papers no. 46. Tempe: Arizona State University.

1998    The Process of Migration in the Late Prehistoric Southwest. In *Migration and Reorganization: The Pueblo IV Period in the American Southwest*, edited by K. A. Spielmann, pp. 31–52. Anthropological Research Papers no. 51. Tempe: Arizona State University.

2000    Scale, Interaction and Regional Analysis in Late Pueblo Prehistory. In *The Archaeology of Regional Interaction: Religion, Warfare, and Exchange across the American Southwest and Beyond*, edited by M. Hegmon, pp. 71–98. Boulder: University Press of Colorado.

2002    *Western Pueblo Identities: Regional Interaction, Migration, and Transformation.* Tucson: University of Arizona Press.

**Duff, A. I., and G. Schachner**
n.d.    Becoming Central: Social Processes in the Emergence of Zuni. In *Hinterlands and Heartlands in Southwestern Prehistory*, forthcoming, edited by A. Sullivan and J. Bayman. Tucson: University of Arizona Press.

**Duff, A. I., and R. H. Wilshusen**
2000    Prehistoric Population Dynamics in the Northern San Juan Region, AD 950–1300. *Kiva* 66(1):167–190.

**Durand, K. R.**
2003    Function of Chaco-Era Great Houses. *Kiva* 69(2):141–169.

**Durand, S. R.**
1992    Architectural Change and Chaco Prehistory. Ph.D. diss., University of Washington, Seattle.

**Durand, S. R., and K. R. Durand**
2000    Notes from the Edge: Settlement Pattern Changes at the Guadalupe
        Community. In *Great House Communities across the Chacoan Landscape*, edited
        by J. Kantner and N. M. Mahoney, pp. 101–110. Anthropological Papers
        no. 64. Tucson: University of Arizona Press.

**Durand, S. R., P. H. Shelley, R. C. Antweiler, and H. E. Taylor**
1999    Trees, Chemistry, and Prehistory in the American Southwest. *Journal of
        Archaeological Science* 26(2):185–203.

**Dykeman, D. D., and K. Langenfeld**
1987    *Prehistory and History of the La Plata Valley, New Mexico.* Contributions to
        Anthropology no. 891. Farmington, NM: Division of Conservation
        Archaeology, San Juan College.

**Earle, T.**
2001    Economic Support of Chaco Canyon Society. *American Antiquity*
        66(1):26–35.

**Eddy, F. W.**
1966    *Prehistory of the Navajo Reservoir District.* Papers in Anthropology no. 15,
        parts 1 and 2. Santa Fe: Museum of New Mexico.

1972    Culture Ecology and the Prehistory of the Navajo Reservoir District.
        *Southwestern Lore* 38(1-2):1–75.

1974    Population Dislocation in the Navaho Reservoir District, New Mexico and
        Colorado. *American Antiquity* 39(1):75–84.

1977    *Archaeological Investigations at Chimney Rock Mesa: 1970–1972.* Memoir no. 1.
        Boulder: Colorado Archaeological Society.

1993    Recent Research at Chimney Rock. In *The Chimney Rock Archaeological
        Symposium, October 20–21, 1990, Durango, Colorado*, edited by J. M. Malville
        and G. Matlock, pp. 14–19. General Technical Report RM-227. Fort
        Collins, CO: Rocky Mountain Forest and Range Experiment Station, US
        Department of Agriculture.

**Ekholm, G. F.**
1942    *Excavations at Guasave, Sinaloa.* Anthropological Papers no. 38, part 2. New
        York: American Museum of Natural History.

**Ekholm, K.**
1972    *Power and Prestige: The Rise and Fall of the Kongo Kingdom.* Upsala: Skriv
        Service.

**Ellis, F. H.**
1950    Big Kivas, Little Kivas, and Moiety Houses in Historical Reconstruction.
        *Southwestern Journal of Anthropology* 6(3):286–302.

**Elson, M. D., and D. R. Abbott**
2000    Organizational Variability in Platform Mound–Building Groups of the
        American Southwest. In *Alternative Leadership Strategies in the Prehispanic
        Southwest*, edited by B. J. Mills, pp. 117–135. Tucson: University of Arizona
        Press.

**English, N. B., J. L. Betancourt, J. S. Dean, and J. Quade**

2001    Strontium Isotopes Reveal Distant Sources of Architectural Timber in Chaco Canyon, New Mexico. *Proceedings of the National Association of Science* 98(21):11891–11896.

**Ezzo, J. A., C. M. Johnson, and T. D. Price**

1997    Analytical Perspectives on Prehistoric Migration: A Case Study from East Central Arizona. *Journal of Archaeological Science* 24(5):447–466.

**Fagan, B.**

2005    *Chaco Canyon: Archaeologists Explore the Lives of an Ancient Society.* Oxford: Oxford University Press.

**Feinman, G. M.**

1992    An Outside Perspective on Chaco Canyon. In *Anasazi Regional Organization and the Chaco System*, edited by D. E. Doyel, pp. 177–182. Anthropological Papers no. 5. Albuquerque: Maxwell Museum of Anthropology, University of New Mexico.

2000    Dual-Processual Theory and Social Formations in the Southwest. In *Alternative Leadership Strategies in the Prehispanic Southwest*, edited by B. J. Mills, pp. 207–224. Tucson: University of Arizona Press.

**Feinman, G. M., K. G. Lightfoot, and S. Upham**

2000    Political Hierarchies and Organizational Strategies in the Puebloan Southwest. *American Antiquity* 65(3):449–470.

**Ferguson, T. J., and E. R. Hart**

1985    *A Zuni Atlas.* Norman and London: University of Oklahoma Press.

**Fernandez-Armesto, F.**

2001    *Civilizations: Culture, Ambition, and the Transformation of Nature.* New York: Free Press.

**Fewkes, J. W.**

1917    A Prehistoric Mesa Verde Pueblo and Its People (Far View House). In *Smithsonian Institution Annual Report for 1916*, pp. 416–488. Washington, DC: Smithsonian Institution Press.

1922    Archaeological Field-work on the Mesa Verde National Park. *Smithsonian Institution Miscellaneous Collections* 72(15):64–83.

**Fish, S. K.**

1999    How Complex Were the Southwestern Great Towns' Polities? In *Great Towns and Regional Polities in the Prehistoric American Southwest and Southeast*, edited by J. E. Neitzel, pp. 45–58. Albuquerque: University of New Mexico Press.

**Flannery, K. V.**

2002    The Origins of the Village Revisited: From Nuclear to Extended Households. *American Antiquity* 67(3):417–433.

**Flannery, K. V., and J. Marcus**

1976    Evolution of the Public Building in Formative Oaxaca. In *Cultural*

*Continuity and Change, Essays in Honor of James B. Griffin*, edited by C. E. Cleland, pp. 205–221. New York: Academic Press.

**Fletcher, R.**
1995    *The Limits of Settlement Growth.* Cambridge: Cambridge University Press.

**Floyd, M. L., and T. A. Kohler**
1990    Current Productivity and Prehistoric Use of Pinyon (*Pinus edulis*, Pinaceae) in the Dolores Archaeological Project Area, Southwestern Colorado. *Economic Botany* 44(2):141–156.

**Folan, W. J., J. M. Hau, J. Marcus, W. F. Miller, and R. González Heredia**
2001    Los Caminos de Calakmul, Campeche. *Ancient Mesoamerica* 12(2):293–298.

**Folan, W. J., J. Marcus, and W. F. Miller**
1995    Verification of a Maya Settlement Model through Remote Sensing. *Cambridge Archaeological Journal* 5(2):277–283.

**Folsom, F., and M. Folsom**
1993    *America's Ancient Treasures.* Albuquerque: University of New Mexico Press.

**Force, E. R., R. G. Vivian, T. C. Windes, and J. S. Dean, eds.**
2002    *Relation of "Bonito" Paleo-channels and Base-Level Variations to Anasazi Occupation, Chaco Canyon, New Mexico.* Archeological Series 194. Tucson: Arizona State Museum, University of Arizona Press.

**Ford, R. I.**
1972    Barter, Gift, or Violence: An Analysis of Tewa Intertribal Exchange. In *Social Exchange and Interaction*, edited by E. Wilmsen, pp. 21–45, Memoirs no. 46. Ann Arbor: University of Michigan.

**Foster, M. K.**
1996    Language and the Culture History of North America. In *Languages*, vol. 17 of *Handbook of North American Indians*, edited by I. Goddard, pp. 64–110. Washington, DC: Smithsonian Institution Press.

**Fowler, A. P., and J. R. Stein**
1992    The Anasazi Great House in Space, Time and Paradigm. In *Anasazi Regional Organization and the Chaco System*, edited by D. E. Doyel, pp. 101–122. Anthropological Papers no. 5. Albuquerque: Maxwell Museum of Anthropology, University of New Mexico.

**Fowler, A. P., J. R. Stein, and R. Anyon**
1987    An Archaeological Reconnaissance of West-Central New Mexico, The Anasazi Monuments Project. Report submitted to State of New Mexico, Office of Cultural Affairs, Historic Preservation Division, Albuquerque.

**Fox, J. W.**
1981    The Late Postclassic Eastern Frontier of Mesoamerica: Cultural Innovation along the Periphery. *Current Anthropology* 22(4):321–346.

1987    *Maya Postclassic State Formation: Segmentary Lineage Migration in Advancing Frontiers.* Cambridge: Cambridge University Press.

REFERENCES

Fox, R.
1967    The Keresan Bridge: A Problem in Pueblo Ethnology. London School of Economics, Monographs on Social Anthropology 35. London: Athlone Press.

Franklin, H.
1980    Salmon Ruin Ceramics Laboratory Report. In *Investigations at the Salmon Site: The Structure of Chacoan Society in the Northern Southwest*, vol. II, edited by C. Irwin-Williams and P. H. Shelley, pp. ii–482. Final Report to Funding Agencies. Portales: Eastern New Mexico University.

Frazier, K.
1986    *People of Chaco: A Canyon and Its Culture*. New York: W. W. Norton.
1999    *People of Chaco: A Canyon and Its Culture*. 2d ed. New York: W. W. Norton.
2005    *People of Chaco: A Canyon and Its Culture*. 3rd ed. New York: W. W. Norton.

Frierman, J. D., ed.
1969    *The Natalie Wood Collection of Pre-Columbian Ceramics from Chupicuaro, Guanajuato, Mexico at UCLA*. Los Angeles: University of California, Los Angeles Museum and Laboratories of Ethnic Arts and Technology.

Fritz, J. M.
1978    Paleopsychology Today: Ideational Systems and Human Adaptation in Prehistory. In *Social Archeology: Beyond Subsistence and Dating*, edited by C. L. Redman, M. J. Berman, E. V. Curtin, W. T. Langhorne Jr., N. M. Versaggi, and J. C. Wanser, pp. 37–59. New York: Academic Press.

Fuller, S. L.
1984    *Late Anasazi Pottery Kilns in the Yellowjacket District, Southwestern Colorado*. CASA Papers no. 4, Cortez, CO: CASA.

Gabriel, K.
1991    *Roads to Center Place: A Cultural Atlas of Chaco Canyon and the Anasazi*. Boulder, CO: Johnson Publishing.
1996    *Gambler Way: Indian Gaming in Mythology, History, and Archaeology in North America*. Boulder, CO: Johnson Publishing.

Ganot Rodríguez, J., and A. A. Peschard Fernández
1995    The Archaeological Site of Cañon del Molino, Durango, México. In *The Gran Chichimeca: Essays on the Archaeology and Ethnohistory of Northern Mesoamerica*, edited by J. E. Reyman, pp. 146–178. Brookfield, VT: Avebury.

García Chávez, R. E.
1991    Desarrollo Cultural en Azcapotzalco y el Area Suroccidental de la Cuenca de México, desde el Preclásico Medio Hasta el Epiclásico. Tesis de Licenciatura, Escuela Nacional de Antropología e Historia, México.

Gaxiola González, M.
1999    Huapalcalco y las tradiciones alfareras del epiclásico. *Arqueología* 21:45–72.

Gillespie, W. B.
1976    *Culture Change at the Ute Canyon Site: A Study of the Pithouse to Kiva Transition in the Mesa Verde Region*. M.A. thesis, University of Colorado, Boulder.

1984    Una Vida. In *Great Pueblo Architecture of Chaco Canyon, New Mexico*, edited by
        S. H. Lekson, pp. 79–94. Publications in Archeology 18B, Chaco Canyon
        Studies. Albuquerque, NM: National Park Service, US Department of the
        Interior.

**Gilman, P. A.**
1987    Architecture as Artifact: Pit Structures and Pueblos in the American
        Southwest. *American Antiquity* 52(3):538–564.

**Gilpin, D.**
2003    Chacoan-Era Site Clustering and the Concept of Communities. *Kiva*
        69(2):171–205.

**Gilpin, D., and L. Benallie Jr.**
2000    Juniper Cove and Early Anasazi Community Structure West of the Chuska
        Mountains. In *Foundations of Anasazi Culture: The Basketmaker-Pueblo
        Transition*, edited by P. F. Reed, pp. 161–173. Salt Lake City: University of
        Utah Press.

**Gilpin, D., D. D. Dykeman, and P. F. Reed**
1996    *Anasazi Community Architecture in the Chuska Valley*. Albuquerque: New
        Mexico Archaeological Council.

**Gilpin, D., and D. E. Purcell**
2000    Peach Springs Revisited: Surface Recording and Excavation on the South
        Chaco Slope, New Mexico. In *Great House Communities across the Chacoan
        Landscape*, edited by J. Kantner and N. M. Mahoney, pp. 28–38.
        Anthropological Papers no. 64. Tucson: University of Arizona Press.

**Gladwin, H. S.**
1945    *The Chaco Branch: Excavations at White Mound and in the Red Mesa Valley*.
        Medallion Papers no. 15. Globe, AZ: Gila Pueblo.

**Glowacki, D. M., H. Neff, M. M. Hegmon, J. W. Kendrick, and W. J. Judge**
2002    Resource Use, Red-Ware Production, and Vessel Distribution in the
        Northern San Juan Region. In *Ceramic Production and Circulation in the
        Greater Southwest*, edited by D. M. Glowacki and H. Neff, pp. 67–73.
        Monograph 44. Los Angeles: The Cotsen Institute of Archaeology,
        University of California at Los Angeles.

**Godelier, M.**
1999    *The Enigma of the Gift*. Translated by N. Scott. Chicago: University of
        Chicago Press.

**González Crespo, N., S. Garza Tarazona, H. de Vega Nova, P. Mayer Guala, and
G. Canto Aguilar**
1995    Archaeological Investigations at Xochicalco, Morelos: 1984 and 1986.
        *Ancient Mesoamerica* 6(2):223–236.

**Gooding, J. C., ed.**
1980    The Durango South Project: Archaeological Salvage of Two Late
        Basketmaker III Sites in the Durango District. Anthropological Papers no.
        34. Tucson: University of Arizona Press.

**Grebinger, P.**

1973    Prehistoric Social Organization in Chaco Canyon, New Mexico: An Alternative Reconstruction. *Kiva* 39(1):3–23.

**Gregory, D. A.**

1991    Form and Variation in Hohokam Settlement Patterns. In *Chaco and Hohokam: Prehistoric Regional Systems in the American Southwest*, edited by P. L. Crown and W. J. Judge, pp. 159–193. School of American Research Advanced Seminar Series. Santa Fe, NM: SAR Press.

**Gumerman, G. J., ed.**

1991    *Exploring the Hohokam*. Albuquerque: University of New Mexico Press.

**Gupta, A., and J. Ferguson**

1997    Discipline and Practice: "The Field" as Site, Method, and Location in Anthropology. In *Anthropological Locations: Boundaries and Grounds of a Field Science*, edited by A. Gupta and J. Ferguson, pp. 1–47. Berkeley: University of California Press.

**Guyer, J., and S. L. Belinga**

1995    Wealth in People as Wealth in Knowledge: Accumulation and Composition in Equatorial Africa. *Journal of African History* (36):91–120.

**Habicht-Mauche, J. A.**

2000    Pottery, Food, Hides, and Women: Labor, Production, and Exchange across the Protohistoric Plains-Pueblo Frontier. In *The Archaeology of Regional Interaction: Religion, Warfare, and Exchange across the American Southwest and Beyond*, edited by M. Hegmon, pp. 209–234. Boulder: University Press of Colorado.

**Hagstrum, M.**

2001    Household Production in Chaco Canyon Society. *American Antiquity* 66(1):47–55.

**Hall, S. A.**

1977    Late Quaternary Sedimentation and Paleoecologic History of Chaco Canyon, New Mexico. *Geological Society of America Bulletin* 88(11):1593–1618.

1983    Holocene Stratigraphy and Paleoecology of Chaco Canyon. In *Chaco Canyon Country: American Geomorphological Field Group 1983 Field Trip Guidebook*, edited by S. G. Wells, D. W. Love, and T. W. Gardner, pp. 219–226. Albuquerque, NM: American Geomorphological Field Group.

**Hallasi, J. A.**

1979    Archeological Excavation at the Escalante Site, Dolores, Colorado, 1975 and 1976. In *The Archeology and Stabilization of the Dominguez and Escalante Ruins*, by A. Reed, J. Hallasi, A. White, and D. Breternitz, pp. 197–425.

Cultural Resource Series 7. Denver: Bureau of Land Management, Colorado State Office.

**Harper, R. A., M. K. Swift, B. J. Mills, and J. Winter**
1988    *The Casamero and Pierre's Outliers Survey: An Archaeological Class III Inventory of the BLM Lands Surrounding the Outliers.* Albuquerque: Office of Contract Archaeology, University of New Mexico.

**Hastorf, C. A.**
1990    One Path to the Heights: Negotiating Political Inequality in the Sausa of Peru. In *The Evolution of Political Systems: Sociopolitics in Small-Scale Sedentary Societies,* edited by S. Upham, pp. 147–177. Cambridge: Cambridge University Press.

**Haury, E. W.**
1945    The Problem of Contacts between the Southwestern United States and Mexico. *Southwestern Journal of Anthropology* 1(1):55–74.

1958    Evidence at Point of Pines for a Prehistoric Migration from Northern Arizona. In *Migrations in New World Culture History,* edited by R. Thompson, pp. 1–6. Social Science Bulletin 27. Tucson: University of Arizona Press.

1976    *The Hohokam: Desert Farmers and Craftsmen.* Tucson: University of Arizona Press.

1985    *Mogollon Culture in the Forestdale Valley, East-Central Arizona.* Tucson: University of Arizona Press.

1986    Thoughts after Sixty Years as a Southwestern Archaeologist. In *E. W. Haury's Prehistory of the American Southwest,* edited by J. J. Reid and D. E. Doyel, pp. 435–464. Tucson: University of Arizona Press.

**Hawkes, J.**
1968    The Proper Study of Mankind. *Antiquity* 42(168):255–262.

**Hayden, B.**
1995    Pathways to Power: Principles for Creating Socioeconomic Inequalities. In *Foundations of Social Inequality,* edited by T. D. Price and G. M. Feinman, pp. 15–86. New York: Plenum Press.

**Hayes, A. C.**
1964    *The Archeological Survey of Wetherill Mesa, Mesa Verde National Park, Colorado.* Archeological Research Series 7-A. Washington, DC: National Park Service, US Department of the Interior.

1981    A Survey of Chaco Canyon Archeology. In *Archeological Surveys of Chaco Canyon, New Mexico,* compiled by A. C. Hayes, D. M. Brugge, and W. J. Judge, pp. 1–68. Publications in Archeology 18A, Chaco Canyon Studies. Washington, DC: National Park Service, US Department of the Interior.

**Hayes, A. C., D. M. Brugge, and W. J. Judge**
1981    *Archeological Surveys of Chaco Canyon, New Mexico.* Publications in Archeology 18A, Chaco Canyon Studies. Washington, DC: National Park Service, US Department of the Interior.

REFERENCES

Hayes, A. C., and J. A. Lancaster
1975    *Badger House Community, Mesa Verde National Park.* Publications in
        Archeology 7E, Chaco Canyon Studies. Washington, DC: National Park
        Service, US Department of the Interior.

Hayes, A. C., and T. C. Windes
1975    An Anasazi Shrine in Chaco Canyon. In *Collected Papers in Honor of Florence
        Hawley Ellis*, edited by T. R. Frisbie, pp. 143–156. Papers of the
        Archaeological Society of New Mexico no. 2. Norman, OK: Hooper Press;
        Santa Fe: Archaeological Society of New Mexico.

Hays-Gilpin, K., and J. H. Hill
2000    The Flower World in Prehistoric Southwestern Material Culture. In *The
        Archaeology of Regional Interaction*, edited by M. Hegmon, pp. 411–428.
        Boulder: University Press of Colorado.

Healan, D. M., J. M. Kerley, and G. J. Bey
1983    Excavation and Preliminary Analysis of an Obsidian Workshop in Tula,
        Hidalgo, Mexico. *Journal of Field Archaeology* 10(2):127–145.

Hegmon, M.
2002    Recent Issues in the Archaeology of the Mimbres Region of the North
        American Southwest. *Journal of Archaeological Research* 10(4):307–357.
2003    Setting Theoretical Egos Aside: Issues and Theory in North American
        Archaeology. *American Antiquity* 68(23):213–243.

Helms, M. W.
1988    *Ulysses' Sail: An Ethnographic Odyssey of Power, Knowledge, and Geographical
        Distance.* Princeton, NJ: Princeton University Press.
1993    *Craft and the Kingly Ideal: Art, Trade, and Power.* Austin: University of Texas
        Press.

Hensler, K. N., and E. Blinman
2002    Experimental Ceramic Technology—Or, The Road to Ruin(s) Is Paved
        with Crack(ed) Pots. In *Traditions, Transitions, and Technologies: Themes in
        Southwestern Archaeology*, edited by S. H. Schlanger, pp. 366–385. Boulder:
        University Press of Colorado.

Herr, S. A.
2001    *Beyond Chaco: Great Kiva Communities on the Mogollon Rim Frontier.*
        Anthropological Papers no. 66. Tucson: University of Arizona Press.

Hers, M.
1989    *Los toltecas en tierras Chichimecas.* Cuadernos de Investigaciones Estéticas,
        no. 35. México, DF: Instituto de Investigaciones Estéticas, Universidad
        Nacional Autónoma de México.

Hill, J. N.
1970    Broken K Pueblo: Prehistoric Social Organization in the American
        Southwest. Anthropological Papers no. 18. Tucson: University of Arizona
        Press.

**Hill, W. D., and J. E. Clark**
2001    Sports, Gambling, and Government: America's First Social Compact? *American Anthropologist* 103(2):331–345.

**Holien, T., and R. Pickering**
1978    Analogues in a Chalchihuites Culture Sacrificial Burial to Late Mesoamerican Ceremonialism. In *Middle Classic Mesoamerica: AD 400–700*, edited by E. Pasztory, pp. 145–157. New York: Columbia University Press.

**Holsinger, S. J.**
1901    Report on Prehistoric Ruins of Chaco Canyon National Monument. Unpublished paper on file, General Land Office, National Archives, Washington, DC.

**Horton, R.**
1971    Stateless Societies in the History of Africa. In *History of West Africa: Volume I*, edited by J. F. A. Ajayi and M. Crowder, pp. 78–119. London: Longmann.

**Hosler, D.**
1994    *The Sounds and Colors of Power: The Sacred Metallurgical Technology of Ancient West Mexico.* Cambridge, MA: MIT Press.

**Hosler, D., and A. MacFarlane**
1996    Copper Sources, Metal Production, and Metals Trade in Late Postclassic Mesoamerica. *Science* 273(5283):1819–1824.

**Hough, W.**
1907    *Antiquities of the Upper Gila and Salt River Valleys in Arizona and New Mexico.* Bureau of American Ethnology Bulletin 35. Washington, DC: Government Printing Office.

1914    *Culture of the Ancient Pueblos of the Upper Gila Region, New Mexico.* Bulletin 87. Washington, DC: United States National Museum.

**Howard, J. B.**
1993    A Paleohydraulic Approach to Examining Agricultural Intensification in Hohokam Irrigation Systems. In *Economic Aspects of Water Management in the Prehispanic New World*, edited by V. Scarborough and B. Isaac, pp. 263–324. Research in Economic Anthropology 7. Greenwich, CT: JAI Press.

1996    Measuring Complexity in Irrigation Societies. In *Debating Complexity: Proceedings of the 26th Annual Chacmool Conference*, edited by D. Meyer, P. Dawson, and D. Hanna, pp. 297–303. Calgary, Alberta: The Archaeological Association of the University of Calgary.

**Huntley, D., N. Mahoney, and K. Kintigh**
1998    Modeling Cibolan Community Interaction through Ceramic Compositional Analysis. Paper presented at the annual meeting of the Society for American Archaeology, Seattle, WA.

**Hurst, W. B.**
2000    Chaco Outlier or "Wannabe?" Comments and Observations on a
        Provincial, Chacoesque Great House at Edge of the Cedars Ruin, Utah. In
        *Great House Communities across the Chacoan Landscape*, edited by J. Kantner
        and N. M. Mahoney, pp. 63–78. Anthropological Papers no. 64. Tucson:
        University of Arizona Press.

**Hurst, W. B., and J. D. Till**
2002    Some Observations Regarding the "Chaco Phenomenon" in the
        Northwestern San Juan Provinces. Paper presented at the annual meeting
        of the Society for American Archaeology, Denver.

**Ingpen, R., and P. Wilkinson**
1990    *Encyclopedia of Mysterious Places*. New York: Viking Press.

**Isbell, W. H.**
2000    What We Should Be Studying: The "Imagined Community" and the
        "Natural Community." In *The Archaeology of Communities: A New World
        Perspective*, edited by M. A. Canuto and J. Yeager, pp. 243–266. London:
        Routledge.

**Jennings, J. D.**
1966    *Glen Canyon: A Summary*. Anthropological Papers no. 81. Glen Canyon
        Series 31. Salt Lake City: University of Utah Press.

**Johnson, C. D.**
2003    Mesa Verde Region Towers: A View from Above. *Kiva* 68(4):323–340.

**Johnson, F.**
1966    Archaeology in an Emergency. *Science* 152(3529):1592–1597.

**Johnson, G. A.**
1982    Organizational Structure and Scalar Stress. In *Theory and Explanation
        in Archaeology: The Southampton Conference*, edited by C. Renfrew,
        M. J. Rowlands, and B. Abbott Segraves, pp. 389–421. New York: Academic
        Press.

1989    Dynamics of Southwestern Prehistory: Far Outside, Looking In. In
        *Dynamics of Southwest Prehistory*, edited by L. S. Cordell and G. J.
        Gumerman, pp. 371–389. Washington, DC: Smithsonian Institution Press.

**Judd, N. M.**
1954    *The Material Culture of Pueblo Bonito*. Smithsonian Miscellaneous
        Collections, vol. 124. Washington, DC: Smithsonian Institution Press.

1959    *Pueblo del Arroyo, Chaco Canyon, New Mexico*. Smithsonian Miscellaneous
        Collections, vol. 138, no. 1. Washington, DC: Smithsonian Institution
        Press.

1964    *The Architecture of Pueblo Bonito*. Smithsonian Miscellaneous Collections,
        vol. 145, no. 1. Washington, DC: Smithsonian Institution Press.

**Judge, W. J.**
1979    The Development of a Complex Cultural Ecosystem in the Chaco Basin,

New Mexico. In *Proceedings of the First Conference on Scientific Research in the National Parks*, vol. II, edited by R. M. Linn, pp. 901–906. Transactions and Proceedings Series 5. Washington, DC: National Park Service, US Department of the Interior.

1981    Transect Sampling in Chaco Canyon—Evaluations of a Survey Technique. In *Archaeological Surveys of Chaco Canyon, New Mexico*, compiled by A. C. Hayes, D. M. Brugge, and W. J. Judge, pp. 107–137. Publications in Archeology 18A, Chaco Canyon Studies. Washington, DC: National Park Service, US Department of the Interior.

1989    Chaco Canyon–San Juan Basin. In *Dynamics of Southwest Prehistory*, edited by L. S. Cordell and G. J. Gumerman, pp. 209–261. Washington, DC: Smithsonian Institution Press.

1991    Chaco: Current Views of Prehistory and the Regional System. In *Chaco and Hohokam: Prehistoric Regional Systems in the American Southwest*, edited by P. L. Crown and W. J. Judge, pp. 11–30. School of American Research Advanced Seminar Series. Santa Fe, NM: SAR Press.

1993    Resource Distribution and the Chaco Phenomenon. In *The Chimney Rock Archaeological Symposium*, edited by J. M. Malville and G. Matlock, pp. 35–37. General Technical Report RM-227. Fort Collins, CO: Rocky Mountain Forest and Range Experiment Station, Forest Service, US Department of Agriculture.

2004    Chaco's Golden Century. In *In Search of Chaco*, edited by D. G. Noble, pp. 1–6. School of American Research. Santa Fe, NM: SAR Press.

**Judge, W. J., and J. M. Malville**
2004    Calendrical Knowledge and Ritual Power. In *Chimney Rock: The Ultimate Outlier*, edited by J. M. Malville, pp. 151–162. New York: Lexington Books.

**Judge, W. J., and J. D. Schelberg**
1984    *Recent Research on Chaco Prehistory*. Reports of the Chaco Center no. 8. Albuquerque, NM: Division of Cultural Research, National Park Service.

**Judge, W. J., H. W. Toll, W. B. Gillespie, and S. H. Lekson**
1981    Tenth-Century Developments in Chaco Canyon. In *Collected Papers in Honor of Erik Kellerman Reed*, edited by A. H. Schroeder, pp. 65–98. Papers of the Archaeological Society of New Mexico no. 6. Albuquerque: Archaeological Society of New Mexico.

**Kane, A. E.**
1984    Prehistory of the Dolores Project Area. In *Dolores Archaeological Program: Synthetic Report 1978–1981*, compiled by D. A. Breternitz, pp. 21–51. Denver, CO: Bureau of Reclamation, Engineering and Research Center.

1986    Social Organization and Cultural Process in Dolores Anasazi Communities, AD 600–900. In *Dolores Archaeological Program: Final Synthetic Report*, compiled by D. A. Breternitz, C. K. Robinson, and G. T. Gross, pp. 633–661. Denver, CO: Bureau of Reclamation, Engineering and Research Center.

1989 Did the Sheep Look Up? Sociopolitical Complexity in Ninth-Century Dolores Society. In *The Sociopolitical Structure of Prehistoric Southwestern Societies*, edited by S. Upham, K. G. Lightfoot, and R. A. Jewett, pp. 307–361. Boulder, CO: Westview Press.

1993 Settlement Analogues for Chimney Rock: A Model of 11th and 12th Century Northern Anasazi Society. In *The Chimney Rock Archaeological Symposium, October 20–21, 1990, Durango, Colorado*, edited by J. M. Malville and G. Matlock, pp. 43–60. General Technical Report RM-227. Fort Collins, CO: Rocky Mountain Forest and Range Experiment Station, US Department of Agriculture.

**Kantner, J.**

1996 Political Competition among the Chaco Anasazi of the American Southwest. *Journal of Anthropological Archaeology* 15(1):41–105.

1997 Ancient Roads, Modern Mapping: Evaluating Prehistoric Chaco Anasazi Roadways Using GIS Technology. *Expedition Magazine* 39(3):49–62.

1999a The Influence of Self-Interested Behavior on Sociopolitical Change: The Evolution of the Chaco Anasazi in the Prehistoric American Southwest. Ph.D. diss., University of California, Santa Barbara.

1999b Anasazi Mutilation and Cannibalism in the American Southwest. In *The Anthropology of Cannibalism*, edited by L. R. Goldman, pp. 75–104. Westport, CT: Bergin and Garvey.

2000 Interaction among Great House Communities: An Elemental Analysis of Cibolan Ceramics. In *Great House Communities across the Chacoan Landscape*, edited by J. Kantner and N. M. Mahoney, pp. 130–146. Anthropological Papers no. 64. Tucson: University of Arizona Press.

2003a Rethinking Chaco as a System. *Kiva* 69(2):207–227.

2003b Biological Evolutionary Theory and Individual Decision Making. In *Essential Tensions in Archaeological Method and Theory*, edited by T. L. VanPool and C. S. VanPool, pp. 67–87. Salt Lake City: University of Utah Press.

2003c Preface: The Chaco World. *Kiva* 69(2):83–92.

2004 Strategies of Authority and Status in a Typical Chaco Anasazi Village. Paper presented at the 69th annual meeting of the Society for American Archaeology, Montreal, Quebec, Canada.

**Kantner, J., N. Bower, J. Ladwig, J. Perlitz, S. Hata, and D. Greve**

2000 Interaction between Great House Communities: An Elemental Analysis of Cibolan Ceramics. In *Great House Communities across the Chacoan Landscape*, edited by J. Kantner and N. M. Mahoney, pp. 130–146. Anthropological Papers no. 64. Tucson: University of Arizona Press.

**Kantner, J., and R. Hobgood**

2003 Digital Technologies and Prehistoric Landscapes in the American Southwest. In *The Reconstruction of Archaeological Landscapes through Digital*

*Technologies*, edited by M. Forte, P. R. Williams, and J. Wiseman, pp. 117–123. Oxford: Archaeopress.

**Kantner, J., and N. M. Mahoney, eds.**
2000    *Great House Communities across the Chacoan Landscape.* Anthropological Papers no. 64. Tucson: University of Arizona Press.

**Keating, E.**
2000    Moments of Hierarchy: Constructing Social Stratification by Means of Language, Food, Space, and the Body in Pohnpei, Micronesia. *American Anthropologist* 102(2):303–320.

**Keeley, L. H.**
1996    *War before Civilization: The Myth of the Peaceful Savage.* New York: Oxford University Press.

**Kelley, J. C.**
1956    Settlement Patterns in North-Central Mexico. In *Prehistoric Settlement Patterns in the New World*, edited by G. R. Willey, pp. 128–202. Viking Fund Publications in Anthropology, vol. 23. New York: Wenner-Gren Foundation.

1986    The Mobile Merchants of Molino. In *Ripples in the Chichimec Sea: New Considerations of Mesoamerican-Southwestern Interactions*, edited by F. J. Mathien and R. H. McGuire, pp. 81–104. Carbondale and Edwardsville: Southern Illinois University Press.

**Kelley, J. C., and E. A. Kelley**
1975    An Alternative Hypothesis for the Explanation of Anasazi Culture History. In *Collected Papers in Honor of Florence Hawley Ellis*, edited by T. R. Frisbie, pp. 178–223. Papers of the Archaeological Society of New Mexico no. 2. Norman, OK: Hooper Press; Santa Fe: Archaeological Society of New Mexico.

**Kelley, J. C., and H. D. Winters**
1960    A Revision of the Archaeological Sequence in Sinaloa, Mexico. *American Antiquity* 25(4):547–561.

**Kelly, I.**
1938    *Excavations at Chametla, Sinaloa.* Iberoamericana 14. Berkeley: University of California Press.

**Kendrick, J. W., and W. J. Judge**
2000    Household Economic Autonomy and Great House Development in the Lowry Area. In *Great House Communities across the Chacoan Landscape*, edited by J. Kantner and N. M. Mahoney, pp. 111–129. Anthropological Papers no. 64. Tucson: University of Arizona Press.

**Kertzer, D. I.**
1988    *Ritual, Politics, and Power.* New Haven, CT: Yale University Press.

**Kidder, A. V.**

1917    Prehistoric Cultures of the San Juan Drainage. In *Proceedings of the International Congress of Americanists, 19th session, Washington, DC, December 27–31, 1915*, edited by F. W. Hodge, pp. 108–113.

1924    *An Introduction to the Study of Southwestern Archaeology with a Preliminary Account of the Excavations at Pecos.* Papers of the Southwest Expedition no. 1. Reprint, New Haven, CT: Yale University Press, 1962.

1927    Southwestern Archaeological Conference. *Science* 66(1716):489–491.

1936    Introduction. In *The Glaze-Paint, Culinary and Other Wares*, vol. 2 of *The Pottery of Pecos*, by A. V. Kidder and A. O. Shepard, pp. xvii–xxxi. Papers of the Phillips Academy Southwest Expedition no. 7. New Haven, CT: Yale University Press.

**Kidder, A. V., and A. O. Shepard**

1936    *The Glaze-Paint, Culinary and Other Wares.* Vol. 2 of *The Pottery of Pecos*, by A. V. Kidder and A. O. Shepard. Papers of the Phillips Academy Southwest Expedition no. 7. New Haven, CT: Yale University Press.

**Kievit, K.**

1998    Seeing and Reading Chaco Architecture at AD 1100. Ph.D. diss., University of Colorado, Boulder.

**Kincaid, C., ed.**

1983    *Chaco Roads Project Phase I: A Reappraisal of Prehistoric Roads in the San Juan Basin.* Albuquerque, NM: Bureau of Land Management, US Department of the Interior.

**King, V. C.**

1996    The Cibola Region in the Post-Chacoan Era. In *The Prehistoric Pueblo World, AD 1150–1350*, edited by M. A. Adler, pp. 131–144. Tucson: University of Arizona Press.

2003    The Organization of Production of Chuska Gray Ware Ceramics for Distribution and Consumption in Chaco Canyon, New Mexico. Ph.D. diss., University of New Mexico, Albuquerque.

2004    Community Specialization in the Production of Chuska Gray Ware Ceramics Consumed in Chaco Canyon. *NewsMAC: Newsletter of the New Mexico Archeological Council* 2004:4–8.

**Kintigh, K. W.**

1985    *Settlement, Subsistence, and Society in Late Zuni Prehistory.* Anthropological Papers no. 44. Tucson: University of Arizona Press.

1990    Protohistoric Transitions in the Western Pueblo Area. In *Patterns of Southwestern Prehistory*, edited by P. E. Minnis and C. L. Redman, pp. 258–275. Boulder, CO: Westview Press.

1994    Chaco, Communal Architecture, and Cibolan Aggregation. In *The Ancient Southwestern Community: Methods and Models for the Study of Prehistoric Social Organizations*, edited by W. W. Wills and R. Leonard, pp. 131–140. Albuquerque: University of New Mexico Press.

1996    The Cibola Area in the Post-Chacoan Era. In *The Prehistoric Pueblo World, AD 1100–1300*, edited by M. Adler, pp. 131–144. Tucson: University of Arizona Press.

2003    Coming to Terms with the Chaco World. *Kiva* 69(2):93–116.

**Kintigh, K. W., T. L. Howell, and A. I. Duff**

1996    Post-Chacoan Social Integration at the Hinkson Site, New Mexico. *Kiva* 61(3):257–274.

**Kirkby, A. V. T.**

1973    *The Use of Land and Water Resources in the Past and Present Valley of Oaxaca, Mexico.* Memoirs of the Museum of Anthropology no. 5. Ann Arbor: University of Michigan.

**Kluckhohn, C.**

1939    Discussion. In *Preliminary Report on the 1937 Excavations, Bc 50–51, Chaco Canyon, New Mexico*, edited by C. Kluckhohn and P. Reiter, pp. 151–162. The University of New Mexico Bulletin 345, Anthropological Series, vol. 3, no. 2. Albuquerque: University of New Mexico. Reprint, Millwood, NY: Kraus, 1977.

**Knight, V. J. Jr., and V. P. Steponaitis**

1998    A New History of Moundville. In *Archaeology of the Moundville Chiefdom*, edited by V. J. Knight Jr. and V. P. Steponaitis, pp. 1–25. Washington, DC: Smithsonian Institution Press.

**Knowles, R. L.**

1974    *Energy and Form: An Ecological Approach to Urban Growth.* Cambridge, MA: MIT Press.

**Kohler, T. A.**

1992    Field Houses, Villages, and the Tragedy of the Commons in the Early Northern Anasazi Southwest. *American Antiquity* 57(4):617–635.

1993    News from the Northern American Southwest: Prehistory on the Edge of Chaos. *Journal of Archaeological Research* 1(4):267–321.

**Kohler, T. A., C. D. Johnson, S. Ortman, M. Varien, R. Reynolds, Z. Kobti, J. Cowan, K. Kolm, S. Smith, and L. Yap**

2005    Settlement Ecodynamics in the Prehispanic Mesa Verde. Unpublished paper.

**Kohler, T. A., and K. Kramer**

2003    Evolutionary Perspectives on Raiding for Women in the Prehispanic Eastern Puebloan Southwest. Paper presented in the Presidential Session "Cooperation and Conflict: Current Studies in Evolutionary Anthropology" at the annual meeting of the American Anthropological Association, Chicago.

**Kohler, T. A., and M. H. Matthews**

1988    Long-Term Anasazi Land Use and Forest Reduction: A Case Study from Southwest Colorado. *American Antiquity* 53(3):537–564.

**Kohler, T. A., J. Orcutt, E. Blinman, and K. L. Petersen**
1986    Anasazi Spreadsheets: The Cost of Doing Business in Prehistoric Dolores. In *Dolores Archaeological Program: Final Synthetic Report*, compiled by D. A. Breternitz, C. K. Robinson, and G. T. Gross, pp. 525–538. Denver, CO: Bureau of Reclamation, US Department of the Interior.

**Kohler, T. A., and M. J. Root**
2004    The Late Coalition and Earliest Classic on the Pajarito Plateau (AD 1250–1375). In *Archaeology of Bandelier National Monument: Village Formation on the Pajarito Plateau, New Mexico*, edited by T. A. Kohler, pp. 173–213. Albuquerque: University of New Mexico Press.

**Kolb, M. J., and J. E. Snead**
1997    It's a Small World After All: Comparative Analyses of Community Organization in Archaeology. *American Antiquity* 62(4):609–628.

**Kopytoff, I.**
1999    Permutations in Patrimonialism and Populism: The Aghem Chiefdoms of Western Cameroon. In *Beyond Chiefdoms: Pathways to Complexity in Africa*, edited by S. K. McIntosh, pp. 88–96. Cambridge: Cambridge University Press.

**Kopytoff, I., and S. Miers**
1977    African "Slavery" as an Institution of Marginality. In *Slavery in Africa: Historical and Anthropological Perspectives*, edited by S. Miers and I. Kopytoff, pp. 3–84. Madison: University of Wisconsin.

**Krader, L., ed.**
1972    *The Ethnological Notebooks of Karl Marx*. Assen: Van Gorcum.

**Kubler, G.**
1962    *The Shape of Time: Remarks on the History of Things*. New Haven, CT: Yale University Press.

**Kuckelman, K. A., R. R. Lightfoot, and D. L. Martin**
2000    Changing Patterns of Violence in the Northern San Juan Region. *Kiva* 66(1):147–165.

2002    The Bioarchaeology and Taphonomy of Violence at Castle Rock and Sand Canyon Pueblos, Southwestern Colorado. *American Antiquity* 67(3):486–513.

**Kuckelman, K. A., ed.**
2003    *The Archaeology of Yellow Jacket Pueblo (Site 5MT5): Excavations at a Large Community Center in Southwestern Colorado*. Cortez, CO: Crow Canyon Archaeological Center. http://www.crowcanyon.org/yellowjacket (accessed April 10, 2005). http://www.crowcanyon.org/ResearchReports/YellowJacket/Text/yjpw_contentsvolume.htm (accessed June 10, 2004).

**Lagasse, P. F., W. B. Gillespie, and K. G. Eggert**
1984    Hydraulic Engineering Analysis of Prehistoric Water-Control Systems at

Chaco Canyon. In *Recent Research on Chaco Prehistory*, edited by W. J. Judge and J. Schelberg, pp. 187–211. Reports of the Chaco Center no. 8. Albuquerque, NM: Division of Cultural Research, National Park Service.

**Lange, F., N. Mahaney, J. B. Wheat, and M. L. Chenault**
1988    *Yellow Jacket: A Four Corners Anasazi Ceremonial Center.* 2d ed. Boulder, CO: Johnson Publishing.

**Laumbach, K. W., and J. L. Wakeman**
1999    Rebuilding an Ancient Pueblo: The Victorio Site in Regional Perspective. In *Sixty Years of Mogollon Archaeology, Papers from the Ninth Mogollon Conference, Silver City, New Mexico, 1996*, edited by S. M. Whittlesey, pp. 183–189. Tucson, AZ: SRI Press.

**LeBlanc, S. A.**
1983    *The Mimbres People, Ancient Painters of the American Southwest.* London: Thames and Hudson.

1989a   Cibola: Shifting Cultural Boundaries. In *Dynamics of Southwest Prehistory*, edited by L. S. Cordell and G. J. Gumerman, pp. 337–369. Washington, DC: Smithsonian Institution Press.

1989b   Cultural Dynamics in the Southern Mogollon Area. In *Dynamics of Southwest Prehistory*, edited by L. S. Cordell and G. J. Gumerman, pp. 179–207. Washington, DC: Smithsonian Institution Press.

1999    *Prehistoric Warfare in the American Southwest.* Salt Lake City: University of Utah Press.

**Lehmer, D. J.**
1971    *Introduction to Middle Missouri Archaeology.* Anthropological Papers no. 1. Washington, DC: National Park Service, US Department of the Interior.

**Lekson, S. H.**
1983a   Chaco Architecture in Continental Context. In *Proceedings of the Anasazi Symposium 1981*, edited by J. E. Smith, pp. 183–194. Cortez, CO: Mesa Verde Museum Association.

1983b   Dating the Hubbard Tri-Wall and Other Tri-Wall Structures. *Southwestern Lore* 49(4):15–23.

1983c   *The Architecture and Dendrochronology of Chetro Ketl, Chaco Canyon, New Mexico.* Albuquerque, NM: Division of Cultural Research, National Park Service.

1984a   *Great Pueblo Architecture of Chaco Canyon, New Mexico.* Publications in Archeology 18B, Chaco Canyon Studies. Albuquerque, NM: National Park Service, US Department of the Interior.

1984b   Standing Architecture at Chaco Canyon and the Interpretation of Local and Regional Organization. In *Recent Research on Chaco Prehistory*, edited by W. J. Judge and J. D. Schelberg, pp. 55–73. Reports of the Chaco Center no. 8. Albuquerque, NM: Division of Cultural Research, National Park Service.

1985    The Architecture of Talus Unit, Chaco Canyon, New Mexico. In *Prehistory and History in the Southwest. Collected Papers in Honor of Alden C. Hayes*, edited by N. Fox, pp. 43–59. Papers of the Archaeological Society of New Mexico no. 11. Santa Fe, NM: Ancient City Press, Inc.

1988a   Sociopolitical Complexity at Chaco Canyon, New Mexico. Ph.D. diss., University of New Mexico, Albuquerque.

1988b   The Idea of the Kiva in Anasazi Archaeology. *Kiva* 53(3):213–234.

1989a   Kivas? In *The Architecture of Social Integration in Prehistoric Pueblos*, edited by W. D. Lipe and M. Hegmon, pp. 161–167. Cortez, NM: Crow Canyon Archaeological Center.

1989b   The Great Pueblo Period in Southwestern Archaeology. In *Pueblo Style and Regional Architecture*, edited by N. C. Markovich, W. F. E. Preiser, and F. G. Sturm, pp. 64–77. New York: Van Nostrand Reinhold.

1991    Settlement Pattern and the Chaco Region. In *Chaco and Hohokam: Prehistoric Regional Systems in the American Southwest*, edited by P. L. Crown and W. J. Judge, pp. 31–55. School of American Research Advanced Seminar Series. Santa Fe, NM: SAR Press.

1992    Mimbres Art and Archaeology. In *Archaeology, Art, and Anthropology: Papers in Honor of J. J. Brody*, edited by M. S. Duran and D. T. Kirkpatrick, pp. 111–122. Papers of the Archaeological Society of New Mexico no. 18. Albuquerque: Archaeological Society of New Mexico.

1993    Chaco, Mimbres, and Hohokam: The 11th and 12th Centuries in the American Southwest. *Expedition* 35(1):44–52.

1996    Southwestern New Mexico and Southeastern Arizona, AD 900–1300. In *The Prehistoric Pueblo World, AD 1100–1300*, edited by M. Adler, pp. 170–176. Tucson: University of Arizona Press.

1999    *The Chaco Meridian: Centers of Political Power in the Ancient Southwest.* Walnut Creek, CA: AltaMira Press.

2000    Great! In *Great House Communities across the Chacoan Landscape*, edited by J. Kantner and N. Mahoney, pp. 157–163. Anthropological Papers no. 64. Tucson: University of Arizona Press.

2002    War in the Southwest, War in the World. *American Antiquity* 67(4):607–624.

**Lekson, S. H., ed.**

1983    *The Architecture and Dendrochronology of Chetro Ketl, Chaco Canyon, New Mexico.* Reports of the Chaco Center no. 6. Albuquerque, NM: Division of Cultural Research, National Park Service.

**Lekson, S. H., and C. M. Cameron**

1995    The Abandonment of Chaco Canyon, The Mesa Verde Migrations, and the Reorganization of the Pueblo World. *Journal of Anthropological Archaeology* 14(2):184–202.

**Lekson, S. H., and P. N. Peregrine**

2004    A Continental Perspective for North American Archaeology. *SAA Archaeological Record* 4(1):15–19.

**Lekson, S. H., T. C. Windes, J. R. Stein, and W. J. Judge**
1988    The Chaco Canyon Community. *Scientific American* 256(7):100–109.

**Lelgemann, A.**
2000    Proyecto Ciudadela de La Quemada, Zacatecas. Informe final al Consejo de Arqueología, Instituto Nacional de Antropología e Historia, Bonn, Germany.

**LeTourneau, P. D.**
1997    Sources and Prehistoric Use of Yellowish Brown Spotted Chert in Northwest-Central New Mexico. Paper presented at the 62nd annual meeting of the Society for American Archaeology, Nashville, TN.

**Levine, F.**
1999    *Our Prayers Are in This Place: Pecos Pueblo Identity over the Centuries.* Albuquerque: University of New Mexico Press.

**Lewis, C. K.**
2002    Knowledge Is Power: Pigments, Painted Artifacts, and Chacoan Ritual Leaders. M.A. thesis, Northern Arizona University, Flagstaff.

**Lightfoot, K. G.**
1979    Food Redistribution among Prehistoric Pueblo Groups. *Kiva* 44(4):319–339.

**Lightfoot, R. R.**
1988    Roofing an Early Anasazi Great Kiva: Analysis of an Architectural Model. *Kiva* 53(3):253–274.
1992    Architecture and Tree-Ring Dating at the Duckfoot Site in Southwestern Colorado. *Kiva* 57(3):213–236.
1994    *The Duckfoot Site.* Vol. 2 of *Archaeology of the House and Household.* Occasional Paper no. 4. Cortez, CO: Crow Canyon Archaeological Center.

**Lipe, W. D.**
1974    A Conservation Model for American Archaeology. *Kiva* 39(3-4):213–245.
1986    Modeling Dolores Area Cultural Dynamics. In *Dolores Archaeological Program: Final Synthetic Report,* compiled by D. A. Breternitz, C. K. Robinson, and G. T. Gross, pp. 439–467. Denver, CO: Bureau of Reclamation, US Department of the Interior.
1989    Social Scale of Mesa Verde Anasazi Kivas. In *The Architecture of Social Integration in Prehistoric Pueblos,* edited by W. D. Lipe and M. Hegmon, pp. 53–71. Occasional Paper no. 1. Cortez, CO: Crow Canyon Archaeological Center.
1995    The Depopulation of the Northern San Juan: Conditions in the Turbulent 1200s. *Journal of Anthropological Archaeology* 14(2):143–169.
1999a    National Register of Historic Places Registration Form for Bass Site Complex (5MT136). Submitted by the Crow Canyon Archaeological Center, Cortez, CO. Denver: Colorado Historical Society.

## References

1999b     History of Archaeology. In *Colorado Prehistory: A Context for the Southern Colorado River Basin*, edited by W. D. Lipe, M. D. Varien, and R. H. Wilshusen, pp. 51–94. Denver: Colorado Council of Professional Archaeologists.

2002a     Chaco: Notes from the North. Paper presented at the Chaco Capstone Conference, Albuquerque, NM.

2002b     Social Power in the Central Mesa Verde Region, AD 1150–1290. In *Seeking the Center Place: Archaeology and Ancient Communities in the Mesa Verde Region*, edited by M. D. Varien and R. H. Wilshusen, pp. 203–232. Salt Lake City: University of Utah Press.

**Lipe, W. D., and S. H. Lekson**

2001     Mesa Verde Pueblo Migration and Cultural Transformations, AD 1250–1350. Paper presented at the 66th annual meeting of the Society for American Archaeology, New Orleans.

**Lipe, W. D., and S. G. Ortman**

2000     Spatial Patterning in Northern San Juan Villages, AD 1050–1300. *Kiva* 66(1):91–122.

**Lipe, W. D., and M. D. Varien**

1999a     Pueblo II (AD 900–1150). In *Colorado Prehistory: A Context for the Southern Colorado Drainage Basin*, edited by W. D. Lipe, M. D. Varien, and R. H. Wilshusen, pp. 242–289. Denver: Colorado Council of Professional Archaeologists.

1999b     Pueblo III (AD 1150–1300). In *Colorado Prehistory: A Context for the Southern Colorado River Basin*, edited by W. D. Lipe, M. D. Varien, and R. Wilshusen, pp. 290–352. Denver: Colorado Council of Professional Archaeologists.

**Lister, F. C.**

1993     *In the Shadow of the Rocks: Archaeology of the Chimney Rock District in Southern Colorado.* Niwot: University Press of Colorado.

**Lister, F. C., and R. H. Lister**

1968     *Earl Morris and Southwestern Archaeology.* Albuquerque: University of New Mexico Press.

**Lister, R. H.**

1978     Mesoamerican Influence on Chaco Canyon, New Mexico. In *Across the Chichimec Sea, Papers in Honor of J. Charles Kelley*, edited by C. L. Riley and B. C. Hedrick, pp. 233–241. Carbondale and Edwardsville: Southern Illinois University Press.

**Lister, R. H., and F. C. Lister**

1969     *The Earl H. Morris Memorial Pottery Collection. An Example of Ten Centuries of Prehistoric Ceramic Art in the Four Corners Country of Southwestern United States.* Studies Series in Anthropology 16. Boulder: University Press of Colorado.

1981     *Chaco Canyon Archaeology and Archaeologists.* Albuquerque: University of New Mexico Press.

1987    *Aztec Ruins on the Animas: Excavated, Preserved, and Interpreted.* Albuquerque: University of New Mexico Press.

1990    *Aztec Ruins National Monument: Administrative History of an Archeological Preserve.* Southwest Cultural Resources Center, Professional Paper no. 24. Santa Fe, NM: Division of History, National Park Service.

**Loebig, D. E.**

2000    Red Willow Hamlet. In *Excavations in the Northern Tohatchi Flats. Pipeline Archaeology 1990–1993: The El Paso Natural Gas North System Expansion Project, New Mexico and Arizona,* vol. V, book 2, edited by S. W. Yost, chapter 5. Western Cultural Resource Management Report no. (F)074. Farmington, NM: Western Cultural Resource Management.

**Loebig, D. E., S. W. Yost, and R. M. Van Dyke**

2000    Flowing Well Hamlet. In *Excavations in the Northern Tohatchi Flats. Pipeline Archaeology 1990–1993: The El Paso Natural Gas North System Expansion Project, New Mexico and Arizona,* vol. V, book 2, edited by S. W. Yost, chapter 4. Western Cultural Resource Management Report no. (F)074. Farmington, NM: Western Cultural Resource Management.

**Logan, W., and Z. Bradley**

1969    Prospectus: Chaco Canyon Studies. Reproduced in the appendix of Mary Maruca's *An Administrative History of the Chaco Project* (1982).

**Loose, R. W., and T. R. Lyons**

1976    The Chetro Ketl Field: A Planned Water Control System in Chaco Canyon. In *Remote Sensing Experiments in Cultural Resource Studies,* edited by T. R. Lyons, pp. 133–156. Reports of the Chaco Center no. 1. Albuquerque, NM: Division of Cultural Research, National Park Service.

**Lowell, J. C.**

1991    *Prehistoric Households at Turkey Creek Pueblo, Arizona.* Anthropological Papers no. 54. Tucson: University of Arizona Press.

**Lyneis, M. M.**

1996    Pueblo II–Pueblo III Change in Southwestern Utah, the Arizona Strip, and Southern Nevada. In *The Prehistoric Pueblo World, AD 1100–1300,* edited by M. Adler, pp. 11–28. Tucson: University of Arizona Press.

**Lyons, T. R., ed.**

1976    *Remote Sensing Experiments in Cultural Resource Studies: Non-destructive Methods of Archeological Exploration, Survey, and Analysis.* Reports of the Chaco Center no. 1. Albuquerque: Division of Cultural Research, National Park Service, and University of New Mexico.

**Lyons, T. R., and R. K. Hitchcock, eds.**

1977    *Aerial Remote Sensing Techniques in Archeology.* Reports of the Chaco Center no. 2. Albuquerque: Division of Cultural Research, National Park Service, and University of New Mexico.

REFERENCES

**Madsen, D. B.**
1989    *Exploring the Fremont.* Salt Lake City: Utah Museum of Natural History.

**Mahoney, N. M.**
2000    Redefining the Scale of Chacoan Communities. In *Great House Communities across the Chacoan Landscape,* edited by J. Kantner and N. M. Mahoney, pp. 17–27. Anthropological Papers no. 64. Tucson: University of Arizona Press.
2001    Monumental Architecture as Conspicuous Display in Chaco Canyon. In *Chaco Society and Polity: Papers from the 1999 Conference,* edited by L. S. Cordell, W. J. Judge, and J. Piper, pp. 13–30. NMAC Special Publication no. 4. Albuquerque: New Mexico Archeological Council.

**Mahoney, N. M., and J. Kantner**
2000    Chacoan Archaeology and Great House Communities. In *Great House Communities across the Chacoan Landscape,* edited by J. Kantner and N. M. Mahoney, pp. 1–17. Anthropological Papers no. 64. Tucson: University of Arizona Press.

**Maldonado Cárdenas, R.**
1980    *Ofrendas Asociadas a Entierros del Infiernillo en el Balsas: Estudio y Experimentación con Tres Métodos de Taxonomía Numérica.* Colección Scientífica—Arqueología. México, DF: Secretaría de Educación Publica, Instituto Nacional de Antropología e Historia, Centro Regional del Sureste.

**Malville, J. M.**
1994    Astronomy and Social Integration among the Anasazi. In *Proceedings of the Anasazi Symposium 1991,* edited by A. Hutchinson and J. E. Smith, pp. 149–164. Mesa Verde, CO: Mesa Verde Museum Association.

**Malville, J. M., and N. J. Malville**
2001    Pilgrimage and Periodical Festivals as Processes of Social Integration in Chaco Canyon. *Kiva* 66(3):327–344.

**Malville, N. J.**
2001    Long-Distance Transport of Bulk Goods in the Pre-Hispanic American Southwest. *Journal of Archaeological Science* 20(2):230–243.

**Mann, M.**
1986    *The Sources of Social Power: Vol. I, A History of Power from the Beginning to AD 1760.* Cambridge: Cambridge University Press.

**Marcus, J.**
2003    Recent Advances in Maya Archaeology. *Journal of Anthropological Archaeology* 11(2):71–148.

**Marshall, J. T.**
2001    Hohokam Regional Ballcourt Data. In appendix J of *The Grewe Archaeological Research Project,* vol. 1, edited by D. B. Craig, pp. 571–585. Anthropological Papers 99-1. Flagstaff, AZ: Northland Research.

**Marshall, M. P.**

1997    The Chacoan Roads: A Cosmological Interpretation. In *Anasazi Architecture and American Design*, edited by B. H. Morrow and V. B. Price, pp. 62–74. Albuquerque: University of New Mexico Press.

**Marshall, M. P., and R. J. Bradley**

1994    El Llano-Escalon and Standing Rock Communities. In *A Study of Two Anasazi Communities in the San Juan Basin*, edited by R. J. Bradley and R. Sullivan, pp. 313–381. Across the Colorado Plateau: Anthropological Studies for the Transwestern Pipeline Project, vol. IX. Albuquerque: University of New Mexico Office of Contract Archeology, Maxwell Museum of Anthropology.

**Marshall, M. P., D. E. Doyel, and C. D. Breternitz**

1982    A Regional Perspective on the Late Bonito Phase. In *Bis sa'ani: A Late Bonito Phase Community on Escavada Wash, Northwest New Mexico*, edited by C. D. Breternitz, D. E. Doyel, and M. P. Marshall, pp. 1227–1240. Navajo Nation Papers in Anthropology no. 14. Window Rock, AZ: Navajo Nation Cultural Resource Management Program.

**Marshall, M. P., and A. Sofaer**

1988    Solstice Project Archaeological Investigations in the Chacoan Province, New Mexico. Unpublished paper on file, Survey Room Library, Laboratory of Anthropology, Santa Fe, NM.

**Marshall, M. P., J. R. Stein, R. W. Loose, and J. Novotny, eds.**

1979    *Anasazi Communities of the San Juan Basin*. Albuquerque: Public Service Company of New Mexico; Santa Fe: New Mexico Historic Preservation Division.

**Martin, D. L.**

1997    Violence against Women in the La Plata River Valley (AD 1000–1300). In *Troubled Times: Violence and Warfare in the Past*, edited by D. L. Martin and D. W. Frayer, pp. 45–75. Amsterdam: Gordon and Breach Publishers.

**Martin, P. S., J. B. Rinaldo, and E. R. Barter**

1957    Late Mogollon Communities: Four Sites of the Tularosa Phase, Western New Mexico. *Fieldiana: Anthropology*, vol. 49, no. 1. Chicago Natural History Museum Publication 823.

**Martin, P. S., J. B. Rinaldo, E. A. Bluhm, and H. C. Cutler**

1956    Higgins Flat Pueblo, Western New Mexico. *Fieldiana: Anthropology*, vol. 45. Chicago Natural History Museum Publication 790.

**Maruca, M.**

1982    *An Administrative History of the Chaco Project*. Washington, DC: National Park Service, US Department of the Interior.

**Mastache, A. G., R. H. Cobean, and D. M. Healan**

2002    *Ancient Tollan: Tula and the Toltec Heartland*. Boulder: University Press of Colorado.

REFERENCES

**Mathien, F. J.**

1981    Neutron Activation of Turquoise Artifacts from Chaco Canyon, New
        Mexico. *Current Anthropology* 22(30):293–294.

1986    External Contacts and the Chaco Anasazi. In *Ripples in the Chichimec Sea,
        New Considerations of Southwestern-Mesoamerican Interaction*, edited by F. J.
        Mathien and R. H. McGuire, pp. 220–243. Carbondale and Edwardsville:
        Southern Illinois University Press.

1993    Ornaments and Minerals from 29SJ629. In *Spadefoot Toad Site: Investigations
        at 29SJ629, Chaco Canyon, New Mexico*, vol. 2, edited by T. C. Windes, pp.
        269–316. Reports of the Chaco Center no. 12. Santa Fe, NM: Division of
        Cultural Research, National Park Service.

1997    Ornaments of the Chaco Anasazi. In *Ceramics, Lithics, and Ornaments of
        Chaco Canyon: Analyses of Artifacts from the Chaco Project, 1971–1978*, vol. III,
        *Lithics and Ornaments*, edited by F. J. Mathien, pp. 1119–1220. Reports of
        the Chaco Center no. 11. Santa Fe, NM: Division of Cultural Research,
        National Park Service.

2001    The Organization of Turquoise Production and Consumption by the
        Prehistoric Chacoans. *American Antiquity* 66(1):103–118.

2003    Artifacts from Pueblo Bonito: One Hundred Years of Interpretation. In
        *Pueblo Bonito: Center of the Chacoan World*, edited by J. E. Neitzel, pp.
        127–142. Washington, DC: Smithsonian Books.

2005    *Culture and Ecology of Chaco Canyon and the San Juan Basin*. Santa Fe, NM:
        National Park Service, US Department of the Interior.

**Mathien, F. J., ed.**

1985    *Environment and Subsistence of Chaco Canyon, New Mexico*. Publications in
        Archeology 18E, Chaco Canyon Studies. Albuquerque, NM: National Park
        Service, US Department of the Interior.

1991    *Excavations at 29SJ633: The Eleventh Hour Site, Chaco Canyon, New Mexico*.
        Reports of the Chaco Center no. 10. Santa Fe, NM: Division of Cultural
        Research, National Park Service.

1992    *Excavations at 29SJ627: Vol. 2, Artifact Analyses*. Reports of the Chaco Center
        no. 11. Santa Fe, NM: Division of Cultural Research, National Park
        Service.

1997    *Ceramics, Lithics, and Ornaments of Chaco Canyon: Analyses of Artifacts from the
        Chaco Project, 1971–1978*. Publications in Archaeology 18G, Chaco Canyon
        Studies. Santa Fe, NM: National Park Service, US Department of the
        Interior.

**Mathien, F. J., and R. H. McGuire, eds.**

1986    *Ripples in the Chichimec Sea: New Considerations of Southwestern-Mesoamerican
        Interactions*. Carbondale and Edwardsville: Southern Illinois University
        Press.

**Mathien, F. J., and T. C. Windes**

1987    *Investigations at the Pueblo Alto Complex, Chaco Canyon: Vol. III, Artifactual and Biological Analyses.* Publications in Archeology 18F, Chaco Canyon Studies. Santa Fe, NM: National Park Service, US Department of the Interior.

1989    Great House Revisited: Kin Nahasbas, Chaco Culture National Historical Park. In *From Chaco to Chaco: Papers in Honor of Robert H. and Florence C. Lister,* edited by M. S. Duran and D. T. Kirkpatrick, pp. 11–34. Papers of the Archaeological Society of New Mexico no. 15. Albuquerque: Archaeological Society of New Mexico.

**Mauss, M.**

1966    *The Gift: Forms and Functions of Exchange in Archaic Societies.* Translated by I. Cunnison. London: Cohen and West.

**McGimsey, C. R., and H. A. Davis**

1977    *The Management of Archaeological Resources: The Airlie House Report.* Special Publication of the Society for American Archaeology. Washington, DC: Society for American Archaeology.

**McGregor, J. C.**

1941    *Southwestern Archaeology.* New York: J. Wiley and Sons.

**McGuire, R. H.**

1980    The Mesoamerican Connection in the Southwest. *Kiva* 46(1-2):3–38.

1992    *A Marxist Archaeology.* Orlando, FL, and San Diego: Academic Press.

**McGuire, R. H., E. C. Adams, B. A. Nelson, and K. A. Spielmann**

1994    Drawing the Southwest to Scale: Perspectives on Macroregional Relations. In *Themes in Southwest Prehistory,* edited by G. J. Gumerman, pp. 239–265. School of American Research. Santa Fe, NM: SAR Press.

**McGuire, R. H., and A. V. Howard**

1987    The Structure and Organization of Hohokam Shell Exchange. *Kiva* 52(2):113–146.

**McIntosh, R. J., and S. K. McIntosh**

2003    Early Urban Configurations on the Middle Niger. In *The Social Construction of Ancient Cities,* edited by M. L. Smith, pp. 103–120. Washington, DC: Smithsonian Books.

**McIntosh, S. K.**

1999    Pathways to Complexity: An African Perspective. In *Beyond Chiefdoms: Pathways to Complexity in Africa,* edited by S. K. McIntosh, pp. 1–30. Cambridge: Cambridge University Press.

**McKenna, P. J.**

1984    *Architecture and Material Culture of 29SJ1360, Chaco Canyon, New Mexico.* Reports of the Chaco Center no. 7. Albuquerque, NM: Division of Cultural Research, National Park Service.

# REFERENCES

1986    A Summary of the Chaco Center's Small Site Excavations: 1973–1978. In *Small Site Architecture of Chaco Canyon, New Mexico*, compiled by P. J. McKenna and M. L. Truell, pp. 5–114. Publications in Archeology 18D, Chaco Canyon Studies. Albuquerque, NM: National Park Service, US Department of the Interior.

**McKenna, P. J., and H. W. Toll**

1984    Ceramics. In *The Architecture and Material Culture of 29SJ1360, Chaco Canyon, New Mexico*, pp. 103–222. Reports of the Chaco Center no 7. Albuquerque, NM: National Park Service.

1992    Regional Patterns of Great House Development among the Totah Anasazi, New Mexico. In *Anasazi Regional Organization and the Chaco System*, edited by D. E. Doyel, pp. 133–143. Anthropological Papers no. 5. Albuquerque: Maxwell Museum of Anthropology, University of New Mexico.

**McKenna, P. J., and M. Truell**

1986    *Small Site Architecture of Chaco Canyon, New Mexico*. Publications in Archeology 18D, Chaco Canyon Studies. Santa Fe, NM: National Park Service, US Department of the Interior.

**Medina González, J. H.**

2000    El paisaje ritual del Valle de Malpaso. Tésis de Licenciatura en Arqueología, Escuela Nacional de Antropología, Instituto Nacional de Antropología y Secretaría de Educación Pública, México.

**Meighan, C. W., ed.**

1976    *The Archaeology of Amapa, Nayarit*. Vol. 2 of *Monumenta Archaeologica*. Los Angeles: Institute of Archaeology, University of California.

**Metcalf, M. P.**

2003    Construction Labor at Pueblo Bonito. In *Pueblo Bonito: Center of the Chacoan World*, edited by J. E. Neitzel, pp. 72–79. Washington, DC: Smithsonian Institution Press.

**Millon, C.**

1973    Painting, Writing, and Polity at Teotihuacan, Mexico. *American Antiquity* 38(3):294–314.

**Millon, R.**

1981    Teotihuacan: City, State, and Civilization. In *Archaeology*, edited by J. A. Sabloff, pp. 198–243. Supplement to the Handbook of Middle American Indians, vol. 1, V. R. Bricker, general editor. Austin: University of Texas Press.

**Mills, B. J.**

1998    Migration and Pueblo IV Community Reorganization in the Silver Creek Area, East-Central Arizona. In *Migration and Reorganization: The Pueblo IV Period in the American Southwest*, edited by K. A. Spielmann, pp. 65–80. Anthropological Research Papers no. 51. Tempe: Arizona State University.

2002      Recent Research on Chaco: Changing Views on Economy, Ritual, and Society. *Journal of Archaeological Research* 10(1):65–117.

**Mills, B. J., ed.**

2000      *Alternative Leadership Strategies in the Prehispanic Southwest.* Tucson: University of Arizona Press.

**Mills, B. J., A. J. Carpenter, and W. Grimm**

1997      Sourcing Chuska Ceramic Production: Petrographic and Experimental Analysis. *Kiva* 62(3):261–282.

**Mills, B. J., S. A. Herr, and S. Van Keuren, eds.**

1999      *Living on the Edge of the Rim: Excavations and Analysis of the Silver Creek Archaeological Research Project, 1993–1998.* Arizona State Museum Archaeological Series 192. Tucson: Arizona State Museum.

**Mindeleff, V.**

1891      *A Study of Pueblo Architecture in Tusayan and Cibola.* Eighth Annual Report of the Bureau of American Ethnology. Reprint, Washington, DC: Smithsonian Institution Press, 1989.

**Mitchell, M. D.**

n.d.      Research Traditions, Public Policy, and the Underdevelopment of Theory in Plains Archaeology: Tracing the Legacy of the Missouri Basin Project. *American Antiquity.* Forthcoming.

**Moorehead, W. K.**

1908      Ruins at Aztec and on the Rio La Plata, New Mexico. *American Anthropologist* n.s. 10(2):255–263.

**Morenon, E. P.**

1977      Summary of Energy Study Results Conducted in Chaco Canyon National Monument. Unpublished paper on file, Division of Cultural Research, National Park Service, Albuquerque, NM.

**Morgan, L. H.**

[1881]     *Houses and Houselife of the American Aborigines.* Vol. IV of *US*
1965      *Geographical and Geological Survey of the Rocky Mountain Region, Contributions to North American Ethnology.* Washington, DC: Government Printing Office. Reprint, Chicago: University of Chicago Press, 1965.

**Morgan, W. N.**

1994      *Ancient Architecture of the Southwest.* Austin: University of Texas Press.
1999      *Precolumbian Architecture in Eastern North America.* Gainsville: University Press of Florida. Originally published 1980, Cambridge, MA: MIT Press.

**Morris, E. A.**

1959      A Pueblo I Site near Bennett's Peak, Northwestern New Mexico. *El Palacio* 66(5):169–175.

**Morris, E. H.**

1919 Preliminary Account of the Antiquities of the Region between the Mancos and La Plata Rivers in Southwestern Colorado. In *Thirty-Third Annual Report of the Bureau of American Ethnology*, pp. 155–206. Washington, DC: Smithsonian Institution Press.

1924 Burials in the Aztec Ruin. *Anthropological Papers of the American Museum of Natural History* XXVI(III):139–225.

1928 Notes on Excavations in the Aztec Ruin. *Anthropological Papers of the American Museum of Natural History* XXVI(V):259–420.

1939 *Archaeological Studies in the La Plata District, Southwestern Colorado and Northwestern New Mexico*. Publication 519. Washington, DC: Carnegie Institution of Washington.

**Mountjoy, J. B., and L. Torres M.**

1985 The Production and Use of Prehispanic Metal Artifacts in the Central Coastal Area of Jalisco, Mexico. In *The Archaeology of West and Northwest Mesoamerica*, edited by M. S. Foster and P. C. Weigand, pp. 133–152. Boulder, CO: Westview Press.

**Nabokov, P.**

1981 *Indian Running: Native American History and Tradition*. Santa Fe, NM: Ancient City Press.

**Nagao, D.**

1989 Public Proclamation in the Art of Cacaxtla and Xochicalco. In *Mesoamerica after the Decline of Teotihuacan, AD 700–900*, edited by R. A. Diehl and J. C. Berlo, pp. 83–104. Washington, DC: Dumbarton Oaks Research Library and Collection.

**National Park Service (NPS)**

1969 *Prospectus: Chaco Canyon Studies*. Washington, DC: National Park Service, US Department of the Interior.

2002 *Federal Historic Preservation Laws*. Washington, DC: National Center for Cultural Resources, National Park Service, US Department of the Interior.

**Neitzel, J. E.**

1989 The Chaco Regional System: Interpreting the Evidence for Sociopolitical Complexity. In *The Sociopolitical Structure of Prehistoric Southwestern Societies*, edited by S. Upham, K. G. Lightfoot, and R. A. Jewett, pp. 509–556. Boulder, CO: Westview Press.

1994 Boundary Dynamics in the Chacoan Regional System. In *The Ancient Southwestern Community: Models and Methods for the Study of Prehistoric Social Organization*, edited by W. H. Wills and R. D. Leonard, pp. 209–240. Albuquerque: University of New Mexico Press.

1995 Elite Styles in Hierarchically Organized Societies: The Chacoan Regional System. In *Style, Society, and Person: Archaeological and Ethnological Perspectives*, edited by C. Carr and J. E. Neitzel, pp. 393–418. New York: Plenum Press.

2000 What Is a Regional System? Issues of Scale and Interaction in the

Prehistoric Southwest. In *The Archaeology of Regional Interaction: Religion, Warfare, and Exchange across the American Southwest*, edited by M. Hegmon, pp. 25–40. Boulder: University Press of Colorado.

2003a    The Organization, Function, and Population of Pueblo Bonito. In *Pueblo Bonito: Center of the Chacoan World*, edited by J. E. Neitzel, pp. 143–149. Washington, DC: Smithsonian Institution Press.

2003b    Artifact Distributions at Pueblo Bonito. In *Pueblo Bonito: Center of the Chacoan World*, edited by J. E. Neitzel, pp. 107–126. Washington, DC: Smithsonian Institution Press.

**Neitzel, J. E., ed.**
2003    *Pueblo Bonito: Center of the Chacoan World*. Washington, DC: Smithsonian Institution Press.

**Neitzel, J. E., and R. L. Bishop**
1990    Neutron Activation of Dogoszhi-Style Ceramics: Production and Exchange in the Chacoan Regional System. *Kiva* 56(1):67–85.

**Neitzel, J. E., H. Neff, M. D. Glascock, and R. L. Bishop**
2002    Chaco and the Production and Exchange of Dogoszhi-Style Pottery. In *Ceramic Production and Circulation in the Greater Southwest*, edited by D. M. Glowacki and H. Neff, pp. 47–65. Monograph 44. Los Angeles: The Cotsen Institute of Archaeology, University of California.

**Nelson, B. A.**
1995    Complexity, Hierarchy, and Scale: A Controlled Comparison between Chaco Canyon, New Mexico, and La Quemada, Zacatecas. *American Antiquity* 60(4):597–618.

1997    Chronology and Stratigraphy at La Quemada, Zacatecas, Mexico. *Journal of Field Archaeology* 24(1):85–109.

2000    Aggregation, Warfare, and the Spread of the Mesoamerican Tradition. In *The Archaeology of Regional Interaction: Religion, Warfare, and Exchange across the American Southwest and Beyond*, edited by M. Hegmon, pp. 317–337. Salt Lake City: University of Utah Press.

**Nelson, B. A., and D. Crider**
2001    Posibles Pasajes Migratorios en el Norte de México y el Suroeste de los EE.UU. durante el Epiclásico y el Postclásico. Paper presented at the XXVI Mesa Redonda of the Sociedad Mexicana de Antropología, Zacatecas, Zac., México.

**Nelson, B. A., J. Millhauser, and D. To**
1998    Burial Excavations in Plaza 1 of Los Pilarillos, Zacatecas, Mexico: 1997 Season. Report to the Foundation for the Advancement of Mesoamerican Studies. Tempe: Department of Anthropology, Arizona State University.

**Nelson, R. S.**
1991    *Hohokam Marine Shell Exchange and Artifacts*. Arizona State Museum Archaeological Series 179. Tucson: Arizona State Museum.

REFERENCES

**Newland, J.**

1999    Ornaments, Rare Rocks, and Miscellaneous. In *The Dolores Legacy: A User's Guide to the Dolores Archaeological Program Data*, compiled by R. Wilshusen, with the assistance of K. Burd, J. Till, C. G. Ward, and B. Yunker, pp. 97–104. www.co.blm.gov/ahc/colprojects.htm (accessed April 15, 2003).

**Nials, F., J. Stein, and J. Roney**

1987    *Chacoan Roads in the Southern Periphery: Results of Phase II of the BLM Chaco Roads Project.* Cultural Resources Series 1. Santa Fe: Bureau of Land Management, New Mexico State Office.

**Nials, F. L.**

1983    Physical Characteristics of Chacoan Roads. In *Chaco Roads Project Phase I: A Reappraisal of Prehistoric Roads in the San Juan Basin*, edited by C. Kincaid, pp. 6-1–6-51. Albuquerque, NM: Bureau of Land Management, US Department of the Interior.

**Noble, D. G., ed.**

1984    *New Light on Chaco Canyon.* School of American Research. Santa Fe, NM: SAR Press.

2004    *In Search of Chaco: New Approaches to an Archaeological Enigma.* School of American Research. Santa Fe, NM: SAR Press.

**Noguera, E.**

1930    *Ruinas Arqueológicas del Norte de México: Casas Grandes (Chihuahua), La Quemada, Chalchihuites (Zacatecas).* Mexico City: Secretaría de Educación Publica.

**Northrup, D.**

1978    *Trade without Rulers: Pre-Colonial Economic Development in Southeastern Nigeria.* Oxford: Clarendon Press.

**Oakes, Y. R.**

1999a    Evaluating Placement of Mogollon Sites. In *Sixty Years of Mogollon Archaeology, Papers from the Ninth Mogollon Conference, Silver City, New Mexico, 1996*, edited by S. M. Whittlesey, pp. 163–172. Tucson: SRI Press.

1999b    *Synthesis and Conclusions.* Vol. 6 of *Archaeology of the Mogollon Highlands*, edited by Y. R. Oakes and D. A. Zamora. Office of Archaeological Studies, Archaeology Notes 232. Santa Fe: Museum of New Mexico.

**Obenauf, M. S.**

1980a    The Chaco Roadway System. M.A. thesis, University of New Mexico, Albuquerque.

1980b    A History of Research on the Chacoan Roadway System. In *Cultural Resources Remote Sensing*, edited by T. R. Lyons and F. J. Mathien, pp. 123–167. Washington, DC: Cultural Resources Management Division, National Park Service.

1983    The Prehistoric Roadway Network in the San Juan Basin. In *Remote Sensing in Cultural Resource Management: The San Juan Basin Project*, edited by

D. L. Drager and T. R. Lyons, pp. 117–122. Washington, DC: Cultural
Resources Management Division, National Park Service.

**Ortiz, A.**
1965     Dual Organization as an Operational Concept in the Pueblo Southwest.
         *Ethnology* 4(4):389–396.
1969     *The Tewa World: Space, Time, Being, and Becoming in a Pueblo Society.* Chicago:
         University of Chicago Press.
1994     The Dynamics of Pueblo Cultural Survival. In *North American Indian
         Anthropology: Essays on Society and Culture*, edited by R. J. DeMallie and A.
         Ortiz, pp. 296–306. Norman: University of Oklahoma Press.

**Ortiz, S.**
1994     What We See: A Perspective on Chaco Canyon and Its Ancestry. In *Chaco
         Canyon: A Center and Its World*, edited by M. Peck, S. H. Lekson, J. R. Stein,
         and S. Ortiz, pp. 65–72. Santa Fe: Museum of New Mexico Press.

**Ortman, S. G., and B. A. Bradley**
2002     Sand Canyon Pueblo: The Container in the Center. In *Seeking the Center
         Place: Archaeology and Ancient Communities in the Mesa Verde Region*, edited by
         M. D. Varien and R. Wilshusen, pp. 41–78. Salt Lake City: University of
         Utah Press.

**Ortman, S. G., D. M. Glowacki, M. J. Churchill, and K. A. Kuckelman**
2000     Pattern and Variation in Northern San Juan Village Histories. *Kiva*
         66(1):123–146.

**Ortman, S. G., M. D. Varien, and M. G. Spitzer**
2003     Changing Settlement Patterns in the Central Mesa Verde Region: The Site
         Database. Paper presented at the 68th annual meeting of the Society for
         American Archaeology, Milwaukee, WI.

**Osborne, D. (assembler)**
1965     *Contributions of the Wetherill Mesa Archeological Project.* Memoirs 19. Salt Lake
         City, UT: Society for American Archaeology.

**Pauketat, T. R.**
1998     Refiguring the Archaeology of Greater Cahokia. *Journal of Archaeological
         Research* 6(1):45–89.
2001     A New Tradition in Archaeology. In *The Archaeology of Traditions: Agency
         and History before and after Columbus*, edited by T. R. Pauketat, pp. 1–16.
         Gainesville: University Press of Florida.
2004     *Ancient Cahokia and the Mississippians.* Cambridge: Cambridge University
         Press.

**Pauketat, T. R., and S. M. Alt**
2003     Mounds, Memory, and Contested Mississippian History. In *Archaeologies of
         Memory*, edited by R. M. Van Dyke and S. E. Alcock, pp. 151–179. Malden,
         MA: Blackwell Publishing, Ltd.

Pauketat, T. R., L. S. Kelly, G. J. Fritz, N. H. Lopinot, S. Elias, and E. Hargrave
2002    The Residues of Feasting and Public Ritual at Early Cahokia. *American Antiquity* 67(2):257–277.

Pepper, G. H.
1920    *Pueblo Bonito.* Anthropological Papers no. 27. New York: American Museum of Natural History. Reprint, Albuquerque: University of New Mexico Press, 1996.

Peregrine, P. N.
2001    Matrilocality, Corporate Strategy, and the Organization of Production in the Chacoan World. *American Antiquity* 66(1):36–46.

Petersen, K. L.
1994    A Warm and Wet Little Climatic Optimum and a Cold and Dry Little Ice Age in the Southern Rocky Mountains, USA. *Climatic Change* 26(1):243–269.

Phillips, D. A.
1993    Rethinking Chaco. Paper presented at the 26th Chacmool Conference, University of Calgary, Calgary, Alberta.

Plog, F. T.
1974    *The Study of Prehistoric Change.* New York: Academic Press.
1979    Prehistory: Western Anasazi. In *Southwest,* edited by A. Ortiz, pp. 108–130. Vol. 9 of *Handbook of North American Indians,* edited by W. C. Sturtevant. Washington, DC: Smithsonian Institution Press.

Plog, S.
1980    *Stylistic Variation in Prehistoric Ceramics: Design Analysis in the American Southwest.* Cambridge: Cambridge University Press.
1990    Sociopolitical Implications of Stylistic Variation in the American Southwest. In *The Uses of Style in Archaeology,* edited by M. W. Conkey and C. A. Hastorf, pp. 61–72. Cambridge: Cambridge University Press.
2003    Exploring the Ubiquitous through the Unusual: Color Symbolism in Pueblo Black-on-White Pottery. *American Antiquity* 68(4):665–695.

Pollard, H. P.
1991    The Construction of Ideology in the Emergence of the Tarascan State. *Ancient Mesoamerica* 2(2):167–179.

Pollard, H. P., and T. A. Vogel
1994    Implicaciones Políticas y Económicas de Intercambio de Obsidiana Dentro del Estado Tarasco. In *Arqueología del Occidente de México: Nuevas Aportaciones,* edited by E. Williams and R. Novella, pp. 159–182. Zamora: El Colegio de Michoacán.

Potter, J. M.
1997    Community Ritual and Faunal Remains: An Example from the Dolores Anasazi. *Journal of Field Archaeology* 24(4):353–364.

2000    Pots, Parties, and Politics: Communal Feasting in the American Southwest. *American Antiquity* 65(3):471–492.

**Powell, S., P. P. Andrews, D. L. Nichols, and F. E. Smiley**

1983    Fifteen Years on the Rock: Archaeological Research, Administration, and Compliance on Black Mesa, Arizona. *American Antiquity* 48(3):228–252.

**Powell, S., G. J. Gumerman, and F. E. Smiley**

2002    A History and Retrospective of the Black Mesa Archaeological Project. In *Prehistoric Culture Change on the Colorado Plateau: Ten Thousand Years on Black Mesa*, edited by S. Powell and F. E. Smiley, pp. 1–11. Tucson: University of Arizona Press.

**Powers, R. P., W. B. Gillespie, and S. H. Lekson**

1983    *The Outlier Survey: A Regional View of Settlement in the San Juan Basin.* Reports of the Chaco Center no. 3. Albuquerque, NM: Division of Cultural Research, National Park Service.

**Proskouriakoff, T.**

[1946]    *An Album of Maya Architecture.* Norman: University of Oklahoma Press.
1963    Originally published 1946, Carnegie Institution of Washington.

**Prudden, T. M.**

1903    The Prehistoric Ruins of the San Juan Watershed in Utah, Arizona, Colorado, and New Mexico. *American Anthropologist* n.s. 5(2):224–288.

1914    The Circular Kiva of Small Ruins in the San Juan Watershed. *American Anthropologist* n.s. 16(1):33–58.

1918    *A Further Study of Prehistoric Small House Ruins in the San Juan Watershed.* American Anthropological Association Memoirs, vol. 5, no. 1.

**Purcell, D. E.**

1993    Pottery Kilns of the Northern San Juan Anasazi Tradition. M.A. thesis, Northern Arizona University, Flagstaff.

**Rapoport, A.**

1982    *The Meaning of the Built Environment: A Nonverbal Communication Approach.* Beverly Hills, CA: Sage Publications.

**Rappaport, R. A.**

1971    Ritual, Sanctity, and Cybernetics. *American Anthropologist* 73(1):59–76.
1974    Obvious Aspects of Ritual. *Cambridge Anthropology* 2(1):3–69.

**Redman, C. L.**

1978    *The Rise of Civilization.* San Francisco: W. H. Freeman and Co.

**Redman, C. L., and A. P. Kinzig**

2003    Resilience of Past Landscapes: Resilience Theory, Society, and the Longue Durée. *Conservation Ecology* 7(1):article 14. http://www.ecologyandsociety.org/vol7/iss1/ (accessed July 1, 2005).

**Reed, E. K.**

1956 Types of Village-Plan Layouts in the Southwest. In *Prehistoric Settlement Patterns in the New World*, edited by G. R. Willey, pp. 11–17. Viking Fund Publications in Anthropology no. 23. New York: Wenner-Gren Foundation for Anthropological Research.

1958 *Excavations in Mancos Canyon, Colorado.* Anthropological Papers no. 35. Salt Lake City: University of Utah Press.

**Reed, P. F., ed.**

2000 *Foundations of Anasazi Culture: The Basketmaker-Pueblo Transition.* Salt Lake City: University of Utah Press

**Reed, P. F., and K. N. Hensler, eds.**

2000 *Anasazi Community Development in Redrock Valley: Final Report on the Cove Archaeological Project along the N33 Road in Apache County, Arizona.* Navajo Nation Papers in Archaeology no. 33. Window Rock, AZ: Navajo Nation Archaeology Department.

**Reents-Budet, D.**

1994 *Painting the Maya Universe: Royal Ceramics of the Classic Period.* Durham, NC: Duke University Press.

**Reid, J. J., J. R. Welch, B. K. Montgomery, and M. N. Zedeño**

1996 A Demographic Overview of the Late Pueblo III Period in the Mountains of East-Central Arizona. In *The Prehistoric Pueblo World, AD 1150–1350*, edited by M. Adler, pp. 73–85. Tucson: University of Arizona Press.

**Renfrew, C.**

1986 Introduction: Peer Polity Interaction and Socio-political Change. In *Peer Polity Interaction and Socio-political Change*, edited by C. Renfrew and J. Cherry, pp. 1–18. Cambridge: Cambridge University Press.

2001 Production and Consumption in a Sacred Economy: The Material Correlates of High Devotional Expression at Chaco Canyon. *American Antiquity* 66(1):14–25.

**Riggs, C. R. Jr.**

2001 *The Architecture of Grasshopper Pueblo.* Salt Lake City: University of Utah Press.

**Rinaldo, J. B.**

1959 Foote Canyon Pueblo, Eastern Arizona. *Fieldiana: Anthropology*, vol. 49, no. 2. Chicago Natural History Museum Publication 864.

**Roberts, F. H. H. Jr.**

1929 *Shabik'eshchee Village, A Late Basket Maker Site in Chaco Canyon, New Mexico.* Bureau of American Ethnology Bulletin 92. Washington, DC: Smithsonian Institution Press.

1931 *The Ruins at Kiatuthlana, Eastern Arizona.* Bureau of American Ethnology Bulletin 100. Washington, DC: Government Printing Office.

1932 *The Village of the Great Kivas on the Zuni Reservation, New Mexico.* Bureau of

American Ethnology Bulletin 111. Washington, DC: Government Printing Office.

1939     *Archaeological Remains in the Whitewater District, Eastern Arizona.* Bureau of American Ethnology Bulletin 121. Washington, DC: Government Printing Office.

**Robertshaw, P.**

1999     Seeking and Keeping Power in Bunyoro-Kitara, Uganda. In *Beyond Chiefdoms: Pathways to Complexity in Africa,* edited by S. K. McIntosh, pp. 124–135. Cambridge: Cambridge University Press.

**Robinson, W. J., and B. G. Harrill**

1974     *Tree-Ring Dates from Colorado V: Mesa Verde Area.* Tucson: Laboratory of Tree-Ring Research, University of Arizona.

**Rogge, A. E.**

1983     Little Archaeology, Big Archaeology: The Changing Context of Archaeological Research. Ph.D. diss., University of Arizona, Tucson.

**Rohn, A. H.**

1963     Prehistoric Soil and Water Conservation on Chapin Mesa, Southwestern Colorado. *American Antiquity* 28(4):441–455.

1971     *Mug House: Mesa Verde National Park, Colorado.* NPS Archeological Research Series 7-D. Washington, DC: National Park Service, US Department of the Interior.

1977     *Cultural Change and Continuity on Chapin Mesa.* Lawrence, KA: Regents Press.

1983     Budding Urban Settlements in the Northern San Juan. In *Proceedings of the Anasazi Symposium 1981,* edited by J. E. Smith, pp. 175–180. Mesa Verde, CO: Mesa Verde Museum Association.

**Roler, K. L.**

1999     The Chaco Phenomenon: A Faunal Perspective from the Peripheries. Ph.D. diss., Arizona State University, Tempe.

**Roney, J. R.**

1992     Prehistoric Roads and Regional Interaction in the Chacoan System. In *Anasazi Regional Organization and the Chaco System,* edited by D. E. Doyel, pp. 123–131. Anthropological Papers no. 5. Albuquerque: Maxwell Museum of Anthropology, University of New Mexico.

1996     The Pueblo III Period in the Eastern San Juan Basin and Acoma-Laguna Areas. In *The Prehistoric Pueblo World, AD 1150–1350,* edited by M. Adler, pp. 145–169. Tucson: University of Arizona Press.

**Rose, M. R., W. J. Robinson, and J. S. Dean**

1982     *Dendroclimatic Reconstruction for the Southeastern Colorado Plateau.* Final report to the Division of Cultural Research, National Park Service, Albuquerque. Contract no. PX7486-7-0121. Tucson: Laboratory of Tree-Ring Research, University of Arizona.

REFERENCES

**Ryan, S. C.**

2003     *Albert Porter Pueblo (Site 5MT123), Montezuma County, Colorado. Annual Report, 2002 Field Season.* Cortez, CO: Crow Canyon Archaeological Center. http://www.crowcanyon.org/ResearchReports/AlbertPorter/Porter2002 season/Text_Tables/Text_2002.htm (accessed December 15, 2003).

2004     *Albert Porter Pueblo (Site 5MT123), Montezuma County, Colorado, Annual Report, 2003 Field Season.* Cortez, CO: Crow Canyon Archaeological Center. http://www.crowcanyon.org/ResearchReports/AlbertPorter/Porter2003 season/Text_Tables/Text_2003.htm (accessed June 10, 2004).

**Sahagún, Fray B. d.**

1950     *Florentine Codex: General History of the Things of New Spain.* Translated and edited by A. J. O. Anderson and C. E. Dibble. Santa Fe, NM: School of American Research; Salt Lake City: University of Utah.

**Saitta, D. J.**

1997     Power, Labor, and the Dynamics of Change in Chacoan Political Economy. *American Antiquity* 62(1):7–26.

**Salzer, M. W.**

2000a     Dendroclimatology in the San Francisco Peaks Region of Northern Arizona, USA. Ph.D. diss., University of Arizona, Tucson. Available at University Microfilms International, Ann Arbor, MI.

2000b     Temperature Variability and the Northern Anasazi: Possible Implications for Regional Abandonment. *Kiva* 65(4):295–318.

**Sanday, P. R.**

1986     *Divine Hunger: Cannibalism as a Cultural System.* Cambridge: Cambridge University Press.

**Sauer, C. O., and D. D. Brand**

1932     *Aztatlán: Prehistoric Mexican Frontier on the Pacific Coast.* Iberoamericana. Berkeley: University of California.

**Schachner, G.**

2001     Ritual Control and Transformation in Middle-Range Societies: An Example from the American Southwest. *Journal of Anthropological Archaeology* 20(2):168–194.

2002     Corporate Group Formation and Differentiation in Early Puebloan Villages of the American Southwest. Unpublished paper in possession of author. Cited with permission.

**Schelberg, J. D.**

1984     Analogy, Complexity, and Regionally Based Perspectives. In *Recent Research on Chaco Prehistory,* edited by W. J. Judge and J. D. Schelberg, pp. 5–21. Reports of the Chaco Center no. 8. Albuquerque, NM: Division of Cultural Research, National Park Service.

1992     Hierarchical Organization as a Short-Term Buffering Mechanism in Chaco Canyon. In *Anasazi Regional Organization and the Chaco System,* edited by

D. E. Doyel, pp. 59–71. Anthropological Papers no. 5. Albuquerque: Maxwell Museum of Anthropology, University of New Mexico.

**Schillaci, M. A.**

2003    The Development of Population Diversity at Chaco Canyon. *Kiva* 68(3):221–245.

**Schillachi, M. A., and C. M. Stojanowski**

2002    A Reassessment of Matrilocality in Chacoan Culture. *American Antiquity* 67(2):343–356.

**Schlanger, S. H.**

1988    Patterns of Population Movement and Long-Term Population Growth in Southwestern Colorado. *American Antiquity* 53(4):773–793.

1992    Recognizing Persistent Places in Anasazi Settlement Systems. In *Space, Time, and Archaeological Landscapes*, edited by J. Rossignol and L. Wandsnider, pp. 91–112. New York: Plenum Press.

**Schlanger, S. H., and R. H. Wilshusen**

1993    Local Abandonments and Regional Conditions in the North American Southwest. In *Abandonment of Settlements and Regions: Ethnoarchaeological and Archaeological Approaches*, edited by C. M. Cameron and S. A. Tomka, pp. 85–98. Cambridge: Cambridge University Press.

**Schroeder, A. H.**

1979    Pecos Pueblo. In *Southwest*, vol. 9 of *Handbook of North American Indians*, edited by A. A. Ortiz, pp. 430–437. Washington, DC: Smithsonian Institution Press.

**Schutt, J. A.**

1997    Prehistoric Settlement at Fort Wingate. In *Cycles of Closure: A Cultural Resources Inventory of Fort Wingate Depot Activity, New Mexico*, edited by J. Schutt and R. Chapman, pp. 149–189. Albuquerque: Office of Contract Archaeology, University of New Mexico.

**Sebastian, L.**

1991    Sociopolitical Complexity and the Chaco System. In *Chaco and Hohokam: Prehistoric Regional Systems in the American Southwest*, edited by P. L. Crown and W. J. Judge, pp. 109–134. School of American Research Advanced Seminar Series. Santa Fe, NM: SAR Press.

1992a   *The Chaco Anasazi: Sociopolitical Evolution in the Prehistoric Southwest.* Cambridge: Cambridge University Press.

1992b   Chaco Canyon and the Anasazi Southwest: Changing Views of Sociopolitical Organization. In *Anasazi Regional Organization and the Chaco System*, edited by D. E. Doyel, pp. 23–31. Anthropological Papers no 5. Albuquerque: Maxwell Museum of Anthropology, University of New Mexico.

2004    Understanding Chacoan Society. In *In Search of Chaco*, edited by D. G. Noble, pp. 93–99. School of American Research. Santa Fe, NM: SAR Press.

**Sebastian, L., and J. H. Altschul**

n.d.     Settlement Pattern, Site Typology, and Demographic Analyses: The Anasazi, Archaic, and Unknown Sites. In *An Archaeological Survey of the Additions to Chaco Culture National Historic Park*, edited by R. M. Van Dyke. Publications in Archeology 13, Chaco Canyon Studies. Santa Fe, NM: National Park Service, US Department of the Interior, in prep.

**Sebastian, L., and H. W. Toll**

1987     Historic Structure Evaluation Report: The Chacoan Outliers of Twin Angels and Kin Nizhoni. Prepared for the Bureau of Land Management, Office of Contract Archeology, University of New Mexico, Albuquerque.

**Sejourné, L.**

1966     *La Arqueología de Teotihuacan: La Cerámica.* México, DF: Fondo de Cultura Económica.

**Sellars, R. W.**

1997     *Preserving Nature in the National Parks: A History.* New Haven, CT: Yale University Press.

**Shafer, H. J.**

1995     Architecture and Symbolism in Transitional Pueblo Development in the Mimbres Valley, SW New Mexico. *Journal of Field Archaeology* 22(1):23–47.

1999     The Classic Mimbres Phenomenon and Some New Interpretations. In *Sixty Years of Mogollon Archaeology, Papers from the Ninth Mogollon Conference, Silver City, New Mexico, 1996*, edited by S. M. Whittlesey, pp. 95–105. Tucson, AZ: SRI Press.

**Shelley, P. H.**

1980     Salmon Ruins Lithic Laboratory Report. In *Investigations at the Salmon Site: The Structure of Chacoan Society in the Northern Southwest*, vol. III, edited by C. Irwin-Williams and P. H. Shelley, pp. xxiii–159. Final Report to Funding Agencies. Portales: Eastern New Mexico University.

**Shepard, A. O.**

1939     Technology of La Plata Pottery. Appendix A in *Archaeological Studies in the La Plata District, Southwestern Colorado and Northwestern New Mexico*, by E. H. Morris, pp. 249–287. Publication no. 519. Washington, DC: Carnegie Institution of Washington.

1956     *Ceramics for the Archaeologist.* Publication no. 609. Washington, DC: Carnegie Institution of Washington.

**Sigleo, A. C.**

1981     Casamero: A Chacoan Site in the Red Mesa Valley, New Mexico, LA 8779. Unpublished paper.

**Smith, M. F., and F. F. Berdan, eds.**

2003     *The Postclassic Mesoamerican World.* Salt Lake City: University of Utah Press.

**Smith, M. L.**

2003     Introduction: The Social Construction of Ancient Cities. In *The Social*

*Construction of Ancient Cities*, edited by M. L. Smith, pp. 1–36. Washington, DC: Smithsonian Books.

**Smith, M. L., ed.**
2003    *The Social Construction of Ancient Cities.* Washington, DC: Smithsonian Books.

**Smith, R. L.**
1998    Kivas of the Northern San Juan and the Northern Rio Grande Regions, AD 1150–1350: A Comparative Analysis. M.A. thesis, Washington State University, Pullman.

**Smith, W. R.**
1973    *The Williams Site: A Frontier Mogollon Village in West-Central New Mexico.* Papers of the Peabody Museum of Archaeology and Ethnology, vol. 39, no. 2. Cambridge, MA: Harvard University.

1977    *The Fiesta System and Economic Change.* New York: Columbia University Press.

**Snyder, L. M., D. Hull-Walski, T. Thiessen, and M. Giesen**
2000    Post-War Partners in Archaeology: The Bureau of Reclamation, the National Park Service, and the River Basin Surveys in the Missouri River Basin (1945–1969). *CRM* 23(1):17–20.

**Snygg, J., and T. Windes**
1998    Long, Wide Roads and Great Kiva Roofs. *Kiva* 64(1):7–25.

**Sofaer, A.**
1997    The Primary Architecture of the Chacoan Culture: A Cosmological Expression. In *Anasazi Architecture and American Design*, edited by B. H. Morrow and V. B. Price, pp. 88–132. Albuquerque: University of New Mexico Press.

1999    *The Mystery of Chaco Canyon.* Oley, PA: Bullfrog Films.

**Sofaer, A. P., M. P. Marshall, and R. M. Sinclair**
1989    The Great North Road: A Cosmographic Expression of the Chaco Culture of New Mexico. In *World Archaeoastronomy*, edited by A. F. Aveni, pp. 365–376. Cambridge: Cambridge University Press.

**Sofaer, A. P., and R. M. Sinclair**
1987    Astronomical Markings at Three Sites on Fajada Butte. In *Astronomy and Ceremony in the Prehistoric Southwest*, edited by J. B. Carlson and W. J. Judge, pp. 43–70. Papers of the Maxwell Museum of Anthropology no. 2. Albuquerque: Maxwell Museum of Anthropology, University of New Mexico.

**Southall, A.**
1998    *The City in Time and Space.* Cambridge: Cambridge University Press.

1999    The Segmentary State and the Ritual Phase in Political Economy. In *Beyond Chiefdoms: Pathways to Complexity in Africa*, edited by S. K. McIntosh, pp. 31–38. Cambridge: Cambridge University Press.

REFERENCES

**Speth, J. D., and S. L. Scott I**
1989    Horticulture and Large-Animal Hunting: The Role of Resource Depletion and the Constraints of Time and Labor. In *Farmers as Hunters*, edited by S. Kent, pp. 71–79. Cambridge: Cambridge University Press.

**Spielmann, K. A.**
1989    Colonists, Hunters, and Farmers: Plains-Pueblo Interaction in the Seventeenth Century. In *Columbian Consequences*, vol. 1, *Archaeological and Historical Perspectives in the Spanish Borderlands West*, edited by D. H. Thomas, pp. 101–114. Washington, DC: Smithsonian Institution Press.

1991    Coercion or Cooperation? Plains-Pueblo Interaction in the Protohistoric Period. In *Farmers, Hunters, and Colonists: Interaction between the Southwest and Southern Plains*, edited by K. A. Spielmann, pp. 36–50. Tucson: University of Arizona Press.

1998    Ritual Craft Specialists in Middle-Range Societies. In *Craft and Social Identity*, edited by C. L. Costin and R. P. Wright, pp. 153–159. Archeological Papers no. 8. Washington, DC: American Anthropological Association.

2004    Communal Feasting, Ceramics and Exchange. In *Identity, Feasting, and the Archaeology of the Greater Southwest*, edited by B. J. Mills, pp. 210–232. Boulder: University Press of Colorado.

**Stanfield, J. H. Jr.**
1996    Multiethnic Societies and Regions. *American Behavioral Scientist* 40(1):8–17.

**Stein, J. R., D. Ford, and R. Friedman**
2003    Reconstructing Pueblo Bonito. In *Pueblo Bonito: Center of the Chacoan World*, edited by J. E. Neitzel, pp. 33–60. Washington, DC: Smithsonian Institution Press.

**Stein, J. R., and A. P. Fowler**
1996    Looking beyond Chaco in the San Juan Basin and Its Peripheries. In *The Prehistoric Pueblo World, AD 1100–1300*, edited by M. Adler, pp. 114–130. Tucson: University of Arizona Press.

**Stein, J. R., R. Friedman, and T. Blackhorse**
n.d.    Revisiting Downtown Chaco. In *Architecture of Chaco Canyon, New Mexico*, edited by S. H. Lekson. Salt Lake City: University of Utah Press, in press.

**Stein, J. R., and S. H. Lekson**
1992    Anasazi Ritual Landscapes. In *Anasazi Regional Organization and the Chaco System*, edited by D. E. Doyel, pp. 87–100. Anthropological Papers no. 5. Albuquerque: Maxwell Museum of Anthropology, University of New Mexico.

**Stein, J. R., J. E. Suiter, and D. Ford**
1997    High Noon in Old Bonito: Sun, Shadow and the Geometry of the Chaco

Complex. In *Anasazi Architecture and American Design*, edited by B. H. Morrow and V. B. Price,

**Steponaitis, V. P.**
1991    Contrasting Patterns of Mississippian Development. In *Chiefdoms: Power, Economy, and Ideology*, edited by T. Earle, pp. 193–228. Cambridge: Cambridge University Press.

**Steward, J. H.**
1937    Ecological Aspects of Pueblo Society. *Anthropos* 32:87–104.

**Stewart, J. D., and K. R. Adams**
1999    Evaluating Visual Criteria for Identifying Carbon and Iron-Based Pottery Paints from the Four Corners Region Using SEM-EDS. *American Antiquity* 64(4):675–696.

**Stoltman, J. B.**
1999    The Chaco-Chuska Connection: In Defense of Anna Shepard. In *Pottery and People: A Dynamic Interaction*, edited by J. M. Skibo and G. M. Feinman, pp. 9–24. Salt Lake City: University of Utah Press.

**Stone, T. T.**
1999    The Chaos of Collapse: Disintegration and Reintegration of Inter-regional Systems. *Antiquity* 73(279):110–118.

**Struever, S.**
1968    Problems, Methods, and Organization: A Disparity in the Growth of Archeology. In *Anthropological Archeology in the Americas*, edited by B. J. Meggers, pp. 131–151. Washington, DC: Anthropological Society of Washington.

**Stuart, D. E.**
2000    *Anasazi America: Seventeen Centuries on the Road from Center Place.* Albuquerque: University of New Mexico Press.

**Stubbs, S. A.**
1950    *Birds-Eye View of the Pueblos.* Norman: University of Oklahoma Press.

**Sullivan, M., and J. M. Malville**
1993    Clay Sourcing at Chimney Rock: The Chemistry and Mineralogy of Feather Holders and Other Ceramics. In *The Chimney Rock Archaeological Symposium*, edited by J. M. Malville and G. Matlock, pp. 29–34. General Technical Report RM-227. Fort Collins, CO: Rocky Mountain Forest and Range Experiment Station, US Department of Agriculture.

**Swanson, S.**
2003    Documenting Prehistoric Communication Networks: A Case Study in the Paquimé Polity. *American Antiquity* 68(4):753–767.

**Szuter, C. R., and F. E. Bayham**
1989    Sedentism and Prehistoric Animal Procurement among Desert Horticulturists of the North American Southwest. In *Farmers as Hunters*, edited by S. Kent, pp. 80–95. Cambridge: Cambridge University Press.

**Teague, L. S.**

1998    *Textiles in Southwestern Prehistory*. Albuquerque: University of New Mexico Press.

**Tennessen, D., R. A. Blanchette, and T. C. Windes**

2002    Differentiating Aspen and Cottonwood in Prehistoric Wood from Chacoan Great House Ruins. *Journal of Archaeological Science* 29(5):521–527.

**Till, J. D.**

2001    Chacoan Roads and Road-Associated Sites in the Lower San Juan Region: Assessing the Role of Chacoan Influences in the Northwestern Periphery. M.A. thesis, University of Colorado, Boulder.

**Till, J. D., and W. B. Hurst**

2002    Trail of the Ancients: A Network of Ancient Roads and Great Houses in Southeastern Utah. Paper presented at the 67th annual meeting of the Society for American Archaeology, Denver.

**Toll, H. W.**

1985    Pottery, Production, Public Architecture, and the Chaco Anasazi System. Ph.D. diss., University of Colorado, Boulder. Available at University Microfilms, Ann Arbor, MI.

1990    A Reassessment of Chaco Cylinder Jars. In *Clues to the Past: Papers in Honor of William Sundt*, edited by M. S. Duran and D. T. Kirkpatrick, pp. 273–305. Archaeological Society of New Mexico Papers no. 16. Albuquerque: Archaeological Society of New Mexico.

1991    Material Distributions and Exchange in the Chaco System. In *Chaco and Hohokam: Prehistoric Regional Systems in the American Southwest*, edited by P. L. Crown and W. J. Judge, pp. 77–108. School of American Research Advanced Seminar Series. Santa Fe, NM: SAR Press.

2001    Making and Breaking Pots in the Chaco World. *American Antiquity* 66(1):56–78.

**Toll, H. W., E. Blinman, and C. D. Wilson**

1992    Chaco in the Context of Ceramic Regional Systems. In *Anasazi Regional Organization and the Chaco System*, edited by D. E. Doyel, pp. 147–157. Anthropological Papers no. 5. Albuquerque: Maxwell Museum of Anthropology, University of New Mexico.

**Toll, H. W., and P. J. McKenna**

1987    The Ceramography of Pueblo Alto. In *Investigations at the Pueblo Alto Complex, Chaco Canyon, New Mexico, 1975–1979: Vol. III, Artifactual and Biological Analyses*, edited by F. J Mathien and T. C. Windes, pp. 19–230. Publications in Archeology 18F, Chaco Canyon Studies. Santa Fe, NM: National Park Service, US Department of the Interior.

1993    The Testimony of the Spadefoot Ceramics. In *The Spadefoot Toad Site: Investigations at 29SJ 629 Chaco Canyon, New Mexico*, edited by T. C. Windes, pp. 15–134. Reports of the Chaco Center no. 12. Santa Fe, NM: Division of Cultural Research, National Park Service.

1997    Chaco Ceramics. In *Ceramics, Lithics, and Ornaments of Chaco Canyon, Analyses of Artifacts from the Chaco Project, 1976–1978*, vol. I, edited by F. J. Mathien, pp. 17–530. Publications in Archeology 18G, Chaco Canyon Studies. Santa Fe, NM: National Park Service, US Department of the Interior.

**Toll, H. W., M. T. Newren, and P. J. McKenna**
2005    Always There, Often Overlooked: The Roles and Significance of Small House Sites in Chaco Canyon. Paper presented at the 70th annual meeting of the Society for American Archaeology, Salt Lake City, Utah.

**Toll, H. W., T. C. Windes, and P. J. McKenna**
1980    Late Ceramic Patterns in Chaco Canyon: The Pragmatics of Modeling Ceramic Exchange. In *Models and Methods in Regional Exchange*, edited by R. E. Fry, pp. 95–117. SAA Papers no. 1. Washington, DC: Society for American Archaeology.

**Toll, M. S.**
1983    Changing Patterns of Plant Utilization for Food and Fuel: Evidence from Flotation and Macrobotanical Remains. In *Economy and Interaction along the Lower Chaco River: The Navajo Mine Archeological Program, Mining Area III*, edited by P. Hogan and J. C. Winter, pp. 331–350. Albuquerque: Office of Contract Archeology, University of New Mexico.

1985    An Overview of Chaco Canyon Macrobotanical Materials and Analyses to Date. In *Environment and Subsistence in Chaco Canyon, New Mexico*, edited by F. J. Mathien, pp. 247–277. Publications in Archeology 18E, Chaco Canyon Studies. Albuquerque, NM: National Park Service, US Department of the Interior.

1986    Flotation and Macrobotanical Evidence of Plant Use through Anasazi Occupation of LA 50337, in the La Plata River Valley, Northwest New Mexico. Castetter Laboratory for Ethnobotanical Studies, Technical Series 158. Unpublished paper on file, Museum of New Mexico, Laboratory of Anthropology, Research Section, Santa Fe.

1987    Plant Utilization at Pueblo Alto, A Chacoan Town Site: Floatation and Macrobotanical Analyses. In *Investigations at the Pueblo Alto Complex, Chaco Canyon, New Mexico, 1975–1979: Vol. III, Artifactual and Biological Analyses*, edited by F. J. Mathien and T. C. Windes, pp. 691–784. Publications in Archeology 18F, Chaco Canyon Studies. Santa Fe, NM: National Park Service, US Department of the Interior.

1993    The Archeobotany of the La Plata Valley in Totah Perspective. Paper presented at the Fifth Occasional Anasazi Symposium, Farmington, NM.

**Trigger, B.**
1972    Determinants of Urban Growth in Pre-Industrial Societies. In *Man, Settlement, and Urbanism*, edited by P. J. Ucko, R. Tringham, and G. W. Dimbleby, pp. 575–599. London: Duckworth.

2003    *Understanding Early Civilizations: A Comparative Study*. Cambridge: Cambridge University Press.

**Trigger, B. G.**
1989    *A History of Archaeological Thought*. Cambridge: Cambridge University Press.

REFERENCES

**Trombold, C. D.**

1991    Causeways in the Context of Strategic Planning in the La Quemada Region, Zacatecas, Mexico. In *Ancient Road Networks and Settlement Hierarchies in the New World*, pp. 145–168. Cambridge: Cambridge University Press.

**Truell, M. L.**

1986    A Summary of Small Site Architecture in Chaco Canyon, New Mexico. In *Small Site Architecture of Chaco Canyon*, eidted by P. J. McKenna and M. L. Truell, pp. 115–502. Publications in Archeology 18D, Chaco Canyon Studies. Santa Fe, NM: National Park Service, US Department of the Interior.

1992    *Excavations at 29SJ627: Vol. 1, The Architecture and Stratigraphy.* Reports of the Chaco Center no. 11. Santa Fe, NM: Division of Cultural Research, National Park Service.

**Turner, C. G. II, and J. A. Turner**

1999    *Man Corn: Cannibalism and Violence in the Prehistoric American Southwest.* Salt Lake City: University of Utah Press.

**Van Dyke, R. M.**

1997a   The Andrews Great House Community: A Ceramic Chronometric Perspective. *Kiva* 63(2):137–154.

1997b   Tracking the Trachyte Boundary: A Southern Perspective on Exchange and Interaction among Chacoan Communities. Paper presented at the 62nd annual meeting of the Society for American Archaeology, Nashville, TN.

1999a   The Andrews Community: A Chacoan Outlier in the Red Mesa Valley, New Mexico. *Journal of Field Archaeology* 26(1):55–67.

1999b   The Chaco Connection: Bonito-Style Architecture in Outlier Communities. Ph.D. diss., University of Arizona, Tucson.

1999c   The Chaco Connection: Evaluating Bonito-Style Architecture in Outlier Communities. *Journal of Anthropological Archaeology* 18(4):471–506.

2000    Chacoan Ritual Landscapes: The View from Red Mesa Valley. In *Great House Communities across the Chacoan Landscape*, edited by J. Kantner and N. M. Mahoney, pp. 91–100. Anthropological Papers no. 64. Tucson: University of Arizona Press.

2001    Andrews Community Archaeological Research Project, 1999–2000. Report prepared for the Bureau of Land Management, Albuquerque, NM, and the State of New Mexico, Santa Fe. Unpublished paper on file, NMCRIS Project no. 65869, Laboratory of Anthropology, Santa Fe, NM.

2003a   Bounding Chaco: Great House Architectural Variability across Time and Space. *Kiva* 69(2):117–139.

2003b   Memory and the Construction of Chacoan Society. In *Archaeologies of Memory*, edited by R. M. Van Dyke and S. E. Alcock, pp. 180–200. Oxford and Malden, MA: Blackwell Publishers.

2004    Memory, Meaning and Masonry: The Late Bonito Chacoan Landscape. *American Antiquity* 69(3):413–431.

n.d.a    Great Kivas in Time, Space, and Society. In *Architecture of Chaco Canyon, New Mexico,* edited by S. H. Lekson. Salt Lake City: University of Utah Press, in press.

n.d.b    *Lived Landscapes, Constructed Pasts: Memory, Phenomenology, and Chacoan Society,* in prep. School of American Research. Santa Fe, NM: SAR Press.

**Van Dyke, R. M., ed.**

n.d.    An Archaeological Survey of the Additions to Chaco Culture National Historical Park. Reports of the Chaco Center no. 13. Unpublished paper on file in Anthropology Projects, Cultural Resources Management, National Park Service, Santa Fe, NM.

**Van Dyke, R. M., and S. E. Alcock**

2003    Archaeologies of Memory: An Introduction. In *Archaeologies of Memory,* edited by R. M. Van Dyke and S. E. Alcock, pp. 1–13. Malden, MA: Blackwell Publishers, Ltd.

**Van West, C. R.**

1994    *Modeling Prehistoric Agricultural Productivity in Southwestern Colorado: A GIS Approach.* Reports of Investigations no. 67. Pullman: Department of Anthropology, Washington State University; Cortez, CO: Crow Canyon Archaeological Center.

**Vansina, J.**

1999    Pathways of Political Development in Equatorial Africa and Neo-Evolutionary Theory. In *Beyond Chiefdoms: Pathways to Complexity in Africa,* edited by S. K. McIntosh, pp. 166–172. Cambridge: Cambridge University Press.

**Vargas, V. D.**

1995    *Copper Bell Trade Patterns in the Prehispanic US Southwest and Northwest Mexico.* Arizona State Museum Archaeological Series 187. Tucson: Arizona State Museum.

2001    Mesoamerican Copper Bells in the Pre-Hispanic Southwestern United States and Northwestern Mexico. In *The Road to Aztlan: Art from a Mythic Homeland,* edited by V. Fields and V. Zamudio-Taylor, pp. 196–211. Los Angeles: Los Angeles County Museum of Art.

**Varien, M. D.**

1999    *Sedentism and Mobility in a Social Landscape: Mesa Verde and Beyond.* Tucson: University of Arizona Press.

2000    Communities and the Chacoan Regional System. In *Great House Communities across the Chacoan Landscape,* edited by J. Kantner and N. M. Mahoney, pp. 149–156. Anthropological Papers no. 64. Tucson: University of Arizona Press.

2001 We Have Learned a Lot, but We Still Have More to Learn. In *Chaco Society and Polity: Papers from the 1999 Conference*, edited by L. S. Cordell, W. J. Judge, and J. Piper, pp. 47–62. Albuquerque: New Mexico Archeological Council.

2002 Persistent Communities and Mobile Households: Population Movement in the Central Mesa Verde Region, AD 950–1290. In *Seeking the Center Place: Archaeology and Ancient Communities in the Mesa Verde Region*, edited by M. D. Varien and R. H. Wilshusen, pp. 163–184. Salt Lake City: University of Utah Press.

**Varien, M. D., W. D. Lipe, M. A. Adler, I. M. Thompson, and B. A. Bradley**
1996 Southwest Colorado and Southeast Utah Mesa Verde Region Settlement Patterns: AD 1100 to 1300. In *The Prehistoric Pueblo World, AD 1150–1350*, edited by M. A. Adler, pp. 86–113. Tucson: University of Arizona Press.

**Vivian, R. G.**
1959 *The Hubbard Site and Other Tri-Wall Structures in New Mexico and Colorado.* Archeological Research Series 5. Washington, DC: National Park Service, US Department of the Interior.

1965 *The Three-C Site, an Early Pueblo II Ruin in Chaco Canyon, New Mexico.* UNM Publications in Anthropology no. 13. Albuquerque: University of New Mexico Press.

1970 An Inquiry into Prehistoric Social Organization in Chaco Canyon, New Mexico. In *Reconstructing Prehistoric Pueblo Societies*, edited by W. A. Longacre, pp. 59–83. School of American Research Advanced Seminar Series. Albuquerque: University of New Mexico Press.

1974 Conservation and Diversion, Water Control Systems in the Anasazi Southwest. In *Irrigation's Impact on Society*, edited by T. E. Downing and M. Gibson, pp. 95–112. Anthropological Papers no. 25. Tucson: University of Arizona Press.

**Vivian, R. G., D. N. Dogden, and G. H. Hartman**
1978 *Wooden Ritual Artifacts from Chaco Canyon, New Mexico: The Chetro Ketl Collection.* Anthropological Papers no. 32. Tucson: University of Arizona Press.

**Vivian, R. G., and T. W. Mathews**
1965 *Kin Kletso: A Pueblo III Community in Chaco Canyon, New Mexico.* Technical Series 6, part 1, pp. 1–115. Globe, AZ: Southwestern Parks and Monuments Association.

**Vivian, R. G., and P. Reiter**
1960 *The Great Kivas of Chaco Canyon and Their Relationships.* Monographs of the School of American Research and the Museum of New Mexico no. 22. Santa Fe, NM: School of American Research.

**Vivian, R. G.**
1990 *The Chacoan Prehistory of the San Juan Basin.* New York and San Diego: Academic Press.

1991      Chacoan Subsistence. In *Chaco and Hohokam: Prehistoric Regional Systems in the American Southwest*, edited by P. L. Crown and W. J. Judge, pp. 57–75. School of American Research Advanced Seminar Series. Santa Fe, NM: SAR Press.

1992      Chacoan Water Use and Managerial Decision Making. In *Anasazi Regional Organization and the Chaco System*, edited by D. E. Doyel, pp. 45–58. Anthropological Papers no. 5. Albuquerque: Maxwell Museum of Anthropology, University of New Mexico.

1996      "Chaco" as a Regional System. In *Interpreting Southwestern Diversity: Underlying Principles and Overarching Patterns*, edited by P. R. Fish and J. J. Rid, pp. 45–53. Anthropological Research Paper no. 48. Tempe: Arizona State University.

1997a     Chacoan Roads: Morphology. *Kiva* 63(1):7–34.

1997b     Chacoan Roads: Function. *Kiva* 63(1):35–67.

2000      Economy and Ecology. *Archaeology Southwest* 14(1):5–7.

2001      Chacoan Water Use and Managerial Decision Making. In *Anasazi Regional Organization and the Chaco System*, 2d ed., edited by D. E. Doyel, pp. 45–57. Anthropological Papers no. 5. Albuquerque: Maxwell Museum of Anthropology, University of New Mexico.

**Vivian, R. G., and B. Hilpert**

2002      *The Chaco Handbook: An Encyclopedic Guide*. Salt Lake City: University of Utah Press.

**Walker, W. H.**

1995      Ceremonial Trash? In *Expanding Archaeology*, edited by J. M. Skibo, W. H. Walker, and A. E. Nielsen, pp. 67–74. Salt Lake City: University of Utah Press.

**Wallace, A. F. C.**

1966      *Religion: An Anthropological View*. New York: Random House.

**Warburton, M., and D. K. Graves**

1992      Navajo Springs, Arizona: Frontier Outlier or Autonomous Great House? *Journal of Field Archaeology* 19(1):51–69.

**Ware, J. A.**

2001      Chaco Social Organization: A Peripheral View. In *Chaco Society and Polity: Papers from the 1999 Conference*, edited by L. S. Cordell, W. J. Judge, and J. Piper, pp. 79–93. NMAC Special Publication no. 4. Albuquerque: New Mexico Archeological Council.

2002a     Descent Group and Sodality: Alternative Pueblo Social Histories. In *Traditions, Transitions, and Technologies: Themes in Southwestern Archaeology*, edited by S. H. Schlanger, pp. 94–112. Boulder: University Press of Colorado.

REFERENCES

2002b     What Is a Kiva? The Social Organization of Early Pueblo Communities. In
          *Culture and Environment in the American Southwest: Essays in Honor of Robert
          C. Euler*, edited by D. A. Phillips Jr. and J. A. Ware, pp. 79–88. SWCA
          Anthropological Research Paper no. 8. Phoenix, AZ: SWCA
          Environmental Consultants.

Ware, J. A., and E. Blinman
2000      Cultural Collapse and Reorganization: Origin and Spread of Pueblo Ritual
          Sodalities. In *The Archaeology of Regional Interaction: Religion, Warfare, and
          Exchange across the American Southwest and Beyond*, edited by M. Hegmon,
          pp. 381–409. Boulder: University Press of Colorado.

Ware, J. A., and G. J. Gumerman
1977      Remote Sensing Methodology and the Chaco Canyon Prehistoric Road
          System. In *Aerial Remote Sensing Techniques in Archaeology*, edited by
          T. R. Lyons and R. K. Hitchcock, pp. 135–167. Reports of the Chaco
          Center no. 2. Albuquerque, NM: Division of Cultural Research, National
          Park Service.

Warren, H. A.
1980      Production and Distribution of Pottery in Chaco Canyon and
          Northwestern New Mexico. Paper on file, NPS Chaco Culture National
          Historical Park Museum Archive, University of New Mexico, Albuquerque.

Warriner, G.
2000      *Chaco.* Seattle, WA: Camera One.

Washburn, D. K.
1980      The Mexican Connection: Cylinder Jars from the Valley of Oaxaca. In *New
          Frontiers in the Archaeology and History of the Southwest*, vol. 72, no. 4, edited
          by C. L. Riley and B. C. Hedrick, pp. 70–85. Springfield: Illinois State
          Academy of Science.

2004      A Symmetry Analysis of Salmon Ruins Ceramics. Paper presented at
          the Salmon Working Conference, Bloomfield, NM. Permission to cite
          requested.

Waters, T.
1995      Towards a Theory of Ethnic Identity and Migration: The Formation of
          Ethnic Enclaves by Migrant Germans in Russia and North America.
          *International Migration Review* 29(2):519–544.

Watrous, L. V.
1987      The Role of the Near East in the Rise of the Cretan Palaces. In *The
          Function of the Minoan Palaces*, edited by R. Hägg and N. Marinatos,
          pp. 65–70. Stockholm: Paul Åströms Förlag.

Weigand, P. C.
1978      The Prehistory of the State of Zacatecas: An Interpretation, Part I.
          *Anthropology* 2(1):67–87.

1982    Mining and Mineral Trade in Prehispanic Zacatecas. In *Mining and Mineral Trade in Prehispanic Zacatecas*. Special Issue of *Anthropology*, vol. 6, edited by P. C. Weigand and G. Gwynne, pp. 87–134. Stony Brook: Department of Anthropology, State University of New York.

**Weigand, P. C., and A. García de Weigand**
2001    A Macroeconomic Study of the Relationships between the Ancient Cultures of the American Southwest and Mesoamerica. In *The Road to Aztlan: Art from a Mythic Homeland*, edited by V. Fields and V. Zamudio-Taylor, pp. 196–211. Los Angeles: Los Angeles County Museum of Art.

**Weigand, P. C., and G. Harbottle**
1993    The Role of Turquoise in the Ancient Mesoamerican Trade Structure. In *The American Southwest and Mesoamerica: Systems of Prehistoric Exchange*, edited by J. E. Ericson and T. G. Baugh, pp. 159–177. New York: Plenum Press.

**Weigand, P. C., G. Harbottle, and E. V. Sayre**
1977    Turquoise Sources and Source Analysis: Mesoamerica and the Southwestern USA. In *Exchange Systems in Prehistory*, edited by T. K. Earle and J. E. Ericson, pp. 15–34. New York: Academic Press.

**Weiner, A. B.**
1992    *Inalienable Possessions: The Paradox of Keeping-While-Giving*. Berkeley: University of California Press.

**Wendorf, F., and E. K. Reed**
1955    An Alternative Reconstruction of Northern Rio Grande Prehistory. *El Palacio* 62(5-6):131–173.

**Whalen, M. E.**
1984    Settlement System Evolution on the Mogollon-Anasazi Frontier. In *Recent Research in Mogollon Archaeology*, edited by S. Upham, F. Plog, D. Batcho, and B. Kauffman, pp. 75–89. NMSU Occasional Papers no. 10. Las Cruces: The University Museum, New Mexico State University.

**Whalen, M. E., and P. E. Minnis**
2001    The Local and the Distant in the Origin of Casas Grandes, Chihuahua, Mexico. *American Antiquity* 68(2):314–332.

**Wheat, J. B.**
1955    *Mogollon Culture prior to AD 1000*. Memoirs of the Society for American Archaeology no. 10. Salt Lake City, UT: Society for American Archaeology.

**Wheatley, P.**
1971    *The Pivot of the Four Quarters; A Preliminary Enquiry into the Origins and Character of the Ancient Chinese City*. Chicago: Aldine.

**Wilcox, D. R.**
1991    The Mesoamerican Ballgame in the American Southwest. In *The Mesoamerican Ballgame*, edited by V. L. Scarborough and D. R. Wilcox, pp. 101–125. Tucson: University of Arizona Press.

1993    The Evolution of the Chacoan Polity. In *The Chimney Rock Archaeological Symposium, October 20–21, Durango, Colorado*, edited by J. M. Malville and G. Matlock, pp. 76–90. General Technical Report RM-227. Fort Collins, CO: Rocky Mountain Forest and Range Experiment Station, US Department of Agriculture.

1999    A Peregrine View of Macroregional Systems in the North American Southwest, AD 750–1250. In *Great Towns and Regional Polities in the Prehistoric American Southwest and Southeast*, edited by J. E. Neitzel, pp. 115–141. Albuquerque: University of New Mexico Press.

**Wilcox, D. R., and J. Haas**

1994    The Scream of the Butterfly: Competition and Conflict in the Prehistoric Southwest. In *Themes in Southwest Prehistory*, edited by G. J. Gumerman, pp. 211–238. School of American Research. Santa Fe, NM: SAR Press.

**Wills, W. H.**

2000    Political Leadership and the Construction of Chacoan Great Houses in Chaco Canyon, New Mexico, AD 1020–1140. In *Alternative Leadership Strategies in the Prehispanic Southwest*, edited by B. J. Mills, pp. 19–44. Tucson: University of Arizona Press.

2001    Ritual and Mound Formation during the Bonito Phase in Chaco Canyon. *American Antiquity* 66(3):433–451.

**Wills, W. H., and P. L. Crown**

2004    Commensal Politics in the Prehispanic American Southwest: An Introductory Review. In *Identity, Feasting, and the Archaeology of the Greater Southwest*, edited by B. J. Mills, pp. 153–172. Boulder: University Press of Colorado.

**Wills, W. H., and T. C. Windes**

1989    Evidence for Population Aggregation and Dispersal during the Basketmaker III Period in Chaco Canyon, New Mexico. *American Antiquity* 54(2):347–369.

**Wilshusen, R. H.**

1986    The Relationship between Abandonment Mode and Ritual Use in Pueblo I Anasazi Protokivas. *Journal of Field Archaeology* 13(2):245–254.

1988a    Architectural Trends in Prehistoric Anasazi Sites during AD 600 to 1200. In *Dolores Archaeological Program: Supporting Studies: Additive and Reductive Technologies*, compiled by E. Blinman, C. J. Phagan, and R. H. Wilshusen, pp. 599–633. Denver, CO: Bureau of Reclamation, US Department of the Interior.

1988b    Sipapus, Ceremonial Vaults, and Foot Drums (or a Resounding Argument for Protokivas). In *Dolores Archaeological Program: Supporting Studies: Additive and Reductive Technologies*, compiled by E. Blinman, C. J. Phagan, and R. H. Wilshusen, pp. 649–671. Denver, CO: Bureau of Reclamation, US Department of the Interior.

1989    Unstuffing the Estufa: Ritual Floor Features in Anasazi Pit Structures and

Pueblo Kivas. In *The Architecture of Social Integration in Prehistoric Pueblos*, edited by W. D. Lipe and M. Hegmon, pp. 89–111. Occasional Paper no. 1. Cortez, CO: Crow Canyon Archaeological Center.

1991    Early Villages in the American Southwest: Cross-cultural and Archaeological Perspectives. Ph.D. diss., University of Colorado, Boulder.

1995    Conclusion, Management Suggestions, and Directions for Future Research. In *The Cedar Hill Special Treatment Project: Late Pueblo I, Early Navajo, and Historic Occupations in Northwestern New Mexico*, compiled by R. H. Wilshusen, pp. 117–120. LAC Research Papers no. 1. Dolores, CO: La Plata Archaeological Consultants.

1999    Pueblo I (AD 750–900). In *Colorado Prehistory: A Context for the Southern Colorado Drainage Basin*, edited by W. D. Lipe, M. D. Varien, and R. H. Wilshusen, pp. 196–241. Denver: Colorado Council of Professional Archaeologists.

2002    Estimating Population in the Central Mesa Verde Region. In *Seeking the Center Place: Archaeology and Ancient Communities in the Mesa Verde Region*, edited by M. D. Varien and R. H. Wilshusen, pp. 101–120. Salt Lake City: University of Utah Press.

**Wilshusen, R. H., M. J. Churchill, and J. M. Potter**

1997    Prehistoric Reservoirs and Water Basins in the Mesa Verde Region: Intensification of Water Collection Strategies during the Great Pueblo Period. *American Antiquity* 62(4):664–681.

**Wilshusen, R. H., and S. G. Ortman**

1999    Rethinking the Pueblo I Period in the Northern Southwest: Aggregation, Migration, and Cultural Diversity. *Kiva* 64(3):369–399.

**Wilshusen, R. H., L. M. Sesler, and T. D. Hovezak**

2000    Understanding Variation in Pueblo I Sites across the San Juan Region: Frances Mesa Compared with Navajo Reservoir, Dolores, Mesa Verde, and Cedar Hill. In *The Frances Mesa Special Treatment Project: New Interpretations of the Ancestral Pueblo and Navajo Occupations in the Navajo Reservoir Area*, compiled by R. H. Wilshusen, T. D. Hovezak, and L. M. Sesler, pp. 111–158. LAC Research Papers no. 3. Dolores, CO: La Plata Archaeological Consultants.

**Wilshusen, R. H., and C. D. Wilson**

1995    Reformatting the Social Landscape in the Late Pueblo I–Early Pueblo II Period: The Cedar Hill Data in Regional Context. In *The Cedar Hill Special Treatment Project: Late Pueblo I, Early Navajo, and Historic Occupations in Northwestern New Mexico*, compiled by R. H. Wilshusen, pp. 43–80. LAC Research Papers no. 1. Dolores, CO: La Plata Archaeological Consultants.

**Wilson, C. D.**

1996    Ceramic Pigment Distributions and Regional Interaction: A Re-examination of Interpretations in Shepard's "Technology of La Plata Pottery." *Kiva* 62(1):83–102.

**Wilson, C. D., and E. Blinman**

1993    *Upper San Juan Region Pottery Typology.* Archaeology Notes no. 80. Santa Fe: Museum of New Mexico.

**Wilson, E.**

[1940]    *To the Finland Station.* New York: Harcourt Brace. Reprint, New York: New
2003    York Review Books, 2003.

**Wilson, P. J.**

1988    *The Domestication of the Human Species.* New Haven, CT: Yale University Press.

**Windes, T. C.**

1978    *Stone Circles of Chaco Canyon, Northwestern New Mexico.* Reports of the Chaco Center no. 4. Albuquerque, NM: Division of Cultural Resources, National Park Service.

1984a    A New Look at Population in Chaco Canyon. In *Recent Research on Chaco Prehistory,* edited by W. J. Judge and J. D. Schelberg, pp. 75–87. Reports of the Chaco Center no. 8. Albuquerque, NM: Division of Cultural Research, National Park Service.

1984b    A View of the Cibola Whiteware from Chaco Canyon. In *Regional Analysis of Prehistoric Ceramic Variation: Contemporary Studies of the Cibola Whitewares,* edited by A. P. Sullivan and J. L. Hantman, pp. 94–119. Anthropological Research Papers no. 31. Tempe: Arizona State University.

1987a    *Investigations at the Pueblo Alto Complex, Chaco Canyon, New Mexico, 1975–1979: Vol. I, Summary of Tests and Excavations at the Pueblo Alto Community.* Publications in Archeology 18F, Chaco Canyon Studies. Santa Fe, NM: National Park Service, US Department of the Interior.

1987b    *Investigations at the Pueblo Alto Complex, Chaco Canyon, New Mexico, 1975–1979: Vol. II, Architecture and Stratigraphy.* Publications in Archeology 18F, Chaco Canyon Studies. Santa Fe, NM: National Park Service, US Department of the Interior.

1991    The Prehistoric Road Network at Pueblo Alto, Chaco Canyon, New Mexico. In *Ancient Road Networks and Settlement Hierarchies in the New World,* edited by C. D. Trombold, pp. 111–131. Cambridge: Cambridge University Press.

1992    Blue Notes: The Chacoan Turquoise Industry in the San Juan Basin. In *Anasazi Regional Organization and the Chaco System,* edited by D. E. Doyel, pp. 159–168. Anthropological Papers no. 5. Albuquerque: Maxwell Museum of Anthropology, University of New Mexico.

1993    *The Spadefoot Toad Site: Investigations at 29SJ629, Chaco Canyon, New Mexico.* Vols. I and II. Reports of the Chaco Center no. 12. Santa Fe, NM: Division of Cultural Research, National Park Service.

2001a    House Location Patterns in the Chaco Canyon Area: A Short Description. In *Chaco Society and Polity: Papers from the 1999 Conference,* edited by

L. S. Cordell, W. J. Judge, and J. Piper, pp. 31–46. NMAC Special Publication no. 4. Albuquerque: New Mexico Archeological Council.

2001b     Map of Casa del Rio. Unpublished paper.

2003     This Old House: Construction and Abandonment at Pueblo Bonito. In *Pueblo Bonito: Center of the Chacoan World*, edited by J. E. Neitzel, pp. 14–32. Washington, DC: Smithsonian Institution Press.

n.d.     Gearing Up and Piling On: Early Great Houses in the San Juan Basin Interior. In *The Chaco Synthesis: Architecture*, edited by S. H. Lekson. Salt Lake City: University of Utah Press, in press.

**Windes, T. C., ed.**

1993     *Spadefoot Toad Site: Investigations at 29SJ629, Chaco Canyon, New Mexico*. Vol. 1. Reports of the Chaco Center no. 12. Santa Fe, NM: Division of Cultural Research, National Park Service.

n.d.     *Early Pueblo Occupations in the Chaco Region: Excavations and Survey of Basketmaker III and Pueblo I Sites, Chaco Canyon, New Mexico*, in prep. Vol. 1. Reports of the Chaco Center no. 14. Santa Fe, NM: Division of Cultural Research, National Park Service.

**Windes, T. C., R. M. Anderson, B. K. Johnson, and C. A. Ford**

2000     Sunrise, Sunset: Sedentism and Mobility in the Chaco East Community. In *Great House Communities across the Chacoan Landscape*, edited by J. Kantner and N. M. Mahoney, pp. 39–59. Anthropological Papers no. 64. Tucson: University of Arizona Press.

**Windes, T. C., and D. Ford**

1992     The Nature of the Early Bonito Phase. In *Anasazi Regional Organization and the Chaco System*, edited by D. E. Doyel, pp. 75–86. Anthropological Papers no. 5. Albuquerque: Maxwell Museum of Anthropology, University of New Mexico.

1996     The Chaco Wood Project: The Chronometric Reappraisal of Pueblo Bonito. *American Antiquity* 61(2):295–310.

**Windes, T. C., and P. J. McKenna**

2001     Going against the Grain: Wood Production in Chacoan Society. *American Antiquity* 66(1):119–140.

**Winter, J. C.**

1978     Anasazi Agriculture at Hovenweep, I: Field Systems. In *Limited Activity and Occupation Sites: A Collection of Conference Papers*, compiled and edited by A. E. Ward, pp. 83–97. Contributions to Anthropological Studies no. 1. Albuquerque, NM: Center for Anthropological Studies.

1993     Environment and Subsistence across the Colorado Plateau. In *Across the Colorado Plateau: Anthropological Studies for the Transwestern Pipeline Expansion Project*, vol. XV, part 5, edited by J. C. Winter, pp. 601–648. ENRON Report. Albuquerque: Office of Contract Archeology and Maxwell Museum of Anthropology, University of New Mexico.

**Wobst, H. M.**
1975    The Demography of Finite Populations and the Origins of the Incest
        Taboo. *American Antiquity* 40(2, part 2):75–81.

**Wright, K. R.**
2003    *Water for the Anasazi.* Essays in Public Works History no. 22. Kansas City:
        Public Works Historical Society.

**Yaeger, J., and M. A. Canuto**
2000    Introducing an Archaeology of Communities. In *The Archaeology of
        Communities: A New World Perspective,* edited by M. A. Canuto and J. Yaeger,
        pp. 1–15. New York: Routledge.

**Yoffee, N.**
2001    The Chaco "Rituality" Revisited. In *Chaco Society and Polity: Papers from the
        1999 Conference,* edited by L. S. Cordell, W. J. Judge, and J. Piper, pp.
        63–78. NMAC Special Publication no. 4. Albuquerque: New Mexico
        Archeological Council.

2005    *Myths of the Archaic State: Evolution of the Earliest Cities, States, and
        Civilizations.* New York and Cambridge: Cambridge University Press.

**Yoffee, N., S. K. Fish, and G. R. Milner**
1999    *Communidades,* Ritualities, and Chiefdoms: Social Evolution in the
        American Southwest and Southeast. In *Great Towns and Regional Polities
        in the Prehistoric American Southwest and Southeast,* edited by J. E. Neitzel,
        pp. 261–271. Albuquerque: University of New Mexico Press.

2001    The Chaco "Rituality" Revisited. In *Chaco Society and Polity: Papers from the
        1999 Conference,* edited by L. S. Cordell, W. J. Judge, and J. Piper. NMAC
        Special Publication no. 4. Albuquerque: New Mexico Archaeological
        Council.

**Zedeño, M. N.**
1994    *Sourcing Prehistoric Ceramics at Chodistaas Pueblo, Arizona: The Circulation of
        People and Pots in the Grasshopper Region.* Anthropological Papers no. 58.
        Tucson: University of Arizona Press.

# Index

Abandonment, of Great Houses, 184–86, 401; of Pueblo I villages, 238–39, 245–46

Acoma. *See* Zuni-Acoma region

Adams, E. C., 268

Adams, K., 300

Adams, R., 299–300

administrative centers, Great Kivas as, 87

African societies, and relationship between ritual and political organization, 412–18

Aghem chiefdoms (Cameroon), 416–18

agriculture: and Casa del Rio, 76; and colonization of Chaco Canyon, 191–92; and droughts in Northern San Juan during Pueblo I, 237; and environment of Classic Bonito phase, 58–62, 442–47; and environment of Early Aggradation period, 52–56, 431–34; and environment of Early Bonito phase, 56–58, 438–39; and environment of Late Aggradation period, 62–65, 451–54; San Juan Basin as environment for, 190–91, 395–96; technology of and Pueblo adjustments to fluctuating climate, 52. *See also* maize; plants; water control systems

*akchin*, and hydrology in Chaco Canyon, 53, 433–34

Akins, N. J., 384, 385

Alkalai Ridge Site 13, 217

Alta Vista, 344, 358, 362, 366, 371n4

*American Antiquity* (vol. 66, no 1), 117, 118, 150n1

American Museum of Natural History, 8

Anasazi: and migrations into Mogollon Highlands, 327; use of term, 6; water in traditions of, 110

*Anasazi America* (Stuart 2000), 40–41

Anasazi Heritage Center, 390

Ancestral Pueblo, use of term, 6

Anderson, D. G., 345

Andrews Great House, 159–60, 162, 163, 230, 235, 251

animals. *See* faunal use

Anyon, R., 322

Aragon Great House, 332

archaeology: and Chaco Project, 373–92; concept of seven sins of, 36, 43n3; and excavation at Chaco Canyon, 420–21; history of in Chaco Canyon, 8; and context of Chacoan Great Houses in Northern San Juan, 271–80; importance of Chaco in development of Southwestern and American, 4; and overview of Bonito phase in Chaco Canyon, 10–17; view of Chaco as city and anthropological, 116

*Archaeology Southwest* (vol. 14, no 1), 65n1

architecture: and cityscape of Chaco, 68, 101–16;

and concept of Chacoan architectural complex, 155; and definition of Chaco culture, 45, 67; and evidence for complexity at Chaco, 281–82; of Great Houses in Zuni-Acoma region, 320; and Hohokam, 333; and Mesoamerican connections at Chaco, 347–48, 358; new forms of public in Northern San Juan in 1200s, 311–12; origin of Chacoan style, 181; and post-Chaco period, 99–101; and Pueblo I Great Houses, 70–77; and Pueblo I villages, 238; and Pueblo II Great Houses, 78–93; research on history of development at Chaco, 67–70; San Juan cultural pattern and symbolism of Chacoan, 263–71; of small sites at Chaco, 93–99; and unity in Chaco World, 175–77; use of terms *public* and *civic*, 312–13n3. *See also* colonnades; Great Houses; Great Kivas; kivas; mounds; plazas

Arizona State University, 21

artifacts: deposition of along roadways, 165; and overview of archaeology of Chaco Canyon, 13–14. *See also* ceramics; lithics

Aztatlan Horizon (West Mexico), 344

Aztec (Mexico), and Toltecs, 345

Aztec hegemony model, 294

Chaco, 401; as evidence for complexity, 31–32, 37, 43–44n4, 283–84; ground plans of, *68*; hiatus in construction of during Early Bonito phase, 57; interpretations of relationship between eleventh- century and others in canyon, 202–203; and mounds, 105–106; organization of production and periodic use of, 144; of Pueblo I, 70–77, 234–35; of Pueblo II, 78–93; and Timeline for Chaco World, 184–86; and unity in Chaco World, 175–78, 397–402; and wood use, 56; in Zuni-Acoma region, 319–23. *See also* architecture; outliers; Pueblo Bonito

Great Kivas: and Basketmaker III communities, 71; and Chacoan influence in Mogollon Highlands, 327; and Chacoan influence in Zuni-Acoma region, 323; and cultural patterns in Northern San Juan, 266–67, 397; and definition of early Great Houses, 248; and overview of archaeology of Chaco Canyon, 13; and Pueblo I villages, 257; social and political organization of Chacoan system and, 198. *See also* kivas

Great North Road, 32–33, 43n2, 108, 164, 272

*Great Pueblo Architecture of Chaco Canyon, New Mexico* (Lekson 1984), 78–93, 385

Grebinger, P., 244

Guadalupe Ruin, 251

Hachure, and styles of ceramics, 125, *126*, 179, 201

Hagstrum, M., 144, 150n1

Hall, S. A., 430

Hamilton, W. D., 18

Haury, E. W., 327, 328, 334, 355–56

Hawkes, J., 387

Hayes, A. C., 18, 70, 94, 381

Haystack site, 171, *172*

Helms, M. W., 368

Herr, S. A., 185, 326, 327

Hewett, E., 15, 28

hierarchy: Great Houses as evidence of, 83, 92–93; and horizontal integration of social and political power, 414–15; and view of Chaco as city, 112. *See also* complexity; elites; social organization

Hohokam: and Chacoan influence on southern neighbors, 330–33, 334, 336–37; and mounds, 106; and shell bracelets, 330, 331, 350–51

Holmes's Group, 107

Holsinger, S. J., 442

Hooper Ranch site, 329

Hopewell earthworks, 106, 107

Hopi: and historical patterns of mobility, 146–47; and legacy of Chaco, 208, 209; and oral history on formation of villages, 137. *See also* Pueblo

Horton, R., 414

Hosler, D., 360, 364, 365, 371n4

Hosta Butte, *163*, 164

Hough, W., 327–28

households, and organization of production, 144, 147–48

*Houses and House-Life of the American Aborigines* (Morgan 1881), 37–38

Howell, T. L., 268

human ecology, and Chaco Project, 378

Hungo Pavi, 79

hunting. *See* faunal use

hydrology: and agriculture in Classic Bonito phase, 58–62, 441–50; and agriculture in Early Aggradation period, 52–56, 433; and agricul-

ture in Early Bonito phase, 56–58, 437–41; and agriculture in Late Aggradation period, 62–65; features of Chaco Canyon, *50*. *See also* sand-dune dam

Ida Jean Site, 275

ideology, and significance of colonnade, 347. *See also* symbolism; themes

imports, long-distance: and Chaco florescence, 285–86; and exchange in Chaco World, 167, 169; increase in eleventh century, 198; and organization of production, 119–31, 135–37; and overview of archaeology of Chaco Canyon, 14; and parallels between Chaco and Mimbres, 334; social and political organization of Chacoan system and, 199–201; and unity of Chaco World, 183. *See also* ceramics; copper bells; macaws; shell; trade; turquoise

*In Search of Chaco* (Noble 2004), 23, 26

interaction: in Chaco World, 161–72; direct and indirect between Mesoamerica and Chaco, 355–63; Mesoamerica and markers of in Chaco's cycle, 345–55

interdependence, in Chaco World, 173–75

Isleta Pueblo, 209

Jemez Pueblo, 209

Johnson, G. A., 27

Judd, N. M., 15, 128, 349–50, 353, 354, 361–62, 386, 442

Judge, W. J., 16, 18, 192, 197, 222, 244–45, 321, 380, 381, 389, 398, 404, 405, 407–408

Kantner, J., 148, 156, 159, 161–62, 174, 291–92

Chaco context, 189–90. *See also* chiefs and chiefdoms; leadership; power
population: and Chaco Synthesis, 396–97; and decline of Chaco, 205; estimates of for Chaco, 82, 84, 112; of Pueblo I villages, 217–18, 220, 230–35; regional in Northern San Juan, 276, 296; and social upheavals of 1200s and 1300s in Northern San Juan, 279–80. *See also* abandonment; demographic network; migration
postprocessual approaches, to interpretation of Bonito phase at Chaco Canyon, 16–17, 18
Potter, J. M., 143
power: beginnings of Chaco and changes in material correlates of, 237–47; and Mesoamerican connections to Chaco, 369–70; in modern and historical Pueblo societies, 406. *See also* control; elites; polity; political organization
Powers, R. P., 19, 20, 22, 383, 387
Prescott College, 379
prestige-goods economy, 169
priest, use of term, 195
primitive communism, theory of, 38, 39
processual approach, and Chaco Project, 378–79
production, organization of: and broad concept of Chaco, 137–42; chronological outline of imports and, 119–31; legacy of Chaco and social economies of Pueblos, 207; and modern economic concepts, 118; and political structure of Chaco, 142–49; trends in, 131–37. *See also* labor
Proskouriakoff, T., 103
Prudden, T. M., 264
Prudden units, 94, 263–64,

265, 269
*Publications in Archaeology* (National Park Service), 19
public education, and Chaco Project, 22–23, 85, 388–90
Public Service Company of New Mexico, 383
Pueblo (modern): concept of "primitive communism" and political power among, 38–40; and dual organization of leadership, 204; flowers in cosmology of, 109–10; historical development of city in past of, 102; inferences from discussions of society and polity of, 190, 406; and interpretations of Bonito phase at Chaco Canyon, 15; languages of and Chaco sphere, 137; and legacy of Chaco, 206–10; 315–16; and memories of Chaco, 100, 135; ritual and ceremony versus political power, 28–30. *See also* Hopi; Tewa; Zuni
Pueblo I: definition of, 6; environment and agriculture during, 52–56; and Great Houses, 70–77; and immigration, 193, 196–97; origins of Chaco system and, 212, 213, 214–37; and sites in Zuni-Acoma region, 318
Pueblo II expansion: and Mimbres area, 334, 335; use of term, 328
Pueblo III: definition of, 6; origins of Chaco system and, 212
Pueblo Alto, 33, 84, 144, 382, 384, 399, 448
Pueblo Bonito: chronology of, 79, 226, 234, 239–40, 242; and copper bells, 349–50; and cylindrical vessels, 352, 353; and exchange, 166; and high-status burials, 282; kivas and rituals at, 86; and maize, 448; and mid-

dens, 76; overview of archaeology of, 11–12; plan of, *241*; and platform mounds, 105; and Pueblo I, 234; and storage, 89, 90–91; and variations in architecture, 68–69
Pueblo del Arroyo, 79, 125, 308, 391–92
Pueblo Indian Cultural Center, 3–4
Pueblo Pintado, 59–60, 74, 77, 96, 447
Pueblo Revolt of 1680, 209
Pueblo Viejo, 332

**R**apoport, A., 114
Rappaport, R. A., 369
redistribution: concept of Chaco as system of, 141; and interdependence in Chaco World, 173–74
Redman, C. L., 345–46
Red Mesa Valley: and boundary between Chaco and Zuni-Acoma region, 317; and ceramics, 120, 121, 124, *125*, 179; and Chaco World, 159–61; and Pueblo I communities, 230
Red Willow Hamlet, 227
Reed, E. K., 265
reformatting, of social landscape, 257
regional pattern: and analysis of origins of Chaco, 212; and Chaco Project, 382–85; and geographic extent of Chacoan polity, 288; and Hohokam, 332; and primacy as evidence for complexity, 32–38; settlement patterns and cultural differences in Pueblo I period and origins of Chaco, 214–37; social power and control of resources in San Juan region, 243–45. *See also* Chaco Halo; Chaco region; Chaco World
Reiter, P., 267
*Relación de Michoacan* (Hosler 1994), 364, 365
Renfrew, C., 27, 143, 149,

# School of American Research Advanced Seminar Series

PUBLISHED BY SAR PRESS

TIKAL: DYNASTIES, FOREIGNERS, & AFFAIRS OF STATE: ADVANCING MAYA ARCHAEOLOGY
*Jeremy A. Sabloff, ed.*

GRAY AREAS: ETHNOGRAPHIC ENCOUNTERS WITH NURSING HOME CULTURE
*Philip B. Stafford, ed.*

AMERICAN ARRIVALS: ANTHROPOLOGY ENGAGES THE NEW IMMIGRATION
*Nancy Foner, ed.*

VIOLENCE
*Neil L. Whitehead, ed.*

LAW & EMPIRE IN THE PACIFIC: FIJI AND HAWAI'I
*Sally Engle Merry &*
*Donald Brenneis, eds.*

ANTHROPOLOGY IN THE MARGINS OF THE STATE
*Veena Das & Deborah Poole, eds.*

PLURALIZING ETHNOGRAPHY: COMPARISON AND REPRESENTATION IN MAYA CULTURES, HISTORIES, AND IDENTITIES
*John M. Watanabe &*
*Edward F. Fischer, eds.*

THE ARCHAEOLOGY OF COLONIAL ENCOUNTERS: COMPARATIVE PERSPECTIVES
*Gil J. Stein, ed.*

COPÁN: THE HISTORY OF AN ANCIENT MAYA KINGDOM
*E. Wyllys Andrews &*
*William L. Fash, eds.*

GLOBALIZATION, WATER, & HEALTH: RESOURCE MANAGEMENT IN TIMES OF SCARCITY
*Linda Whiteford & Scott Whteford, eds.*

COMMUNITY BUILDING IN THE TWENTY-FIRST CENTURY
*Stanley E. Hyland, ed.*

A CATALYST FOR IDEAS: ANTHROPOLOGICAL ARCHAEOLOGY AND THE LEGACY OF DOUGLAS W. SCHWARTZ
*Vernon L. Scarborough, ed.*

AFRO-ATLANTIC DIALOGUES: ANTHROPOLOGY IN THE DIASPORA
*Kevin A. Yelvington, ed.*

THE ANASAZI IN A CHANGING ENVIRONMENT
*George J. Gumerman, ed.*

REGIONAL PERSPECTIVES ON THE OLMEC
*Robert J. Sharer & David C. Grove, eds.*

THE CHEMISTRY OF PREHISTORIC HUMAN BONE
*T. Douglas Price, ed.*

THE EMERGENCE OF MODERN HUMANS: BIOCULTURAL ADAPTATIONS IN THE LATER PLEISTOCENE
*Erik Trinkaus, ed.*

THE ANTHROPOLOGY OF WAR
*Jonathan Haas, ed.*

THE EVOLUTION OF POLITICAL SYSTEMS
*Steadman Upham, ed.*

CLASSIC MAYA POLITICAL HISTORY: HIEROGLYPHIC AND ARCHAEOLOGICAL EVIDENCE
*T. Patrick Culbert, ed.*

TURKO-PERSIA IN HISTORICAL PERSPECTIVE
*Robert L. Canfield, ed.*

CHIEFDOMS: POWER, ECONOMY, AND IDEOLOGY
*Timothy Earle, ed.*

RECONSTRUCTING PREHISTORIC PUEBLO SOCIETIES
*William A. Longacre, ed.*

WRITING CULTURE: THE POETICS
AND POLITICS OF ETHNOGRAPHY
*James Clifford &*
*George E. Marcus, eds.*

THE COLLAPSE OF ANCIENT STATES AND
CIVILIZATIONS
*Norman Yoffee &*
*George L. Cowgill, eds.*

NEW PERSPECTIVES ON THE PUEBLOS
*Alfonso Ortiz, ed.*

STRUCTURE AND PROCESS IN LATIN
AMERICA
*Arnold Strickon &*
*Sidney M. Greenfield, eds.*

THE CLASSIC MAYA COLLAPSE
*T. Patrick Culbert, ed.*

METHODS AND THEORIES OF
ANTHROPOLOGICAL GENETICS
*M. H. Crawford & P. L. Workman, eds.*

SIXTEENTH-CENTURY MEXICO:
THE WORK OF SAHAGUN
*Munro S. Edmonson, ed.*

ANCIENT CIVILIZATION AND TRADE
*Jeremy A. Sabloff &*
*C. C. Lamberg-Karlovsky, eds.*

PHOTOGRAPHY IN ARCHAEOLOGICAL
RESEARCH
*Elmer Harp, Jr., ed.*

MEANING IN ANTHROPOLOGY
*Keith H. Basso & Henry A. Selby, eds.*

THE VALLEY OF MEXICO: STUDIES IN
PRE-HISPANIC ECOLOGY AND SOCIETY
*Eric R. Wolf, ed.*

DEMOGRAPHIC ANTHROPOLOGY:
QUANTITATIVE APPROACHES
*Ezra B. W. Zubrow, ed.*

THE ORIGINS OF MAYA CIVILIZATION
*Richard E. W. Adams, ed.*

EXPLANATION OF PREHISTORIC CHANGE
*James N. Hill, ed.*

EXPLORATIONS IN ETHNOARCHAEOLOGY
*Richard A. Gould, ed.*

ENTREPRENEURS IN CULTURAL CONTEXT
*Sidney M. Greenfield, Arnold Strickon,*
*& Robert T. Aubey, eds.*

THE DYING COMMUNITY
*Art Gallaher, Jr. &*
*Harlan Padfield, eds.*

SOUTHWESTERN INDIAN RITUAL DRAMA
*Charlotte J. Frisbie, ed.*

LOWLAND MAYA SETTLEMENT PATTERNS
*Wendy Ashmore, ed.*

SIMULATIONS IN ARCHAEOLOGY
*Jeremy A. Sabloff, ed.*

CHAN CHAN: ANDEAN DESERT CITY
*Michael E. Moseley & Kent C. Day, eds.*

SHIPWRECK ANTHROPOLOGY
*Richard A. Gould, ed.*

ELITES: ETHNOGRAPHIC ISSUES
*George E. Marcus, ed.*

THE ARCHAEOLOGY OF LOWER CENTRAL
AMERICA
*Frederick W. Lange &*
*Doris Z. Stone, eds.*

LATE LOWLAND MAYA CIVILIZATION:
CLASSIC TO POSTCLASSIC
*Jeremy A. Sabloff &*
*E. Wyllys Andrews V, eds.*

Participants in the School of American Research Advanced seminar "Chaco Synthesis," Santa Fe, New Mexico, May 4–7, 2003. Seated from left: Ruth Van Dyke, Timothy R. Pauketat, Stephen H. Lekson, Ben Nelson, John Kantner, W. James Judge. Standing from left: Richard Levanthal, Norm Yoffee, Lynne Sebastian, Tom Windes, H. Wolcott Toll, Linda Cordell

Printed in the USA
CPSIA information can be obtained
at www.ICGtesting.com
CBHW031141300424
7768CB00018B/92